A Modern Guide to Macroeconomics

To our families

A Modern Guide to Macroeconomics

An Introduction to Competing Schools of Thought

Brian Snowdon
Principal Lecturer in Economics
School of Social, Political and Economic Sciences
University of Northumbria
Newcastle-upon-Tyne, UK

Howard Vane
Reader in Economics
School of Social Science
Liverpool John Moores University
Liverpool, UK

and Peter Wynarczyk
Senior Lecturer in Economics
School of Social, Political and Economic Sciences
University of Northumbria
Newcastle-upon-Tyne, UK

Edward Elgar
Cheltenham, UK • Northampton, MA, USA

Published by
Edward Elgar Publishing Limited
8 Lansdown Place
Cheltenham
Glos GL50 2HU
UK

Edward Elgar Publishing, Inc.
6 Market Street
Northampton
Massachusetts 01060
USA

Reprinted 1995, 1996, 1998

British Library Cataloguing in Publication Data
Snowdon, B.
    Modern Guide to Macroeconomics:
    Introduction to Competing Schools of
    Thought
    I. Title
    339.3

Library of Congress Cataloging-in-Publication Data
Snowdon, Brian.
    A modern guide to macroeconomics: an introduction to competing
    schools of thought / by Brian Snowdon, Howard Vane and Peter
    Wynarczyk.
        p.   cm.
    Includes bibliographical references (p.) and index.
    1. Macroeconomics.   2. Keynesian economics.   3. Comparative
    economics.   I. Vane, Howard R.   II. Wynarczyk, Peter.   III. Title.
    HB172.5.S85   1994
    339–dc20   94–8255
                                                                                    CIP

ISBN 1 85278 884 4
        1 85278 882 8 (paperback)

Printed in Great Britain at the University Press, Cambridge

Contents

Figures

Preface

Until the early 1970s there was a generally accepted broad consensus in macroeconomics which revolved around the orthodox Keynesian model. By the mid-1980s the received conventional wisdom had been shattered and replaced by a number of competing schools of thought. The main aim of this book is to provide a comprehensive *introduction* to the central tenets underlying, and the policy implications of, these various schools of thought in macroeconomics. This book is primarily aimed at *intermediate* undergraduates taking courses in macroeconomics and we have assumed that such students will have a firm grasp of basic economic principles and be familiar with introductory macroeconomic theories and models. The book should also prove useful to students taking courses in monetary economics and the history of economic thought, as well as postgraduate students in their preliminary year of study. For intermediate students we have marked with an asterisk within the bibliography those references which are particularly recommended, while postgraduates should find the extensive bibliography especially useful.

While written in such a way as to allow students on a range of degree courses to read individual chapters in isolation, according to their interests and needs, the book follows a structured direction, tracing the origins and development of modern macroeconomics in historical perspective. After an introductory chapter on visions of the macroeconomy, Chapter 2 considers the debate between Keynes and the old classical model before tracing the development of the orthodox Keynesian school and the re-interpretation of Keynes (Chapter 3), the orthodox monetarist school (Chapter 4), the new classical school (Chapter 5), the real business cycle school (Chapter 6), the new Keynesian school (Chapter 7), and, finally the contributions of the Austrian and Post-Keynesian Schools (Chapter 8). Following the pattern of individual chapters, the overall book is self-contained and could be used either as a main text for a macroeconomics course or read alongside a standard macro text such as Dornbusch and Fischer (1994). While in the former case we have sought to provide extensive references which provide more detailed treatment of the issues covered, the reader should be aware that constraints of space have forced us to limit our discussion of some important areas of macroeconomic analysis, most notably that relating to the open economy and economic growth.

In order to help bring the subject matter alive and capture the imagination of the reader, included at the end of each chapter are interviews with some leading exponents of the main schools of macroeconomic thought. We are extremely grateful to (listed in the order the interviews appear in the book) Stanley Fischer, Robert Skidelsky, James Tobin, Milton Friedman, David Laidler, Robert Lucas Jr, Patrick Minford, Robert Barro, Charles Plosser, Gregory Mankiw, Edmund Phelps, Roger Garrison and Victoria Chick, for the time and care they took in answering our questions. Their illuminating and contrasting answers demonstrate that modern macroeconomics is both an exciting and controversial subject.

Our final thanks go to a number of individuals, in particular Jenny Burke, Cecilia Dalrymple and Joanne Steward, for their patience, humour and cooperation in typing various parts of the final manuscript. Any remaining errors (few in number, it is hoped) are our responsibility.

Brian Snowdon
Howard Vane
Peter Wynarczyk

1. Visions of the macroeconomy

> My mind is a raging torrent, flooded with rivulets of thought, cascading into a waterfall of creative alternatives. (Hedley Lamarr, from the film, *Blazing Saddles*, 1974).

1.1 Macroeconomics: Issues and Ideas

Macroeconomics is concerned with the structure, performance and behaviour of the economy as a whole. The prime concern of macroeconomists is to analyse and attempt to understand the underlying determinants of the main aggregate trends in the economy with respect to the total output of goods and services, unemployment, inflation and the balance of payments. Obviously the subject matter of macroeconomics is of crucial importance because in one way or another macroeconomic events influence the lives and welfare of all of us. Because macroeconomic performance and policies are closely connected, the major macroeconomic issues are also the subject of constant media attention and inevitably play a central role in political debate. The influence of the performance of the economy on political events is particularly important and pertinent during election campaigns and research has confirmed that in the post-war period the outcome of elections has in many cases been affected by the state of the economy as measured by three main macroeconomic indicators – inflation, unemployment and economic growth (see Frey and Schneider, 1988; Alesina, 1989; Harrington, 1993).

An understanding by government policy makers of the factors which determine the long-run growth of an economy and the short-run fluctuations that constitute the business cycle is essential in order to design and implement economic policies which have the potential vastly to improve economic welfare. The primary aim of macroeconomic research is to develop as comprehensive an understanding as possible about the way the economy functions and how it is likely to react to specific policies and the wide variety of demand and supply shocks which can cause instability. Macroeconomic theory, consisting of a set of views about the way the economy operates, organised within a logical framework (or model), forms the basis upon which economic policy is designed and implemented. However economists differ over what they regard as the 'correct' model of the economy and as a result substantial disagreement exists over the role and conduct of macroeconomic policy.

1

The great ungluing of the Keynesian conventional wisdom in the early 1970s allowed a proliferation of alternative views on macroeconomics to develop and this diversity and richness has been sustained by the failure of any contender to achieve such widespread acceptance or rejection that it either firmly established a new dogma or was totally dispatched from the scene. Any adequate account of the current state of macroeconomics needs to explore the rise and fall of the old ideas and the state of the new within a comparative and historical context. This book examines, compares and evaluates the major rival accounts comprising contemporary macroeconomic thought. We would maintain that the coexistence of alternative explanations is a sign of strength rather than weakness, since it permits gains from intellectual trade and improved understanding. It was John Stuart Mill who recognized, more than one hundred years ago, that *all* parties gain from the comparative interplay of ideas. Alternatives not only protect us from intellectual slavery and complacency where 'teachers and learners go to sleep at their post as soon as there is no enemy in the field' (Mill, 1982, p. 105) but they also provide a catalyst for improved understanding whereby the effort to comprehend our competitors allows us to judge ourselves more earnestly. We would endorse Mill's imperative for continued dialogue, in this case within macroeconomics, between the alternative frameworks and suggest that they all have something to learn from each other since the macroeconomic problems they address and endeavour to solve are often shared.

That there are a wide variety of schools of thought in economics in general, and macroeconomics in particular, should not surprise us given the intrinsic difficulty and importance of the issues under investigation. Readers should also note that the degree of permissiveness in economics discourse appears to be greater in macroeconomics than in microeconomics; while economists disagree, they tend to do so more frequently, vociferously, and at greater length, in the former area. Wicksell's contention (1958, pp. 51–2) that within economics 'the state of war seems to persist and remain permanent' seems more appropriate for contemporary macroeconomics where the diverse neoclassical research traditions of Marshall, Menger and Walras continue to do battle at the aggregative level alongside the unorthodox Keynes. Although microeconomists have their own important and controversial debates, these receive much less attention in the media than those taking place between macroeconomists which are regularly played out on the public stage. To a large extent this reflects the importance of the issues which macroeconomists deal with but it also supports the findings of a recent survey of economists which shows that 'consensus is stronger on microeconomic than on macroeconomic propositions' (see Alston *et al.*, 1992).

A significant factor accounting for the prolonged length of debate and controversy within macroeconomics is that it seems more sensitive to external influences than microeconomics; this is brought out clearly if one compares a key component from each, monetary theory from macro, value theory from micro. Monetary theory is more open to external influences, being less abstract, more topical and policy-oriented, displaying a concern for monetary institutions and their evolution (see Hicks, 1967a, pp. 156–9, 1976, p. 216; Deane, 1978, p. 46). An indication of this increased sensitivity (and openness to the challenge of events as well as new ideas) is given by the way in which the loss of professional confidence in what we now call macroeconomics during the interwar period was not matched by a similar response in microeconomics (see King, 1988, p. 239). The latter appeared better insulated against the discovery of widespread excess capacity and administered pricing than the former, which was rocked by the length and severity of the Great Depression (and other events subsequently).

While it is certainly true that the contemporary state of macroeconomic theory appears like a battlefield, with regiments of economists grouped under different banners, it is our view that economists should resist the temptation to embrace a one-sided or restrictive consensus 'because the right answers are unlikely to come from any pure economic dogma' (Deane, 1983). In addition the very nature of scientific research dictates that disagreements and debate are most vocal at the frontier and this is further complicated by the 'strong incentives that exist in academia to differentiate products' (Blanchard and Fischer, 1989).

1.2 Objectives, Instruments and the Role of Government

Although macroeconomics appears to have been in a state of crisis during the past quarter-century and there is no denying the significant conflicts of opinion which exist between the different schools of thought, it should also be noted that economists tend to disagree more over theoretical issues, empirical evidence and the choice of policy instruments than they do over the ultimate objectives of policy. In the opening statement of what turned out to be one of the most influential articles written in the post-war period, Milton Friedman (1968a) gave emphasis to this very issue:

> There is wide agreement about the major goals of economic policy: high employment, stable prices, and rapid growth. There is less agreement that these goals are mutually compatible or, among those who regard them as incompatible, about the terms at which they can and should be substituted for one another. There is least agreement about the role that various instruments of policy can and should play in achieving the several goals.

The choice of appropriate instruments in order to achieve the 'major goals' of economic policy will depend on a detailed analysis of the causes of specific macroeconomic problems. Here we encounter two main intellectual traditions in macroeconomics which we can define broadly as the classical and Keynesian approaches. It is when we examine how policy objectives are interconnected and how different economists view the role and effectiveness of markets in coordinating economic activity that we find the fundamental issue which underlies disagreements between economists on matters of policy, namely, what is the proper role of government in the economy? The extent and form of government intervention in the economy was a major concern of Adam Smith (1776) in the *Wealth of Nations* and the rejection of uncontrolled *laissez-faire* by Keynes is well documented. In a radio broadcast in 1934, Keynes presented a talk entitled 'Poverty and Plenty: is the economic system self adjusting?' In it he distinguished between two warring factions of economists:

> On the one side are those that believe that the existing economic system is, in the long run, a self-adjusting system, though with creaks and groans and jerks and interrupted by time lags, outside interference and mistakes ... On the other side of the gulf are those that reject the idea that the existing economic system is, in any significant sense, self-adjusting. The strength of the self-adjusting school depends on it having behind it almost the whole body of organised economic thinking of the last hundred years ... Thus, if the heretics on the other side of the gulf are to demolish the forces of nineteenth-century orthodoxy... they must attack them in their citadel ... Now I range myself with the heretics. (Keynes, 1973, Vol. XIII, pp. 485–92)

Despite the development of more sophisticated and quantitatively powerful techniques during the past half-century, these two basic views identified by Keynes have persisted. Witness the opening comments of Stanley Fischer in a recent survey of developments in macroeconomics:

> One view and school of thought, associated with Keynes, Keynesians and new Keynesians, is that the private economy is subject to co-ordination failures that can produce excessive levels of unemployment and excessive fluctuations in real activity. The other view, attributed to classical economists, and espoused by monetarists and equilibrium business cycle theorists, is that the private economy reaches as good an equilibrium as is possible given government policy. (Fischer, 1988, p. 294)

It is clear that modern debates bear an uncanny resemblance to those which took place between Keynes and his critics in the 1930s, a clear case of 'back to the future'.

In this book we are primarily concerned with an examination of the intellectual influences which have shaped the development of macroeconomic theory and the conduct of macroeconomic policy in the period since the publication of Keynes's *General Theory of Employment, Interest and Money*

(1936). The first 25 years following the end of the Second World War were halcyon days for Keynesian macroeconomics. The new generation of macroeconomists generally accepted Keynes's central message that a *laissez-faire* capitalist economy could possess equilibria characterized by excessive involuntary unemployment. The main policy message to come out of the *General Theory* was that active government intervention in order to regulate aggregate demand was necessary, indeed unavoidable, if a satisfactory level of aggregate output and employment were to be maintained. That the *General Theory* was written in the early 1930s should be of no surprise, given the cataclysmic events associated with the Great Depression. The lessons from the history of economic thought teach us that one of the main driving forces behind the evolution of new ideas is the march of events. While theoretical ideas can help us understand historical events, it is also true that 'the outcome of historical events often challenges theorists and overturns theories, leading to the evolution of new theories' (Gordon, 1993, p. 560). The Great Depression gave birth to modern macroeconomics as surely as accelerating inflation in the late 1960s and early 1970s facilitated the monetarist counter-revolution (see Johnson, 1971).

1.3 The Great Depression

Prior to the 1930s the dominant view in what we now call macroeconomics was the 'old' classical approach the origins of which go back more than two centuries. In 1776, Adam Smith's celebrated *An Inquiry into the Nature and Causes of the Wealth of Nations* was published, in which he set forth the invisible-hand theorem. The main idea here is that profit and utility-maximizing behaviour under competitive conditions will translate the activities of millions of economic agents into a social optimum via market forces. Following Smith, political economy had an underlying bias towards *laissez-faire*, and the classical vision of macroeconomics found its most famous expression in the dictum 'supply creates its own demand'. This view, popularly known as Say's Law, denies the possibility of general overproduction or underproduction. With the notable exception of Malthus, Marx and a few other heretics, this view dominated both classical and early neoclassical (post 1870) contributions to macroeconomic theory (see Chapter 2).

In contrast to this prevailing orthodoxy, the most revolutionary aspect of Keynes's work from the early 1930s onwards was his clear and unambiguous message that with regard to the general level of output and employment, there was no invisible hand channelling self-interest into some social optimum. The most objectionable feature of capitalism for Keynes was the intolerable levels of unemployment which emerged in the UK economy during the 1920s and on a global scale in the 1930s. The extent and magnitude of the depression can be appreciated by referring to the data contained in Table 1.1, which indicates the extent of the collapse of industrial production and GDP for the major capitalist market economies between 1929 and 1932. The most severe downturn was in the USA, which experienced a 44.7 per cent decline in industrial production and a 28 per cent decline in GDP. The most severe recessions outside the USA were in Austria, Germany, France, Italy, Czechoslovakia and Poland, with the Scandinavian countries, the UK, Spain, Romania and the Netherlands less severely affected. Accompanying the decline in economic activity was an alarming rise in unemployment and a collapse of commodity and wholesale prices (see Aldcroft, 1993). The classical theory clearly appeared to be inconsistent with these events and created the need for a new approach which was provided by Keynes in his *General Theory*. For Keynes these traumatic events of the 1930s were symptomatic of a fundamental flaw in the operation of the price mechanism as a coordinating device.

Table 1.1   Percentage change in industrial production and GDP, 1929–32

Country	Industrial production	GDP
Austria	–34.3	–22.5
Belgium	–27.1	–7.1
Denmark	–5.6	4.0
Finland	–20.0	–5.9
France	–25.6	–11.0
Germany	–40.8	–15.7
Italy	–22.7	–6.1
Netherlands	–9.8	–8.2
Norway	–7.9	–0.9
Spain	–11.6	–8.0
Sweden	–11.8	–8.9
UK	–11.4	–5.8
USA	–44.7	–28.0
Czechoslovakia	–26.5	–18.2
Hungary	–19.2	–11.5
Poland	–37.0	n.a.
Romania	–11.8	n.a.

Source: Aldcroft (1993, p. 64).

To confront this problem Keynes needed to challenge the classical economists from within their citadel. The flaw, as he saw it, lay in the existing classical theory whose teaching Keynes regarded as not only 'misleading' but 'disastrous' if applied to the real-world problems facing the capitalist economies during the interwar period. For Keynes, capitalism was not terminally ill but unstable. His objective was to modify the rules of the game within the capitalist system in order to preserve and strengthen it. He wanted full employment to be the norm rather than the exception and his would be a conservative revolution. As Galbraith (1977) has noted, Keynes never sought to change the world out of personal dissatisfaction: 'for him the world was excellent'. Although the republic of Keynes's political imagination lay on the 'extreme left of celestial space', he was no socialist. Despite the prompting of George Bernard Shaw, Keynes remained notoriously blind to Marx. In his opinion, *Das Kapital* contained nothing but 'dreary out of date academic controversialising' which added up to nothing more than complicated *hocus pocus*. At one of Keynes's Political Economy Club meetings he admitted to having read Marx in the same spirit as reading a detective story. He had hoped to find some clue to an idea but had never succeeded in doing so (see Skidelsky, 1992, pp. 514–23). But Keynes's contempt for Marxist analysis did not stop those on the right of the political spectrum from regarding his message as dangerously radical. For Keynes the ultimate political problem was how to combine economic efficiency, social justice and individual freedom. But questions of equity were always secondary to questions of efficiency, stability and growth. His solution to the economic malaise which was sweeping the capitalist economies in the early 1930s was to accept 'a large extension of the traditional functions of government'. But as Keynes argued in *The End of Laissez-Faire* (1926), if the government is to be effective it should not concern itself with 'those activities which private individuals are already fulfilling' but attend to 'those functions which fall outside the private sphere of the individual, to those decisions which are made by no one if the state does not make them' (Keynes, 1972, Vol. IX, p. 291).

The Great Depression was the most significant economic catastrophe of modern times to affect capitalist market economies. In the USA, despite rapid growth after 1933 (with the exception of 1938), output remained substantially below normal until about 1942. The behaviour of US unemployment during this period is consistent with the movement of GDP. Unemployment reached its peak at 25 per cent in 1933 and despite rapid output growth in most of the subsequent period this proved insufficient to return the US economy to full employment. The economy had fallen so far below capacity (which continued to expand as the result of technological improvements, investment in human capital and rapid labour force growth) that, despite a 47 per cent increase in output between 1933 and 1937, unemployment failed to fall below 9 per cent and, following the impact of the 1938 recession, was still almost 10 per cent when the USA entered the Second World War in December 1941 (see Lee and Passell, 1979; Romer, 1992). Although the

Great Depression was a truly global phenomenon affecting the developing countries of Africa, Asia and Latin America as well as the major industrial economies, few countries could match the real losses experienced by the US economy. In comparison the recession in the UK was mild (see Aldcroft, 1986).

The causes of the Great Depression are still the subject of considerable dispute. What is certain and important for our purposes is that the explanation provided by Keynes, which placed emphasis on the instability of aggregate demand, was to change and influence the development of macroeconomics to this day. Following Keynes a consensus view emerged that the Great Depression had been caused by a dramatic decline of aggregate demand rather than by supply-side factors. The balance of evidence as far as the USA is concerned is that the stock market crash led to a series of domestic spending shocks which were subsequently reinforced by monetary shocks (C.D. Romer, 1993). Keynes himself placed a great deal of emphasis on the instability of investment expenditure 'occasioned by a cyclical change in the marginal efficiency of capital', a hypothesis later supported by the work of R.A. Gordon (1974). Other subsequent explanations have focused attention on the deflationary monetary policy implemented in the USA during the period 1929–33 (Friedman and Schwartz, 1963), the lack of world leadership exhibited by both the US and UK governments in not preventing the move towards increasing protectionism (Kindleberger, 1973) and independent changes in consumption demand (Temin, 1976). Temin's work is particularly important because it not only provides a comprehensive critique of Friedman and Schwartz but also calls into question the traditional Keynesian explanations based on independent shifts of the investment function (for a critique of Temin, see Mayer, 1978a).

Although Keynes did meet Roosevelt in May 1934, he appears to have had little influence on the President. Roosevelt thought Keynes some kind of mathematician while Keynes had 'supposed the President was more literate economically speaking' (Lekachman, 1969, p. 105). The analysis of E. Carey Brown buried the myth that Roosevelt was the first American Keynesian (Brown, 1956). Brown's analysis, which made use of the concept of the full employment budget surplus, showed that on balance the net impact of government fiscal policy on aggregate demand was negative in four out of seven years between 1932 and 1939. Thus fiscal expansion seems to have been an unsuccessful recovery device in the 1930s, not because it did not work, but because it was not tried. More recent research by Christina Romer has confirmed this view, demonstrating that fiscal policy contributed almost nothing to the US recovery before 1942. Romer's work suggests that 'the rapid rates of growth of real output in the mid- and late 1930s were largely due to conventional aggregate demand stimulus primarily in the form of monetary expansion'. Furthermore Romer's calculations indicate that 'in the absence of these stimuli the economy would have remained depressed for longer and far more deeply than it actually did' (Romer, 1992). In the end it was war that brought the Keynesian remedy. In a cynical comment on these events, J.K. Galbraith (1977) writes that 'Hitler, having ended unemployment in Germany, had gone on to end it for his enemies'. What is common in all this work is the emphasis given to aggregate demand as the driving force behind business fluctuations. This view was to remain dominant, both within Keynesian, monetarist and early new classical approaches to the analysis of macroeconomic fluctuations until the early 1980s, when a number of economists began to place emphasis on supply-side explanations (see Chapter 6).

1.4   The Rise and Fall of the Keynesian Consensus

The elimination of mass unemployment during the Second World War had a profound influence on the spread and influence of Keynesian ideas concerning the responsibility of government for maintaining full employment. In the UK, William Beveridge's *Full Employment in a Free Society* was published in 1944 and in the same year the government also committed itself to the maintenance of a 'high and stable level of employment' in a White Paper on *Employment Policy*. In the USA the *Employment Act* of 1946 dedicated the Federal Government to the pursuit of 'maximum employment, production and purchasing power'. These commitments in both the UK and the USA were of great symbolic significance although they lacked specific discussion of how such objectives were to be attained. In the case of the UK, Keynes thought that the Beveridge target of an average level of unemployment of 3 per cent was far too optimistic although there was 'no harm in trying' (see Hutchison, 1977). Nevertheless the post-war prosperity enjoyed in the advanced economies was assumed to be in large part the direct result of Keynesian stabilization policies. In the words of James Tobin, the United States' most prominent Keynesian economist:

> A strong case can be made for the success of Keynesian policies. Virtually all advanced democratic capitalist societies adopted, in varying degrees, Keynesian strategies of demand management after World War Two. The period, certainly until 1973, was one of unparalleled prosperity, growth, expansion of world trade, and stability. Unemployment was low, and the business cycle was tamed. (Tobin, 1987)

In a similar vein Michael Stewart (1986) has argued that:

> the common sense conclusion is that Britain and other Western countries had full employment for a quarter of a century after the war because their governments

were committed to full employment, and knew how to secure it; and they knew how to secure it because Keynes had told them how.

Underlying these statements is the implicit acceptance of the consensus view that the severity of business cycles in the period since 1945 has actually declined compared to previous periods. Recently research carried out by Christina Romer has challenged this conventional wisdom. In a series of papers Romer (1986a, 1986b, 1986c) has argued that the available historical data give a misleading picture, overstating the volatility of pre-war unemployment, GNP and industrial production. If Romer is right then obviously post-war Keynesian policies have not achieved as much as has been claimed for them and the stabilization of the unemployment rate 'between the pre 1930 and post 1948 eras is an artefact of improvements in data collection procedures' (Romer, 1986a, p. 1). Romer's work, not surprisingly, has come in for a great deal of criticism. DeLong and Summers (1986) suggest that 'deficiencies in the data lead us to *underestimate* rather than overestimate the extent of cyclical variation in the pre-World War I [US] economy'. In a comprehensive analysis of historical data, Balke and Gordon (1989) have also provided effective support for the traditional view. Sheffrin's (1989) comparative study shows that for the USA, by all measures, the pre-war period is more volatile than the post-war period, even when the Great Depression is excluded. However, in examining the evidence outside the USA Sheffrin finds that, except for Sweden, 'the data do not exhibit the dramatic decrease in the volatility of real economic activity that is present in the original data for the United States'. In a recent survey of business cycle research, Zarnowitz (1992a) provides support for the conventional view and concludes that the available evidence indicates that 'Even though economic growth decreased and cyclical instability increased in the latter part of the post-war era (since the early 1970s) business cycles remained moderate in comparison to the pre-World War I and, *a fortiori*, the interwar periods.' Furthermore, compared to the US economy, the 'post-war recessions are much fewer and generally milder still in France, Italy and particularly West Germany and Japan'.

Even if we accept the conventional view that the post-war economy has been more stable, not everyone would agree that there was a Keynesian revolution in economic policy (the opposing views are well represented in Stein, 1969; Robinson, 1972; Tomlinson, 1984; Booth, 1985; Salant, 1988). Some authors have also questioned whether it was the traditional Keynesian emphasis on fiscal policy that made the difference to economic performance in the period after 1945 (Matthews, 1968). What is not in doubt is that from the end of the Second World War until 1973 the industrial market economies enjoyed a golden age of unparalleled prosperity. Angus Maddison (1979,

1980) has identified several special characteristics which contributed to this 'golden age' of economic performance:

1. increased liberalization of international trade and transactions,
2. favourable circumstances and policies which contributed to producing low inflation in conditions of very buoyant aggregate demand,
3. active government promotion of buoyant domestic demand,
4. a backlog of growth possibilities following the end of the Second World War.

Whatever the causes, this golden age came to an end after 1973 and the economic problems of the 1970s brought the Keynesian bandwagon to an abrupt (but temporary) halt. The acceleration of inflation, rising unemployment and low economic growth (see Tables 1.2–1.4 and Figures 1.1–1.3) during the 1970s were attributed by Keynesian critics to the expansionary policies carried out in the name of Keynes. The legacy of the golden age of demand management was seen to be stagflation (see Cairncross and Cairncross, 1992, for a discussion of the legacy of the 1960s).

1.5 Theoretical Schizophrenia in Post-War Economics

What Keynes would have made of the Keynesian policies carried out in his name we can only speculate. What is now clear, with the benefit of hindsight and experience, is that at the theoretical level Keynesian economics created schizophrenia in the way that economics was taught, with courses in microeconomics typically concentrating on issues relating to allocation, production and distribution (questions of efficiency and equity) and courses in macroeconomics focusing on problems associated with the level and the long-term trend of aggregate output and employment, and the rate of inflation (questions of growth and stability). The Keynesian propositions of market failure and involuntary unemployment expounded within macroeconomics did not rest easily alongside the Walrasian theory of general competitive equilibrium where the actions of rational optimizing individuals ensure that all markets, including the labour market, are cleared by flexible prices. In the Walrasian model, which dominated microeconomics, lapses from full employment cannot occur. Although Paul Samuelson and others attempted to reconcile these two strands of economics, producing a 'neoclassical synthesis', Keynesian macroeconomics and orthodox neoclassical microeconomics integrated about as well as oil and water. During the 'golden age' this problem could be ignored. By 1973 it could not. As Greenwald and Stiglitz (1987) have argued, there were two ways in which the two sub-disciplines could be reconciled. Either macro theory could be adapted to micro theory (the new

A modern guide to macroeconomics

Table 1.2   Unemployment rates, 1964–92

	USA	Canada	Japan	France	Germany	Italy	UK
1964	5.0	4.3	1.1	1.4	0.4	4.3	2.6
1965	4.4	3.6	1.2	1.5	0.3	5.3	2.3
1966	3.6	3.3	1.3	1.8	0.2	5.7	2.2
1967	3.7	3.8	1.3	1.9	1.3	5.3	3.3
1968	3.5	4.4	1.2	2.7	1.5	5.6	3.1
1969	3.4	4.4	1.1	2.3	0.9	5.6	2.9
1970	4.8	5.6	1.1	2.5	0.8	5.3	3.0
1971	5.8	6.1	1.2	2.7	0.9	5.3	3.6
1972	5.5	6.2	1.4	2.8	0.8	6.3	4.0
1973	4.8	5.5	1.3	2.7	0.8	6.2	3.0
1974	5.5	5.3	1.4	2.8	1.6	5.3	2.9
1975	8.3	6.9	1.9	4.0	3.6	5.8	4.3
1976	7.6	7.1	2.0	4.4	3.7	6.6	5.6
1977	6.9	8.0	2.0	4.9	3.6	7.0	6.0
1978	6.0	8.3	2.2	5.2	3.5	7.1	5.9
1979	5.8	7.4	2.1	5.9	3.2	7.6	5.0
1980	7.0	7.4	2.0	6.3	2.9	7.5	6.4
1981	7.5	7.5	2.2	7.4	4.2	7.8	9.8
1982	9.5	10.9	2.4	8.1	5.9	8.4	11.3
1983	9.5	11.8	2.6	8.3	7.7	8.8	12.4
1984	7.4	11.2	2.7	9.7	7.1	9.4	11.7
1985	7.1	10.4	2.6	10.2	7.1	9.6	11.2
1986	6.9	9.5	2.8	10.4	6.4	10.5	11.2
1987	6.1	8.8	2.8	10.5	6.2	10.9	10.3
1988	5.4	7.7	2.5	10.0	6.2	11.0	8.6
1989	5.2	7.5	2.3	9.4	5.5	10.9	7.1
1990	5.4	8.1	2.1	8.9	4.9	10.3	6.8
1991	6.6	10.2	2.1	9.4	4.4	9.9	8.7
1992	7.3	11.2	2.2	10.2	4.8	10.5	9.9

Notes: Standardized unemployment rates (percentage of total labour force).

Source: OECD, *Economic Outlook*, various issues.

Table 1.3 Inflation rates, 1964–92

	USA	Canada	Japan	France	Germany	Italy	UK
1964	1.3	1.8	3.8	3.1	2.3	5.9	3.2
1965	1.7	2.5	6.6	2.7	3.2	4.4	4.8
1966	3.0	3.7	5.1	2.6	3.6	3.2	3.9
1967	2.8	3.6	4.0	2.8	1.6	0.5	2.4
1968	4.2	4.1	5.4	4.6	1.6	1.5	4.7
1969	5.4	4.5	5.2	6.1	1.9	2.4	5.5
1970	5.9	3.4	7.7	5.9	3.4	5.0	6.4
1971	4.3	2.8	6.4	5.5	5.2	4.9	9.4
1972	3.3	4.8	4.9	6.2	5.5	5.8	7.1
1973	6.2	7.6	11.7	7.3	7.0	10.8	9.2
1974	11.0	10.9	23.1	13.7	7.0	19.1	15.9
1975	9.1	10.8	11.8	11.8	5.9	16.9	24.2
1976	5.7	7.5	9.4	9.6	4.3	16.8	16.5
1977	6.5	8.0	8.2	9.4	3.7	18.3	15.9
1978	7.6	8.9	4.1	9.1	2.7	12.1	8.2
1979	11.3	9.1	3.8	10.8	4.1	14.8	13.5
1980	13.5	10.2	7.8	13.3	5.4	21.2	18.0
1981	10.3	12.5	4.9	13.4	6.3	19.5	11.9
1982	6.2	10.8	2.7	11.8	5.3	16.5	8.6
1983	3.2	5.8	1.9	9.6	3.3	14.7	4.6
1984	4.3	4.3	2.2	7.4	2.4	10.8	5.0
1985	3.6	4.0	2.0	5.8	2.2	9.2	6.1
1986	1.9	4.2	0.6	2.5	–0.1	5.8	3.4
1987	3.7	4.4	0.1	3.3	0.2	4.7	4.1
1988	4.0	4.0	0.7	2.7	1.3	5.1	4.9
1989	4.8	5.0	2.3	3.5	2.8	6.3	7.8
1990	5.4	4.8	3.1	3.4	2.7	6.4	9.5
1991	4.2	5.6	3.3	3.2	3.5	6.4	5.9
1992	3.0	1.5	1.7	2.4	4.0	5.2	3.7

Notes: Percentage change over previous year of consumer prices (calculated from indexes).

Source: International Monetary Fund, *International Financial Statistics: Yearbook*, 1993.

A modern guide to macroeconomics

Table 1.4   Growth rates, 1964–92

	USA	Canada	Japan	France	Germany	Italy	UK
1964	5.7	6.7	11.4	6.5	6.6	2.8	5.2
1965	5.6	6.6	5.8	4.8	5.3	3.3	2.3
1966	5.9	6.8	10.5	5.2	2.9	6.0	2.1
1967	2.6	2.9	10.9	4.7	−0.2	7.2	2.8
1968	4.1	5.4	12.1	4.3	5.6	6.5	4.2
1969	2.7	5.4	12.1	7.0	7.6	6.1	1.4
1970	−0.1	2.6	10.3	5.7	5.1	5.3	2.4
1971	3.2	5.8	4.4	4.8	3.1	—	2.8
1972	4.8	5.7	8.3	4.4	4.2	4.3	2.4
1973	5.4	7.7	7.7	5.4	4.7	7.1	7.9
1974	−0.5	4.4	−0.8	3.1	0.1	5.0	−1.0
1975	−1.1	2.6	2.9	−0.3	−1.2	−2.7	−0.7
1976	5.1	6.2	4.2	4.2	5.5	6.3	3.7
1977	4.6	3.6	4.8	3.2	2.5	3.7	1.0
1978	4.8	4.6	5.0	3.3	3.5	3.7	3.8
1979	2.8	3.9	5.6	3.2	4.1	6.0	2.3
1980	−0.6	1.5	3.5	1.6	1.0	4.2	−1.9
1981	1.6	3.7	3.4	1.2	—	0.5	−1.1
1982	−2.3	−3.2	3.4	2.5	−1.1	0.3	1.3
1983	3.8	3.2	2.8	0.7	1.8	−0.4	3.8
1984	6.0	6.3	4.3	1.3	3.1	4.1	1.6
1985	2.9	4.8	5.1	1.9	2.1	2.7	3.7
1986	2.8	3.3	2.7	2.5	2.2	2.8	4.0
1987	3.0	4.3	4.4	2.3	1.4	3.1	4.6
1988	4.0	4.9	6.2	4.5	3.7	4.1	4.4
1989	2.4	2.3	4.8	4.3	4.0	2.9	2.1
1990	1.1	−0.5	4.8	2.5	4.9	2.1	0.5
1991	−1.2	−1.7	4.1	0.7	3.6	1.3	−2.2
1992	2.0	0.9	1.5	1.3	0.8	0.9	−0.6

Note: Percentage change over previous year of GDP at constant prices (calculated from indexes).

Source: International Monetary Fund, *International Financial Statistics: Yearbook*, 1993.

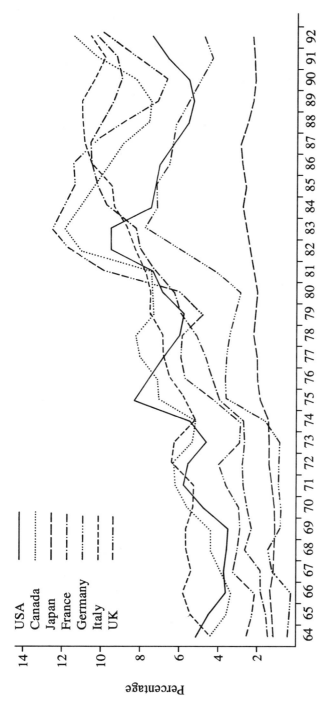

Note: Standardized unemployment rates (percentage of total labour force).

Source: OECD, *Economic Outlook*, various issues.

Figure 1.1 Unemployment rates, 1964–92

15

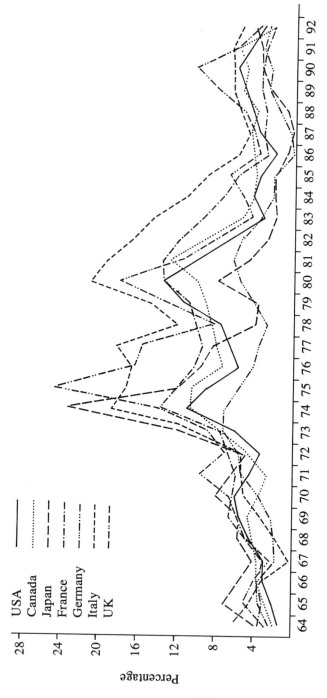

Notes: Percentage change over previous year of consumer prices (calculated from indexes).

Source: International Monetary Fund, *International Financial Statistics: Yearbook*, 1993.

Figure 1.2 Inflation rates, 1964–92

16

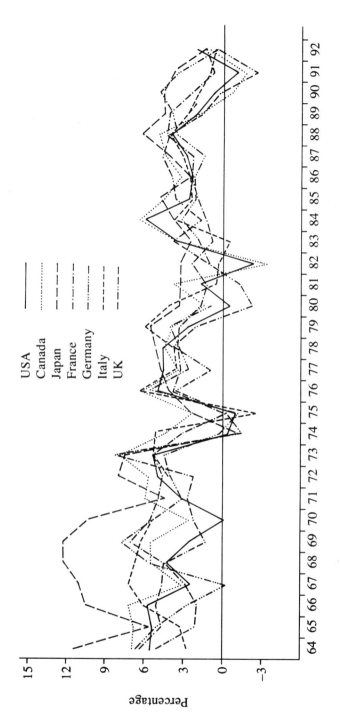

Note: Percentage change over previous year of GDP at constant prices (calculated from indexes).

Source: International Monetary Fund, *International Financial Statistics: Yearbook,* 1993.

Figure 1.3 Growth rates, 1964–92

classical approach) or micro theory could be adapted to macro theory (the new Keynesian approach). As we shall see, these attempts at reconciliation have dominated macroeconomic theorizing during the past two decades.

Keynes himself had contributed to this dichotomy because he saw 'no reason to suppose that the existing system seriously misemploys the factors of production which are in use... It is in determining the volume, not the direction, of actual employment that the existing system has broken down' (Keynes, 1936, p. 379). In other words, the apparent inability of the capitalist system to provide for full employment was the main blemish on an economic system which Keynes otherwise held in high regard. Once this major defect was remedied and full employment restored, 'the classical theory comes into its own again from this point onwards' and there 'is no objection to be raised against classical analysis of the manner in which private self-interest will determine what in particular is produced, in what proportions the factors of production will be combined to produce it, and how the value of the final product will be distributed between them' (Keynes, 1936, pp. 378–9). Thus Keynes can be viewed as attempting to reconcile two opposing views of a capitalist market economy. First, we have the classical–neoclassical view which extols the efficiency of the price mechanism in solving the fundamental allocation and production problems which arise from the scarcity of resources. Second, we have Keynes's iconoclastic vision which highlights the shortcomings of the invisible hand, at least with respect to the general level of output and employment. Keynes was optimistic that this later problem could be solved with limited government intervention, and capitalism could be saved from itself.

1.6   The Neoclassical Synthesis

The synthesis of the ideas of the classical economists with those of Keynes dominated mainstream economics at least until the early 1970s. The standard textbook approach to macroeconomics from the period following the Second World War until the early 1970s relied heavily on the interpretation of the *General Theory* provided by Hicks (1937) and modified by the contributions of Modigliani (1944), Patinkin (1956) and Tobin (1958). Samuelson's best-selling textbook popularized the synthesis of Keynesian and classical ideas, making them accessible to a wide readership and successive generations of students. It was Samuelson who introduced the label 'neoclassical synthesis' into the literature in the third edition of *Economics*, in 1955. This synthesis of classical and Keynesian ideas became the standard approach to macroeconomic analysis, both in textbooks and in professional discussion (see Chapter 3). The orthodox Keynesian model provided the foundation for the large-scale macroeconometric models developed by Lawrence Klein and also those associated with the Cowles Commission. Such models were used for forecasting purposes and to enable economists to assess the likely impact on the economy of alternative economic policies. Lucas and Sargent (1978) have attributed the 'dominant scientific position' that orthodox Keynesian economics attained by 1960 to the fact that it 'lent itself so readily to the formulation of explicit econometric models'. As far as macroeconomics was concerned, for the majority of researchers in the 1960s, the 'Keynesian model was the only game in town' (Barro, 1989a).

The orthodox Keynesian argument that government intervention, in the form of activist monetary and fiscal policy, could correct the aggregate instability exhibited by market economies also influenced political decision makers. Both Labour and Conservative parties in the UK adhered to Keynesian principles. In the USA it was not until the early 1960s that the Keynesian approach (known as the 'New Economics') was adopted with any real enthusiasm. The Council of Economic Advisors (CEA) appointed by President Kennedy was dominated by Keynesian economists. Chaired by Walter Heller, the CEA also included James Tobin and Robert Solow. Paul Samuelson served as an unofficial advisor. By 1971 even President Nixon had declared 'we are all Keynesians now!'

Prior to the 1970s the Keynesian approach gave emphasis to demand-side factors. Keynes had reversed Say's Law and Keynesianism based on the IS–LM interpretation of Keynes was the established orthodoxy in macroeconomics (see Chapter 3, and Patinkin, 1990a, for a discussion of the IS–LM interpretation of Keynes). Initially Keynesianism was associated with fiscalism but by the late 1960s the importance of monetary factors was widely recognized by Keynesians (see Tobin, 1987). The most important Keynesian development during this period was the incorporation of the Phillips curve into the prevailing macroeconomic model (see Phillips, 1958; Lipsey, 1978). By the early 1960s the IS–LM model was being used to explain the determination of output and employment, while the Phillips curve enabled the policy maker to predict the rate of inflation which would result from different target levels of unemployment. The simultaneous increase in both unemployment and inflation (shown in Figures 1.1 and 1.2) in the major industrial economies in the early 1970s proved fatal to the more simplistic versions of 'hydraulic' Keynesianism and prepared the way for the monetarist and new classical counter-revolutions (see Johnson, 1971; Bleaney, 1985; Colander, 1988). The 1970s witnessed a significant renaissance of the pre-Keynesian belief that the market economy is capable of achieving macroeconomic stability and rapid growth providing the visible (and palsied) hand of government is prevented from conducting activist discretionary fiscal and monetary policies. The stagflation of the 1970s gave increasing credibility and influence to those economists who had for many years warned that Keynesian macroeconomic policies were both over-ambitious and, more importantly, predicated on theories which were fundamentally flawed (see Friedman, 1968a; Hayek, 1978a; Buchanan, Burton and Wagner, 1978; Lucas and Sargent, 1978).

The demise of the neoclassical synthesis mainstream position signalled the beginning of a period when the dominance of Keynesian macroeconomics came to an end and, as we have seen, the breakdown of this consensus position was due to both empirical and theoretical flaws (see Mankiw, 1990). For the more extreme critics the task facing the new generation of macroeconomic theorists was to 'sort through the wreckage determining which features of that remarkable intellectual event called the Keynesian revolution can be salvaged and put to good use and which others must be discarded' (Lucas and Sargent, 1978). In the process of sorting through the wreckage no one school has managed to dominate the others in terms of theoretical and empirical success. But according to Hoover (1988) there is no question that the 'undisputed reign of Keynesian economics is over'.

1.7   Methodological Issues

Economists have been keen to draw on ideas imported from the philosophy of science in order to account for the historical development and current standing of their discipline (or aspects of it). A leading conclusion of these 'growth of knowledge' theories is that the evaluation and appraisal of theories, paradigms, research programmes or traditions is a comparative matter that must be done within a comparative context and that effective criticism and appreciation can only be carried out when there exist real alternatives for comparison (see Laudan, 1977; Lakatos, 1978; Feyerabend, 1978). Within economics itself, Caldwell's (1982) argument in favour of methodological pluralism places a premium upon dialogue between rival frameworks since comparative methodological evaluation depends upon a willingness to examine one's opponents critically on their own terms and to open oneself up to criticism from without. Arguments such as these support and sustain the rationale behind the present book that an improved understanding of contemporary macroeconomics can only be gleaned by attending to such matters as diversity and disagreement head-on.

The 'growth of knowledge' theories associated with Popper (1959), Kuhn (1970) and Lakatos (1978) have been applied by economists as models for the development of their subject. That they have proved useful in highlighting certain aspects of our intellectual experience merits our attention. Popper (1959) pointed to a logical asymmetry between verification and falsification, arguing that, whilst we cannot prove theories by means of confirmation, we can disprove theories by refutation. The practice of critical rationalism and falsification is eventually what demarcates science from non- or pseudoscience. However the growth of economic knowledge has not followed the falsificationist path – there is no evidence of serious Popperian falsificationism in economics, no major crucial experiments or sustained attempted refutations. In economics there appear to be no quick methodological kills, rather we observe the acceptance of new ideas *without* the complete rejection of the old.

Kuhn's (1970) central thesis that the development of science is characterized by periods of continuity and progress (normal science) leading to the recognition of serious anomaly (crisis) and the possibility of discontinuity (revolution) has been widely adopted and applied by economists to their own discipline. This is hardly surprising, given that economists, long before Kuhn, often cast the development of their subject in revolutionary terms (see Johnson, 1971). The most fundamental (and ambiguous) concept advanced in Kuhn's thesis on the way science develops is his notion of the *paradigm*. He has tended to stress and uphold two important aspects of the term, namely, *disciplinary matrix* and *exemplars*, with the former standing for 'the entire constellation of beliefs, values, techniques, and so on shared by members of a given community' and the latter representing the concrete problem or puzzle solutions (see Kuhn, 1970, p. 175). We may view a paradigm as a worldview, vision or framework. In Kuhn's approach, a discipline reaches maturity when there is a transition toward a consensus of approach and shared group commitment to an agreed outlook. What was once marked by dispute, discord and competing schools is now unity, harmony and agreement. The development of science involves the successive transition from one monopoly (or dominant) paradigm to another via revolution. Such revolutions are seen as a reaction to the malfunctioning of normal science. Kuhn's theoretical innovation is both constructive as well as destructive, given that paradigm replacement involves complete surrender of the old and victory of the new. Another feature is the communication failure which exists between paradigms which represent fundamentally different ways of seeing the world. The participants talk past each other since they face insurmountable translation difficulties. Unlike Popper's methodology, where criticism is to be welcomed and there is permanent revolution, Kuhn emphasizes tenacity and the commitment to defend a paradigm from attack. No paradigm is surrendered lightly or until a viable alternative exists. Revolutions are seen to be occasional occurrences marked by a temporary period of intense competition between paradigms.

Economics appears to fit Kuhn's model of art rather better than his model of science (see Kuhn, 1977, pp. 340–51). In economics the end of controversy is more usually marked by an acceptance of the new without the destruction of the old. Complete victory is rare, which allows the possibility of a comeback or revival of the old, for example the recent classical revival led by Robert Lucas. Economics, not unlike Kuhn's presentation of art, supports more readily a number of simultaneously incompatible traditions or schools. Since economic ideas display a great deal of tenacity and as it is terribly difficult to kill an economic theory, we have a tendency to retain rather than reject. What seem to be outmoded ideas never appear to be totally displaced (with regard to the Keynesian experience, see, for example, Rowley, 1983, 1984; Snowdon and Wynarczyk, 1984, 1985).

Attempts to apply Kuhn to economics in general (Routh, 1977) or to macroeconomics (Dow, 1985) or to the Keynesian episode (Mehta, 1977) have not been entirely successful, since they fail to apply Kuhn strictly on his own terms where he is unable to account for important concrete developments in the discipline, such as the rehabilitation of Say's Law or the revival of the quantity theory of money. Kuhn's framework is too extreme in arguing for both the totality of communication failure and the totality of paradigm replacement. A Kuhnian interpretation of contemporary macroeconomics would have to conclude either that the subject was in a period of crisis following the breakdown of the Keynesian consensus or that it had never achieved the status of a mature science, given the continued existence of rival positions both before and after Keynes.

In Lakatos's (1978) methodology of scientific research programmes, attention is shifted away from an isolated theory or hypothesis towards a series or succession of theories which are genetically linked together. Lakatos provides an objective reconstruction of Kuhn's paradigm by presenting the structure of a scientific research programme composed of the main building-blocks of hard core, positive heuristic and a vast protective belt of auxiliary hypotheses. Research programmes are characterized by their hard core, which spells out a fundamental set of statements about the world, consisting of deep and fertile hypotheses which are conventionally accepted as irrefutable (see Worrall, 1978; Musgrave, 1976). No internal investigation of the hard core is permitted: it is forbidden by the negative heuristic of the programme which tells us what paths of research to avoid. One cannot test the hard core directly, although testable theories are built around it. Examples of hard core propositions within macroeconomics are Keynes's replacement of the classical and neoclassical belief in rational economic calculation based upon certainty equivalence with pervasive uncertainty, or the Keynesian and monetarist hard core disagreements over the self-adjusting ability of the private sector, the virtues of state intervention, and the impact and potency of fiscal and monetary policy (see Blaug, 1976). As Leijonhufvud (1976, p. 71) recognizes, monetarism includes the 'belief' or hard core proposition that 'the economic system will exhibit strong tendencies to converge relatively rapidly to the equilibrium values of its real variables and that the equilibrium values, most specifically of employment and real interest rates, are (to a first approximation, at least) independent of general monetary and fiscal stabilization policies'. The *positive heuristic* of a research programme tells us what paths of research to pursue; it is the driving force which guides the production of specific theories by providing a future research outline, strategy or agenda. The basic positive heuristic of orthodox Keynesianism is seen as the endeavour to 'explain fluctuations in output and employment by analysing fluctuations in the aggregate demand for output' whilst that of orthodox monetarism is to explain 'sustained variations in the rate of inflation by sustained prior variations in the rate of monetary expansion' (Cross, 1982a, pp. 18–19). The hard core and positive heuristic provide the metaphysical principles which define the research programme, whilst the negative and positive heuristics furnish us with a rough definition of a conceptual framework.

Research programmes can be either progressive or degenerative. The notion of progress is crucially linked to the concept of *novel fact*, which plays the decisive role in the Lakatosian enterprise. In order for a research programme to be appraised as progressive or degenerative it is necessary to assess not only whether it is theoretically progressive – does it display excess empirical content over its rivals by predicting novel facts? – but also whether it is empirically progressive – is some of the excess empirical content corroborated so that new novel facts are actually discovered? The growth of objective knowledge occurs when progressive research programmes are able to triumph over degenerating ones. For example, Cross (1982b, p. 329) has suggested that monetarism was both theoretically and empirically progressive in the early 1970s, given its general incorporation of the open economy dimension, whilst Keynesian economics became theoretically degenerate in the late 1960s, following its attempt to explain inflation in non-economic terms after the demise of the simple Phillips curve. Unfortunately the concept of novel fact, not unlike that of paradigm, has proved to be especially problematical (for an interesting illustration of this point in connection with the Keynesian episode, see the debate between Hands, 1985 and Blaug, 1991). This is serious for the Lakatosian framework which links the production of novel facts to progress so that 'the idea of growth and the concept of empirical character are soldered into one' (Lakatos, 1978, p. 35). Further Lakatos lacks a robust historical time dimension for appraisal to work to the extent that he expects.

Leaving aside such problems as these, the Lakatosian methodology has proved to be popular amongst economists for several reasons, not least of which is its emphasis upon competition between rivals and their fluctuating fortunes, with its allowance of comebacks for previously degenerating programmes. The numerous interpretations and applications of Lakatos to economics remain a matter of some disagreement (Fulton, 1984; Hands, 1985), but we have had, amongst others, Lakatosian interpretations of the Keynesian revolution (Leijonhufvud, 1976; Blaug, 1976, 1991), the controversy and debate in macroeconomics (Cross, 1982a, 1982b) as well as application at the discipline-wide level (Blaug, 1980). Lakatos, unfortunately, has a strictly empirical criterion of progress which does not fit economics because it is unable to capture some of its best gambits as progressive, given its neglect of conceptual matters.

Laudan's (1977) problem-solving orientation offers greater promise, although its detailed application to economics remains generally underexplored (see Wynarczyk, 1990, pp. 333–404). His approach emphasizes the comparative and historical context of appraisal by drawing attention to the contemporaneous competition between rivals. Laudan's problem-solving model acknowledges both the coexistence and equal importance of conceptual and empirical problems, with progress measured in terms not only of increasing empirical support but also of the elimination of conceptual difficulties. According to Laudan the value of a theory or research tradition depends upon how many problems it solves relative to its competitors, solved problems acting as assets and unresolved problems as liabilities. There is a need to weigh up the gains and losses. To that end, Laudan (1981, p. 149) has proposed that we adopt a cost–benefit approach where we weigh the relative importance of the problems being faced and the adequacy of the proposed solutions.

Whilst the solved empirical or conceptual problem is the basic unit of scientific progress, Laudan makes the research tradition, rather than the individual theory, the primary focus of attention. Each research tradition 'exhibits certain metaphysical and methodological commitments' and provides guidelines for theory development and the legitimate methods of inquiry. Although a research tradition is composed of a number of specific theories, it is more comprehensive and general than a Lakatosian research programme (different research programmes can belong to the same research tradition) and suffers from less ambiguity than a Kuhnian paradigm. Research traditions tend to be enduring entities displaying considerable longevity and an ability to survive the demise of some of their constituent theories (the latter are considerably more prone to replacement and abandonment). Laudan's research traditions and their constituent theories coexist with their rivals in an environment of permanent competition and continuous appraisal and evaluation. Attention is shifted away from periods of intellectual continuity or discontinuity towards the permanent coexistence of a variety of rival conflicting research traditions. Emphasis upon successful knowledge communication between rivals partly depends upon the fact that different theories and research traditions can deal with the same problems. Laudan maintains that it is far more usual to find problems which are common to a number of competing theories or research traditions than to find those which are strictly exclusive. This is certainly the case within macroeconomics, where we find the continuing coexistence of rival explanations of fluctuations in output, employment and the price level.

We shall find that some of the insights provided by the methodology literature can help us in our understanding of the complex developments which have characterized the evolution of macroeconomics in the post-war era.

1.8 The Use of Rhetoric in Economists' Discourse

Alongside the importing of these ideas into economics there has also been a growth of interest in the language of economists, what Klamer, McCloskey and Solow (1988) refer to as the 'new conversation' about economics. According to Klamer and McCloskey (1988, p. 10) the *rhetoric* of economists refers to 'the whole art and science of argument, the honest persuasion that is good conversation'. By taking into account the importance of rhetoric in economists' discourse we are recognizing the importance of the persuasiveness of an argument which is often not just a matter of appeal to logic or available empirical evidence. McCloskey's (1983, 1985) work has stimulated interest in the study of the way people persuade and Goodwin (1988) has drawn attention to the heterogeneity of the economists' discourse. In relation to this point, David Laidler (1992a), in commenting on the rise of real business cycle theory during the 1980s, notes that rhetoric has been central to the debate between equilibrium theorists and economists who prefer monetary explanations of the business cycle. He notes with some cynicism that 'recent developments in business cycle theory provide a striking example of the power of the right words to draw attention to an idea. Who ... could resist the appeal of a "real" theory of the business cycle? How could it fail to be better than, shall we say, a "mythical" theory?'

The use of rhetoric, or the art of persuasion, is not new in economics. After all it was Keynes, more than any other economist, who wrote in the spirit of persuasion in order to try and influence opinion. His *Economic Consequences of the Peace* (1919) and *Essays in Persuasion* (1931) contain ample evidence to support Skidelsky's (1992) observation that the 'mastery of science *and* words was to be the basis of all his achievements'. Keynes's powers of persuasion and rhetoric are legendary and it is no surprise to find him confident in the anticipation that his *General Theory* would 'largely revolutionise ... the way the world thinks about economics'. In his concluding comments in that book, Keynes made clear his conviction 'that the ideas of economists and political philosophers ... are more powerful than is normally understood' and it is 'ideas not vested interests which are dangerous for good or evil' (Keynes, 1936, p. 384). Skidelsky writes that Keynes's greatness as an economist was his 'combination of intellect and charm of incantation in the service of moderation' (Skidelsky, 1992, p. 521). Keynes was the supreme example of a literary craftsman who believed that 'words ought to be a little wild', given that they are 'the assault of thought on the unthinking' (Johnson, 1973, p. 15). It is perhaps paradoxical that the *General Theory*, Keynes's most influential work, should draw the most criticism for its style. The *General Theory* is 'not what one settles down to in anticipation of a good read in bed' (Johnson, 1978).

Despite Keynes's mathematical background his hostility to the mathematization of economic analysis is well known. Neither was he an enthusiastic advocate of the general equilibrium methodology of Walras. It is ironic that within months of publication the language of the *General Theory* was being translated into determinate simultaneous equations by Hicks, Harrod and Meade (see Skidelsky, 1992, p. 613). For once Keynes's powers of persuasion had failed. That the mathematically elegant IS–LM curves might be mere straws in the winds of uncertainty could not prevent Keynes's younger disciples from interpreting his ideas in a language which he viewed with great suspicion. In order to digest the *General Theory*, the qualifications and complexities which Keynes was careful to point out were pushed to one side so that the mathematical language of general equilibrium theory could be unleashed. To the technically minded younger generation of economists the emergence of quantitative Keynesian macroeconomics was a form of language with great appeal. Thirty years later the rhetoric of 'rational' as opposed to 'irrational' expectations also played a large part in persuading the new generation of technically equipped economists to forge a new classical revolution.

Klamer (1984) has explored some of the communication problems which clearly exist between macroeconomists, especially appertaining to the new classical developments. His conversations with leading macroeconomists, which took place over a decade ago, provide some fascinating insights into the major areas of disagreement, diversity of argument and lack of communication which exist at the highest level. Klamer's main contention is that 'economists are not at all wholly detached, but are committed from the start to a point of view which they will support with different types of argument'. The present work follows this line of inquiry and traces the evolution and development of macroeconomics following Keynes's contribution. By presenting interviews with some of the leading figures in modern macroeconomics, we wish to highlight some of the important divisions which exist. In our comparative approach we endeavour to draw out and identify the connections and divides between the various schools of thought as well as the potential areas of communication success and failure.

1.9 Schools of Thought in Modern Macroeconomics

According to Johnson (1971), 'by far the most helpful circumstance for the rapid propagation of a new revolutionary theory is the existence of an established orthodoxy which is clearly inconsistent with the most salient facts of reality'. As we have seen, the inability of the classical model to account adequately for the collapse of output and employment in the 1930s paved the way for the Keynesian revolution. During the 1950s and 1960s the neoclassical synthesis became the accepted wisdom for the majority of economists (see Chapter 3). The work of Nobel Laureates, James Tobin, Lawrence Klein, Robert Solow, Franco Modigliani, James Meade, John Hicks and Paul Samuelson dominated the Keynesian school and provided intellectual support for the view that government intervention in the form of demand management can significantly improve the performance of the economy. The 'New Economics' adopted by the Kennedy administration demonstrated the influence of Keynesian thinking and the 1962 *Economic Report of the President* explicitly advocated stabilization policies with the objective of keeping 'overall demand in step with the basic production potential of the economy'.

However, in turn, Keynesianism also became ripe for attack and the monetarist counter-revolution based its comeback on the apparent failure of orthodox Keynesian theory to account adequately for the growing problem of inflation (see Chapter 4). To trace the origins of the monetarist counter-revolution and the subsequent classical revival in macroeconomics it is necessary to examine the influential work of Nobel Laureate Milton Friedman and his followers. From the late 1950s onwards his ideas were exerting an increasing influence on fellow economists. In the UK during the early 1970s the work of David Laidler and Michael Parkin, together with the influence of Harry Johnson, helped the propagation of monetarist ideas (see Johnson, 1972b; Laidler and Parkin, 1975). Other notable advocates of the monetarist approach include Karl Brunner, Alan Meltzer and Mrs Thatcher's economic advisor, Alan Walters. During this period, especially in the USA, it seemed that Keynesians under the age of 40 were becoming an endangered species (see Blinder, 1988a). But soon the monetarist critiques were overtaken by a tidal wave of new classical contributions. So powerful was this new anti-Keynesian virus that by the mid-1970s new classical macroeconomics had become the main alternative to Keynesianism (see Chapter 5). One important reason for the decline in the prominence of monetarism within the theoretical debate is that most of the plausible monetarist ideas had been absorbed, in a diluted form, into mainstream Keynesian analysis (see Mayer, 1990; Blinder, 1992a; Laidler, 1992a). Notwithstanding this development, by the late 1970s, particularly in the USA, it even began to look as though new classical macroeconomics might become the new mainstream position. The new

classical school, inspired by the pioneering and innovative work of Robert
Lucas (1972, 1973) includes among its leading advocates Thomas Sargent,
Neil Wallace, Robert Barro, Edward Prescott and Patrick Minford (see Hoover, 1988). Initially new classical macroeconomics was regarded as a variant
of monetarism, with James Tobin (1981) referring to this school as monetarism mark II (see also Hoover, 1984). It is now evident that the new classical
school is best regarded as a separate body of thought, particularly with
respect to the methodology and assumptions adopted. This is especially true
of the more recent varieties of new classical macroeconomics associated with
the real business cycle school which give emphasis to real supply-side factors
rather than to monetary impulses in their explanation of aggregate instability
(see Chapter 6). The most recent real equilibrium business cycle theories are
particularly associated with the pioneering work of Kydland and Prescott
(1982) and Long and Plosser (1983).

The new classical equilibrium approach has in turn been challenged by a
revitalized group of new Keynesian theorists who prefer to adapt micro to
macro theory rather than accept the new classical approach of adapting
macro theory to orthodox neoclassical market-clearing microfoundations.
Important figures here include George Akerlof, Janet Yellen, Olivier Blanchard,
Gregory Mankiw, Edmund Phelps, David Romer, Joseph Stiglitz and Ben
Bernanke (see Mankiw and Romer, 1991 and Chapter 7).

Finally we can identify two further groups or schools of thought. The work
of Ludwig von Mises and Nobel Laureate Friedrich von Hayek has inspired a
distinctly Austrian approach to economic analysis and in particular to the
explanation of business cycle phenomena (see Chapter 8). Modern advocates
of the Austrian approach include Israel Kirzner, Karen Vaughn and Roger
Garrison. There is also a school of thought descended from some of Keynes's
more radical contemporaries and disciples. The Post-Keynesian school has
derived its inspiration and distinctive approach from the writings of Joan
Robinson, Nicholas Kaldor, Michael Kalecki, George Shackle and Piero
Sraffa (see Chapter 8). Modern advocates of this approach include Paul
Davidson, Jan Kregel, Victoria Chick and Hyman Minsky.

To recap, we identify the following schools of thought in modern
macroeconomics: (1) Orthodox Keynesianism (Chapter 3), (2) Monetarism
(Chapter 4), (3) New Classical Macroeconomics Mark I (Chapter 5), (4) New
Classical Macroeconomics Mark II – Real Business Cycle Theory (Chapter
6), (5) New Keynesian Economics (Chapter 7) and (6) Austrian and Post-
Keynesian Economics (Chapter 8). No doubt other economists would choose
a different classification, and some have done so (see Cross, 1982a; Phelps,
1990). We are also acutely aware of the dangers of categorizing particular
economists in ways which are bound to oversimplify the sophistication and
breadth of their own views. As Kevin Hoover (1988) has observed in a

similar enterprise, 'Any economist is described most fully by a vector of characteristics' and any definition will 'emphasise some elements of this vector, while playing down related ones'. With these caveats in mind we will examine in the chapters which follow the competing schools of macroeconomic thought identified above. We also include interviews with some of the economists who are generally recognized as being leading representatives of each group and prominent in the development of macroeconomic analysis in the post-war period. In discussing these various schools of thought it is important to remember that the work of Keynes remains the 'main single point of reference, either positive or negative, for all the schools of macroeconomics'. All of the schools define themselves in relation to the ideas originally put forward by Keynes in his *General Theory*, 'either as a development of some version of his thought or as a restoration of some version of pre-Keynesian classical thought' (Vercelli, 1991, p. 3).

Before considering the important features of the old classical model and Keynes's critique, we will finally review the main business cycle 'stylized facts' which play an important part in the evaluation of alternative macroeconomic theories.

1.10 Explaining the 'Stylized Facts'

As we have noted earlier, the main objective of macroeconomic analysis is to explain the phenomena of aggregate movements of output, employment and the price level. We have also drawn attention to the variety of research programmes or schools of thought which have emerged during the past 25 years which attempt to explain such movements. Any assessment of a particular theory must take into account its ability to explain the 'stylized facts' which characterize macroeconomic phenomena (see Greenwald and Stiglitz, 1988). By 'stylized facts' we mean the broad regularities which have been identified in the statistical property of economic time series. The identification of the major 'stylized facts' relating to business cycle phenomena is a legitimate field of enquiry in its own right (see Zarnowitz, 1992b). In the USA the National Bureau of Economic Research, founded in 1920, has pioneered research into business cycle phenomena, the landmark work being *Measuring Business Cycles* by Arthur Burns and Wesley Mitchell, published in 1946. In this book Burns and Mitchell provide the classic definition of business cycles:

> Business cycles are a type of fluctuation found in the aggregate economic activity of nations that organise their work mainly in business enterprises. A cycle consists of expansions occurring at about the same time in many economic activities, followed by similarly general recessions, contractions, and revivals which merge into the expansion phase of the next cycle; this sequence of changes is recurrent

but not periodic, in duration business cycles vary from more than one year to ten or twelve years.

The identification by Burns and Mitchell and subsequent research of co-movements of economic variables behaving in a predictable way over the course of the business cycle has led some researchers to claim that 'business cycles are all alike' and this is attractive to the theorist because 'it suggests the possibility of a unified explanation of business cycles grounded in the general laws governing market economies' (Lucas, 1977, p. 10). Although many economists would not go this far it is obvious that theoretical explanations of business cycle phenomena must be generally guided by the identified statistical properties of the co-movements of deviations from trend of the various economic aggregates with those of real GDP. How well a particular theory is capable of accounting for the major stylized facts of the business cycle will be a principal means of evaluating that theory. As Abel and Bernanke (1992, p. 331) have argued, 'to be completely successful, a theory of the business cycle should be able to explain not just the cyclical behaviour of a few variables such as output and employment but also the cyclical patterns found in other important economic variables'. What are these key business cycle 'stylized facts' which any viable macroeconomic theory must confront? Here we present only a brief summary of the findings (for a more detailed discussion, see Lucas, 1981; Blanchard and Fischer, 1989; Abel and Bernanke, 1992; Zarnowitz, 1992a).

Within macroeconomics there is a great deal of controversy about the causes of aggregate fluctuations in economic activity. However, according to Abel and Bernanke (1992), 'there is a reasonable amount of agreement about the basic empirical business cycle facts'. However, as we shall see, this 'agreement' about the 'stylized facts' has in recent years been seriously challenged, with important implications for our assessment of the competing theories. The main 'stylized facts' as summarized by Abel and Bernanke (1992), are as follows:

1. Output movements tend to be correlated across all sectors of the economy.
2. Industrial production, consumption and investment are procyclical and coincident. Government purchases also tend to be procyclical.
3. Investment is much more volatile over the course of the business cycle than consumption, although spending on consumer durables is strongly procyclical.
4. Employment is procyclical and unemployment counter-cyclical.
5. The real wage and average labour productivity are procyclical, although the real wage is only slightly procyclical.
6. The money supply and stock prices are procyclical and lead the cycle.

7. Inflation (and by implication the price level) and nominal interest rates are procyclical and lagging.
8. The real interest rate is acyclical.

In what follows we will return to some of these important issues, which in recent years have become an important source of controversy (see Kydland and Prescott, 1990; Barro, 1993; and Chapter 6). We will next review the essential features of the 'old' classical model which Keynes attacked in his *General Theory*. This important debate between Keynes and the classics sets the scene for the remaining chapters of this book.

STANLEY FISCHER

Stanley Fischer was born in Zambia in 1943 and took his BSc (Econ) and MSc (Econ) at the LSE during 1962–6, before obtaining his PhD at MIT in 1969. He taught at the University of Chicago until 1973, when he returned to MIT and where he became Professor of Economics in 1977. He has also held visiting positions at the Hebrew University, Jerusalem and at the Hoover Institution.

Among his best known books are: *Indexing, Inflation and Economic Policy* (MIT Press, 1986), *Economics* (McGraw-Hill, 2nd edn, 1988) co-written with Rudiger Dornbusch and Richard Schmalensee, *Lectures on Macroeconomics* (MIT Press, 1989) co-written with Olivier Blanchard, and the best-selling text *Macroeconomics* (McGraw-Hill, 6th edn, 1994) co-written with Rudiger Dornbusch.

His best known articles include: 'Long-Term Contracts, Rational Expectations, and the Optimal Money Supply Rule', *Journal of Political Economy* (1977), 'Towards an Understanding of the Real Effects and Costs of Inflation', *Weltwirtschaftliches Archiv* (1978) co-written with Franco Modigliani, 'Stopping Hyperinflation: Past and Present', *Weltwirtschaftliches Archiv* (1986) co-written with Rudiger Dornbusch, and 'Recent Developments in Macroeconomics', *Economic Journal* (1988).

We interviewed Professor Fischer in his office at MIT on 19 February 1993.

What are the important business cycle 'stylized facts' which a good macro-economic theory needs to explain?
Well the first fact is that there is a business cycle – that there are periods of booms and recessions. The second is that inflation moves up and down over the cycle and sometimes moves quite independently of it. The third is that unemployment fluctuates – and that unemployment is much higher in some recessions than in others.

Do you feel that the main differences between macroeconomists today are over empirical or theoretical matters?
Oh I think a very large part of it is theoretical. There is widespread agreement on certain facts, like the ones we have just been through. But then there are very different ways of interpreting the facts. Some people insist as a meth-odological precept on doing it 'right' and other people insist there's a meth-odological precept of giving some sort of realistic – in terms of what they or their grandmother can understand – description of what's going on. So I think of the differences as more methodological/theoretical than an argument about the basic facts. Of course there are also disagreements about facts – like does deficit-financed fiscal policy have any impact? – but they are somewhere lower down the food chain.

What do you consider to be the key papers/books which have had a major impact on the post-war development of macroeconomics?
Well after the *General Theory* I would point to the contributions of the Chicago School summarized in *Studies in the Quantity Theory of Money* [1956]. Patinkin's *Money, Interest and Prices* [1956] was very important in drawing together everything that had gone before. The Phillips [1958] article was obviously very important and everything that came out as a result of that. Friedman and Schwartz's [1963] book is extraordinarily important – part of the Chicago tradition. Then Lucas's [1973] article in the *AER* seems to me quite crucial in continuing the Phelps/Friedman Phillips curve analysis. After that I give an important role to the Kydland and Prescott [1982] real business cycle article and the Akerlof and Yellen [1985a] paper and everything that followed from that.

Why do you think there is more consensus amongst economists over microeconomic issues compared to macroeconomic issues?
In part because micro is less important and in part because, believe it or not, I think that the empirical standards are lower in microeconomics. Let me justify what I mean. When Rudi Dornbusch and I came to write our princi-ples book I knew macro well but hadn't done much micro for a long time. I thought it was going to be a breeze, the macro part we know and the micro

part is all clear – there would be a thousand empirical equations out there to illustrate demand and supply curves. Well the empirical backing isn't around very much – there are lots of stories and models but I don't think micro focuses on a set of issues in the same way that macro does. Microeconomists are not called upon to explain real-world phenomena to anything like the extent that macroeconomists are. They don't have a daily confrontation with policy makers, the newspapers and the capital markets. One of the very successful micro fields is finance, partly because they are really pushed to come up with something that will stand the test of a lot of very sceptical people.

How important do you think it is for macroeconomic models to have choice-theoretic micro foundations?
All else equal, I'd much rather have choice-theoretic foundations in any model. Furthermore I push my students very hard to do that. However I think it is more important than being methodologically right to have a model that you believe can fly in the real world. You know the House of the Lord has many rooms, so part of the profession can be busy doing one thing while other people can be doing other things. What I don't think is smart is to go out and use, say, an overlapping generations model to model monetary policy because that's the only way to get money in the model rigorously.

In the introduction to the book you wrote with Olivier Blanchard [Lectures on Macroeconomics] you suggest that on the surface macroeconomics appears to be a field divided among schools, but that this represents public relations gimmicks and the strong incentives that exist in academia to differentiate products. What made you take this view?
Oh I think a lot of what's going on is people differentiating themselves. The new Keynesians are essentially the mid-1970s Keynesians. As between, say, Lucas and the Keynesians there is more to it than mere product differentiation.

Where do you see yourself in the spectrum of opinion?
Well at the business end I am a pretty straightforward Keynesian. I am very eclectic in how I teach and how I think of the value of the activities of different people in the profession. There are some very respected people who regard the real business cycle stuff as a waste of time, saying it doesn't lead anywhere, its basic premises are ridiculous and so on. Actually I think that they are developing a lot of material and a methodology which is very useful. So methodologically I am very eclectic, but at the policy end I am quite Keynesian.

Does the Hicksian IS–LM model still have a useful role to play in introducing students to the work of Keynes?
It is useful for two reasons. One as a historical device and two it's still the basic model that people use – in fact I use it – in understanding the economy. We teach our incoming graduate students the IS–LM model and I don't think that there is a better model for getting the intuition of the short-run adjustment of the economy right.

How influential have Keynesian ideas actually been in the conduct of macroeconomic policy in the United States since 1960?
You know they are really so simple and intuitive that even people who rail against them believe them. We've had Keynesian-style policies repeatedly. In 1975 there was a cash rebate to households, which was one of the Keynesian policies implemented to help us get out of the 1973–5 recession. The credit policies under Volcker in 1980–81 were very Keynesian and Bush knew the tax increases he was proposing would have an impact on slowing down the economy. The notion that fiscal policy has an effect on demand and growth is believed right across the spectrum and has always been taken into account. Deep down most people believe that deficits matter, although it is politically convenient for some politicians to pretend that they don't.

How important do you think the discovery of the Phillips curve was for macroeconomic policy making in the United States?
That's tough. If you read what people were saying before that, you realize that they understood the fact that you tend to get more inflation as you get closer to full employment. It's one of those many cases where economists managed to get a formal expression of something that was already widely understood. When I gave the Frank Paish lecture a few years ago I went back and read Paish. He already knew when he was writing, in the late forties, that there were problems with inflation as you got close to full employment – so did Keynes in the *General Theory*. I think that the way the profession works is that there is a small group at the top, who have fantastic intuition and after their initial training can operate without formal models. Then you have the great bulk of the profession who have to be taught to think within a formal model. The Phillips curve was very important in formalizing price adjustment, but the intuition was around.

Do you think unemployment is a more important problem than inflation?
You know it's clear that politically things have changed completely. When I was a student at the LSE in the early sixties unemployment was 'the' problem and the notion that you could have a government re-elected in Britain with unemployment in excess of two million would have been considered

insane. So politically it's clear that the whole thing has shifted both in Europe and in the United States. Personally I still worry a great deal about unemployment. However there are two facts. One, we have much better social welfare systems than we used to, and the lot of the unemployed is not what it was in the thirties. Two, there is a much more sophisticated understanding of the problems of inflation than there was 25 years ago.

What do you think of Lucas's idea [1978, AER] *that macroeconomists should abandon the concept of involuntary unemployment?*
Well, that's an example of somebody differentiating their product. Patinkin has a great line in his chapter on involuntary unemployment in *Money, Interest and Prices* where he quotes the Talmudic ruling that in certain cases where a person's consent is required for a ruling you may coerce him to give his consent. In that sense people are always in a position they would like to be in. However I don't find it very useful to imagine that 25 per cent unemployment is a situation in which people are unemployed voluntarily. In one sense people don't offer to work for one cent per hour so they are voluntarily unemployed but I can't see the use of a definition like that.

Does fiscal policy still have a useful role in stabilizing the economy?
Yes, in extreme situations when you are in a deep recession, but not very often. The 1975 income tax rebate of 50 dollars per head across the board was very useful. But the political process in the States is so messy when getting a tax bill through that it is very hard to think of it being used for short-term purposes. One thing is clear, lousy fiscal policy decisions can make the task of monetary policy much harder. Germany's current cyclical problems derive from inappropriate fiscal policy.

Did the monetarist counter-revolution serve a useful scientific purpose?
I think so. There was a great underplaying of monetary policy. Friedman really put the issue on the front burner and into the public domain in a way that simply couldn't be overlooked. Nobody now doubts that monetary policy matters – that is due largely to Friedman. Bob Solow had a good line at the recent Clinton Economic Summit, when he told us that, when he was in the army, one of the enlisted men said that the trouble with their lieutenant was that he knew everything and realized nothing. Well, before Friedman, the profession knew money mattered – afterwards we realized that.

Do you think that there is a natural rate of unemployment towards which the economy inevitably converges following a demand or supply shock?
Yes, in the very longest of long runs.

In your view, has empirical research settled any significant issues in the macroeconomic debate relating to the role of money in the business cycle?
I think so. I thought that the Friedman and Schwartz [1963] book made a very very strong case. The hyperinflation empirical research also tells you a lot about the role of money in the extreme cases.

Given all the criticisms of the public choice school and the contributions from the political business cycle literature, can we trust politicians, when implementing policy, not to try and maximize their own welfare?
No [*laughter*]. What you have to hope is that you have a constitutional system in which, when that's what politicians do, something reasonable comes out at the other end. I don't think ours is terrific because we lack the British party system. We don't have a mechanism which transforms the interests of the individual Congressman – which is to keep his constituents happy by giving them goodies – with the interests of the country. There is another thing that comes out of that literature: what advice should economists give when they know their views will be used for purposes they don't intend? There's a very nice game that weather forecasters play – they always forecast snow if there is any chance of it snowing because the loss function is asymmetric. Economists shouldn't play that game – they should say what they think will happen if XYZ happens. They should say what they think ought to be done on purely technical grounds.

Macroeconomic controversy in the 1950s and 1960s revolved mainly around issues relating to aggregate demand. What caused the shift of emphasis to the supply side in the 1970s?
It was the oil shock and the failure to understand it. I remember discussions at the time where I, and my monetarist friends, didn't understand at all what was going to happen to inflation as a result of the supply shock. People said that you just keep the quantity of money constant, it's 1 per cent of GNP, $MV = PT$, prices will go up by 1 per cent. That was the level of understanding if you came either from the quantity theory or an aggregate demand model.

What do you regard as being the most serious criticisms that have been raised in the literature against new classical macroeconomics?
Well let me try and define what I mean by new classical macroeconomics. When it's just the methodological precept of trying to explain everything from first principles then I don't think there are any serious criticisms you could make of that – except that it's too often used as an excuse for not giving policy advice. Beyond the methodological approach, which I generally agree with, the most serious criticism arises when new classical macroeconomics crosses over into talking about the real world. When you come up with a model which has

nothing of much to do with reality – like a real business cycle model in which monetary policy has no effect on anything or everything that happens in the economy is as a result of technology shocks – it's at that point I part company. It's not that starting from first principles is bad, it's just that believing that you don't have to do a reality check every now and again is very bad.

Over the years the rational expectations hypothesis has been presented in the literature in a number of different forms and versions. What do you regard as being the essence of the hypothesis?
The hypothesis, narrowly put, is simply that people form expectations using all available information and process it optimally. That seems to me a very nice methodological assumption.

Do you think the evidence supports the Ricardian equivalence theorem?
No, not at all [*laughter*].

What do you consider to be the most significant impact that the new classical approach has had on macroeconomics?
If we are talking about Lucas, one massive impact was to give people an excuse to throw away 30 years of empirical work in the econometric policy evaluation critique. After Lucas's [1976] paper it was perfectly acceptable for people to say econometric models are useless. In fact the Lucas critique just tells you what may happen, not what does happen. That's number one. Number two is a complete change in the methodological approach for doing macroeconomics. Whereas it used to be acceptable to do partial equilibrium stuff, now almost everybody uses general equilibrium analysis with a complete model where everything is explained somewhere in some way.

What do you think has been the main contribution that the new Keynesian literature has made to the development of macroeconomics?
Firstly, I associate the efficiency wage hypothesis with that and that's a very important notion. All the work trying to explain why labour markets don't work like the simple demand and supply model strikes me as being very important and really getting at something. I like the Akerlof and Yellen result that small costs of price change could have big effects – but the [1987] paper by Caplin and Spulber, which shows that stickiness at the micro level doesn't translate into stickiness at the macro level, seems to have greatly reduced the importance of that approach. At the more general level, the most important thing it's done is to make it respectable for very smart people like Greg Mankiw and David Romer to become Keynesians and have a research programme which can ask questions about the real world raised by the Keynesian revolution.

Is the crux of the difference between Keynesians and new classicists the speed at which markets clear?
Yes, but I hesitate a little because you can always say that markets clear, subject to the fact that people are constrained by contracts they have signed. But the forces of demand and supply don't register in the market at every moment, so you can also say that markets don't clear – although you don't necessarily see excess demand or supply in a non-clearing market.

What contribution has real business cycle theory made to macroeconomics? Has it taken macroeconomics down a dead-end?
I think it was going down a dead-end for a long time, but everything comes around. At the first conference I came back to after working with the World Bank for three years, Bob King, who is a neoclassical economist from Rochester, gave a paper in which he said you couldn't explain the role of money without sticky prices. So here we have a real business cycle model with sticky prices. If they had insisted that the original Kydland and Prescott model was it and money had nothing to do with anything then it would have been a dead end – but they've come back to the real world [*laughter*].

Can you elaborate on the view you expressed in your [1988] Economic Journal article, that the views of Friedman, Brunner and Meltzer are closer to those of Keynesians than those of equilibrium business cycle theorists?
If you take Friedman's views of rational expectations you get some sense of what I mean. Friedman really doesn't think that expectations are rational – he really thinks people adjust their views pretty slowly. If you read Friedman's account of why there are long and variable lags in monetary policy, it's a completely Keynesian account. You can read Friedman's and Tobin's statement of the transmission mechanism and you can't tell who wrote which. The analogy I use is that when I was a kid I could tell cars apart coming down the road. Then the differences between say a Chev and a Ford were enormous. Now if I look at an old car I know it's a 1950s model but I don't have any idea whether it's a Ford or a Chev because they look practically identical. In that sense the methods and models they used and the issues they looked at were very similar.

In view of the attacks on the desirability and effectiveness of activist fiscal and monetary policy by monetarists, new classicists and public choice theorists, should we adopt a policy regime based on rules?
On a monetary rule, definitely not because the monetary system keeps changing. There really is something to Goodhart's Law/Murphy's Law/the Lucas critique view, that when you adopt a target you change behaviour. I don't think we have seen a monetary rule successfully applied anywhere. Simons's

monetary rule in the 1930s was to stabilize the price level – a rule about the objective, not the instrument, of policy. That seems to me to be a good way of proceeding. Trying to keep the money supply growing at a constant rate strikes me as a bad idea and one that has never worked.

Is Keynesian economics a lot healthier now than it was in the 1970s?
I think so. We have integrated exchange rates into the system. We now have a much better understanding of the Phillips curve and the role of expectations. Although Keynesian economics has a much better base than it had in the past you sit around knowing that some other damn thing is going to come up, which you have been overlooking [*laughter*].

How healthy is the current state of macroeconomics, given the level of controversy?
There is a very unhealthy element in the gap between what the practitioners do and what the profession talks about. If you want to take part in the policy debate, you will find that almost everything that is being done at the frontier is quite useless. The guys who are good at policies know the basic AD–AS model (dynamized) and a lot about the real world. But that's not what we teach. What's missing are attempts to get us back to real-world phenomena – focusing on empirical issues. When I started the *NBER Macroeconomics Annual* it was to try and bring theoretical and policy issues together. Over the eight years since it started in 1986, I have noticed that a lot of the papers which are supposedly front-line theory are more about the real world. So there has been a welcome change.

Do you see any signs of an emerging consensus in macroeconomics?
No. I don't see any convergence, judging by what I hear coming out of Minnesota or Chicago.

Do you think that to be a good macroeconomist you need to know some fairly simple models well, like the IS–LM and AD–AS models? Is that sufficient to give you a good understanding of many real-world problems?
Marty Weitzman has this line that what you learn in the first course of economics is basically all you need to know. But then you have to go on learning for about eight years to understand just what it is you've learned in the first course and what the qualifications are. Unless you have a decent education you are going to make a lot of mistakes because the model is too simple. It's only when you've thought through the growth and expectations issues that you are sophisticated enough to say when you can use these models.

If you were advising President Clinton about economic strategy over the next four years, what would your advice be?

I thought his State of the Union Address was pretty good, although he has underdone the fiscal correction and we are still going to be left with quite a large budget deficit in 1997. The basic approach of starting with a short-term fiscal stimulus and ending with a fiscal contraction seems to me right, and that's the advice I would have given. The proportions aren't quite right, and I can't understand why he went to all the trouble of introducing an energy tax, and then made it raise only $20 billion per year. But the big approach is right.

2.   Keynes v. the 'old' classical model

> To understand my state of mind ... you have to know that I believe myself to be writing a book on economic theory which will largely revolutionise ... in the course of the next ten years ... the way the world thinks about economic problems. (Keynes, 1935, letter to George Bernard Shaw)

2.1   Introduction

In order to better understand current controversies within macroeconomics it is necessary to trace their origin back to the 'Keynes v. Classics' debate which began in the 1930s and has continued in various forms ever since. Today the two schools of thought at the centre of the mainstream debate are represented by the new classical (real) equilibrium business cycle theorists and the new Keynesian school. The former carry on the tradition of the classical economists and emphasize the optimizing power of economic agents acting within a framework of free market forces. The latter 'believe that understanding economic fluctuations requires not just studying the intricacies of general equilibrium, but also appreciating the possibility of market failure on a grand scale' (Mankiw, 1989).

Classical economics is that body of thought which existed prior to the publication of Keynes's (1936) *General Theory*. For Keynes the classical school not only included Adam Smith, David Ricardo and John Stuart Mill, but also 'the *followers* of Ricardo, those, that is to say, who adopted and perfected the theory of Ricardian economics' (Keynes, 1936, p. 3). Keynes was therefore at odds with the conventional history of economic thought classification, particularly with his inclusion of both Alfred Marshall and Arthur Cecil Pigou within the classical school. However, given that most of the theoretical advances which distinguish the neoclassical from the classical period had been in microeconomic analysis, Keynes perhaps felt justified in regarding the macroeconomic ideas of the 1776–1936 period as being reasonably homogeneous in terms of their broad message. This placed great faith in the natural market adjustment mechanisms as a means of maintaining full employment equilibrium

Before moving on to examine the main strands of macroeconomic thought associated with the classical economists, the reader should be aware that, prior to the publication of the *General Theory*, there was no single unified or formalized theory of aggregate employment, and substantial differences existed between economists on the nature and origin of the business cycle (see Haberler, 1963). The structure of classical macroeconomics mainly emerged *after* 1936 and did so largely in response to Keynes's own theory in order that comparisons could be made. Here we take the conventional approach of presenting a somewhat artificial summary of classical macroeconomics, a body of thought that in reality was extremely complex and diverse (see O'Brien, 1975).

Although no single classical economist ever held *all* the ideas presented below, there are certain strands of thought running through the pre-Keynes literature which permit us to characterize classical theory as a coherent story with clearly identifiable building-blocks. To do so will be analytically useful, even if 'historically somewhat inaccurate' (see Ackley, 1966, p. 109). Even an 'Aunt Sally' version of the classical theory can, by comparison, help us better understand post-1936 developments in macroeconomic theory. We accept that, whilst the major presentations of the 'Keynes v. Classics' debate consist of ahistorical fictions – especially those of Hicks (1937) and Leijonhufvud (1968) – and serve as straw men, they aid our understanding by overtly simplifying both the Keynes and the classics positions.

2.2 Classical Macroeconomics

Classical economists were well aware that a capitalist market economy could deviate from its equilibrium level of output and employment. However they believed that such disturbances would be temporary and very short-lived. Their collective view was that the market mechanism would operate quickly and efficiently to restore full employment equilibrium. If the classical economic analysis was correct then government intervention, in the form of stabilization policies, would be neither necessary nor desirable. Indeed such policies were more than likely to create greater instability. As we shall see later, modern champions of the old classical view (that is, new classical equilibrium business cycle theorists) share this faith in the optimizing power of market forces and the potential for active government intervention to create havoc rather than harmony. It follows that the classical writers gave little attention to either the factors which determine aggregate demand or the policies which could be used to stabilize aggregate demand in order to promote full employment. For the classical economists full employment was the normal state of affairs. That Keynes should attack such ideas in the 1930s should come as no surprise. But how did the classical economists reach such an optimistic conclusion? In what follows we will present a 'stylized' version of the classical model which seeks to explain the determinants of an economy's level of real output (Y), real (W/P) and nominal (W) wages, the price level (P) and the real rate of interest (r). In this model it is assumed that:

1. all economic agents (firms and households) are rational and aim to maximize their profits or utility; furthermore, they do not suffer from money illusion;
2. all markets are perfectly competitive so that agents decide how much to buy and sell on the basis of a given set of prices which are perfectly flexible;
3. all agents have perfect knowledge of market conditions and prices before engaging in trade;
4. trade only takes place when market-clearing prices have been established in all markets, this being ensured by a fictional Walrasian auctioneer whose presence prevents *false trading*;
5. agents have stable expectations.

These assumptions ensure that in the classical model markets, including the labour market, always clear. To see how the classical model explains the determination of the crucial macro variables, we will follow their approach and divide the economy into two sectors; a *real* sector and a *monetary* sector. To simplify the analysis we will also assume a closed economy, that is, no foreign trade sector.

In examining the behaviour of the real and monetary sectors we need to consider the following three components of the model: (i) the classical theory of employment and output determination, (ii) Say's Law of markets, and (iii) the quantity theory of money. The first two components show how the equilibrium values of the real variables in the model are determined exclusively in the labour and commodity markets. The third component explains how the nominal variables in the system are determined. Thus in the classical model there is a *dichotomy*. The real and monetary sectors are separated. As a result, changes in the quantity of money will not affect the equilibrium values of the real variables in the model. With the real variables invariant to changes in the quantity of money, the classical economists argued that the quantity of money was *neutral*.

2.3 Employment and Output Determination

The classical neutrality proposition implies that the level of real output will be independent of the quantity of money in the economy. We now consider what determines real output. A key component of the classical model is the *short-run production function*. In general terms at the micro level a production function expresses the *maximum* amount of output that a firm can produce from any given amounts of factor inputs. The more inputs of labour (L) and capital (K) that a firm uses then the greater will be the output produced (providing the inputs are used effectively). However, in the short run, it is assumed that the only variable input is labour. The amount of capital input and the state of technology are taken as constant. When we consider the economy as a whole the quantity of aggregate output ($GDP = Y$) will also depend on the amount of inputs used and how efficiently they are used. This relationship, known as the short-run *aggregate* production function, can be written in the following form:

$$Y = AF(K,L) \tag{2.1}$$

where   (1) Y = real output per period,
          (2) K = the quantity of capital inputs used per period,
          (3) L = the quantity of labour inputs used per period,
          (4) A = an index of total factor productivity, and
          (5) F = a function which relates real output to the inputs of K and L.

The symbol A represents an autonomous growth factor which captures the impact of improvements in technology and any other influences which raise the overall effectiveness of an economy's use of its factors of production. Equation (2.1) simply tells us that aggregate output will depend on the amount of labour employed, given the existing capital stock, technology and organization of inputs. This relationship is expressed graphically in panel (a) of Figure 2.1.

The short-run aggregate production function displays certain properties. Three points are worth noting. First, for given values of A and K there is a positive relationship between employment (L) and output (Y), shown as a movement along the production function from, for example, point a to b. Second, the production function exhibits *diminishing returns* to the variable input, labour. This is indicated by the slope of the production function ($\Delta Y/ \Delta L$) which declines as employment increases. Successive increases in the amount of labour employed yield less and less additional output. Since $\Delta Y/ \Delta L$ measures the *marginal product of labour* (MPL) we can see by the slope of the production function that an increase in employment is associated with a declining marginal product of labour. This is illustrated in panel (b) of Figure 2.1, where D_L shows the MPL to be both positive and diminishing (MPL declines as employment expands from L_0 to L_1; that is, $MPL_a > MPL_b$). Third, the production function will shift upwards if the capital input is increased and/or there is an increase in the productivity of the inputs represented by an increase in the value of A (for example, a technological improvement). Such a change is shown in panel (a) of Figure 2.1 by a shift in the production function from Y to Y^* caused by A increasing to A^*. In panel (b) the impact of the upward shift of the production function causes the MPL schedule to shift up from D_L to D_L^*. Note that following such a change the

(a)

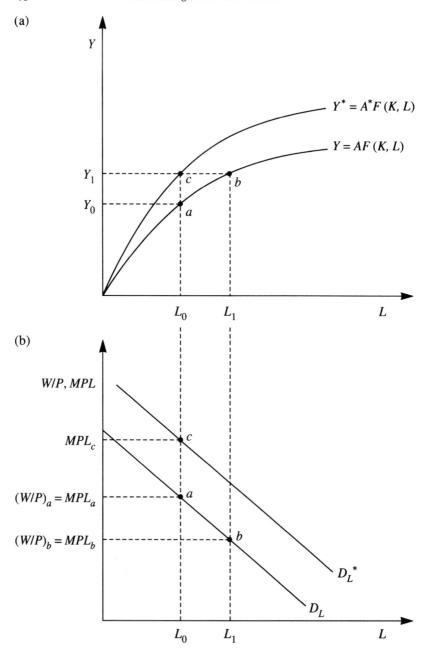

Figure 2.1　The aggregate production function (a) and the marginal product of labour (b)

productivity of labour increases (L_0 amount of labour employed can now produce Y_1 rather than Y_0 amount of output). We will see in Chapter 6 that such production function shifts play a crucial role in the most recent new classical real business cycle theories (see Plosser, 1989).

Although equation (2.1) and Figure 2.1 tell us a great deal about the relationship between an economy's output and the inputs used, they tell us nothing about how much labour will actually be employed in any particular time period. To see how the aggregate level of employment is determined in the classical model, we must examine the classical economists' model of the labour market. We first consider how much labour a profit-maximizing firm will employ. The well-known condition for profit maximization is that a firm should set its marginal revenue (MR_i) equal to the marginal cost of production (MC_i). For a perfectly competitive firm, $MR_i = P_i$, the output price of firm $_i$. We can therefore write the profit-maximizing rule as equation (2.2):

$$P_i = MC_i \tag{2.2}$$

If a firm hires labour within a competitive labour market, a money wage equal to W_i must be paid to each extra worker. The additional cost of hiring an extra unit of labour will be $W_i \Delta L_i$. The extra revenue generated by an additional worker is the extra output produced (ΔQ_i) multiplied by the price of the firm's product (P_i). The additional revenue is therefore $P_i \Delta Q_i$. It pays for a profit maximising firm to hire labour as long as $W_i \Delta L_i < P_i \Delta Q_i$. To maximize profits requires satisfaction of the following condition:

$$P_i \Delta Q_i = W_i \Delta L_i \tag{2.3}$$

This is equivalent to:

$$\frac{\Delta Q_i}{\Delta L_i} = \frac{W_i}{P_i} \tag{2.4}$$

Since $\Delta Q_i / \Delta L_i$ is the marginal product of labour, a firm should hire labour until the marginal product of labour equals the real wage rate. This condition is simply another way of expressing equation (2.2). Since MC_i is the cost of the additional worker (W_i) divided by the extra output produced by that worker (MPL_i) we can write this relationship as:

$$MC_i = \frac{W_i}{MPL_i} \tag{2.5}$$

Combining (2.5) and (2.2) yields equation (2.6):

$$P_i = \frac{W_i}{MPL_i} = MC_i \qquad (2.6)$$

Because the MPL is a declining function of the amount of labour employed, owing to the influence of diminishing returns, the MPL curve is downward-sloping (see panel (b) of Figure 2.1). Since we have shown that profits will be maximized when a firm equates the MPL_i with W_i/P_i, the marginal product curve is equivalent to the firm's demand curve for labour (D_{Li}). Equation (2.7) expresses this relationship:

$$D_{Li} = D_{Li}(W_i/P_i) \qquad (2.7)$$

This relationship tells us that a firm's demand for labour will be an inverse function of the real wage: the lower the real wage the more labour will be profitably employed.

In the above analysis we considered the behaviour of an individual firm. The same reasoning can be applied to the economy as a whole. Since the individual firm's demand for labour is an inverse function of the real wage, by aggregating such functions over all the firms in an economy we arrive at the classical postulate that the *aggregate* demand for labour is also an inverse function of the real wage. In this case W represents the economy-wide average money wage and P represents the general price level. In panel (b) of Figure 2.1 this relationship is shown as D_L. When the real wage is reduced from $(W/P)_a$ to $(W/P)_b$, employment expands from L_0 to L_1. The aggregate labour demand function is expressed in equation (2.8):

$$D_L = D_L(W/P) \qquad (2.8)$$

So far we have been considering the factors which determine the demand for labour. We now need to consider the supply side of the labour market. It is assumed in the classical model that households aim to maximize their utility. The market supply of labour is therefore a positive function of the real wage rate and is given by equation (2.9) and is shown in panel (b) of Figure 2.2 as S_L.

$$S_L = S_L(W/P) \qquad (2.9)$$

How much labour is supplied for a given population depends on household preferences for consumption and leisure, both of which yield positive utility. But in order to consume, income must be earned by replacing leisure time with working time. Work is viewed as yielding disutility. Hence the preferences of workers and the real wage will determine the equilibrium amount of

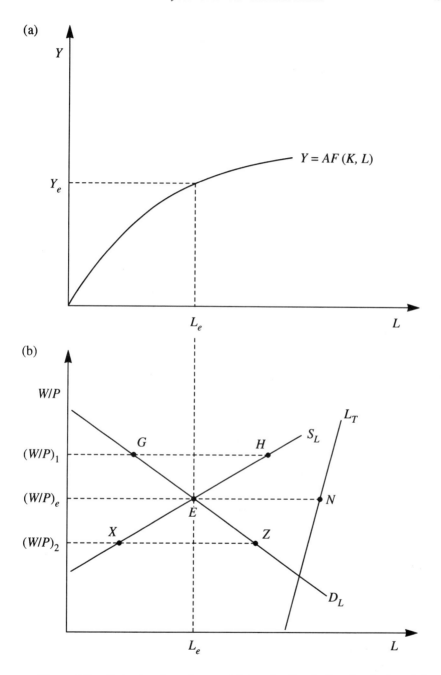

Figure 2.2   Output and employment determination in the classical model

labour supplied. A rise in the real wage makes leisure more expensive in terms of forgone income and will tend to increase the supply of labour. This is known as the *substitution* effect. However a rise in the real wage also makes workers better off, so they can afford to choose more leisure. This is known as the *income* effect. The classical model assumes that the substitution effect dominates the income effect so that the labour supply responds positively to an increase in the real wage. For a more detailed discussion of these issues, see, for example, Begg, Dornbusch and Fischer (1991, chap. 11); Stiglitz (1993, chap. 11).

Now that we have explained the derivation of the demand and supply curves for labour, we are in a position to examine the determination of the competitive equilibrium output and employment in the classical model. The classical labour market is illustrated in panel (b) of Figure 2.2, where the forces of demand and supply establish an equilibrium market-clearing real wage $(W/P)_e$ and an equilibrium level of employment (L_e). If the real wage was lower than $(W/P)_e$, such as $(W/P)_2$, then there would be excess demand for labour of ZX and money wages would rise in response to the competitive bidding of firms, restoring the real wage to its equilibrium value. If the real wage was above equilibrium, such as $(W/P)_1$, there would be an excess supply of labour equal to HG. In this case money wages would fall until the real wage returned to $(W/P)_e$. This result is guaranteed in the classical model because the classical economists assumed perfectly competitive markets, flexible prices and full information. The level of employment in equilibrium (L_e) represents 'full employment', in that all those members of the labour force who desire to work at the equilibrium real wage can do so. Whereas the schedule S_L shows how many people are prepared to accept job offers at each real wage, the schedule L_T indicates the total number of people who wish to be in the labour force at each real wage rate. L_T has a positive slope, indicating that at higher real wages more people wish to enter the labour force. In the classical model labour market equilibrium is associated with unemployment equal to the distance EN in panel (b) of Figure 2.2. Classical full employment equilibrium is perfectly compatible with the existence of *frictional* and *voluntary* unemployment, but does not admit the possibility of *involuntary* unemployment. Friedman (1968a) later introduced the concept of the *natural rate* of unemployment when discussing equilibrium unemployment in the labour market (see section 4.3). Once the equilibrium level of employment is determined in the labour market, the level of output is determined by the position of the aggregate production function. By referring to panel (a) of Figure 2.2, we can see that L_e amount of employment will produce Y_e level of output.

So far the simple stylized model we have reproduced here has enabled us to see how the classical economists explained the determination of the equilibrium level of real output, employment and real wages as well as the equilibrium level of unemployment. Changes in the equilibrium values of the above variables can obviously come about if the labour demand curve shifts and/or the labour supply curve shifts. For example, an upward shift of the production function due to technological change would move the labour demand curve to the right. Providing the labour supply curve has a positive slope, this will lead to an increase in employment, output and the real wage. Population growth, by shifting the labour supply curve to the right, would increase employment and output but lower the real wage. Readers should verify this for themselves.

We have seen in the analysis above that competition in the labour market ensures full employment in the classical model. At the equilibrium real wage no person who wishes to work at that real wage is without employment. In this sense 'the classical postulates do not admit the possibility of involuntary unemployment' (Keynes, 1936, p. 6). However the classical economists were perfectly aware that persistent unemployment in excess of the equilibrium level was possible if artificial restrictions were placed on the equilibrating function of real wages. If real wages are held above equilibrium (such as $(W/P)_1$, in panel (b) of Figure 2.2) by trade union monopoly power or minimum wage legislation then obviously everyone who wishes to work at the 'distorted' real wage will not be able to do so. For classical economists the solution to such 'classical unemployment' was simple and obvious. Real wages should be reduced by cutting the money wage.

Keynes regarded the equilibrium outcome depicted in Figure 2.2 as a 'special case' which was not typical of the 'economic society in which we actually live' (Keynes, 1936, p. 3). The full employment equilibrium of the classical model was a special case because it corresponded to a situation where aggregate demand was just sufficient to absorb the level of output produced. Keynes objected that there was no guarantee that aggregate demand would be at such a level. The classical economists denied the possibility of a deficiency of aggregate demand by appealing to 'Say's Law' which is 'equivalent to the proposition that there is no obstacle to full employment' (Keynes, 1936, p. 26). It is to this proposition that we now turn.

2.4 Say's Law

In 1803, Jean-Baptiste Say's *Treatise of Political Economy* was published. The simplest version of the law associated with this economist is that labour will only offer itself for employment in order to obtain income which is then used to purchase the output produced. In his own words, Say puts forward the proposition in the following way.

> 'A product is no sooner created, than it, *from that instant*, affords a market for other products to the full extent of its own value ... the mere circumstance of the creation of one product immediately opens a vent for other products. (Say, 1821)

In other words, because the act of production simultaneously creates income and purchasing power there could be no impediment to full employment caused by a deficiency of aggregate demand. The dictum 'supply creates its own demand' captures the essence of Say's Law, which aimed to characterize the *essential* feature of exchange within a specialized economy. That the act of supply created an equivalent demand seemed obvious to the classical writers. The law does not deny the possibility that a misallocation of re-sources can occur and that a glut of certain commodities can develop, but this problem would be temporary and no such excess supply could occur for goods as a whole. For a detailed discussion of Say's contribution, see Sowell (1972) and Baumol (1977).

Say's Law was originally set forth in the context of a barter economy where, by definition, the act of supplying one good unavoidably implies the demand for some other good. In general classical economists, notably Ricardo and Mill, gave support to Say's Law, which they believed also held true for a monetary exchange economy. Money was nothing more than a convenient medium of exchange which enabled market participants to avoid the awk-wardness and inconvenience of barter. If Say's Law applies to a money-using economy then the implication is that a market is guaranteed for whatever level of output is produced, although market forces will obviously lead to changes in the composition of aggregate output. If aggregate demand and aggregate supply are always guaranteed equality then money is nothing more than a 'veil' covering the underlying real forces in the economy.

At this point it is important to distinguish between two versions of Say's Law. According to Trevithick (1992) the *weak* version is taken to imply that each act of production and supply necessarily involves the creation of an equivalent demand for output in general. But this version of Say's Law does not guarantee that the output produced will be consistent with full employ-ment. It merely states that whatever level of aggregate output happens to be forthcoming will find a market. This weak version of Say's Law applies to both depressed and buoyant levels of output. The *strong* version of Say's Law states that in a competitive market economy there will be an automatic tendency for full employment to be established (see panel (b) of Figure 2.2). Since the strong version of Say's Law implies an equality of aggregate demand and supply which is consistent with labour market equilibrium, it is equivalent to the proposition that there is no obstacle to the achievement of full employment in terms of a deficiency of aggregate demand. To see how the classical economists justified their belief that aggregate spending in the economy will always be sufficient to purchase the full employment level of output, we need to examine their ideas relating to investment, saving and the rate of interest.

The classical theory of interest rate determination plays a crucial role in ensuring that a deficiency of aggregate demand does not occur. If we imagine an economy consisting of two sectors, firms and households, we can write down the following equation, which tells us that in equilibrium aggregate expenditure (E) must equal aggregate output (Y).

$$E = C(r) + I(r) = Y \qquad (2.10)$$

Furthermore aggregate expenditure consists of two components: investment expenditure (I) which arises from firms and consumption expenditure (C) which arises from households. The planned demand for goods (E) is the sum of the planned demand for consumption goods plus the planned demand for investment goods. In the classical model the demand for both types of goods is a function of the interest rate (r). Since households do not automatically spend all of their income, we can also write down equation (2.11):

$$Y - C(r) = S(r) \qquad (2.11)$$

Combining (2.10) and (2.11) yields the equilibrium condition given by (2.12):

$$S(r) = I(r) \qquad (2.12)$$

We can see from (2.11) that in the classical model saving (S) is also a function of the interest rate. The higher the rate of interest the more willing will savers be to replace present consumption with future consumption. Hence the classical economists viewed the interest rate as a real reward for absti-nence or thrift. The flow of saving therefore represents a *supply of loanable funds* in the capital market. Since household saving responds positively to the rate of interest $(\Delta S/\Delta r > 0)$ household consumption must be negatively re-lated to the rate of interest $(\Delta C/\Delta r < 0)$. Investment expenditure on capital goods is negatively related to the rate of interest in the classical model $(\Delta I/\Delta r < 0)$ and represents a *demand for loanable funds* in the capital market. Investment spending by firms can only be justified if the expected rate of return from the expenditure is greater than, or at least equal to, the cost of acquiring the funds used to purchase the capital goods. The higher the rate of interest the higher the explicit (and implicit cost) of the funds used to pur-chase the capital goods. We can therefore represent business expenditure (I) as a declining function of the interest rate. The relationship between invest-ment, saving and the interest rate in the classical model is shown in panel (a) of Figure 2.3. The twin forces of productivity and thrift determine the real rate of interest and variations in the interest rate act as an equilibrating force which maintains equality between the demand for and supply of loanable funds, ensuring that aggregate demand is never deficient. By referring to Figure 2.3 we can see how important flexibility in the interest rate was to the classical equilibration process. In panel (a) we represent the classical theory of interest rate determination, with the interest rate on the vertical axis and the flows of saving and investment measured on the horizontal axis. In panel (b) real output is measured on the vertical axis with the overall demand for commodities $(C + I)$ measured on the horizontal axis. From Figure 2.2 we know that competition in the labour market will yield an equilibrium real

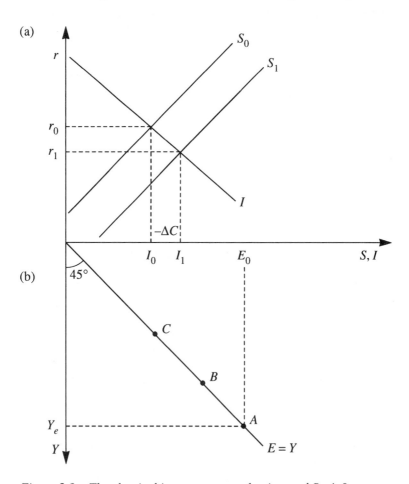

Figure 2.3   The classical interest rate mechanism and Say's Law

wage and level of employment which when combined with the production function give a level of full employment output of Y_e. Panel (b) of Figure 2.3 indicates that aggregate expenditures of an amount equal to E_0 are necessary to purchase the output of Y_e. Since output and demand are identical at all points along the 45° line, any point such as B and C is consistent with the weak version of Say's Law. Point A in panel (b) corresponds to the strong version of Say's Law. Not only are aggregate expenditure and output in equality, Y_e corresponds to the level of output associated with full employment labour market equilibrium.

We can best see the importance of interest rate flexibility in this model by asking what would happen if households suddenly decided to save more (consume less). This is represented in panel (a) of Figure 2.3 by a rightward shift of the saving function from S_0 to S_1. The initial excess supply of loanable funds would lead to a fall in the rate of interest from r_0 to r_1. This would encourage an increase in investment expenditure from I_0 to I_1. Since $E_0 - I_0$ equals consumption expenditure, it is clear that the rise in investment expenditure, $I_1 - I_0$, exactly offsets the fall in consumption expenditure equal to $-\Delta C$ in the diagram. Aggregate expenditure would remain at E_0, although its composition would change.

Even though in the classical model the decisions to save and invest can be carried out by different sets of people, the rate of interest will change so as to reconcile the desires to save and invest. In Keynesian theory divergences between S and I cause a *quantity* response. In the case of an increase in saving, the Keynesian model predicts a decline in aggregate spending, output and employment; that is, Keynes's paradox of thrift. The classical model, armed with Say's Law, flexible wages, prices and the interest rate, can experience changes in the structure of final demand but no prolonged demand deficiency and involuntary unemployment. A remarkable result.

Not all the classical economists accepted Say's Law and its implications. Robert Thomas Malthus argued that a general glut of commodities was possible. Whereas Ricardo, Mill and the followers of Say believed that the conditions of supply determine aggregate output, Malthus, anticipating Keynes, gave emphasis to demand as the determining factor (see Dorfman, 1989). But 'Ricardo conquered England as completely as the Holy Inquisition conquered Spain' (Keynes, 1936, p. 32). For Keynes the completeness of the Ricardian victory was something of a curiosity and a mystery. For this reason Keynes gave high praise to Malthus for anticipating his own ideas with respect to a general deficiency of aggregate demand (see Keynes, 1936, pp. 362–71). Although Ricardo appeared to be stone deaf to what Malthus was saying, part of the disagreement had its origin in the time horizon adopted by each writer. Ricardo had his eyes fixed firmly on the long run, whereas Malthus, like Keynes, was more concerned with the short run.

In our discussion of the classical model so far we have concentrated on the real sector. The operation of the labour and capital markets, buttressed by Say's Law, provided the classical economists with a theoretical system capable of explaining the determination of the real variables in the system. But what determines the price level in the classical model? The final component which explains the determination of the price level and the other nominal values in the classical economists' system is the quantity theory of money.

2.5   The Quantity Theory of Money

The hallmark of classical macroeconomic theory is the separation of real and nominal variables. This classical dichotomy enables us to examine the behaviour of the real variables in the economic system while ignoring the nominal variables. In the stylized classical model we have developed, the quantity of money is irrelevant for the determination of the real variables. *Long-run money neutrality is a crucial property of the classical model.*

To explain the determination of the nominal variables in the system, the classical economists subscribed to the quantity theory of money. A long line of famous economists have either contributed to the development of this theory or have been associated with its policy prescriptions. The list includes Cantillon, Hume, Ricardo, Mill, Marshall, Fisher, Pigou, Hayek and even Keynes. More recently the quantity theory of money has been associated with the development of monetarism and the work of Milton Friedman, perhaps the most influential economist in the past quarter-century. Although the term 'monetarism' did not emerge until 1968 (see Brunner, 1968) its main core proposition, the quantity theory of money, was well established in classical macroeconomics following the publication of David Hume's influential essay, *Of Money*, in 1752. Indeed Mayer (1980) has argued that the salient date for the birth of monetarist ideas was 1752, since most of the fundamental propositions which characterize monetarism date back to Hume's essay. Here we will present only a short exposition of the quantity theory in order to complete the classical scheme. For a more detailed discussion, see Laidler (1991).

The dominant macroeconomic theory prior to the 1930s was the quantity theory of money. Two highly influential versions of the quantity theory can be identified in the literature. The first version, associated with Marshall and Pigou, is known as the Cambridge cash-balance approach. The second version is associated with Irving Fisher.

The Cambridge economists drew a clear distinction in their version of the quantity theory between the demand for money (Md) and the supply of money (M). The demand for money was *primarily* determined by the need to conduct transactions which will have a positive relationship to the money value of aggregate expenditure. Since the latter is equal to money national income we can represent the Cambridge money demand function as equation (2.13):

$$Md = kPY \qquad (2.13)$$

where Md is the demand to hold nominal money balances, and k is the fraction of the annual value of money national income (PY) that agents (firms and households) *wish* to hold. The reader should be aware that the Cambridge monetary approach did recognize that k could vary in the short run (see Laidler, 1993) but, in the stylized presentation we consider in equation (2.13), the coefficient k is assumed to be constant. As it stands, the Cambridge equation is a theory of the demand for money. In order to explain the price level we must introduce the supply of money. If we assume that the supply of money is determined by the monetary authorities (that is, M is exogenous) then we can write the condition for monetary equilibrium as equation (2.14):

$$M = Md \qquad (2.14)$$

Substituting (2.14) into (2.13) we obtain (2.15):

$$M = kPY \qquad (2.15)$$

To obtain the quantity theory result that changes in the quantity of money have no real effects in the long run but will determine the price level, we simply need to remember from our earlier discussion that Y is predetermined at its full employment value by the production function and the operation of a competitive labour market. With k and Y constant, M determines P. If the money market is initially in equilibrium then an increase in the money supply creates disequilibrium ($M > Md$). Since the values of Y and k are fixed, equilibrium in the money market can only be restored if the price level rises. The reason why prices rise in the classical model is that, if households and firms find themselves holding more money than they desire, the excess money balances are used to purchase goods and services. Since the supply of goods and services is constrained by the predetermined full employment level of output, excess demand in the goods market causes the general price level to rise in proportion to the initial increase in the money supply.

The second approach uses the *income version* of Fisher's equation of exchange. This relationship is given by equation (2.16):

$$MV = PY \qquad (2.16)$$

where V is the income velocity of circulation of money and represents the average number of times a unit of money is used in the course of conducting final transactions which constitute nominal GDP. Since V can be defined as the reciprocal of k, the constancy of V can be justified because institutional factors which determine the frequency of the transactions carried out by agents are likely to change slowly over time. That V is the reciprocal of k can be seen by comparing (2.15) with (2.16) and noting that both V and $1/k$ equal PY/M. That the price level is dependent on the nominal money supply is clearly brought out if we examine equation (2.17), which rearranges (2.16):

$$P = MV/Y \qquad\qquad (2.17)$$

With V and Y constant, it is easy to see that P depends on M and that ΔM equals ΔP.

To see how the price level is determined in the classical model and how real output, real wages and employment are invariant to the quantity of money, consider Figure 2.4. In quadrants (a) and (b) we reproduce Figure 2.2. Here a competitive labour market generates equilibrium employment of L_0 and an equilibrium real wage of W_0/P_0. From the production function we can see that full employment in this model leads to an output of Y_0. In quadrant (c) we have the classical aggregate demand (AD) and aggregate supply (AS) functions. The AS function is perfectly inelastic, indicating that real output is invariant to the general price level. The classical AD curve is derived from equation (2.16). With a constant supply of money (for example, M_0) and V constant, a higher price level must be associated with a lower level of real output. $AD_0(M_0)$ shows how, for a given money supply, MV can be split up among an infinite number of combinations of P and Y. Since we have assumed V is fixed, the nominal value of all transactions in the economy is determined by the supply of money. With higher prices each transaction requires more units of currency and therefore the quantity of goods and services that can be bought must fall. Since the AD curve is drawn for a given quantity of money, an increase in the money supply will shift the AD curve to the right, as shown by $AD_1(M_1)$. Finally in quadrant (d) we show the relationship between the real wage and the price level for a given nominal wage. If the nominal wage is W_0 then a higher price level will reduce the real wage.

Let us assume that the initial equilibrium values in the model associated with the quantity of money M_0 are Y_0, W_0/P_0, and L_0. Suppose the monetary authorities increase the supply of money to M_1 in an attempt to increase real output and employment. We can see that such a policy will be completely ineffectual in the classical model. The increase in the quantity of money, by creating disequilibrium in the money market ($Md < M$), will lead to an increase in the demand for goods and services. Since Y is constrained at Y_0 by

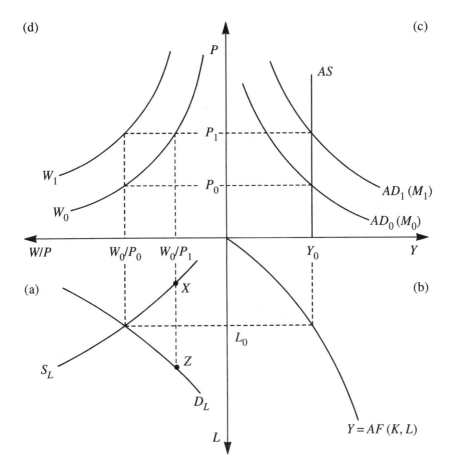

Figure 2.4   The determination of the price level in the classical model

labour market equilibrium employment (L_0), prices rise to P_1. For a given nominal wage of W_0, an increase in the price level lowers the real wage and creates disequilibrium in the labour market. An excess demand for labour of ZX emerges at a real wage of W_0/P_1. Competitive bidding by employers will drive the nominal wage up until it reaches a value of W_1, which restores the real wage to its equilibrium value (that is, $W_0/P_0 = W_1/P_1$). Irving Fisher (1907) also demonstrated how monetary expansion would raise the nominal rate of interest through the '*Fisher effect*'. In the classical model, the real interest rate adjusts to equate saving and investment in the loanable funds market. Since the real rate of interest is equal to the nominal interest rate minus the inflation rate and is determined by the real forces of productivity and thrift, the nominal rate of interest will adjust to reflect the influence of variations in both the real interest rate and the rate of inflation. Monetary expansion, by raising the rate of inflation, will also raise the nominal interest rate. To summarize, the end result of a monetary expansion is that the price level, nominal wages and the nominal interest rate will increase but all the real values in the system remain unaffected (that is, money is neutral) . In the language of David Hume (1752) ''tis evident that the greater or less plenty of money is of no consequence since the prices of commodities are always proportional to the plenty of money'.

Before moving on to examine Keynes's objections to the classical model we should note that the stylized version of the quantity theory presented above does not do justice to the complexities and sophistication of the theories developed by pre-Keynesian economists working in the quantity theory tradition. Classical economists such as Ricardo were concerned with long-run equilibrium states and utilized a comparative-static method of analysis in order to compare one equilibrium state with another. Some classical economists were well aware that the neutrality of money proposition would not hold in the short run (see Corry, 1962). Indeed Ralph Hawtrey, who strayed from the classical nest even earlier than Keynes, throughout his career advocated a purely monetary theory of the business cycle where money was far from neutral in the short run (see Haberler, 1963; Deutscher, 1990). But viewed from the vantage point of the early 1930s, during the depths of the Great Depression, the Ricardian long-run equilibrium might just as well have been located on Mars. In his *Tract on Monetary Reform* (1923), Keynes declared, 'In the long run we are all dead. Economists set themselves too easy, too useless a task if in tempestuous seasons they can only tell us that when the storm is long past the ocean is flat again.' We now turn to consider Keynes's objections to classical theory, which culminated in the publication of his most influential book.

2.6 Keynes's *General Theory*

Keynes's contribution to economic theory remains a matter of considerable debate, despite over half a century having gone by since the publication of the *General Theory*, in February 1936. Few economists would challenge Samuelson's (1988) view that Keynes's influence on the course of economics has been 'the most significant event in twentieth-century economic science' or that macroeconomics was his creation. Opponents are convinced that Keynes was fundamentally mistaken (Hayek, 1983). Keynesians themselves are divided between those who regard the policy implications of the *General Theory* as being moderately conservative (Tobin, 1987) and others who see Keynes's magnum opus as representing a revolutionary break from mainstream classical and neoclassical doctrines (Robinson, 1971). That the *General Theory* has had a profound influence on the conduct of macroeconomic policy-making, for good or ill, is beyond question.

Keynes was essentially an applied economist brought up in the Cambridge tradition of Alfred Marshall, where the attraction of economics lay in the prospect it held out to its practitioners for making the world a better place. But for Keynes to write the *General Theory* involved a 'long struggle to escape ... from habitual modes of thought and expression'. The old ideas from which Keynes sought to escape were the *laissez-faire* doctrines associated with the liberal tradition of nineteenth-century classical economics. Following Adam Smith, political economy had an underlying bias towards *laissez-faire*. The classical economists, with some exceptions, were preoccupied with government failure. In their view the state should confine its activities to ensuring a peaceful, competitive environment within which citizens could pursue their individual objectives as fully as possible. Only the evils of monopoly power or too much state involvement in economic affairs could prevent the price mechanism from yielding maximum national output, given the constraint of scarce but fully employed resources. In contrast to this orthodoxy, the most revolutionary aspect of Keynes's work, which we can detect in his writings from the mid-1920s onwards, was his clear and unambiguous message that with regard to the general level of employment and output there was no invisible hand channelling self-interest into some social optimum. Although Keynes's iconoclastic vision emerges time and time again in his critiques of UK government policy during the 1920s, many of his policy recommendations lacked the theoretical structure from which they could logically be derived. For example, in 1929 Keynes was arguing forcefully for government programmes to expand demand via deficit financing in full support of Lloyd George's Liberal programme of recovery. But he was doing so without a theory of effective demand and a multiplier mechanism which are so important to the argument (see Keynes, 1972, Vol. IX). In order effectively to confront the existing classical orthodoxy head-on, Keynes needed to provide an alternative theory. We therefore find him from 1930 onwards groping towards his *General Theory*, a book which, unlike many of his earlier writings, was addressed to his fellow economists. By late 1932, and certainly no later than early 1933, the initial vision or 'grey fuzzy woolly monster' in his mind was beginning to appear in his Cambridge lectures (see Skidelsky, 1992; Patinkin, 1993). To his critics the *General Theory* has remained a 'monster'. Lucas, a leading modern critic of Keynesianism, finds it a book 'he can't read' which is 'carelessly written' and represents a 'political response to the Depression' (see Klamer, 1984). Even Samuelson, one of Keynes's earliest converts, describes the book as a 'poorly organised' and 'badly written' book. But for Samuelson 'it is a work of genius' which, because of its obscurity and polemical character, will remain a long-run influence on the development of economics (Samuelson, 1946). Galbraith (1977), reaching a similar conclusion, sees the ambiguity contained in the *General Theory* as a feature guaranteed to win converts, for:

> When understanding is achieved after much effort, readers hold tenaciously to their belief. The pain, they wish to think, was worthwhile. And if there are enough contradictions and ambiguities, as there are also in the Bible and Marx, the reader can always find something he wants to believe. This too wins disciples.

Hardly surprising that it was mainly the younger generation of economists at Cambridge UK and Cambridge USA that took quickly to the new ideas. Whereas economists over the age of 50 were on the whole immune from Keynes's message, the *General Theory* 'caught most economists under the age of thirty-five with the unexpected virulence of a disease first attacking and decimating an isolated tribe of South Sea islanders' (Samuelson, 1946). That change in economics comes with the changing generations also played an important role some 40 years later when the rise of new classical economics infected mainly the younger generation of economists, so much so that Keynesians appeared to be threatened with extinction (see Colander, 1988; Blinder, 1988a).

2.7   Interpreting the *General Theory*

One of the great problems in discussing the content of the *General Theory* is that, being a highly complex, controversial and influential book, it has enabled economists of widely different persuasions to find statements within it which support their own vision of Keynes's essential message. The Keynesiology literature, already vast, continues to grow exponentially! The diverse range of views is a source of confusion and enlightenment. E. Roy Weintraub (1979), for example, has a chapter entitled 'The 4,827th re-examination of Keynes's system'! To get some idea of the contrasting theoretical interpretations of the *General Theory* the reader should consult Hicks (1937), Modigliani (1944), Klein (1947), Patinkin (1956, 1976, 1990b), Leijonhufvud (1968), Davidson (1978), Chick (1983), Coddington (1983), Kahn (1984) and Meltzer (1988). The papers collected in the edited volumes by Cunningham Wood (1983) give some idea of the critiques and developments which emerged after 1936. To understand the development of Keynes's contributions in the wider context of his life and philosophy, the reader should consult the excellent biographies of Keynes by Harrod (1951), Moggridge (1992) and Skidelsky (1983 and 1992). The Collected Works of John Maynard Keynes, edited by Donald Moggridge, run to 30 volumes.

There is no definitive interpretation of Keynes which commands universal support; nor could there ever be, given the non-mathematical style of the book. The turbulence he has caused in economics shows no sign of abatement and the *General Theory* remains a text which is 'not yet fully mined' (Phelps, 1990). One of the reasons for this is that the very issue with which Keynes was concerned, namely the effectiveness of market forces in generating a stable full employment equilibrium without active government intervention, is still at the centre of economic debate (the same issue relating to government v. market failure lies at the heart of controversy elsewhere in economics – see Roper and Snowdon, 1987).

Bill Gerrard (1991) attempts to analyse the reasons why different interpretations occur. These include confusions generated by Keynes himself due to 'technical incompetence', 'stylistic difficulties', 'inconsistencies' and 'mistakes' . Other possible sources of confusion are 'reader-generated' and result from 'selective reading', 'inappropriate framing' and 'reliance on secondary sources'. A further problem arises in the sheer quantity of material which Keynes produced in addition to the *General Theory*; for example, some recent contributors have shifted emphasis towards Keynes's earlier and neglected philosophical papers (O'Donnell, 1989). Gerrard concludes that the achievement of Keynes's *General Theory* is mainly in 'its ability to generate a diversity of research programmes' reflecting a number of possible ways of looking at the macroeconomy. In short, Gerrard suggests that we should stop worrying about multiple interpretations, since this confirms the fertility of Keynes's work and its 'reference power'.

Since we cannot hope to do justice to the wide variety of interpretations of Keynes here, we will present a conventional account of some of the main arguments associated with the *General Theory*.

2.8 Keynes's Main Propositions

In the *General Theory* Keynes sets out to 'discover what determines at any time the national income of a given system and (which is almost the same thing) the amount of its employment' (Keynes, 1936, p. 247). In the framework he constructs, 'the national income depends on the volume of employment'. In developing his theory Keynes attempted to prove that macroeconomic equilibrium was consistent with *involuntary* unemployment. The theoretical novelty and central proposition of the book is the principle of *effective demand*, together with the equilibrating role of changes in output rather than prices. The emphasis given to *quantity* rather than price adjustment in the *General Theory* is in sharp contrast to the classical model and Keynes's own earlier work contained in his *Treatise on Money* (1930), where discrepancies between saving and investment decisions cause the price level to oscillate.

The principle of effective demand states that in a closed economy with spare capacity the level of output (and hence employment) is determined by aggregate planned expenditure, which consists of two components, consumption expenditure from the household sector (C) and investment expenditure from firms (I). In the *General Theory* there is no explicit analysis of the effects of variations in spending stimulated either directly by government expenditure or indirectly via changes in taxation. Hence in the *General Theory* there are two sectors (households and firms) and planned expenditure is given by equation (2.18):

$$E = C + I \qquad\qquad (2.18)$$

The reader will recall that in the classical model consumption, saving and investment are all functions of the interest rate – see equations (2.10) and (2.11). In Keynes's model, consumption expenditure is endogenous and essentially passive, depending as it does on income rather than the interest rate. Keynes's theory of the consumption function develops this relationship.

Investment expenditure depends on the *expected* profitability of investment and the interest rate which represents the cost of borrowing funds. Keynes called expected profits the *marginal efficiency of capital*. Thus, unavoidably, in Keynes's model employment becomes dependent on an unstable factor, investment expenditure, which is liable to wide and sudden fluctuations. The dependency of output and employment on investment would not be so important if investment expenditure was stable from year to year. Unfortunately the investment decision is a difficult one because machinery and buildings are bought now to produce goods that will be sold in a future which is inevitably uncertain. Expectations about future levels of demand and costs are involved in the calculation, allowing hopes and fears, as well as hard facts, to influence the decision. Given the volatility of expectations, often driven by 'animal spirits', the expected profitability of capital must also be highly unstable. That investment decisions could be influenced by tides of irrational optimism and pessimism, causing large swings in the state of business confidence, led Keynes to question the efficacy of interest rate adjustments as a way of influencing the volume of investment. Expectations of the future profitability of investment are far more important than the rate of interest in linking the future with the present because: 'given the psychology of the public, the level of output and employment as a whole depends on the amount of investment' and 'it is those factors which determine the rate of investment which are most unreliable, since it is they which are influenced by our views of the future about which we know so little' (Keynes, 1937).

The 'extreme precariousness' of a firm's knowledge concerning the prospective yield of an investment decision lies at the heart of Keynes's explanation of the business cycle. In his analysis of instability, 'violent fluctuations' in the marginal efficiency of capital form the shocks which shift *real* aggregate demand, that is, the main source of economic fluctuations comes from the real side of the economy, as described by the *IS* curve; see section 3.3.1. From his analysis of the consumption function Keynes developed the concept of the *marginal propensity to consume* which plays a crucial role in determining the size of the *multiplier*. Because of the multiplier any disturbance to investment expenditure will have a magnified impact on aggregate output. This can be shown quite easily as follows. Letting *c* equal the marginal propensity to consume ($\Delta C/\Delta Y$) we can write the behavioural equation for consumption as (2.19):

$$C = cY \tag{2.19}$$

Remember in Keynes's model the amount of aggregate consumption is (mainly) dependent on the amount of aggregate income. Substituting (2.19) into (2.18) we get the equilibrium condition given by (2.20):

$$Y = cY + I \tag{2.20}$$

Since $Y - cY = I$ and $Y - cY = Y(1 - c)$ we obtain the familiar reduced-form equation (2.21):

$$Y = I\,(1/1 - c) \tag{2.21}$$

where $1/1 - c$ represents the multiplier. It follows that

$$\Delta Y = \Delta I(1/1 - c) \tag{2.22}$$

Equation (2.22) tells us that income (output) changes by a multiple of the change in investment expenditure. The size of the multiplier will depend on the value of *c*, and $1 > c > 0$. The multiplier effect shows that for an autonomous demand shift (ΔI) income will initially rise by an equivalent amount. But this rise in income in turn raises consumption by $c\Delta I$. The second round increase in income again raises expenditure by $c(c\Delta I)$ which further raises expenditure and income. So what we have here is an infinite geometric series such that the full effect of an autonomous change in demand on output is given by (2.23):

$$\Delta Y = \Delta I + c\Delta I + c^2\Delta I + = \Delta I(1 + c + c^2 + c^3 + \ldots) \tag{2.23}$$

and $(1 + c + c^2 + c^3 + ...) = 1/1 - c$. Throughout the above analysis it is assumed that we are talking about an economy with spare capacity where firms are prepared to respond to extra demand by producing more output. Since more output requires more labour input, the output multiplier implies an employment multiplier (Kahn, 1931). Hence an increase in autonomous spending raises output and employment. In the early Keynesian theories of the business cycle developed by Harrod, Samuelson and Hicks, the interaction of the multiplier with an *accelerator* mechanism (where investment depends on the change in output) played a crucial role and the models developed viewed the cycle as an 'entirely real phenomenon' (Laidler, 1992a).

Keynes's explanation of interest rate determination also marked a break with his classical predecessors. Keynes rejected the idea that the interest rate was determined by the real forces of thrift and the marginal productivity of capital. In the *General Theory* the interest rate is a purely monetary phenomenon determined by the liquidity preference (demand for money) of the public in conjunction with the supply of money determined by the monetary authorities. To the *transactions* motive for holding money, Keynes added the *precautionary* and *speculative* motives, the latter being sensitive to the rate of interest (see section 3.3.2). Keynes rejected the classical notion that interest was the reward for postponed current consumption. For him the rate of interest is the reward for parting with liquidity or not hoarding for a specified period. In a world characterized by uncertainty there will always be a speculative motive to hold cash in preference to other financial assets (such as bonds) and in Keynes's view liquidity preference will always exert a more powerful influence on the rate of interest than saving decisions. By introducing the speculative motive into the money demand function, Keynes made the rate of interest dependent on the state of confidence as well as the money supply. If liquidity preference can vary, this undermines the classical postulate relating to the stability of the money demand function. This in turn implies that the velocity of circulation of money is liable to vary.

The basic structure of Keynes's theory of effective demand can be understood with reference to Figure 2.5. From this the reader can see that the dependence of aggregate output and employment on aggregate expenditure $(C + I)$ creates the potential for instability, since investment expenditure is typically unstable owing to the influence of business expectations relating to an uncertain future. An uncertain future also creates the desire for liquidity, so that variations in the demand for money as well as changes in the money supply can influence output and employment. Therefore in Keynes's model the classical proposition that the quantity of money is neutral is rejected. An increase in the money supply, by reducing the rate of interest, can stimulate aggregate spending via an increase in investment and the subsequent multiplier effect – see equation (2.22). The relationship can be depicted as follows:

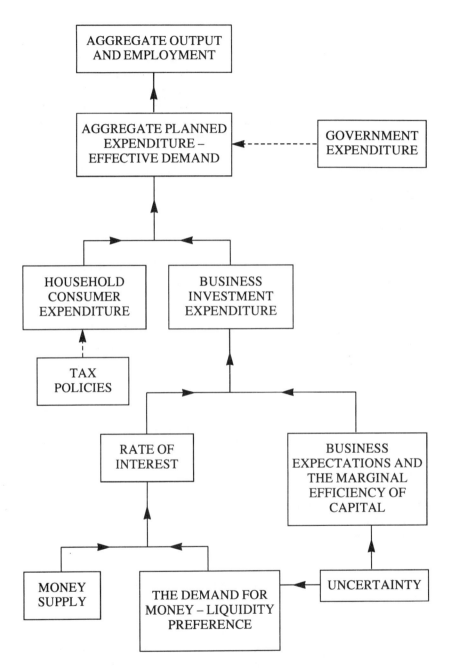

Figure 2.5   The determination of output and employment

$$+\Delta M \rightarrow -\Delta r \rightarrow +\Delta I \rightarrow +\Delta Y, \ +\Delta L$$

It should now be obvious why the title of Keynes's book is *The General Theory of Employment, Interest and Money*. For Keynes it was *General* because full employment was a special case and the characteristics of this special case assumed by classical theory 'happen not to be those of the economic society in which we actually live' (Keynes, 1936, p. 3). However Keynes recognized that the power of monetary policy may be limited, particularly in a deep recession, and there 'may be several slips between the cup and the lip' (Keynes, 1936, p. 173). Should monetary policy prove to be weak or ineffective, aggregate expenditure could be stimulated directly via government expenditure or indirectly via tax changes which stimulate consumer spending by raising household disposable income. In the concluding notes of the *General Theory* we get some hints on Keynes's policy conclusions: 'The State will have to exercise a guiding influence on the propensity to consume partly through its scheme of taxation, partly by fixing the rate of interest, and partly, perhaps, in other ways' (Keynes, 1936, p. 378).

But what are the 'other ways'? In Keynes's view, because of the chronic tendency for the propensity to save to exceed the inducement to invest, the key to reducing aggregate instability was to find ways of stabilizing investment expenditure at a level sufficient to absorb the full employment level of savings. Keynes's suggestion that 'a somewhat comprehensive socialisation of investment' would prove the 'only means of securing an approximation to full employment' is open to a wide variety of interpretations (see Meltzer, 1988). That Keynes saw his theory as having 'moderately conservative' implications and at the same time implying a 'large extension of the traditional functions of government' is a perfect example of the kind of ambiguity found in the *General Theory* which has allowed for considerable variation of interpretation in subsequent work.

In our discussion of the classical model we drew attention to three main aspects of their work: the theory of employment and output determination, Say's Law of markets and the quantity theory of money. We can now briefly examine how Keynes rejected the basic ideas relating to each of these foundations of classical economics.

2.9 Keynes's Analysis of the Labour Market

We have already seen (section 2.3) that full employment is guaranteed in the classical model providing that competition prevails in the labour market, and prices and wages are perfectly flexible (see Figures 2.2 and 2.4). In sharp contrast, Keynes did not accept that the labour market worked in a way which would always ensure market clearing. Involuntary unemployment is likely to be a feature of the labour market if money wages are rigid. But Keynes went further than this and argued that flexibility of nominal wages would be unlikely to generate powerful enough forces which could lead the economy back to full employment. Let us examine each of these cases.

2.9.1   Rigidity of nominal wages

In the *General Theory*, to begin with, Keynes assumes that the money wage is 'constant' in order to 'facilitate the exposition' while noting that the 'essential character of the argument is precisely the same whether or not money-wages are liable to change' (Keynes, 1936, p. 27). We can see the impact of a negative demand shock on real output and employment in the case of nominal wage rigidity by referring to Figure 2.6. Suppose an economy which is initially in equilibrium at full employment (L_e and Y_F) experiences a fall in aggregate demand illustrated by a shift of the AD curve from AD_0 to AD_1. If prices are flexible but nominal wages are rigid the economy moves from e_0 to e_1 in panel (b). With nominal wage rigidity the aggregate supply curve becomes W_0AS. With a fall in the price level to P_1, and nominal wages remaining at W_0 the real wage increases to W_0/P_1 in panel (a). At this real wage the supply of labour (L_d) exceeds the demand for labour (L_c) and involuntary unemployment of cd emerges.

According to Keynes (1936, p. 15) workers are involuntarily unemployed if 'in the event of a small rise in the price of wage-goods relatively to the money-wage, both the aggregate supply of labour willing to work for the current money-wage and the aggregate demand for it at that wage would be greater than the existing volume of employment'. This makes sense when we remember that the labour supply curve indicates the *maximum* amount of labour supplied at each real wage. Since $L_e - L_c$ part of the involuntarily unemployed workers are prepared to work for the equilibrium real wage W_0/P_0 a fall in the real wage from W_0/P_1 to W_0/P_0 is acceptable to them since they would have been prepared to work for a lower real wage, as indicated by the supply curve for labour between b and e. A fall in the real wage will also induce profit-maximizing firms to demand more labour.

But how can the real wage be reduced? There are basically two ways. Either money wages must fall relative to the price level, or the price level must rise relative to the nominal wage. Keynes favoured the latter and he advocated expansions of aggregate demand in order to exert upward pressure on the price level. In terms of Figure 2.6 panel (b), policies are required which will shift AD from AD_1 to AD_0. The rise in the price level from P_1 to P_0 reduces the real wage back to its equilibrium level of W_0/P_0 and involuntary unemployment is eliminated. Keynes rejected the alternative policy of wage cutting as a method of stimulating employment on both practical and theo-

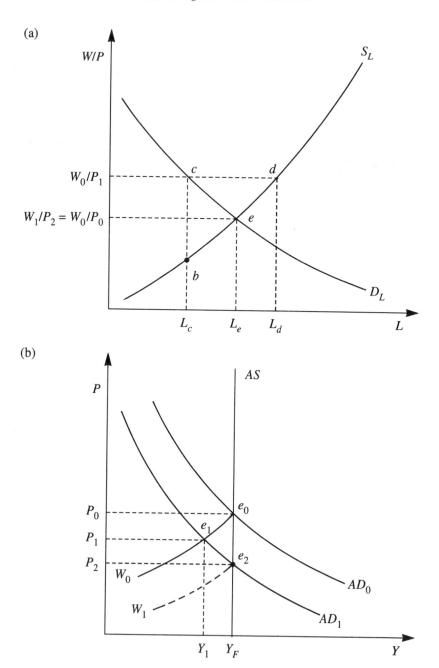

Figure 2.6 Keynes and involuntary unemployment

retical grounds. The practical reason was that in a democracy characterized by decentralized wage bargaining wage reductions are only likely to occur after 'wasteful and disastrous struggles' producing an end result which is not justifiable on any criterion of social justice or economic expediency (see Chapters 3 and 19 of the *General Theory*). Keynes also argued that workers will not resist real wage reductions brought about by an increase in the general price level, since this will leave *relative* real wages unchanged and this is a major concern of workers. We should note that this does not imply *money illusion* on the part of workers. The resistance to money wage cuts and acceptance of reductions in the real wage via a general rise in the cost of living has the advantage of preserving the existing structure of relativities (see Trevithick, 1975; Keynes, 1936, p. 14). In any case, since labour can only bargain over money wages and the price level is outside their control, there is no way in which labour as a whole can reduce its real wage by revising money wage bargains with entrepreneurs (Keynes, 1936, p. 13). But Keynes went further in his objections to nominal wage cutting than these practical issues. He rejected wage and price flexibility as a reliable method of restoring equilibrium on theoretical grounds also. Indeed in many circumstances extreme flexibility of the nominal wage in a *monetary economy* would in all probability make the situation worse.

2.9.2 Flexibility of nominal wages

Keynes demonstrated in the *General Theory* that the way in which nominal wage cuts would cure unemployment would operate primarily through their impact on the interest rate. If wage cuts allowed further reductions of the price level this would increase the real value of the money supply, lower interest rates and stimulate investment spending. In terms of Figure 2.6 panel (b), the falling money wage shifts the aggregate supply curve from $W_0 AS$ to $W_1 AS$ (where $W_1 < W_0$). The economy would return to full employment at e_2. The price mechanism has allowed aggregate demand to increase without government intervention in the form of an aggregate demand stimulus. However, as we will see more clearly in section 3.4.2, Keynes introduced two reasons why this 'Keynes effect' might fail. The existence of a *liquidity trap* which prevents the interest rate from falling or an *interest-inelastic investment schedule* could prevent falling prices from stimulating aggregate demand via changes in the interest rate. In terms of Figure 2.6 panel (b), these possible limitations of deflation as a route to recovery would show up as an *AD* curve which becomes vertical below e_1, that is, the economy is prevented from moving from e_1 to e_2.

For Keynes the policy of allowing money wages to fall for a given money supply could, in theory, produce the same effects as a policy of expanding the money supply with a given nominal wage. But since this was the case, monetary policy was subject to the same limitations as wage cutting as a method of securing full employment. However a severe deflation of prices would also be likely to have adverse repercussions on business expectations, which could lead to further declines of aggregate demand (see Keynes, 1936, p. 269). The impact of severe deflation on the propensity to consume via distributional effects was also likely to be 'adverse' (Keynes, 1936, p. 262). In summing up these issues, Keynes took a pragmatic stance.

> Having regard to human nature and our institutions, it can only be a foolish person who would prefer a flexible wage policy to a flexible money policy... to suppose that a flexible wage policy is a right and proper adjunct to a system which on the whole is one of *laissez-faire*, is the opposite of the truth. (Keynes, 1936, pp. 268–9)

Because of these various limitations of the price mechanism, Keynes was convinced that the authorities would need to take positive action in order to eliminate involuntary unemployment. Unless they did so the system could find itself caught in a situation of *underemployment equilibrium*, by which he meant the tendency of market economies to remain in a chronic condition of subnormal activity for a considerable period 'without any marked tendency either towards recovery or towards complete collapse' (Keynes, 1936, p. 249).

2.10   Keynes's Rejection of Say's Law

Say's Law, if accepted, makes macroeconomic demand management policies redundant. We have seen earlier that in the classical model a decision to refrain from current consumption is equivalent to a decision to consume more in the future. This decision therefore automatically implies that re-sources need to be diverted to the production of investment goods which will be needed to provide the flow of future consumption goods. An increase in saving automatically becomes an increase in investment expenditure via adjustment of the interest rate. In the classical model, saving is in effect just another form of spending. The principles underlying Say's Law raised their head during discussions relating to anti-depression economic policy during the interwar period. Ralph Hawtrey, a strong advocate of the 'Treasury View', argued forcefully that public works programmes would be useless since such expenditures would simply 'crowd out' an equivalent amount of private spending. Such views only make sense in the context of a fully employed economy (Deutscher, 1990).

A principle objective of writing the *General Theory* was to provide a theoretical refutation of Say's Law, something Malthus over a century earlier had tried and failed to do. In Keynes's model output and employment are determined by effective demand and the operation of the labour market cannot guarantee full employment. The interest rate is determined in the money market rather than by saving and investment decisions. Variations in the marginal efficiency of investment bring about variations in real output via the multiplier effect and as a result saving adjusts to investment through changes in income. Hence in Keynes's model any inequality between planned investment and planned saving leads to quantity adjustments rather than equilibrating adjustments of the rate of interest. By demonstrating the flaws inherent in wage and price flexibility as a method of returning the economy to full employment following a negative demand shock, Keynes effectively reversed Say's Law. In Keynes's world of underemployment equilibrium, demand creates supply!

2.11 Keynes and the Quantity Theory of Money

In the classical model a monetary impulse has no real effects on the economy. Money is neutral. Since the quantity of real output is predetermined by the combined impact of a competitive labour market and Say's Law, any change in the quantity of money can only affect the general price level. By rejecting both Say's Law and the classical model of the labour market, Keynes's theory no longer assumes that real output is predetermined at its full employment level. In Chapter 21 of the *General Theory*, Keynes discusses the various possibilities. If the aggregate supply curve is perfectly elastic then a change in effective demand brought about by an increase in the quantity of money will cause output and employment to increase with no effect on the price level until full employment is reached. However, in the normal course of events, an increase in effective demand will 'spend itself partly in increasing the quantity of employment and partly in raising the level of prices' (Keynes, 1936, p. 296). In other words, the supply response of the economy in Keynes's model can be represented by an aggregate supply function such as $W_0 AS$ in Figure 2.6, panel (b). Therefore for monetary expansions carried out when $Y < Y_F$ both output and the price level will rise. Once the aggregate volume of output corresponding to full employment is established, Keynes accepted that 'the classical theory comes into its own again' and monetary expansions will produce 'true inflation' (Keynes, 1936, pp. 378, 303). A further complication in Keynes's model is that the linkage between a change in the quantity of money and a change in effective demand is indirect, coming as it does via its influence on interest rates, investment and the size of the multiplier. We should also note that, once Keynes had introduced the theory of liquidity preference, the possibility that the demand for money function might shift about unpredictably, causing velocity to vary, implies that changes in M may be offset by changes in V in the opposite direction.

With Y and V no longer assumed constant in the equation $MV = PY$, it is clear that changes in the quantity of money may cause V, P or Y to vary. The neutrality of money is no longer guaranteed.

2.12   Three Important Interpretations of Keynes

In the vast literature relating to Keynes's contribution since 1936 we can identify three distinct interpretations which command varying degrees of support (see Coddington, 1983): (i) The 'hydraulic' interpretation, (ii) The 'fundamentalist' interpretation, and (iii) The modified general equilibrium approach.

2.12.1   The 'hydraulic' interpretation

This is the orthodox interpretation of Keynes initiated and inspired by Hicks (1937), Modigliani (1944), Klein (1947), Samuelson (1948) and Hansen (1953). The IS–LM model formed the backbone of theorizing within this approach and it dominated thinking in the emerging neoclassical synthesis during the 1950s and 1960s. Samuelson's textbook played a very important role here, popularizing Keynes with the aid of the 45° Keynesian cross diagram. Following Modigliani's contribution, Keynesian economics was seen to be the economics of wage and price rigidities. The destabilizing impact of unstable expectations was played down in this approach. Although Keynesians such as Modigliani and Tobin worked on improving the microfoundations of Keynes's model, a major weakness of hydraulic Keynesianism was the lack of a convincing reason for wage and price rigidities. The ideas associated with this hydraulic variety of Keynesianism are developed in Chapter 3, while the recent attempts by new Keynesian theorists to rectify the theoretical shortcomings of the neoclassical synthesis model are examined in Chapter 7.

2.12.2   The 'fundamentalist' interpretation

This interpretation of the *General Theory* regards Keynes's work as a frontal assault on neoclassical orthodoxy. Fundamentalists regard the influence of unstable expectations due to uncertainty as a key feature of Keynes's work, particularly as expressed in Chapters 12 and 17 of the *General Theory*, where he discusses *The State of Long-Term Expectations* and *The Essential Properties of Interest and Money*. Fundamentalists also point to Keynes's (1937) *Quarterly Journal of Economics* article entitled 'The General Theory of Employment', which Keynes wrote in response to his critics, as evidence that the problems of decision making under conditions of uncertainty lay at the heart of his system. The key figures in this school include George Shackle (1967, 1974) and Joan Robinson (1962), although a very early statement can be found in Townshend (1937). Fundamentalists reject the hydraulic interpretation as a 'bastardization' of Keynes's contribution. The ideas and development of this Post-Keynesian school are explored in Chapter 8.

2.12.3 The modified general equilibrium approach

Alan Coddington (1983) refers to this view as 'reconstituted reductionism' (reductionists are those economists whose method of analysis consists of 'analysing markets on the basis of the choices made by individual traders'; see Coddington, 1983, p. 92). This approach initially received stimulus from Patinkin's (1956) suggestion that Keynesian economics is the economics of *unemployment disequilibrium* and that involuntary unemployment should be viewed as a problem of dynamic disequilibrium. In Patinkin's analysis, involuntary unemployment can exist in a perfectly competitive economy with flexible wages and prices. The emphasis given by Patinkin to the speed with which markets are able to absorb and rectify shocks shifted attention away from the degree of price and wage flexibility to the issue of *coordination*. This line of enquiry was followed by Clower (1965) and Leijonhufvud (1968) who developed a modified general equilibrium approach along Walrasian lines in order to make sense of coordination problems which inevitably emerge in a market economy operating without the fictional 'auctioneer'. If the hydraulic interpretation played down Keynes's contribution *as a theorist*, the reconstituted, reductionist approach attempts to rehabilitate the *General Theory* as a pioneering exercise in disequilibrium dynamics. We explore these ideas in the second half of Chapter 3.

2.13 The 'New Keynes Scholarship'

In recent years there has been a growth of interest in the early Keynes in order to better understand the later Keynes of the *General Theory*. There is an increasing recognition and acceptance that Keynes's philosophical and methodological framework had a significant influence upon his economic analysis as well as his politics. Whilst much has been written about the alleged content of Keynes's economics, very little has dealt with Keynes's method and philosophy. Littleboy and Mehta (1983) argue that 'The great stimulus to macroeconomic theory provided by Keynes is well recognised but much less is said about his views on scientific methodology', and Lawson and Pesaran (1985, p. 1) concede that 'Keynes's methodological contribution has been neglected generally'. The only major exception to the charge, until the recent contributions of, for example, Carabelli (1988), Fitzgibbons (1988) and O'Donnell (1989), was the latter's earlier study which endeavoured to provide a serious extended analysis of the connection between Keynes's philosophy and his economics (O'Donnell, 1982). These recent attempts to explore the methodological and philosophical foundations of Keynes's political economy may be termed 'the new Keynes scholarship' (see Skidelsky, 1992, pp. 82–9).

The main theme of the new scholarship is to highlight the need to recognize that Keynes's economics is based upon a strong philosophical base and to provide a detailed examination of Keynes's rich and elaborate treatment of uncertainty, knowledge, ignorance and probability. The new scholarship also gives prime importance to Keynes's lifelong fascination with the problem of decision making under conditions of uncertainty. Carabelli (1988) has argued that the general epistemological premises of Keynes's method have been generally overlooked, even though they were systematically presented, albeit in a very refined state, in his *A Treatise on Probability* (1921). Fitzgibbons (1988) maintains that economists have been guilty of suppressing Keynes's philosophy because of its lack of systematization and anti-modernist stance. For Fitzgibbons, Keynes provided a radical alternative to long-run thinking firmly based within the flux and temporary nature of the short run. It is argued that the *General Theory* is centred upon a radical economics of uncertainty organized around 'animal spirits' and creative impulses, alongside the constant threat of economic breakdown: within such a world, money has a rationale and impact on the real side of the economy. Keynes is seen to be concerned with the problems of economic indeterminacy and the abandonment of equilibrium. Likewise Carabelli has placed stress upon Keynes's focus upon the close relation between time and change and the need to analyse and attend to the problems of the short period. O'Donnell (1982, pp. 222–9) attempted to reconcile the long-period and short-period interpretations of Keynes by acknowledging Keynes's interest in both periods, but with greater emphasis being placed on the latter. In O'Donnell's interpretation of Keynes, a universal role for uncertainty and expectations regardless of the period dimension has to be granted.

Although the new scholarship has increased awareness of the linkages between Keynes's philosophy and his economics, it can be argued that, in locating the core of Keynes's method in *A Treatise on Probability*, a work which largely predates much of his serious and scholarly economic writing, authors such as Carabelli fail to consider adequately the reciprocal influence of the economic upon the philosophical and their interaction and continued development. Nevertheless the new scholarship does add weight to the 'fundamentalist' Keynesian position that Keynes's ideas on uncertainty were central to his vision (see Shackle, 1974; Davidson, 1978; and Chapter 8).

2.14 The Classical Revival

Throughout the period after 1936 there have been numerous developments and contributions which reflect a hostile response to Keynes's *General Theory* and have ultimately contributed to a classical revival. The influence of Friedman and the monetarist counter-revolution represented a major challenge to the more simplistic versions and policy conclusions associated with hydraulic Keynesianism. In Friedman's (1983) opinion, 'While the *General Theory* is a great book, I do not regard it as his best ... I have been led to reject it ... because I believe that it has been contradicted by the evidence.'

In Chapter 4 we examine the important challenge to the Keynesian orthodoxy posed by monetarist analysis. Following this we examine the emergence of the new classical school, which launched a much more fundamental attack against Keynesianism during the 1970s. To many, this critique represents the most important challenge to date for the Keynesian conventional wisdom. For Lucas and Sargent, it is a simple matter of 'fact' that the predictions of Keynesian models were 'wildly incorrect' and based on a doctrine which is 'fundamentally flawed'. The 'spectacular failure' of Keynesian models in the 1970s has led to more attention and respect being accorded to 'the theoretical casualties of the Keynesian revolution, to the ideas of Keynes's contemporaries and of *earlier economists whose thinking has been regarded for years as outmoded*' (Lucas and Sargent, 1978, emphasis added).

Charles Plosser, a leading advocate of the new classical real business cycle approach to macroeconomic fluctuations, is also of the view that the Keynesian model is fundamentally flawed. In his opinion, 'the underpinnings of our understanding of economic fluctuations are likely to be found somewhere other than a suitably modified version of the Keynesian model' (Plosser, 1989). Patrick Minford and David Peel (1983), in commenting on the impact of rational expectations on macroeconomics, feel that 'It has turned a body of knowledge – macroeconomics based on the neo-Keynesian or neo-classical systems of the late 1960s – upside down; virtually every topic ... has been found to be in need of rethinking.' In Chapters 5 and 6 we examine the development of the new classical ideas particularly associated with Lucas, Sargent, Barro, Prescott, Kydland and Plosser.

From the Austrian viewpoint, Friedrich von Hayek throughout his life remained a stern critic of Keynes and Keynesians. In Hayek's own words, Keynes was: 'wholly wrong in the scientific work for which he is chiefly known (Hayek, 1983). The powerful Austrian critique associated with the work of Hayek and his followers is reviewed in Chapter 8.

Although we do not deal with the 'Public Choice' school specifically, the perspective offered by James Buchanan and Richard Wagner (1978) is worth noting, given the influence such ideas have had on popular opinion in recent years. Buchanan and Wagner accuse Keynes of 'Intellectual error of monumental proportions' and assert that Keynesian economics 'has turned politicians loose; it has destroyed the effective constraint on politicians' ordinary appetites to spend and spend without the apparent necessity to tax'.

Only a great economist could stir up such reactions. In writing to Roy Harrod in 1935, Keynes made it clear that his attack on the classical economists in his forthcoming book was quite deliberate because he wanted 'to force the classicals to make a rejoinder'. His objective was, 'so to speak, to raise a dust' (see Skidelsky, 1992, p. 534). We can only conclude that in this objective Keynes was spectacularly successful!

In the remaining chapters as well as the interviews we will explore the reasons why economists have reached such a wide variety of conclusions.

ROBERT SKIDELSKY

Robert Skidelsky was born in 1939 in China and graduated in 1960 from Jesus College, Oxford, where he also obtained his MA and DPhil, in 1961 and 1967, respectively. He was a research fellow at Nuffield College, Oxford (1965–8) and at the British Academy (1968–70), Associate Professor of History at Johns Hopkins University (1970–76), Head of Department of History, Philosophy and European Studies, Polytechnic of North London (1976–8), Professor of International Studies, University of Warwick (1978–90) and is currently Professor of Political Economy, University of Warwick (since 1990). He was made a life peer in 1991.

Professor Skidelsky is one of the leading authorities on Keynes and the Interwar Period. Among his best known books are: *Politicians and the Slump* (Macmillan, 1967), *The End of the Keynesian Era* (editor) (Macmillan, 1977), *John Maynard Keynes, Vol. 1 Hopes Betrayed, 1883–1920,* (Macmillan, 1983) and *John Maynard Keynes, Vol. 2 The Economist as Saviour, 1920–1937* (Macmillan, 1992).

Some of his recent articles are: 'Keynes's Political Legacy' and 'Some Aspects of Keynes the Man', in O.F. Hamouda and J.N. Smithin (eds), *Keynes and Public Policy After Fifty Years, Vol. 1, Economics and Policy* (New York University Press, 1988), 'Keynes and the State', in D. Helm (ed.) *The Economic Borders of the State* (Oxford University Press, 1989).

We interviewed Professor Skidelsky in his office at Warwick University on 9 March 1993.

Why did you decide to write a biography of Keynes?
It evolved out of my earlier historical work relating to the interwar years. Keynes was a major presence in my previous books and a major source of inspiration for my view of that period. I thought he was an interesting person and I had better write about him. I came to that conclusion after reading the biography of Roy Harrod in which I thought there were things which were left too vague and unclear.

Does your interpretation of Keynes's life and work differ in any fundamental way from that offered by Harrod and Moggridge?
I am more historically minded. That may be the major difference. There are historical ways of thinking about phenomena and economic ways of thinking about them. Now I do not think you must draw a very sharp divide but economists tend to be generalizers and historians tend to concentrate on the idiosyncratic and unexpected. Historians make better biographers, on balance, than economists. For many economists, evidence is simply data rather than being history – the stuff of illumination. They treat history like statisticians. That is not a very illuminating approach to understanding a man's life or work.

Why are there so many varied interpretations of Keynes's General Theory*? Does this demonstrate the strength or weakness of the book?*
Probably the main reason is that Keynes was a fertile rather than a systematic thinker. He was much better over the short essay than over the treatise. His mind was always brimming with ideas, and he could not really stick to one line for any length of time. Too many things kept coming in. The second reason is that there was, in all his work, a strong polemical element. He wanted very much to do things. You have to sort out the polemics from the theory and it is not always very clear where one begins and the other ends. Keynes would always overemphasize one part of an argument in order to clinch a policy conclusion. The third reason is that Keynes operated on many different levels. You can pick and choose which level you find most attractive. That is why there are these different interpretations.

Do you see this multidimensional picture as a strength?
Yes, because, in the end, fertility is what lasts, not rigour. Rigour is for its own time, fertility is for all time.

What elements of Marshall did Keynes reject and which did he retain in his intellectual journey from The Tract *to the* General Theory*?*

The most obvious thing is that he took from Marshall his particular method of dealing with time. He made a clear distinction, in many of his writings, between the short period and the long period – that came straight out of Marshall. But one must not take that too rigidly because Keynes retained a fairly open mind about the analytic method he would use till quite late in the writing of the *General Theory* – whether to use a short period equilibrium framework or to use a disequilibrium framework. Secondly, he probably never deviated much from Marshall's theory of the firm and he always, rather illogically, accepted Marshall's perfect competition models, despite Marshall's acceptance of increasing returns. Keynes never thought much beyond that, which is why he was really very uninterested in the imperfect competition revolution. I always found that fascinating, paradoxical and odd. The evidence is that although he was a great admirer of Piero Sraffa, he never took on board that element of the Cambridge revolution starting with Sraffa's [1926] article leading through to Joan Robinson's [1933] contribution. This was partly because he remained very Marshallian on the supply side of microeconomics and perhaps as confused as Marshall was on one or two of these issues. Keynes believed in a third-generation theory of the firm and tended to assume that firms decayed naturally before they established any serious monopolistic position in the market. The third influence was the idea that you should not take wants as given and that there were higher value wants. But, unlike Marshall, he thought that these higher value wants were derived from philosophy rather than from evolution. Fourthly, Keynes took from Marshall the cash-balances version of the quantity theory of money. He always thought about the quantity theory in that way and not in the Fisher way. That's how he got into the *Treatise on Money* and beyond that into the *General Theory*. These legacies of Marshall were enormously important.

How would you characterize Keynes's methodological stance?

I think Keynes was only weakly verificationist. He would not have much favoured the view that hypotheses can be verified by tests of one kind or another – certainly not hypotheses in the social or moral sciences. In fact that was the root cause of his opposition to econometrics. He thought that the most important thing about a theory is that it must be fertile and atuned to one's intuitions. He thought data was very important in forming these intuitions: you should not ignore the real world. You should be a vigilant observer, this was one of the economist's most important tasks, but it was raw stuff, it was not doctored or predigested. The kind of stuff modern economists look at is all pre-done, the curves are already there. Keynes hated economic data presented as graphs – that is why he never used graphs in any of his writings, and the one diagram contained in the *General Theory* was provided by Harrod. He always wanted the actual figures. The figures were not to verify hypotheses, they were to indicate the sort of limits of the validity of our intuitions. If the figures were totally contrary to your intuitions then probably your intuition is wrong – but it was a rough and ready kind of testing: nothing that could claim to be verificationist theory. What he would have said about Popper's falsifiability method I do not know. He may have been more interested in that.

Given your detailed biographical work on Keynes, were there any real surprises which you unearthed in your research?
The surprises, if at all, arise from the historical treatment itself, by embedding Keynes's ideas very carefully in historical and biographical situations, including values and, therefore, paying greater attention to the more ephemeral writings. It is usually there that one can see the mind in action and at the edge of things. I find his lectures from the period 1931–3 to be much more interesting, in a way, than the *General Theory* itself, because you can see the whole thing raw. You can actually see more clearly what was going into it. When he was writing his *Treatise on Probability*, he wrote to Lytton Strachey and said, 'I am now turning my stuff into a more formal treatise and everything original that I have thought is going to be snuffed out in the course of doing it because that is what academic life is like.' Now that is not quite true; of course, the *General Theory* was thought to be a revolutionary book when it came out. But I think some of the raw energy that went into the creation of it was lost.

You have written that 'Keynes's inspiration was radical, his purpose conservative' – how did Keynes reconcile these conflicting forces?
Well, the best answer to that was given by Galbraith, who said people who are radical in monetary matters are usually social conservatives. In other words, there is a certain kind of therapy for an economy which is non-structural, which serves the purpose of preserving the existing structures. That does not give rise to a problem in my mind. If you think of some of the competing radicalisms of Keynes's time, particularly Marxism, you do see that Keynes's theory was, by comparison with that, very conservative about the social order, and deliberately so. He said, time and again, if you do not accept my modest remedies you will be faced with having to accept much more disagreeable ones sooner or later. I do not think his theory was simply instrumental to preserving the existing social order but he had that as an aim in his mind. He also really did believe that, with some small changes in the way things were run, you could avoid the worst of business fluctuations and stabilize the economy. You could do this by improvements in economic

science. So in terms of economic theory he was eventually very radical, but in terms of the concluding notes of the *General Theory* he maintains that his theory is moderately conservative.

What exactly did Keynes mean when he talked about the 'socialisation of investment'?
Keynes was a political operator and it was one of those phrases tossed out to the Labour Party. That phrase comes out of the 1920s when he was talking about the growth of socialistic institutions in the womb of capitalism. By the late 1920s he was really arguing that a large part of private enterprise was not properly private any longer; it was, in some sense, socialized because its managers paid more attention to stability than short-run profit maximization. Once firms reached a certain size they also started developing public motives and responsibilities and they tended to be run by people who are much more like civil servants and dons than old-style thrusting Schumpeterian entrepreneurs. So I think the socialization of investment minimally meant simply a growing tendency for investment criteria to be social, arising from the natural evolution of the capitalist system. I think Galbraith has something of the same thought in his *New Industrial State* [1967].

How would you account for the very rapid spread of Keynesian ideas, especially in the United States of America?
Well, did they spread very rapidly in the United States? Within academia you find a very patchy picture if you look at the United States as a whole. Harvard, yes, certainly. The Harvard–Washington nexus has been very well explored. Once Keynesianism could take a tax remission form rather than a public spending form, then, of course, you got quite a lot of conservative business support. You could always give it a supply-side justification. That is why you had a Reagan version of Keynes in the 1980s. There was a much more modest built-in stabilizers version in the 1940s and 1950s. I personally think Keynes had more effect on Roosevelt's New Deal than he has latterly been given credit for, especially in the first phase of the New Deal, the pre-*General Theory* phase. But, as in Britain, Keynesianism really arrived in connection with wartime finance.

Would you draw a clear separation between the work of Keynes and the contributions of Keynesians? In particular, what is your view of the IS–LM interpretation?
You always have to draw a distinction between the work of an original pioneer and that of his followers. The fertility, innocence and sharpness of the original version is modified and made acceptable for the ordinary business of life. Keynes was always quite careful to have a portion of his theory

that could be modelled, even though he did not particularly spend much time modelling it himself. It was left for others to do that, not only Hicks, but Harrod and Meade; the whole thing was reduced to a set of simultaneous equations, an approach which was not true to Keynes's own spirit. He was much more a chain equation person, being far more interested in chains of causation, and trying to work those out. Hicks emptied the *General Theory* of its real bite, he generalized and increased its acceptability, whilst laying the basis for the neoclassical synthesis. It was a very important PR job but I do not think it captured the essence of what Keynes was trying to say. In fact, Hicks conceded this. The interesting point is Keynes's reaction to Hicks's interpretation. Here I do differ somewhat from Don Patinkin, who has always argued that Keynes accepted the Hicks version as an entirely accurate representation of his theory. That Keynes never criticized it is perfectly true. My own feeling is that Keynes, although it sounds odd to say this, never grasped the significance of it and never thought it particularly interesting. He never reacted to it, that is the important point. It is not that he said that this is marvellous or awful, he just never reacted and that is puzzling. He was a punctilious correspondent. Hicks sent it to him, yet he did not reply for six months, and then said 'I have got nothing to say about this', apart from one or two points which seemed rather unimportant. But it does seem to me he thought Hicks was not a very interesting thinker. He said Hicks had got a good beta plus mind. That was a mistake. There was something about Hicks Keynes did not respond to – in exactly the same way Kaldor never did. Kaldor once said to me that Hicks was not a great economist because 'a great economist has to be a pamphleteer – Hicks is a judge, he weighs up everything and takes a middle view. That is not the tradition of Adam Smith at all. Keynes was in that tradition, I, Kaldor, am in that tradition, Hicks is not'. There was some lack of sympathy between Keynes and Hicks which meant that Keynes tended to ignore anything which Hicks did.

Did Keynes give the classics a rough deal in the General Theory*?*
Yes. He set up an Aunt Sally. No classical economist ever believed in the things Keynes claimed that classical economics stood for and none of his associates did really. Neither Robertson, Hawtrey nor Hayek were classical economists. The only classical economist was someone like Pigou. Keynes was quite deliberate. He said the things he was describing as classical economics were not what the economists of his day actually believed in, but the things they would need to believe to make sense of what they were saying. Keynes was challenging them to make their premises consistent with their conclusions.

If the General Theory *had been written in 1926, could the economic disaster experienced in the 1930s have been avoided?*

No, I do not think that the *General Theory* could have been published ten years earlier. That particular indictment of classical economics and, indeed, of the way the economy behaved needed the great slump to crystallize it. Keynes's books were very good reflections of the experience of the different decades. The *Treatise on Money* sums up the 1920s and had nothing to do with the great slump. It is an open economy model where one country is not doing very well. The *General Theory* is a book about a world slump and, therefore, there is no escape except through the government. But your question, in addition, seems to be asking: if people had been equipped with better theory would they have had better policy? You needed not only the better theory but also the better theory *to be accepted*, and that is very different. My hunch is that all theories of a Keynesian type, paradoxically, start to wilt a bit if things get very, very bad. They are most acceptable when they are least needed. In other words, everyone was Keynesian in the 1950s and 1960s when there was no pressure. As soon as the pressure starts you find that orthodoxy has a habit of coming back and here is a psychological puzzle: when people are under great stress and there is a great increase in nervousness then people do cling to the oldest of their verities, not the newfangled ones.

Do you think too much has been made of the Pigou effect as a way of diminishing Keynes's theoretical contribution? Did he not anticipate but reject this idea himself?

In the 1920s it came under the rubric of 'induced lacking' which Keynes added to Dennis Robertson's *Banking Policy and the Price Level* [1926]. This is where you increase your saving in order to restore the real value of your cash balances eroded by inflation, and that is an equilibrating mechanism, and Keynes suggested this real balance effect to Robertson. Why did Keynes not see it working in reverse, in a situation of deflation? I think the answer is that he was not thinking along those equilibrium lines. I know Presley [1986] makes out the case that he was, but I did not find his argument persuasive. In the case of the Pigou effect, why did not Keynes admit it as a sort of theoretical possibility and then simply discount it as irrelevant or very weak? I do not know. Keynes was greatly concerned about the consequences of a community becoming increasingly impoverished, rather than mechanical adjustments of balances.

To what extent was there a Keynesian revolution in the UK and USA in the post-Second World War period? Do you think Keynes would have approved of the policies so often carried out in his name?

It is hard to say that there was not a revolution. Some commentators have doubted whether there was. It still seems to me that if you commit yourself to maintain a high and stable level of employment you are saying something new, and governments had not said that before. How much you intend to do about it is another matter. But once you have produced a form of words, even politicians are somewhat constrained by them. And, of course, they would only have made that pledge, had they had a somewhat different model of the economy than they had before the war, and some experience of Keynesian fiscal management, which came in the Second World War. So there was a worldwide Keynesian revolution which was obviously different in different countries. Everyone took what they wanted from Keynes and added it to their own traditions.

How fundamental are the 'presuppositions of Harvey Road' to Keynes the political economist? Surely the contributions made by the Public Choice school and from the political business cycle literature have shown Keynes to have been politically naive?
No, I would not accept that. You cannot really say that someone was naive unless they lived through the relevant period and failed to register the findings of that period. It is not the right word to use about Keynes and I think his political views would have developed had he lived through the 1960s and 1970s. The assumptions that he made at the time probably fitted the facts of the time rather better than they fitted the facts of later times.

*Other than Keynes, who in your view has had the most important influence on the post-*General Theory *development of macroeconomics?*
Undoubtedly Friedman. Both as a challenger to Keynes and as a leader of thought in his own right. The Friedmanite challenge to Keynes also led into the rational expectations revolution. It is very, very, important to understand that Friedman is a macroeconomist and shares many of Keynes's presuppositions of the role of macroeconomics in stabilizing economies. Friedman has always given high praise to Keynes's *Tract on Monetary Reform*. The other great economist of the twentieth century was Hayek, but Hayek disbelieved in macroeconomics, he did not believe it to be a valid science because he was a methodological individualist of a very extreme kind.

Given Keynes's emphasis upon the importance of expectations in the General Theory, *what do you think he would have made of the rational expectations hypothesis and the new classical models developed by Lucas and others?*
Again, it is terribly difficult, because you are really asking a question about Keynes's epistemology and that takes you into his *Treatise on Probability* and how you talk about the rationality of beliefs. There are flashes of rational

expectations in Keynes – you could tell a rational expectations story about the instantaneous multiplier if you wanted to, since you expect or anticipate all of the effects immediately – but on the whole, surely, his leading idea was uncertain expectations.

David Laidler [1992b] has recently drawn attention to the low standards of historical scholarship amongst economists. As a historian and an economist would you agree with this view?

Yes, I think so, partly for the reasons I have outlined earlier. Economists are not very good historians and I believe this comes out particularly in connection with Keynesian studies which emphasize or pay exclusive attention to a single book – the *General Theory* – and which show a lack of interest as to how it fits into the whole of his thought and the history of the time. One of the few economists who understood that was Axel Leijonhufvud [1968], who took the *Treatise on Money* seriously and tried to build up a picture of Keynesian theory that was halfway between the *Treatise on Money* and the *General Theory*. That was a very interesting exercise. The new scholarship has taken seriously the problem of linking Keynes's later economic writings to his earlier philosophical writing, but this approach is curiously unhistorical. They do not, for example, see the *Treatise on Probability* as a work of before 1914, which is what a historian would instinctively see it as, and root it there. These new scholars simply set it side-by-side with the *General Theory* and explore the differences and similarities. That is not history.

Which non-economic elements most influenced Keynes's economics?

I would have thought there were three key non-economic elements. First, the classics, which he studied at school, and his sense of the classical world and its methods. There are lots of classical and fairy-tale allusions in his writings. Second, theology. A lot of his language, and the way he used it, was quite theological. After all, economics was theology's successor and retains many of its characteristics. Third, the arts. What is economic activity for? This comes out especially in essays like 'Economic Possibilities for our Grand-children' [1930]. Aesthetics influenced his view of the role of economics.

The vehement opposition to the UK's membership of the ERM expressed by leading British monetarists such as Alan Walters and Patrick Minford bears an uncanny resemblance to Keynes's attack upon Churchill in the 1920s. Are the two episodes similar?

The two episodes are similar in many ways. In both cases the pound was overvalued and insufficient attention was paid to the adjustment process. Keynes's opposition to the gold standard was based upon the argument of the *Tract on Monetary Reform*, which is very monetarist. It has to do with the lag system in the adjustment to new sets of prices or exchange rates. But I do not think that Keynes was ever a currency floater in the 1970s monetarist sense. He wanted a managed system, and remember he was one of the main architects of the Bretton Woods system. In a world in which there were no controls on capital and where you had a financial system that was much more deregulated than it was even in Keynes's day, one may conjecture whether he would have thought that we cannot win the game against speculators, hence the attempt to maintain fixed exchange rates is doomed to failure.

Despite the crisis in Keynesianism, widely recognized in the 1970s, such ideas are now experiencing something of a resurgence. How do you account for this? Do you see an emerging consensus, perhaps, where Keynesianism again has a focal point in macroeconomics?
Well yes. Keynes said two things that seem to me of permanent value and must be part of anyone's thinking about the way economies work. Firstly, he emphasized uncertainty leading to volatility. Speculation is the balancer of economies and the way it balances is through extreme volatility in other markets. Secondly, he emphasized repercussions on income, output and prices, rather than prices alone. These two things are very important and any modern understanding of the way economies work must bear those two things in mind. If you believe economies are volatile, that recessions are sufficiently severe and that their effects do not go away automatically, then that dictates some role for government. Other economists say that government should not play very much of a role, just follow a few rules. This is where the real debate is and I am on Keynes's side. That does not mean that we shall exactly follow Keynes's own prescriptions. Times change and his policies would have changed with them.

If Keynes had still been alive in 1969, do you think he would have received the first Nobel Prize in Economics?
Ah [*laughter*]. Well, all one can say is yes [*further laughter*].

3. The orthodox Keynesian school and the reinterpretation of Keynes

The Keynesian revolution was the most significant event in 20th-century economic science. (Samuelson, 1988)

3.1 Introduction

The main purpose of this chapter is twofold: first, to review briefly one interpretation of Keynes's *General Theory*, the familiar Hicksian IS–LM model, before considering more fully the theoretical debate on underemployment equilibrium; second, to consider the reinterpretation of Keynes by a number of economists who have argued that the orthodox Keynesian IS–LM model seriously misrepresents Keynes's contribution to economic theory and aborts his fundamental message. The reader should be aware that throughout this and subsequent chapters two recurrent and interrelated issues arise, concerning (i) the controversy over the self-equilibrating properties of the economy and (ii) the role for interventionist government policies. We begin our discussion with the orthodox Keynesian approach to these central issues within macroeconomics.

3.2 The Orthodox Keynesian School

The central distinguishing beliefs within the orthodox Keynesian school can be listed as follows:

1. The economy is *inherently unstable* and is subject to erratic shocks. The shocks are attributed primarily to changes in the marginal efficiency of investment following a change in the state of business confidence, or what Keynes referred to as a change in investors' 'animal spirits' (see section 2.8).
2. Left to its own devices the economy can take a long time to return to the neighbourhood of full employment after being subjected to some disturbance; that is, the economy is not rapidly self-equilibrating.
3. The aggregate level of output and employment is essentially determined by aggregate demand and the authorities can intervene to influence the

level of aggregate 'effective' demand to ensure a more rapid return to full employment.

4. In the conduct of stabilization policy, fiscal as opposed to monetary policy is generally preferred as the effects of fiscal policy measures are considered to be more direct, predictable and faster acting on aggregate demand than those of monetary policy. These beliefs found expression in the orthodox Keynesian model, known as the IS–LM model, to which we now turn.

3.3   The IS–LM Model

The orthodox Keynesian model which has had such an important bearing on the development of macroeconomics, right through to the present day, initially stemmed from Hicks's (1937) famous article entitled 'Mr Keynes and the Classics: A Suggested Interpretation'. This Hicksian model was subsequently elaborated upon by Modigliani (1944) and was popularized in the United States by Hansen (1949, 1953). Indeed over the next half-century the Hicksian IS–LM model became the established model for macroeconomic theorizing and it had a tremendous influence on the direction of macroeconomic policy right up to the mid-1960s.

It is assumed that most readers will at least be familiar with the derivation of the IS–LM model, so that in what follows we merely review the main features of the model for a closed economy, in particular the way the model integrates real and monetary factors in determining aggregate demand and therefore the level of output and employment. Those readers who are unfamiliar with the derivation of the model (or the extension of the model to an open economy) should refer to any standard macroeconomics text, such as Dornbusch and Fischer (1994). We begin our review with the goods market and the IS curve.

3.3.1   The goods market and the IS curve

Equilibrium in the goods market occurs where the aggregate demand for and aggregate supply of goods are equal. In the orthodox Keynesian model the level of output and employment is assumed to be determined entirely by aggregate demand; that is, supply constraints are ignored. In a closed economy aggregate demand is comprised of the sum of consumption, government expenditure and investment. In order to simplify the analysis, consumption expenditure is held to depend positively on disposable income, government expenditure is taken as being exogenously determined, while investment is treated as being inversely related to the rate of interest, a variable determined within the model by the interaction of the goods and money markets.

The *IS* curve traces out a locus of combinations of interest rates and income associated with equilibrium in the goods market. The *IS* curve derives its name from the equilibrium condition in the goods market where, in a closed economy with no government sector, investment (*I*) equals savings (*S*). Given the assumption that investment is inversely related to the rate of interest, the *IS* curve is downward sloping (see Figure 3.2). *Ceteris paribus*, as the rate of interest falls, investment increases, resulting in a higher level of income. The slope of the *IS* curve depends on the interest elasticity of investment expenditure and the value of the multiplier. The *IS* curve will be steeper (flatter) the less (more) investment responds to a change in the rate of interest and the smaller (greater) is the value of the multiplier. For example, *ceteris paribus*, the less investment increases for a given fall in the rate of interest, the less income will increase, generating a steeper *IS* curve. Similarly the smaller the value of the multiplier the less income will increase following a given increase in investment, and hence the steeper the *IS* curve will be. In the limiting (extreme Keynesian) case where investment is perfectly interest-inelastic, the *IS* curve will be vertical.

Finally it is important to remember that the *IS* curve is drawn for a given level of government expenditure, taxation and expectations, so that expansionary fiscal policy (that is, an increase in government expenditure and/or a reduction in taxation, or a more optimistic business outlook) shifts the *IS* curve outwards to the right, and vice versa. For example, an increase in government expenditure will be associated with a higher level of income at any given level of the rate of interest, the outward shift of the *IS* curve being equal to the increase in government expenditure times the value of the multiplier. We now turn to the money market and the *LM* curve.

3.3.2 The money market and the *LM* curve

Equilibrium in the money market occurs where the demand for and supply of money are equal. The money supply is assumed to be exogenously determined by the authorities. Within the model three main motives for holding money are identified: the transactions, the precautionary and the speculative motives. The demand for transactions and precautionary balances is assumed to vary positively with income. The demand for speculative or idle balances depends on the current level of the rate of interest relative to the normal rate of interest. By assuming that different people have different expectations about the future course of the rate of interest, it is possible to postulate that the demand for speculative balances will vary inversely with the rate of interest (see Figure 3.1). The higher the current level of the rate of interest (relative to the level regarded as normal) the greater the number of individuals who expect future reductions in the rate of interest (and therefore rising bond prices) and the less speculative balances demanded, and vice versa. Of particular importance is the theoretical possibility that, at low interest rates, which would be expected to prevail in conditions of underemployment equilibrium, the demand for money could become perfectly elastic with respect to the rate of interest. This is illustrated by the horizontal section of the curve at r^* in Figure 3.1. At r^* expectations converge as everyone expects that the only future course of the rate of interest is upwards, so that the demand for money becomes perfectly interest-elastic: the so-called 'liquidity trap'. With regard to the liquidity trap, it is interesting to note that Keynes put it forward only as a theoretical possibility and even commented that he was not aware of it ever having been operative in practice (see Keynes, 1936, p. 207). Nevertheless, as we will discuss in section 3.4.2, it became especially important to the analysis of underemployment equilibrium in the orthodox Keynesian model.

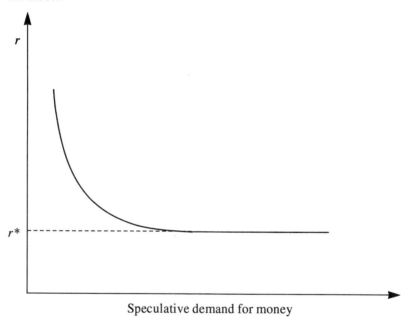

Figure 3.1   Demand for speculative balances

The *LM* curve traces out a locus of combinations of interest rates and income associated with equilibrium in the money market. The *LM* curve derives its name from the equilibrium condition in the money market where the demand for money, or what Keynes called liquidity preference (*L*), equals the supply of money (*M*). Given the assumption that the demand for money is positively/negatively related to income/interest rate, the *LM* curve is upward-sloping (see Figure 3.2). *Ceteris paribus*, as income rises the transactions and precautionary demand for money increase which, given the supply of money, necessitates a higher rate of interest to reduce the speculative demand for money and maintain equilibrium in the money market. The slope of the *LM* curve depends on the income elasticity and the interest elasticity of the demand for money. The *LM* curve will be steeper (flatter) the higher (smaller) the income elasticity and the smaller (greater) the interest elasticity of the demand for money. For example, *ceteris paribus*, the more the demand for money increases following a given increase in income, the larger will be the rise in the rate of interest required to maintain equilibrium in the money market, generating a steeper *LM* curve. In the limiting cases of (i) the so-called 'classical range' (where the demand for money is perfectly interest-inelastic) and (ii) the liquidity trap (where the demand for money is perfectly elastic with respect to the rate of interest) the *LM* curve will be vertical and horizontal respectively.

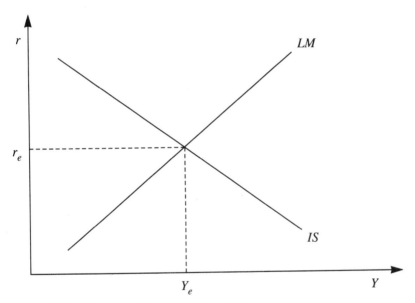

Figure 3.2   The generalized IS–LM model

Finally it is important to remember that the *LM* curve is drawn for a given money supply, price level and expectations, so that expansionary monetary policy (that is, an increase in the supply of money) shifts the *LM* curve downwards to the right, and vice versa. Following an increase in the money supply, and a given income elasticity of the demand for money, any given level of income must be associated with a lower interest rate to maintain equilibrium in the money market. The extent to which the *LM* curve shifts depends on the interest elasticity of the demand for money. A given increase in the supply of money will cause a small/large shift in the *LM* curve where the demand for money is relatively interest-elastic/inelastic as equilibrium in the money market will be restored by a small/large fall in the interest rate. Readers should verify this for themselves.

3.3.3   The complete model and the role of fiscal and monetary policy

Equilibrium in both the goods and money markets is simultaneously attained where the *IS* and *LM* curves intersect, that is, at $r_e Y_e$ in Figure 3.2. Two points are worth emphasizing. First, the intersection of the two curves in Figure 3.2 represents the *only* value of the rate of interest and income which is consistent with equilibrium in both markets. Second, if the level of income is below that of full employment then both fiscal and monetary policy have a potentially important role to play in stabilizing the economy. We now briefly review what determines the relative effectiveness of fiscal and monetary policy in influencing aggregate demand and therefore the level of output and employment.

In Figure 3.3, the economy is initially in equilibrium at $r_0 Y_0$ (the intersection of IS_0 and *LM*) at less than full employment. Expansionary fiscal policy (for example, an increase in government expenditure) shifts the *IS* curve outwards to the right, from IS_0 to IS_1 and results in an increase in both the equilibrium rate of interest (from r_0 to r_1) and the equilibrium level of income

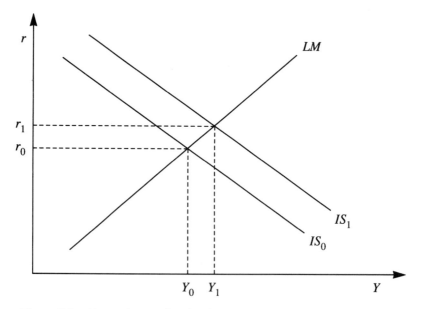

Figure 3.3   Expansionary fiscal policy

(from Y_0 to Y_1). As spending and income increases, the transactions and precautionary demand for money increase, which, with a fixed money supply, results in an increase in the rate of interest. The rise in the rate of interest in turn leads to a reduction in private sector investment spending, the extent of which depends on the interest elasticity of investment. Readers should verify for themselves that fiscal policy will be more effective in influencing aggregate demand and therefore the level of output and employment (i) the more interest-elastic is the demand for money; that is, the flatter is the *LM* curve, and (ii) the less interest-elastic is investment; that is, the steeper is the *IS* curve. In the limiting cases of (i) a vertical *LM* curve (classical range) fiscal expansion will have no effect on income, as the rise in the rate of interest will reduce private investment by an amount identical to the increase in government expenditure; that is, complete (100 per cent) crowding out or the so-called 'Treasury View'; and (ii) a horizontal *LM* curve (liquidity trap) fiscal expansion will result in the full multiplier effect of the simple Keynesian 45° or cross model.

In Figure 3.4, the economy is again initially in equilibrium at r_0Y_0 (the intersection of LM_0 and *IS*) at less than full employment. Expansionary monetary policy shifts the *LM* curve downwards to the right, from LM_0 to LM_1 and results in a fall in the equilibrium rate of interest (from r_0 to r_1) and an increase in the equilibrium level of income (from Y_0 to Y_1). Within the

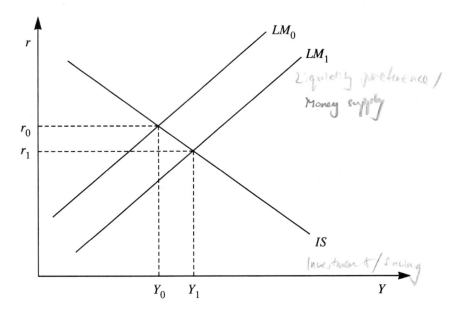

Figure 3.4   Expansionary monetary policy

orthodox Keynesian transmission mechanism the strength of monetary policy depends on (i) the degree to which the rate of interest falls following an increase in the money supply; (ii) the degree to which investment responds to a fall in the rate of interest; and (iii) the size of the multiplier. Readers should verify for themselves that monetary policy will be more effective in influencing aggregate demand and therefore the level of output and employment (i) the more interest-inelastic is the demand for money; that is, the steeper is the *LM* curve, and (ii) the more interest-elastic is investment; that is, the flatter is the *IS* curve. In the limiting (extreme Keynesian) cases of either (i) a horizontal *LM* curve (liquidity trap) or (ii) a vertical *IS* curve (that is, where investment is completely interest-inelastic) the transmission mechanism breaks down and monetary policy will have no effect on the level of income.

From the above discussion it should be evident that, while both fiscal and monetary policies can, in normal circumstances, be used to influence the level of output and employment, the relative effectiveness of these two policy instruments depends on the structural parameters of the model, that is, the relative slopes of the *IS* and *LM* curves. Within the orthodox Keynesian approach, the demand for money has traditionally been viewed as being highly responsive to changes in the rate of interest (generating a relatively flat *LM* curve), while investment has been taken as being fairly unresponsive to changes in the rate of interest (generating a relatively steep *IS* curve). Indeed there was early empirical support for orthodox Keynesianism associated with the elasticities of the *IS* and *LM* curves, with Klein referring to its 'solid empirical basis' (see Klein, 1968, pp. 65–6, pp. 71–2) – a basis, we hasten to add, which became increasingly questionable in the early 1960s. In these circumstances disturbances from the real side of the economy (that is, stochastic shifts in the *IS* curve) tend to dominate changes in income. Furthermore fiscal policy is generally preferred as it is relatively powerful, while monetary policy is relatively weak. At this point the reader should note that by the end of the 1950s the belief in the efficacy of fiscal policy relative to monetary policy was much stronger amongst British as compared to American Keynesians.

This analysis can also be summarized in algebraic terms. In what follows it is assumed that the price level is fixed when the economy is at less than full employment. Aggregate real expenditure (E) is equal to an autonomous component (A), a component dependent on real income (cY) and an interest-sensitive component (ar).

$$E = A + cY - ar \qquad (3.1)$$

Equilibrium in the goods market occurs where the aggregate demand for and aggregate supply of goods are equal.

$$E = Y \tag{3.2}$$

Turning to the money market, the demand for real money balances (M/P) has a component dependent on real income (mY) and an interest-sensitive component (br).

$$\frac{M}{P} = mY - br \tag{3.3}$$

The supply of nominal money balances is assumed to be exogenously determined ($\overline{M}_s$). Equilibrium in the money market occurs where the demand for and supply of money are equal.

$$\frac{M}{P} = \frac{\overline{M}_s}{P} \tag{3.4}$$

Rearranging these relationships and solving the system for Y gives:

$$Y = \frac{1}{1 - (c - \frac{a}{b}m)} A + \frac{1}{m + \frac{b}{a}(1 - c)} \frac{\overline{M}_s}{P} \tag{3.5}$$

Within this framework, orthodox Keynesians can be characterized as low a and high b people. Reference to equation (3.5) reveals that, where the ratio a/b is small, (i) disturbances from the real side of the economy tend to dominate changes in income, and (ii) fiscal policy is relatively powerful with the autonomous expenditure multiplier tending to $1/1-c$, while monetary policy is relatively weak with the money multiplier tending to zero. These central distinguishing beliefs of orthodox Keynesians were noted earlier, in section 3.2.

The orthodox Keynesian faith in the effectiveness of fiscal policy has been challenged by, amongst others, monetarists who typically argue that in the long run 'pure' fiscal expansion (that is, expansion without any accommodating changes in the money supply) will result in the crowding out or replacement of components of private expenditure with relatively minor effects on aggregate demand, the level of income and employment. A number of reasons as to why crowding out can occur in the IS–LM framework have been put forward in the literature, which do not rely on the demand for money being perfectly interest-inelastic (a vertically-sloped *LM* curve), including expectations and wealth effects (see Carlson and Spencer, 1975). In what follows we outline the Keynesian response which reasserted the importance of fiscal policy (see Blinder and Solow, 1973) focusing on the wealth effects

of a bond-financed increase in government expenditure. This analysis involves an extended version of the Keynesian IS–LM model incorporating the
government budget constraint.

The top panel of Figure 3.5 depicts the conventional IS–LM model and the
lower panel the government budget position determined by the relationship
between government expenditure (G), which is assumed to be independent of
income, and tax receipts (T), which are endogenous to the level of income. At
Y_0 (the intersection of IS_0 and LM) both the goods and money markets are in
equilibrium and the government budget is balanced ($G_0=T$); that is, a stable
equilibrium position prevails. Suppose the authorities now seek to raise the

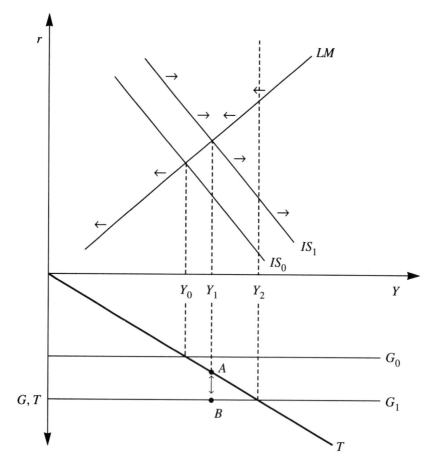

Figure 3.5   *The government budget constraint and bond-financed fiscal
expansion*

level of income and employment by increasing their expenditure. An increase in government expenditure shifts the *IS* curve outwards to the right, from IS_0 to IS_1, and the government expenditure function downwards, from G_0 to G_1. At Y_1 (the intersection of IS_1 and *LM*) there is a budget deficit equal to AB. As long as the deficit persists, the authorities will have to issue more bonds, which will lead to an increase in private sector wealth (owing to increased bond holdings) and an increase in private consumption expenditure and the demand for money. If the wealth effect on consumption (which shifts the *IS* curve further outwards to the right, as indicated by the arrows) outweighs that on the demand for money (which shifts the *LM* curve upwards to the left) then in the long run bond-financed fiscal expansion will result in income increasing to Y_2, where the deficit will be removed; that is, crowding out will be absent. Furthermore if increased interest payments arising from bond finance are taken into account (shifting the government expenditure function downwards beyond G_1) income will have to rise above Y_2 in order to balance the government budget. It is evident therefore that incorporating wealth effects and the government budget constraint into the IS–LM model makes a bond-financed increase in government expenditure potentially very effective in raising the level of income and employment.

One particular objection to the predictions of this analysis concerning the efficacy of fiscal policy worth commenting on is that which derives from what has come to be known as the Ricardian debt equivalence theorem (see, for example, Buchanan, 1976). In short this theorem states that the burden of government expenditure on the private sector is equivalent whether it is financed by an increase in taxation or by bond sales. The sale of government bonds places a burden on the private sector involving a future tax liability in order to meet interest payments on and, where the bonds are not perpetuities, redemption of the bonds. Assuming the private sector takes this future tax liability fully into account, government bonds will be not regarded as net wealth. Future tax liabilities will be discounted and their present value will be perceived to exactly offset the value of the bonds sold. Barro's (1974) influential paper presents an elegant exposition of the controversial view that government bonds should not be regarded as net wealth. In these circumstances it would make no difference whether the government sold bonds or raised taxes to finance expenditure, as selling bonds will not affect the private sector's wealth. The private sector would merely react to a bond-financed increase in government expenditure by saving more in the present period in order to meet future tax liabilities. In other words the effect of an increase in government expenditure will be the same whether it is financed by increased taxation or bond sales, in line with the so-called 'balanced-budget' multiplier. A bond-financed increase in government expenditure will only be more effective than a tax-financed increase in expenditure if government bonds are regarded as net wealth.

Several arguments have been raised against the Ricardian debt equivalence theorem and in what follows we briefly mention two of the main criticisms of it. The reader is referred to Tobin (1980a) and Feldstein (1982) for accessible and critical discussions of the Ricardian doctrine and its implications, and to Barro (1989b) for a spirited defence against the main theoretical objections that have been raised to the approach. First, if the future tax liability arising out of bond-financed fiscal expansion falls on a future generation then it can be argued that the present generation will be wealthier. Barro has argued, however, that the existence of bequests implies that the present generation will raise their saving so as to increase their bequests to their children in order to pay for the future tax liability. Barro's argument that the existence of bequests implies concern by parents about the tax burden their children will face has itself been subjected to a number of criticisms. For example, it is open to debate as to whether or not all parents will be so far-sighted, or concerned enough, to take into account the expected tax liability of their children. Second, given imperfect capital markets, government bonds may be regarded as net wealth. The rate of interest the government pays on bonds establishes the magnitude of the future tax liability. If, as a result of the government having more favourable access to capital markets than individuals, the rate of interest is less than the discount rate appropriate to the private sector when estimating the present value of the future tax liability, government bonds will be regarded as net wealth. In this situation a bond-financed increase in government expenditure will increase private sector wealth and consumption, and be more expansionary that a tax-financed increase in government expenditure.

We now turn to consider the Keynesian belief that the economy can take a long time to return to full employment after being subjected to some disturbance. This involves a discussion of the debate on underemployment equilibrium and in what follows we examine the circumstances under which the IS–LM model will fail to self-equilibrate at full employment.

3.4 Underemployment Equilibrium in the Keynesian Model

3 4.1 The general case
Within the IS–LM model the existence of underemployment equilibrium can be attributed to the existence of 'rigidities' in the system, especially two key prices, the money wage and the interest rate. We begin with that of the 'Keynesian' assumption of downward rigidity in money wages. This case can be illustrated using the four-quadrant diagram of Figure 3.6. Quadrant (a) depicts the standard IS–LM model. Quadrant (c) shows the short-run produc-

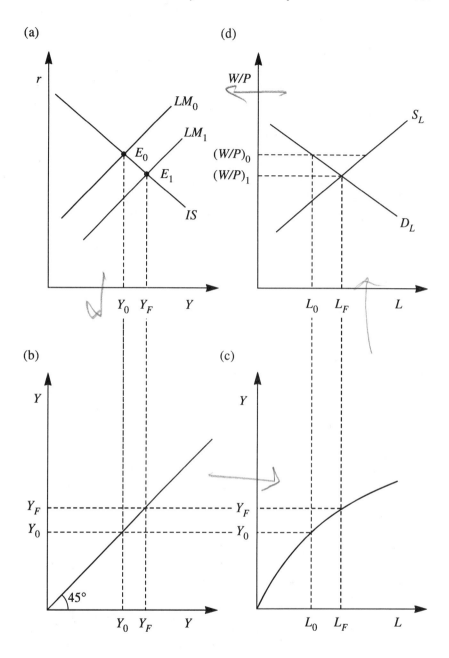

Figure 3.6   The general case with the Keynes effect

tion function where, with the capital stock and technology taken as given, the level of output/income (Y) depends on the level of employment (L) – see section 2.3. Quadrant (d) depicts the labour market in which it is assumed that the demand for/supply of labour is negatively/positively related to real wages (W/P). Finally quadrant (b) shows, via a 45° line, equality between the two axes, both of which depict income. The inclusion of this quadrant allows us to see more easily the implications of a particular equilibrium level of income, established in the goods and money markets in quadrant (a), for the level of employment shown in quadrant (d). In other words in what follows the reader should always start in quadrant (a) and move in an anti-clockwise direction to trace the implications of the level of income (determined by aggregate demand) in terms of the level of employment in quadrant (d).

Suppose the economy is initially at point E_0; that is, the intersection of LM_0 and IS in quadrant (a). While both the goods and money markets are in equilibrium, the income level of Y_0 is below the full employment income level Y_F. Reference to quadrant (d) reveals that with a fixed money wage (set exogenously) and a price level consistent with equilibrium in the money market (that is, the curve LM_0) the resultant level of real wages (W/P)$_0$ is inconsistent with the labour market clearing. In other words there is no guarantee that the demand-determined level of employment (L_0) will be at full employment (L_F). The excess supply of labour has no effect on the money wage, so that it is possible for the economy to remain at less than full employment equilibrium with persistent unemployment. We now consider what effect combining the IS–LM model with the classical assumption of flexible prices *and* money wages has on the theoretical possibility of under-employment equilibrium.

Again suppose the economy is initially at point E_0; that is, the intersection of IS and LM_0 in quadrant (a). As before, while both the goods and money markets are in equilibrium, the income level of Y_0 is below the full employment income level Y_F. Reference to quadrant (d) reveals that this implies that the level of employment (L_0) is below its full employment level (L_F) with real wages (W/P)$_0$ above their market clearing level (W/P)$_1$. As long as prices and money wages are perfectly flexible, the macroeconomy will, however, self-equilibrate at full employment. At (W/P)$_0$ the excess supply of labour results in a fall in money wages (W) which reduces firms' costs and causes a fall in prices (P). The fall in prices increases the real value of the money supply, causing the LM curve to shift downwards to the right. Excess real balances are channelled into the bond market where bond prices are bid up and the rate of interest is bid down. The resultant fall in the rate of interest in turn stimulates investment expenditure, increasing the level of aggregate demand and therefore output and employment. The 'indirect' effect of falling money wages and prices which stimulates spending via the interest rate is referred to as the *Keynes effect.* The increase in aggregate demand moderates the rate of fall in prices so that as money wages fall at a faster rate than prices (an unbalanced deflation) the real wage falls towards its (full employment) market-clearing level, that is $(W/P)_1$ in quadrant (d). Money wages and prices will continue to be bid down and the LM curve will continue to shift downwards to the right until full employment is restored and the excess supply of labour is eliminated. This occurs at point E_1, the intersection of LM_1 and *IS*. It is important to stress that it is the increase in aggregate demand, via the Keynes effect, which ensures that the economy returns to full employment.

Within this general framework there are, however, two limiting or special cases where, despite perfect money wage and price flexibility, the economy will fail to self-equilibrate at full employment. The two special cases of (i) the liquidity trap and (ii) that where investment expenditure is interest-inelastic are illustrated in Figures 3.7 and 3.8, respectively.

3.4.2 The limiting or special cases

In the liquidity trap case illustrated in Figure 3.7, the economy is initially at point E_0, the intersection of IS_0 and LM_0. Although both the goods and money markets are in equilibrium, the income level of Y_0 is below the full employment income level Y_F. Reference to quadrant (d) reveals that this implies that the level of employment (L_0) is below its full employment level (L_F) with real wages $(W/P)_0$ above their market-clearing level $(W/P)_1$. At $(W/P)_0$ the excess supply of labour results in a fall in money wages (W) which reduces firms' costs and causes a fall in prices. Although the fall in prices increases the real value of the money supply (which shifts the LM curve outwards, from LM_0 to LM_1) the increased real balances are entirely absorbed into idle or speculative balances. In other words, in the liquidity trap where the demand for money is perfectly elastic with respect to the rate of interest at r^* (see also Figure 3.1), the excess balances will not be channelled into the bond market and this prevents a reduction in the rate of interest to r_1 (at point E_2) which would be required to stimulate aggregate demand and restore full employment. With no increase in aggregate demand to moderate the rate of fall in prices, prices fall proportionately to the fall in money wages (a balanced deflation) and real wages remain at $(W/P)_0$, above their market-clearing level $(W/P)_1$. Aggregate demand is insufficient to achieve full employment and the economy remains at less than full employment equilibrium with persistent 'involuntary' unemployment. Finally, as noted earlier, in section 3.3.3, in the case of the liquidity trap monetary policy becomes impotent, while fiscal policy becomes all-powerful, as a means of increasing aggregate demand and therefore the level of output and employment.

In the interest-inelastic investment case illustrated in Figure 3.8, the economy will also fail to self-equilibrate at full employment. As before, we assume the

liquidity trap

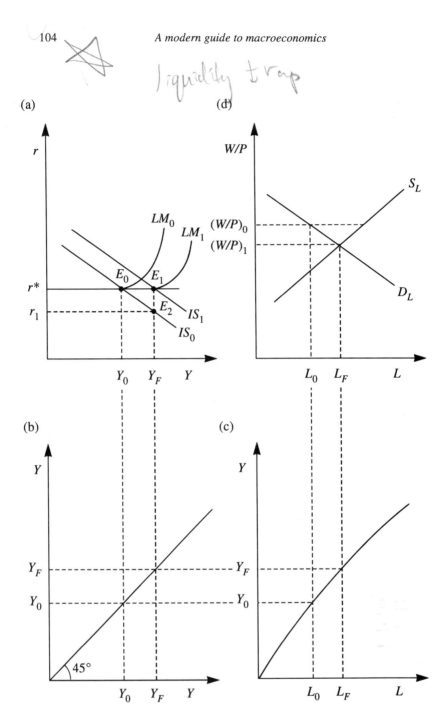

Figure 3.7   The liquidity trap case

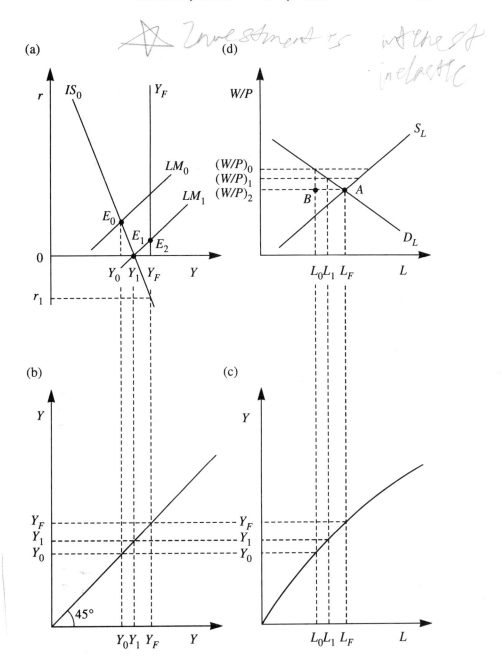

Figure 3.8 The interest-inelastic investment case

economy is initially at point E_0 (the intersection of IS_0 and LM_0) at an income level (Y_0) which is below its full employment level (Y_F). This implies that the level of employment (L_0) is below its full employment level with real wages $(W/P)_0$ above their market clearing level $(W/P)_2$. The excess supply of labour results in a fall in money wages and prices. Although the increase in real balances (which shifts the LM curve from LM_0 to LM_1) through the Keynes effect results in a reduction in the rate of interest, the fall in the rate of interest is insufficient to restore full employment. Reference to Figure 3.8 reveals that, with investment expenditure being so interest-inelastic, full employment equilibrium could only be restored through the Keynes effect with a negative rate of interest at r_1. In theory the economy would come to rest at E_1 (with a zero rate of interest) a point of underemployment equilibrium (Y_1) with persistent involuntary unemployment.

At this stage it would be useful to highlight the essential points of the above analysis. In summary, reductions in money wages and prices will fail to restore full employment unless they succeed in increasing aggregate demand via the Keynes effect. In the liquidity trap and interest-inelastic investment cases, aggregate demand is insufficient to achieve full employment and persistent involuntary unemployment will only be eliminated if the level of aggregate demand is increased by expansionary fiscal policy. The effect of combining the comparative-static IS–LM model with the classical assumption of flexible prices and money wages is to imply that Keynes failed to provide a robust 'general theory' of underemployment equilibrium and that the possibility of underemployment equilibrium rests on two highly limiting/special cases.

The above *equilibrium* analysis, which owes much to the work of Modigliani, implies, as we have seen, that it is possible for the economy to come to rest with persistent (involuntary) unemployment due to 'rigidities' in the system; that is, rigid money wages, the liquidity trap or the interest-inelastic investment case. In contrast Patinkin (1956) has argued that unemployment is a *disequilibrium* phenomenon and can prevail even when money wages and prices are perfectly flexible. To illustrate the argument, assume an initial position of full employment and suppose that there then occurs a reduction in aggregate demand. This reduction will result in a period of disequilibrium in which both prices and money wages will tend to fall. Patinkin assumes that money wages and prices will fall at the same rate: a balanced deflation. In consequence the fall in the level of employment is not associated with a rise in real wages but with the fall in the level of aggregate 'effective' demand. In other words, firms would be forced off their demand curves for labour. In terms of panel (d) of Figure 3.8, this would entail a movement from point A to B. Nevertheless in Patinkin's view this disequilibrium will not last indefinitely because, as money wages and prices fall, there will be a 'direct' effect stimulating an increase in aggregate demand, via the value of money balances, thereby restoring full employment; that is, a movement back from point *B* to *A*. This particular version of the wealth effect on spending is referred to as a 'real-balance' effect. More generally, as we discuss in the next section, the introduction of the wealth or Pigou effect on expenditure into the analysis ensures that, in theory, as long as money wages and prices are flexible, even in the two special cases noted above the macroeconomy will self-equilibrate at full employment. We now turn to discuss the nature and role of the Pigou effect with respect to the possibility of underemployment equilibrium in the Keynesian IS–LM model.

3.4.3 The Pigou effect

Pigou was one of the last great classical economists who spoke for the classical school in the 1940s (for example, 1941, 1943, 1947) arguing that, providing money wages and prices were flexible, the orthodox Keynesian model would not come to rest at less than full employment equilibrium. The Pigou effect (see, for example, Patinkin, 1948, for a classic discussion of the Pigou effect) concerns the effect that falling prices have on increasing real wealth, which in turn increases consumption expenditure. Suppose, as is the case in Figure 3.7, the economy is at underemployment equilibrium (Y_0) in the liquidity trap at point E_0, the intersection of IS_0 and LM_0. As prices fall, not only will the *LM* curve shift outwards to the right (from LM_0 to LM_1) as the real value of the money supply increases, but the *IS* curve will also shift to the right, from IS_0 to IS_1, as the resultant increase in real wealth increases consumption expenditure. In theory the economy cannot settle at underemployment equilibrium but will automatically adjust until full employment is achieved at point E_1, the intersection of IS_1 and LM_1. The reader should verify that, once the Pigou or wealth effect on expenditure is incorporated into the analysis, in the special interest–inelastic investment case illustrated in Figure 3.8 the economy will automatically adjust to restore full employment, at point E_2. The importance of the Pigou effect at the *theoretical* level has been neatly summarized by Johnson (1964): 'the Pigou effect finally disposes of the Keynesian contention that underemployment equilibrium does not depend on the assumption of wage rigidity. It does.'

Over the years a number of reservations have been put forward which question whether, in practice, the Pigou or wealth effect will ensure a quick return to full employment (see, for example, Tobin, 1980a). In what follows we consider two of the main criticisms of the effect. First, dynamic considerations may invalidate the Pigou effect as a rapid self-equilibrating mechanism. For example, if individuals expect a further future fall in prices, they may postpone consumption, causing unemployment to rise. At the same time, if firms expect a recession to continue, they may postpone their investment plans, again causing unemployment to rise. Furthermore in a deep recession bankruptcies are likely to increase, reducing expenditure still further (see, for example, Fisher, 1933). In terms of the diagrammatic analysis we have been considering, falling prices may cause the *IS* curve to shift to the left, driving the economy further away from full employment equilibrium. In these circumstances expansionary fiscal policy would ensure a more rapid return to full employment.

Second, we need to consider briefly the debate on which assets constitute 'net' wealth. Net wealth can be defined as total wealth less outstanding liabilities. In the Keynesian model wealth can be held in money and bonds. Consider first money, which is widely accepted as comprising currency plus bank deposits. Outside money can be defined as currency, plus bank deposits which are matched by banks' holdings of cash reserves or reserves at the central bank. Outside money may be considered as net wealth to the private sector as there is no offsetting private sector liability. In contrast inside money can be defined as bank deposits which are created by lending to the private sector. As these bank deposits are matched by a corresponding private sector liability (bank loans) it can be argued that inside money cannot be regarded as net wealth. It is worth noting that the argument that inside money does not constitute net wealth has been challenged by, among others, Pesek and Saving (1967) and Johnson (1969). While this is an interesting debate within monetary economics it goes beyond what is required for our purposes. Suffice it to say that, if one accepts the argument that only outside money unambiguously constitutes net wealth, the wealth effect of falling prices on consumption expenditure is greatly diminished. Next, as noted earlier, in section 3.3.3, there is debate over whether government bonds can be regarded as net wealth. It could be argued that the private sector will realize that, following a fall in prices, the increase in the real value of government debt outstanding will necessitate future increases in taxes to meet the increased value of interest payments on, and redemption of, government bonds. If the rise in the present value of future tax liabilities exactly offsets the increase in the real value of government debt outstanding there would be no wealth-induced shift in the *IS* curve. Again, while this view is not one that is universally accepted, it does nevertheless cast doubt on the self-equilibrating properties of the economy via the Pigou effect. The empirical evidence for the strength of the Pigou effect shows it to be extremely weak. For example, both Glahe (1973, pp. 213–14) for the USA and Morgan (1978, pp. 55–7) for the UK found that the Pigou effect was not strong enough to restore full employment in the interwar period, with actual price level falls taking place alongside a *decline* in expenditure and output. Furthermore, on reasonable assumptions, Stiglitz (1992) has shown that, if prices were to fall by 10 per cent per year, then *ceteris paribus* 'to increase consumption by 25 per cent would take roughly 400 years' and 'it is hard to see even under the most optimistic view, the quantitative significance of the real balance effect for short-run macroeconomic analysis'. Given such doubts, orthodox Keynesians prescribe expansionary fiscal policy to ensure a more rapid return to full employment.

Finally it is interesting to quote Pigou (1947), who suggested that the 'puzzles we have been considering ... are academic exercises, of some slight use perhaps for clarifying thought, but with very little chance of ever being posed on the chequer board of actual life'.

3.4.4 The neoclassical synthesis

From the discussion of sections 3.4.1–3.4.3 it will be apparent that, if money wages and prices are flexible, the Keynesian IS–LM model can in theory, via the Pigou or wealth effect, automatically adjust to achieve full employment, the main prediction of classical economics. In terms of pure analytical theory, Pigou was said to have won the intellectual battle, establishing a triumph for classical theory. Some writers (for example, Wilson, 1980; Presley, 1986; Bridel, 1987) have suggested that Keynes anticipated the wealth effect but rejected it on theoretical and practical grounds. Notwithstanding this neglected point, Keynesians regarded themselves as having won the policy debate in that the process of adjustment via the Pigou effect might be so slow that interventionist policies (notably expansionary fiscal policy) would be required to ensure a more rapid return to full employment. During the late 1950s and early 1960s a consensus view emerged, the so-called 'neoclassical synthesis', in which the *General Theory* was seen as a special case of a more general classical theory (that is, the case where downward money wage rigidity prevents the classical automatic adjustment to full employment), while the need was recognized for Keynesian interventionist policies to ensure a more rapid return to full employment. In the mid-1960s a number of economists reacted against the neoclassical synthesis which minimized Keynes's status as an economic theorist and, in reinterpreting the *General Theory*, sought to re-establish Keynes's contribution to economic theory. It is to this reinterpretation of Keynes we now turn. We begin by considering the work of Robert Clower and Axel Leijonhufvud, who in the 1960s led a movement to restore Keynes's credibility as a theorist by reconstructing his work on the basis of a rejection of the classical theory of market-clearing equilibrium.

3.5 The Reinterpretation of Keynes: Disequilibrium Models

3.5.1 The work of Clower and Leijonhufvud

Clower (1965) opened the attack on the standard presentation of Keynes in his seminal paper. This was followed by Leijonhufvud's criticisms (1967,

1968) of the income-expenditure model and his elaboration of the 'economics of Keynes'. Their work has been characterized as *disequilibrium* Keynesianism since it presents unemployment and effective demand failure as a disequilibrium problem brought about by information and coordination deficiencies. It has also been called 'reconstituted reductionism' (see Coddington, 1976) as it maintains that Keynes accepted many of the key microtheoretic assumptions of orthodoxy, such as atomistic competition and price signals, but wished to extend the specification of the choice constraints on individual behaviour by including both price and quantity factors.

The Clower–Leijonhufvud reinterpretation suggests that Keynes's revolution was directed at Walras. The neoclassical synthesis failed to recognize that the logic of Keynes's case is based upon a rejection of the key Walrasian coordinating mechanism, namely, the auctioneer. His theoretical contribution only becomes understandable in that context. To comprehend the enormity of Keynes's intellectual achievement in the *General Theory* we need to explore both Walras's old world and Keynes's brave new world and recognize that they exist independently of each other.

The Walrasian general equilibrium framework attaches a pivotal role to the auctioneer who guarantees, via the tâtonnement mechanism, that *all* markets succeed in achieving optimal trades. In this world there is neither disappointment nor surprise, no false trading ever occurs. The auctioneer searches for the correct price vector which will clear all markets and does not permit trading at non-equilibrium prices since that would result in either buyers or sellers being rationed in their purchases or sales. Economic agents allow the auctioneer-cum-price mechanism to establish and police the array of relative prices (that is, they are price takers) and they decide upon the quantities they wish to sell (that is, they are quantity makers). In this world *all goods are equally liquid* in the sense that, once you accept the equilibrium prices, you can realize all your assets. It is a paradoxical world, since all goods are both money goods (in the sense of being acceptable in all markets – what we may term, super-barter) and non-money goods (in the sense of lacking a differentiable liquidity spectrum).

We present such a world in Figure 3.9 where, for simplicity, we assume two *interdependent* markets, the labour and goods markets. For example, let us presume that the auctioneer initially sets prices at $(W/P)_1$ in the labour market and P_1 in the goods market. With this array of relative prices only L_1 of labour would be notionally purchased whilst L_2 would be offered, that is, $L_2 - L_1$ would represent an excess supply (*ES*) of labour. Likewise, in the goods market, only Q_1 would be notionally offered for sale whilst Q_2 would be demanded; that is, $Q_2 - Q_1$ would represent an excess demand (*ED*) for goods. Of course the Walrasian auctioneer would not permit such false trades at these disequilibrium prices and the tâtonnement or groping process would

(a)

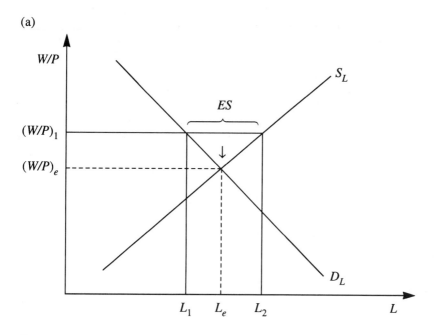

(b)

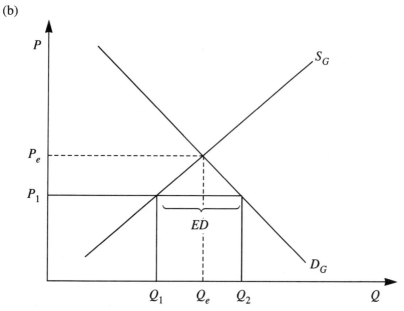

Figure 3.9   The labour (a) and goods (b) markets

allow the real wage to fall in the labour market and the price level to rise in the goods market until equilibrium prices and hence market-clearing quantities were established. Within such a world the excess supply is matched by an excess demand; with the establishment of equilibrium prices we find that effective and notional trades must be equal, since *the decision to supply labour is automatically also the decision to demand goods* (what Clower calls the unitary decision hypothesis). The auctioneer takes account of the transmission of notional desires or signals and turns them into effective messages by only permitting equilibrium prices and trades to take place. The auctioneer-cum-price mechanism controls and coordinates economic actions in order to guarantee optimal trades between parties.

As Clower and Leijonhufvud both recognized, to make the transition from this world of Walras to that of Keynes all one has to do is dispense with the above smooth functioning (deviation-counteracting) tâtonnement mechanism by removing the Walrasian auctioneer:

> The only thing which Keynes *removed* from the foundations of classical theory was the *deux ex machina* – the auctioneer which is assumed to furnish, without charge, all the information needed to obtain the perfect co-ordination of the activities of all traders in the present and through the future. (Leijonhufvud, 1967, pp. 308–9)

Keynes's mission was to kill off the auctioneer myth in order to raise the profile of information and coordination difficulties within real economies. What the neoclassical synthesis did was to raise up the auctioneer fiction to its former glory and totally abort the purpose of Keynes's escape from the classics.

Once we enter Keynes's world, a whole host of relevant problems present themselves. Without the auctioneer, economic agents have to become price makers and the control mechanism which prohibited sub-optimal trades is no longer in force, since non-equilibrium prices may become established. In such a world the short end of the market will determine effective trades, with the long end displaying the degree of rationing. This can be seen in Figure 3.10, where an above-equilibrium price of P_1 generates the offer of Q_2 with only Q_1 being purchased since actual trades are demand-determined. Likewise with a below-equilibrium price of P_2 we have a demand for Q_2 with only Q_1 being sold since actual trades are supply-determined ($Q_2 - Q_1$ measures the degree of disappointment or rationing when the market fails to clear). In non-clearing markets there is a need to distinguish between notional and effective demands/supplies, with the former representing unconstrained desires (based upon the assumption that sales/purchases can always be realized) and the latter representing constrained opportunities (limited by one's ability to buy or sell). In effect, the line *abc* represents the

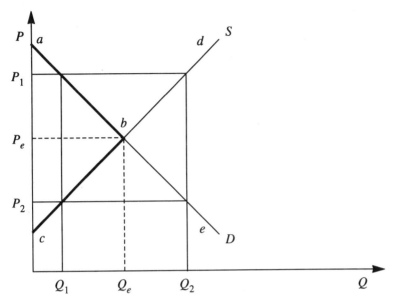

Figure 3.10 Effective trades and notional preferences

effective trade curve, with the line *dbe* as the notional trade curve. It is only in the special Walrasian world of market clearing prices that notional and effective demands/supplies are equal, that is at point *b*. In the general Keynes world, where non-equilibrium prices generate false trades and disequilibrium, the effective demand (the short end) is below the notional supply (the long end).

In such a world as this the decision to sell is not automatically transformed into a decision to buy, since the sale has first to be realized before a purchase can be made. This is the essential point of Clower's dual decision hypothesis. Planned (notional) purchases will not be made unless intended sales have been realized (made effective). The only signals transmitted from one market to another are the effective messages backed by the wherewithal to pay. If the labour market, for example, were to find itself with a non-equilibrium real wage of $(W/P)_1$, as in Figure 3.9, then it would only employ L_1 (there would be an excess supply of labour equivalent to $L_2 - L_1$) and many sellers of labour would find that being rationed in this market would also constrain their purchases in the goods market. An inability to sell or realize one's labour would transform itself into an inability to purchase or command commodities, since the sellers of such goods are *only* interested in a demand backed by an ability to pay; that is, an effective rather than a notional demand. The seller of champagne would quickly tire of the unemployed coming to the store to state how much they liked champagne if only they could afford it. Notional demands do not convey any useful information or signals. Only effective demands and supplies count.

Acceptance of the dual decision hypothesis is so crucial to Clower's argument that he maintains that 'Keynes either had a dual-decision hypothesis at the back of his mind, or most of the *General Theory* is theoretical nonsense' (Clower, 1969, p. 290). The fact that one has to sell before one can buy suggests that there is a realization problem within decentralized market systems such that the super-barter fiction under the Walrasian auctioneer also needs to be abandoned. It is no longer correct in Keynes's world to uphold that all goods are equally liquid, equally marketable. One needs to distinguish money from non-money commodities and recognize a spectrum of salability, with money as the only truly acceptable asset across all markets. As Clower has so succinctly put it, 'Money buys goods and goods buy money; but goods do not buy goods' (1969, pp. 207–8). Abandonment of the barter fiction means the rejection of the unitary decision hypothesis.

Leijonhufvud elaborates upon the Clower theme by building an 'economics of Keynes' distinct from the Walrasian Keynesianism of the neoclassical synthesis. Like Clower, he suggests that the neoclassical synthesis got the formal basis of the Keynesian revolution wrong. He argues that Keynes recognized the difficulties, within decentralized capitalism, of finding the appropriate market-clearing price vector. It is argued that in Keynes's world the initial response to shocks upon the system is via quantities rather than prices, with the relative speed of adjustment of the latter tending to lag behind the former (a reversal of Walras). In the absence of the Walrasian auctioneer, the key question is focused upon the control mechanisms and relates to the generation and dissemination of information. For Keynes, information and coordination deficiencies lead to deviation-amplifying (positive feedback) processes, such as the multiplier, which were played down by the Walrasian synthesis which highlighted the deviation-counteracting (negative feedback) mechanisms.

According to Leijonhufvud, the neoclassical synthesis totally misunderstood and misinterpreted Keynes. Its telling of the Keynesian story highlighted elements which played no real part in the argument of the *General Theory* but a significant part in the work of the Keynesians – such as the claims that wages are rigid; the liquidity trap exists in actuality; and that investment is interest-inelastic. Leijonhufvud maintains that none of these Keynesian building-blocks are to be found in the economics of Keynes. In addition, he argues that the neoclassical claims that Keynes neglected the wealth effect in the *General Theory* cannot be sustained – Keynes attended to the wealth effect and to the mechanisms which were later highlighted by Pigou and Patinkin.

Much of the problem is seen to reside in the income–expenditure (IS–LM) model itself. The standard model is presented as a misleading framework or guide to Keynes because it is based upon a different aggregative structure. Whilst Keynesians and Keynes both have five goods (consumer goods, capital goods, labour, money and bonds) in their respective models they only solve for three relative prices. This means that there is a need to assimilate one good into another. The standard model combines consumer goods with capital goods under the heading of commodities, whilst Leijonhufvud argues that Keynes combines bonds with capital goods under the heading of non-money assets, which in turn suggests a more pronounced interest sensitivity of investment expenditure. In attacking the IS–LM apparatus, Leijonhufvud also attacks the inherent elasticity pessimism of the model and the rationalization of its functional relationships. For further discussion of these matters see, for example, Jackman (1974) .

Leijonhufvud develops Clower's insights that Keynes's departure from the classics involved nothing more than the removal of the auctioneer, with many of the inherited microtheoretic building-blocks retained (especially those related to pricing signals and incentives). In this world economic agents make both price and quantity decisions and display inelastic expectations; that is, they establish reservation prices for their labour (and other commodities) which are based upon past experiences. When such markets fail to clear, potential traders are slow to adjust their prices and engage in a search of the market in the hope of achieving previously obtainable prices. The problem appears to be one of sluggish price adjustments lagging behind those required for market clearing.

Leijonhufvud accepts Clower's claim that this disequilibrium problem only arises within a truly monetary economy with goods being exchanged for money and money for goods. In Keynes's world the market signals presupposed in Walrasian general equilibrium are not transmitted. There are two key problems which appear to prevent an economy suffering from effective demand failures from bouncing back towards equilibrium and which only arise once the auctioneer and super-barter fiction are removed. First, in Keynes's world, as argued above, the offer of labour services by the unemployed does not constitute effective demand for goods *until such sales are realized*. Prospective workers are unwilling to be paid in real terms in a monetary economy – the output of firms is an unattractive means of payment since workers will have to bear many of the risks and transactions costs of business. If producers found that their output *was* a suitable means of payment for labour inputs – as in the Walrasian world – then the offer of labour services *would* automatically translate into an effective demand for the output of the firm.

Second, there is a temporal problem related to a change in the time preference of individual economic agents. In Walras's world an increase in saving is transmitted via the loanable funds market into a reduction in the interest rate and a matching rise in investment, so that the new output mix reflects the changed desires (see section 2.4). Signals are transmitted to the production sector that it should switch its output mix away from consumption towards investment. In Keynes's world, however, the situation is decidedly different because no such signals are transmitted. Not only is the interest rate mechanism slow to adjust, but an increase in saving primarily feeds through a reduction in effective demand, since economic agents only signal what they do not want, rather than what they do want. The production sector fails to receive information on where it is to re-employ freed resources because savers do not wish to transmit (hence commit themselves). As Keynes recognized in the *General Theory*, savers want to have 'the potentiality of consuming an unspecified product at an unspecified time'. Such future demands are not effective demands.

With regard to the Pigou effect, Leijonhufvud argues that there is a critical ratio of the demand price for productive assets to money wages which is low during a depression, not because money wages are too high, but because the price of assets is too low – the reason being that either the interest rate is too high or entrepreneurs are too pessimistic about the rates of return on such assets. In this case there is a need to increase the critical ratio by monetary and/or fiscal policy. The wealth effect, since it is based upon a *balanced* deflation, cannot restore full employment equilibrium because it would affect the two components of the critical ratio *equally* rather than differentially.

Although the economics of Keynes presented by Clower and Leijonhufvud presents a fruitful line of interpretation, a great deal of doubt remains over whether they have correctly identified Keynes's contribution. It can be argued that both authors struggle to find sufficient textual support in Keynes for their claims. As one critic put it (Coddington, 1976, p. 1268), Clower does 'not so much read between the lines as off the edge of the page'. One crucial flaw in their respective presentations is that they both assume Keynes's revolt was against Walras. They both invent a formalized and systematic Walrasian fiction as representative of the classics. Unfortunately Keynes's long struggle to escape was not directed at Walras (who is only cited once, on a relatively trivial matter, in the *General Theory*) but rather the Cambridge of Marshall and Pigou (as well as the Vienna of Mises and Hayek). The highly developed Walrasian world model with which they compare Keynes's theoretical break and achievement was an after-Keynes product (rigorously defined in the USA after the Second World War) and could not have been the target of Keynes's revolt against orthodoxy (although it *was* the target of both Clower's and Leijonhufvud's separation of Walrasian (auctioneer) Keynesianism and their (auctioneerless) economics of Keynes). The arguments of Clower and Leijonhufvud are only really addressed to the neoclassical synthesis debate;

they tell us very little about the actual Keynes episode, since they fail to separate the economics of the classics from the classical economics fictions created after Keynes. This point has been more recently admitted by Leijonhufvud (1976) when conceding that Keynes's revolution was actually directed at Marshall whilst his and Clower's aim was to debunk elements of Walras to *re-establish* Keynes's message. Hicks (1967a, p. vii) also became dissatisfied with his IS–LM depiction of classical theory, admitting that he was unable 'to get his predecessors at all right'. Since Leijonhufvud did not address the issue of the economics of the classics correctly, it can be argued that his demarcation criterion between Keynes and pre-Keynes thought (with quantity adjustments in the former but not in the latter) fails since it is not robust enough to discount the achievements of Hawtrey or Robertson (both of whom are given almost no role in his telling of the Keynesian story).

3.5.2   The microfoundations of the macroeconomics of non-clearing markets

Orthodox Keynesianism appeared to lack a clear and robust choice-theoretic micro base for the macro adjustments it endeavoured to explain. Clower's and Leijonhufvud's reappraisal of Keynesian theory in the light of general equilibrium analysis focused a great deal of its attention upon the microfoundations of Keynes and the Keynesians (as well as the classics) and the micro–macro link between price signals, expectations and quantity adjustments. The work of Phelps *et al.* (1970) maintained that no self-respecting macroeconomic theory was complete without a thorough examination of its microeconomic credentials. More recently the contributions of Barro and Grossman (1976) and Malinvaud (1977), amongst others, have attempted to provide a reconsideration of the theory of unemployment in terms of rationing models within a framework of the macroeconomics of non-clearing markets. There was an increasingly recognized need for a carefully elaborated price choice-theoretic account of the quantity adjustments taking place. Barro and Grossman pointed to the weak foundations of conventional macroeconomic analysis and the need for re-examination and restructuring of the microeconomic foundations to deal with the problem of exchange under non-market-clearing conditions. Likewise Malinvaud endorsed both the reconsideration of the basic foundations and the development of the general equilibrium approach with sticky prices and rationing in the short run.

One of the key theoretical ambitions of those engaged in the microfoundations of macroeconomics is to bridge the gulf that developed between micro and macro theory on the basis of a distinction between those models which worked well and those which worked badly. E. Roy Weintraub (1979, p. 76) has drawn attention to the need for microfoundations of macroeconomics which can explain both coordination successes and failures.

Given the limited space at our disposal, in what follows we shall concentrate our analysis upon the work of Malinvaud (1977) which provides a succinct outline and typology of different equilibria appertaining to an economy facing rationing. Attention will be focused upon rationing in a two-market model (consumer goods and labour). Malinvaud maintains that the theory of unemployment is closely tied to the theory of rationing since the very existence of involuntary unemployment demonstrates that suppliers of labour are being rationed (given that labour market supply is greater than labour market demand). In addition it is argued that a general equilibrium approach is superior to partial equilibrium, as any rationing in the labour market is closely related to rationing taking place in the goods market (and vice versa). One needs to adopt a general interdependency framework in order to examine the constraints that are effective and the simultaneous determination of quantities traded in both markets. A Hicksian distinction is drawn between fix-price (industrial) and flex-price (agricultural) markets in the short run, with the acceptance of downward price rigidities in the former allowing for the dominance of quantity adjustments. Malinvaud states, 'The classical teaching, according to which prices quickly react to excess supplies or demands, is more and more inadequate for short run macroeconomic analysis as we move into ever-higher degrees of organisation of society' (1977, p. 9). Concern is with short-run intertemporal equilibria and the model assumes that prices and wages are determined exogenously. Emphasis switches to quantities being traded rather than prices and (following our discussion of Clower and Leijonhufvud) in each market it is the short side which determines the amount transacted and the long side the amount being rationed (see discussion of Figure 3.10 earlier). This allows Malinvaud to conclude: 'In a Walrasian equilibrium, in which prices are supposed to have adjusted, demand is equal to purchase or supply to sale. But in an equilibrium with fixed prices and quantity adjustments, the equality no longer holds' (1977, p. 13).

Malinvaud provides a typology of different equilibria with rationing where the markets for labour and consumer goods are unbalanced in the sense that they can be either a seller's market (with the rationing of at least one buyer) or a buyer's market (with the rationing of at least one seller) – see Figure 3.11. Keynesian unemployment is characterized by sellers being rationed in both markets; that is, there is an excess supply in both the labour and goods markets, with workers rationed in employment and firms in sales of goods. Classical unemployment takes place when buyers are rationed in the goods market and sellers are rationed in the labour market; that is, firms have less desire to trade than households in each market and the high level of wages makes it unprofitable either to employ more workers or to sell more goods. Repressed inflation is characterized by buyers being rationed in both markets; that is, the excess demand in both markets means that the quantities

		MARKET FOR GOODS	
		BUYERS	SELLERS
MARKET FOR LABOUR	BUYERS	KEYNESIAN UNEMPLOYMENT	CLASSICAL UNEMPLOYMENT
	SELLERS	UNDER-CONSUMPTION	REPRESSED INFLATION

Figure 3.11   Typology of rationing equilibria

actually being traded are the effective supplies. An increase in the wage rate and price level would help to reduce or eliminate the prevailing excess demands. Finally underconsumption takes place when sellers are rationed in the goods market and buyers rationed in the labour market; that is, a low wage level means that there is an excess supply in the goods market along-side an excess demand in the labour market. Malinvaud pays little attention to this case in his approach, finding it of little interest and reducing its importance in his analysis by enlarging the significance of the Keynesian case.

One can present the above typology in diagrammatic terms in *W,P* space; that is, in terms of the different money wage and price level regions, as shown in Figure 3.12. For a concise and accessible discussion of the deriva-tion and manipulation of the curves depicted in Figure 3.12, see Trevithick (1978) and Muellbauer and Portes (1978, pp. 809–10). The *AB* line repre-sents equilibrium in the labour market, and the *CD* line equilibrium in the

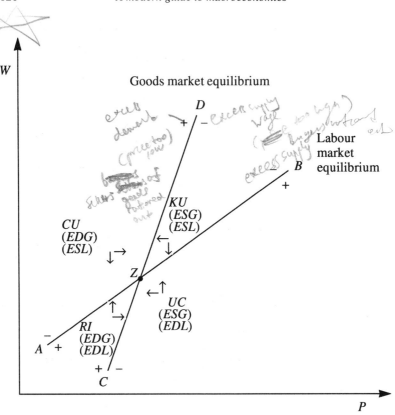

Figure 3.12   Non-clearing markets and W,P space (I)

consumer goods market. The point Z refers to the Walrasian equilibrium
where the two markets have cleared. The classical unemployment case is
given by *CU*, Keynesian unemployment by *KU*, repressed inflation by *RI*,
and underconsumption by *UC*. This is because below the *AB* line we have an
excess demand for labour and above it an excess supply. Likewise to the left
of the *CD* line we have an excess demand for goods, and to the right an
excess supply. The conditions prevailing in the labour and goods markets
define our different *W,P* regions (see brackets, with *ES* and *ED* representing
excess supply and demand, respectively, followed by a *L* or a *G* referring to
the labour and goods markets). The arrows indicate the direction of the
equilibrating forces *if* prices and wages were able to adjust. For example, in
the case of classical unemployment, wages should be falling (given *ESL*) and
prices rising (because of *EDG*). There is nothing to stop the two regions of
classical unemployment and Keynesian unemployment from coexisting within
an actual economy. Malinvaud (1977, pp. 110–11) concedes that, once one

moves away from an aggregated commodity and recognizes the multiplicity of goods, there is the possibility of *mixed* unemployment (that is, both Keynesian and classical varieties) and much else besides. Indeed a recent re-examination of the interwar episode suggested that a singular monocausal explanation of a multiple problem may be inappropriate and that classical and Keynesian unemployment may have prevailed simultaneously (see Booth and Glynn, 1975, 1983).

As stated earlier, it is more usual to present the non-clearing markets and the W,P space without attaching such significance to the underconsumption region. Indeed some authors (such as Grandmont, 1990, pp. 50–51) reduce the underconsumption region to the curve L_3 shown in Figure 3.13. The Keynesian case is the area to the right of L_2 and L_3, the classical case to the left of L_2 and above L_1, with repressed inflation corresponding to the region between L_1 and L_3.

Within the rationing approach the type of government policy depends upon the region the economy is in. You do not use Keynesian policies to deal with classical unemployment, for example. This can be easily demonstrated. Any increase in government spending raises the AB line (in Figure 3.12) and causes a rightward shift of the CD line; that is, there will be an overall movement in a north-easterly direction; both firms and households find themselves competing with the government for resources: labour in the former case, consumer goods in the latter. As Malinvaud (1977, p. 59) maintains, 'Increasing government demand increases employment and lowers excess supply both in the goods market and in the labour market.' There is a crowding-out effect in the goods market alongside a fall in the labour supply (given the latter's inverse relationship with non-wage wealth – see Barro and Grossman, 1976, pp. 14–15, pp. 18–20). The new regions are given by the dotted lines in Figure 3.13. If the economy suffered from either classical unemployment or repressed inflation the increase in state activity would make the situation worse rather than better, whilst it would probably improve the Keynesian situation (points a and b are further removed from the new Walrasian equilibrium of Z^1, whilst point c is closer to it). Of course, whilst government demand for goods and services represents one instrument of economic policy, Malinvaud's approach also highlights that P and W may become instruments themselves to steer the economy towards the equilibrium path. Take classical unemployment, for instance; appropriate manipulation of the real wage through either cuts in W or rises in P (or some combination thereof) will lead to improvement, that is a reduction in the supply and demand discrepancies.

Those who adopt such a framework as the above are forced to conclude that the Keynesian case is *one* amongst a number of others. Indeed Malinvaud makes the point most eloquently when he is forced to assert that 'the "Keynes-

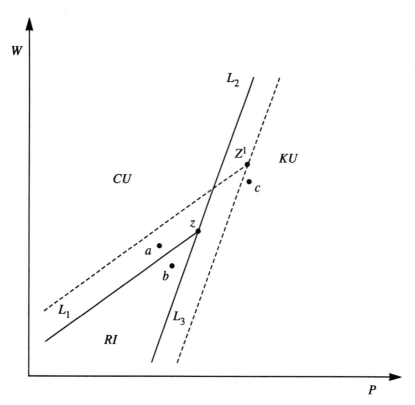

Figure 3.13   Non-clearing markets and W,P space (II)

ian revolution" was a shift of emphasis from one type of short-run equilibrium to another type as providing the appropriate theory for actual unemployment situations' (1977, pp. 29–30). Keynesian economics, once again, is
presented as no longer representing the genuinely general theory (with classical, or others, as special cases). However it needs to be stated that Malinvaud
concedes that Keynesian unemployment and repressed inflation are much
more frequent than the classical unemployment case, although it is also
suggested that conventional Walrasian equilibrium is appropriate for long-
run economic analysis, given that prices regain their required flexibility
(Malinvaud, 1977). The approach of Malinvaud (as well as that of others
adopting the non-clearing framework) has been criticized by several authors
for ignoring several key concerns of Keynes – not least such matters as
expectations, uncertainty and capital. For example, Kahn (1983) has argued
that it provides a 'very thin representation of Keynes's theory'. Trevithick
(1978, p. 116) also raises objections to Malinvaud's approach on the grounds

that it accords 'unwarranted prominence' to the real balance effect. However it must be conceded that the disequilibrium theorists have developed an important area of macroeconomics which emphasizes false trading and the need to bridge the divide separating micro and macro. They therefore provide a more sophisticated approach to the microfoundations of the macroeconomics of non-clearing markets. The theoretical contributions of the disequilibrium theorists resulted in a growing realization that the orthodox Keynesian framework had inadequate microfoundations. One result of this was the revival of interest in the market-clearing approach developed by adherents of the new classical school. Another consequence was the more elaborate micro approach (concerned with rationalizing both sticky wages and prices) of the new Keynesians in explaining coordination difficulties. Before proceeding to discuss these developments we need to consider the orthodox monetarist school, which also regarded the orthodox Keynesian framework as having serious weaknesses at both the theoretical and empirical levels.

JAMES TOBIN

Photograph courtesy of T. Charles Erickson,
Yale University, Office of Public Information

James Tobin was born in 1918 in Champaign, Illinois and obtained his BA, MA and PhD from Harvard University in 1939, 1940 and 1947, respectively. He began teaching while a graduate student at Harvard University in 1946. In 1950, he moved to Yale University where he has remained ever since as Professor of Economics, with the exception of one and a half years in Washington as a member of President Kennedy's Council of Economic Advisers (1961–2), and academic leaves including a year as Visiting Professor at the University of Nairobi Institute for Development Studies in Kenya (1972–3).

James Tobin is one of America's most prominent Keynesian economists. In 1981, he was awarded the Prize in Economic Science in Memory of Alfred Nobel. Among his best known books are: *National Economic Policy* (Yale University Press, 1966), *Essays in Economics: Macroeconomics* (Markham, 1971; North-Holland 1974), *The New Economics One Decade Older* (Princeton University Press, 1974), *Essays in Economics: Consumption and Econometrics* (North-Holland, 1975), *Asset Accumulation and Economic Activity* (Basil Blackwell, 1980), *Policies for Prosperity: Essays in a Keynesian Mode* (Harvester Wheatsheaf, 1987) edited by Peter Jackson, and *Essays in Economics: Theory and Policy* (MIT Press, 1982).

Among the numerous articles he has written, the best known include: 'The Interest-Elasticity of Transactions Demand for Cash', *Review of Economics and Statistics* (1956), 'Liquidity Preference as Behaviour Towards Risk',

Review of Economic Studies (1958), 'Money and Economic Growth', *Econometrica* (1965), 'A General Equilibrium Approach to Monetary Theory', *Journal of Money, Credit and Banking* (1969), 'Money and Income: Post Hoc, Ergo Propter Hoc', *Quarterly Journal of Economics* (1970), 'Inflation and Unemployment', *American Economic Review* (1972), 'How Dead is Keynes?', *Economic Inquiry* (1977), 'Are New Classical Models Plausible Enough to Guide Policy?', *Journal of Money, Credit and Banking* (1980) and 'The Monetarist Counter-Revolution: An Appraisal', *Economic Journal* (1981)

We interviewed Professor Tobin in his office at Yale University on 17 February 1993.

You began your study of economics at Harvard the very year that the General Theory *was published. What attracted you to economics?*
It was an unbelievably happy combination of a subject that promised to save the world and was fascinating from an intellectual puzzle-solving point of view. I was also very much worried about the Great Depression and had every reason to think that the massive failure of our economies was the key to many other of the world's ills, political as well as economic.

The General Theory *is a very difficult book and reflects Keynes's 'long struggle to escape' previous ideas. What were your first impressions of the* General Theory*?*
I didn't know enough to know it was a difficult book which I had no business reading. I was 19 years old. My tutor at Harvard, who had been in England for a year, just said at our first one-on-one tutorial meeting, 'Why don't you and I read this new book I've heard about for our tutorial this year?' I didn't know any better so I read it, and I didn't feel it was that difficult. One of the exciting things, of course, for a 19-year-old was the sense of intellectual revolution, overturning the obsolete wisdom encrusted in the past, especially when the new theory was on the side of promising to do something constructive about the main problems that concerned me and people of my generation.

Skidelsky in his biography of Keynes (Volume II) has argued that 'Keynes's inspiration was radical but his purpose conservative'. How did Keynes reconcile these two opposing forces?
I think that what Skidelsky says is essentially right. Compare Keynes's remedies for the problems of the world at the time to those of Marxians and Spengler's *Decline of the West* – all those apocalyptic warnings of the death of capitalism, because capitalism can't ever succeed. Keynes comes along and says that the basic problem is not really the organization of the economy

but rather the way that aggregate demand is controlled. Keynes had no great complaint about the way the economy allocates the resources that it does employ, that it just doesn't employ them all.

It only took about 12 years for the General Theory *to capture the hearts and minds of the vast majority of the economics profession. Why did Keynes's ideas spread so quickly?*
Well, because it did look as if they would work to remedy the problems of the Great Depression. There was a lot of anxiety in all countries that after the Second World War we would revert to the depression conditions of the pre-war period. Keynes's ideas looked like a pretty good way to avoid that possibility. In the United States, consider the spending for mobilization even before we got in the war, and what it did to GNP and employment. That was a dramatic living vindication of Keynes's ideas.

You are widely recognized as being America's most distinguished Keynesian economist. Are you happy with the label 'Keynesian' and what does being a Keynesian mean to you?
If you'd asked me that, let's say 25 years ago, I would have said that I don't like any label and that I'm just an economist working on problems that I happen to be interested in: macroeconomic problems, monetary–fiscal policy and all those things. There appeared to be a considerable practical consensus about these matters. A lot of my work had been fixing up Keynes in various ways where I found theoretical problems or a lack of 'micro foundations'. In fact the first thing I wrote and got published (in 1941) was a piece of anti-Keynesian theory on his problem of the relation of money wage and employment. So at that time I would have said let's not label people, let's just do our work. After the counter-revolutions, when all these schools and labels arose, I certainly would be proud to be regarded as a Keynesian, considering the alternatives [*laughter*].

What are the fundamental propositions which Keynesians adhere to?
One way to put it is to say that there is a two-regime model of the economy. Sometimes the economy is in a classical situation where markets are clearing (demand equals supply) and the economy's ability to produce output is supply-constrained. You can't produce any more because there are essentially no idle resources (I exaggerate to simplify). Therefore the constraint on output is *capacity*. That capacity constraint results in a price and income structure that equalizes demand and supply at those prices. At other times the economy is in a Keynesian situation in which the constraint on actual output is *demand* – aggregate spending. Extra output would he produced if there were extra aggregate real demand, and the inputs to make it are available at

real returns which won't exceed what the factors of production could earn by their productivity if they were employed. That situation obtains lots of the time, not always, and there are then demand-increasing policies that will eliminate the social waste involved. That I think is the distinction. Whereas for the real business cycle theorists (like Ed Prescott) and new classical guys (like Robert Barro) you are always supply-constrained. There is just one regime, and the observed cyclical fluctuations are fluctuations in the voluntary willingness to be employed.

Some interpretations of the neoclassical synthesis which emerged in the late 1950s and early 1960s suggest that the General Theory *represents a special case of a more general classical model. What is your view on that particular interpretation?*
I wouldn't interpret it that way. Rather there was a consensus on the two-regime model just mentioned. I thought there was also a normative consensus, in the sense that you shouldn't regard any output that you get from putting unemployed resources to work as free, because you have alternative ways of putting unemployed resources to work. The same classical opportunity cost considerations that determine allocation of resources in a classical equilibrium determine the allocation of resources as among different ways of returning to that supply-constrained regime. So I think that in that sense there is no excuse for wasteful projects to increase employment, like digging holes in the ground, because you can arrange to employ people by investments or other projects that are socially beneficial. In that sense the classical opportunity cost considerations apply in either regime. But that's only if you're prepared to do something to get out of the wasteful situation that you're in.

Has too much been made of the Pigou effect as a way of diminishing Keynes's contribution to economic theory?
Of course. I've said that all the time in print. It's a very slender reed on which to assert the efficacy of self-adjusting mechanisms. For one thing the accounting aggregation of credits and debts doesn't necessarily imply behavioural netting out of credits and debts. I believe that the effects of deflation on aggregate demand can be perverse if debtors have a bigger propensity to spend from wealth than creditors do – a reasonable expectation. Then there's the whole issue how you get to the lower price level from where you are. The immaculate conception effect of getting there suggests there's no real time involved – it's just the static comparison of one price level to another price level. As Keynes himself observed, although he didn't make of it a point of theoretical principle, the process of deflation – or disinflation for that matter – involves an increase in the real interest rate and certainly produces perverse effects.

Do you think that, if Keynes had still been alive in 1969 (aged 86), he would have been awarded the first Nobel Prize in economics?

Very likely. He would have got my vote. As for Keynes versus Tinbergen and Frisch, the actual recipients, I don't know. The prize says for economic *science*. In some senses they might have been considered to have made identifiable innovations more similar to those of Nobel-winning natural scientists. But JMK would have been an early award-winner.

How do you feel about your award of the Nobel Prize in 1981? What do you consider to be your most important contributions to macroeconomics?

They gave me the award. I didn't ask for it! I don't think I need to defend what they did. I never thought I was going to get it. I was interested in straightening out macroeconomics and the neoclassical synthesis as I understood them, in generalizing monetary models to take account of the variety of assets, in portfolio theory and its macroeconomic implications – that's what I was trying to do.

Why do you think there are so many conflicting interpretations of the General Theory?

Well, I suppose one reason is that the book is ambiguous in many ways and has a number of strands that could be cited to support different messages. They allow people a variety of different views about the world. In particular, on the one hand, since people interpret the *General Theory* as a kind of general equilibrium model of the determination of output, employment, interest rates, that could be used in both of the two regimes I referred to above. That's what J.R. Hicks was doing in his famous article. On the other hand, you have Chapter 12 on long-run expectations, which suggests that maybe there is not an investment function at all. In the Hicks general equilibrium model you have got to have an investment function. The second approach, stressing the conventionality of expectations and animal spirits, may be seen as opening the way to a different kind of model. This would be supported by Keynes's own tentative advocacy of the socialization of investment, his suspicion that maybe investment wouldn't be adequately stabilized by monetary and fiscal policy, his feeling that you need some central planning to get it right. I guess those ambiguities allow us to interpret it one way or the other. Of course, some people hoped to extract from Keynes a much more radical position with regard to the social and political institutions than he had explicitly expressed. I have in mind Mrs Robinson and others who claim to be the true heirs of Keynes. I never could get that excited about this kind of battle over Keynes's mantle, so to speak. The central part of the book, the central core of the modelling is on the other side, Hicks's side, in my opinion.

Certainly that's in practice the model that has been taught and has influenced policy making and macroeconomic theorizing for more than 50 years.

Do you think teaching the IS–LM model is still an important part of an undergraduate's understanding of the macroeconomy, given the criticisms of the IS–LM model by people like Robinson, Clower and Leijonhufvud ?
Yes, I think the IS–LM model is the tool of first resort. If you're faced with a problem of interpretation of the economy – policy or events – probably the most useful first thing you can do is to try to see how to look at it in these terms. Since students are in that position, yes they need to know it. It's not the end of the matter by any means. I don't say that it's enough. I doubt if Keynes or Hicks would have thought it enough. But it's a start and lots of times it's exactly right.

Would you accept that many of the theoretical changes made in the 1970s, and inspired by people like Lucas, were the inevitable consequence of defects in the Keynesian model?
No, I wouldn't accept that. I do think the idea of model-consistent expectations is a good idea. It would be a bad feature of any equilibrium model that people chronically perpetuate mistaken expectations about variables, mistaken in the sense that they are different than those that the model persistently creates itself. But I think that applying that idea to dynamic situations where learning is going on and people can have a lot of different opinions about the world is carrying it too far.

How important do you think it is for macroeconomics to have neoclassical choice – theoretic foundations?
Well, I think it's important for the behavioural equations of a macroeconomic model not to contradict choice-theoretic considerations, to be in principle consistent with them. But I think the stronger version of 'micro foundations' is a methodological mistake, one that has produced a tremendous amount of mischief. I refer to the now orthodox requirement of postulating representative agents whose optimizations generate 'macroeconomic' behavioural equations. That is a considerable sacrifice of the essence of much of macroeconomics. Suppose you have a lot of different types of agents, who are all maximizing. Then it's their aggregation into a behavioural equation that you want for a macro model. That aggregation won't necessarily be the solution for any single agent. To insist that it must be seems to me very wrong-headed. It has put us on the wrong track in macroeconomics, or what passes for macroeconomics.

In the late 1960s you had a considerable debate with Friedman, who at one stage argued that the main differences between macroeconomists were over

empirical matters. Surely the 1970s demonstrated that there were some fundamental theoretical differences between macroeconomists ?
What Friedman was saying was disingenuous. He had a theory of the demand for money which put a lot of variables in the demand function, including various interest rates, and yet his monetary policy propositions were based on the assumption that interest rates were not in the function. He asserted empirical results that he was unique in finding – that the interest elasticity of the demand for money was negligible. When he was really stuck by the weight of evidence, he then wrote that the question of the size of interest elasticity of the demand for money had nothing to do with anything. The only way one could make sense of that particular proposition was that you were going to be at full employment anyway, no matter what the stock of money was, and so the interest rate would have to be what was consistent with the demand and supply of savings at full employment. But that was a complete evasion of the original issues of our debate. He had never before said that monetary policy would have *no* effects on real variables. He said they have a lot of effects on real variables. He had some kind of Phillips curve (although he didn't call it that) in his mind, and even when he invented the natural rate he still did. He didn't deny that monetary policy would have some effects on real output during cyclical fluctuations – so he was caught between being a true new classical economist, in which case he was going to have to say that money doesn't ever matter, or being a pragmatic monetarist, where he didn't have a good theoretical or empirical basis for what he had been saying.

What exactly is the difference between Friedman's concept of the natural rate of unemployment and NAIRU – the non accelerating inflation rate of unemployment? Is there some important difference between these two concepts?
I don't think there is a big practical difference. Maybe what was in the mind of Modigliani, when he started that acronym, was that Friedman said that the natural rate was the amount of unemployment that was the solution to Walrasian general equilibrium equations – a proposition that neither he nor anybody else ever proved as far as I know – complete speculation. I mean, why would Walrasian equations have any unemployment at all in their solution [*laughter*]? That identification of the natural rate doesn't make any sense, and it's certainly not true. When Modigliani and others started talking about NAIRU, they were talking more about a pragmatic empirical idea.

At the end of the day politicians make economic policy. The Public Choice school, as well as the work of your colleague William Nordhaus on political business cycles, suggests that politicians may actually use economic policy for their own gain. Do you think that Keynes was perhaps naive in thinking that we could hand over policy making to politicians and they would follow the advice of economists?

I won't quote the last paragraph of the *General Theory*, which says that in the long run ideas matter. I think that's true, but I think my point would be a little different. If we are advising government officials, politicians, voters, it's not for us economists to play games with them. It's not for Keynes to say, I am not going to suppress the *General Theory* and not tell the House of Commons, the Labour Party, the Tories, whomever, that it would be possible to reduce unemployment by public works expenditure. If I am giving advice to them about war finance – or whatever else my advice will be not to do bad things – I am not going to decide myself that they are so evil and irresponsible that I don't give them advice about what actions will do what. I don't think that Jim Buchanan has, or I have, the right to withhold advice from Presidents of the United States or Members of Congress or the electorate on the grounds that, if they knew what we know, they would misuse it. I don't think that is for us to decide.

You have said that good papers in economics contain surprises and stimulate further work. On this criterion the 1970s contributions of people like Lucas, Sargent, Wallace and Barro were good. Do you feel that new classical macroeconomics has changed macroeconomics for the better?

In some respects I think Lucas's ideas about policies' being anticipated by actors, so you can't be sure that behaviour will stay put when you change policy, is an important idea, one we have to worry about. I don't think it is as important an idea as he seemed to think it was. I thought his ingenious explanation of how you can have observations that look like Phillips curves yet have none of the operational policy implications of the curve – that was neat. However I think it turned out not to be a good idea. It didn't survive because of the implausible notion that people are confused about what the money supply is. If they're confused, why don't we publish the money supply data every Friday afternoon – which in the US we do of course, and have been doing for a long time. I observe that the new classicals no longer pay any attention to this misperception story. They have become much more extreme. Barro's [1974] paper was provocative and stimulated a lot of theoretical and empirical work. I had a paper in my Jahnsson lectures that gave, I don't know, say 15 reasons why Barro's neutrality proposition doesn't work, and I think there have been numerous articles since on each of them.

We have seen a lot of contributions recently from what are called new Keynesian economists. What is the central difference between your view of Keynesian economics and the new Keynesian contributions? Is it that they accept rational expectations and a lot of monetarist ideas?

Yes, they accept rational expectations. Moreover they accept the methodology of choice-theoretic foundations and representative agents, much more than I would. They accept market clearing, except as it is modified by imperfect competition, much more than I would. They regard their task as to give a rationale for the alleged rigidity of money wages and money prices, a rationale that allows nominal shocks to create real consequences. I think that was *not* Keynes's idea. Keynes was primarily concerned, not with nominal demand shocks, but real demand shocks, which would create problems even if prices were flexible. They have said that all they are going to do is show how it is rational for nominal prices to be inflexible and derive unemployment results from that. I don't find it extremely convincing – and I'm sure Keynes would have not – that the whole effective demand problem is that there are real costs of changing nominal prices on the menu at the restaurant. I think Keynes would have laughed at the idea that menu costs are a big enough resource-using problem to cause the Great Depression or any other substantial losses of economic activity. It's not credible. If I had a copyright on who could use the term 'Keynesian' I wouldn't allow them to use it [*laughter*].

What do you think of the real business cycle approach?
That's really the enemy at the other extreme of macroeconomics. Real business cycle theory suggests that society is a moving equilibrium responding continuously to technological productivity–supply shocks all the time, and that the economy is doing the best job possible in responding to them. It's those benign responses that generate the fluctuations we call business cycles. There isn't any unemployment in the Keynesian sense. There are simply intertemporal substitutions of employment now and employment later, which are rational responses to the stochastic environment in which people live. I don't see any credibility to the idea that people are doing a lot of intertemporal substitution as to how much they want to work. To interpret the rise in unemployment in this country from 5.7 per cent in 1978 to 11 per cent in 1982 as a desire on the part of workers to take leisure in preparation for working when real wages will be higher – that is ridiculous [*laughter*].

When in office Mrs Thatcher repeatedly stated that in her view inflation was the most important target for macroeconomic policy. How do you react to this view?
Well, that's substituting a subordinate target for a real target. To the extent that inflation is damaging to real standards of living now or in the future, then inflation is something to worry about. But you could easily make greater sacrifices of real output and real consumption in the name of inflation than the benefits of reducing inflation are worth.

Should we take Lucas's [1978] advice and abandon the concept of involuntary unemployment?
Certainly not. Any time that you don't have supply and demand equal at existing prices then there is involuntary something. Some people would like to supply more, or some people might like to demand more, at those prices but are not able to do so. The only way you can say that everything must be voluntary is to assume market clearing all the time – that at every moment in time the economy is in market-clearing equilibrium.

In new classical models, full employment is equated with actual employment. How should we define full employment?
I would define it in a classical way at the point where, as Keynes did, people are on the supply curve for labour, getting all the work they are willing to accept at real wages that employees can and will pay for them. Keynes himself allows for intersectoral flux and frictional unemployment, but essentially I wouldn't define equilibrium full employment any differently from a classical model.

Structural budget deficits have been a feature of the US economy in the 1980s and indeed at the moment there is a lot of talk of the problem of growing budget deficits. Are budget deficits damaging? Do you think that the structural budget deficit of the US economy is a real problem, and what should be done about it?
Well, again you have to keep your eye on the ball and not confuse ends and means. When you think about the objectives to which fiscal policy may be relevant, it is the growth of our capacity to provide higher standards of living to people in the future. For the United States we are talking about a deficit that is in dollars, a debt that is in the currency that we print. It's not a debt in sterling, in yen, or anything else. It's largely an internally held debt and when you think about international wealth balance sheets it's not important whether foreigners hold our federal public debt, or hold other assets. There is a burden, however, in that the public debt diverts some private wealth that could be placed in privately owned productive capital to holding government paper that was generated to finance private or collective consumption. In that sense deficits which increase the debt have been using savings that could have been used for productive investments in capital that would have raised real wages that our grandchildren would earn. But that doesn't mean we need a deficit reduction this year, when the economy is in a slump. Today GDP is not supply-constrained; the amount of investment in the economy is not constrained by the supply of saving. In fact deficit reduction in a weak economy would be counter-productive, reduce GDP, reduce investment. We would be doing not as well for our children and their children as we would if

we did some spending on public investment or cut taxes in ways that stimulate private investment. All this is terribly mixed up in the political discussion about deficits. I have been one of the principal opponents of the kind of fiscal policy that the Reagan and Bush administrations ran for 12 years. And at the same time, to rush into a blind policy of deficit reduction that begins too soon, before we are out of the slump – I wouldn't do that either. It all gets back to trying to suit the medicine to the circumstances of the patient.

Are you still an advocate of incomes policies? Some Keynesians like Alan Blinder have little enthusiasm for such policies, whereas you seem to think that incomes policy has a role to play in addition to demand management.
Well, I thought incomes policy did have a role in the 1970s, and especially in the disinflation that was going to take place beginning in 1979. I think we could have done that disinflation with less loss in output and employment if we'd used some kind of incomes policy then. Right now, I'm not very excited about incomes policy. One thing that has come out well in the 1980s, partly a matter of good fortune, is that we haven't had any more oil shocks. Wage pressures are also very moderate. In 1979/80 there were very few economists who would have said it was possible to get unemployment down to almost 5 per cent in 1988 and have virtually no inflationary consequences. I wouldn't have said that 10 years earlier – yet it happened. We don't have an inflation problem right now. If it comes back, then incomes policy may be a possible thing to do, but I wouldn't muddy the waters and get excited about it right now.

Why has Keynesian economics experienced something of a restoration in the last decade?
Well, it's because you have had Keynesian problems for the last five years. Keynesian economics got a bum rap in the 1970s. I see it all the time. People say, 'Why do you want to go back to the failed policies of the 1970s and the late 1960s?' Keynesian policies were thought to be responsible for inflation and stagflation – people never mention, or erase from the memory, the oil shocks and the Vietnam War. Now we are back to a more normal environment and the new classical ideas are not so appealing to a new generation of economists, who have grown up subsequent to the high tides of the counter-revolutions.

Do you see any signs of an emerging consensus in macroeconomics?
It may be coming, but I don't see it. There is still great conflict.

There seems to be more consensus amongst economists on microeconomic issues than on macroeconomic issues. Why do you think this is the case?

Let's go back to what Keynes said. He didn't have any big reservations about the way the market economy allocates the resources it does employ. I think myself, and many microeconomists and economists in general would say, that Keynes gave away too much. He should have recognized more externalities in the ordinary market allocation of resources, and he should have worried more about the possible social wastes of monopolistic competition, than he did. In many areas of microeconomics, like rent control and minimum wages, choice-theoretic opportunity-cost methodology is being used the way we are trained to use it. That's the secret that we know, and sociologists and other social scientists don't know. We are a more scientific discipline, but I don't think that all is well in those respects. What rational expectations has done to macroeconomics is what game theory has been doing to microeconomics. Game theory has the problem that it leads to multiple solutions all the time, so it doesn't seem to get results. It's got the same fascination for people looking for ways to use their mathematical and puzzle-solving prowess as rational expectations has, and that comes at the expense of more pragmatic, and empirical, and institutional industrial organization studies. So I am not so sure that all is well in microeconomics either. A lot of good policy work continues in more applied areas.

If you were advising Clinton about the economic strategy to be pursued over the next four years what are the important things you think he should do?
Well, that's a tricky thing, for reasons we already discussed. The problem he has right now is to pep up the economy and the recovery. The economy is doing a little better than it was six months ago, but it is still not doing great. At the same time there is all this pressure to do something about the federal deficit. He is trying to do both. Since one really requires more deficit while the other requires less deficit, it's rather difficult. I'm afraid the stimulus he is going to give is not very big, and it's not going to last long enough. There is going to be a deficit-increasing phase of his programme this year and maybe next year [1994] his budget is going to be deficit-neutral. Thereafter tax increases and cuts in entitlements and other outlays are going to be phased in, so eventually for the fiscal year 1997 he will be able to say that he will have done what he said. He is asking for both these things at once. It's sort of like saying we're going to have to perform some surgery on this patient, but right now the patient is a little weak, so we'll have to build the patient up first. There are two difficulties. One is that the dual approach is a rather subtle point to explain – why we do one thing now when we are going to do the opposite later. In fact, he hasn't even explained it yet.

Maybe he doesn't understand it.
Oh he does, this is a smart guy. This is as smart a politician as I have ever met – he understands it.

4. The orthodox monetarist school

Money is honey. (Max Bialystock, from the film, *The Producers*, 1967)

4.1 Introduction

The main purpose of this chapter is twofold. First, to trace the historical development of orthodox monetarism (see Figure 4.1) beginning with the quantity theory of money approach (section 4.2) as it evolved from the mid-1950s to the mid-1960s; through to the expectations-augmented Phillips curve analysis (section 4.3) which was absorbed into monetarist analysis after the mid-to-late 1960s; finally to the monetary approach to balance of payments theory and exchange rate determination (section 4.4) which was incorporated into monetarist analysis in the early 1970s. Second, in the light of this discussion, to summarize the central distinguishing beliefs commonly held within the orthodox monetarist school (section 4.5).

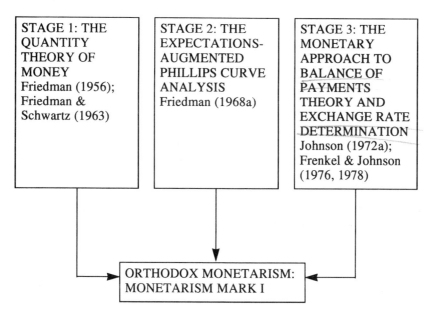

Figure 4.1   The evolution of orthodox monetarism

4.2   The Quantity Theory of Money Approach

The first stage in the development of orthodox monetarism can be traced from the mid-1950s to the mid-1960s, and involved an attempt to re-establish the quantity theory of money approach to macroeconomic analysis which had been usurped by the Keynesian revolution. Within the quantity theory approach (see also Chapter 2, section 2.5) changes in the money stock are regarded as the predominant, though not the only, factor explaining changes in money or nominal income.

Orthodox Keynesian analysis (see Chapter 3, section 3.3) emphasized real disturbances (notably fluctuations in investment and autonomous consumption) as the main cause of fluctuations in money income, predominantly in the form of changes in real income. In terms of the stylized quantity theory of money outlined in Chapter 2, section 2.5, Keynes's *General Theory* was interpreted as implying that in conditions of underemployment (which could prevail for protracted periods) income velocity (V) would be highly unstable and would passively adapt to whatever changes occurred independently in the money supply (M) or money income (PY). In these circumstances money was regarded as being relatively unimportant. For example, in the two extreme cases of the liquidity and investment traps, money does not matter inasmuch as monetary policy would be completely ineffective in influencing economic activity. In the liquidity trap case, an increase in the money supply would be exactly and completely offset by an opposite change in velocity. The increase in the money supply would be absorbed entirely into idle/speculative balances at an unchanged rate of interest and level of income. In the investment trap case, where investment is completely interest-inelastic, an increase in the money supply would again have no effect on the level of real income. The money supply would be powerless to influence real income because investment is insensitive to interest rate changes. Velocity would fall as the demand for money increased relative to an unchanged level of income. Readers should verify for themselves that, in either of these two extreme Keynesian cases where money does not matter, any change in autonomous consumption, investment or government expenditure would result in the full multiplier effect of the simple Keynesian cross or 45° model. Under such conditions, although the quantity theory relationship (equation 2.16) would be valid, orthodox Keynesians argued it would be useless in terms of monetary policy prescription.

4.2.1   The quantity theory as a theory of the demand for money
It was against this orthodox Keynesian background that Milton Friedman sought to maintain and re-establish across the profession what he regarded as the oral tradition of the University of Chicago, namely the quantity theory

approach to macroeconomic analysis (for a criticism of this interpretation, see Patinkin, 1969). Although the traditional quantity theory is a body of doctrine concerned with the relationship between the money supply and the general price level, Friedman (1956) initially presented his restatement of the quantity theory of money as a theory of the demand for money, rather than a theory of the general price level or money income.

Friedman postulated that the demand for money (like the demand for any asset) yields a flow of services to the holder and depends on three main factors: (i) the wealth constraint, which determines the maximum amount of money that can be held; (ii) the return or yield on money in relation to the return on other financial and real assets in which wealth can be held; and (iii) the asset-holder's tastes and preferences. The way total wealth is allocated between various forms depends on the relative rates of return on the various assets. These assets include not just money and bonds but also equities and physical goods. In equilibrium wealth will be allocated between assets such that marginal rates of return are equal. Although Patinkin (1969) has suggested that Friedman's restatement should be regarded as an extension of Keynesian analysis, there are three important differences worth highlighting. First, Friedman's analysis of the demand for money can be regarded as an application of his permanent income theory of consumption to the demand for a particular asset. Second, he introduced the expected rate of inflation as a potentially important variable into the demand for money function. Third, he asserted that the demand for money was a stable function of a limited number of variables.

A *simplified* version of Friedman's demand function for real money balances can be written in the following form:

$$\frac{M_d}{P} = f(Y^p;\ r,\ \dot{P}^e;\ u) \tag{4.1}$$

where Y^p represents permanent income which is used as a proxy for wealth, the budget constraint;

       r represents the return on financial assets,

       $\dot{P}^e$ represents the expected rate of inflation, and

       u represents individual's tastes and preferences.

This analysis predicts that, *ceteris paribus*, the demand for money will be greater (i) the higher the level of wealth; (ii) the lower the yield on other assets; (iii) the lower the expected rate of inflation, and vice versa. Utility-maximizing individuals will reallocate wealth between different assets whenever marginal rates of return are not equal. This portfolio adjustment process is central to the monetarist specification of the transmission mechanism whereby changes in the stock of money affect the real sector. This can be illustrated by examining the effects of an increase in the money supply brought about by open market operations by the monetary authorities. An initial equilibrium is assumed where wealth is allocated between financial and real assets such that marginal rates of return are equal. Following open market purchases of bonds by the monetary authorities, the public's money holdings will increase. Given that the marginal return on any asset diminishes as holdings of it increase, the marginal rate of return on money holdings will in consequence fall. As excess money balances are exchanged for financial and real assets (such as consumer durables) their prices will be bid up until portfolio equilibrium is re-established when once again all assets are willingly held and marginal rates of return are equal. In contrast to orthodox Keynesian analysis, monetarists argue that money is a substitute for a wide range of real and financial assets, and that no single asset or group of assets can be considered to be a close substitute for money. A much broader range of assets and associated expenditures is emphasized and in consequence monetarists attribute a much stronger and more direct effect on aggregate spending to monetary impulses.

4.2.2 The quantity theory and changes in money income: empirical evidence

The assertion that there exists a stable functional relationship (behaviour) between the demand for real balances and a limited number of variables that determine it lies at the heart of the modern quantity theory approach to macroeconomic analysis. If the demand for money function is stable then velocity will also be stable, changing in a predictable manner if any of the limited number of variables in the demand for money function should change. Friedman (1968b, p. 434) has postulated the quantity theory as

> the empirical generalisation that changes in desired real balances (in the demand for money) tend to proceed slowly and gradually or to be the result of events set in train by prior changes in supply, whereas, in contrast, substantial changes in the supply of nominal balances can and frequently do occur independently of any changes in demand. The conclusion is that substantial changes in prices or nominal income are almost invariably the result of changes in the nominal supply of money.

In this section we discuss various empirical evidence put forward in support of the quantity theory of money approach to macroeconomic analysis, beginning with the demand for money function. Constraints of space preclude a detailed discussion of the empirical evidence on the demand for money. Nevertheless two points are worth highlighting. First, although Friedman (1959) in his early empirical work on the demand for money claimed to have found that the interest rate was insignificant, virtually all studies undertaken thereafter have found the interest rate to be an important variable in the function. Indeed in a subsequent paper Friedman (1966) acknowledged this. Furthermore there also appears little evidence that the interest elasticity of the money demand increases as the rate of interest falls, as the liquidity trap requires. This means that both the extreme quantity theory and Keynesian cases of vertical and horizontal *LM* curves, respectively, can be ruled out. The static IS–LM model can, however, still be used to illustrate the quantity theory approach to macroeconomic analysis if both the real rate of interest and real income are determined by real, not monetary, forces and the economy automatically tends towards full employment (see Friedman, 1968a). Second, although the belief in a stable demand for money function was well supported by empirical evidence up to the early 1970s, since then a number of studies, both in the US and other economies, have found evidence of apparent instability of the demand for money. A number of possible explanations have been put forward to explain this apparent instability, including institutional change within the financial system which took place in the 1970s and 1980s. The reader is referred to Laidler (1993) for a detailed and very accessible discussion of the empirical evidence on the demand for money, and the continuing controversy over the question of the stability of the demand for money function.

Friedman (1958) sought to re-establish an important independent role for money through a study of time series data comparing rates of monetary growth with turning-points in the level of economic activity for the USA. On the average of 18 non-war cycles since 1870, he found that peaks (troughs) in the rate of change of the money supply had preceded peaks (troughs) in the level of economic activity by an average of 16 (12) months. Friedman concluded that this provided strong *suggestive* evidence of an influence running from money to business. Friedman's study was subsequently criticized by Culbertson (1960, 1961) and by Kareken and Solow (1963) on both methodological and statistical grounds. First, the question was raised as to whether the timing evidence justified the inference of a causal relationship running from money to economic activity (see also Kaldor, 1970; Tobin, 1970; Sims, 1972). What appears to be a positive relation with a lead may be an inverted relation with a lag, in that the lead may be simply a reflection of an earlier influence of business on money. Monetary and business changes might also be the result of some other influences which have their effect on money more promptly than on business activity. Second, statistical objections to Friedman's procedure were raised in that he had not compared like with like. When Kareken and Solow reran the tests with Friedman's data using rates of change for both money and economic activity, they found no uniform lead of monetary changes over changes in the level of economic activity.

In 1963, Friedman and Schwartz (1963) presented more persuasive evidence to support the monetarist belief that changes in the stock of money play a largely independent role in cyclical fluctuations. In their influential study of the *Monetary History of the United States 1867–1960*, they found that, while the stock of money had tended to rise during both cyclical expansions and contractions, the *rate of growth* of the money supply had been slower during contractions than during expansions in the level of economic activity. Within the period examined, the only times when there was an appreciable *absolute* fall in the money stock were also the six periods of major economic contraction identified: 1873–9, 1893–4, 1907–8, 1920–21, 1929–33 and 1937–8. Furthermore, from studying the historical circumstances underlying the changes that occurred in the money supply during these major recessions, Friedman and Schwartz argued that the factors producing monetary contraction were mainly independent of contemporary or prior changes in money income and prices. In other words, monetary changes were seen as the cause, rather than the consequence, of major recessions. For example, Friedman and Schwartz argued that the absolute decline in the money stock which took place during both 1920–21 and 1937–8 was a consequence of highly restrictive policy actions undertaken by the Federal Reserve System: for example, reserve requirements were doubled in 1936 and early 1937. These actions were themselves followed by sharp declines in the money stock, which were in turn followed by a period of severe economic contraction.

Even more controversial was the reinterpretation of the Great Depression as demonstrating the potency of monetary change and monetary policy. Friedman and Schwartz argued that an initial mild decline in the money stock from 1929 to 1930 was converted into a sharp decline by a wave of bank failures which started in late 1930 (see also Bernanke, 1983). Bank failures produced an increase in both the currency-to-deposit ratio, owing to the public's loss of faith in the banks' ability to redeem their deposits and the reserve-to-deposit ratio, owing to the banks' loss of faith in the public's willingness to maintain their deposits with them. In Friedman and Schwartz's view, the consequent decline in the money stock was further intensified by the Federal Reserve System's restrictive action of raising the discount rate in October 1931, which in turn led to further bank failures. In this interpretation the depression only became great as a consequence of the failure of the Federal Reserve to prevent the dramatic decline in the money stock – between October 1929 and June 1933, the money stock fell by about a third. By adopting alternative policies the Federal Reserve System, they argued, could have prevented the banking collapse and the resulting fall in the money stock and severe economic contraction. Friedman and Schwartz further justified their view that changes in the stock of money play a largely independent role in cyclical fluctuations from the evidence that cyclical movements in money had much the same relationship (both in timing and amplitude) as cyclical movements in business activity, even under substantially different monetary arrangements that had prevailed in the USA over the period 1867–1960. For further discussion of these issues, see Romer and Romer (1989).

A more intense exchange was triggered by the publication of the study undertaken by Friedman and Meiselman (1963) for the Commission on Money and Credit. Although the ensuing Friedman–Meiselman debate occupied economists for a lengthy period of time, the debate itself is now generally regarded as largely only being of interest to students of the history of economic thought. In brief, Friedman and Meiselman attempted to estimate how much of the variation in consumption (a proxy variable for income) could be explained by changes in (i) the money supply, in line with the quantity theory approach, and (ii) autonomous expenditure (investment), in line with Keynesian analysis. Using two test equations (one using money and the other autonomous expenditure as the independent variable) for US data over the period 1897–1958, they found that, apart from one sub-period dominated by the Great Depression, the money equation gave much the better explanation. These results were subsequently challenged, most notably by De Prano and Mayer (1965) and Ando and Modigliani (1965), who showed that a change in the definition of autonomous expenditure improved the performance of the autonomous expenditure equation.

On reflection it is fair to say that these tests were ill devised to discriminate between the quantity theory and the Keynesian view, so that they failed to establish whether it was changes in the supply of money or autonomous expenditure that were causing changes in income. This can be illustrated by reference to the IS–LM model for a closed economy. In general within the Hicksian IS–LM framework, monetary and fiscal multipliers each depend on both the consumption function and the liquidity preference function. Equally good results can be obtained using the two equations when income determination is either purely classical or Keynesian. The classical case is illustrated in Figure 4.2, where the demand for money is independent of the rate of interest. The economy is initially in equilibrium at a less than full employment income level of Y_0 and a rate of interest r_0; that is, the intersection of LM_0 and IS. An increase in the money supply (which shifts the LM curve from LM_0 to LM_1) would result in a lower rate of interest (r_1) and a higher level of income (Y_1). As the interest rate falls, investment expenditure is stimulated, which in turn, through the multiplier, affects consumption and income. In the classical case, empirical studies would uncover a stable relationship between autonomous expenditure and the level of income, even though the direction of causation would run from money to income.

The Keynesian case is illustrated in Figure 4.3. The economy is initially in equilibrium at an income level of Y_0 and a rate of interest of r^*; that is, the intersection of IS_0 and LM_0. Following an expansionary real impulse (which

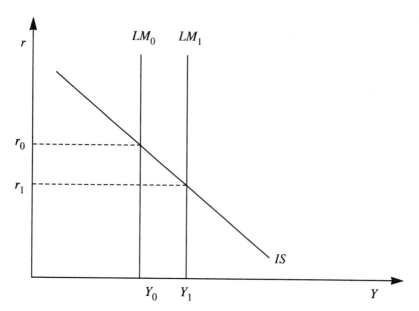

Figure 4.2   The classical case

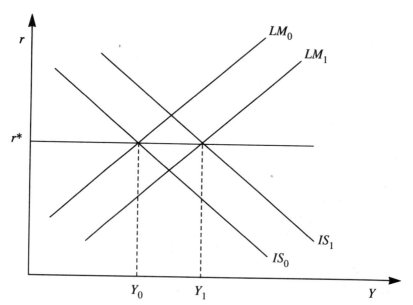

Figure 4.3   The Keynesian case

shifts the *IS* curve outwards to the right, from IS_0 to IS_1) the authorities could stabilize the interest rate at r^* by expanding the money supply (shifting the *LM* curve downwards to the right, from LM_0 to LM_1). In the Keynesian case, empirical studies would uncover a stable relationship between the money supply and the level of income, even though in this particular case the direction of causation would run from income to money. In conclusion, what the Friedman–Meiselman tests appeared to demonstrate was that (i) the marginal propensity to consume had been relatively stable and (ii) contrary to the extreme Keynesian view, the economy had not been in a liquidity or investment trap because if it had the tests would not have found such good fits for the money equation.

4.2.3 Concluding remarks

At this point it would be useful to draw together the material presented in this section and summarize the central tenets that proponents of the quantity theory of money approach to macroeconomic analysis generally adhered to by the mid-1960s (see Purvis, 1980). The central distinguishing beliefs at that time could be listed as follows:

1. Changes in the money stock are the predominant factor explaining changes in money income.
2. In the face of a stable demand for money, most of the observed instability in the economy could be attributed to fluctuations in the money supply induced by the monetary authorities.
3. The authorities can control the money supply if they choose to do so and when that control is exercised the path of money income will be different from a situation where the money supply is endogenous.
4. The lag between changes in the money stock and changes in money income is long and variable, so that attempts to use discretionary monetary policy to fine-tune the economy could turn out to be destabilizing.
5. The money supply should be allowed to grow at a fixed rate in line with the underlying growth of output to ensure long-term price stability.

The Keynesian–monetarist debate, relating to the importance of changes in the money stock as the predominant factor explaining changes in money income, reached a climax in 1970, when Friedman, in response to his critics, attempted to set forth his 'Theoretical Framework for Monetary Analysis' (see Friedman, 1970a, 1972; Tobin, 1972a). Until the publication of this paper there existed no *explicit, formal* and coherent statement of the theoretical structure underlying monetarist pronouncements. In opening up the monetarist 'black box' for theoretical scrutiny, Friedman intended to demonstrate that 'the basic differences among economists are empirical not theoretical'. His theoretical statement turned out to be a generalized IS–LM model which helped to place the monetarist approach *within* the mainstream position. According to Tobin (1981), the central issue for both macroeconomic theory and policy is the supply response of the economy to monetary impulses. The division of such impulses between prices and quantities was referred to by Friedman as 'the missing equation'. In Tobin's view, Friedman's solution to this problem 'was not different in spirit from the wage/price/output mechanisms of mainstream eclectic Keynesian theory and econometrics' (Tobin, 1981, p. 36).

In retrospect we can now see that Friedman's debate with his critics demonstrated that their differences were more *quantitative* than *qualitative*, and contributed towards an emerging synthesis of monetarist and Keynesian ideas. This emerging synthesis, or theoretical accord, was to establish that the Keynesian-dominated macroeconomics of the 1950s had *understated* (but not neglected) the importance of monetary impulses in generating economic instability (see Laidler, 1992a). This was perhaps especially true in the UK in the period culminating in the Radcliffe Report (1959) on the working of the monetary system in the UK. According to Samuelson, a leading US Keynesian, 'the contrast between British and American Keynesianism had become dramatic' by 1959 because many of Keynes's admirers in Britain 'were still frozen in the Model T version of his system' (see Samuelson, 1983, 1988; Johnson, 1978).

4.3   The Expectations-augmented Phillips Curve Analysis

The second stage in the development of orthodox monetarism came with a more precise analysis of the way the effects of changes in the rate of monetary expansion are divided between real and nominal magnitudes. This analysis involved the independent contributions made by Friedman (1968a) and Phelps (1967) to the Phillips curve literature. In order to understand the significance of these contributions, we begin with a brief discussion of the original Phillips curve analysis and comment on the importance of the curve to orthodox Keynesian analysis.

4.3.1   The Phillips curve
The Phillips curve is concerned with the controversy over the relationship between inflation and unemployment and is one of the most famous relationships in macroeconomics. The curve was derived from a *statistical* investigation undertaken by A.W. Phillips (1958) into the relationship between unemployment (U) and the rate of change of *money* wages ($\dot{W}$) in the UK over the period 1861–1957. As depicted in Figure 4.4, the estimated average relationship was found to be non-linear and inverse. At an unemployment level of approximately 5.5 per cent, the rate of change of money wages was zero per

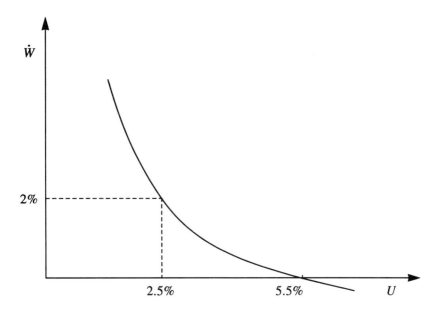

Figure 4.4   The Phillips curve

cent, while at an unemployment level of approximately 2.5 per cent the rate
of change of money wages was 2.0 per cent.

   Following Phillips's pioneering work, there developed two strands to the
literature, one theoretical, the other empirical. On the empirical front, economists were interested to establish whether a stable relationship between inflation and unemployment prevailed in other market economies. For a discussion of the empirical literature, see Santomero and Seater (1978). As far as
the simultaneous achievement of low inflation and low unemployment was
concerned, the discovery of a stable trade-off between these two objectives
implied a policy dilemma, one which might be overcome if the curve could
be shifted to the left by appropriate economic policies. This in turn would
necessitate a coherent theoretical explanation of the economic forces which
lay behind the relationship. The first major attempt to provide a robust theoretical underpinning to the curve was provided by Lipsey (1960) through the
combination of two postulated relationships: (i) a positive linear relationship
between the rate of increase in money wages and excess demand, and (ii) a
negative non-linear relationship between excess demand and unemployment.
The relationship between wage change and excess demand for labour is
illustrated in Figure 4.5. Panel (a) shows that at any wage rate below W_e
wages will rise as a result of there being excess demand in the labour market.
Panel (b) shows that the rate of increase in money wage rates will be greater

(a)

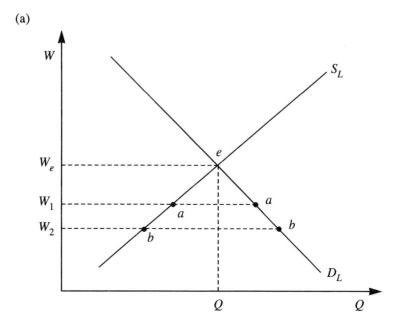

(b)

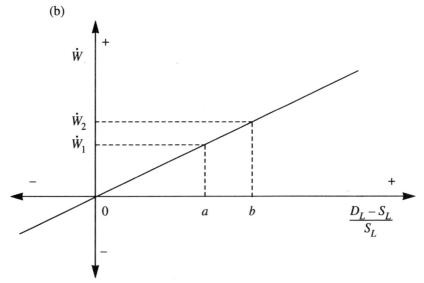

Figure 4.5   The relationship between wage change and excess demand for labour

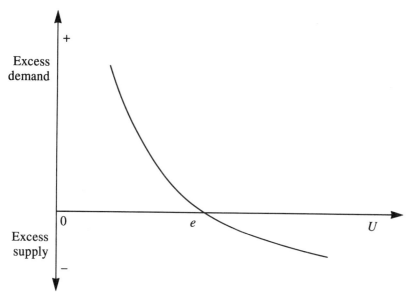

Figure 4.6   The relationship between excess demand for labour and unemployment

the larger the excess demand for labour. For example, at a wage rate W_1 in panel (a) there is an excess demand for labour of *aa*. This excess demand is equal to 0*a* in panel (b) and results in a rate of increase in money wage rates of $\dot{W}_1$. The relationship between excess demand for labour and unemployment is illustrated in Figure 4.6. Even when the labour market clears (that is to say, there is neither excess demand nor excess supply) there will be some positive amount of unemployment as people change jobs and search for new employment; that is, 0*e* in Figure 4.6. Lipsey argued that, although unemployment would fall in response to positive excess demand (for example, jobs become easier to find as vacancies increase), unemployment would only asymptotically approach zero. In other words, steadily increasing excess demand would be accompanied by increasingly smaller reductions in unemployment. By combining these two postulated relationships, Lipsey was able to provide an economic rationale for Phillips's observed non-linear inverse relationship between the rate of change of money wages and unemployment shown in Figure 4.4. In summary, Lipsey's rationale suggests that the rate of change of money wages depends on the degree of excess demand (or supply) in the labour market as proxied by the level of unemployment. This can be expressed by the equation:

$$\dot{W} = f(U) \tag{4.2}$$

The Phillips curve was quickly adopted by orthodox Keynesians as it provided an explanation of price determination and inflation which was missing in the then prevailing macroeconomic model. The reader will recall from the discussion contained in section 3.3 that within the IS–LM model the price level is assumed to be fixed at less than full employment, with the result that up to full employment changes in aggregate demand affect the level of real income and employment. Up to full employment money wages are assumed to be fixed and unresponsive to changes in aggregate demand. Only when full employment is reached will changes in aggregate demand affect the price level. The Phillips curve allowed the orthodox Keynesian theory of output and employment determination to be linked to a theory of wage and price inflation. Following Lipsey (1978) this is illustrated in Figure 4.7. The top panel of Figure 4.7 depicts the standard IS–LM model, while the bottom panel shows the Phillips curve with the modified axes of price inflation ($\dot{P}$) and output/income (Y). Panel (b) is derived by assuming (i) that the level of output depends on the level of employment and that the level of unemployment is inversely related to the level of employment, and (ii) a hypothesis that prices are set by a mark-up to unit costs of production, the main component of which is wages. Put in its simplest form, the mark-up pricing hypothesis suggests that price inflation depends on money wage inflation minus productivity growth. In this context it is interesting to note that the estimated Phillips curve (Figure 4.4) showed that an unemployment level of approximately 2.5 per cent was compatible with stable prices because at this level of unemployment the rate of change of money wages was approximately equal to the then average growth of productivity of 2 per cent. Suppose the economy is initially operating at a full employment level of income (Y_{FE}); that is, the intersection of IS_0 and LM_0 in panel (a) of Figure 4.7. Reference to panel (b) reveals that the full employment level of income is compatible with stable prices; that is, $\dot{P} = 0$. Following a once-and-for-all expansionary real impulse, the IS curve shifts outwards to the right, from IS_0 to IS_1, and real income rises above its full employment level of Y_{FE} to Y_1. Reference to panel (b) reveals that as income rises above its full employment level price inflation increases to $\dot{P}_1$. As prices increase the real value of the money supply is reduced, causing the LM curve to shift to the left, from LM_0 to LM_1 and the economy returns to full employment; that is, the intersection of IS_1 and LM_1 in panel (a). At full employment stable prices prevail; that is, $\dot{P} = 0$ in panel (b).

The Phillips curve was interpreted by many orthodox Keynesians as implying a stable *long-run* trade-off which offered the authorities a menu of possible inflation–unemployment combinations for policy choice (see, for

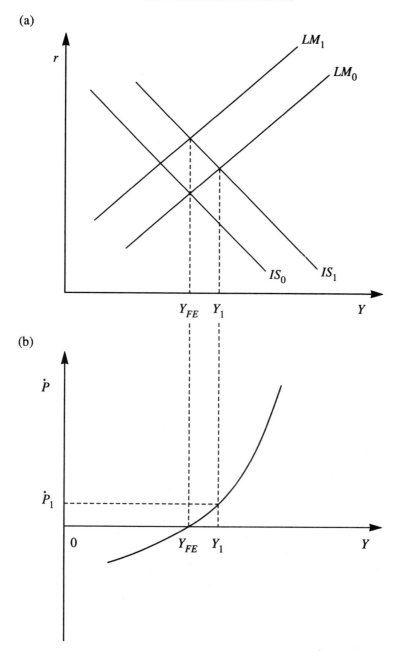

Figure 4.7   The link between the Keynesian model and wage and price inflation

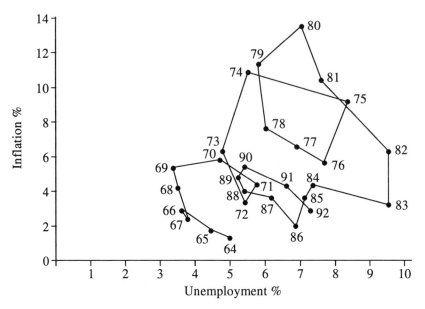

Notes:　As for Tables 1.2 and 1.3.

Sources:　As for Tables 1.2 and 1.3.

Figure 4.8　Inflation and unemployment in the USA, 1964–92

example, Samuelson and Solow, 1960). However, by the late 1960s/early 1970s, both inflation and unemployment had begun to increase, as is evident from Figures 4.8 and 4.9. The notion of a stable relationship was challenged independently by Friedman and Phelps, who both denied the existence of a permanent (long-run) trade-off between inflation and unemployment. The problem with the original specification of the Phillips curve as reflected in equation (4.2) is that the rate of change of money wages is determined quite independently of the rate of inflation. This in turn implies that workers are irrational and suffer from complete money illusion, in that they base their labour supply decisions on the level of money wages quite independently of what is happening to prices. In what follows we focus on the highly influential arguments put forward by Friedman (1968a) in his 1967 Presidential Address to the American Economic Association.

4.3.2　The expectations-augmented Phillips curve
According to Friedman, the original Phillips curve which related the rate of change of *money* wages to unemployment was misspecified. Although money

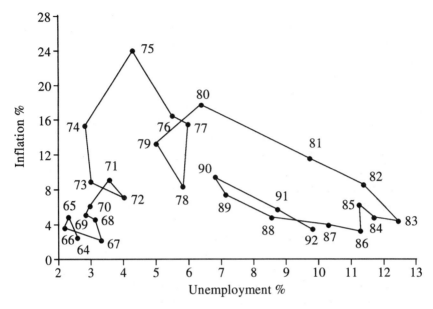

Notes: As for Tables 1.2 and 1.3.

Sources: As for Tables 1.2 and 1.3.

Figure 4.9   Inflation and unemployment in the UK, 1964–92

wages are set in negotiations, both employers and employees are interested in real, not money, wages. Since wage bargains are negotiated for discrete time periods, what affects the anticipated real wage is the rate of inflation expected to exist throughout the period of the contract. Friedman argued that the Phillips curve should be set in terms of the rate of change of *real* wages. He therefore augmented the basic Phillips curve with the anticipated or expected rate of inflation as an additional variable determining the rate of change of money wages. The expectations-augmented Phillips curve can be expressed mathematically by the equation:

$$\dot{W} = f(U) + \dot{P}^e \tag{4.3}$$

Equation (4.3) shows that the rate of money wage increase is equal to a component determined by the state of excess demand (as proxied by the level of unemployment) plus the expected rate of inflation.

Introducing the expected rate of inflation as an additional variable to excess demand which determines the rate of change of money wages implies that, instead of one unique Phillips curve, there will be a family of Phillips curves, each associated with a different expected rate of inflation. Two such curves are illustrated in Figure 4.10. Suppose the economy is initially in equilibrium at point A along the short-run Phillips curve ($SRPC_1$) with unemployment at U_N, its natural level (see below) and with a zero rate of increase of money wages. For simplification purposes in this, and subsequent, analysis we assume a zero growth in productivity so that with a zero rate of money wage increase the price level would also be constant and the expected rate of inflation would be zero; that is, $\dot{W} = \dot{P} = \dot{P}^e = 0$ per cent. Now imagine the authorities reduce unemployment from U_N to U_1 by expanding aggregate demand through monetary expansion. Excess demand in goods and labour markets would result in upward pressure on prices and money wages, with commodity prices typically adjusting more rapidly than wages. Having recently experienced a period of price stability ($\dot{P}^e = 0$), workers would misinterpret their money wage increases as real wage increases and supply more labour; that is, they would suffer from temporary money illusion. Real wages would, however, actually fall and, as firms demanded more labour, unemployment would fall, with money wages rising at a rate of $\dot{W}_1$; that is, point B on the short-run Phillips curve ($SRPC_1$). As workers started slowly to adapt their inflation expectations in the light of the actual rate of inflation experienced ($\dot{P} = \dot{W}_1$), they would realize that, although their money wages had risen, their real wages had fallen, and they would press

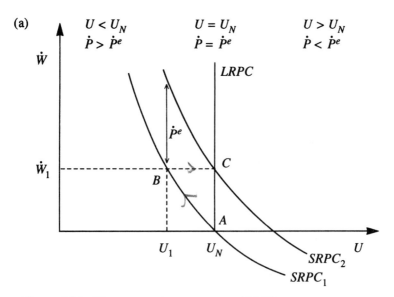

(a)

Figure 4.10   The expectations-augmented Phillips curve

for increased money wages, shifting the short-run Phillips curve upwards from $SRPC_1$ to $SRPC_2$. Money wages would rise at a rate of $\dot{W}_1$ plus the expected rate of inflation. Firms would lay off workers as real wages rose and unemployment would increase until, at point C, real wages were restored to their original level with unemployment at its natural level. This means that, once the actual rate of inflation is completely anticipated ($\dot{P}_1 = \dot{P}^e$) in wage bargains ($\dot{W}_1 = \dot{P}^e$, that is to say there is no money illusion), there will be no long-run trade-off between unemployment and wage inflation. It follows that if there is no excess demand (that is, the economy is operating at the natural rate of unemployment) then the rate of increase of money wages would equal the expected rate of inflation and only in the special case where the expected rate of inflation is zero would wage inflation be zero; that is, at point A in Figure 4.10. By joining points such as A and C together, a long-run vertical Phillips curve is obtained at the natural rate of employment (U_N). At U_N the rate of increase in money wages is exactly equal to the rate of increase in prices, so that the real wage is constant. In consequence there will be no disturbance in the labour market. At the natural rate the labour market is in a state of equilibrium and the actual and expected rates of inflation are equal; that is, inflation is fully anticipated. Friedman's analysis helped reconcile the classical proposition with respect to the *long-run* neutrality of money (see section 2.5), while still allowing money to have real effects in the short run.

Following Friedman's attack on the Phillips curve numerous empirical studies of the expectations-augmented Phillips curve were undertaken using the type of equation:

$$\dot{W} = f(U) + \beta \dot{P}^e \qquad (4.4)$$

Estimated values for β of unity imply no long-run trade-off. Conversely estimates of β of less than unity, but greater than zero, imply a long-run trade-off but one which is less favourable than in the short run. This can be demonstrated algebraically in the following manner. Assuming a zero growth in productivity so that $\dot{W} = \dot{P}$, equation (4.4) can be written as:

$$\dot{P} = f(U) + \beta \dot{P}^e \qquad (4.5)$$

Rearranging equation (4.5) we obtain:

$$\dot{P} - \beta \dot{P}^e = f(U) \qquad (4.6)$$

Starting from a position of equilibrium where unemployment equals U^* (see Figure 4.11) and the actual and expected rates of inflation are both equal to zero (that is, $\dot{P} = \dot{P}^e$) equation (4.6) can be factorized and written as:

$$\dot{P}(1-\beta) = f(U) \tag{4.7}$$

Finally dividing both sides of equation (4.7) by $1 - \beta$ we obtain

$$\dot{P} = \frac{f(U)}{1-\beta} \tag{4.8}$$

Now imagine the authorities initially reduce unemployment below U^* (see Figure 4.11) by expanding aggregate demand through monetary expansion. From equation (4.8) we can see that, as illustrated in Figure 4.11, (i) estimated values for β of zero imply both a stable short- and long-run trade-off between inflation and unemployment in line with the original Phillips curve; (ii) estimates of β of unity imply no long-run trade-off; and (iii) estimates of β of less than unity, but greater than zero, imply a long-run trade-off but one which is less favourable than in the short run. Early evidence from a wide range of studies that sought to test whether the coefficient (β) on the inflation expectations term is equal to one proved far from clear-cut. In consequence, during the early 1970s, the subject of the possible existence of a long-run vertical Phillips curve became a controversial issue in the monetarist–Keynesian debate. While there was a body of evidence that monetarists could draw on to justify their belief that β equals unity, so that there would be no trade-

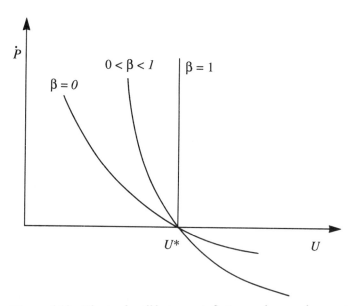

Figure 4.11   The trade-off between inflation and unemployment

off between unemployment and inflation in the long run, there was insufficient evidence to convince all the sceptics. However, according to one prominent American Keynesian economist, 'by 1972 the "vertical-in-the-long-run" view of the Phillips curve had won the day' (Blinder, 1992a). The reader is referred to Santomero and Seater (1978) for a very readable review of the vast literature on the Phillips curve up to 1978. By the mid-to-late 1970s, the majority of mainstream Keynesians (especially in the USA) had come to accept that the long-run Phillips curve is vertical. There is, however, still considerable controversy on the time it takes for the economy to return to the long-run solution following a disturbance.

Before turning to discuss the policy implications of the expectations-augmented Phillips curve, it is worth mentioning that in his Nobel Lecture Friedman (1977) offered an explanation for the existence of a positively-sloped Phillips curve for a period of several years, which is compatible with a vertical long-run Phillips curve at the natural rate of unemployment. Friedman noted that inflation rates tend to become increasingly volatile at higher rates of inflation. Increased volatility of inflation results in greater uncertainty and unemployment may rise as market efficiency is reduced and the price system becomes less efficient as a coordinating/communication mechanism (see Hayek, 1948). Increased uncertainty may also cause a fall in investment and result in an increase in unemployment. Friedman further argued that, as inflation rates increase and become increasingly volatile, governments tend to intervene more in the price-setting process by imposing wage and price controls, which reduces the efficiency of the price system and results in an increase in unemployment. The positive relationship between inflation and unemployment results then from an unanticipated increase in the rate *and* volatility of inflation. While the period of transition could be quite long, extending over decades, once the economy had adjusted to high and volatile inflation, in Friedman's view, it would return to the natural rate of unemployment.

4.3.3 The policy implications of the expectations-augmented Phillips curve

The scope for short-run output–employment gains The monetarist belief in a long-run vertical Phillips curve implies that an increased rate of monetary expansion can reduce unemployment below the natural rate only because the resulting inflation is unexpected. As we have discussed, as soon as inflation is fully anticipated it will be incorporated into wage bargains and unemployment will return to the natural rate. The assumption underlying orthodox monetarist analysis is that expected inflation adjusts to actual inflation only gradually in line with the so-called 'adaptive' or error-learning expectations hypothesis. The main idea behind this hypothesis, which was first modelled by Cagan (1956) in the context of hyperinflation, is that economic agents adapt their inflation expectations in the light of past inflation rates and that they learn from their errors. Workers are assumed to adjust their inflation expectations by a fraction of the last error made: that is, the difference between the actual rate of inflation and the expected rate of inflation. This can be expressed by the equation:

$$\dot{P}_t^e - \dot{P}_{t-1}^e = \alpha(\dot{P}_t - \dot{P}_{t-1}^e) \qquad (4.9)$$

where α is a constant fraction. By repeated back substitution expected inflation can be shown to be a geometrically weighted average of past actual inflation rates with greater importance attached to more recent experience of inflation:

$$\dot{P}_t^e = \alpha\dot{P}_t + \alpha(1-\alpha)\dot{P}_{t-1} \ldots \alpha(1-\alpha)^n \dot{P}_{t-n} \qquad (4.10)$$

In this 'backward-looking' model, expectations of inflation are based solely on past actual inflation rates. The existence of a gap in time between an increase in the actual rate of inflation and an increase in the expected rate permits a temporary reduction in unemployment below the natural rate. Once inflation is fully anticipated, the economy returns to its natural rate of unemployment but with a higher equilibrium rate of wage and price inflation equal to the rate of monetary growth. As we will discuss in section 5.4.1, if expectations are formed according to the rational expectations hypothesis and economic agents have access to the same information as the authorities then the expected rate of inflation will rise immediately in response to an increased rate of monetary expansion. In the case where there was no lag between an increase in the actual and expected rate of inflation the authorities would be powerless to influence output and employment even in the short run.

The accelerationist hypothesis   A second important policy implication of the belief in a vertical long-run Phillips curve concerns the so-called 'accelerationist' hypothesis. This hypothesis implies that any attempt to maintain unemployment permanently below the natural rate would result in accelerating inflation and require the authorities to increase continuously the rate of monetary expansion. Reference to Figure 4.10 reveals that, if unemployment was held permanently at U_1 (that is, below the natural rate U_N), the continued existence of excess demand in the labour market would lead to a higher actual rate of inflation than expected. As the actual rate of inflation increased, people would revise their inflation expectations upwards (that is, shifting the short-run Phillips curve upwards) which would in turn lead to a higher actual rate of inflation and so on, leading to hyperinflation. In other words, in order to maintain unemployment below the natural rate, real wages would have to be kept below their equilibrium level. For this to happen actual prices would have to rise at a faster rate than money wages. In such a situation employees would revise their expectations of inflation upwards and press for higher money wage increases, which would in turn lead to a higher actual rate of inflation. The end result would be accelerating inflation which would necessitate continuous increases in the rate of monetary expansion to validate the continuously rising rate of inflation. Conversely, if unemployment is held permanently above the natural rate, accelerating deflation will occur. Where unemployment is held permanently above the natural rate the continued existence of excess supply in the labour market will lead to a lower actual rate of inflation than expected. In this situation people would revise their inflation expectations downwards (that is, the short-run Phillips curve would shift downwards) which would in turn lead to a lower actual rate of inflation and so on. It follows from this analysis that the natural rate is the only level of unemployment at which a constant rate of inflation may be maintained. In other words, in long-run equilibrium with the economy at the natural rate of unemployment, the rate of monetary expansion will determine the rate of inflation (assuming a constant growth of output and velocity) in line with the quantity theory of money approach to macroeconomic analysis.

The output–employment costs of reducing inflation   Friedman (1970b) has suggested that: 'inflation is always and everywhere a monetary phenomenon in the sense that it can be produced only by a more rapid increase in the quantity of money than in output'. Given the orthodox monetarist belief that inflation is essentially a monetary phenomenon propagated by excessive monetary growth, monetarists argue that inflation can only be reduced by slowing down the rate of growth of the money supply. Reducing the rate of monetary expansion results in an increase in the level of unemployment. The policy dilemma the authorities face is that, the more rapidly they seek to reduce inflation through monetary contraction, the higher will be the costs in terms of unemployment. Recognition of this fact has led some orthodox monetarists (such as David Laidler) to advocate a gradual adjustment process whereby the rate of monetary expansion is slowly brought down to its desired level in order to minimize the output–employment costs of reducing inflation. The costs of the alternative policy options of gradualism versus cold turkey are illustrated in Figure 4.12.

In Figure 4.12 we assume the economy is initially operating at point *A*, the intersection of the short-run Phillips curve (*SRPC*$_1$) and the long-run vertical Phillips curve (*LRPC*). The initial starting position is then both a short- and long-run equilibrium situation where the economy is experiencing a constant

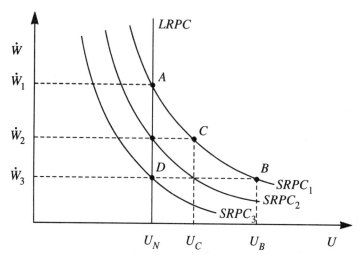

Figure 4.12   The output–employment costs of reducing inflation

rate of wage and price inflation which is fully anticipated (that is, $\dot{W}_1 = \dot{P} = \dot{P}^e$) and unemployment is at the natural rate (U_N). Now suppose that this rate of inflation is too high for the authorities' liking and that they wish to reduce the rate of inflation by lowering the rate of monetary expansion and move to position D on the long-run vertical Phillips curve. Consider two alternative policy options open to the authorities to move to their preferred position at point D. One (cold turkey) option would be to reduce *dramatically* the rate of monetary expansion and raise unemployment to U_B, so that wage and price inflation quickly fell to $\dot{W}_3$; that is, an initial movement along $SRPC_1$ from point A to B. The initial cost of this option would be a relatively large increase in unemployment from U_N to U_B. As the actual rate of inflation fell below the expected rate, expectations of future rates of inflation would be revised in a downwards direction. The short-run Phillips curve would shift downwards and a new short- and long-run equilibrium would eventually be achieved at point D, the intersection of $SRPC_3$ and $LRPC$ where $\dot{W}_3 = \dot{P} = \dot{P}^e$ with unemployment at U_N. Another (gradual) policy option open to the authorities would be to begin with a much smaller reduction in the rate of monetary expansion and initially increase unemployment to, say, U_C so that wage and price inflation fell to $\dot{W}_2$; that is, an initial movement along $SRPC_1$ from point A to C. Compared to the cold turkey option, this gradual option would involve a much smaller initial increase in unemployment, from U_N to

U_c. As the actual rate of inflation fell below the expected rate (but to a much lesser extent than in the first option), expectations would be revised downwards. The short-run Phillips curve would move downwards as the economy adjusted to a new lower rate of inflation. The short-run Phillips curve ($SRPC_2$) would be associated with an expected rate of inflation of $\dot{W}_2$. A further reduction in the rate of monetary expansion would further reduce the rate of inflation until the inflation target of $\dot{W}_3$ was achieved. The transition to point D on the $LRPC$ would, however, take a much longer time span than under the first policy option. Such a policy entails living with inflation for quite long periods of time and has led some economists to advocate supplementary policy measures to accompany the gradual adjustment process to a lower rate of inflation. Before we consider the potential scope for such supplementary measures as indexation and prices and incomes policy, it is important to stress the importance of the credibility of any anti-inflation strategy (this issue is discussed more fully in section 5.4.2). If the public believes that the authorities are committed to contractionary monetary policies to reduce inflation, economic agents will adjust their inflation expectations downwards more quickly, thereby reducing the output–employment costs associated with the adjustment process.

Some monetarists (for example, Friedman, 1974) have suggested that some form of indexation would be a useful supplementary policy measure to accompany the gradual adjustment process to a lower rate of inflation. It is claimed that indexation would reduce, not only the cost of unanticipated inflation incurred through arbitrary redistribution of income and wealth, but also the output–employment costs that are associated with a reduction in the rate of monetary expansion. With indexation, money wage increases would automatically decline as inflation decreased, thereby removing the danger that employers would be committed, under existing contracts, to excessive money wage increases when inflation fell. In other words, with indexation wage increases would be less rapid and unemployment would therefore rise by a smaller amount. Further some economists (for example, Tobin, 1977, 1981; Trevithick and Stevenson, 1977) have suggested that a prices and incomes policy could have a role to play, as a temporary and supplementary policy measure to monetary contraction, to assist the transition to a lower rate of inflation by reducing inflationary expectations. In terms of Figure 4.12, to the extent that a prices and incomes policy succeeded in reducing inflationary expectations, the short-run Phillips curves would shift downwards more quickly. This in turn would enable adjustment to a lower rate of inflation to be achieved both more quickly and at a lower cost in terms of the extent and duration of unemployment that accompanies monetary contraction. However one of the problems of using prices and incomes policy is that, even if the policy initially succeeds in reducing inflationary expectations, once the policy begins to break down or is ended inflationary expectations may be revised upwards. As a result the short-run Phillips curve will shift upwards, thereby offsetting the initial benefit of the policy in terms of lower unemployment and wage inflation. For example, Henry and Ormerod (1978) concluded that:

> Whilst some incomes policies have reduced the rate of wage inflation during the period in which they operated, this reduction has only been temporary. Wage increases in the period immediately following the ending of policies were higher than they would otherwise have been, and these increases match losses incurred during the operation of the incomes policy.

In summary, within the orthodox monetarist approach the output–employment costs associated with monetary contraction depend upon three main factors: first, whether the authorities pursue a rapid or gradual reduction in the rate of monetary expansion; second, the extent of institutional adaptations – for example, whether or not wage contracts are indexed; third, the speed with which economic agents adjust their inflationary expectations downwards.

The monetarist view that inflation can only be reduced by slowing down the rate of growth of the money supply had an important bearing on the course of macroeconomic policy pursued both in the USA (see Brimmer, 1983) and in the UK during the early 1980s. For example, in the UK the Conservative government elected into power in 1979 sought, as part of its medium-term financial strategy, to reduce progressively the rate of monetary growth (with pre-announced target ranges for four years ahead) in order to achieve its overriding economic policy objective of permanently reducing the rate of inflation. Furthermore the orthodox monetarist contention that inflation cannot be reduced without output–employment costs appears to have been borne out by the recessions experienced in the US and UK economies in 1981–2 and 1980–81, respectively (see section 5.4.2). For well written and highly accessible accounts of the background to, execution and effects of what the media dubbed 'Thatcher's monetarist experiment', the interested reader is referred to Keegan (1984) and Smith (1987).

The role and conduct of monetary policy   The belief in a long-run vertical Phillips curve and that aggregate-demand management policies can only affect the level of output and employment in the short run has important implications for the role and conduct of monetary policy. Before discussing the rationale for Friedman's policy prescription for a fixed monetary growth rule, it is important to stress that, even if the long-run Phillips curve is vertical, arguments justifying discretionary monetary intervention to stabilize the economy in the short run can be made on the grounds of either the potential to identify and respond to economic disturbances or the length of time required for the economy to return to the natural rate following a disturbance. Friedman's policy prescription for a fixed rate of monetary growth, in line with the trend/long-run growth rate of the economy, is based on a number of arguments. These arguments include the beliefs that: (i) if the authorities expand the money supply at a steady rate over time the economy will tend to settle down at the natural rate of unemployment with a steady rate of inflation; that is, at a point along the long-run vertical Phillips curve; (ii) the adoption of a monetary rule would remove the greatest source of instability in the economy; that is, unless disturbed by erratic monetary growth, advanced capitalist economies are inherently stable around the natural rate of unemployment; (iii) in the present state of economic knowledge, discretionary monetary policy could turn out to be destabilizing and make matters worse rather than better, owing to the long and variable lags associated with monetary policy; and (iv) because of ignorance of the natural rate itself (which may change over time), the government should not aim at a target unemployment rate for fear of the consequences noted earlier, most notably accelerating inflation.

We finally consider the implication of the belief in a natural rate of unemployment for employment policy.

The natural rate of unemployment and supply-side policies   As we have discussed earlier, the natural rate of unemployment is associated with equilibrium in the labour market and hence in the structure of real wage rates. Friedman (1968a) has defined the natural rate as:

> the level that would be ground out by the Walrasian system of general equilibrium equations provided there is embedded in them the actual structural characteristics of the labor and commodity markets, including market imperfections, stochastic variability in demands and supplies, the cost of gathering information about job vacancies and labor availabilities, the costs of mobility and so on.

What this approach implies is that, if governments wish to reduce the natural rate of unemployment in order to achieve higher output and employment levels, they should pursue supply-management policies which are designed to improve the structure and functioning of the labour market and industry, rather than demand-management policies. Examples of the wide range of (often highly controversial) supply-side policies which have been pursued over recent years both in the UK (see for example, Vane, 1992) and elsewhere include measures designed to increase: (i) the incentive to work, for example through reductions in marginal income tax rates, and reductions in unemployment and social security benefits; (ii) the flexibility of wages and working practices, for example by curtailing trade union power; (iii) the occupational and geographical mobility of labour, for example in the former case through greater provision of government retraining schemes; and (iv) the efficiency of markets for goods and services, for example by privatization.

4.4   The Monetary Approach to Balance of Payments Theory and Exchange Rate Determination

The third stage in the development of orthodox monetarism came in the 1970s, with the incorporation of the monetary approach to balance of payments theory and exchange rate determination into monetarist analysis. Until the collapse of the Bretton Woods system of fixed exchange rates against the United States dollar in 1971, the US economy could be treated as a reasonably close approximation to a closed economy. The monetary approach was particularly important in that it made monetarist analysis, which had been implicitly developed in this closed economy context, relevant to open economies such as the UK.

4.4.1   The monetary approach to the balance of payments under fixed exchange rates

During the 1970s, a large number of different monetary models of the balance of payments appeared in the literature. However common to all monetary models is the view that the balance of payments is essentially a monetary phenomenon. As we will discuss, the approach concentrates primarily on the money market in which the relationship between the stock demand for and supply of money is regarded as the main determinant of balance of payments flows. Furthermore, despite different specifications, in most of the monetary models of the balance of payments four key assumptions are generally made. First, the demand for money is a stable function of a limited number of variables. Second, in the long run output and employment tend towards their full employment or natural levels. Third, the authorities cannot sterilize or neutralize the monetary impact of balance of payments deficits/surpluses on the domestic money supply in the long run. Fourth, after due allowance for tariffs and transport costs, arbitrage will ensure that the prices of similar traded goods will tend to be equalized in the long run.

The most influential contributions to the development of the monetary approach to balance of payments theory have been made by Johnson (1972a) and Frenkel and Johnson (1976). Following Johnson (1972a) we now consider a simple monetary model of the balance of payments for a small open economy. Within this model it is assumed that: (i) real income is fixed at its full employment or natural level; (ii) the law of one price holds in both commodity and financial markets, and (iii) both the domestic price level and interest rate are pegged to world levels.

The demand for real balances depends on real income and the rate of interest.

$$M_d = Pf(Y,r) \tag{4.11}$$

The supply of money is equal to domestic credit (that is, money created domestically) plus money associated with changes in international reserves.

$$M_s = D + R \tag{4.12}$$

In money market equilibrium, M_d must be equal to M_s so that:

$$M_d = D + R \tag{4.13}$$

or

$$R = M_d - D \tag{4.14}$$

Assuming the system is initially in equilibrium, we now examine the consequence of a once-and-for-all increase in domestic credit (D) by the authorities. Since the arguments in the demand for money function (equation 4.11) are all exogenously given, the demand for money cannot adjust to the increase in domestic credit. Individuals will get rid of their excess money balances by buying foreign goods and securities, generating a balance of payments deficit. Under a regime of fixed exchange rates, the authorities are committed to sell foreign exchange for the home currency to cover a balance of payments deficit which results in a loss of international reserves (R). The loss of international reserves would reverse the initial increase in the money supply, owing to an increase in domestic credit, and the money supply would continue to fall until the balance of payments deficit was eliminated. The system will return to equilibrium when the money supply returns to its original level, with the increase in domestic credit being matched by an equal reduction in foreign exchange reserves (equation 4.12). In short any discrepancy between actual and desired money balances results in a balance of payments deficit/surplus which in turn provides the mechanism whereby the discrepancy is eliminated. In equilibrium actual and desired money balances are again in balance and there will be no changes in international reserves; that is, the balance of payments is self-correcting.

The analysis can also be conducted in dynamic terms. To illustrate the predictions of the approach, we again simplify the analysis, this time by assuming that the small open economy experiences continuous real income growth while world (and hence domestic) prices and interest rates are constant. In this case the balance of payments position would reflect the relationship between the growth of money demand and the growth of domestic credit. A country will experience a persistent balance of payments deficit, and will in consequence be continually losing international reserves, whenever domestic credit expansion is greater than the growth in the demand for money balances (owing to real income growth). Clearly the level of foreign exchange reserves provides a limit to the duration of time a country could finance a persistent balance of payments deficit. Conversely a country will experience a persistent balance of payments surplus whenever the authorities fail to expand domestic credit in line with the growth in the demand for money balances. While a country might aim to achieve a balance of payments surplus in order to build up depleted international reserves in the short run, in the long run it would be irrational for a country to pursue a policy of achieving a continuous balance of payments surplus, thereby continually acquiring international reserves.

4.4.2 The policy implications of the monetary approach under fixed exchange rates

Automatic adjustment and the power of expenditure switching policies The monetary approach predicts that there is an automatic adjustment mechanism that operates, without discretionary government policy, to correct balance of payments disequilibria. As we have discussed, any discrepancy between actual and desired real balances results in balance of payments disequilibria as people try to get rid of or acquire real money balances through international markets for goods and securities. The adjustment process operates through balance of payments flows and continues until the discrepancy between actual and desired real money balances has been eliminated. Closely linked to the belief in an automatic adjustment mechanism is the prediction that expenditure switching policies will only temporarily improve the balance of payments if they induce an increase in the demand for money by raising domestic prices. For example, devaluation would raise the domestic price level, which would in turn reduce the level of real money balances below their equilibrium level. Reference to equation (4.13) reveals that, assuming there is no increase in domestic credit, the system will return to equilibrium once the money supply has increased, through a balance of payments surplus and an associated increase in the level of foreign exchange reserves, to meet the increased demand for money.

The power of monetary policy From the above analysis it will be apparent that, in the case of a small country maintaining a fixed exchange rate with the rest of the world, the country's money supply becomes an endogenous variable. *Ceteris paribus,* a balance of payments deficit leads to a reduction in a country's foreign exchange reserves and the domestic money supply, and vice versa. In other words, where the authorities are committed to buy and sell foreign exchange for the home currency at a fixed price, changes in the money supply can arise not only from domestic sources (that is, domestic credit) but also from balance of payments intervention policy to maintain a fixed exchange rate. Reference to equation (4.12) reveals that domestic monetary policy only determines the division of the country's money supply between domestic credit and foreign exchange reserves, not the money supply itself. *Ceteris paribus*, any increase in domestic credit will be matched by an equal reduction in foreign exchange reserves, with no effect on the money supply. Monetary policy, in a small open economy, is completely impotent to influence any variable, other than foreign exchange reserves, in the long run. For an open economy operating under fixed exchange rates, the rate of growth of the money supply ($\dot{M}$) will equal domestic credit expansion ($\dot{D}$) plus the rate of change of foreign exchange reserves ($\dot{R}$), reflecting the balance of payments position. Domestic monetary expansion will have no influence on the domestic rate of inflation, interest rates or the rate of growth of output. Monetary expansion by a large country relative to the rest of the world can, however, influence the rate of world monetary expansion and world inflation.

Inflation as an international monetary phenomenon In a world of fixed exchange rates, inflation is viewed as an international monetary phenomenon which can be explained by an excess-demand expectations model. Excess demand depends on world, rather than domestic, monetary expansion. An increase in the world rate of monetary expansion (due to rapid monetary expansion by either a large country or a number of small countries simultaneously) would create excess demand and result in inflationary pressure throughout the world economy. In this context it is interesting to note that monetarists have argued that the acceleration of inflation that occurred in western economies in the late 1960s was primarily the consequence of an increase in the rate of monetary expansion in the USA to finance increased spending on the Vietnam War (see, for example, Johnson, 1972b; Laidler, 1976). Under the regime of fixed exchange rates that existed up to 1971, it is claimed that the inflationary pressure initiated in the USA was transmitted to other western economies via changes in their domestic money supplies originating from the US balance of payments deficit. In practice the USA determined monetary conditions for the rest of world. This situation eventually proved unacceptable to other countries and helped lead to the breakdown of the Bretton Woods system.

4.4.3   The monetary approach to exchange rate determination

The monetary approach to exchange rate determination is a direct application of the monetary approach to the balance of payments to the case of flexible exchange rates (see Frenkel and Johnson, 1978). Under a system of perfectly flexible exchange rates, the exchange rate adjusts to clear the foreign exchange market so that the balance of payments is always zero. In the absence of balance of payments deficits/surpluses there are no international reserves changes so that domestic credit expansion is the only source of monetary expansion. In contrast to a regime of fixed exchange rates where, *ceteris paribus,* an increase in domestic credit leads to a balance of payments deficit and a loss of international reserves, under flexible exchange rates it leads to a depreciation in the nominal exchange rate and an increase in the domestic price level. In the flexible exchange rate case of the monetary approach, 'the proximate determinants of exchange rates ... are the demand for and supply of various national monies' (Mussa, 1976).

The monetary approach to exchange rate determination can be illustrated using the simple monetary model first introduced in section 4.4.1. Assuming the system is initially in equilibrium, we again examine the consequence of a once-and-for-all increase in the domestic money supply (that is, domestic credit) by the authorities which disturbs the initial money market equilibrium. Reference to equation (4.11) reveals that, with real income fixed at its full employment or natural level, and the domestic rate of interest pegged to the world rate, the excess supply of money can only be eliminated by an increase in the domestic price level. The discrepancy between actual and desired money balances results in an increased demand for foreign goods and securities and a corresponding excess supply of domestic currency on the foreign exchange market, which causes the domestic currency to depreciate. The depreciation in the domestic currency results in an increase in the domestic price level, which in turn leads to an increased demand for money balances, and money market equilibrium is restored when actual and desired money balances are again in balance. In this simple monetary model, the nominal exchange rate depreciates in proportion to the increase in the money supply. In other words the exchange rate is determined by relative money supplies. For example, in a two country world, *ceteris paribus* there would be no change in the (real) exchange rate if both countries increased their money supplies together by the same amount.

The analysis can also be conducted in dynamic terms using slightly more complicated monetary models which allow for differential real income growth and differential inflation experience (due to different rates of monetary expansion). These models predict that the rate of change of the exchange rate depends on relative rates of monetary expansion and real income growth. Two examples will suffice. First, *ceteris paribus*, if domestic real income growth is lower than in the rest of the world, the exchange rate will depreciate, and vice versa. Second, *ceteris paribus*, if the domestic rate of monetary expansion is greater than in the rest of the world, the exchange rate will depreciate, and vice versa. In other words the monetary approach predicts that, *ceteris paribus*, a slowly growing country or a rapidly inflating country will experience a depreciating exchange rate, and vice versa. The important policy implication that derives from this approach is that exchange rate flexibility is a necessary, but not a sufficient, condition for the control of the domestic rate of inflation via control of the domestic rate of monetary expansion. In the case of perfectly flexible exchange rates, the domestic rate of inflation is held to be determined by the domestic rate of monetary expansion relative to the domestic growth of real income.

4.5 The Orthodox Monetarist School

In conclusion it would be useful to comment briefly on the development of orthodox monetarism. The development of orthodox monetarism can be appraised in a positive light, given that it displayed both theoretical and empirical progress over the period of the mid-1950s to the early 1970s (see, for example, Cross, 1982a, 1982b). The reformulation of the quantity theory of money approach, the addition of the expectations-augmented Phillips curve analysis and the incorporation of the monetary approach to the balance of payments theory and exchange rate determination, generated a large amount of real-world correspondence and empirical support (see Laidler, 1976). In contrast, towards the close of this period, the orthodox Keynesian position was looking increasingly degenerative given (i) its failure to explain theoretically the breakdown of the Phillips curve relationship and (ii) its willingness to retreat increasingly into non-economic explanations of accelerating inflation and rising unemployment.

Finally we can draw together the discussion contained in sections 4.2–4.4 and seek to summarize the central distinguishing beliefs within the orthodox monetarist school of thought (see also Brunner, 1970; Friedman, 1970b; Mayer, 1978b; Purvis, 1980; Laidler, 1981). These beliefs can be listed as follows:

1. Changes in the money stock are the predominant, though not the only, factor explaining changes in money income.
2. The economy is *inherently stable*, unless disturbed by erratic monetary growth, and when subjected to some disturbance, will return fairly rapidly to the neighbourhood of long-run equilibrium at the natural rate of unemployment.
3. There is no trade-off between unemployment and inflation in the long run; that is, the long-run Phillips curve is vertical at the natural rate of unemployment.

4. Inflation and the balance of payments are essentially monetary phenomena.

5. In the conduct of economic policy the authorities should follow some rule for monetary aggregates to ensure long-run price stability, with fiscal policy assigned to its traditional roles of influencing the distribution of income and wealth, and the allocation of resources. In the former case, Laidler (1993, p. 187) has argued that the authorities must be prepared to adapt the behaviour of the supply of whatever monetary aggregate they chose to control (that is, in response to shifts in the demand for money resulting from, for example, institutional change) rather than pursue a rigid (legislated) growth rule for a chosen monetary aggregate.

The monetarist aversion to activist stabilization policy, both monetary and fiscal policy (and prices and incomes policy), which derives both from the interrelated theoretical propositions and from empirical evidence discussed in sections 4.2–4.4, is the central issue which distinguishes orthodox monetarists from Keynesians. The debate over the role and conduct of stabilization policy is neatly summarized in the following passage, taken from Modigliani's (1977) Presidential Address to the American Economic Association, a comment which is as relevant today as when it was made over a decade and a half ago:

> Nonmonetarists accept what I regard to be the fundamental practical message of *The General Theory*: that a private enterprise economy using an intangible money *needs* to be stabilized, *can* be stabilized, and therefore *should* be stabilized by appropriate monetary and fiscal policies. Monetarists by contrast take the view that there is no serious need to stabilize the economy; that even if there were a need, it could not be done, for stabilization policies would be more likely to increase than decrease instability.

During the 1970s, developments in macroeconomics associated with the new classical school cast further doubt on whether traditional stabilization policies can be used to improve the overall performance of the economy. Before turning to these developments and the new classical case against activist policy in the next chapter it is worth noting that for many economists

> the monetarist school of thought is alive and well. Only when inflation is eliminated from the world economy will the journeyman monetarist be able to lay down his tools. Where else can you find a professional group who will only rest easy when they have made themselves redundant? (Chrystal, 1990, p. xix)

MILTON FRIEDMAN

Milton Friedman was born in 1912 in New York City and graduated from Rutgers University with a BA in 1932, before obtaining his MA from the University of Chicago in 1933 and his PhD from Columbia University in 1946. Between 1946 and 1977 (when he retired) he taught at the University of Chicago and he has lectured at universities throughout the world. He is currently a Senior Research Fellow at the Hoover Institution (on War, Revolution and Peace) at Stanford University, California.

Milton Friedman is the most famous living economist in the world and has a truly outstanding record and reputation at the international level, both as a scholar and as a debater. In 1976 he won the Nobel Prize in Economics. Among his best known books are: *Essays in Positive Economics* (University of Chicago Press, 1953), *Studies in the Quantity Theory of Money* (University of Chicago Press, 1956), *A Theory of the Consumption Function* (Princeton University Press, 1957), *Capitalism and Freedom* (University of Chicago Press, 1962), *A Monetary History of the United States, 1867–1960* (Princeton University Press, 1963), co-authored with Anna Schwartz, *Free to Choose* (Harcourt Brace Jovanovich, 1980), co-authored with his wife Rose Friedman, *Monetary Trends in the United States and the United Kingdom* (University of Chicago Press, 1982), co-authored with Anna Schwartz, and *Monetarist Economics* (Basil Blackwell, 1991).

Among the numerous articles he has written, the best known include: 'The Methodology of Positive Economics', in *Essays in Positive Economics* (University of Chicago Press, 1953), 'The Quantity Theory of Money: A Restatement', in *Studies in the Quantity Theory of Money* (ed. M. Friedman) (University of Chicago Press, 1956), 'The Role of Monetary Policy', *American Economic Review* (1968) – his presidential address to the American Economic Association, 'A Theoretical Framework for Monetary Analysis', *Journal of Political Economy* (1970), and ' Inflation and Unemployment', *Journal of Political Economy* (1977) – his Nobel Lecture.

We corresponded with Milton Friedman in February 1993.

Why do you think there is more consensus among economists over microeconomic issues compared to macroeconomic issues?
Primarily because there has not been in the microeconomic area anything comparable to the Keynesian revolution in the macroeconomic area. For a time it looked as if the imperfect competition developments of Chamberlin and Robinson would play the same role in the microeconomic area, but they turned out to be more readily absorbed in the traditional classical body of microeconomic theory as presented in Marshall's *Principles*. A second reason, indeed the one that gave rise to the Keynesian revolution, was that the issues of employment/unemployment and business cycles became major political issues.

How important do you think it is for macroeconomic models to have choice-theoretic micro foundations?
I think it is less important for macroeconomic models to have choice-theoretic micro foundations than it is for them to have empirical implications that can be subjected to refutation. Choice-theoretic micro foundations may provide hypotheses for improving macroeconomic models, but the key macroeconomic models have been of long standing and have had a great deal of success without the more recent emphasis on choice-theoretic micro foundations.

What do you consider to be the key papers/books which have had a major impact on the development of your ideas with respect to macroeconomics during the past 25 years?
As I said in a comment at the American Economic Association meeting in 1974, 'it is far harder to specify what "we" – meaning the profession of economics – have learned in the past 200 years than what we have learned in the past 25 years' ['Twenty-five Years after the Rediscovery of Money: What Have We Learned? Discussion', *American Economic Review, Papers and*

Proceedings, 65 (May 1975), 176]. The major impact on my own ideas with respect to macroeconomics during the past 25 years has come primarily from the accumulation of data and studies for many different countries of the relation between monetary and other magnitudes than from any of the papers or books during that period.

You were a graduate student at Chicago during the early 1930s. How was Keynes's General Theory *received by Chicago economists, and in particular what were your first impressions?*
Keynes's *General Theory* was not published until after I had ended my period as a graduate student at Chicago during the early 1930s. My last year of graduate study was 1934–5; the *General Theory* appeared in 1936. The Keynes book we studied was *A Treatise on Money*. I cannot at this late date truly say with any confidence what my first impressions were. I do know that early in the 1940s I wrote a review in which I was very critical of the Keynesian analysis. But also, in 1942, I published an analysis of the wartime inflation problem that was strictly Keynesian – see *Essays in Positive Economics*, pp. 251–62, especially p. 253, n. 2.

Do you think that the distinction made by Keynes between voluntary and involuntary unemployment has been a useful one for the development of macroeconomics?
I have not myself found it a terribly useful distinction, but I cannot speak for others.

From your many publications it is evident that you have a great admiration and respect for J.M. Keynes. If he had still been living in 1969 when the first Nobel Prize was awarded, would he have received your vote?
Yes.

What importance do you personally attach to being awarded the Nobel Prize in Economics?
Obviously it is extremely rewarding. However, when I first learned of the award from a reporter in a parking lot in Detroit who stuck a microphone in my face and asked, 'Do you regard this as the high point of your career?', I answered, 'I care more what my successors 50 years from now will think about my professional work than I do about the judgement of seven people from Sweden who happen to be serving on the Nobel Committee.' I do not mean to denigrate the Nobel Committee. They have been doing a very conscientious and good job on the whole, but at the same time what really matters to a scientist is the long-run effect of his work on his science.

Which book and/or article do you consider to be your most important/influential work?

I believe that my best scientific work was *The Theory of the Consumption Function*; my most influential work, *A Monetary History of the United States*, jointly authored with Anna J. Schwartz.

What are the fundamental propositions of monetarism?

I listed some fundamental propositions of monetarism in a talk I gave at the Institute of Economic Affairs in 1970 – see Friedman, M. (1970) *The Counter-Revolution in Monetary Theory*, pp. 22–6 (IEA Occasional Paper 33, London, Institute of Economic Affairs).

You have been a lifelong advocate of floating exchange rates. Has the experience since the breakdown of the Bretton Woods system in the early 1970s confirmed that opinion?

Yes. Every attempt to re-establish a system of fixed exchange rates has broken down in turn. That happened to the European Payments Union, the snake, and most recently the European Monetary System. Britain in particular would be in a far better shape today if no attempt had been made to peg the British pound to the German mark.

Some economists, perhaps most, would argue that the fundamental difference between monetarists and Keynesians is not so much their respective views on the influence of the money supply but their differing views on the equilibrating powers of the market mechanism. Whereas monetarists have faith in the equilibrating tendencies of market forces, Keynesians argue that there is substantial market failure requiring some sort of activist intervention at the macro level. Would you agree with this view?

I do not agree with this view. There are monetarists of all kinds, some who stress market failure and some who do not. All economists – monetarists, Keynesians, or what-not – recognize that there is such a thing as market failure. I believe that what really distinguishes economists is not whether they recognize market failure, but how much importance they attach to government failure, especially when government seeks to remedy what are said to be market failures. That difference in turn is related to the time perspective that economists bring to various issues. Speaking for myself, I do not believe that I have more faith in the equilibrating tendencies of market forces than most Keynesians, but I have far less faith than most economists, whether Keynesians or monetarists, in the ability of government to offset market failure without making matters worse.

What do you see as the important differences between your monetarism and the new classical and Austrian varieties?

Re the Austrian variety, the major difference is methodological. The Austrians believe their theories are aprioristic, not subject to contradiction by evidence. I believe that the views I have expressed are attempts to state generalizations capable of being contradicted by evidence. The new classical theory is a special case of the quantity theory of money that all monetarists accept. However, as a hypothesis about the real world, it has been contradicted by experience.

One of the policy implications of new classical analysis is that there will be no trade-off between inflation and unemployment even in the short run following announced/anticipated monetary expansion. How do you view this policy ineffectiveness proposition?

I answered this in the previous question. It is simply an unsuccessful empirical hypothesis.

What importance do you attach to the rational expectations hypothesis?

The basic ideas underlying the rational expectations hypothesis are of long standing. However formalizing them, giving them a name, has been exceedingly useful and has been of considerable importance in promoting a fuller understanding of real-world phenomena.

Do you feel that the Kydland/Prescott time-inconsistency argument has added anything significant to the monetarist case for rules rather than discretion?

The Kydland/Prescott argument is important, but I believe that it has not added much to the case for rules rather than discretion. That case has always been very strong.

Real business cycle theory evolved out of the monetary surprise version of new classical macroeconomics. However this new approach treats the money supply as endogenous and unimportant as a major explanatory factor in business cycle analysis. Has this undermined the orthodox monetarist position?

Real business cycle theory is a tentative hypothesis intended to explain empirical phenomena. So far it has not been very successful. Nothing about the theory requires treating the money supply as endogenous and unimportant. Disturbances of all kinds may produce fluctuations in economic activity. Those disturbances may be monetary or they may be real. There is no reason why they should be consistently one or the other. As a matter of experience, monetary disturbances seem to predominate, though other disturbances have been important from time to time. However one proposition that I feel the evidence strongly supports is that there cannot be a major collapse of the economy without a major collapse of the financial system.

What is your opinion of the Austrian view that the monetary authorities should have as their objective a target of zero inflation?
I favour a target of zero inflation.

In 'A Theoretical Framework for Monetary Analysis,' Journal of Political Economy *(1970) you concluded that it was your belief that the basic differences among economists are empirical, not theoretical. In view of the subsequent developments of new classical economics, real business cycle theory, and the new Keynesian response to these, would you now accept that there are some fundamental theoretical differences between macroeconomists?*
I do not believe that there are fundamental theoretical differences among macroeconomists. The so-called 'new classical' economics does not differ in any theoretical way whatsoever from the kind of theoretical framework I outlined in my article, nor does the new Keynesian response. Both differ in respect of the kind of empirical presumptions they append to their theoretical structure.

In your view, has empirical research settled any significant issues in the macroeconomic debate relating to the role of money in the business cycle?
I believe it has. There is hardly anyone involved in the macroeconomic debate who will today maintain that the demand curve for money has infinite elasticity, that is, the liquidity trap, or, what is equivalent, that monetary velocity is a will-o'-the-wisp that is infinitely malleable, a position that was strongly maintained at one time. The argument has shifted from whether money matters to how does money matter and what are the quantitative characteristics of the demand curve for money.

It was interesting to see that you chose the relationship between inflation and unemployment as the topic for your Nobel Lecture. What now is your view on the nature of this relationship in the light of the recent experience of the US economy?
Recent experience of the US economy is entirely consistent with the view I expressed in my Nobel Lecture, namely, that unanticipated inflation will temporarily reduce unemployment below its natural level, but that, once inflation becomes anticipated, unemployment is likely to be raised rather than lowered. Similarly in reverse, unanticipated disinflation will be consistent with a higher than natural level of unemployment. That has certainly been the experience in the USA.

What important lessons can be drawn from the monetary policy experiment carried out in the USA in the period 1979–82? Could this experiment be described as monetarist?

No monetarist experiment was carried out in the period 1979–82. Monetarist rhetoric was accompanied by wider fluctuations in the quantity of money than had occurred earlier. The only important lesson that can be drawn from that experience is one we knew before: that a sufficiently restrictive rate of monetary growth will break the back of inflation.

What approximate rate of unemployment do you believe at present (1993) corresponds to the natural rate in the USA? Has this rate changed significantly since the start of the 1970s and, if so, what factors have been most influential?

I do not have any numerical estimate of the rate of unemployment that currently corresponds to the natural rate in the USA. I believe that the rate has gone up since the early 1970s because of increased governmental intervention into the labour market, particularly through so-called 'affirmative' action.

What policies do you personally favour to reduce the natural rate of unemployment?

The policies I personally favour are freeing the labour market, in particular eliminating the kind of affirmative action that has led to quotas in employment; repealing the minimum wage; and allowing the market to set rates of wages.

Do you think the case for a steady rate of monetary growth is at least as much political as it is economic?

I hardly know how to compare the political with the economic case. I believe there are strong economic arguments for a steady rate of monetary growth that derive from our limited knowledge about the short-term relation between the rate of monetary growth and economic activity. There is also a strong political case because it is a policy which is simply, easy to understand, and can be used to hold the monetary authorities accountable for their behaviour.

Politics is sometimes referred to as the 'art of persuasion'. Could that same definition be applied to economics?

Economics viewed as a positive science is an attempt to construct generalizations about the relations among economic variables that have implications that are capable of being contradicted by experience but that are not in fact contradicted. This definition will apply to any science – physical, biological or social. There is also an art of economics that is the capacity to judge the particular economic generalizations that are most relevant to understanding a specific set of events. Finally there is a politics of economics that could be regarded as the art of persuading the public at large or policy makers to follow specified policies.

Over the years monetarism has often been associated with conservative politics. Is this alleged association inevitable?
The alleged association is not inevitable. Karl Marx was a quantity theorist. The Bank of China (communist China) is monetarist. Moreover I am not myself a conservative. I am a liberal in the classical sense or, in the terminology that has become common in the United States, a libertarian in philosophy. In any event, monetarism properly interpreted is an objective set of propositions about the relation between monetary magnitudes and other economic variables. Conservative, radical, communist, socialist, any ruling authorities can only achieve their objectives if they can predict what the consequences of their action will be. A correct body of monetarist propositions is as necessary to authorities of one stripe as of another.

DAVID LAIDLER

David Laidler was born in 1938 in Tynemouth, England and graduated from the London School of Economics with a BSc Econ in 1959, before obtaining his MA from the University of Syracuse in 1960 and his PhD from the University of Chicago in 1964. He has taught at a number of universities including the LSE, 1961–2, the University of California, Berkeley 1963–6, the University of Essex, 1966–9 and the University of Manchester, where he was Professor of Economics from 1969 to 1975. Since 1975 he has taught at the University of Western Ontario where he is currently Professor of Economics.

Before emigrating to Canada, David Laidler was widely recognized as being one of Britain's leading proponents of the gradualist monetarist approach in the UK and, through his key role in the Manchester University Inflation Workshop (set up in 1971), he was influential in disseminating monetarist views in the UK.

His books include: *Labour Markets and Inflation* (Manchester University Press, 1974), co-edited with David Purdy; *Essays on Money and Inflation* (Manchester University Press, 1975), *Monetarist Perspectives* (Philip Allan, 1982), *Introduction to Microeconomics* (Philip Allan, 3rd edn, 1989), co-written with Saul Estrin, *Taking Money Seriously* (Philip Allan, 1990), *The Golden Age of the Quantity Theory* (Philip Allan, 1991) and *The Demand for Money: Theories, Evidence and Problems* (Harper Collins, 4th edn, 1993).

His best known articles include: 'Inflation – A Survey', *Economic Journal* (1975), co-authored with Michael Parkin, 'Inflation in Britain: A Monetarist Perspective', *American Economic Review* (1976), 'Monetarism: An Interpretation and An Assessment', *Economic Journal* (1981), 'The New Classical Contribution to Macroeconomics', *Banca Nazionale Del Lavoro* (1986) and 'Taking Money Seriously', *Canadian Journal of Economics* (1988).

We corresponded with David Laidler in January 1993.

How important do you think it is for macroeconomic models to have choice-theoretic micro foundations?
Not very: macroeconomic models are about aggregate behaviour, and to insist upon explicit choice-theoretic foundations without worrying about aggregation problems seems to me to be silly, if that means refusing to take seriously a macroeconomic hypothesis that is not explicitly derived from choice theory. The ultimate test of any economic hypothesis is its empirical performance, not its conformity to *a priori* principles. There are, though, certain characteristics that I would like models to have. I do not think long-run money illusion is a very sensible property for a macro model to display, and the reasons I would give for this do, I suppose, have to do with choice theory. And the application of choice-theoretic models has sometimes been helpful in particular cases – the application of the Permanent Income Hypothesis to the consumption function, for example.

What do you consider to be the key papers/books which have had a major impact on the development of your ideas with respect to macroeconomics during the past 25 years?
The Phelps 1967 Phillips curve piece in *Economica* and Friedman's Presidential Address to the AEA of the same year were very important. I also learned an enormous amount from Peter Jonson. His 1976 *Kredit und Kapital* article for example. My colleague Peter Howitt has also been very influential – the key papers are in his *Keynesian Recovery* book. Also John Hicks, notably his *Market Theory of Money*, and of course Axel Leijonhufvud's *Information and Coordination* essays.

If Keynes had still been alive in 1969, do you think he would have been awarded the first Nobel Prize in Economics?
I very much doubt that Keynes would have been awarded the first Nobel Prize in Economics. You must remember that the Nobel Prize is a Swedish institution and that throughout the 1930s the Swedes were, with considerable justice, extremely critical of what they regarded as Keynes's 'unnecessary originality'. Bertil Ohlin was still alive and influential in 1969, and in light of

his *Economic Journal* commentary on *The General Theory* I doubt that he would have been all that anxious to single Keynes out for the first Nobel Prize.

In your view, how important was the discovery of the Phillips curve for macroeconomic policy making in the UK and USA?
I do not think it was very important in the UK: so-called 'Keynesian' policy analysis there was based on a cost-push view of inflation, grounded in pop sociology. That had nothing to do with the Phillips curve. It probably was a bit more important in the USA in the Kennedy administration, but I am bound to say that the Vietnam War seems to me to have had a lot more to do with the inflationary problems of the world economy in the 1970s than the Phillips curve did. Americans do not like to talk about Vietnam, and that is why, I think, they put so much emphasis on attempts to exploit the Phillips curve when they discuss the policy failures of the late 1960s– early 1970s.

You are known and referred to as a monetarist economist. Are you happy with the label 'monetarist'?
Not entirely, but one learns to live with the label, and I always do my best to make it mean what I want it to mean.

What are the fundamental propositions of monetarism?
A demand-for-money function that is rather stable in the long run (but not in the short run); the absence of the long-run inflation–unemployment trade-off; a belief that the monetary authorities can control the money supply's behaviour; to these many would add belief in a monetary rule – but I do not believe in monetary rules, so I would just as soon leave that off the list.

Are there any fundamental differences between the views of British and American monetarists?
I think American monetarists might, on the whole, be politically a little more conservative than British monetarists. And I suspect that they are on average much more sceptical about fiscal policies as stabilization devices.

If money is neutral why should we worry about inflation?
Money might be neutral, in the sense that if we change the quantity of nominal money and change all prices in proportion nothing real happens, but money is not super-neutral: its rate of change does matter. And I do not just mean the inflation tax: I mean the way in which ongoing inflation disrupts money's role as a unit of account, distorts the structure of taxation, etc., etc.

What role does fiscal policy have in stabilizing the economy?
If we put it in IS–LM terms, I do not believe that the LM curve is vertical. Nor do I believe in the 'Ricardian equivalence' theorem. It follows from these two propositions that I have to believe that fiscal policy can shift the IS curve and have effects on income and employment. Having said that, I think there are problems in getting fiscal policies designed and implemented fast enough to be helpful, and though I do not believe in Ricardian equivalence, I do believe that a fair bit of crowding out goes on through expectations mechanisms when government spending and/or taxes are changed. I am not, therefore, a big fan of activist stabilization policies in practice.

In your paper on 'The Phillips Curve, Expectations and Incomes Policy', in The Current Inflation *(eds H.G. Johnson and A.R. Nobay, Macmillan, 1971) you argued that 'we know so little about how to design a successful incomes policy that it would probably be better to forget about it altogether'. James Tobin has argued the case for incomes policies on the basis that they would reduce the real costs of disinflationary policies. In the light of the high unemployment experienced as a result of the Thatcher and Volcker deflations have you changed your views on this issue?*
Not really: you might have mentioned the Canadian experience with incomes policies in the late 1970s. In the light of that experience, it does seem as though incomes policies can sometimes be a useful supplement to monetary policies in reducing the costs of disinflation. But I do think that they lead to all kinds of unfairness between the public and private sector, between unionized and non-unionized workers, between the employed and self-employed, between those whose employers can easily change the payment-in-cash payment-in-kind mix and those whose employers cannot, etc. I still do not like incomes policies, very much, therefore. And I am an adamant opponent of using them as a substitute for monetary policy. That is what Nixon tried in the USA and Heath in Britain, and in both cases a lot of damage was done.

What do you regard as the essential difference(s) between monetarism and new classical macroeconomics?
Monetarism seems to me to have been largely a set of empirical propositions that could be encompassed within the structure of a variation on a fairly standard post-Keynesian model of the IS–LM family. It also has plenty of room for price stickiness and markets that do not clear. New classical economics is just another name for flexible-price Walrasian general equilibrium analysis applied to macroeconomic issues, and represents a completely different – and in my view fundamentally misconceived – set of doctrines.

As an economist you have worked in both the UK and the USA. Why do you think that monetarism and new classical economics both exerted less influence in UK academic circles than they did in the USA?

I suspect that a lot of this has to do with the fact that two very important US journals, namely the *JPE* and the *JME*, both originated in departments where these two schools of thought were successively prominent. There really was no British equivalent to this institutional detail.

Professor Alan Blinder [1988a] in commenting on the new classical economics has noted that 'By about 1980 it was hard to find an American academic macroeconomist under the age of 40 who professed to be a Keynesian.' This was not the case in the UK and, as a monetarist working in North America, you also remained highly critical of the new classical approach. What are your main objections to the new classical models?

The insistence on clearing markets seems to me to be empirically untenable. It is surely the case that monetary fluctuations are followed first by quantity responses and then by wage and price responses. New classical models, with their insistence on clearing markets, have prices and quantities fluctuating simultaneously, and that is simply empirically wrong.

In your survey of monetarism in the Economic Journal *(1981) you described the work of the new classical economists such as Lucas, Sargent and Barro as neo-Austrian. How do you justify this comparison, given the fundamental differences which exist between these two schools of thought? For example, Hayek favoured a target of zero inflation, whereas new classical models do not seem to provide any justification for such a target.*

What I was getting at here was the fact that both the Austrians of the 1930s and the new classicals of the 1970s insisted on methodological individualism and Walrasian general equilibrium analysis as a basis for macro modelling. There are of course differences on other matters between the two groups. Hayek, by the way, favoured a constant level of money income, and therefore falling, not stable, prices in a growing economy. You are right that new classical models do not justify any specific inflation target. Hayek at least was sensible enough to understand that monetary policy could have serious effects on the economy!

Real business cycle theory evolved out of the monetary surprise version of new classical macroeconomics. However this new approach treats the money supply as endogenous and unimportant as a major explanatory factor in business cycle analysis. Has this undermined the orthodox monetarist position?

The orthodox monetarist position can be undermined by empirical evidence which refutes it. It cannot be undermined by *a priori* theoretically based assertions about its alleged irrelevance. Any fool with a high enough IQ can produce an analytic model in which money is irrelevant, but what has that got to do with money's role in the real world?

Macroeconomic controversy in the 1950s and 1960s revolved mainly around issues relating to aggregate demand. Since the 1970s, emphasis has shifted to the supply side. What caused this shift of emphasis?
The major problem surely had to do with finding an explanation of the interaction of inflation and unemployment. As soon as you locate the key to this puzzle in the labour market you begin to talk about the economy's supply side.

Keynesian economics has been attacked by monetarists, new classicists, Austrians, supply-siders and public choice theorists. Despite this we seem to be witnessing a Keynesian restoration. What are you views on the 'new Keynesian' contributions?
What nowadays is called 'new Keynesian' economics has been very heavily influenced by 'old monetarist' ideas. What the new Keynesians are doing that is very useful is showing that nominal rigidities of various kinds can be compatible with maximizing behaviour, at least at the level of partial equilibrium analysis. That is helpful, because it stops new classicals scoring cheap debating points about macro models which incorporate such rigidities being devoid in 'micro foundations'.

What do you think of Professor Blinder's claim that 'Keynesian economics now seems to be on the ascendancy in academia' ('The Fall and Rise of Keynesian Economics', The Economic Record (1988))?
It all depends on what you mean by 'Keynesian economics'. I do think that the new classical revolution, so called, is played out. I also, however, think that what is nowadays called 'Keynesian economics', particularly of the kind taught by Alan Blinder, would make old-line British Keynesians such as Nicholas Kaldor, Joan Robinson, or even Richard Sayers, turn in their graves.

How important was the Manchester University Inflation Workshop in promoting and developing monetarist views in the early 1970s in the UK?
You had better get someone else to answer this question – I was too close to it to be objective. I hope we were important, of course, particularly in helping to adapt what started out as American closed economy monetarist ideas to the open economy case which fitted the UK better. But Harry Johnson made a huge contribution here too.

Why do you think the natural unemployment rate in the UK has risen since the early 1970s, when in 1975 ('The End of Demand Management: How to Reduce Unemployment', in Unemployment and Inflation, *IEA Paper) you suggested that it was as low as 2 per cent?*

I am sorry you reminded me about that estimate! I am afraid I have been away from the UK since 1975, except as a visitor from time to time, and I am not well enough informed to give a sensible answer to this question.

What important lessons can be drawn from the monetary policy experiments carried out in the UK in the period 1979–82? Could these experiments be described as monetarist?

The first lesson is surely that, even if the choice of a monetary aggregate for targeting purposes is not very important if the policy problem is to sustain an already satisfactorily low inflation rate, that same choice is absolutely crucial when one is trying to turn things around. The British authorities should have paid much closer attention to the narrow aggregates at that time. High interest rates led to a shift along the demand curve for interest-bearing bank liabilities, and made the broad aggregates very unreliable policy indicators at this time. Their rapid growth was demand- rather than supply-driven. The government's focus on broad money meant that the turnaround in monetary policy was much more drastic and less gradualist than a monetarist like myself would have wanted. Also, the way in which the Public Sector Borrowing Requirement became a centrepiece of monetary policy was very odd indeed: I sometimes think that money growth targets were popular among Conservative politicians because they provided a means of imposing discipline on fiscal policy. That might have been good Conservative politics, but it certainly was not monetarist economics in any sense at all.

You have argued that monetarist analysis suggests that it is the tools of high employment policy, rather than its goals, which must be changed. Do you feel that the Thatcher government's policies in the UK were monetarist in this sense?

You must remember that I was not around in Britain during the Thatcher years. From a purely economic point of view, though, I think policies to free up the labour market should have been implemented earlier and more vigorously than they were. That was easier said than done, though, from a political point of view.

How would you use monetarist views to explain the current recession in the UK economy?

Britain entered the exchange rate mechanism with an overvalued currency, and an inflation rate that was quite a bit above the German rate. That, in and of itself, was bound to provoke some kind of recession. Add to that the real shock to the EMS imparted by German reunification, which required a real appreciation of the Deutschmark, and you have a ready-made recipe for the current British mess. I am not sure if that analysis is monetarist – but there is a monetarist moral to it, namely that, if monetary policy is to be adapted to domestic problems, the economy must have a flexible exchange rate.

You have recently argued that old-fashioned monetarist models with adaptive expectations have provided a better guide to the outcomes of macroeconomic policies in the early 1980s than new classical models which at that time were very influential, particularly in the USA. How do you explain this?
There is a great deal of inertia in the economy, coming from nominal rigidities of one sort or another. The lagged dependent variables which adaptive expectations introduce into macroeconomics systems capture quite a bit of this inertia. Also, though perhaps it is not fashionable to say so, I do think that quite a lot of expectations formation is backward-looking, and that the adaptive expectations hypothesis captures this fact as well.

In 1971 Professor H.G. Johnson, in an article, 'The Keynesian Revolution and the Monetarist Counter-Revolution', American Economic Review, *anticipated that the monetarist counter-revolution would eventually 'peter out' because 'the Keynesians are right in their view that inflation is a far less serious social problem than mass unemployment'. Is unemployment a more important problem than inflation and, in the light of Johnson's comments, has the monetarist counter-revolution served a useful scientific purpose?*
Harry Johnson was still writing at a time when people thought there might be something to the notion of a trade-off between inflation and unemployment, and he therefore treated them as alternatives. We now understand, I think, that the interaction of these two policy problems is much more subtle. Inflation did not peter out in the 1970s as Johnson expected, it got much worse. As a result of that experience, we understand that inflation itself can contribute to the creation of longer-run structural unemployment problems.

You have recently drawn attention to the appallingly low standards of historical scholarship amongst economists. Is it really important for an economist to be a competent historian?
Economists should not only teach about the division of labour, they should practise it too. There is not enough time for anyone simultaneously to be a competent theorist, econometrician, historian, etc. But there should be some competent historians in the economics profession, and their colleagues should respect them and take notice of them. The problem at the moment is not that mainstream economists do not know much history: it is the appalling arro-

gance which those mainstream economists display towards historical studies. Lionel Robbins used to say that provincialism in time is the very worst sort of provincialism. By his standards, most modern economists are worse than provincials, they are hayseeds!

To what extent will a future history of economic thought look upon monetarism as simply a sophisticated elaboration of Keynes's basic macroeconomic framework?
I think that this is a very good first approximation to describing monetarism: if we regard 'Keynes's basic macroeconomic framework' as being captured in something like an IS–LM model – not every Keynesian would agree with that – then the main difference between 'Keynesianism' and 'monetarism' is that Friedman used the Permanent Income Hypothesis to undermine the notion of a stable marginal propensity to save out of current income, and then replaced the stable multiplier hypothesis which relied on this parameter with a stable demand-for-money function. But monetarists are also much more aware of the problems presented by lags in the effects of policy than was Keynes.

How healthy is the current state of macroeconomics, given the level of controversy? Do you see any signs of an emerging consensus in macroeconomics and, if so, what form will it take?
Even the new classicals these days are beginning to study models with nominal rigidities in them: that is surely healthy, because we have known for a long time that nominal rigidities do matter (and I do mean for a long time, since the 1870s at least!). I would, though, like to see more attention paid to empirical content, and policy relevance and less to theoretical rigor when it comes to judging contributions to macroeconomic knowledge.

5. The new classical school

Highbrow opinion is like a hunted hare; if you stand in the same place, or nearly the same place, it can be relied upon to come round to you in a circle. (Robertson, 1954)

5.1 Introduction

The main purpose of this chapter is threefold. First, to discuss the central theoretical propositions which underlie new classical models (section 5.2). Second, in the light of this discussion, to consider the new classical theory of the business cycle (section 5.3). Third, to examine the main policy implications that derive from the new classical approach to macroeconomics (section 5.4). In conclusion (section 5.5) we comment on the impact the new classical school has made on the development of macroeconomics.

5.2 The Structure of New Classical Models

At the outset it is important to stress that, while new classical macroeconomics evolved out of monetarist macroeconomics during the 1970s and incorporates certain elements of that approach (such as the monetarist explanation of inflation), it should be seen as a separate school of thought from orthodox monetarism (see, for example, Hoover, 1984). The new classical approach itself is often taken to be synonymous with the work of Robert Lucas Jr. (University of Chicago) whom Michael Parkin (1992) recently described as 'the leading macro mountaineer of our generation'. Other leading American exponents of new classical macroeconomics include Thomas Sargent (Stanford University), Robert Barro (Harvard University), and Edward Prescott and Neil Wallace (University of Minnesota). In the UK the approach is mainly associated with the work of Patrick Minford, Professor of Economics at the University of Liverpool.

Underlying the new classical approach to macroeconomics is the joint acceptance of three main sub-hypotheses involving (i) the rational expectations hypothesis; (ii) the assumption of continuous market clearing; and (iii) the aggregate supply hypothesis. In discussing these hypotheses individually in what follows, the reader should bear in mind that each hypothesis can be used and judged in isolation on its own merits. Although new classicists accept all three hypotheses (see Figure 5.1) it is possible for economists of different persuasions to support one or other of the hypotheses without necessarily accepting all three together.

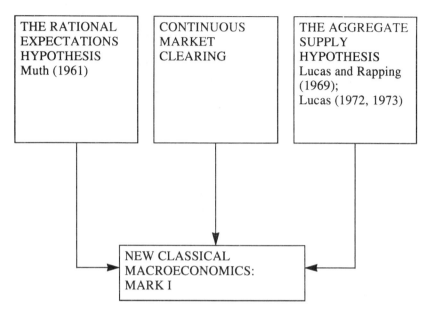

Figure 5.1   The structure of new classical models

5.2.1   The rational expectations hypothesis

One of the central tenets underlying new classical macroeconomics is the rational expectations hypothesis associated with the work of John Muth (1961) in the context of microeconomics. It is, however, interesting to note that Keuzenkamp (1991) has suggested that Tinbergen was a precursor to Muth, having presented a model of rational expectations nearly 30 years earlier. In his seminal article, Muth (1961) suggested 'that expectations since they are informed predictions of future events are essentially the same as the predictions of the relevant economic theory'. Muth's idea was not immediately taken up by other economists and it took almost ten years before Lucas, Sargent and other leading new classical economists began to incorporate the hypothesis into their macroeconomic models.

The rational expectations hypothesis has over the years been presented in the literature in a number of different forms and versions. At the outset it is important to note the distinction between weak and strong versions of the hypothesis. The main idea behind the *weak* version of the hypothesis is that, in forming forecasts or expectations about the future value of a variable, rational economic agents will make the *best* (most efficient) use of *all* publicly available information about the factors which they believe determine that variable. In other words, expectations are assumed to be formed 'rationally' in line with utility-maximizing behaviour on the part of individual economic agents. For example, if economic agents believe that the rate of inflation is determined by the rate of monetary expansion then they will make the best use of all publicly available information on rates of monetary expansion in forming their expectations of future rates of inflation. The *strong* version of the rational expectations hypothesis is captured in the above quotation taken from Muth's (1961) article and it is the Muthian version that has been taken up by leading exponents of the new classical school and incorporated into their macroeconomic models. In the Muthian 'strong' version, economic agents' *subjective* expectations of economic variables will coincide with the true or objective mathematical conditional expectations of those variables. Using the example of economic agents' expectations of inflation, the rational expectations hypothesis may be expressed algebraically in the following way:

$$\dot{P}_t^e = E(\dot{P}_t | I_{t-1}) \tag{5.1}$$

where $\dot{P}_t^e$ is the expected rate of inflation from t to $t+1$, and $E(\dot{P}_t | I_{t-1})$ is the expected rate of inflation conditional on the set of information available to economic agents at time period $t-1$. It is important to emphasize that rational expectations does not mean that agents can foresee the future exactly. Rational expectations is not the same as perfect foresight. In order to form a rational expectation of inflation, agents will need to take into account what they believe to be the 'correct' macroeconomic model of the economy. Agents will make errors in their forecasts, since available information will be incomplete. Indeed this is an essential element of Lucas's monetary surprise model – see sections 5.2.3 and 5.4.1. However such forecast errors will be unrelated to the information set at the time the expectation (for example of inflation) was formed. With rational expectations, agents' expectations of economic variables on average will be correct; that is, will equal their true value. Furthermore the hypothesis implies that agents will not form expectations which are systematically wrong (biased) over time. If expectations were systematically wrong, agents would, it is held, learn from their mistakes and change the way they formed expectations, thereby eliminating systematic errors. More formally the strong version of the rational expectations hypothesis implies that:

$$\dot{P}_t^e = \dot{P}_t + \varepsilon_t \tag{5.2}$$

where $\dot{P}_t^e$ = expected rate of inflation from t to $t + 1$;

$\dot{P}_t$ = actual rate of inflation from t to $t + 1$; and

ε_t = random error term, which (i) has a mean of zero, and (ii) is uncorrelated with the information set available at the time when expectations are formed, otherwise economic agents would not be fully exploiting all available information.

In summary, the forecasting errors from rationally formed expectations will (i) be essentially random with a mean of zero; (ii) be unrelated to those made in previous periods, revealing no discernible pattern: that is, they will be serially uncorrelated over time; and (iii) have the lowest variance compared to any other forecasting method. In other words, rational expectations is the most accurate and efficient form of expectations formation.

The rational expectations hypothesis contrasts with the adaptive expectations hypothesis initially used by orthodox monetarists in their explanation of inflation expectations and the Phillips curve (see section 4.3.3). In the adaptive expectations hypothesis, economic agents base their expectations of future values of a variable (such as inflation) only on past values of the variable concerned. One of the main problems with this 'backward-looking' approach to forming expectations is that, until the variable being predicted is stable for a considerable period of time, expectations formed of it will be repeatedly wrong. For example, following the discussion of section 4.3.3, on the accelerationist hypothesis, if unemployment is held below the natural rate inflation will accelerate and inflation expectations will be biased in a downward direction. This problem results from (i) the assumption that economic agents only partially adjust their expectations by a fraction of the last error made; and (ii) the failure of agents to take into consideration additional information available to them other than past values of the variable concerned, despite making repeated errors. In contrast, in the 'forward-looking' approach, rational expectations are based on the use of all publicly available information with the crucial implication of the strong version of the hypothesis being that economic agents will not form expectations which are systematically wrong over time; that is, such expectations will be unbiased.

A number of criticisms have been raised against the rational expectations hypothesis and we now briefly consider two common ones. The first of these concerns the costs (in time, effort and money) of acquiring and processing all publicly available information in order to forecast the future value of a variable, such as inflation. It is important to note that the weak version of the hypothesis *does not* require, as some critics have suggested, that economic agents actually use 'all' publicly available information. Given the costs involved in acquiring and processing information, it is unlikely that agents would ever use all publicly available information. What proponents of the weak version of the hypothesis suggest is that 'rational' economic agents will have an incentive to make the 'best' use of all publicly available information in forming their expectations. In other words, agents will have an incentive to use information up to the point where the marginal benefit (in terms of improved accuracy of the variable being forecast) equals the marginal cost (in terms of acquiring and processing all publicly available information). In this case, expectations would be less efficient than they would be if *all* available information was used. Furthermore the weak version of the hypothesis *does not* require, as some critics have suggested, that all individual agents directly acquire and process available information personally. Economic agents can derive information indirectly from, for example, published forecasts and commentaries in the news media. Given that forecasts frequently differ, the problem then arises of discerning which is the 'correct' view.

A far more serious objection concerns the problem of how agents actually acquire knowledge of the 'correct' model of the economy, given that economists themselves display considerable disagreement over the correct model. The issue of whether individual agents operating in decentralized markets will be able to 'learn' the true model of the economy has been the subject of considerable debate (see, for example, Frydman and Phelps, 1983). With regard to this particular criticism, it is important to note that the strong version of the hypothesis *does not* require that economic agents actually know the correct model of the economy. What the hypothesis implies is that rational agents will not form expectations which are systematically wrong over time. In other words, expectations, it is suggested, will resemble those formed 'as if' agents did know the correct model to the extent that they will be unbiased and randomly distributed over time. Critics of the hypothesis are not, however, convinced by arguments such as these and suggest that, owing to such problems as the costs of acquiring and processing all available information, and uncertainty over which is the correct model, it 'is' possible for agents to form expectations which are systematically wrong. In point of fact there is some evidence that agents do make systematic errors in expectations (see, for example, Lovell, 1986).

Two final points are worth making. First, the use of the word 'rational' in the presentation of the hypothesis proved to be an important 'rhetorical' weapon in the battle to win the minds of macroeconomists during the 1970s. As Barro (1984) has pointed out:

> One of the cleverest features of the rational expectations revolution was the application of the term 'rational'. Thereby, the opponents of this approach were forced into the defensive position of either being irrational or of modelling others as irrational, neither of which are comfortable positions for an economist.

Second, it is interesting to note that rational expectations has an alleged connection with the Austrian school. This view will be explored, and challenged, in Chapter 8, where Austrian and Post-Keynesian criticisms of rational expectations will be considered. For a more detailed discussion of the rational expectations hypothesis and its application in macroeconomics, the reader is referred to Begg (1982); Sheffrin (1983); Carter and Maddock (1984); Shaw (1984); and Attfield, Demery and Duck (1985).

5.2.2 Continuous market clearing

A second key assumption in new classical models is that all markets in the economy continuously clear in line with the Walrasian tradition. At each point of time all observed outcomes are viewed as 'market-clearing', and are the result of the optimal demand and supply responses of economic agents to their perceptions of prices. As a result the economy is viewed as being in a continuous state of (short- and long-run) equilibrium. New classical models are in consequence often referred to as *equilibrium* models.

When markets clear as a result of the equilibration of demand and supply, all possible gains from trade have been exploited (see Barro, 1979). The assumption of continuous market clearing is the most critical assumption underlying new classical analysis and is highly contentious, as it implies that prices are free to adjust instantaneously to clear markets. The assumption stands in bold contrast to the approach adopted in both orthodox Keynesian and monetarist models. As we have discussed in the two previous chapters, orthodox Keynesians and monetarists disagree about the time it takes for markets to clear. Keynesian models incorporate the assumption that markets may fail to clear because of the slow adjustment of prices, so that the economy is viewed as being in a possible state of continuous disequilibrium. In contrast, orthodox monetarist models incorporate the assumption that prices adjust fairly rapidly to clear markets and, while accepting that the economy may be in disequilibrium in the short run, monetarists assume that the economy will automatically return to a state of macroeconomic equilibrium in the long run at the natural rate of output and employment.

The assumption of continuous market clearing is far more controversial than the rational expectations hypothesis. As we shall discuss in Chapter 7, new Keynesians have put forward a number of arguments to explain why both prices and wages will be slow to adjust to clear markets following a disturbance. Serious objections can be raised as to the reality of the new classical assumption, especially with respect to the labour market, where new classicists hold that anyone wishing to work can find employment at the market-clearing equilibrium wage; that is to say, the new classical equilibrium approach treats unemployment entirely as a voluntary phenomenon. For example, given efficiency wage considerations (see section 7.6.2) it can be argued that it is both profitable and rational for a firm to pay an efficiency wage above the market-clearing wage. In such a situation equilibrium in the labour market can occur where supply exceeds demand, with the existence of involuntary unemployment as an equilibrium phenomenon.

We now consider the final main tenet of new classical macroeconomics, the aggregate supply hypothesis.

5.2.3   The aggregate supply hypothesis

As with the rational expectations hypothesis, various explanations of the aggregate supply hypothesis can be found in the literature. Having said this, two main approaches to aggregate supply can be identified. Underlying these approaches are two orthodox microeconomic assumptions, namely, that (i) rational decisions taken by workers and firms reflect optimizing behaviour on their part; and (ii) the supply of labour/output by workers/firms depends upon relative prices.

The first new classical approach to aggregate supply focuses on the supply of labour and derives from the work of Lucas and Rapping (1969). This analysis is discussed more fully in section 6.6.2 and in what follows we merely outline the essence of the approach. During any period, workers have to decide how much time to allocate between work and leisure. Workers, it is assumed, have some notion of the normal or expected average real wage. If the current real wage is above the normal real wage, workers will have an incentive to work more (take less leisure time) in the current period in the anticipation of taking more leisure (working less) in the future, when the real wage is expected to be lower. Conversely, if the current real wage is below the norm, workers will have an incentive to take more leisure (work less) in the current period in the anticipation of working more (taking less leisure) in the future, when the real wage is expected to be higher. The supply of labour is postulated, therefore, to respond to perceived temporary changes in the real wage. This behavioural response of substituting current leisure for future leisure and vice versa is referred to as *intertemporal substitution*. Within the intertemporal substitution model, changes in employment are explained in terms of the 'voluntary' choices of workers who change their supply of labour in response to perceived temporary changes in the real wage.

The second new classical approach to aggregate supply again derives from the highly influential work of Lucas (1972, 1973). In what follows we illustrate the spirit of Lucas's arguments by focusing on the goods market and the supply decisions of firms. An important element of Lucas's analysis concerns the structure of the information set available to producers. It is assumed that, while a firm knows the current price of its own goods, the general price level for other markets only becomes known with a time lag. When a firm experiences a rise in the current market price of its output it has to decide whether the change in price reflects (i) a real shift in demand towards its product, in which case the firm should respond (rationally) to the increase in the price of its output relative to the price of other goods by increasing its output, or (ii) merely a nominal increase in demand across all markets, producing a general increase in prices which would not require a supply response. Firms are faced by what is referred to as a 'signal extraction' problem, in that they have to distinguish between relative and absolute price changes. Indeed the greater the variability of the general price level, the more difficult it will be for a producer to extract a correct signal and the smaller the supply response is likely to be to any given change in prices.

The analysis of the behaviour of individual agents in terms of the supply of both labour and goods has led to what is referred to as the Lucas 'surprise' supply function:

$$Y - Y_N = \alpha(P - P^e) \tag{5.3}$$

Equation (5.3) states that output (Y) deviates from its natural level (Y_N) only in response to deviations of the actual price level (P) from its expected value (P^e); that is, in response to an unexpected (surprise) increase in the price level. For example, when the actual price level turns out to be greater than expected, individual agents are 'surprised' and mistake the increase as an increase in the relative price of their own output, resulting in an increase in the supply of output and employment in the economy. In the absence of price surprises, output will be at its natural level (see Figure 5.2 and section 5.4.1). An alternative specification of the Lucas surprise function states that output only deviates from its natural level in response to a deviation of actual from expected inflation (that is, in response to errors in inflation expectations) so that:

$$Y - Y_N = \alpha(\dot{P} - \dot{P}^e) \tag{5.4}$$

In effect this specification of the surprise supply function amounts to a restatement of the expectations-augmented version of the Phillips curve (see section 4.3.2). Only when inflation expectations are exactly correct (that is, in the absence of price surprises) will output and employment be at its natural level (see Figure 4.8).

5.3 Equilibrium Business Cycle Theory

Before Keynes's *General Theory* many economists were actively engaged in business cycle research (see Haberler, 1963). However one of the important consequences of the Keynesian revolution was the redirection of macroeconomic research towards questions relating to the *level* of output at a point in time, rather than the dynamic evolution of the economy over time. To Keynesians business cycles looked like disequilibrium phenomena. But in the early 1930s Hayek had set forth a research agenda which, 40 years later, Lucas was to take up. For Hayek (1933) 'the crucial problem of Trade Cycle Theory' was to produce a solution which would allow 'incorporation of cyclical phenomena into the system of economic equilibrium theory, with which they are in apparent contradiction'. By equilibrium theory, Hayek meant that which had been 'most perfectly expressed by the Lausanne School of theoretical economics'. While Keynesian economists regarded the quest for an equilibrium theory of the business cycle as unattainable, it was one of Lucas's most notable achievements to demonstrate that it was possible to develop an equilibrium account of aggregate instability. As Hoover (1988) notes, 'To explain the related movements of macroeconomic aggregates and prices without recourse to the notion of disequilibrium is the *desideratum* of new classical research on the theory of business cycles.'

The hypothesis that aggregate supply depends upon relative prices is central to the new classical explanation of fluctuations in output and employment (see, for example, Lucas, 1975, 1977). In new classical analysis, unanticipated aggregate demand shocks (resulting mainly from unanticipated changes in the money supply) which affect the whole economy cause errors in (rationally formed) price expectations and result in output and employment deviating from their long-run (full information) equilibrium (natural) levels. These errors are held to result from workers and firms who both have *incomplete/ imperfect* information, so that they mistake general price changes for relative price changes and react by changing the supply of labour and output, respectively.

Consider, for example, an economy which is initially in a position where output and employment are at their natural levels. Suppose an unanticipated monetary disturbance occurs which leads to an increase in the general price level, and hence individual prices, in all markets throughout the economy. As noted in the previous section, firms are assumed to have information only on prices in the limited number of markets in which they trade. If individual firms interpret the increase in the price of their goods as an increase in the relative price of their output, they will react by increasing their output. Workers are also assumed to have incomplete information. If workers mistakenly perceive an increase in money wages (relative to their expected value) as an increase in real wages they will respond by increasing the supply of labour. In contrast to Friedman's model (see section 4.3.2) where workers are fooled, Lucas's model *does not* rely on any asymmetry of information between workers and firms. Both firms and workers are inclined to make expectational errors and respond positively to misperceived global price increases by increasing the supply of output and labour, respectively. As a result aggregate output and employment will rise temporarily above their natural levels. Once agents realize that there has been no change in relative prices, output and employment return to their long-run (full information) equilibrium (natural) levels.

In the new classical approach, deviations in output and employment from their natural levels are due to 'random shocks' (mainly unanticipated changes in the money supply) which cause errors in price expectations. As we discussed earlier, in section 5.2.1, the rational expectations hypothesis implies that these expectational errors will be essentially random and reveal no discernible pattern. The combination of the rational expectations hypothesis and the surprise supply function in turn implies that output and employment will fluctuate randomly around their natural levels. Further assumptions are therefore required to explain why during the business cycle output and employment remain persistently above (upswing) or below (downswing) their trend values for a succession of time periods. The observed serially correlated movements in output and employment (that is, where output and employment levels in any one time period are correlated with their preceding values) have been explained in the literature in a number of ways. These explanations include reference to lagged output and the durability of capital goods, the existence of contracts inhibiting immediate adjustment and adjustment costs. For example, in the field of employment firms face costs both in hiring and in firing labour: costs associated with interviewing and training new employees, making redundancy payments and so on. In consequence their optimal response may be to adjust their employment and output levels gradually over a period of time following some unanticipated shock.

We now turn to consider the main policy implications of the new classical approach to macroeconomics.

5.4 The Policy Implications of the New Classical Approach

The combination of the rational expectations, continuous market clearing and aggregate supply hypotheses produces a number of important policy conclusions. In what follows we discuss the main policy implications of the new classical approach, namely (i) the policy ineffectiveness proposition; (ii) the output–employment costs of reducing inflation; (iii) dynamic time inconsistency, credibility and monetary rules; (iv) the role of microeconomic policies to increase aggregate supply; and (v) the Lucas critique of econometric policy evaluation. We begin with a discussion of the strong policy conclusion that fully anticipated changes in monetary policy will be ineffective in influencing the level of output and employment even in the short run; that is, the super-neutrality of money.

5.4.1 The policy ineffectiveness proposition

The new classical policy ineffectiveness proposition was first presented in two influential papers by Sargent and Wallace (1975, 1976). The proposition can best be illustrated using the aggregate demand/supply model shown in Figure 5.2. Those readers unfamiliar with the derivation of this model should refer to any standard macroeconomics text, such as Dornbusch and Fischer (1994). In Figure 5.2, the economy is initially operating at point A, the triple intersection of AD_0 $SRAS_0$ and $LRAS$. At point A, in line with equation (5.3), the price level (P_0) is fully anticipated (that is, the actual and expected price levels coincide) and output and employment are at their long-run (full information) equilibrium (natural) levels. Suppose the authorities announce that they intend to increase the money supply. Rational economic agents would take this information into account in forming their expectations and fully anticipate the effects of the increase in the money supply on the general price level, so that output and employment would remain unchanged at their natural levels. The rightward shift of the aggregate demand curve from AD_0 to AD_1 would be offset by an upward shift to the left of the positively-sloped aggregate supply curve from $SRAS_0$ to $SRAS_1$, as money wages were increased following an immediate upward revision of price expectations. In this case the economy would move straight from point A to C, remaining on

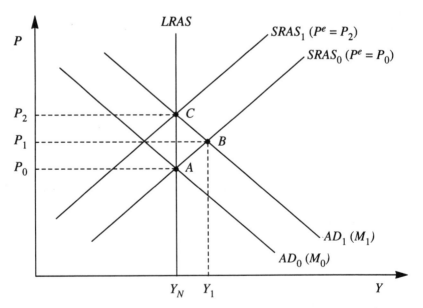

Figure 5.2   The effects of anticipated and unanticipated changes in the money supply on the level of output and the price level

the vertical long-run aggregate supply curve with no change in output and employment even in the short run; that is, money is super-neutral.

In contrast, suppose the authorities surprise economic agents by increasing the money supply without announcing their intentions. In this situation firms and workers with incomplete information would misperceive the resultant increase in the general price level as an increase in relative prices and react by increasing the supply of output and labour. In other words, workers and firms would mistakenly perceive this as a real (as opposed to a nominal) increase in the demand for their services/goods and respond by increasing the supply of labour/output. In terms of Figure 5.2, the aggregate demand curve would shift to the right from AD_0 to AD_1 to intersect the positively-sloped aggregate supply curve $SRAS_0$ at point B. In line with equation (5.3), output (Y_1) would deviate from its natural level (Y_N) as a consequence of deviations of the price level (P_1) from its expected level (P_0); that is, as the result of expectational errors by agents. Any increase/decrease in output/unemployment would, it is argued, only be temporary. Once agents realized that there had been no change in relative prices, output and employment would return to their long-run equilibrium (natural) levels. In terms of Figure 5.2, as agents fully adjusted their price expectations the positively-sloped aggregate supply curve would shift upwards to the left, from $SRAS_0$ to $SRAS_1$ to intersect AD_1 at point C. It is interesting to note that the former new classical adjustment process discussed above (from A to C) corresponds to the orthodox monetarist case in the long run, while the latter adjustment process (from A to B to C) corresponds to the orthodox monetarist case in the short run, regardless of whether the increase in the money supply is anticipated or unanticipated. To summarize, the new classical analysis suggests that (i) an anticipated increase in the money supply will raise the price level and have no effect on real output and employment, and (ii) only unanticipated monetary surprises can affect real variables in the short run.

This strong policy ineffectiveness proposition has major implications for the controversy over the role and conduct of macroeconomic stabilization policy. If the money supply is determined by the authorities according to some 'known' rule then the authorities will be unable to influence output and employment even in the short run by pursuing a systematic monetary policy as it can be anticipated by agents. For example, the authorities might adopt a monetary rule which allows for a given fixed rate of monetary growth of 6 per cent per annum. In forming their expectations of inflation, rational economic agents would include the anticipated effects of the 6 per cent expansion of the money supply. Consequently the systematic component (that is, 6 per cent) of the monetary rule would have no effect on real variables. If, in practice, the money supply grew at a rate of 8 per cent per annum, the non-systematic (unanticipated) component of monetary expansion (that is, 2 per cent per annum) would cause output and employment to rise temporarily above their long-run equilibrium (natural) levels, owing to errors in inflation expectations. Alternatively the authorities might allow the money supply to be determined by a feedback rule (for example, in response to changes in unemployment and output). Again changes in the rate of monetary growth which arise from a known feedback rule will be anticipated by agents, making the feedback policy rule ineffective. Only departures from a known monetary rule (such as policy errors made by the monetary authorities or unforeseen changes in policy) which are unanticipated will influence output.

The policy ineffectiveness proposition can be expressed algebraically in the following way (see Gordon, 1976). We begin by rewriting the Friedman–Phelps equation in modified linear form as:

$$\dot{P}_t = \dot{P}_t^e - \phi(U_t - UN_t) + \phi\theta S_t \tag{5.5}$$

where θS_t represents an 'exogenous' supply shock (with zero mean) and $U_t - UN_t$ represents the deviation of unemployment from its natural rate. Equation (5.5) can be rewritten as:

$$U_t = UN_t - \frac{1}{\phi}(\dot{P}_t - \dot{P}_t^e) + \theta S_t \tag{5.6}$$

The structural relationship between inflation ($\dot{P}_t$) and the rate of monetary growth ($\dot{M}_t$) is given by:

$$\dot{P}_t = \dot{M}_t + \theta D_t \tag{5.7}$$

where θD_t represents 'unpredictable' demand shocks (such as shocks from the private sector) which also have a zero mean. If $\dot{M}_t^e$ is the *expected* rate of growth of the money supply, the rational expectation of inflation will be:

$$\dot{P}_t^e = \dot{M}_t^e \tag{5.8}$$

Suppose a Keynesian-inspired monetary authority attempts to control monetary growth so that it grows at some constant rate (λ_0) plus some proportion (λ_1) of the previous period's deviation of unemployment from its natural rate. In this case the *actual* rate of monetary growth will be:

$$\dot{M}_t = \lambda_0 + \lambda_1(U_{t-1} - UN_{t-1}) + \theta\dot{M}_t \tag{5.9}$$

where $\theta\dot{M}_t$ signifies a *random* or *unanticipated* element in monetary growth. Equation (5.9) indicates that the monetary authorities are operating a *system-*

atic feedback monetary rule which can be predicted by rational economic agents as it becomes part of their information set (I_{t-1}) in equation (5.1). Rational economic agents will therefore have expectations of inflation based on the expected rate of monetary growth, shown in equation (5.10).

$$\dot{M}_t^e = \lambda_0 + \lambda_1(U_{t-1} - UN_{t-1}) \tag{5.10}$$

By subtracting (5.10) from (5.9) we obtain:

$$\dot{M}_t - \dot{M}_t^e = \theta\dot{M}_t \tag{5.11}$$

Subtracting (5.8) from (5.7) and substituting from (5.11) we derive equation (5.12):

$$\dot{P}_t - \dot{P}_t^e = \theta\dot{M}_t + \theta D_t \tag{5.12}$$

Finally substituting (5.12) into (5.6) gives us:

$$U_t = UN_t - \frac{1}{\phi}(\theta\dot{M}_t + \theta D_t) + \theta S_t \tag{5.13}$$

The important point to notice about equation (5.13) is that the systematic component of monetary growth ($\lambda_0 + \lambda_1(U_{t-1} - UN_{t-1})$), which the government was attempting to use in order to prevent unemployment from deviating from its natural rate, does not enter into it. The only component of equation (5.13) which the monetary authorities can influence directly is $\theta\dot{M}_t$, the random component of monetary growth. Therefore equation (5.13) tells us that, in a Sargent and Wallace world, unemployment can deviate from its natural rate as the result of unpredictable demand (θD_t) and supply (θS_t) shocks or *unanticipated* monetary surprises ($\theta\dot{M}_t$). Any systematic feedback monetary rule, by becoming part of economic agents' information set, cannot cause inflation to deviate from its expected rate. Only departures from a known monetary rule (such as policy errors made by the monetary authorities or unforeseen changes in policy) which are unanticipated will influence output and employment.

In summary, the approach predicts that, as rational economic agents will take into account any known monetary rule in forming their expectations, the authorities will be unable to influence output and employment even in the short run by pursuing a systematic monetary policy. Furthermore any attempt to affect output and employment by random or non-systematic monetary policy will, it is argued, only increase the variation of output and employment around their natural levels. It can be seen, therefore, that the argument advanced by new classicists against policy activism is subtly different from those put forward by orthodox monetarists (see section 4.3.3, on the role and conduct of monetary policy).

The policy ineffectiveness proposition that only unanticipated monetary surprises have real output effects (or what is sometimes referred to as the 'anticipated–unanticipated money debate') has been the subject of a number of empirical studies. Early work, in particular the seminal papers by Barro (1977a, 1978) seemed to support the proposition. Using annual data for the US economy over the period 1941–76, Barro used a two-stage method in first estimating anticipated and unanticipated money growth before regressing output and unemployment on unanticipated money growth. In general, Barro's studies provided support for the viewpoint that, while output and unemployment are significantly affected by unanticipated money growth, anticipated money growth has no real effects. However subsequent studies, most notably by Mishkin (1982) and Gordon (1982a), found evidence that suggested that both unanticipated and anticipated monetary policy affect output and employment. Overall, while the empirical evidence is mixed, it does not appear to support the view that systematic monetary policy has no real effects.

5.4.2 The real costs of disinflation

The second main policy implication of the new classical approach concerns the output–employment costs of reducing inflation. New classical economists share the monetarist view that inflation is essentially a monetary phenomenon propagated by excessive monetary growth. However substantial disagreement exists between economists over the real costs of disinflation. Here we will compare the new classical view with that of Keynesians and monetarists.

The amount of lost output that an economy endures in order to reduce inflation is known as the *sacrifice ratio*. In Keynesian models the sacrifice ratio tends to be large, even if agents have rational expectations, owing to the sluggish response of prices and wages to reductions in aggregate demand. Given gradual price adjustment, a deflationary impulse will inevitably lead to significant real losses which can be prolonged by hysteresis effects; that is, where a recession causes the natural rate of unemployment to increase (see Cross, 1988; Gordon, 1988 and Chapter 7). Some Keynesians have advocated the *temporary* use of incomes policy as a *supplementary* policy measure to accompany monetary restraint as a way of increasing the efficiency of disinflation policies (see section 4.3.3, and Lipsey, 1981). It should also be noted that Post-Keynesian economists regard incomes policy as a crucial *permanent* anti-inflationary weapon. Monetary disinflation alone will tend to produce a permanently higher level of unemployment in Post-Keynesian models (see Cornwall, 1984).

The orthodox monetarist view, discussed in section 4.3.3, is that unemployment will rise following monetary contraction, the extent and duration of which depends on the degree of monetary contraction, the extent of institutional adaptations and how quickly people adjust downwards their expectations of future rates of inflation. The critical factor here is the responsiveness of expectations to the change of monetary regime and this in turn implies that the *credibility* and *reputation* of the monetary authority will play a crucial role in determining the sacrifice ratio.

In contrast to both the Keynesian and monetarist models, the new classical approach implies that announced/anticipated changes in monetary policy will have no effect on the level of output and employment even in the short run, provided the policy is credible. An announced monetary contraction which is believed will cause rational agents immediately to revise downwards their inflation expectations. The monetary authorities can in principle reduce the rate of inflation without the associated output and employment costs predicted by Keynesian and monetarist analysis; that is, the sacrifice ratio is zero! As one critic has noted, 'in a Sargent–Wallace world the Fed could eliminate inflation simply by announcing that henceforth it would expand the money supply at a rate compatible with price stability' (Gordon, 1978, p. 338). In terms of Figure 4.12, the rate of inflation could be reduced from *A* to *D* without any increase in unemployment. In such circumstances there is no necessity to follow a policy of gradual monetary contraction advocated by orthodox monetarists. Given the absence of output–employment costs, new classicists argue that the authorities might just as well announce a dramatic reduction in the rate of monetary expansion to reduce inflation to their preferred target rate.

With respect to the output–employment costs of reducing inflation, it is interesting to note briefly the *prima facie* evidence provided by the Reagan (USA) and Thatcher (UK) deflations in the early 1980s. Following the restrictive monetary policy pursued in both economies during this period, both the US economy (1981–2) and the UK economy (1980–81) experienced deep recessions. Between 1979 and 1983, inflation fell from 11.3 per cent to 3.2 per cent in the US economy and from 13.5 per cent to 4.6 per cent in the UK economy, while over the same period unemployment rose from 5.8 per cent to 9.5 per cent in the USA and from 5.0 to 12.4 per cent in the UK (see Tables 1.2 and 1.3). In commenting on the UK experience, Matthews and Minford (1987) attribute the severity of the recession in this period primarily to adverse external and supply-side shocks. However the monetary disinflation initiated by the Thatcher government was also a factor. This disinflation was unintentionally severe and as a result 'expectations were quite unprepared for it'. Because initially the Thatcher government had a credibility problem, the 'accidental shock treatment' produced painful effects on output and employment. An important influence on credibility in new classical models is the growth path of government debt. New classical economists insist that in order to engineer a disinflation without experiencing a severe sacrifice ratio, a fiscal strategy is required which is compatible with the announced monetary policy, otherwise agents with rational expectations will expect a policy reversal ('U-turn') in the future. As Matthews and Minford (1987) point out, 'A key feature of the Thatcher anti-inflation strategy was a parallel reduction in government budget deficits.' This 'Medium Term Financial Strategy' was aimed at creating long-run credibility (see also Minford, Brech and Matthews, 1980; Sargent and Wallace, 1981; Sargent, 1993).

In the USA a 'monetary policy experiment' was conducted between October 1979 and the summer of 1982. This Volcker disinflation was also associated with a severe recession, although the influence of the second oil shock must also have been a contributory factor. In commenting on this case, Milton Friedman (1984) has argued that the relevant economic agents did not have any widespread belief in the new disinflationary policy announced by the Fed in October 1979. In a similar vein, Poole (1988) has observed that 'a recession may be necessary to provide the evidence that the central bank is serious'. For a discussion of the US 'monetarist experiment', the reader is referred to Brimmer (1983) and B. Friedman (1988). Useful surveys relating to the issue of disinflation are provided by Dalziel (1991), Ball (1991, 1994) and Chadha *et al.* (1992).

From the above discussion it is clear that, for painless disinflation to occur, the public must believe that the monetary authority is prepared to carry through its announced monetary contraction. If policy announcements lack credibility, inflationary expectations will not fall sufficiently to prevent the economy from experiencing output–employment costs. Initially the arguments relating to the importance of credibility were forcefully presented by Fellner (1976, 1979). A second line of argument, closely related to the need for policy credibility, is that associated with the problem of dynamic time inconsistency. This matter was first raised in the seminal paper of Kydland and Prescott (1977) and we next examine the policy implications of this influential theory.

5.4.3 Dynamic time inconsistency, credibility and monetary rules
The case for a constant monetary growth rate rule has been well articulated within an orthodox monetarist framework by Milton Friedman. This case is based on a number of arguments, including the informational constraints facing policy makers; problems associated with time lags and forecasting; uncertainty with respect to the size of fiscal and monetary policy multipliers; the inflationary consequences of reducing unemployment below the natural rate; and a basic distrust of the political process compared to market forces.

The Lucas–Sargent–Wallace policy ineffectiveness proposition calls into question the power of anticipated monetary policy to influence real variables, adding further weight to Friedman's attack on discretionary policies. In 1977, Kydland and Prescott provided a reformulation of the case against discretionary policies by developing an analytically rigorous new classical model where the policy maker is engaged in a strategic dynamic game with sophisticated forward-looking private sector agents.

The theory of economic policy which Kydland and Prescott attack in their paper is that which evolved during the 1950s and 1960s. The conventional approach, inspired by Tinbergen (1952), consists of three crucial steps. First, the policy maker must specify the *targets* or goals of economic policy (for example, low inflation and unemployment). Second, given this *social welfare function* which the policy maker is attempting to maximize, a set of *instruments* (monetary and fiscal) are chosen which will be used to achieve the targets. Finally, the policy maker must make use of an economic model so that the instruments may be set at their optimal values. This *normative* approach to economic policy is concerned with how policy makers *should* act and, within the context of optimal control theory, economists sought to identify the optimal policy in order to reach the best outcome, given the decision takers' preferences (see Chow, 1975). Kydland and Prescott argue that there is 'no way' that 'optimal control theory can be made applicable to economic planning when expectations are rational'. Although optimal control theory had proved to be very useful in the *physical* sciences, Kydland and Prescott deny that the control of *social* systems can be viewed in the same way. Within social systems there are intelligent agents who will attempt to anticipate policy actions. As a result, in dynamic economic systems where policy makers are involved with a sequence of actions over a period of time, 'discretionary policy, namely the selection of that decision which is best, given the current situation, does not result in the social objective function being maximised' (Kydland and Prescott, 1977, p. 463). This apparent paradox results because 'economic planning is not a game against nature but, rather, a game against rational economic agents'. This argument has very important implications both for the conduct of monetary policy and for the institutional structure most likely to generate credibility with respect to the stated objective of low inflation.

The fundamental insight provided by Kydland and Prescott relating to the evaluation of macroeconomic policy is that when economic agents are forward-looking the policy problem emerges as a dynamic game between intelligent players – the government (or monetary authorities) and the private sector (see Blackburn, 1987). Suppose a government formulates what it considers to be an optimal policy which is then announced to private agents. If this policy is believed then in subsequent periods it may not remain optimal since, in the new situation, the government finds that it has an incentive to renege or cheat on its previously announced optimal policy. The difference between *ex ante* and *ex post* optimality is known as *time inconsistency*. As Blackburn (1992) notes, an optimal policy computed at time t is time-inconsistent if reoptimization at $t + n$ implies a different optimal policy. Kydland and Prescott demonstrate how time-inconsistent policies will significantly weaken the credibility of announced policies.

The demonstration that optimal plans are time-inconsistent is best illustrated in the macroeconomic context by examining a strategic game played between the monetary authorities and private economic agents, utilizing the Lucas monetary surprise version of the Phillips curve trade-off between inflation and unemployment to show how a consistent equilibrium will involve an inflationary bias. In the Kydland and Prescott model discretionary policies are incapable of achieving an optimal equilibrium. In what follows we assume that the monetary authorities can control the rate of inflation perfectly, that markets clear continuously and that economic agents have rational expectations. Equation (5.14) indicates that unemployment can be reduced by a positive inflation surprise:

$$U_t = UN + \psi(\dot{P}_t^e - \dot{P}_t) \tag{5.14}$$

Here, as before, U_t is unemployment in time period t, UN is the natural rate of unemployment, ψ is a positive constant, $\dot{P}_t^e$ is the expected and $\dot{P}_t$ the actual rate of inflation in time period t. Equation (5.14) represents the constraint facing the policy maker. Kydland and Prescott assume that there is some social objective function which rationalizes the policy choice and is of the form shown in equation (5.15):

$$S = S(\dot{P}_t, U_t), \text{ where } S'(\dot{P}_t) < 0 \text{ and } S'(U_t) < 0 \tag{5.15}$$

The social objective function (5.15) indicates that inflation and unemployment are 'bads' since a reduction in either or both increases social welfare. A *consistent* policy will seek to maximize (5.15) subject to the Phillips curve constraint given by equation (5.14). Figure 5.3 illustrates the Phillips curve trade-off for two expected rates of inflation, $\dot{P}_{to}^e$ and $\dot{P}_{tc}^e$. The contours of the social objective function are indicated by the indifference curves $S_1 S_2 S_3$ and S_4. Given that inflation and unemployment are 'bads', $S_1 > S_2 > S_3 > S_4$. In Figure 5.3, all points on the vertical axis are potential equilibrium positions, since at points O and C unemployment is at the natural rate (that is, $U_t = UN$) and agents are correctly forecasting inflation (that is, $\dot{P}_t^e = \dot{P}_t$). The indifference curves indicate that the *optimal* position is at point O where a combination of $\dot{P}_t$ = zero and $U_t = UN$ prevails. While the monetary authorities in this

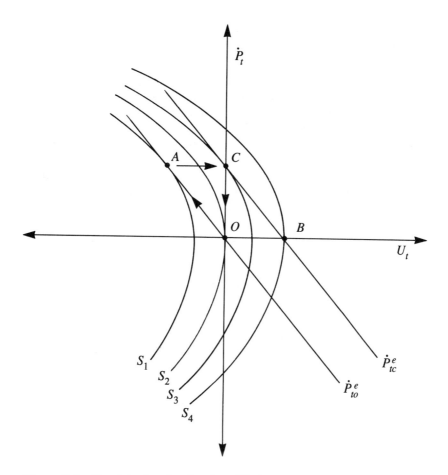

Figure 5.3   Consistent and optimal equilibrium

model can determine the rate of inflation, the position of the Phillips curves in Figure 5.3 will depend on the inflationary expectations of private economic agents. In this situation a *time-consistent equilibrium* is achieved where the indifference curve S_3 is at a tangent to the Phillips curve passing through point C. Since C lies on S_3, it is clear that the time-consistent equilibrium is sub-optimal. Let us see how such a situation can arise in the context of a dynamic game played out between policy makers and private agents.

In a dynamic game, each player chooses a strategy which indicates how they will behave as information is received during the game. The strategy chosen by a particular player will depend on their perception of the strategies likely to be followed by the other participants, as well as how they expect other participants to be influenced by their own strategy. In a dynamic game, each player will seek to maximize their own objective function, subject to their perception of the strategies adopted by other players. The situation where the game is between the government and private agents is an example of a non-cooperative *Stackelberg* game. Stackelberg games have a hierarchical structure, with the dominant player acting as *leader* and the remaining participants reacting to the strategy of the leader. In the monetary policy game discussed by Kydland and Prescott, the government is the dominant player. When the government decides on its optimal policy it will take into account the likely reaction of the *followers* (private agents). In a Stackelberg game, unless there is a precommitment from the leader with respect to the announced policy, the optimal policy will be dynamically inconsistent because the government can improve its own pay-off by cheating. Since the private sector players understand this, the time consistent equilibrium will be a *Nash* equilibrium. In such a situation each player correctly perceives that they are doing the best they can, given the actions of the other players, with the leader relinquishing the dominant role. For a non-technical discussion of game theory, see Davis (1983).

Suppose the economy is initially at the sub-optimal but time-consistent equilibrium indicated by point C in Figure 5.3. In order to move the economy to the optimal position indicated by point O, the monetary authorities announce a target of zero inflation which will be achieved by reducing the growth rate of the money supply from $\dot{M}_c$ to $\dot{M}_o$. If such an announcement is credible and believed by private economic agents then they will revise downwards their inflationary expectations from $\dot{P}^e_{tc}$ to $\dot{P}^e_{to}$, causing the Phillips curve to shift downwards from C to O. But once agents have revised their expectations in response to the declared policy, what guarantee is there that the monetary authorities will not renege on their promise and engineer an inflationary surprise? As is clear from Figure 5.3, the optimal policy for the authorities to follow is *time-inconsistent*. If they exercise their discretionary powers and increase the rate of monetary growth in order to create an 'inflation surprise', the economy can reach point A on S_1, which is clearly superior to point O. However such a position is unsustainable, since at point A unemployment is below the natural rate and $\dot{P}_t > \dot{P}^e_t$. Rational agents will soon realize they have been fooled and the economy will return to the time-consistent equilibrium at point C. What this example illustrates is that, if the monetary authorities have discretionary powers, they will have an incentive to cheat. Announced policies which are time-inconsistent will not be credible. Because the other players in the inflation game know the authorities' objective function, they will not adjust their inflationary expectations in response to announcements which lack credibility and in the absence of binding rules the economy will not be able to reach the optimal but time inconsistent position indicated by point O. The non-cooperative Nash equilibrium indicated by point C demonstrates that discretionary policy produces a sub-optimal outcome exhibiting an inflationary bias. Because rational agents can anticipate the strategy of monetary authorities which possess discretionary powers, they will anticipate inflation of $\dot{P}_{tc}$. Hence policy makers must also supply inflation equal to that expected by the private sector in order to prevent a squeeze on output. An optimal policy which lacks credibility because of time inconsistency will therefore be neither optimal nor feasible.

The various outcomes which can arise in the game played between the monetary authorities and wage negotiators has been neatly captured by Taylor (1985). Figure 5.4, which is adapted from Taylor (1985), shows the four

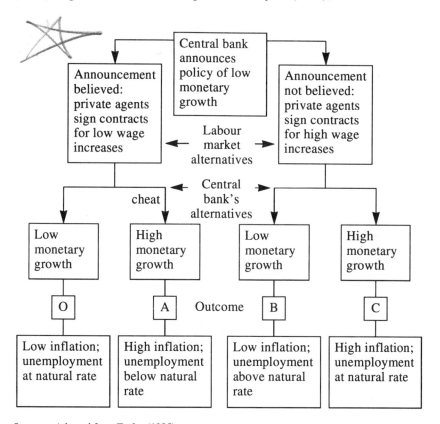

Source: Adapted from Taylor (1985).

Figure 5.4 Game played between the monetary authorities and wage negotiators

possible outcomes in a non-cooperative game between private agents and the central bank. The time-consistent outcome is shown by *C*, whereas the optimal outcome of low inflation with unemployment at the natural rate is shown by *O*. The temptation for a government to stimulate the economy because of time inconsistency is indicated by outcome *A*, whereas the decision not to validate a high rate of expected inflation and high wage increases will produce a recession and is indicated by outcome *B*.

The credibility problem identified by Kydland and Prescott arises most clearly in the situation of a one-shot full information non-cooperative Stackelberg game where the government has discretion with respect to monetary policy. However, in the situation of economic policy making, this is unrealistic since the game will be repeated. In the case of a repeated game (a super-game) the policy maker is forced to take a longer-term view since the future consequences of current policy decisions will influence the *reputation* of the policy maker. In this situation the government's incentive to cheat is reduced because they face an intertemporal trade-off between the current gains from reneging and the future costs which inevitably arise from riding the Phillips curve.

In their development and popularization of the time inconsistency model, Barro and Gordon (1983a, 1983b) have explored the possibilities of substituting the policy maker's reputation for more formal rules. The work of Barro and Gordon represents a significant contribution to the *positive* analysis of monetary policy which is concerned with the way policy makers *do* behave, rather than how they *should* behave. If economists can agree that inflation is primarily determined by monetary growth, why do governments allow excessive monetary growth? In the Barro–Gordon model an inflationary bias results because the monetary authorities are not bound by rules. However even a government exercising discretion will be influenced by reputational considerations if it faces punishment from private agents and it must consequently weigh up the gains from cheating on its announced policy, against the future costs of the higher inflation which characterizes the discretionary equilibrium. Given this intertemporal trade-off between current gains (in terms of lower unemployment and higher output) and the future costs, the equilibrium of this game will depend on the discount rate of the policy maker. The higher the discount rate the closer the equilibrium solution is to the time consistent equilibrium of the Kydland–Prescott model (point *C* in Figure 5.3). If the discount rate is low, the equilibrium position will be closer to the optimal zero inflation precommitment outcome.

One problem with the above analysis is that private agents do not know what type of government behaviour they face since they have incomplete information (see Driffill, 1988). Given uncertainty with respect to government intentions, private agents will carefully analyse various signals in the form of policy actions and announcements. In this scenario it is difficult for private agents to distinguish 'hard-nosed' (zero inflation) administrations from 'wet' (high inflation) administrations, since 'wets' have an incentive to masquerade as 'hard-nosed'. But as Blackburn (1992) has observed agents 'extract information about the government's identity by watching what it does, knowing full well that what they do observe may be nothing more than the dissembling actions of an imposter'. Backus and Driffill (1985) have extended the Barro and Gordon framework to take into account uncertainty on the part of the private sector with respect to the true intentions of the policy maker. Given this uncertainty, a dry, hard-nosed government will inevitably face a high sacrifice ratio if it initiates disinflationary policies and engages in a game of 'chicken' with wage negotiators. For detailed surveys of the issues discussed in this section, the reader should consult Barro (1986), Persson (1988), Blackburn and Christenson (1989) and Fischer (1990).

The dynamic inconsistency theories of inflation initiated by Kydland and Prescott and developed by Barro and Gordon, and Backus and Driffill, provide a strong case for the establishment of independent central banks which act as a precommitment device. Since the problem of credibility has its source in the discretionary powers of the government with respect to monetary policy, this could be overcome by transferring the responsibility for anti-inflationary policy to a non-political independent central bank. Rogoff (1985) has suggested that the appointment of conservative inflation-averse central bankers will prevent the excessive use of activist discretionary stabilization policies and the consequent inflationary bias that these policies imply. Recently a considerable amount of research has been carried out which has examined the relationship between central bank independence and economic performance (see Grilli *et al.*, 1991; Bernanke and Mishkin, 1992; Alesina and Summers, 1993; Eijffinger and Schaling, 1993).

The central difficulty recognized by researchers into the economic impact of central bank independence is the problem of constructing an index of independence. Alesina and Summers (1993) identify the ability of the central bank to select its policy objectives without the influence of government, the selection procedure of the governor of the central bank, the ability to use monetary instruments without restrictions and the requirement of the central bank to finance fiscal deficits as key indicators which can be used to construct a measure of central bank independence. Using a composite index derived from Parkin and Bade (1982) and Grilli *et al.* (1991), Alesina and Summers have examined the correlation between an index of independence and some major economic indicators. Table 5.1 indicates that, 'while central bank independence promotes price stability, it has no measurable impact on real economic performance' (Alesina and Summers, 1993, p. 151). The 'near perfect' negative correlation between inflation and central bank independence is clearly

Table 5.1	*Central bank independence and economic performance*

Country	Average index of central bank independence	Average inflation 1955–88	Average unemployment rate 1958–88	Average real GNP growth 1955–87
Spain	1.5	8.5	n/a	4.2
New Zealand	1	7.6	n/a	3.0
Australia	2.0	6.4	4.7	4.0
Italy	1.75	7.3	7.0	4.0
United Kingdom	2	6.7	5.3	2.4
France	2	6.1	4.2	3.9
Denmark	2.5	6.5	6.1	3.3
Belgium	2	4.1	8.0	3.1
Norway	2	6.1	2.1	4.0
Sweden	2	6.1	2.1	2.9
Canada	2.5	4.5	7.0	4.1
Netherlands	2.5	4.2	5.1	3.4
Japan	2.5	4.9	1.8	6.7
United States	3.5	4.1	6.0	3.0
Germany	4	3.0	3.6	3.4
Switzerland	4	3.2	n/a	2.7

Source:	Alesina and Summers (1993).

visible in Figure 5.5. However, as Alesina and Summers recognize, the excellent anti-inflationary performance of Germany may have more to do with the public aversion to inflation following the disastrous experience of the hyperinflation in 1923 than the existence of an independent central bank. In this case the independent central bank could be an effect of the German public aversion to inflation rather than a cause of low inflation. Indeed the reputation established by the German Bundesbank for maintaining low inflation was one important reason given by the UK government for joining the ERM in October 1990. The participation of the UK in such a regime, where monetary policy is determined by an anti-inflationary central bank which has an established reputation and credibility, was intended to tie the hands of domestic policy makers and help lower inflationary expectations (see Alogoskoufis *et al.*, 1992)

While monetary rules which avoid the dynamic time inconsistency problems are likely to produce lower average rates of inflation, many economists doubt that, overall, rules are superior to discretion, given the possibility of

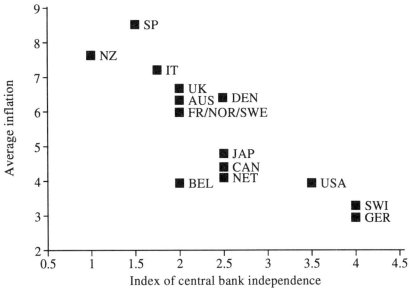

Source: Alesina and Summers (1993).

Figure 5.5   The relationship between average inflation and central bank
independence

large unforeseen shocks. A central bank, independent of political control, which could exercise discretion in the face of large shocks may be a more attractive alternative to rule-based policies. The recent research of Bernanke and Mishkin also confirms that 'Central banks never and nowhere adhere to strict, ironclad rules for monetary growth' (Bernanke and Mishkin, 1992, p. 186). It is also recognized that the separation of fiscal and monetary management can lead to coordination problems which can undermine credibility. As Blackburn (1992) concludes, 'the credibility of monetary policy does not depend upon monetary policy alone but also upon the macroeconomic programme in its entirety'.

We finally draw the reader's attention in this section to the considerable research which has been conducted into the role played by politics in influencing economic performance. The *political business cycle* or *monetary politics* literature was stimulated by the seminal work of Nordhaus (1975) and Hibbs (1977). In the Nordhaus model, politicians aim to maximize their re-election prospects. Hence in this model booms are created in the pre-election period. Hibbs argued that policies are also guided by ideological (partisan) considerations and this gives rise to the prediction that left-wing governments are likely to favour more expansionary (inflationary) policies than right-wing governments. Although the political business cycle literature is a separate development from new classical economics (Nordhaus is a Keynesian), the burgeoning literature in the last few years has been heavily influenced by the rational expectations revolution and the issues related to time inconsistency, credibility and reputation. The work by Alesina has shown that the imposition of rational expectations does not remove the importance of political factors in business cycle analysis and in general the political business cycle literature provides more ammunition to those economists who favour taking monetary policy out of the hands of elected politicians. Excellent surveys of the monetary politics literature can be found in Frey and Schneider (1988), Alesina (1989), Nordhaus (1989), Whynes (1989) and Alesina and Roubini (1992).

5.4.4 Microeconomic policies to increase aggregate supply
The next policy implication of the new classical approach we consider concerns what policies the authorities should pursue if they wish to increase output/reduce unemployment permanently. As we have seen, changes in output and employment are held to reflect the equilibrium supply decisions of firms and workers, given their perceptions of relative prices. Unemployment is regarded as an equilibrium outcome reflecting the optimal decisions of workers who substitute work/leisure in response to movements in current and expected future real wages. The labour market continuously clears so that anyone wanting to work at the current real wage can do so. Those who are unemployed voluntarily choose not to work at the current real wage. It follows from this view that the appropriate policy measures to increase output/reduce unemployment are those that increase the microeconomic incentives for firms and workers to supply more output and labour (see, for example, Minford *et al.*, 1985, Minford, 1991). Examples of the wide range of (often highly controversial) supply-side policies which have been pursued over recent years can be found in section 4.3.3, on the natural rate and supply-side policies.

5.4.5 The Lucas critique of econometric policy evaluation
The final implication of the new classical approach for the formulation of macroeconomic policy concerns what is popularly known as the 'Lucas critique', after the title of Lucas's seminal paper in which the proposition first appeared. Lucas (1976) attacked the established practice of using large-scale macroeconometric models to evaluate the consequences of alternative policy scenarios, given that such policy simulations are based on the assumption that the parameters of the model remain unchanged when there is a change in policy. Lucas argued that the parameters of large-scale macroeconometric

models may not remain constant in the face of policy changes, since economic agents may adjust their behaviour to the new environment. The Lucas critique has profound implications for the formulation of macroeconomic policy. Since policy makers cannot predict the effects of new and different economic policies on the parameters of their models, simulations using existing models cannot in turn be used to predict the consequences of alternative policy regimes. In Lucas's view the invariability of parameters in a model to policy changes cannot be guaranteed in Keynesian-type disequilibrium models. In contrast, the advantage of equilibrium theorizing is that by, focusing attention on individuals' objectives and constraints, it is much more likely that the resulting model will consist entirely of *structural* relations which are invariant to changes in policy. Lucas identified the treatment of expectations as a major defect of the standard large-scale macroeconometric models. With rational expectations, agents will react quickly to announced policy changes. The underprediction of inflation during the late 1960s and early 1970s seemed to confirm Lucas's argument. However some direct tests of the Lucas critique have not provided strong support for the proposition that policy changes lead to shifts of the coefficients on behavioural equations. Blanchard (1984) has shown that 'there is no evidence of a major shift of the Phillips curve' during the Volcker disinflation. However other economists have pointed out that the Volcker disinflation involved a lower sacrifice ratio than would have been expected before October 1979, when the policy was implemented (see Mankiw, 1994). Finally it should be noted that even the structural parameters of new classical 'equilibrium' models may not be invariant to policy changes if economic agents' tastes and technology change following a shift in the rules of economic policy. In practice it would seem that the significance of the Lucas critique depends upon the stability of the parameters of a model following the particular policy change under consideration.

5.5 Conclusion

The contributions made by leading new classicists such as Lucas, Sargent and Wallace dominated macroeconomics discussion throughout the 1970s, particularly in the United States. However, by the close of the decade, several weaknesses of the new classical equilibrium approach were becoming apparent. These deficiencies were mainly the consequence of utilizing the twin assumptions of continuous market clearing and imperfect information. Critics drew attention to aggregate price and money supply data readily available to agents at relatively low cost and questioned how this could be reconciled with the magnitude and length of actual business cycles supposedly caused by informational gaps. In addition, as we have discussed, the proposition that only unanticipated monetary surprises have real output effects became the subject of intense debate and empirical testing. In general the results did not provide any strong support for the view that systematic monetary policy had been ineffective with respect to real variables in the short run. The depth of the recessions in both the USA and the UK in the 1980–82 period following the Reagan and Thatcher deflations provided the critics with further ammunition.

These criticisms led some economists sympathetic to the new classical approach (such as Finn Kydland and Edward Prescott) to develop a mark II version of the new classical model, known as equilibrium real business cycle theory (see Figure 5.6). While proponents of the real business cycle approach have abandoned the monetary surprise approach to explaining business cycles, they have retained components of the equilibrium approach and the propagation mechanisms (such as adjustment costs) used in mark I versions. Before turning to discuss this approach in the next chapter, in concluding the

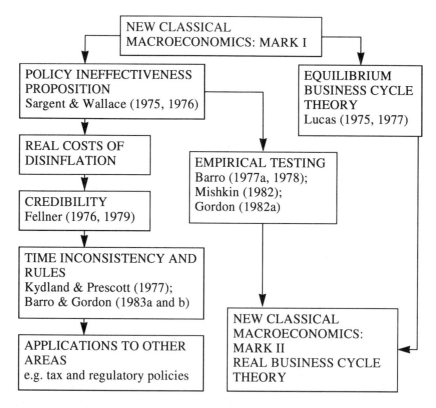

Figure 5.6   The evolution of new classical macroeconomics

present chapter we consider the impact new classical macroeconomics mark I has made on the development of macroeconomics.

Despite the controversy that surrounds the approach, new classical economics has had a significant impact on the development of macroeconomics over the last decade and a half. This impact can be seen in a number of areas. First, it has led to much greater attention being paid to the way that expectations are modelled, resulting in a so-called 'rational expectations revolution' in macroeconomics. Second, the insight of rational expectations that a change in policy will almost certainly influence expectations (which in turn is likely to influence the behaviour of economic agents) is now fairly widely accepted. This in turn has led economists to reconsider the role and conduct of macroeconomic stabilization policy. Much of the controversy that surrounds new classical macroeconomics is directed, not at the rational expectations hypothesis *per se*, but at the policy implications that derive from the structure of new classical models. In this context it is interesting to note that Keynesian-like disequilibrium models (where markets do not clear continuously) but which allow agents to have rational expectations, as well as incorporating the natural rate hypothesis, still predict a role for demand management policies to stabilize the economy. If, in the face of random shocks to aggregate demand, the government is able to adjust its policies more quickly than the private sector can renegotiate money wages then there is still a role for aggregate demand management to stabilize the economy and offset fluctuations in output and employment around their natural levels. Furthermore, given the gradual adjustment of prices and wages in new Keynesian models, any policy of monetary disinflation, even if credible and anticipated by rational agents, will lead to a substantial recession in terms of output and employment, with hysteresis effects raising the natural rate of unemployment (see section 7.8).

Finally, in trying to come to an overall assessment of the impact of new classical macroeconomics on the debate concerning the role and conduct of macroeconomic stabilization policy, three conclusions seem to suggest themselves. First, it is fairly widely agreed that the conditions necessary to render macroeconomic stabilization policy completely powerless to influence output and employment in the short run are unlikely to hold. Having said this, the possibility that economic agents will anticipate the effects of changes in economic policy does imply that the authorities' scope to stabilize the economy is reduced. Second, new classical macroeconomics has brought the possibility of using aggregate supply policies to stimulate output and employment much more to the forefront. Lastly, new Keynesians have been forced to respond to the challenge of new classical macroeconomics and in doing so, in particular explaining why wages and prices tend to adjust only gradually, have provided a more sound theoretical base to justify interventionist policies (both demand and supply management policies) to stabilize the economy. Before discussing these developments in Chapter 7, we next consider equilibrium real business cycle theory.

ROBERT LUCAS, JR

Photograph courtesy of Lloyd De Grane

Robert Lucas was born in 1937 in Yakima, Washington and obtained his BA (in history) and his PhD from the University of Chicago in 1959 and 1964, respectively. He taught at Carnegie-Mellon University from 1964 to 1975, becoming Professor of Economics in 1970. In 1975, he moved to the University of Chicago, to become the John Dewey Distinguished Service Professor of Economics, and he has remained there ever since.

Robert Lucas is widely acknowledged as being the central figure in the development of the new classical approach to macroeconomics. Among his best known books are: *Studies in Business Cycle Theory* (MIT Press, 1981), *Rational Expectations and Econometric Practice* (University of Minnesota Press, 1981; Allen & Unwin, 1982), co-edited with Thomas Sargent, *Models of Business Cycles* (Basil Blackwell, 1987) and *Recursive Methods in Economic Dynamics* (Harvard University Press, 1989), co-written with Nancy Stokey and Edward Prescott.

His best known articles include: 'Real Wages, Employment and Inflation', *Journal of Political Economy* (1969), co-written with Leonard Rapping, 'Expectations and the Neutrality of Money', *Journal of Economic Theory* (1972), 'Some International Evidence on Output–Inflation Trade-Offs', *American Economic Review* (1973), 'An Equilibrium Model of the Business Cycle', *Journal of Political Economy* (1975), 'Methods and Problems in Business

Cycle Theory', *Journal of Money, Credit and Banking* (1980) and 'Making a Miracle', *Econometrica* (1993).

We corresponded with Robert Lucas in March 1993.

As an undergraduate you were a student of history. Why did you switch your interest towards economics as a postgraduate?
I became interested in economic forces in history, began studying economic history, and found I needed to learn some economics. I'm still working on it.

David Laidler [1992b] has recently drawn attention to what he described as 'the appallingly low standards of historical scholarship amongst economists'. Is it important for an economist to be a competent historian?
No. It is important that some economists be competent historians, just as it is important that some economists be competent mathematicians, competent sociologists, and so on. But there is neither a need nor a possibility for everyone to be good at everything. Like Stephen Dedalus, none of us will ever be more than a shy guest at the feast of the world's culture.

How do you view Keynes as a macroeconomist?
I suppose Keynes, via Hicks, Modigliani and Samuelson, was the founder of macroeconomics, so one has to view him as a leading figure in the field!

Should students of macroeconomics still read the General Theory*?*
No.

Had Keynes still been living in 1969, do you think he would have been awarded the first Nobel Prize in Economics? Would he have received your vote?
I thought Joan Robinson would get the first one, so my credentials as a Nobel forecaster have been dubious from the start. But certainly Keynes would have got one early on. Since I am not a member of the Swedish Academy, I do not have a vote to cast.

Prior to your own contributions in the 1970s which papers/books do you feel most influenced the development of macroeconomics after Keynes?
I've already mentioned Hicks, Modigliani and Samuelson. I have in mind Hicks's review of the *General Theory*, Modigliani's 1944 paper, and many of Samuelson's writings, including his *Principles*. Lawrence Klein and James Tobin have both influenced me a great deal as well. Personally, I first learned Keynesian economics from Martin Bailey, using his excellent graduate text.

For me, though, Milton Friedman is by far the most important teacher. His *Theory of the Consumption Function* and his *Monetary History* with Anna Schwartz are central, but I'm sure I've read everything he's ever written.

What do you consider to be the key papers/books which have had a major impact on the development of your ideas with respect to macroeconomics during the past 25 years?
Friedman's AEA Presidential address and Edmund Phelp's parallel work initiated the rethinking that so many of us went through in the 1970s. Sargent's work was central. In the 1980s, Kydland and Prescott's work reoriented everyone's thinking, certainly including mine.

Do you think that it is crucial for macroeconomic models to have neoclassical choice-theoretic micro foundations?
No. It depends on the purposes you want the model to serve. For short-term forecasting, for example, the Wharton model does very well with little in the way of theoretical foundations, and Sims, Litterman and others have had pretty good success with purely statistical extrapolation methods that involve no economics at all. But if one wants to know how behaviour is likely to change under some change in policy, it is necessary to model the way people make choices. If you see me driving north on Clark Street, you will have good (though not perfect) predictive success by guessing that I will still be going north on the same street a few minutes later. But if you want to predict how I will respond if Clark Street is closed off, you have to have some idea of where I am going and what my alternative routes are – of the nature of my decision problem.

Why do you think there is more consensus among economists over microeconomic issues compared to macroeconomic issues?
What is the microeconomic consensus you are referring to? Does it just mean that microeconomists agree on the Slutsky equation, or other purely mathematical propositions? Macroeconomists all take derivatives in the same way, too. On matters of application and policy, microeconomists disagree as vehemently as macroeconomists – neither side in an antitrust action has any difficulty finding expert witnesses.

I think there is a tremendous amount of consensus on macroeconomic issues today. But there is much that we don't know, and so – necessarily – a lot to argue about.

When and how did you first realize the significance and implications of the rational expectations hypothesis for macroeconomic analysis?
In 1970, when I wrote 'Econometric Testing of the Natural Rate Hypothesis'.

Over the years the rational expectations hypothesis has been presented in the literature in a number of different forms and versions. What do you regard as being the essence of the hypothesis ?

Rational expectations is the principle that agents in an economic model use the correct conditional expectations, given their information. In different models, this principle is made explicit in different ways, so of course it appears in different forms in the literature.

You are widely recognized as the founder of new classical macroeconomics. Are you happy with the label 'new classicist' and what do you see as being the fundamental propositions of new classical macroeconomics?

I don't feel an urgent need for a label, but if I have to have one I will stay with 'monetarist', so as to identify my opinions on macroeconomic policy with those of people like Milton Friedman, Karl Brunner and Allan Meltzer. Compared to those economists, though, I have a strong preference for mathematically explicit general equilibrium models. Does this preference necessitate a new label, or can we just conclude that there are many styles for doing economics?

Do you regard the new classical approach as having resulted in a revolution in macroeconomic thought?

Sargent once wrote that you can interpret any scientific development as continuous evolution or discontinuous revolution, at your pleasure. For myself, I do not have any romantic associations with the term 'revolution'. To me, it connotes lying, theft and murder, so I would prefer not to be known as a revolutionary.

To what extent did the work of the Austrians (Hayek etc.) influence your ideas?

I once thought of myself as a kind of Austrian, but Kevin Hoover's book persuaded me that this was just a result of my misreading of Hayek and others.

In your Yrjö Jahnsson lectures you argued that the rational expectations revolution in macroeconomics was not primarily a reaction to Keynes and Keynesians. Does this also apply to the other components of new classical economics, such as the market clearing assumption ?

Yes.

One of the policy implications of new classical analysis is that there will be no trade-off between inflation and unemployment even in the short run following announced/anticipated monetary expansion. How do you now view this policy ineffectiveness proposition in the light of the disinflationary experiences of both the UK and the US economies in the early 1980s?

It is nearly impossible to tell what was and was not anticipated in any particular episode, so the 1980s did not offer a crucial test of anything. Sargent's two essays on disinflation in his book, *Rational Expectations and Inflation*, provide the best analysis of this issue, and a serious discussion of what is meant by an 'anticipated' policy change.

David Laidler [1992b] has recently argued that old-fashioned monetarist models with adaptive expectations have provided a better guide to the outcomes of macroeconomic policies in the early 1980s than new classical models, which at that time were very influential, particularly in the USA. What is your reaction to this view?

I haven't even *seen* a monetarist model with adaptive expectations for 20 years! I'm not familiar with the comparison you attribute to Laidler.

Real business cycle theory evolved out of the monetary surprise version of new classical macroeconomics. However the models which have been developed give little importance to the money supply as an explanatory factor in business cycle analysis. Would you say that this work represents a serious challenge to the orthodox monetarist position represented by Friedman and Schwartz?

Yes, it certainly does. Many economists who formerly believed that monetary shocks are central to business cycles now believe they play no role at all. But I would not like to have the task of rewriting Friedman and Schwartz's chapter on the 1930s with productivity shocks playing the lead.

Do you feel that the main differences between macroeconomists today are over empirical or theoretical matters?

There is no disagreement over a purely theoretical issue, like how many real roots a given quadratic has. If by 'theoretical matters' you mean something other than mathematics, then I don't see the distinction. Theory is what we use to make sense out of data. When I say I don't like your theory, I either mean that I think you made a mathematical error in working it out, or else I don't think it works empirically. In the latter case, is our disagreement empirical or theoretical?

A key propagation mechanism in real business cycle theories is the intertemporal substitution of labour. Doesn't the available evidence on labour supply elasticity suggest only a minimal response of labour to temporary wage changes?

I don't know what you mean by the 'available evidence'. The degree of intertemporal substitution of labour assumed in real business cycle models is *selected* to generate employment fluctuations of the magnitude we observe, which is to say, to be consistent with some of the 'available evidence'. Economists who have used survey data on individuals have been unsuccessful in explaining employment fluctuations at the individual level – we just haven't learned anything about preferences from their work. This is a disappointment, but no good purpose is served by reinterpreting this failure as though it were a successful attempt to estimate something.

In his recent survey of the macroeconomics literature, Stanley Fischer (EJ, 1988) has argued that 'real wages simply do not show the movements that are needed for real business cycle theory to explain the facts'. What is your response to this?
I haven't seen Fischer's paper. Real wage movements pose problems for any business cycle theory I know about.

Is it your view that the traditional approach of distinguishing between short-run and long-run forces in macroeconomics has been misconceived and counter-productive? Did Keynes send everyone off down the wrong track?
The short-run–long-run distinction is Marshall's, not Keynes's. Indeed Keynes is quite explicit in the *General Theory* that he thinks that permanent stagnation can result from demand deficiencies. Samuelson's neoclassical synthesis reclaimed the long run for neoclassical analysis, at least here in the States. Now Samuelson's students – my whole generation – are trying to get the short run back, too! It's hard going, I know, but Samuelson already did the easy part, and we have to make a living somehow.

The 1930s sent all of us off on the wrong track, starting with Keynes. Even today, 50 years after the depression ended, public figures talk about every little wiggle in the GNP figures as though it were the end of capitalism. If Keynes were alive today, he would take pride in his role in setting up the system that permitted the recovery of Europe and the Japanese miracle, and he would be excited about the prospects for integrating the second and third worlds into the world economy. I think he would be as impatient with the overemphasis on short-term fine-tuning as I am.

The US federal budget deficits since the early 1980s have been exceptionally large. Opinions concerning the likely welfare consequences of these deficits seem to vary considerably. Is it your view that these large deficits have been damaging to the US economy or would you share the view of Robert Barro and others that deficits are relatively unimportant? Should President Clinton regard the reduction of the budget deficit as a top priority?
I was a deficit alarmist in the early 1980s, not because I disagreed with Barro that deficits are just postponed taxes – which is obviously correct – but

because I feared the tax that would make present values add up would be the inflation tax. Now I think it is more likely that it will be defaults on social security promises that will do it. Either way, I think Clinton is right to try to get us to face the issue (if that is what he is doing).

Does the argument that money is super-neutral imply that inflation is an unimportant problem?
No one ever argued that money is super-neutral, any more than anyone ever argued that people consume only two goods. These are just simplifying assumptions made for specific purposes. If one's purpose is to study the costs of inflation, then obviously one would work with a model that doesn't have the super-neutrality property.

In 1978 (AER) you suggested that macroeconomic analysis would make more progress if the concept of involuntary unemployment was abandoned. Subsequently Alan Blinder (AER, 1988) and Robert Solow (AER, 1980) have defended Keynes's position on involuntary unemployment. Given the very high average European unemployment rates since 1980, can we really view all unemployment as a voluntary phenomenon?
I haven't seen any work by either Alan Blinder or Robert Solow that contradicts my 1978 opinion. Have they made a lot of progress in understanding unemployment?

Why do you refer to unemployment as an activity identical in character in both booms and slumps?
Why not?

How important has the 'Lucas critique' actually been in practice?
It's had an enormous influence, I think, and all for the good.

In commenting on recent developments in new classical economics, Gregory Mankiw (1989) has argued that, although real business cycle theory has 'served the important function of stimulating and provoking scientific debate, it will [he predicts] *ultimately be discarded as an explanation of observed fluctuations'. What are your predictions for the future development of macroeconomics?*
I agree with Mankiw, but I don't think he understands the implication of his observation. We are now seeing models in the style of Kydland and Prescott with nominal rigidities, imperfect credit markets, and many other features that people thinking of themselves as Keynesians have emphasized. The difference is that within an explicit equilibrium framework we can begin to work out the quantitative implications of these features, not just illustrate them with textbook diagrams.

Do you see any signs of an emerging consensus in macroeconomics, and if so what form will it take?

When a macroeconomic consensus is reached on an issue (as it has been, say, on the monetary sources of inflation) the issue passes off the stage of professional debate, and we argue about something else. Professional economists are primarily scholars, not policy managers. Our responsibility is to create new knowledge by pushing research into new, and hence necessarily controversial, territory. Consensus can be reached on specific issues, but consensus for a research area as a whole is equivalent to stagnation, irrelevance and death.

PATRICK MINFORD

Patrick Minford was born in 1943 in Shrewsbury, England and graduated from Oxford University with a BA in 1964, before obtaining his MSc and PhD from the University of London in 1970 and 1973, respectively. Since 1976 he has taught at the University of Liverpool, where he is currently Professor of Applied Economics.

Patrick Minford is widely recognized as being the leading exponent of new classical economics in the UK. Among his best known books are: *Rational Expectations and the New Macroeconomics* (Martin Robertson, 1983), co-written with David Peel, *Unemployment: Cause and Cure* (Basil Blackwell, 1985), *The Supply Side Revolution in Britain* (Edward Elgar, 1991) and *Rational Expectations Macroeconomics: An Introductory Handbook* (Basil Blackwell, 1992).

His best known articles include: 'The Nature and Purpose of UK Macro-economic Models', *Three Banks Review* (1980), 'The Role of Monetary Stabilisation Policy Under Rational Expectations', *Manchester School* (1981), co-written with David Peel, 'The Political Theory of the Business Cycle', *European Economic Review* (1982), co-written with David Peel, 'The Microfoundations of the Phillips Curve with Rational Expectations', *Oxford Economic Papers* (1982), co-written with David Peel, 'Labour Market Equi-librium in An Open Economy', *Oxford Economic Papers* (1983) and 'Mrs

Thatcher's Economic Policies 1979–1987', in *Economic Policy* (1987), co-written with Kent Matthews.

We interviewed Professor Minford in his office at the University of Liverpool on 18 March 1993.

What do you consider to be the key papers/books which have had a major impact on the development of macroeconomics during the past 25 years?
Well, Friedman's (1968) article and then a series of papers incorporating rational expectations: Lucas and Rapping (1969); Lucas (1972, 1973, 1975); Sargent and Wallace (1975). Since then the various attempts to build representative agent models, again by Lucas and the real business cycle models of Prescott. The main progress in macroeconomics has been made on rational expectations and the representative agent models with rigorous micro foundations. I haven't said anything about new-Keynesian work on menu costs. I am not terribly impressed by this work. It's not clear that there is much of a menu cost and the work still suffers from an awful lot of unsatisfactory features. I don't think new-Keynesians have come up with anything yet that is terribly persuasive [*laughter*].

Why do you think there seems to be more consensus among economists over microeconomic issues compared to macroeconomic issues?
Well obviously there is an agreed paradigm in micro of maximizing agents and the idea of the clearing micro market is not really controversial. With macro there is a disagreement on whether there is a failure of markets to clear. I personally think that this is a misunderstanding. People come up with things like menu costs, contracts, lack of liquidity, which in my opinion are nothing to do with whether markets clear or not. What people are saying is that they can conceive of a model in which there are certain constraints, which they could specify. For example, you build menu costs into the model, then try and get out of those models features that look like sticky prices or sticky quantity behaviour. Markets function subject to constraints of various sorts. The disagreement is really about the relevance of particular constraints. There has always been a frustration on the Keynesian side because they find it extremely hard to model these constraints in such a way as to produce real-world behaviour satisfactorily.

Do you think is it crucial for macroeconomic models to have choice-theoretic micro foundations?
In principle, yes. But when you get down to practical modelling quite often you have a particular problem in that you haven't got the time, the theoretical sophistication, or the mathematical tools, to produce the microeconomic

foundation in detail. For example, suppose we were evaluating the impact of the Budget on the British economy. There is no way that anyone is going to sit down and build a representative agent model of the British economy that is going to be capable of answering that question. All one can do is come up with a model that is as far as possible soundly based in microeconomic foundations. Most of the standard macroeconomic models that we use today to answer questions of that sort have not got completely spelt out micro foundations.

If Keynes had still been living in 1969, do you think he would have been awarded the first Nobel Prize in Economics?
Certainly. It is quite clear that we all live in the shadow of Keynes, because he invented macroeconomics, he drew attention to the fact that there was a macroeconomic set of issues. New classical economists have to deal with the phenomenon that the world does not adjust instantaneously and there are various sorts of lags and rigidities. Keynes was the first to cope with that and to produce a set of ideas which dealt with it. He got us quite a long way along the road of confronting the issues and his models were clearly sensible for the time.

Your outspoken criticism of the UK's decision to join the ERM in 1990 sounds very similar to Keynes's opposition to the restoration of the gold standard in 1925. Are these two events similar?
Yes, in a way. The work that has been done since suggests that, while the pound was overvalued in 1925, there were a lot of supply-side problems in the 1930s which have been drawn attention to since by people like Benjamin and Kochin. Keynes stressed the demand side of the gold standard overvaluation which certainly had a role but probably not as great in fact as the general deflation of the 1920s. Because we were overvalued, we never really had the roaring 1920s; here we had the rather depressed 1920s [*laughter*]. So undoubtedly Keynes had a point and there is a definite parallel with the ERM on the demand side. We have had with our membership of the ERM a tremendous deflation because of the fact that we were on an overvalued parity and it wasn't just the competitiveness that affected that, but the fact that we were trying to rebut very large speculative pressure by high interest rates.

Does the Hicksian IS–LM model still have a useful role to play in introducing students to macroeconomic analysis?
Well, if it is derived from an aggregate demand and supply set-up, then it is useful. The main problem has been that it has tended to be presented as an extension of a purely Keynesian world and that makes it difficult for students to readjust their mental sights on a world of aggregate demand and supply

and clearing markets, a classical world. It is a very useful framework if you can treat the IS–LM curves as an aggregate demand sub-model and then bring in aggregate supply.

How important was the discovery of the Phillips curve for macroeconomic policy making in the UK?
In terms of macroeconomic policy making, it was 'the' great eye-opener for the British economics establishment. In fact outside commentators picked it up faster than the economic establishment in Whitehall. The economics profession as a whole was rather slow in this country to pick up the policy implications of the Phillips curve. It took a big campaign by Michael Parkin and David Laidler to wake people up. It had such a big impact because it was the point at which people started to understand the supply side, the natural rate and the lack of a long-run trade-off. All these ideas were absorbed through the expectations-augmented Phillips curve with the Friedman (1968) and Phelps (1967) articles. Their ideas spread faster here than in the States, thanks to people like Parkin and Laidler, Samuel Brittan and Alan Walters.

Macroeconomic controversy in the 1950s and 1960s mainly revolved around issues relating to aggregate demand. Since the 1970s emphasis has shifted to the supply side of the economy. What do you think caused this shift of emphasis?
The Phillips curve and the lack of a long-run trade-off. I would also like to say a bit more than that, because it is slightly autobiographical in my case. At the beginning of the 1980s I was helping to push the incoming Tories towards the idea of a medium-term financial strategy to control inflation and I tended to think of the natural rate of unemployment as something that would be not too outrageous a number. I don't think it ever crossed my mind that it was anything like three million. Then it began to dawn on me at the beginning of the 1980s that we had a tremendous unemployment problem and, given my ideas about demand management, I couldn't account for it in terms of purely demand shocks. Clearly the 1980–81 recession was a terrific deflation, but it was pretty obvious at the time that it couldn't possibly account for three million unemployed. So I went off and did a lot of work on the natural rate of unemployment and rigidities in the labour market. That didn't happen in the States because they didn't have the same unemployment problem. Unemployment was never as serious a policy problem there. The Thatcher experience, which was well ahead of the deflationary policies in the rest of Europe, got people like myself thinking about supply-side problems. So it was a combination of the Phillips curve and rational expectations, which of course brings the vertical trade-off forward in time rather dramatically.

You are recognized as being a leading exponent of new classical macro-economics. Are you happy with the label 'new classicist'?
Well, I never quarrel with labels because I don't invent them [*laughter*]. Although my work has come from the new classical school, there are flavours of other things in it which people like Sargent and Lucas have never bothered with – like the role of unions and the contracts which unions sign – largely because their implicit model is of the US economy where unions have no power. In that sense, some people have said that there is a fair amount of Keynesian baggage in the Liverpool model because there is a unionized labour market and there are large nominal contracts which unions clearly sign. But when one realizes that these unions are operating within a total labour market where there is a non-union sector which clears in the normal way then I think it is actually clear that the Liverpool model is basically new classical.

What are the fundamental propositions of new classical macroeconomics?
Well, rational expectations is the most important element and the rest I would say is simply good microeconomics. My models have microeconomic agents, maximizing subject to normal constraints under rational expectations. Once you integrate the rigidities due to unions you get Keynesian-type properties such as a long adjustment period. That comes about from the fact that unions are signing contracts which are trying to maximize their members' utility, which endogenizes in the real wage the adjustment lags that come from the employers' side. They sign a contract which takes into account the fact that employers slowly adjust their labour force and that makes them slowly adjust the real wage through the wage bargain. That's an example of something where good microeconomics leads you to a property which looks quite Keynesian and yet is simply the result of rational expectations and a certain structure of institutions, in this case unions.

Do you regard new classical macroeconomics as a separate school of thought from monetarism?
No, except that there is an older school of monetarism which is represented by Friedman which has nothing to do with rational expectations.

Why do you think that both monetarism and new classical macroeconomics exerted less influence in UK academic circles than they did in the USA?
Well, if I am honest I think the reason is politics. The UK academic profession has had a tendency to be quite left-wing, and has disliked the policy implications of monetarism and has liked even less the policy implications of new classical macroeconomics. It has therefore resisted this type of thinking and has hankered after the basically interventionist policy conclusions of

Keynesianism. Keynesianism found a tremendous welcome from Bloomsbury and the centre-left intellectual climate of the 1930s and the post-war period. Monetarism and new classical economics came into this little party as a most unwelcome guest. Macroeconomics is deeply embedded in the policy process, so if you don't like certain sets of policies you argue like hell against them. One could add rather unkindly that the UK economics profession found it hard to retrain. There is an element of that as well; they had not invested any intellectual capital in monetarism. I was at Oxford in the early 1960s and was lucky that my tutor, Paul Streeten, introduced me to Friedman's work. I actually read Hayek out of intellectual curiosity, but he was regarded as a complete theoretical curiosum. In addition to the political aspect, the British economics profession had been brought up on the reverse L-shaped Keynesian aggregate supply curve and found it incredibly difficult intellectually to grasp this other world. They were just not intellectually prepared for it.

One of the policy implications of new classical analysis is that there will be no trade-off between inflation and unemployment even in the short run following announced/anticipated monetary expansion. How do you view this policy ineffectiveness proposition in the light of the disinflationary experiences of the UK economy in the early 1980s?

Well, as you know, the policy ineffectiveness proposition is now regarded as a very special case. Well-understood feedback policies will have an impact on the economy under quite a wide variety of circumstances. That's in a sense a separate issue because what you are talking about here is an announced change in money supply targets quite separate from any feedback policy. We have to consider two things. First, even if it is fully announced and believed there are going to be some significant nominal long-term contracts outstanding which it will have an impact on. Second, there is no such thing as something that has been announced and believed in from eternity. There has got to be some point that it became a surprise. The issue of time inconsistency and the credibility of these announcements has given rise to an enormous literature. I think an awful lot of nonsense is talked about credibility. Ultimately the credibility of politicians in making announcements of any sort, about future inflation policies, can only come from the people themselves. For example, the German people quite clearly have endowed the Bundesbank with tremendous credibility. In Germany, if you inflate you get into trouble with the people. In Britain in the mid-1970s, that did not appear to be the case. I would suggest that the British people have gone on a tremendous learning curve on this issue of time inconsistency and politicians reflating. They are now rather like the German people, pretty anti-inflationary. Pre-announcing anti-inflationary policies is worthless without credibility.

At the end of the day, the only way to solve this problem of credibility of politicians is for the people themselves to actually punish inflationary politicians. I think the European electorates have moved very much towards the Germanic end of that spectrum.

Do you regard the new classical approach as having resulted in a revolution in macroeconomic thought?
Yes, undoubtedly. We now think quite differently about macroeconomics than we did in the mid-1970s both in this country and in the United States. The key element in the revolution has been rational expectations, the rest is just good microeconomics. Under rational expectations the idea of market failure goes out of the window. Because people have rational expectations there is no reason why markets should fail. Adaptive expectations went nicely with the idea of some non-specific market failure. In the early Phillips curve models, prices were just not clearing the market for an unspecific reason. Adaptive expectations completed the picture of a world in which individuals were at sea basically. They didn't know what was hitting them and they were groping about in a fairly undirected way. What rational expectations did was to focus on the idea of informational rationality and efficiency and this non-specific groping became unacceptable theoretically. It then became impossible to get away with bad microeconomics

Do you agree with Lucas [1978] that we should abandon Keynes's concept of involuntary unemployment?
Yes. I can't make any sense of the concept except where you have unions who may not represent some of their members properly. Suppose you would like to work but your union pushes for a wage increase. A person can be involuntarily unemployed in that sector because their vote didn't count in the way it would have done in a free market. If the welding union raises the price of welders, a person could become involuntarily unemployed as a welder and then have to find their way in the world as a taxi driver or a dishwasher. So I would specifically say that, where you have got some collective agency that 'represent workers' in some way, you can get an important element of involuntariness coming into the labour market situation. It is not at all the idea of involuntary unemployment that Keynes had. It's simply an effect of an institutional set-up that you can't do anything about.

What do you think of efficiency wage theories and insider–outsider theories?
Well, implicit in all those theories is a reservation wage among the unemployed which is a given real amount. I do not object to the idea that some employers may have monitoring problems. There are all sorts of efficiency wage stories which lead to somewhat higher wages being paid in some firms.

Some people don't get jobs within those firms because they are willing to put up with unemployment rather than bid the aggregate real wage down. If they were desperate to work at any price, their supply curve of labour was vertical, then they would simply bid the real wage down. The aggregate wage is not prevented from dropping, so implicit in all these stories is a rigid reservation wage. I have no objection to these models at all, they provide a little bit of colour, a little bit of detail. The basic reason for European unemployment is that crucial rigidity which I have associated with the benefit system. Hysteresis is another case. People lose their human capital because of the period of long-term unemployment. The reason this occurs is because there is a benefit system which induces them to stay for long periods on the dole. People then start to lose their human capital in terms of normal labour-market behaviour and so on. They can't get up in the morning, rather like academics in some cases. We work such unsocial hours [*laughter*].

Do you regard inflation as a more important problem than unemployment?
Certainly not, far less important. They are both important problems but you use different tools to tackle each. If I was forced to choose between an economy in which the natural rate was 2 per cent and the inflation rate was 15 per cent, and an economy in which the natural rate was 15 per cent and the inflation rate was 2 per cent, I would have no doubt which economy I would choose to be in [*laughter*]. Having said that, I'd like to have an inflation rate and an unemployment rate of 2 per cent, so I want both tough labour market and inflation measures.

Is there any essential difference between the concepts of the natural rate of unemployment and NAIRU?
They are the same concept. NAIRU comes from the adaptive-expectations Phillips curve model. When unemployment is above the natural rate, inflation is falling and when it is below it, inflation is rising. In that model inflation is above expected inflation when unemployment is below the natural rate and because of adaptive expectations that makes expected inflation rise, which in turn leads to rising inflation, hence NAIRU. In a rational expectations model that isn't true any more. You can have high unemployment and nevertheless expect a tremendous inflation because of budget deficits and out-of-control printing of money. You can have accelerating inflation with high unemployment. In fact many hyperinflation economies have had that. Rational expectations breaks the link between this acceleration of inflation and where the unemployment rate is relative to the natural rate. Hence I try to censor the use of the term 'NAIRU'.

What approximate rate of unemployment do you believe at present [1993]
corresponds to the natural rate in the UK economy ?
Well, I would say it is quite low because we have had a decade of ferocious
labour market reform. We have got a very flexible labour market today and
therefore I put the natural rate down at about 3 or $3^1/_2$ per cent. However, it's
going to take us a long time to get there because that natural rate, I must
make it clear, is not contingent on a capital stock. It's the rate that comes
about from the potential profitability of business in the UK because people
are keen to work and there's a more flexible labour market. That makes the
UK a prime candidate for inward investment because we now have a cheap,
highly productive and cooperative labour force. That is going to bring in an
enormous amount of investment which will take a decade to put into place.
That makes me very bullish, long term, about the British economy.

What contribution has real business cycle theory made to macroeconomics?
I am a big fan of real business cycle theory. However I'm an à-la-carte real
business cycle man. I take my real business cycles and embed them shame-
lessly in models with nominal inertia coming from various sources. Real
business cycle theory is part and parcel of the supply-side revolution.

Don't real business cycle theorists play down the role of money?
That's what they say. I say they have a good case but they spoil it by
overstatement. In our model we have two major sources of shocks which are
very important, supply-side and demand-side shocks. I am eclectic, à-la-carte
[*laughter*].

Do you see any signs of an emerging consensus in macroeconomics?
Yes. I can remember all these great controversies in the 1970s – if you think
back to 1979 and all the controversy over the medium-term financial strategy.
Today everyone agrees that we need tough medium-term policies for the
PSBR, yet ten years ago that would have been highly controversial. To give
another example: I can't find anyone today who doesn't think it was a good
thing that we left the ERM [*laughter*].

6. The real business cycle school

If these theories are correct, they imply that the macroeconomics developed in
the wake of the Keynesian revolution is well confined to the ashbin of history.
(Summers, 1986)

6.1 Introduction: the Demise of New Classical Macroeconomics Mark I

As we have seen in Chapter 5, the dominant new classical theory during the
period 1972–82 was the monetary surprise model initially developed by
Lucas (1972, 1973). By combining the Friedman–Phelps natural rate hypothesis with the assumption of continuous market clearing and the rational
expectations hypothesis, the Lucas model was able to demonstrate rigorously
how a short-run Phillips curve would result if inflation was unanticipated.
Since inflation is governed by the rate of monetary expansion and because
agents with rational expectations cannot be systematically surprised, anticipated monetary policy will be ineffective. This Sargent–Wallace policy ineffectiveness proposition implies that the mean value of real variables cannot
be influenced by anticipated variations in the money supply and constitutes a
remarkable, if highly controversial, anti-Keynesian result.

Despite the enormous influence of the Barro–Lucas–Sargent–Wallace monetary surprise explanation of the business cycle, by 1982 such models had
reached both a theoretical and an empirical impasse. On the theoretical front,
the implausibility of the assumption relating to information confusion was
widely recognized (Okun, 1980; Tobin, 1980b). With sticky prices ruled out
on methodological grounds, new classical models were left without an acceptable explanation of business cycles involving money to output causality.
The doubts cast by Sims (1980) on the causal role of money in money–output
correlations raised further question marks with respect to monetary explanations of the business cycle. On the empirical front, despite some early success, the evidence in support of the proposition that anticipated money was
neutral did not prove to be robust (see Barro, 1993). As a consequence of
these twin difficulties, the monetary surprise model 'has come to be widely
regarded as inapplicable to the industrial nations of today' (McCallum, 1990).
Since the early 1980s the leading new classical explanation of aggregate
instability has focused on real rather than monetary shocks and is called real
business cycle theory. The most well known advocates or contributors to this

approach are Edward Prescott of the University of Minnesota, Finn Kydland of Carnegie-Mellon University, and Charles Plosser, John Long, Robert King, Alan Stockman, Sergio Rebelo and Robert Barro, who are, or have been, associated with the University of Rochester.

6.2 The Transition from Monetary to Real Business Cycle Theory

In response to these developments some new classical theorists have sought to provide a rigorous equilibrium account of the business cycle which is both free from the theoretical weaknesses of the earlier new classical models and empirically robust. The result has been the development of real business cycle theory which replaces the *impulse* mechanism of the earlier models (that is, unanticipated money) with supply-side shocks in the form of random changes in technology. The *propagation* mechanisms of the earlier new classical models are, however, retained and developed. Ironically it was Tobin (1980b) who was one of the first to recognize this unlikely escape route for equilibrium theorists. In criticizing the monetary misperception stories of Lucas, Tobin noted that the 'real equilibrium of a full information model could move around, driven by fluctuations in natural endowments, technologies and tastes' and, if such fluctuations were seriously persistent random processes, the observations generated 'may look like business cycles'. Two years after these comments were published, Kydland and Prescott (1982) launched their non-monetary equilibrium model which, following the subsequent contribution of Long and Plosser (1983), has come to be known as real business cycle theory.

Before moving on to consider real business cycle theory in more detail, it is interesting to note the reaction of two of the leading pioneers of the new classical mark I approach to this second phase of equilibrium theorizing. In Robert Lucas's view, Kydland and Prescott have taken macroeconomic modelling 'into new territory' (Lucas, 1987). However he does regard the exclusive focus of such models on *real* as opposed to *monetary* considerations 'a mistake' and suggests a 'hybrid' model as a fruitful way forward. Nevertheless Lucas warmly approves of the methodology adopted by real business cycle theorists who have followed his own earlier recommendation that an understanding of business cycles is best achieved 'by constructing a *model* in the most literal sense: a fully articulated artificial economy which behaves through time so as to imitate closely the time series behaviour of actual economies' (Lucas, 1977). Such artificial economic systems can serve as laboratories 'in which policies that would be prohibitively expensive to experiment with in actual economies can be tested out at much lower cost' (Lucas, 1980). This is exactly what real business cycle theorists established as their research agenda during the 1980s. As far as Lucas's own work is concerned, his interests have recently been diverted towards the establishment of more coherent micro foundations for monetary theory (the 'new monetary economics') and the analysis of economic growth, an area which has been enjoying a revival of interest following the seminal work of Paul Romer (see P. Romer, 1986; Lucas, 1988, 1993). Lucas now appears to regard the business cycle as a relatively 'minor' problem, at least at the level experienced since 1945. In his view it is far more important to understand the process of economic growth if we are really interested in raising living standards, rather than trying to devise ever more intricate stabilization policies in order to remove the residual amount of business cycle risk (see Lucas, 1987, pp. 30–31). For a discussion of the new monetary economics, the reader is referred to Hoover (1988) who provides a comprehensive survey. Most of the important new classical papers are collected in Hoover (1992).

Robert Barro (1989a, 1989c) now regards the emphasis given by new classical economists during the 1970s to explaining the non-neutrality of money as a priority which was 'misplaced' because the 'new classical approach does not do very well in accounting for an important role for money in business fluctuations'. By the mid-1980s, Barro regarded the contributions of real business cycle theorists as 'especially promising' and representing 'real progress' (Barro, 1984). Furthermore his own work had provided a bridge between the mark I and mark II versions of new classical macroeconomics (see Barro, 1981). In any case the lack of robust empirical success of the earlier models does not invalidate the achievements of the new classical theorists in the 1970s which in Barro's view led to 'superior methods of theoretical and empirical analysis' (Barro, 1984). The three main achievements identified by Barro (1989a) are (i) the application of equilibrium modelling to macroeconomic analysis, (ii) the adoption and promotion of the rational expectations hypothesis, and (iii) the application of game theory to policy making and evaluation.

The first two contributions satisfy the objectives of building macro models on choice-theoretic micro foundations, as well as providing an analytical framework which can better withstand the Lucas (1976) critique. The third area relating to dynamic games has drawn out the importance in policy analysis of the roles of commitment, credibility and reputation as well as clarifying the distinction between rules and discretion. The insights gained relating to the time inconsistency of policy have now been applied to a wide variety of areas other than the conduct of monetary policy. Although Barro is enthusiastic about real business cycle theory, he, like Lucas, has redirected his recent research work towards issues related to economic growth (see Barro, 1991).

For detailed surveys of recent developments in equilibrium business cycle theory, the reader is referred to Walsh (1986), Rush (1987), Plosser (1989), Mullineux and Dickinson (1992), McCallum (1992) and Stadler (1993).

6.3   Real Business Cycle Theory in Historical Perspective

Real business cycle theory, as developed by its modern proponents, is built on the assumption that there are large random fluctuations in the rate of technological progress. These supply-side shocks to the production function generate fluctuations in aggregate output and employment as rational individuals respond to the altered structure of *relative* prices by changing their labour supply and consumption decisions. While this development is in large part a response to the demise of the earlier monetary misperception models and Lucas's call to construct 'artificial economies', it also represents a general revival of interest in the supply side of the macro equation. The idea that business cycles might be driven by *real* rather than *monetary* forces is certainly not a new idea. The real business cycle models inspired by Kydland and Prescott's (1982) seminal paper belong to a long line of analysis which was prominent in the literature prior to Keynes's *General Theory* (see Haberler, 1963, for a superb survey of the interwar business cycle literature). Whereas some economists such as Ralph Hawtrey held to the extreme monetary interpretation of the business cycle, the work of others, in particular Dennis Robertson, emphasized real forces as the engine behind business fluctuations (see Deutscher, 1990; Goodhart and Presley, 1991). While the work of Robertson was not as dismissive of monetary forces as modern real business cycle theory, according to Goodhart and Presley there is a great deal of similarity between the emphasis given by Robertson to technological change and the recent work of the equilibrium theorists. Technological change also played a pivotal role in Joseph Schumpeter's analysis of the short-run instability and long-run dynamics of capitalist development. Since the introduction of new technology influences the long-run growth of productivity as well as causing short-run disequilibrating effects, Schumpeter, like modern real business cycle theorists, viewed cycles and growth as inseparably interrelated (see Schumpeter, 1939).

Following the publication of Keynes's *General Theory*, models of the business cycle were constructed which emphasized the interaction of the multiplier–accelerator mechanism (Samuelson, 1939; Hicks, 1950). These models were also 'real' in that they viewed fluctuations as being driven by *real* aggregate demand, mainly unstable investment expenditures, with monetary factors downgraded and supply-side phenomena providing the constraints which give rise to business cycle turning-points (see Laidler, 1992a). Whatever their merits, multiplier–accelerator models ceased to be a focus of active research by the early 1960s. To a large extent this reflected the impact of the Keynesian revolution, which shifted the focus of macroeconomic analysis away from business cycle phenomena to the development of methods and policies which could improve macroeconomic performance. Such was the confidence of some economists that the business cycle was no longer a major problem that by 1969 some were even considering the question: *Is the Business Cycle Obsolete?* (Bronfenbrenner, 1969). We have already seen that during the 1970s and 1980s the business cycle returned with a vengeance and how dissatisfaction with Keynesian models led to monetarist and new classical counter-revolutions. The most recent developments in business cycle research inspired by equilibrium theorists during the 1980s have proved to be a challenge to *all* the earlier models relying on aggregate demand fluctuations as the main source of instability. Hence real business cycle theory is not only a competitor to the 'old' Keynesian macroeconomics of the synthesis but also represents a serious challenge to all monetarist and early new classical models.

In addition to the above influences, the transition from *monetary* to *real* theories of the business cycle was stimulated by two other important developments. First, the supply shocks associated with the two oil price increases during the 1970s made macroeconomists more aware of the importance of supply-side factors in explaining macroeconomic instability. These events, together with the apparent failure of the demand-oriented Keynesian model to account adequately for rising unemployment accompanied by accelerating inflation, forced *all* macroeconomists to devote considerable research effort to the construction of macroeconomic theories where the supply side has coherent micro foundations (see Chapter 7). Second, the seminal work of Nelson and Plosser (1982) suggested that real shocks may be far more important than monetary shocks in explaining the path of aggregate output over time. Nelson and Plosser argue that the evidence is consistent with the proposition that output follows a path which could best be described as a *random walk*.

6.4   Cycles versus Random Walks

During the 1970s, with the rebirth of interest in business cycle research, economists became more involved with the statistical properties of economic time series. One of the main problems in this work is to separate trend from cycle. The conventional approach has been to imagine that the economy evolves along a path reflecting an underlying trend rate of growth described by Solow's neoclassical model (Solow, 1956). This approach assumes that the long-run trend component of GNP is smooth, with short-run fluctuations about trend being primarily determined by demand shocks. This conventional wisdom was accepted by Keynesian, monetarist and new classical economists alike until the early 1980s. The demand-shock models of all three groups interpret output deviations from trend as *temporary*. Whereas Keynesians feel that such deviations could be severe and prolonged and therefore justify the need for corrective action, monetarists, and especially new classical economists, reject the need for activist stabilization policy, having greater faith in the equilibrating power of market forces. In 1982, Nelson and Plosser published an important paper which challenged this conventional wisdom. The research of Nelson and Plosser into macroeconomic time series led them to conclude that 'macroeconomic models that focus on monetary disturbances as a source of purely transitory fluctuations may never be successful in explaining a large fraction of output variation and that stochastic variation due to real factors is an essential element of any model of macroeconomic fluctuations'.

Nelson and Plosser reached this important conclusion because in their research into US data they were *unable to reject* the hypothesis that GNP follows a *random walk*. How does this conclusion differ from the conventional approach? The view that reversible cyclical fluctuations can account for most of the short-term movements of real GNP can be represented by equation (6.1).

$$Y_t = g_t + bY_{t-1} + z_t \tag{6.1}$$

where t represents time, g and b are constants and z represents random shocks which have a zero mean. In equation (6.1) g_t represents the underlying average growth rate of GNP which describes the deterministic trend. Suppose there is some shock to z_t which causes output to rise above trend at time t. We assume that the shock lasts one period only. Since Y_t depends on Y_{t-1} the shock will be transmitted forward in time, generating serial correlation. But since in the traditional approach $0 < b < 1$ the impact of the shock on output will eventually die out and output will eventually return to its trend rate of growth. In this case output is said to be 'trend reverting' or 'trend stationary' (see Blanchard and Fischer, 1989).

The impact of a shock on the path of income in the trend stationary case is illustrated in Figure 6.1, where we assume an expansionary monetary shock occurs at time t_1. Notice that Y eventually reverts to its trend path and therefore this case is consistent with the natural rate hypothesis which states that deviations from the natural level of output caused by unanticipated monetary shocks will be temporary.

In contrast to the above, Nelson and Plosser argue that most of the changes in GNP that we observe are *permanent*, in that there is no tendency for output to revert to its former trend following a shock. In this case GNP is said to evolve as a statistical process known as a *random walk*. Equation (6.2) shows a random walk with drift for GNP.

$$Y_t = g_t + Y_{t-1} + z_t \tag{6.2}$$

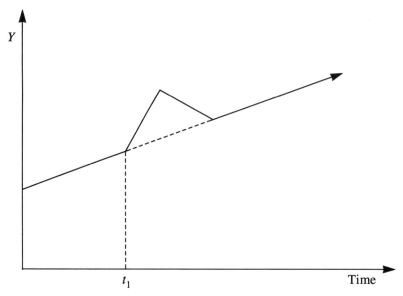

Figure 6.1   The path of output in the 'trend reverting' case

In equation (6.2) g_t reflects the 'drift' of output and, with Y_t also being dependent on Y_{t-1} any shock to z_t will raise output permanently. Suppose a shock raises the level of output at time t_1 in Figure 6.2. Since output in the next period is determined by output in period t_1, the rise in output persists in every future period. In the case of a random walk with drift, output is said to have a '*unit root*; that is, the coefficient on the lagged output term in equation (6.2) is set equal to unity, $b = 1$. The identification of unit roots is assumed to be a manifestation of shocks to the production function.

These findings of Nelson and Plosser have radical implications for business cycle theory. If shocks to productivity growth due to technological change are frequent and random then the path of output following a random walk will exhibit features which resemble a business cycle. *In this case, however, the observed fluctuations in GNP are fluctuations in the natural (trend) rate of output, not deviations of output from a smooth deterministic trend.* What looks like output fluctuating around a smooth trend is in fact fluctuations in the trend itself due to a series of permanent shocks, with each permanent productivity shock determining a new growth path. Whereas, following Solow's seminal work, economists have traditionally separated the analysis of growth from the analysis of fluctuations, the work of Nelson and Plosser suggests that the economic forces determining the trend are not different from those causing fluctuations. *Since permanent changes in GNP*

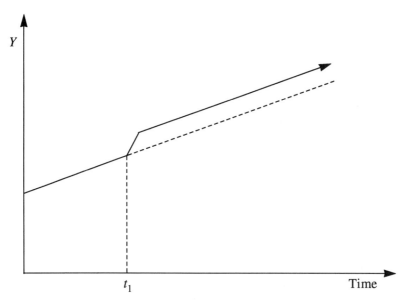

Figure 6.2   The path of output where shocks have a permanent influence

cannot result from monetary shocks in a new classical world because of the neutrality proposition, the main forces causing instability must be real shocks. Nelson and Plosser interpret their findings as placing limits on the importance of monetary theories of the business cycle and that real disturbances are likely to be a much more important source of output fluctuations. If there are important interactions between the process of growth and business cycles, the conventional practice of separating growth theory from the analysis of fluctuations is illegitimate. By ending the distinction between trend and cycle, real business cycle theorists have begun to integrate the theory of growth and fluctuations (see King *et al.*, 1988a, 1988b; Plosser, 1989).

6.5 Supply-side Shocks

Cyclical instability can arise because of shocks to aggregate demand or shocks to aggregate supply, or some combination of the two. On the demand side, the shocks may originate from instability in some component of the *IS* curve, as stressed by Keynes and most of the earlier Keynesian models, or they may originate from instability on the monetary side, as described by the *LM* curve and emphasized by monetarists. On the supply side, we can imagine a variety of shocks which could result in significant changes in productivity:

1. Unfavourable developments in the physical environment which adversely affect agricultural output. This type of shock would include natural disasters such as earthquakes, drought and floods, such as those in the Mississippi basin during 1993.
2. Significant changes in the price of energy, such as the oil price 'hikes' of 1973 and 1979 and the subsequent reduction in 1986. James Hamilton (1983) has argued that most US recessions since 1945 have been preceded by energy price increases.
3. War, political upheaval, or labour unrest which disrupts the existing performance and structure of the economy, as with the disruption experienced in the former Yugoslavia and Soviet Union or the strikes and labour unrest in the UK during the 1970s and 1984.
4. Government regulations, such as import quotas, which damage incentives and divert entrepreneurial talent towards rent-seeking activities.
5. Productivity shocks generated by changes in the quality of the capital and labour inputs, new management practices, the development of new products and the introduction of new techniques of production.

While some or all of the above may be important at specific points in time, it is the fifth category which we can broadly define as 'technological change' and which under normal circumstances we can expect to be the driving-force on the supply side over the longer term for advanced industrial economies. It should not be forgotten that politically stable economies which are normally free from natural disasters are still characterized by aggregate fluctuations.

6.6 Real Business Cycle Theory

Although the second phase of new classical macroeconomics has switched emphasis away from monetary explanations of the business cycle, the more recently developed equilibrium models have retained and refined the other new classical building blocks. The new brand of equilibrium theories have the following general features:

1. Agents aim to maximize their utility or profits, subject to prevailing resource constraints.
2. Agents form expectations rationally and do not suffer informational asymmetries. Agents may still face a signal extraction problem (for example, whether a particular productivity shock is temporary or permanent) but information concerning the path of the general price level is publicly available.
3. Price flexibility ensures continuous market clearing so that equilibrium *always* prevails.

4. Fluctuations in aggregate output and employment are driven by large random changes in the available production technology and a variety of propagation mechanisms carry forward the impact of the initial impulse.
5. Fluctuations in employment reflect *voluntary* changes in the number of hours people want to work. Work and leisure are assumed to be highly substitutable over time.
6. Monetary policy is irrelevant, having no influence on real variables, that is, money is neutral.
7. The distinction between the short run and the long run in the analysis of economic fluctuations and trends is abandoned.

It can be seen from the above that the major changes are with respect to (i) the dominant impulse factor, with technological shocks replacing monetary shocks; (ii) the abandonment of the emphasis given to imperfect information as regards the general price level which played such a crucial role in the earlier monetary misperception models inspired by Lucas; and (iii) the breaking down of the short run–long run dichotomy in macroeconomic analysis by integrating the theory of growth with the theory of fluctuations. The lack of clear supporting evidence from econometric work on the causal role of money in economic fluctuations was generally interpreted as providing a strong case for shifting the direction of research towards models where real forces play a crucial role. As we have already seen, this case was further strengthened by the findings of Nelson and Plosser (1982) that most macroeconomic time series are better described as a random walk, rather than as fluctuations or deviations from deterministic trends. Real business cycle theorists also claim that their theories provide a better explanation of the 'stylized facts' which characterize aggregate fluctuations. Indeed they have challenged much of the conventional wisdom with respect to what are the stylized facts (see section 1.10, and section 6.11 below).

6.6.1 Technological shocks
Following Frisch (1933) real business cycle theorists distinguish between *impulse* and *propagation* mechanisms. An impulse mechanism is the initial shock which causes a variable to deviate from its steady state value. A propagation mechanism consists of those forces which carry the effects of the shock forward through time and cause the deviation from the steady state to persist. Although some versions of real business cycle theory allow for real demand shocks, such as changes in preferences or government expenditures, to act as the impulse mechanism, these models are more typically driven by exogenous productivity shocks. These stochastic fluctuations in factor productivity are the result of large random variations in the rate of technological change. The conventional Solow neoclassical growth model postulates that the growth of

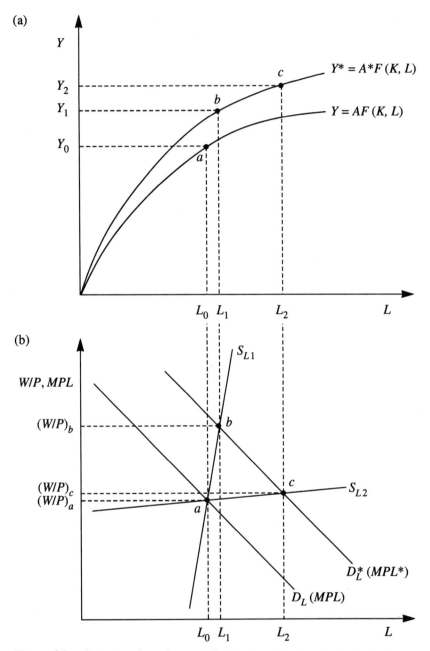

Figure 6.3   Output and employment fluctuations due to a technological shock

output per worker over prolonged periods depends on technological progress which is assumed to take place *smoothly* over time. Real business cycle theorists reject this view and emphasize the *erratic* nature of technological change which they regard as the major cause of changes in aggregate output.

To see how aggregate output and employment vary in a real business cycle model, consider Figure 6.3. Panel (a) of Figure 6.3 illustrates the impact of a beneficial technological shock which shifts the production function from Y to Y^*. The impact of this shift on the marginal product of labour and hence the demand for labour is shown in panel (b). By increasing the demand for labour a productivity shock raises employment as well as output. How much employment expands will depend on the elasticity of labour supply with respect to the current real wage. The 'stylized facts' of the business cycle indicate that *small* procyclical variations in the *real wage* are associated with *large* procyclical variations of *employment*. Thus a crucial requirement which is necessary for real business cycle theory to be consistent with these facts is for the labour supply schedule to be highly elastic with respect to the real wage, as indicated in panel (b) by S_{L2}. In this case a technology shock will cause output to expand from Y_0 to Y_2 with the real wage increasing from $(W/P)_a$ to $(W/P)_c$, and employment increasing from L_0 to L_2. If the labour supply schedule is relatively inelastic, as shown by S_{L1} large variations of the real wage and small changes in employment would result from a technological shock. However this does not fit the stylized facts.

It is clear that, in order for real business cycle theories to explain the substantial variations in employment observed during aggregate fluctuations, there must be significant *intertemporal substitution of leisure*. Since in these models it is assumed that prices and wages are completely flexible, the labour market is always in equilibrium. In such a framework workers *choose* unemployment or employment in accordance with their preferences and the opportunities which are available.

6.6.2   The intertemporal labour substitution hypothesis

According to real business cycle theorists, the large response of the labour supply to small changes in the real wage results from the intertemporal substitution of labour which acts as a powerful propagation mechanism. According to this hypothesis, first introduced by Lucas and Rapping (1969), households shift their labour supply over time, being more willing to work when real wages are *temporarily* high and working fewer hours when real wages are *temporarily* low. Why should this be the case?

Since the aggregate supply of labour depends on the labour supply decisions of individuals, we need to consider the various factors which influence the amount of labour individuals choose to supply. The benefits of current employment relate primarily (but obviously not entirely) to the income earned which allows the individual worker to consume goods and services. In order to earn income, workers will need to allocate less of their time to leisure, a term used to encapsulate all non-income-producing activities. The utility function for the representative worker indicates that consumption and leisure both yield utility. But in making their labour supply decisions workers will consider future as well as current consumption and leisure. In taking into account the future when deciding how much labour to supply in the current period, workers will need to consider how much the current real wage offers are above or below the norm. The *substitution* effect of a higher real wage offer will tend to increase the quantity of labour supplied. However, since higher real wages also make workers feel wealthier, this will tend to suppress the supply of labour. This *wealth* or *income* effect works in the opposite direction to the substitution effect. The impact of an increase in the current real wage on the amount of labour supplied will clearly depend on which of the above effects predominates. Real business cycle theorists distinguish between *permanent* and *temporary* changes in the real wage in order to analyse how rational maximizing individuals respond over time to changes in their economic circumstances which are brought about by technological shocks. The intertemporal labour substitution hypothesis suggests two things. First, if a technological shock is transitory, so that the current above-normal real wage offers are temporary, workers will 'make hay while the sun shines' and substitute work for current leisure. Less work will be offered in the future when the real wage is expected to be lower and hence the decision to supply more labour now is also a decision to consume more leisure in the future and less leisure now. Therefore real business cycle theory predicts a *large* supply response from *temporary* changes in the real wage. Permanent technological shocks, by raising the future real wage, induce wealth effects which will tend to lower the current labour supply (see Abel and Bernanke, 1992, pp. 363–81).

Second, some theorists have stressed the importance of real interest rates on labour supply in flexible price models (see Barro, 1981, 1993). An increase in the real interest rate encourages households to supply more labour in the current period, since the value of income earned from working today relative to tomorrow has risen. This effect would show up as a shift of the labour supply curve to the right (see Hall and Taylor, 1993, pp. 451–61).

We can therefore express the general form of the labour supply function in the real business cycle model as equation (6.3), where r = real interest rate:

$$S_L = S_L (W/P, r) \tag{6.3}$$

The appropriate intertemporal relative price is given by (6.4):

$$(1 + r)(W/P)_1/(W/P)_2 \tag{6.4}$$

According to (6.4) any shocks to the economy which cause either the real interest rate to rise or the current real wage $(W/P)_1$ to be temporarily high relative to the future real wage $(W/P)_2$ will increase labour supply and hence employment (see Mankiw, 1994).

6.7   The Real Business Cycle Aggregate Demand and Supply Model

In a world of rational expectations, perfect price flexibility and full informa-tion relating to the money supply, the neutrality of money is guaranteed. Since nominal variables do not influence real variables, output and employ-ment are entirely determined by the real forces which underlie the production function and supply of factors of production. An IS–LM model which con-forms to such a world is shown in Figure 6.4. The *IS* curve shows that real aggregate demand (*RAD*) is a declining function of the real interest rate. The *LM/P* curve will always shift so as to intersect the *IS* curve at the full employment level of output, providing prices are perfectly flexible. The position of the real aggregate supply curve (*RAS*) is determined by the posi-tion of the production function and the willingness of workers to supply labour (see Figure 6.3). A technological improvement which shifts the pro-duction function will cause the *RAS* curve to shift to the right and any point on *RAS* represents a position of equilibrium (full) employment. Because the

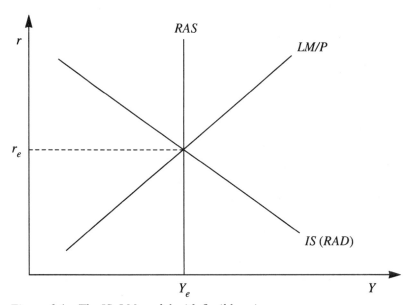

Figure 6.4   The IS–LM model with flexible prices

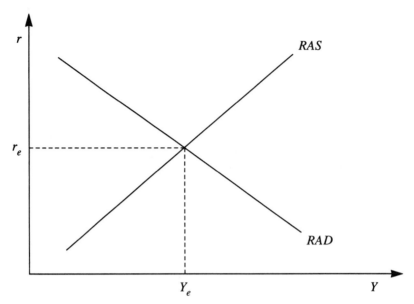

Figure 6.5   The real business cycle aggregate demand and supply model

price level will automatically adjust so that the *LM/P* curve will always intersect the *RAD* curve at the full employment level of output, we need only consider the *RAD* and *RAS* curves. The real business cycle aggregate demand and supply model is shown in Figure 6.5.

The *RAS* curve is now shown as a positive function of the real interest rate, since this influences the intertemporal relative price of labour. Equation (6.4) indicates that the current supply of labour will increase if the real interest rate rises. Several important points are worth noting:

1. This model is entirely real, since the quantity of money and the aggregate price level have no impact on aggregate output or employment.
2. The distinction between the long-run and short-run aggregate supply curves which play an important role in monetarist, early new classical and new Keynesian models is abandoned.
3. The RAS schedule traces out a range of equilibrium positions which are all consistent with full employment.
4. The assumption of price flexibility allows the real interest rate to equilibrate the goods market, so that *RAD* = *RAS*.
5. In explaining fluctuations in output, real business cycle theorists have emphasized *shifts* of the *RAS* curve due to technological shocks (see Kydland and Prescott, 1982; Plosser, 1989).

6. Some equilibrium theorists have shown that real aggregate demand shocks can also be important during some periods as an explanation of aggregate fluctuations. For example, Barro has shown how a *temporary* increase in government expenditure can cause output to expand (see Barro, 1993, chap. 12). He concludes that 'variations in government purchases play a major role during wartime but not in peacetime business fluctuations'.

Figure 6.6 represents the basic market clearing diagram which is central to the modern new classical equilibrium approach to macroeconomic analysis. Following Barro (1993), let Ys represent real aggregate supply and Cd represent real aggregate demand in the commodity market. The market clearing condition is given by (6.5)

$$Cd\ (r,\ldots) = Ys\ (r,\ldots) \tag{6.5}$$

In equation (6.5) variables omitted and indicated by ... include the various wealth and substitution effects which result from shocks to the production function or government expenditure and so on. The response of Cd and Ys to changes in the real rate of interest is illustrated by movements *along* the

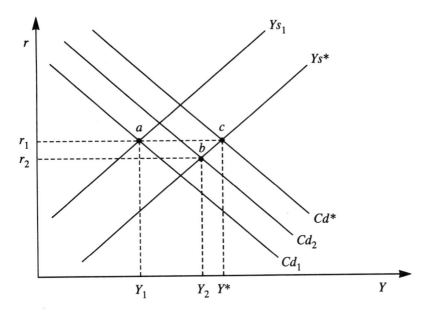

Figure 6.6   The impact of temporary and permanent technological shocks in the real business cycle model

aggregate demand and supply curves. The *Cd* and *Ys* curves will *shift* if any of the other variables which influence *Cd* and *Ys* change, as with a shock to the production function or an increase in government expenditure.

To see how a technological shock will influence aggregate output in this model, consider Figure 6.6 where, starting from point *a*, we assume a beneficial technological change takes place of the type considered in Figure 6.3. Such a shock will clearly shift the *Ys* curve to the right from Ys_1 to Ys^*. If the technology shock is seen to be *temporary*, the impact on consumer demand of the wealth effect is likely to be small and the resultant rightward shift of *Cd* will be less than the shift of *Ys*: a movement from point *a* to *b*. Output rises from Y_1 to Y_2 and the real interest rate falls to r_2. If the technology shock is seen to be *permanent* then the wealth effect of the shock on consumption is more powerful. In this case the rightward shifts of *Ys* and *Cd* are likely to be of a similar magnitude, leading to a rise in output from Y_1 to Y^* but with the real interest rate remaining at r_1: a movement from point *a* to *c*. According to Barro, this model does reasonably well in accounting for the stylized facts of business fluctuations. For a detailed discussion of these issues, see Barro (1993), especially pp. 232–41. Readers should confirm for themselves the likely outcome of a negative shock to the production function.

6.8 Calibrating the model

Real business cycle theorists have not generally attempted to provide models capable of conventional econometric testing but have instead tended to focus on providing numerical examples of a more general theory of fluctuations. In order to examine the *quantitative* implications of their models, real business cycle theorists have developed a method known as *calibration* (see Kydland and Prescott, 1982; Plosser, 1989; Abel and Bernanke, 1992). The calibration method involves the following exercise:

1. Construct a classical equilibrium model of the aggregate economy such as the one represented in Figures 6.5 and 6.6.
2. Provide specific algebraic forms of the functions used to represent production and consumption decisions. For example, a specific Cobb–Douglas production function is used by Plosser (1989).
3. The calibration exercise then involves simulating the effect of subjecting the model to a series of random technology shocks created by a computer with a random number generator.
4. The impact that these shocks have on the key macroeconomic variables is then traced out so that the results can be compared with the actual behaviour of the main macroeconomic time series.

These simulations indicate that a competitive economy hit by repeated technology shocks can exhibit the kind of fluctuations which are actually observed, and those carried out by Prescott and Plosser have produced some impressive results in that the model is able to mimic an actual economy with respect to some important time series data. Indeed real business cycle theorists claim that recent research relating to the stylized facts of the business cycle supports the general predictions of 'real' as opposed to 'monetary' theories of fluctuations. But, as we noted earlier, the correlation between money and output is an accepted stylized fact. How do real business cycle theories deal with the *apparent* causal influence of money?

6.9 Real Business Cycle Theory and the Neutrality of Money

Monetary neutrality is an important property of real business cycle models. In such models neutrality applies to the short run as well as the long run. In the late 1970s, leading representatives from the other major schools of thought, such as Tobin, Friedman and Lucas, all agreed that the rate of growth of the money supply has real effects on the economy and plays an important role in any explanation of output fluctuations. There was of course considerable disagreement on the nature and strength of the relationship between money and output and on the relative power of monetary and fiscal policy, but economists of all persuasions took it for granted that monetary phenomena were crucial to business cycle research. The accepted business cycle stylized fact that money and output exhibit positive correlation, with money leading output, was taken by many as strong evidence of causality running from money to output (Sims, 1972). The research of Friedman and Schwartz (1963, 1982) added further weight to the monetarist claim that monetary instability lay at the heart of real instability. However the well established positive association between money and aggregate output may simply indicate that the money supply is responding to economic activity rather than the reverse. In such a situation money is *endogenous* and the money to output correlations that we observe is evidence of *reverse causation*; that is, expectations of *future* output expansion lead to *current* increases in the money supply. According to real business cycle theories, the demand for money expands during business expansions and elicits an accommodating response from the money supply, especially if the monetary authorities are targeting interest rates (see Barro, 1993, chap. 18). The impetus to downgrade the causal role of money was also given support from the evidence emerging from vector autoregression analysis which indicated that, once interest rates were included among the variables in the estimated system, money ceased to have strong predictive power. The contributions from Sims (1980, 1983) and Litterman and Weiss (1985) provided important evidence which advocates of the real business cycle approach point to in support of their preference for a non-monetary approach to business cycle modelling (see also Eichenbaum and Singleton, 1986).

Initially real business cycle models were constructed without monetary features. Kydland and Prescott (1982) originally set out to construct a model which included only real variables but which could then be extended to take into account nominal variables. But after building their real model Kydland and Prescott concluded that the addition of a monetary sector may not be necessary since business cycles can be explained almost entirely by real quantities (see Prescott, 1986). Although the Long and Plosser (1983) model contains no monetary sector, King and Plosser (1984) explain the historical association between money and output as reflecting an endogenous response of money to output. Building on the work of Black (1987) and Fama (1980), King and Plosser reject the orthodox monetarist interpretation of money to output causality. In their model, 'monetary services are privately produced intermediate goods whose quantities rise and fall with real economic developments'. King and Plosser view the financial industry as providing a flow of accounting services that help to facilitate market transactions. By grafting a financial sector onto a general equilibrium model of production and consumption, King and Plosser show how a positive correlation between real production, credit and transaction services will arise with the timing paths in these co-movements dependent on the source of the variation in real output. Their model implies that the volume of *inside* money (bank deposits) will vary positively with output. Furthermore the fact that financial services can be produced more rapidly than the final product means that an expansion of financial services is likely to occur *prior* to the expansion of output. The stock of bank deposits is therefore highly correlated with output and a *leading* indicator in the business cycle.

This corresponds with the evidence presented by Friedman and Schwartz (1963) but from an entirely different perspective. Whereas in monetarist models *exogenous* changes in the quantity of money play an important role in causing movements in output, King and Plosser stress the *endogenous* response of deposits to *planned* movements in output. In effect the output of the financial sector moves in line with the output of other sectors. *Paradoxically the argument that money is endogenous is a major proposition of the Post-Keynesian school* (see Chapter 8, and Kaldor, 1970). For example, with respect to this very issue of money to output causality, Joan Robinson (1971) suggested that the correlations could be explained 'in quantity theory terms if the equation were read right-handed. Thus we might suggest that a marked rise in the level of activity is likely to be preceded by an increase in the supply of money'. In an unholy alliance, both Post-Keynesian and real business cycle theorists appear to agree with Robinson that the quantity theory

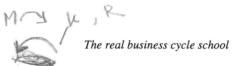

equation ($MV = PY$) should be read in causal terms from right to left. Orthodox Keynesians have also raised the issue of timing in questioning money to output causality. Tobin (1970) showed how an ultra-Keynesian model could be constructed where the money supply is an endogenous response to income changes. In this model changes in real economic activity are *preceded* by expansions of the money supply as firms borrow funds from the banking sector in order to finance their planned expansions. Tobin demonstrated that to infer from the timing evidence that changes in the money supply are causing changes in real economic activity was to fall foul of the *post hoc ergo propter hoc* (after this therefore because of this) fallacy. However, although Tobin used this argument to challenge what he considered to be the exaggerated claims of monetarists relating to the power of monetary forces, he certainly did not conclude that money does not matter for business fluctuations (see also Cagan, 1993).

More recently Kydland and Prescott (1990) have questioned the whole basis of this debate relating to timing and causality by rejecting one of the 'established' stylized facts of the business cycle relating to monetary aggregates. They argue, 'There is no evidence that either the monetary base or M1 leads the cycle although some economists still believe this monetary myth.' Clearly such claims represent a serious challenge to conventional views concerning the role of money. This 'blasphemy' has been rejected by Keynesian and monetarist economists alike who, as a result of real business cycle analysis, have been thrown into an alliance which would have seemed unthinkable during the intense debates which took place between Tobin and Friedman during the 1960s and early 1970s. (For a defence of the earlier Friedman and Schwartz research, see Schwartz, 1992.)

In concluding this section we should note Plosser's (1989) view that 'the role of money in an equilibrium theory of growth and fluctuations is not well understood and thus remains an open issue'.

6.10   Measuring Technological Shocks: the Solow Residual

If technological shocks are the primary cause of business cycles then it is important to identify and measure the rate of technological progress. Given the structure of real business cycle models, the key parameter is the variance of the technology shock. Prescott (1986) suggests that Solow's method of measuring this variance is an acceptable and reasonable approach. Solow's (1957) technique was to define technological change as changes in aggregate output minus the sum of the weighted contributions of the labour and capital inputs. In short, the *Solow residual* measures that part of a change in aggregate output which cannot be explained by changes in the measurable quantities of capital and labour inputs. The derivation of the Solow residual can be shown as follows. The aggregate production function in equation (6.6) shows that output (Y) is dependent on the inputs of capital (K), labour (L) and the currently available technology (A) which acts as an index of *total factor productivity*:

$$Y = AF(K, L) \qquad (6.6)$$

Output will change if A, K or L change. One specific type of production function frequently used in empirical studies relating to growth accounting is the Cobb–Douglas production function, which is written as follows:

$$Y = AK^\delta L^{1-\delta}, \text{ where } 0 < \delta < 1 \qquad (6.7)$$

In equation (6.7) the exponent on the capital shock δ measures the *elasticity of output with respect to capital* and the exponent on the labour input $(1 - \delta)$ measures the *elasticity of output with respect to labour*. The weights δ and $1 - \delta$ measure the income shares of capital and labour, respectively (see Dornbusch and Fischer, 1994, pp. 292–3 for a simple derivation). Since these weights sum to unity this indicates that this is a constant returns to scale production function. Hence an equal percentage increase in both factor inputs (K and L) will increase Y by the same percentage. By rearranging equation (6.7) we can represent the productivity index which we need to measure as equation (6.8):

$$A = \frac{Y}{K^\delta L^{1-\delta}} \qquad (6.8)$$

Because there is no direct way of measuring A, it has to be estimated as a *residual*. Data relating to output and the capital and labour inputs are available. Estimates of δ and hence $1 - \delta$ can be acquired from historical data. Since the growth rate of the product of the inputs will be the growth rate of A plus the growth rate of K^δ plus the growth rate of $L^{1-\delta}$, equation (6.8) can be rewritten as (6.9) which is the basic growth accounting equation which has been used in numerous empirical studies of the sources of economic growth (see Dennison, 1985; Maddison, 1987).

$$\frac{\Delta Y}{Y} = \frac{\Delta A}{A} + \delta \frac{\Delta K}{K} + (1-\delta) \frac{\Delta L}{L} \qquad (6.9)$$

Equation (6.9) is simply the Cobb–Douglas production function written in a form representing rates of change. It shows that the growth of output ($\Delta Y/Y$) depends on the contribution of changes in total factor productivity ($\Delta A/A$), changes in the weighted contribution of capital ($\delta \Delta K/K$) and changes in the weighted contribution of labour $(1 - \delta)(\Delta L/L)$. By writing down equation (6.8) in terms of rates of change or by rearranging equation (6.9), which amounts to the same thing, we can obtain an equation from which the growth of total factor productivity (technological change) can be estimated as a residual. This is shown in equation (6.10).

$$\frac{\Delta A}{A} = \frac{\Delta Y}{Y} - \left[\delta \frac{\Delta K}{K} + 1 - \delta \frac{\Delta L}{L} \right] \qquad (6.10)$$

In equation (6.10) the Solow residual equals $\Delta A/A$. Real business cycle theorists have used estimates of the Solow residual as a measure of technological progress. Prescott's (1986) analysis suggests that 'the process on the percentage change in the technology process is a random walk with drift plus some serially uncorrelated measurement error'. Plosser (1989) also argues that 'it seems acceptable to view the level of productivity as a random walk'. Figure 6.7 reproduces Plosser's estimates for the annual growth rates of technology and output for the period 1955–85 in the USA. These findings *appear* to support the real business cycle view that aggregate fluctuations are

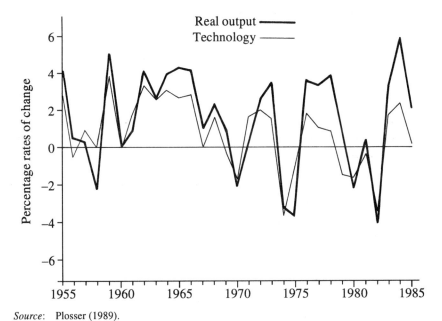

Source: Plosser (1989).

Figure 6.7 *The annual growth rates of technology and output in the USA, 1955–85*

induced, in the main, by technological disturbances. In a more recent study. Kydland and Prescott (1991) find that about 70 per cent of the variance in US output in the post-war period can be accounted for by variations in the Solow residual. We will consider criticisms of the work in this area in section 6.13 below. In particular Keynesians offer an alternative explanation of the observed procyclical behaviour of productivity.

6.11   Real Business Cycle Theory and the Stylized Facts

The rapidly expanding business cycle literature during the 1980s provoked considerable controversy and discussion with respect to the ability of different macroeconomic models to explain the 'stylized facts'. As Danthine and Donaldson (1993) point out, the real business cycle programme 'has forced theorists to recognise how incomplete our knowledge of business cycle phenomena actually was' and a major achievement of this recent literature has been to 'free us to reconsider what we know about the business cycle'. Recent work in this area has called into question much of the conventional wisdom with respect to what are the established stylized facts. Controversy also exists over which model of the business cycle best explains the agreed stylized facts. For a detailed discussion of these issues, the reader is referred to Greenwald and Stiglitz (1988), Kydland and Prescott (1990), Hoover (1991), Blackburn and Ravn (1992), Smith (1992), Zarnowitz (1992b) and Danthine and Donaldson (1993). Here we will briefly discuss the controversy relating to the cyclical behaviour of real wages and prices.

In both orthodox Keynesian and monetarist macroeconomic theories where aggregate demand disturbances drive the business cycle, the real wage is predicted to be *counter-cyclical*. In the *General Theory* an expansion of employment is associated with a decline in the real wage and the Keynesian models of the neoclassical synthesis also assume that the economy is operating along the aggregate labour demand curve so that the real wage must vary counter-cyclically. The theories associated with Friedman's monetarism, as well as some early new classical and new Keynesian models, also incorporate features which imply a counter-cyclical real wage (see Fischer, 1977; Phelps and Taylor, 1977). In Gordon's (1993) view, apart from the big oil shocks of the 1970s, there is no systematic movement of real wages but, if anything, 'there is slight tendency of prices to rise more than wages in booms, implying counter-cyclical real wages'. However Kydland and Prescott (1990) find that the real wage behaves in a 'reasonably strong' procyclical manner, a finding which is consistent with shifts of the production function. The current consensus (see Fischer, 1988) is that the real wage is 'slightly procyclical', and this poses problems for both traditional monetary explanations of the business cycle and real business cycle theory. If the real wage is moderately procyclical then shocks to the production function can significantly influence employment only if the labour supply curve is highly elastic (see panel (b) of Figure 6.3). However the empirical evidence does not offer strong support for the significant intertemporal substitution required for real business cycles to mimic the large variations in employment which characterize business cycles (see Mankiw *et al.*, 1985; Altonji, 1986; Nickell, 1990).

While the behaviour of the real wage over the cycle has been controversial ever since Dunlop (1938) and Tarshis (1939) debated this issue with Keynes (1939), the assumption that prices (and inflation) are generally procyclical was accepted by economists of varying persuasions. The procyclical behaviour of prices is a fundamental feature of Keynesian, monetarist and the monetary misperception version of new classical models. Mankiw (1989) has argued that, in the absence of recognizable supply shocks, such as the OPEC oil price rises in the 1970s, the procyclical behaviour of the inflation rate is a 'well documented fact'. Lucas (1981) also lists the procyclical nature of prices and inflation as a basic stylized fact. In sharp contrast to these views, Kydland and Prescott (1990) show that, in the USA during the period 1954–89, 'the price level has displayed a clear *counter-cyclical* pattern'. This leads them to the following controversial conclusion: 'We caution that any theory in which procyclical prices figure crucially in accounting for postwar business cycle fluctuations is doomed to failure.' This conclusion is supported in a recent study of UK data by Blackburn and Ravn (1992) who describe the conventional wisdom with respect to the procyclical behaviour of the price level as 'a fiction'. In their view the traditional presumption that prices are procyclical is overwhelmingly contradicted by the evidence and they interpret their findings as posing a 'serious challenge' for monetary explanations of the business cycle. The evidence presented by Backus and Kehoe (1992) and Smith (1992) is also supportive of the real business cycle view. (For a defence of the conventional view, see Chadha and Prasad, 1993.)

To see why evidence of a counter-cyclical price level is supportive of real business cycle models, consider Figure 6.8. Here we utilize the conventional aggregate demand and supply framework with the price level on the vertical axis. Because prices and wages are perfectly flexible, the aggregate supply curve (AS) is completely inelastic with respect to the price level. The economy is initially operating at the intersection of AD and AS_0. If the economy is hit by a negative supply shock which shifts the AS curve from AS_0 to AS_2, the equilibrium level of output falls from Y_0 to Y_2 for a *given* money supply. Aggregate demand and supply are brought into equilibrium by a rise in the price level from P_0 to P_2. A favourable supply shock which shifts the AS curve from AS_0 to AS_1 will lead to a fall in the price level for a *given* money supply. The equilibrium positions a, b and c indicate that the price level will be counter-cyclical if real disturbances cause an aggregate supply curve to

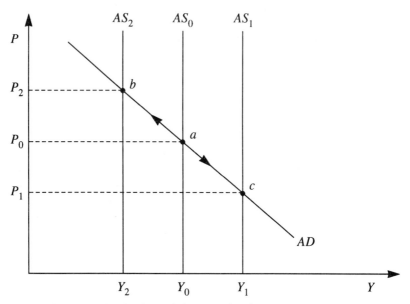

Figure 6.8 Supply shocks and the price level

shift along a given aggregate demand curve. Referring back to panel (b) of Figure (2.6), it is clear that fluctuations brought about by shifts of the aggregate demand curve generate observations of a procyclical price level. Keynesians argue that the counter-cyclical behaviour of the price level following the clearly observable oil shocks of the 1970s does not present a problem for the conventional aggregate demand and supply model and that such effects had already been incorporated into their models by 1975 (see Gordon, 1975; Phelps, 1978; Blinder, 1988a). What Keynesians object to is the suggestion that the business cycle is *predominantly* caused by supply shocks. The consensus view that prices are sometimes procyclical and sometimes counter-cyclical indicates to an eclectic observer that both demand and supply shocks are important in different periods.

6.12 The Policy Implications of Real Business Cycle Theory

Before 1980, although there was considerable intellectual warfare between macroeconomic theorists, there was an underlying consensus relating to three important issues. First, economists viewed fluctuations in aggregate output as *temporary* deviations from some underlying trend rate of growth. An important determinant of this trend was seen to be an exogenously determined smooth rate of technological progress. Second, aggregate instability in the form of business cycles was assumed to be socially undesirable since they reduced economic welfare. Instability could and therefore should be reduced by appropriate policies. Third, monetary forces are an important factor when it comes to explaining the business cycle. Orthodox Keynesian, monetarist and new classical economists accepted all three of these pillars of conventional wisdom. Of course these same economists did not agree about *how* aggregate instability should be reduced. Neither was there agreement about the transmission mechanism which linked money to real output. In Keynesian and monetarist models, non-neutralities were explained by adaptive expectations and the slow adjustment of wages and prices to nominal demand shocks. In the new classical market-clearing models of the 1970s, non-neutralities were explained as a consequence of agents having imperfect information. When it came to policy discussions about how to stabilize the economy, monetarists and new classical economists favoured a fixed monetary growth rate *rule*, whereas Keynesian economists argued in favour of *discretion* (see Modigliani, 1986). The main impact of the first wave of new classical theory on policy analysis was to provide a more robust theoretical case against activism (see Kydland and Prescott, 1977). The political business cycle literature also questioned whether politicians could be trusted to use stabilization policy in order to reduce fluctuations, rather than as a means for maximizing their own interests (Nordhaus, 1975).

During the 1980s everything changed. The work of Nelson and Plosser (1982) and Kydland and Prescott (1982) caused economists to start asking the question, 'Is there a business cycle?' Real business cycle theorists find the use of the term 'business cycle' unfortunate (Prescott, 1986) because it suggests there is a phenomenon to explain which is independent of the forces determining economic growth. Real business cycle theorists, by providing an integrated approach to growth and fluctuations, have shown that large fluctuations in output and employment over relatively short time periods are 'what standard neoclassical theory predicts'. Indeed it 'would be a puzzle if the economy did not display large fluctuations in output and employment' (Prescott, 1986). Since instability is the outcome of rational economic agents responding optimally to changes in the economic environment, observed fluctuations should *not* be viewed as welfare-reducing deviations from some ideal trend path of output. In a competitive theory of fluctuations the equilibria are Pareto optimal (see Long and Plosser, 1983; Plosser, 1989). The idea that the government should in any way attempt to reduce these fluctuations is therefore anathema to real business cycle theorists. Such policies are almost certain to reduce welfare. As Prescott (1986) has argued: 'The policy implication of this research is that costly efforts at stabilisation are likely to be counter-productive. Economic fluctuations are optimal responses to uncertainty in the rate of technological progress.' *This turns conventional thinking about economic fluctuations completely on its head.* If fluctuations are Pareto efficient responses to shocks to the production function largely resulting from technological change, then monetary factors are no longer relevant in order to explain such instability; nor can monetary policy have any real effects. Money is super-neutral. Since workers can decide how much they want to work, observed unemployment is always voluntary. Indeed the observed fluctuating path of GNP is nothing more than a continuously moving full employment equilibrium. In real business cycle theory there can be no meaning to a stated government objective such as 'full employment' because the economy is already there! Of course the real business cycle view is that the government can do a great deal of harm if it creates various distortions through its taxing and spending policies. It should also be noted that in real business cycle models a temporary increase in government purchases will increase output and employment because the labour supply increases in response to the higher real interest rate brought about by higher (real) aggregate demand (see Barro, 1993, chap. 12, for a detailed discussion of this view).

If technological change is the key factor in determining both growth and fluctuations, we certainly need to develop a better understanding of the factors which determine the rate of technological progress, including institutional structures and arrangements. To real business cycle theorists the emphasis given by Keynesian and monetarist economists to the issue of stabilization has been a costly mistake. In a dynamic world instability is as desirable as it is inevitable.

6.13   Criticisms of Real Business Cycle Theory

In this section we will briefly review some of the more important criticisms of real business cycle theory. For a critical review of the literature, the reader is referred to Summers (1986), Hoover (1988), Sheffrin (1989), Mankiw (1989), McCallum (1989), Phelps (1990), Eichenbaum (1991) and Stadler (1993).

As we have already noted, the available evidence relating to the intertemporal elasticity of substitution in labour supply indicates a weak response to transitory wage changes. The variations in employment observed over the business cycle seem to be too large to be accounted for by intertemporal substitution. In addition Mankiw (1989) has argued that the real interest rate is not a significant consideration in labour supply decisions.

A second major criticism of real business cycle theory relates to the reliance of these models on mainly unobservable technological shocks. Many economists doubt whether the technological shocks required in order to generate business cycle phenomena are either large enough or frequent enough.

In these models large movements in output require significant aggregate disturbances to technology. In relation to this issue, Summers (1986) rejects Prescott's use of variations in the Solow residual as evidence of significant shocks to technology. Large variations in the Solow residual can be explained as the outcome of 'off the production function behaviour' in the form of *labour hoarding*. Whereas real business cycle theorists interpret procyclical labour productivity as evidence of shifts in the production function, the traditional Keynesian explanation attributes this stylized fact to the quasi-fixity of the labour input. The reason why productivity falls in recessions is because firms retain more workers than they need, owing to short-run adjustment costs. In such circumstances it will pay firms to smooth the labour input over the cycle, which implies the hoarding of labour in a cyclical downturn. This explains why the percentage reduction in output typically exceeds the percentage reduction in the labour input during a recession. As the economy recovers, firms utilize their labour more intensively, so that output increases by a larger percentage than the labour input (see Fay and Medoff, 1985; Rotemberg and Summers, 1990; Bernanke and Parkinson, 1991) .

A third line of criticism relates to the idea of recessions being periods of technological regress. As Mankiw (1989, p. 85) notes, 'Recessions are important events; they receive widespread attention from the policy-makers and the media. There is, however, no discussion of declines in the available technology. If society suffered some important adverse technological shock we would be aware of it.' Recently, in response to this line of criticism, Hansen and Prescott (1993) have widened the interpretation of technological shocks so that any 'changes in the production functions, or, more generally, the production possibility sets of the profit centres' can be regarded as a potential source of disturbance. In their analysis of the 1990–91 recession in the USA, they suggest that changes to the legal and institutional framework can alter the incentives to adopt certain technologies; for example, a barrage of government regulations could act as a negative technological shock.

An important fourth criticism relates to the issue of unemployment. In real business cycle models unemployment is voluntary. Critics find this argument unconvincing and point to the experience of the Great Depression, where 'it defies credulity to account for movements on this scale by pointing to intertemporal substitution and productivity shocks' (Summers, 1986). Carlin and Soskice (1990) argue that a large proportion of the unemployment in the 1980s was *involuntary* and this represents an important stylized fact which cannot be explained within a new classical framework. In Blinder's view, the challenge of high unemployment in recent years has not been met by either policy makers or economists. In a comment obviously directed at real business cycle theorists, Blinder (1988a, p. 3) notes: 'We will not contribute much toward alleviating unemployment while we fiddle around with theories of Pareto optimal recessions – an avocation that might be called Nero-Classical Economics.' Although the intersectoral shifts model associated with Lilien (1982) introduces unemployment into a model where technological shocks motivate the need to reallocate resources across sectors, the critics regard the neglect of unemployment in real business cycle theory as a major weakness (see Hoover, 1988).

A fifth objection to real business cycle theory relates to the neutrality of money and the irrelevance of monetary policy for real outcomes. It is a matter of some irony that these models emerged in the early 1980s when in both the USA and the UK the monetary disinflations initiated by Volcker and Thatcher were followed by deep recessions in both countries. More recently the 1990–92 economic downturn in the UK appears to have been the direct consequence of another dose of monetary disinflation. In response to this line of criticism, real business cycle theorists point out that the recessions experienced in the early 1980s were preceded by a second major oil shock in 1979. However the majority of economists remain unconvinced that money is neutral in the short run (see Romer and Romer, 1989; Blanchard, 1990a; Ball, 1994).

A sixth line of criticism relates to the important finding by Nelson and Plosser that it is hard to reject the view that real GNP is as persistent as a random walk with drift. This finding appeared to lend support to the idea that fluctuations are caused by supply-side shocks. The work of Nelson and Plosser (1982) showed that aggregate output does not appear to be trend-reverting. If fluctuations were trend-reverting then a temporary deviation of output from its natural rate would not change a forecaster's estimate of output in ten years' time. Campbell and Mankiw (1987, 1989), Stock and Watson (1988) and Durlauf (1989) have confirmed the findings of Nelson and Plosser. As a result the persistence of shocks is now regarded as a 'stylized fact' (see Durlauf, 1989, p. 71). However Campbell, Mankiw and Durlauf do not accept that the discovery of a near unit root in the GNP series is clear evidence of real shocks, or that explanations of fluctuations based on demand disturbances should be abandoned. Aggregate demand could have permanent effects if technological innovation is affected by the business cycle or if hysteresis effects are important (see Chapter 7). Durlauf has shown how, in the presence of coordination failures, substantial persistence in real activity can result from aggregate demand shocks. This implies that demand-side policies can have long-lasting effects on output. Stadler (1990) has also shown how the introduction of *endogenous* technological change fundamentally alters the properties of both real and monetary theories of the business cycle. The dependence of technological progress on economic factors such as demand conditions, research and development expenditures and 'learning by doing' effects (Arrow, 1962) implies that changes on the supply side of the economy are not independent of changes on the demand side. Hence an unanticipated increase in nominal aggregate demand can *induce* technological changes on the supply side which *permanently* increase output. In such a model the natural rate of unemployment will depend on the history of aggregate demand as well as supply-side factors. A purely monetary model of the business cycle where technology is endogenous can also account for the Nelson and Plosser finding that output appears to follow a random walk.

A seventh criticism relates to the pervasive use of the representative agent construct in real business cycle theory. Real business cycle theorists sidestep the aggregation problems inherent in macroeconomic analysis by using a representative agent whose choices are assumed to coincide with the aggregate choices of millions of heterogeneous individuals. Such models therefore avoid the problems associated with asymmetric information, exchange and coordination. To many economists the most important questions in macroeconomic theory relate to problems associated with coordination. If the coordination question and the associated possibility of exchange failures lie at the heart of economic fluctuations then to by-pass the problem by assuming that an economy is populated only by Robinson Crusoe is an unacceptable research strategy for many economists (see Summers, 1986; Kirman, 1992).

A final important criticism relates to the lack of robust empirical testing (see Fair, 1992; Laidler, 1992a). As far as the stylized facts are concerned, both new Keynesian and real business cycle theories can account for a broad pattern of time series co-movements (see Greenwald and Stiglitz, 1988). In a recent assessment of the empirical plausibility of real business cycle theory, Eichenbaum (1991) finds the evidence put forward by its proponents as 'too fragile to be believable'.

6.14 An Assessment

In his Yrjo Jahnsson lectures, given in 1978, James Tobin noted that 'There is no economic business cycle theory, new or old, involved in assuming that waves of economic activity simply mirror waves in underlying technology and taste' (Tobin, 1980a, p. 37). This state of affairs was to change dramatically during the 1980s when, following the widespread rejection of the monetary misperception version of equilibrium theory, real business cycle models proliferated. The research initiated by Nelson and Plosser provides substantial support for the view that shocks to aggregate output tend to have long-lasting effects. Output does not appear to revert to a deterministic trend. This finding has had a profound influence on business cycle research, in that it suggests that much of the disturbance to aggregate output that we witness is caused by supply-side influences. By demonstrating that equilibrium models are not inconsistent with aggregate instability, real business cycle theorists have challenged the conventional wisdom and forced theorists on all sides to recognize how deficient our knowledge is of business cycle phenomena. The real business cycle approach has therefore performed a useful function in raising profound questions relating to the meaning, significance and characteristics of economic fluctuations. Integrating the theory of growth and fluctuations has irreversibly changed the direction of business cycle research. New insights have been gained, along with innovative modelling techniques, and recent work has also begun to extend this line of research into an open economy framework (see Mendoza, 1991; Backus *et al.*, 1992). We should also note that the real business cycle approach has furthered the cause of those economists who insist that macro models need to be based on a firmer microeconomic base. This in turn has strengthened the general move to improve our understanding of the supply side. If anyone seriously questioned it before, no one now doubts that macroeconomics is about demand and supply and their interaction. As Blinder (1987) notes, 'Events in the 1970's and 1980's demonstrated to Keynesian and new classical economists alike that Marshall's celebrated scissors also come in a giant economy size.'

While recognizing the achievements of the real business research programme, the critics remain convinced that this approach has serious deficiencies. A majority of economists believe that the short-run aggregate demand disturbances which arise from monetary policy can have significant real effects because of the nominal price and wage rigidities which characterize actual economies. This important line of criticism challenges the new classical assumption that markets continuously clear, even in a recession. If markets do not clear quickly and the world is characterized by aggregate demand and aggregate supply disturbances, the actual fluctuations that we observe will consist of a stochastic trend around which output deviates as the result of demand shocks. This new consensus view is well represented in a recent paper by Blanchard and Quah (1989) where they 'interpret fluctuations in GNP and unemployment as due to two types of disturbances: disturbances that have a permanent effect on output and disturbances that do not. We interpret the first as supply disturbances, the second as demand disturbances'. Clearly the role of stabilization policy in such a world is immensely complicated, even if we accept that demand disturbances are important. How, for example, can a government make the requisite distinction between demand and supply shocks, especially when such shocks are not independent but interdependent (see Friedman, 1992)?

For those economists who reject the real business cycle view that stabilization policy has no role to play, there remains the theoretical difficulty of explaining in a coherent way why markets fail to clear. Beginning in the late 1970s and continuing during the 1980s and 1990s, many economists have taken up this challenge of attempting to explain why the adjustment of prices and wages in many markets is sluggish. 'The rationality of rigidities' theme is a major feature of the research of new Keynesian economists and it is to this work that we turn in the next chapter.

ROBERT BARRO

Robert Barro was born in 1944 in New York City and graduated with a BSc (physics) from Cal Tech in 1965. He obtained his PhD in economics from Harvard University in 1969. Professor Barro has taught at a number of universities, including Brown University, 1968–72, the University of Chicago, 1973–5 and 1982–4 and the University of Rochester, 1975–82 and was Visiting Fellow at the Hoover Institution, Stanford University 1977–8. Since 1988 he has been Professor of Economics at Harvard University.

Professor Barro is widely recognized as one of the United States' leading macroeconomists and an exponent of new classical macroeconomics. Among his best known books are: *Money, Employment and Inflation* (Cambridge University Press, 1976), co-authored with Herschel Grossman, *Money, Expectations and Business Cycles* (Academic Press, 1981), *Modern Business Cycle Theory* (Harvard University Press, 1989), edited by Robert Barro, and *Macroeconomics* (Wiley, 4th edn, 1993).

Among the numerous articles he has written, his best known include: 'A General Disequilibrium Model of Income and Employment', *American Economic Review* (1971), co-authored with Herschel Grossman, 'Are Government Bonds Net Wealth?', *Journal of Political Economy* (1974), 'Unanticipated Money Growth and Unemployment in the United States', *American Economic Review* (1977), 'A Positive Theory of Monetary Policy in a Natural Rate Model', *Journal of Political Economy* (1983), co-authored with

David Gordon, 'Recent Developments in the Theory of Rules Versus Discretion', *Economic Journal* (1986) and 'The Ricardian Approach to Budget Deficits', *Journal of Economic Perspectives* (1989).

We interviewed Robert Barro in his office at Harvard University on 16 February 1993.

As an undergraduate you studied physics at Cal Tech. Why did you switch your interest towards economics as a postgraduate student at Harvard?
I guess I liked the combination of quantitative analysis with applied social science policy issues. I started from a quantitative background and so it was an easy transition, maybe too easy because if you had some technique you could do better than you should in the Harvard graduate programme at that time.

What do you consider to be the key papers/books which have had a major influence on the development of macroeconomics in the last 25 years?
The right way to do this is to look at the Social Sciences Citation Index and find the ones that are cited the most. That index is the opinion of the profession weighted by publications and I assume people cite work because they think it's had some influence, even if they do not like it.

What have been the main influences on your own work?
I remember in the early 1970s I had done this work on Keynesian economics with Herschel Grossman [AER, 1971] and I felt we had made some progress there, but eventually it was a dead end in terms of actual explanatory power. Then for a period of maybe a year or two I didn't know what was a good direction to go in having decided that the existing framework wasn't right but not having a substitute. At that point I was heavily influenced by Bob Lucas's work on rational expectations macroeconomics. That work had a lot of impact on me and it came just at the right time when I had been frustrated with the kind of work I had been doing within the profession. Lucas's [1972, 1973 and 1976] papers all had a lot of influence on me. Those are very heavily cited papers. A little later the work by Sargent and Wallace [1975] was also influential.

Did you initially regard yourself as a Keynesian economist?
I did not regard myself as a Keynesian economist in the sense that I thought that activist government policy intervention was going to be very helpful. But it seemed to be the only game in town in terms of macroeconomics and I wanted to understand it. In graduate school two papers in particular had an influence on me, a paper by Robert Clower [1965] and the related chapter in

Patinkin's [1965] book. They seemed like two complementary pieces in terms of how excess supply spills over from one market to another. I remember thinking about trying to put these two papers together and that's what Herschel and I did, I think successfully. It helped me understand the sticky price, sticky nominal wage Keynesian framework and what determined quantities of output and employment. I think we resolved that, but since then the Keynesian part of the profession has regressed, in that there is now a poorer understanding of Keynesian macroeconomics than there was 20 years ago. People have forgotten or do not know that work and as a result are making the same kind of mistakes that I thought we had corrected at that time.

What in your view were the crucial weaknesses of the Keynesian model in the early 1970s?
Well I guess not being able to deal with price determination and inflation was a key embarrassment of the model. But also it reflected an inability to deal with the supply side of the economy, it was a completely demand-side model. That meant productivity, technological advance and incentives for working were not part of the framework. The oil shock made it clear that those kinds of matters had to be brought into the model.

How important do you think it is for macroeconomic models to have neoclassical choice-theoretic foundations?
The alternative to the Keynesian model seems to encompass a market-clearing setting and the things that underlie supply and demand come from the usual price-theoretic foundations. I am not sure it is all that crucial to have a highly technical mathematical theory, but it is important to have something that is consistent with the framework of utility and profit maximization underlying the axioms of the actors in the model. That does not mean high-level technique.

You are known as a leading new classical economist. Are you happy with the label 'new classicist'?
I guess its all right if it suggests bringing in micro foundations to a macro framework and thinking of market clearing.

Do you regard new classical macroeconomics as a separate school of thought from monetarism?
I have never quite understood the term 'monetarism'. It is often used in contradictory ways. Friedman used to refer to the quantity theory of money as an organizing principle of how to analyse price determination and inflation, and that's fine. It certainly allows for important real effects on the economy from monetary disturbances in the short run. But the framework

that Milton laid out in 1970 was actually quite Keynesian – it didn't look all that different from the conventional IS–LM model. On other occasions, monetarism is used to suggest that you do not want a lot of government intervention, that the government messes things up. But the framework that generates those results is not that clear.

What do you regard as the central propositions of new classical macroeconomics?

First, there are some positive results about what is supposed to matter for business fluctuations and second, there are some important implications for government policy – whether policy intervention is useful or matters at all. Some of Lucas's positive results about what matters for business cycles have not borne up that well. Initially there was a lot of stress on monetary disturbances even within an equilibrium framework. In fact that is what made it so hard. To get important real effects from monetary shocks was a struggle because they should be fairly close to being neutral. Lucas accepted the idea that money was empirically important, so he wanted a theoretical framework that would be consistent with that. It was a great intellectual achievement. But my own thinking on this has evolved over time because now I think that monetary shocks are less important as an empirical matter as a driver of business cycles. So that whole exercise was a little misplaced. Why go through the big challenge of explaining why money is very important and make it consistent with an equilibrium-style framework when it turns out that money is in fact not so important?

In your macroeconomics textbook you argue the case for a market-clearing approach because it avoids internal inconsistencies and because it provides a better understanding of the real world. Is the influence of new classical macroeconomics growing in other textbooks?

I think it is growing. The latest vintages have more elements of the new classical and real business cycle material than in any of the previous macro books. But in doing a macro book I think that you need one basic approach. It does not work to give equal time to all the alternatives. Students just get confused; they want a single coherent story. I do not know how that reflects on your book, but that is what I always thought [*laughter*]. The publishers always want to have more of the orthodox Keynesian stuff, IS–LM, etc. But the main purpose of a macro book is to evaluate events and policies and I do not think that you can do that satisfactorily with more than one approach.

Do you not think it is healthy to subject students to a breadth of perspectives, even at undergraduate level, so that they realize that there is so much controversy within the discipline?

Maybe when you have gone through one model systematically – later on you can do that, presenting a parallel treatment. Otherwise I think students will just turn off from that – at least US students will. I may not be right. But I do not know any other satisfactory way to do it.

Alan Blinder [1987] has argued that the weight of evidence is overwhelming against the rational expectations hypothesis. How do you react to this line of criticism?

It is true that we do not have very good theories of how people learn about the world. But there is no other satisfactory theory of expectations; there is only one competitor in this game, that is why it is so awkward. In fact, rational expectations has won the day with respect to macro theory. Most Keynesians basically use it and of course it's true that you can still get Keynesian results even using rational expectations. It used to be thought that rational expectations macroeconomics was somehow synonymous with new classical macroeconomics. Well that's not right, in the sense that you can imbed rational expectations into Keynesian-style models. However this seems to be inconsistent because the notion of rational expectations implies that people act efficiently in terms of how they formulate supply and demand decisions, so it is puzzling to have that efficient mode of operation in one place and yet argue that prices are sticky.

How do real business cycle theories deal with money?

Money is basically a side-show in those models, but they do need to be consistent with a number of empirical regularities. One set of facts has to do with the procyclical character of monetary aggregates. To show how those models can be consistent with these facts, even though money does not really do anything much in those models, you need some kind of endogenous money story, either through the banking system or the method of operation of the monetary authorities. You end up generating a pattern where money and output move together and maybe with money moving first. People clearly accept that already in certain contexts. For example, around Christmas time there is a tremendous demand for money and the monetary authority basically supplies it and thereby reacts to the economy. So in those contexts endogenous money is completely accepted. People also accept the idea that if the monetary authority is targeting interest rates then that is going to generate a pattern in which monetary aggregates are endogenous and react to output and other variables that affect the demand for money.

The so-called 'monetarist experiments' both in the UK and the USA in the period 1979–82 provide a rich source of controversy. How do you interpret what happened in this period?

I've never been sure, especially in the context of the USA, whether you can really interpret that period as one where monetary aggregates were being targeted. I did a long study about the character of money supply, interest rates and the price level in the United States and in that statistical work I was not able to detect something dramatically different in that interval. I have not studied the UK.

How do you view the new Keynesian attempts to rectify the weak micro foundations of Keynesian economics?
I really think that they have made no important advance there. One result which is of some interest comes from the menu cost work of Akerlof and Mankiw. But one of the criticisms is that the direct costs of changing prices seem to be trivial, so it is hard to see why you would want to stake a theory on this. The result is that the individual cost of changing prices is trivial yet the macro implications can be more substantial. But that doesn't really work because, as soon as you get away from full employment, it is no longer true that the private costs are trivial. There was a parallel problem in new classical models in terms of how money matters. It all depends on informational gaps such as not knowing what the money supply is. For countries like the USA that does not look very important, just as the cost of changing prices in the new Keynesian theory does not look too important. I guess both criticisms are valid and both theories are missing something important. There are some other strands of this new Keynesian work, such as the efficiency wage theories, but I do not think there is anything too much in that – it is not a monetary theory at all and does not relate to the question of whether money is important in business cycles.

Blanchard and Fischer in their Lectures on Macroeconomics [1989] *suggest that on the surface macroeconomics appears to be a field divided by schools, but that this represents public relations gimmicks and the strong incentives that exist in academia to differentiate products. Do you agree with their view?*
I accept the idea that people like to differentiate their products to make it look like what they are doing is important and unique, but still views are often very different. There is a real difference in substance between these schools, particularly when you start talking about policy recommendations. Some support activism of various kinds, monetary and fiscal, or even direct intervention. There is also a vast difference in terms of what is viewed as a good way to look at the economy or what is an interesting research issue.

What role does fiscal policy have?
The Ricardian view I think has been a great triumph [*laughter*]. I've given up a lot of my previous views but not that one. I think that was basically

accurate. Despite the great attention that has been given to budget deficits and public debt, the empirical evidence shows that it does not look like it has been very important for explaining interest rates, current account balances and the evolution of investment.

Don't you think that large budget deficits are damaging to the US economy?
I think the argument over the last decade has really been over the size of the government. Reagan wanted to have a smaller Federal government and his approach to achieving that was to cut taxes and try to use that as a lever to bring down expenditure. I think that was right. The argument was really between people who wanted to raise taxes and have bigger government versus those who wanted to keep taxes low in order to bring down expenditure. That was the real argument, not how big the budget deficit was.

Is this not a political rather than an economic argument?
Maybe we can apply economic tools in thinking about whether government expenditure is useful or not, but I agree it is partly a political argument. Bush basically gave up on this programme by raising taxes, accepting that the government will be larger. Clinton is now eagerly pursuing the idea of having a larger government. When he says he is going to be courageous and raise taxes and he cares about the debt and the budget deficit, what he is really saying is that he likes bigger government, maybe because he thinks it's useful.

What do you think are the most important stylized facts of the business cycle that any good macro theory needs to explain?
Investment is a key element in the business cycle. Most of the movement of output in the business cycle is in a component which we call investment or, more broadly, durables – I'd want to include consumer durables and business inventories. If you look at consumption of non-durables and services it moves very little, so you would want to explain those facts. Productivity and real wage rates tend to be procyclical, whereas many theories generate opposite implications. The price level in the post-war period for the main countries is actually counter-cyclical, whereas most people tend to view it as procyclical and then try to explain this. In some of these cases there has been a basic misunderstanding of the facts.

Many critics of new classical economics have argued that there is a lack of supporting evidence of strong intertemporal labour substitution effects. How do you react to this line of criticism?
It is hard to get direct evidence on that, just as it is hard to get evidence on how sensitive investment is to the cost of funds – it's the same kind of

problem. Just as you can see that investment is very sensitive over the business cycle, the labour input also moves a lot. If you take an equilibrium perspective and you observe that the labour input is moving, you need to think about what incentives are making it move a lot. But to get direct evidence of intertemporal substitution has been difficult to isolate. The same holds for consumption. It is hard to pin down the intertemporal effects, even though people are more willing to believe that these effects exist. Actually pinning down supply and demand curves is a difficult exercise; there is a hard identification problem there.

Do you think we should still use the term 'business cycle' after the contributions of the real business cycle theorists?
Real business cycle models are compatible with transitory movements of output and employment. Now it is possible to have a theory driven only by permanent technological disturbances, then output might look like a random walk relative to trend and there would be only permanent movements. But it is not inevitable that this line of theory would produce that result.

During the 1980s, despite all the criticisms from new classical economists, Keynesianism seemed to be making some form of comeback. Is this how you see recent developments?
Well there is some validity in that as a factual statement. The new classical work was new and exciting in the middle 1970s and everyone wanted to learn it and teach it to graduate students. Inevitably there was going to be a period where there was less progress, although the real business cycle work did come along together with new work on economic growth. I guess there is some tendency to actually move away from something that's no longer new and fresh. I don't think a Keynesian comeback has anything to do with new empirical evidence or indications that the theory is working better. Certainly the President and his administration are more sympathetic to interventionist lines of thinking. We are going to spend 15 billion dollars and everything is going to be fine [*laughter*].

Why does equilibrium business cycle theory seem to treat unemployment as a secondary issue?
To explain unemployment within an equilibrium-style framework you need some search and incomplete information stories, some kind of framework where it is costly to shift from one activity to another; for example the sectoral shift idea that David Lilien [1982] has stressed. I think that work is interesting but I've never been sure about the best way to treat unemployment within the equilibrium-style framework.

How do you view Keynes as an economist? Do you think he would have been worthy of a Nobel Prize in Economics?
Absolutely. Keynes was a brilliant economist. He came up with an ingenious theory within the context of an economic crisis. Even if I think in the end that the theory is not right what does that prove? Most theories are not right. He also did some very interesting monetary work earlier which has nothing to do with what we now call Keynesianism – the *Tract On Monetary Reform*, for example.

Does the political business cycle and time inconsistency literature provide a clear case for monetary and fiscal rules, or should we trust politicians with discretionary policy?
I think it is a very interesting line of work. Some of the best work has been done by my colleague, Alberto Alesina. He has some interesting empirical results about the interplay between political events, macro policies and business fluctuations. The time inconsistency literature says something useful about the desirable ways of framing policies and why it would be useful for monetary policy to be committed to price stability and not get distracted into other things. A similar kind of constitutional perspective applies to fiscal policy. The idea that governments have an incentive to renege or surprise after the fact is pervasive. For example, Clinton now wants to dump on the drug companies because their prices are too high, but their prices are high as an incentive to do the research and invent new drugs. It's an exact parallel with what comes up with monetary policy, or debt policy where there is an incentive to inflate away the debt. These are all the same problems. As another example, we had a hurricane disaster in Miami and the government came in and bailed people out. Thus the government subsidizes people to live in the wrong place where they are subject to these dangers.

Do you think having an independent central bank is crucial for price stability?
Well, independence seems to be a matter of degree. Some people have looked at this empirically and it seems that more independence delivers lower inflation without costs in terms of growth performance. Alex Cukierman and some of his colleagues have a book on this in which they look at various developing countries. They found that you not only get less inflation but those countries with independent central banks also do better on growth performance. To say it is crucial is probably going too far because no doubt there are lots of different routes to getting price stability.

Do you think that discretionary monetary and fiscal policies inevitably impart an inflationary bias to an economy?

It clearly goes in that direction. To some extent governments are not completely vulnerable to this temptation. They do not always give in to it, for reasons that I do not fully understand.

Have the new classical contributions resulted in a revolution in macroeconomics?
Yes, I think it completely changes the way people who use that framework look at macro determinants of policy. Firstly, it's a positive story about what happens when there is some disturbance to the economy. Secondly, it's a completely different way of looking at policy evaluation. There is a tendency to look at these issues from a constitutional perspective.

Is new classical macroeconomics more robust than monetarism?
I do not know whether it will be the single overriding framework that everybody believes in, but there are clearly aspects of it that are permanent in terms of how one thinks about macroeconomics, such as rational expectations. The Ricardian view of public debt is important. Even if people do not think it's right they feel obliged to know what it is. The interplay between supply and demand in a macro framework is central and tends to push you towards market forces and market clearing.

Would you agree with Stanley Fischer's comment that the views of Milton Friedman, Karl Brunner and Alan Meltzer are closer to those of Keynesians than those of the equilibrium business cycle school?
Yes that's probably right [*laughter*]. I like Milton better when he does applied price theory and relates this to social issues, although the *Monetary History* is a great book.

Would you agree that the last 20 years of research suggests that macroeconomists should take an eclectic approach to their model building?
I do not know what this eclectic view would be, or how you would proceed along such lines. How would you mix the best features of different macro models? The real business cycle literature has the virtue of relating the theory to the empirical regularities in an organized way. It views empirical behaviour as a test of the theory. The Keynesians do not take that approach, at least not now. There is not that much subjecting of the theory to empirical testing. What does the IS–LM model imply about the cyclical behaviour of investment, productivity, real wages and interest rates and how does this match with the data? The Keynesians do not usually take that approach.

Do you see any signs of an emerging consensus in macroeconomics, and if so, what form is it likely to take?

I do not really see it. Olivier Blanchard would like me to say yes. He thinks it is very unpleasant not to see consensus, but I do not see it.

If you were advising President Clinton, what would be your advice with respect to macroeconomic policy in the 1990s?

The notion of my advising President Clinton is, of course, quite amusing. Anyway, one important concern is price stability. People have become overly optimistic about it, taking it for granted now that we have low inflation. I think that it is quite fragile. Fortunately Alan Greenspan is reliable and it is lucky that President Clinton has him in the Federal Reserve. I do not think that fiscal policy issues are central. You cannot run budget deficits forever with the debt–GDP ratio rising continually. At some point you have to have taxes matching expenditure, but it is not a crisis. I would like to see a cut in a lot of government expenditure programmes because many of those programmes are not very useful and the financing of these programmes is distortionary. I thought Reagan was going in the right direction there, but he did not go far enough. The other thing I would like to say is that in terms of macro policy one should take a long-run perspective. What really matters is the rate of growth and productivity expansion over the longer term and the government ought to be geared to doing things that are useful in that context. Apart from price stability, there should be a more favourable treatment of income from capital. It is possible that some infrastructure investment would be useful, but not some of the grandiose programmes that Clinton thinks about.

CHARLES PLOSSER

Charles Plosser was born in 1948 in Birmingham, Alabama and graduated from Vanderbilt University in 1970 with a BE. He received his MBA (1972) and PhD (1976) degrees from the University of Chicago. Charles Plosser has served on the faculties of Standford University Graduate School of Business and the University of Chicago Graduate School of Business. Since 1978 he has taught at the University of Rochester, where he is currently the Dean and John M. Olin Distinguished Professor of Economics and Public Policy and Professor of Economics in the William E. Simon Graduate School of Business Administration and the Department of Economics, respectively.

Professor Plosser is one of the leading figures responsible for the development of 'real business cycle' theory, which is now generally recognized as being the main new classical explanation of economic fluctuations. Among his best known and most influential articles are: 'Government Financing Decisions and Asset Returns', *Journal of Monetary Economics* (1982), 'Trends and Random Walks in Macroeconomics Time Series: Some Evidence and Implications', *Journal of Monetary Economics* (1982), co-authored with Charles Nelson, 'Real Business Cycles', *Journal of Political Economy* (1983), co-authored with John Long, 'Money, Credit and Prices in a Real Business Cycle', *American Economic Review* (1984), co-authored with Robert King; 'Production Growth and Business Cycles I, The Basic Neoclassical Model' and 'Production Growth and Business Cycles II, New Directions', both in the

Journal of Monetary Economics (1988), co-authored with Robert King and Sergio Rebelo, 'Understanding Real Business Cycles', *Journal of Economic Perspectives* (1989) and 'Stochastic Trends and Economic Fluctuations', *American Economic Review* (1991), co-authored with Robert King, James Stock and Mark Watson.

We corresponded with Charles Plosser in October 1993.

What do you consider to be the key papers/books which have had a major impact on the development of macroeconomics in recent years, and in particular which papers have influenced your work?
Such a list is always hard to develop. Macroeconomics is very broad and many articles have been important for different strands in the literature. The work that had the most influence on my thinking includes the writings of Milton Friedman and Edmund Phelps on the Phillips curve in the late 1960s, as well as the work of Robert Lucas on rational expectations and business cycles. Lucas's more general discussions of business cycles (for example, *Understanding Business Cycles*) I found more interesting than his specific monetary models. Interestingly, a textbook, *Macroeconomics: A Neoclassical Introduction*, written by Merton Miller and Charles Upton in the mid-1970s, that attempted to integrate growth theory into a more traditional macroeconomic text had a major impact on my thinking because of the way it forced systematic thinking of dynamic equilibrium concepts. It had its roots, of course, in the work of Sir John Hicks and others, but it was quite a departure from the standard fare at the time. I suppose the other literature that influenced my thinking was modern finance. In particular, the work by Eugene Fama and others on efficient markets affected my own work and how I looked at macroeconomics.

Do you think that it is crucial for macroeconomic models to have neoclassical choice-theoretic micro foundations?
At some levels the answer is yes. The choice-theoretic framework is an important disciplining device along with the concept of equilibrium. Without such a discipline, economic analysis ceases to have much content and ultimately resorts to description. That does not mean, however, that every concept and idea must be developed from these first principles. But they ought to be lurking somewhere in the background.

Macroeconomic controversy in the 1950s and the 1960s mainly revolved around issues relating to aggregate demand. Why has the emphasis now shifted to the supply side?
Equilibrium has always been the balancing of supply and demand. For macroeconomics to have so long focused almost exclusively on demand is

unfortunate. One way to think about it is that the supply side is finally getting the attention it deserves. In any event, I am not convinced that thinking about aggregate supply and demand schedules is the most useful way to think about macroeconomics.

What role have calibration exercises played in the development of real business cycle models? Would you not agree that such models need to pass more stringent empirical tests before they can pose an effective challenge to more conventional Keynesian and monetarist models?
Calibration exercises have played an important role in helping us understand in a quantitative manner how these real business cycle models perform. But such exercises are not the ultimate test of the models. Much more work must be done in developing richer models that can be subjected to more strenuous empirical testing. On the other hand, to say that conventional models have more empirical support is a gross exaggeration. The reason researchers have looked for alternative models has been that conventional models have repeatedly failed to explain the facts. For example, this is certainly true of Keynesian models and of the monetary models as proposed by Robert Lucas and Robert Barro in the 1970s.

Given the central thrust of your work, do you think that we should continue to use the term 'business cycle' when we refer to aggregate economic fluctuations?
I prefer to talk about economic fluctuations.

Your work provides an integrated approach to the theory of growth and fluctuations. Is it your view that the traditional approach of distinguishing between short-run and long-run forces in macroeconomics has been misconceived and counter-productive? Did Keynes send everyone off down the wrong track?
The objective of economics is to improve our understanding of how the economy works. The usefulness of short-term or long-term distinctions depends entirely on what set of questions one is interested in asking. It also becomes an issue of what questions we have the capability to answer. I think we have generally used short-term analysis as an excuse to avoid the challenges of understanding equilibrium dynamics (as opposed to arbitrary adjustment mechanisms).

Do aggregate demand forces have any important role to play in your models?
In the dynamic general equilibrium models of the sort I have proposed I do not find it useful to talk in terms of aggregate demand and aggregate supply shocks. There are shocks to tastes, endowments and technology/productivity.

Many people make the leap to associate technology/productivity shocks with supply shocks, and taste shocks with demand shocks. This may seem natural enough, but I feel it imposes an artificial characterization on our thinking and on the power of the model. For example, in general equilibrium multi-sector models such as those considered by John Long and me, productivity shocks in one sector may show up as demand shocks in other sectors. Furthermore real business cycle models can easily consider shocks that are often thought of as impacting aggregate demand such as government spending. Recently some researchers are trying to incorporate money into these models, although there is no agreement on the appropriate mechanism. The point is that an important contribution of the early real business cycle models was to describe a more coherent way of thinking about economic fluctuations. As we understand these models better, researchers have gradually added features to enrich the sorts of phenomena they are able to address.

In your 1983 paper with John Long you concluded that the fluctuations exhibited by real business cycle models 'should not be confused with welfare-reducing deviations from some ideal path ... Efforts to stabilise this economy can only serve to make consumers worse off'. How do you view stabilization policies in practice?
In the 1983 paper with John Long, our model was characterized by perfect competition and complete markets. Consequently the equilibrium was Pareto optimal and there was no scope for welfare-increasing stabilization short of eliminating the exogenous shocks. In practice I view stabilization policies as largely inappropriate for the usual reasons that have been offered by everyone from Milton Friedman to Edward Prescott and Robert Lucas.

Real business cycle theory evolved out of the monetary surprise version of new classical macroeconomics associated with Lucas, Barro and others. However the models which you have developed give little importance to the money supply as an explanatory factor in business cycle analysis. Would you say that your work represents a serious challenge to the orthodox monetarist position represented by Friedman and Schwartz?
I don't really view real business cycle models as evolving from the monetary models of Lucas and Barro. Certainly those models preceded our work and had some of the same emphasis on equilibrium and rational expectations, but otherwise they are quite different. Indeed real business cycle models are, in part, a response to the unsatisfactory nature of models that relied so heavily on monetary impulses. To the extent that real business cycle models can explain the business cycle without relying on monetary shocks, they do raise questions regarding the relative importance of money as the dominant business cycle impulse. In addition, my research has led me to *think* differently

about money, as reflected in my work with Robert King in the *American Economic Review* and more recently in a *St Louis Federal Reserve Bank* volume. These papers attempt to distinguish banking regulation and taxation (for example, changes in reserve requirements) from monetary policy (for example, open market operations) and between endogenous and exogenous factors influencing the money stock.

The monetary policy experiments carried out in both the US and UK econo-mies in the period 1979–82 would seem to support the view that, at least in the short run, money is not neutral. Recent work by Christina Romer [Journal of Economic History, December 1992] *supports the view that economic recovery in the USA after 1933 was dependent on monetary expansion. How do real business cycle theorists explain these episodes?*

I do not think it is appropriate to validate or invalidate a particular economic model or theory by citing one or two examples as evidence for or against. One of our biggest challenges in testing our economic theories is 'holding other things constant', so anecdotal evidence is rarely compelling. For exam-ple, during the period 1979–82 there are a number of events critical to a complete understanding of the period. First, there was an oil price shock equal or greater in magnitude to the shock in 1973. In addition, President Carter imposed an extensive set of credit controls, affecting everything from banks to retail establishments, that dramatically disrupted financial interme-diation of all sorts. Either of these factors could have accounted for the subsequent recession, whether the federal reserve exogenously contracted the money supply or not. It seems essential that any test that purports to identify *the* cause of economic fluctuations must do so within the context of a model that permits other shocks that may be important.

Critics of real business cycle theories point out that inflation should move counter-cyclically if the business cycle is really driven by supply-side shocks. In the absence of well documented supply-side shocks, such as the OPEC oil price changes, inflation does seem to move procyclically. How do you re-spond to this line of criticism?

Again, real business cycles do not have to be driven solely by so-called 'supply-side' shocks. Thus any argument about the procyclical or counter-cyclical behaviour of prices is largely irrelevant. Moreover there is an impor-tant distinction between the behaviour of prices and that of inflation that your question confuses. The early arguments for demand shocks stemmed from the apparent procyclical behaviour of prices (not inflation) in the pre-WWII period. In the post-war era most people have focused on the behaviour of inflation and real growth (that is, a version of the Phillips curve). In the USA this correlation is marginally negative. Finally the issue of the behaviour of inflation relative to real growth can only be analysed in the context of the operating rules of the monetary authorities. Without an assumption regarding how they behave, one can generate almost any correlation you like between inflation and real growth or between prices and real output.

Equilibrium business cycle theory seems to treat unemployment as a secondary issue. Do you agree with Lucas [1978] that Keynes's concept of involuntary unemployment should be abandoned by macroeconomists?
'Involuntary unemployment' is a very overused and imprecise term that does little to discipline our thinking. In this sense it is much like the term 'disequilibrium', which is similarly useless. It would be much more constructive, for example, to talk in terms of equilibrium subject to constraints and then be forced to explain and justify the existence of the constraints.

During the 1980s, despite the important progress made by new classical economists, Keynesianism appears to be making something of a comeback compared with the situation in the 1970s. How do you account for this? Is it because new Keynesian economists have taken on board many of the new classical criticisms of earlier Keynesian models?
The Keynesians certainly like to think they are making a comeback, but if you judge by the relative number of articles in major economic journals, you might reach a different conclusion. Nevertheless it is true that many of the 'new' Keynesians have adopted many of the principles long advocated by classical economists. This has forced them to be more articulate regarding the sources of market failure that are often critical to their analyses. This has improved the quality of the debate and can only be viewed as positive.

In commenting on recent developments in new classical economics, Gregory Mankiw [1989] has argued that, although real business cycle theory has 'served the important function of stimulating and provoking scientific debate, it will [he predicts] *ultimately be discarded as an explanation of observed fluctuations'. What are your predictions for the future development of macroeconomics?*
Real business cycle models have changed the way many macroeconomists approach economic fluctuations. I do not believe that the profession will ever go back. The models have stressed the importance of analysing dynamic general equilibrium models and have advanced our technical abilities in ways that make quantitative investigations feasible. The future lies not in going back to the old ways, but elaborating and enriching these new models in ways that make them better representations of economic phenomena.

Do you think Keynes would have been worthy of a Nobel Prize in Economics?

The success of Keynes's *General Theory* was, in large part, due to the work of John Hicks and others who took Keynes's unstructured and sometimes rambling arguments and fashioned them into an operational IS–LM framework. Without that framework, Keynes would surely have been much less influential. Moreover it is difficult to answer this question in the abstract without considering several other great 20th-century economists who would be worthy of such recognition. The first one that comes to mind is Irving Fisher. Fisher's contributions and influence, I believe, clearly dominate those of Keynes. What about Pareto or Wicksell? Would Keynes be worthy? Perhaps, but without Hicks it seems unlikely, and he should probably have to stand in line behind several other more distinguished colleagues.

7. The new Keynesian school

The Keynesian promised land is not yet in sight but we may at long last be emerging from the arid desert and looking over the Jordan. (Blinder, 1988b)

7.1 A Keynesian Crisis?

We have seen in the previous chapters how the orthodox Keynesian model associated with the neoclassical synthesis came under attack during the 1970s. It soon became apparent to the Keynesian mainstream that the new classical critique represented a much more powerful and potentially damaging challenge than the one launched by the monetarists, which was of longer standing. Although orthodox monetarism presented itself as an *alternative* to the standard Keynesian model, it did not constitute a radical theoretical challenge to it (see Laidler, 1986). The poor performance of Keynesian wage and price adjustment equations based on the idea of a stable Phillips curve made it imperative for Keynesians to modify their models so as to take into account both the influence of inflationary expectations and the impact of supply shocks. This was duly done and once the Phillips curve was suitably modified it performed 'remarkably well' (Blinder, 1986). The important work of Gordon (1972, 1975), Phelps (1968, 1972, 1978) and Blinder (1979), all of whom are 'Keynesians', was particularly important in creating the necessary groundwork which has subsequently allowed the Keynesian model to adapt and evolve in a way which enabled monetarist influences to be absorbed *within* the existing framework. Moreover this transition towards a synthesis of ideas did not require any *fundamental* change in the way economists viewed the economic machine.

Despite these positive developments within Keynesian economics, by 1978 Lucas and Sargent were contemplating life 'After Keynesian Macroeconomics'. In their view the Keynesian model could not be patched up. The problems were much more fundamental and related in particular to (i) inadequate micro foundations which assume non-market clearing; and (ii) the incorporation in both Keynesian and monetarist models of a hypothesis concerning the formation of expectations which was inconsistent with maximizing behaviour; that is, the use of an adaptive rather than rational expectations hypothesis. In an article entitled 'The Death of Keynesian Economics: Issues and Ideas', Lucas (1980) went so far as to claim that 'people even take offence if referred to as Keynesians. At research seminars people don't take Keynesian theorising seriously anymore; the audience starts to whisper and giggle to one another' (cited in Mankiw, 1992). In a similar vein, Blinder (1988a) has confirmed that 'By about 1980, it was hard to find an American academic macroeconomist under the age of 40 who professed to be a Keynesian. That was an astonishing intellectual turnabout in less than a decade, an intellectual revolution for sure.' By this time the United States' most distinguished 'old' Keynesian economist had already posed the question, 'How dead is Keynes'? (see Tobin, 1977).

7.2 A Keynesian Resurgence?

Lucas's obituary of Keynesian economics can now be seen to have been premature because the 'bad guys' appear to have been making a comeback in recent years. Blinder has talked of 'Keynes after Lucas' (1986), the 'Fall and Rise of Keynesian Economics' (1988a) and most recently has claimed that 'A Keynesian Restoration is Here' (1992b). Howitt (1986) has commented on 'The Keynesian Recovery', Mankiw (1992) claims that Keynesian economics has been 'reincarnated' and Thirlwall (1993) believes that we are witnessing a 'Keynesian Renaissance'. In answering his own (1977) question, Tobin (1987) has provided an unequivocal answer in his essay, 'The Future of Keynesian Economics':

> One reason Keynesian economics has a future is that rival theories of economic fluctuations do not. ... I hazard the prediction that neither of the two species of business cycle theory offered by new classical macroeconomics will be regarded as serious and credible explanations of economic fluctuations a few years from now. Whatever cycle theory emerges in a new synthesis will have important Keynesian elements. ... Yes, Keynesian economics has a future because it is essential to the explanation and understanding of a host of observations and experiences past and present, that alternative macroeconomic approaches do not illuminate.

The persistence of high unemployment in Europe during the 1980s and 1990s also provided increasing 'credibility to Keynesian theory and policy' (Tobin, 1989). When Paul Samuelson was asked whether Keynes was dead he replied 'Yes, Keynes is dead; and so are Einstein and Newton' (see Samuelson, 1988).

We have seen in Chapter 5 and 6 how new classical macroeconomists resolved the tension between neoclassical microeconomics and Keynesian macroeconomics by abandoning the latter. An alternative approach to this problem has been put forward by those economists who feel that the neoclassical synthesis contained some fundamental truths and that, suitably modified, Keynesian economics could once again dominate macroeconomics. However, as we shall see, the 'new' Keynesian models are very different in many aspects from their distant (1960s) cousins. By rebuilding the micro foundations of Keynesian economics new Keynesian theorists have established a research programme aimed at rectifying the theoretical flaws which permeated the supply-side of the 'old' Keynesian model (see Snowdon and Vane, 1994).

For a detailed and critical discussion of the new Keynesian literature, we refer the reader to McCallum (1986), Greenwald and Stiglitz (1987, 1993a), Rotemberg (1987), Fischer (1988), Barro (1989a), Blanchard (1990a), Gordon (1990), Phelps (1990), Hargreaves-Heap (1992), Stiglitz (1992), King (1993), D. Romer (1993) and Tobin (1993). Most of the important papers are collected in the twin volumes edited by Mankiw and Romer (1991), who also provide an excellent tour of the literature in their introductory survey.

7.3   New Keynesian Economics

Although the term 'new Keynesian' was first used by Parkin in 1984, it is clear that this line of thought had been conceived in the 1970s during the first phase of the new classical revolution. The burgeoning new Keynesian literature since then has been primarily concerned with the 'search for rigorous and convincing models of wage and/or price stickiness based on maximising behaviour and rational expectations' (Gordon, 1990). New Keynesian economics developed in response to the perceived theoretical crisis within Keynesian economics which had been exposed by Lucas during the 1970s. The paramount task facing Keynesian theorists is to remedy the theoretical flaws and inconsistencies in the old Keynesian model and this involves the construction of a theory of aggregate supply in which wage and price rigidities can be rationalized.

Both the old and new versions of classical economics assume continuous market clearing and in such a world the economy can never be constrained by a lack of effective demand. To many economists the hallmark of Keynesian economics is the absence of continuous market clearing. In both the old (neoclassical synthesis) and new versions of Keynesian models the failure of prices to change quickly enough to clear markets implies that demand and supply shocks will lead to substantial real effects on the economy's output and employment. In a Keynesian world, deviations of output and employment from their equilibrium values can be substantial and prolonged, and are certainly interpreted as damaging to economic welfare. As Gordon (1993) points out, 'The appeal of Keynesian economics stems from the evident unhappiness of workers and firms during recessions and depressions. Workers and firms *do not act as if they were making a voluntary choice to cut production and hours worked.'*

New Keynesians argue that a theory of the business cycle based on the failure of markets to clear is more realistic than the new classical or real business cycle alternatives. The essential difference between the old and new versions of Keynesian economics is that the models associated with the neoclassical synthesis tended to *assume* a fixed nominal wage, while the attraction of the new Keynesian approach is that it attempts to provide acceptable micro foundations to explain the phenomena of wage and price stickiness.

The reader should be aware that *new Keynesian economists are an extremely heterogeneous group*, so much so that the use of the term 'school' is more convenient than appropriate. Nevertheless economists who have made significant contributions to the new Keynesian literature include Gregory Mankiw and Lawrence Summers (Harvard); Olivier Blanchard and Stanley Fischer (MIT); Bruce Greenwald and Edmund Phelps (Colombia); Ben Bernanke and Laurence Ball (Princeton); George Akerlof, Janet Yellen and David Romer (Berkeley); Joseph Stiglitz, Robert Hall and John Taylor (Stanford); Dennis Snower (Birkbeck, London) and Assar Lindbeck (Stockholm). The proximity of US new Keynesians to the east and west coasts inspired Robert Hall to classify these economists under the general heading of '*Saltwater*' economists. By a strange coincidence new classical economists tend to be associated with '*Freshwater*' academic institutions: Chicago, Rochester, Minnesota and Carnegie-Mellon (see Blanchard, 1990b).

At this point it should be noted that some writers have identified a 'European' brand of macroeconomic analysis which has also been called 'new Keynesian'. The European variant emphasizes imperfect competition in the labour market as well as the product market, reflecting the higher unionization rates which characterize European economies. The appropriateness of a bargaining approach to wage determination as a micro foundation to Keynesian macroeconomics is much more contentious in the USA, where only one in five workers belong to a union. The use of the imperfect competition macro model to examine the problem of unemployment is best represented in the work of Richard Layard (LSE), Stephen Nickell (Oxford) and Richard Jackman (LSE). Wendy Carlin (London) and David Soskice (Oxford) provide the most comprehensive introduction to the European brand of new Keynesianism (see Layard *et al.*, 1991; Carlin and Soskice, 1990). There is of course considerable overlap between the two brands of new Keynesianism, especially when it comes to the issue of real wage rigidity (see section 7.6.2). Economists such as Bénassy, Drèze, Grandmont and Malinvaud have also continued to develop general equilibrium models where non-market-clearing and price-making agents give such models Keynesian features, and in a recent survey of this literature Bénassy (1993) suggests that 'it would certainly be worthwhile to integrate the most relevant new Keynesian insights' into this general equilibrium approach.

At the beginning of the 1980s, three alternative explanations of the business cycle were on offer within mainstream economics (there were others outside the mainstream such as Austrian, Post-Keynesian and Marxian). The mainstream alternatives were (i) flexible price, monetary misperception equilibrium business cycle theories developed and advocated by Lucas (see Chapter 5); (ii) sticky price expectational models emphasizing some element of wage and price rigidity (for example, Fischer, 1977; Phelps and Taylor, 1977; Taylor, 1980); and (iii) real business cycle models which increasingly became the main flagship of the new classical equilibrium theorists during the 1980s (see Chapter 6). By the mid-1980s the 'Saltwater–Freshwater' debate was essentially between the sticky price and real business cycle varieties. However the major concern of new Keynesian theorists has been to explain how nominal rigidities arise from optimizing behaviour. Ball, Mankiw and Romer (1988) consider the decline of Keynesian economics during the 1970s to have been mainly due to a failure to solve this problem.

In the remainder of this chapter we will examine the main elements of this very diverse literature. First we identify the essential characteristics of what is commonly understood to be the new Keynesian approach.

7.4 Core Propositions and Features of New Keynesian Economics

Mankiw and Romer (1991) define new Keynesian economics with reference to the answer a particular theory gives to the following pair of questions.

Question 1 Does the theory violate the classical dichotomy? That is, is money non-neutral?

Question 2 Does the theory assume that real market imperfections in the economy are crucial for understanding economic fluctuations?

Of the mainstream schools only new Keynesians answer both questions in the affirmative. Non-neutralities arise from sticky prices, and market imperfections explain this behaviour of prices. Real business cycle theory gives a negative response to both questions. The disequilibrium Keynesian models of the 1970s (for example, Barro and Grossman, 1976) *imposed* wage and price rigidities on a Walrasian system, whereas more traditional Keynesian and monetarist models did not regard the *explanation* of price rigidities as crucial. The latter two groups regard empirical evidence as being far more important than theoretical purity; for example, speaking from a monetarist perspective, Laidler (1992b) has argued emphatically that 'better and more explicit microfoundations do not guarantee more accurate empirical predictions about the outcome of any macropolicy experiment'.

During the 1980s new Keynesian developments had a distinctly non-empirical flavour. Those younger-generation economists seeking to strengthen the Keynesian model did so primarily by developing and improving the micro foundations of 'Fort Keynes' which had come under theoretical attack (see Blinder, 1992a). Those Keynesian commanders who allocated scarce research resources to the theoretical, rather than empirical, front in defence of 'Fort Keynes' did so because they felt that the modified Keynesian model incorporating both the Phelps–Friedman expectations-augmented Phillips curve and the impact of supply shocks was sufficiently resilient to hold its own on the empirical front. The theoretical defences having now been reinforced, resources are gradually being reallocated to the empirical front in order to test the new Keynesian models.

A crucial difference between new classical and new Keynesian models arises with regard to price setting behaviour. In contrast to the *price takers* who inhabit new classical models, new Keynesian models assume *price-making monopolistic*, rather than perfectly competitive, firms. Although the theory of monopolistic competition had been developed independently by Robinson (1933) and Chamberlain (1933) *prior* to the publication of Keynes's *General Theory*, it is only recently that mainstream Keynesian theorists have begun seriously to incorporate imperfect competition into non-market-clearing models. In this matter Post-Keynesians were first off the mark (see Chapter 8 and Dixon and Rankin, 1994).

Most new Keynesian models assume that expectations are formed rationally. This is clearly one area where the new classical revolution of the 1970s has had a profound effect on macroeconomists in general. However some prominent Keynesians (Blinder, 1987; Phelps, 1992) as well as some economists within the orthodox monetarist school (Laidler, 1992b) remain critical of the theoretical foundations and question the empirical support for the rational expectations hypothesis. Hence, although the incorporation of rational expectations in new Keynesian models is the norm, this need not always be the case.

Although new Keynesian economists share a common interest in improving the supply side of Keynesian models, they hold a wide diversity of views relating to policy issues such as the debate over the importance of discretion, rather than rules, in the conduct of fiscal and monetary policy. New Keynesians regard both supply and demand shocks as potential sources of instability (see Blanchard and Quah, 1989) but part company with real business cycle theorists particularly when it comes to an assessment of a market economy's capacity to absorb such shocks so that full employment is maintained. New Keynesians also share Keynes's view that involuntary unemployment is both possible and likely.

New Keynesian economists inhabit a brave new theoretical world characterized by imperfect competition, incomplete markets, heterogeneous labour and asymmetric information, and where agents are frequently concerned with fairness. As a result the 'real' macro world, as seen through new Keynesian eyes, is characterized by coordination failures and macroeconomic externalities. One problem with the new Keynesian developments is that the research programme has proved to be *article-laden* (Colander, 1988). Hence *there is no single unified new Keynesian model*, rather there are a multiplicity of explanations of wage and price rigidities and their macroeconomic consequences.

Different elements within the new Keynesian school emphasize various aspects and causes of market imperfections and their macroeconomic effects. However the numerous explanations are not mutually exclusive and often complement each other. In short, as Leslie's (1993) recent comment captures so well, 'New Keynesianism throws bucketfuls of grit into the smooth-running neoclassical paradigms.'

Because the literature reviewed here is so wide-ranging, it is convenient to divide the explanations of rigidities between those which focus on *nominal* rigidities and those which focus on *real* rigidities. A nominal rigidity occurs if something prevents the nominal price level from adjusting so as exactly to mimic nominal demand disturbances. A real rigidity occurs if some factor prevents real wages from adjusting or there is stickiness of one wage relative to another, or of one price relative to another (see Gordon, 1993). First we will examine nominal rigidities.

7.5 Nominal Rigidities

Both orthodox and new Keynesian approaches assume that prices adjust slowly following a disturbance. But, unlike the Keynesian cross or IS–LM approaches, which arbitrarily assume fixed nominal wages and prices, the new Keynesian approach seeks to provide a microeconomic underpinning for the slow adjustment of both wages and prices. In line with the choice-theoretical framework of new classical analysis, the new Keynesian approach assumes that workers and firms are rational utility and profit maximizers, respectively.

As we have seen, new classicists adopt the flexible price auction model and apply this to the analysis of transactions conducted in all markets including the labour market. In contrast, new Keynesians argue that it is important to utilize the Hicksian (1974) distinction between markets which are essentially fix-price, predominantly the labour market and a large section of the goods market, and markets which are flex-price, predominantly financial and commodity markets. In fix-price markets price setting is the norm, with price and wage inertia a reality. In order to generate monetary non-neutrality (real effects) Keynesian models rely on the failure of nominal wages and prices to adjust promptly to their new market-clearing levels following an aggregate demand disturbance. Keynesians have traditionally concentrated their attention on the labour market and nominal wage stickiness in order to explain the tendency of market economies to depart from full employment equilibrium. However it is important to note that for any given path of nominal aggregate demand it is price, not wage, stickiness which is necessary to generate fluctuations in real output. Providing profits are sufficiently flexible nominal prices could adjust to exactly mimic changes in nominal aggregate demand, leaving real output unaffected (see Gordon, 1990).

Nevertheless the first wave of new Keynesian reaction to the new classical critique concentrated on nominal wage rigidity.

7.5.1 Nominal wage rigidity

In traditional Keynesian models the price level is prevented from falling to restore equilibrium by the failure of money wages (costs) to adjust (see Figure 2.6). In the new classical models developed by Lucas, Sargent, Wallace and Barro during the 1970s any anticipated monetary disturbance will cause an immediate jump of nominal wages and prices to their new equilibrium values, so preserving output and employment. In such a world, systematic monetary policy is ineffective. Initially it was widely believed that this new classical policy unnecessary proposition was a direct implication of incorporating the rational expectations hypothesis into macroeconomic models. Fischer (1977) and Phelps and Taylor (1977) showed that nominal disturbances were capable of producing real effects in models incorporating rational expectations, providing the assumption of continuously clearing markets was dropped (see also Buiter, 1980). Following these contributions it became clear to everyone that *the rational expectations hypothesis did not imply the end of Keynesian economics*. The crucial feature of new classical models was exposed to be the assumption of continuous market clearing, that is, perfect and instantaneous wage and price flexibility. But, as Phelps (1985) reminds us, it is often through the rejection of a theoretically interesting model that a science progresses and 'even if dead wrong, the new classical macroeconomics is still important because it demands Keynesians to fortify their theoretical structure or reconstruct it'.

The early Keynesian attempts to fortify their theoretical structure concentrated on nominal wage rigidities. The models developed by Fischer (1977) and Taylor (1980) introduced nominal inertia in the form of long-term wage contracts. In developed economies wages are not determined in spot markets but tend to be set for an agreed period in the form of an explicit (or implicit) contract. The existence of these long-term contracts can generate sufficient nominal wage rigidity for monetary policy to regain its effectiveness. Because the monetary authorities can change the money supply more frequently than labour contracts are renegotiated, monetary policy can have real effects in the short run although it will be neutral in the long run. Fischer (1977) makes the 'empirically reasonable' assumption that economic agents negotiate contracts in nominal terms for 'periods longer than the time it takes the monetary authority to react to changing economic circumstances'. It should be noted, however, that neither Fischer nor Phelps and Taylor pretend to have a rigorous micro foundation for their price and wage setting assumptions. Instead they take it for granted that there are disadvantages from too frequent adjustments to wages and prices. For a recent innovative attempt to explain nominal wage inflexibility, see Laing (1993).

The argument presented by Fischer can be understood with reference to Figure 7.1. The economy is initially operating at point A. Suppose in the *current* period an unexpected nominal demand shock occurs (such as a fall in velocity) which shifts the aggregate demand curve from AD_0 to AD_1. If prices are flexible but nominal wages are temporarily rigid (and set $= W_0$) as the result of contracts negotiated in the *previous* period and which extend beyond the current period, the economy will move to point B, with real output falling from Y_N to Y_1. With flexible wages and prices the short-run aggregate supply curve would shift down to the right from $SRAS$ (W_0) to $SRAS$ (W_1), to re-establish the natural rate level of output at point C. However the existence of

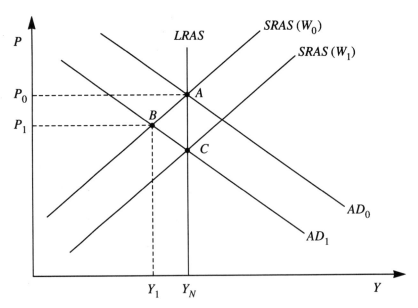

Figure 7.1   Nominal wage contracts, rational expectations and monetary policy

long-term nominal wage contracts prevents this and provides the monetary authorities with an opportunity to expand the money supply which, even if anticipated, shifts the *AD* curve to the right and re-establishes equilibrium at point *A*. Providing the authorities are free to react to exogenous shocks at every time period, while workers are not, there is scope for demand management to stabilize the economy *even if agents have rational expectations.* In effect, if the monetary authorities can react to nominal demand shocks more quickly than the private sector can renegotiate nominal wages, there is scope for discretionary intervention. The fixed nominal wage gives the monetary authorities a handle on the real wage rate and hence employment and output. The non-neutrality of money in the Fischer model is not due to an unanticipated monetary surprise. Anticipated monetary policy has real effects because it is based on information which only becomes available *after* the contract has been made.

Wage contracts are a significant feature in all major industrial market economies. However there are significant differences between countries with respect to both contract duration and the timing of contract renegotiations. For example, in Japan nominal wage contracts typically last for one year and expire simultaneously. The synchronized renegotiation of contracts (the *shunto* system) in Japan is consistent with greater macroeconomic stability than is the case in the US economy, which has a system of non-synchronized overlapping (staggered) contracts, many of which last for three years (see Gordon, 1982b; Hall and Taylor, 1993). In the UK contracts are overlapping but are typically shorter than in the USA, usually lasting for one year. When contracts are staggered, nominal wages will exhibit more inertia in the face of shocks than would be the case if existing contracts are renegotiated in a synchronized way so as to accommodate new information. Taylor (1980) demonstrated that if workers are concerned with their nominal wage *relative* to others then staggered contracting will allow the impact of monetary policy on real variables to persist well beyond the length of the contracting period. More recently Taylor (1992) has shown that the responsiveness of wages to supply and demand conditions in Japan is much greater than in the USA, Canada and other major European countries and this accounts for the more stable macroeconomic performance in Japan since the early 1970s.

An immediate question arises from the above discussion. Why are long-term wage agreements formed if they increase macroeconomic instability? According to Phelps (1985, 1990) there are private advantages to both firms and workers from entering into long-term wage contracts:

1. Wage negotiations are costly in time for both workers and firms. Research must be carried out with respect to the structure of wage relativities both within and outside the negotiating organization. In addition fore-

casts are required with respect to the likely future paths of key variables such as productivity, inflation, demand, profits and prices. The longer the period of the contract the less frequently are such transaction costs incurred and in any case management will always tend to prefer a pre-set schedule for dealing with the the complex issues associated with pay negotiations.

2.   There always exists the potential for such negotiations to break down, with workers feeling that they may need to resort to strike action in order to strengthen their bargaining position. Such disruption is costly to both firms and workers.

3.   It will not be an optimal strategy for a firm to 'jump' its wage rates to the new 'ultimate' equilibrium following a negative demand stock because if other firms do not do likewise the firm will have reduced its relative wage, which would be likely to increase labour turnover, which is costly to the firm.

Thus the responsiveness of wage rates during a recession does not follow the new classical 'precision drill process'; rather we observe a 'ragged, disorderly retreat' as new information becomes available (Phelps, 1985, p. 564).

Another important question raised by this discussion relates to the absence of indexing. Why are labour contracts not indexed to the rate of inflation? Full cost of living agreements (COLAs) are simply too risky for firms (see Gordon, 1993). The danger for firms is that not all shocks are nominal demand shocks. If a firm agreed to index its wage rates to the rate of inflation then supply shocks, such as occurred in the 1970s, would drive up the price level and with it a firm's wage costs, so preventing the necessary fall in real wages implied by the energy shock.

Finally we should also note that the staggering of wage contracts does have some *microeconomic* purpose even if it causes macroeconomic problems. In a world where firms have imperfect knowledge of the current economic situation, they can gain vital information by observing the prices and wages set by other firms. According to Hall and Taylor (1993), staggered wage setting provides useful information to both firms and workers about the changing structure of wages and prices. In a decentralized system without staggering, 'tremendous variability' would be introduced into the system. Ball and Cecchetti (1988) show how imperfect information can make staggered price and wage setting socially optimal by helping firms set prices closer to full information levels, leading to efficiency gains which outweigh the costs of price level inertia. Thus staggered price adjustment can arise from rational economic behaviour. In contrast, the case of wage setting in a synchronized system would seem to require some degree of active participation from the government.

7.5.2 Nominal price rigidity

Keynesian models based on nominal wage contracting soon came in for considerable criticism (see Barro, 1977b). Critics pointed out that the existence of such contracts is not explained from solid microeconomic principles. A further problem relates to the counter-cyclical path of the real wage in models with nominal wage contracts. In Fischer's model, a monetary expansion increases employment by lowering the real wage. Yet, as we have seen, the stylized facts of the business cycle do not provide strong support for this implication since real wages appear to be mildly procyclical (see Mankiw, 1990).

As a result of these and other criticisms, some economists sympathetic to the Keynesian view that business cycles can be caused by fluctuations of aggregate demand switched their attention to nominal rigidities in the goods market, rather than continue with research into nominal wage inertia. Indeed the term 'new Keynesian' emerged in the mid-1980s as a description of those new theories which attempted to provide more solid micro foundations for the phenomena of nominal price rigidity (see Rotemberg, 1987).

If the process of changing prices was a costless exercise and if the failure to adjust prices involved substantial changes in a firm's profitability we would certainly expect to observe a high degree of nominal price flexibility. A firm operating under conditions of perfect competition is a *price taker* and prices change automatically to clear markets as demand and supply conditions change. Since each firm can sell as much output as it likes at the going market price, a perfectly competitive firm which attempted to charge a price above the market-clearing level would have zero sales. There is also no profit incentive to reduce price independently, given that the firm's demand curve is perfectly elastic at the prevailing market price. Thus in this world of perfect price flexibility it makes no sense to talk of the individual firm having a pricing decision.

When firms operate in imperfectly competitive markets a firm's profits will vary differentially with changes in its own price because its sales will not fall to zero if it marginally increases price. Price reductions by such a firm will increase sales but also result in less revenue per unit sold. In such circumstances any divergence of price from the optimum will only produce 'second order' reductions of profits. Hence the presence of even small costs to price adjustment can generate considerable aggregate nominal price rigidity. This observation, due to Akerlof and Yellen (1985a), Mankiw (1985) and Parkin (1986), is referred to by Rotemberg (1987) as the 'PAYM insight'.

The PAYM insight makes a simple but powerful point. The private cost of nominal rigidities to the individual firm is much smaller than the macroeconomic consequences of such rigidities. A key ingredient of the PAYM insight is the presence of frictions or barriers to price adjustment known as *menu costs*. These menu costs include the physical costs of resetting prices, such as the printing of new price lists and catalogues, as well as expensive management time used up in the supervision and renegotiation of purchase and sales contracts with suppliers and customers. To illustrate how small menu costs can produce large macroeconomic fluctuations, we will review the arguments made by Mankiw and by Akerlof and Yellen.

In imperfectly competitive markets a firm's demand will depend on (i) its relative price and (ii) aggregate demand. Suppose following a decline in aggregate demand the demand curve facing an imperfectly competitive firm shifts to the left. A shift of the demand curve to the left can significantly reduce a firm's profits. However, faced with this new demand curve, the firm may gain little by changing its price. The firm would prefer that the demand curve had not shifted but, given the new situation, it can only choose some point on the new demand curve. This decline in demand is illustrated in Figure 7.2 by the shift of demand from D_0 to D_1. Before the decline in demand the profit-maximizing price and output are P_0 and Q_0, since marginal revenue (MR_0) is equal to marginal cost (MC_0) at point X. For convenience we assume that marginal cost does not vary with output over the range shown. Following the decline in demand, the firm suffers a significant reduction in its profits. Before the reduction in demand profits are indicated in Figure 7.2 by the area SP_0YX. If the firm does not initially reduce its price

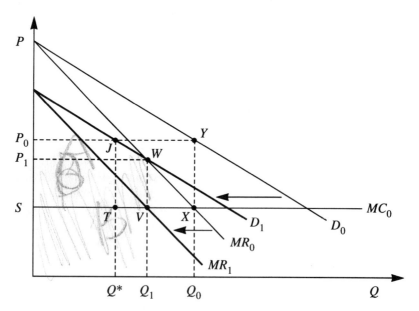

Figure 7.2   Price adjustment under monopolistic competition

following the decline in demand profits fall to the area indicated by SP_0JT. Because this firm is a 'price maker' it must decide whether or not to reduce price to the new profit-maximizing point indicated by W on the new demand curve D_1. The new profit-maximizing level of output is determined where $MR_1 = MC_0$. With a level of output of Q_1, the firm would make profits of SP_1 WV. If there were no adjustment costs associated with changing price, a profit-maximizing firm would reduce its price from P_0 to P_1. However, if a firm faces non-trivial 'menu costs' of z, the firm may decide to leave price at P_0; that is, the firm moves from point Y to point J in Figure 7.2.

Figure 7.3 indicates the consequences of the firm's decision. By reducing price from P_0 to P_1 the firm would increase its profits by $B - A$. There is no incentive for a profit-maximizing firm to reduce price if $z > B - A$. The loss to society of producing an output of Q^* rather than Q_1 is indicated by $B + C$, which represents the loss of total surplus. If following a reduction of demand $B + C > z > B - A$, then the firm will not cut its price even though doing so would be socially optimal. The flatter the MC schedule the smaller are the menu costs necessary to validate a firm's decision to leave the price unchanged. Readers should confirm for themselves that the incentive to lower prices is therefore greater the more marginal cost falls when output declines (see Gordon, 1990; Romer, 1993).

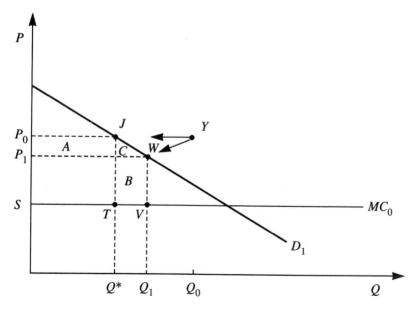

Figure 7.3   Menu costs v. price adjustment

In the Akerlof and Yellen (1985a, 1985b) model, inertial wage-price behaviour by firms 'may be near rational'. Firms that behave sub-optimally in their price-setting behaviour may suffer losses but they are likely to be second order (small). The idea of near rationality is illustrated in Figure 7.4. As before the profit-maximizing price following a decline in demand is indicated by P_1. The reduction in profits ($\pi_1 - \pi^*$) that results from failure to reduce price from P_0 to P_1 is small (second order) even without taking into account menu costs (that is, in Figure 7.3, $B - A$ is small). Akerlof and Yellen (1985a) also demonstrate that, when imperfect competition in the product market is combined with efficiency wages in the labour market, aggregate demand disturbances will lead to cyclical fluctuations.

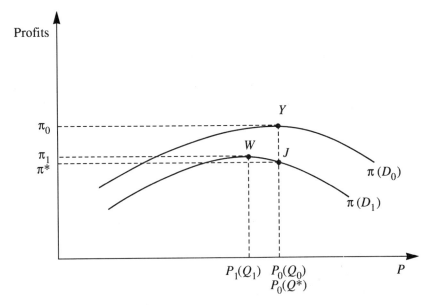

Figure 7.4   Near rationality

Although the firm may optimally choose to maintain price at P_0, the impact of their decision, if repeated by all firms, can have significant macroeconomic effects. Blanchard and Kiyotaki (1987), in their interpretation of the PAYM insight, show that the macroeconomic effects of nominal price rigidity differ from the private costs because price rigidity generates an *aggregate demand externality*. Society would be considerably better off if all firms cut their prices, but the private incentives to do so are absent. As before, assume that a firm's demand curve has shifted left as a result of a decline in aggregate demand. If firms did not face menu costs then profit maximizing-behaviour would dictate that *all* firms lowered their prices; that is, in terms of Figures 7.2 and 7.3, each firm would move from Y to W. Because all firms are lowering their prices, each firm will find the cost of its inputs are falling, including money wages. Hence each firm will find that its marginal cost curve begins to shift down. This allows firms to reduce prices further. In Figure 7.3, as MC_0 shifts down output will expand. Since all firms are engaged in further price reductions, input prices will fall again, producing another reduction of MC. Since this process of price deflation will increase real money balances, thereby lowering interest rates, aggregate demand will increase. This will shift the demand curves facing each firm to the right, so that output will return to Q_0.

If the presence of menu costs and/or near rational behaviour cause nominal price rigidity, shocks to nominal aggregate demand will cause large fluctuations in output and welfare. Since such fluctuations are inefficient this indicates that stabilization policy is desirable. Obviously if money wages are rigid (because of contracts) the marginal cost curve will be sticky, thus reinforcing the impact of menu costs in producing price rigidities.

We noted earlier that there are several private advantages to be gained by both firms and workers from entering into long-term wage contracts. Many of these advantages also apply to long-term agreements between firms with respect to product prices. Pre-set prices not only reduce uncertainty but also economize on the use of scarce resources. Gordon (1981) argues that *persuasive heterogeneity* in the types and quality of products available in a market economy would create 'overwhelming transaction costs' if it were decided that every price was to be decided in an auction. Auction markets are efficient where buyers and sellers do not need to come into physical contact (as with financial assets) or the product is homogeneous (as with wheat). The essential feature of an auction market is that buyers and sellers need to be present simultaneously. Because time and space are scarce resources it would not make any sense for the vast majority of goods to be sold in this way. Instead numerous items are made available at suitable locations where consumers can choose to conduct transactions at their own convenience. The use of 'price tags' (goods available on fixed terms) is a rational response to the problem of heterogeneity. Typically when prices are pre-set the procedure used is a *mark-up pricing* approach (see Okun, 1981).

7.6 Real Rigidities

One important criticism of the menu cost literature noted by Ball, Mankiw and Romer (1988) is that models with nominal frictions can in theory produce large nominal rigidities but 'do so for implausible parameter values'. However Ball and Romer (1990) have demonstrated that substantial nominal

rigidities can result from a *combination* of real rigidities and small frictions
to nominal adjustment. Indeed Mankiw and Romer (1991) identify the interaction between nominal and real imperfections as 'a distinguishing feature of
the new Keynesian economies'.

If all nominal prices in an economy were completely and instantaneously
flexible a purely nominal shock would leave the real equilibrium of an
economy unchanged. As Ball and Romer (1990) note, 'Real rigidity does not
imply nominal rigidity: without an independent source of nominal stickiness
prices adjust fully to nominal shocks regardless of the extent of real rigidities.'
However rigidity of *real* prices and wages will magnify the non-neutralities
which result from small nominal frictions. The importance of this point can
be made by considering the impact of a decline in the money supply. Suppose
initially that the presence of menu costs deters firms from reducing their
prices in response to this nominal disturbance. With the price level unchanged real output will decline. Each monopolistically competitive firm will
find that its demand curve has shifted to the left. Because each firm is
producing less output the *effective* demand for labour declines (see Abel and
Bernanke, 1992, pp. 462–3). If labour supply is relatively inelastic the shift
of labour demand implied by the decline in output will cause a large fall in
real wages; that is, the nominal wage rate declines to bring this about (see
Ball *et al.*, 1988; Gordon, 1990; Romer, 1993). This decline in the real wage
rate implies a decline in marginal cost, a decline which will be strongly
reinforced if the marginal product of labour rises sharply as the labour input
decreases. As is evident from Figure 7.2, an upward-sloping marginal cost
curve would greatly increase the incentive to reduce price and would 'swamp
any plausible barriers to nominal adjustment' unless the elasticity of demand
at the existing price falls as the firm's demand curve shifts to the left. *The
greater the decline in the elasticity of demand at the existing price as output
falls the more the marginal revenue curve facing a firm shifts to the left and
the less incentive there is for a firm to reduce its price.*

Romer (1993) sums up the essence of this issue as follows: 'Thus if the
classical dichotomy is to fail, it must be that marginal cost does not fall
sharply in response to a demand-driven output contraction, or that marginal
revenue does fall sharply, or some combination of the two.' Real price
rigidity is high the greater is the cyclical sensitivity of the elasticity of
demand and the smaller is the cyclical sensitivity of marginal cost. Hence
nominal shocks have large real consequences the greater the degree of real
rigidity.

The points discussed above can be more easily understood by referring to
the familiar mark-up pricing equation facing a profit-maximizing
monopolistically competitive firm (see Pindyck and Rubinfeld, 1989). Profit
maximization requires that the firm produces that level of output where

marginal revenue (*MR*) equals cost (*MC*). Marginal revenue can be expressed in the form shown by equation (7.1):

$$MR = P + P(1/\eta) \qquad (7.1)$$

where *P* is the firm's price and η is the price elasticity of demand. Profit maximization therefore requires that:

$$P + P(1/\eta) = MC \qquad (7.2)$$

By rearranging equation (7.2) we get equation (7.3)

$$\frac{P - MC}{P} = -1/\eta \qquad (7.3)$$

This equation can also be rearranged so as to express price as a mark-up on marginal cost. The mark-up equation is given by (7.4):

$$P = MC \frac{1}{1 + 1/\eta} \qquad (7.4)$$

Since marginal cost is the nominal wage (*W*) divided by the marginal product of labour (*MPL*) we finally get equation (7.5):

$$P = \frac{W}{MPL}\left(\frac{1}{1 + 1/\eta}\right) \qquad (7.5)$$

The term inside the brackets represents the mark-up, the size of which varies *inversely* with the elasticity of demand (remember η is negative). Equation (7.5) indicates that *P* will not fall when *MC* declines if the mark-up rises sufficiently to offset this decline (see Stiglitz, 1984). If the elasticity of demand does not decline then equation (7.5) also indicates that the incentive to change price will be small in the presence of menu costs if *MPL* does not rise strongly as the labour input is reduced (see Hall, 1991). Rotemberg and Woodford (1991) suggest that desired mark-ups over marginal cost fall during a boom because it becomes increasingly difficult to maintain oligopolistic collusion; that is, industries become more competitive in periods of high economic activity. During recessions implicit collusion increases, leading to a counter-cyclical mark-up which acts as a real rigidity, magnifying the impact on nominal rigidity of relatively small menu costs.

7.6.1   Other sources of real price rigidity

We have already noted that mild sensitivity of marginal cost to variations in output and procyclical elasticity of demand will contribute towards real price rigidity. The new Keynesian literature has also identified several other potential sources of real price rigidity.

Thick market externalities   In the real world buyers and sellers are not brought together without incurring search costs. Consumers must spend time searching the market for the goods they desire and firms advertise in order to attract customers. Workers and employers must also spend time and resources searching the market. When markets are '*thick*' during periods of high economic activity it seems plausible that search costs will be lower than is the case in a '*thin*' market characterized by a low level of trading activity (see Diamond, 1982). It may also be the case that people are much more willing to participate in thick markets where a lot of trade is taking place and this leads to *strategic complementary;* that is, the optimal level of activity of one firm depends on the activity of other firms. If these *thick market externalities* help to shift the marginal cost curve up in recessions and down in booms then this will contribute to real price rigidity.

Customer markets   The distinction between auction and customer markets has been developed by Okun (1975, 1981). The crucial characteristic of a customer market is a low frequency of search relative to the frequency of purchase (McDonald, 1992). Most products are sold through a process of shopping and, providing the costs of searching the market are non-trivial, the buyer will always have imperfect (limited) information concerning the lowest price in the market place. Because of the search costs associated with the shopping process, sellers have some monopoly power even though there may be a large number of firms in the market, each selling a similar product. Since a large number of customers make repetitive purchases it is in the interests of any firm to discourage its customers from searching the market in order to find a better deal. Firms are therefore discouraged from frequently changing their prices, a practice which will provide an incentive for customers to look elsewhere. Whereas an increase in price will be noticed immediately by customers, a decrease in price will produce a much smaller initial response as it takes time for this new information to reach the buyers at other firms. This difference in the response rates of customers to price increases and decreases, and the desire of a firm to hold on to its regular customers, will tend to produce *relative* price stickiness (see Phelps, 1985, for an excellent discussion of customer markets).

Price rigidity and the input–output table Gordon (1981, 1990) has drawn attention to the complexity of decision making in a world where, typically, thousands of firms buy thousands of components containing thousands of ingredients from numerous other firms, many of which may reside overseas. 'Once decentralisation and multiplicity of supplier–producer relationships are recognised, no single firm can perform an action that would eliminate the aggregate business cycle' (Gordon, 1981, p. 525).

Because a firm is linked to thousands of other firms via a complex input–output table it is impossible for it to know the identity of all the other agents linked together in the web of supplier–producer relationships. Because of this complexity there is no certainty that marginal revenue and marginal cost will move in tandem following an aggregate demand shock. There is no certainty for an individual firm that, following a decline in aggregate demand, its marginal cost will move in proportion to the decline in demand for its products. Many of its suppliers may be firms in other countries facing different aggregate demand conditions. To reduce price in these circumstances is more likely to produce bankruptcy for the particular firm than it is to contribute to the elimination of the business cycle because *a typical firm will be subject to both local and aggregate demand shocks as well as local and aggregate cost shocks*. As Gordon (1990) argues, in such a world no firm would be likely to take the risk of nominal GNP indexation which would inhibit its freedom and flexibility of action in responding to the wide variety of shocks which can influence the position of its marginal revenue and cost curves. Since indexation is undesirable when there is substantial independence of marginal cost and aggregate demand, Gordon's input–output theory not only provides an explanation of *real* price rigidity but also translates into a theory of *nominal* rigidity. The fundamental reason for the gradual adjustment of prices is that this represents the safest course of action for firms operating in an uncertain world where information is inevitably imperfect.

Clearly the informational requirements necessary for rational pricing behaviour in every period are enormous for price setting-firms. Not only do they need to know the position and shape of their demand and cost curves, they also need to predict the pricing behaviour of all the other firms in the input–output table. Since the firm's demand and cost curves are influenced by aggregate demand, it is also necessary for firms to predict the value of all the relevant macro variables that influence aggregate demand. In short, the decision makers within monopolistically competitive firms need to be first-class general equilibrium theorists with perfect information! Given these complications, the tendency of firms to follow simple mark-up pricing rules may be close to optimal. The incentive to follow such rules is reinforced if other firms do likewise, since this ensures that a firm will maintain its relative price, which will tend to minimize its losses (see Naish, 1993). Another simple rule which a firm can follow in a complex input–output world is to wait until other firms raise or lower their price before initiating a change. This produces *staggering* in price setting, which implies that the price level will take longer to adjust to an aggregate demand shock.

Capital market imperfections   An important obstacle to firms seeking external finance is the problem of asymmetric information between borrowers and lenders; that is, borrowers are much better informed about the viability and quality of their investment projects than lenders. One consequence of this will be that *external* finance will be more expensive to a firm than *internal* finance. During booms when firms are making higher profits there are more internal funds to finance various projects. Hence during recessions the cost of finance rises as the result of a greater reliance on external sources. If the cost of capital is counter-cyclical this too will tend to make a firm's costs rise during a recession (see Bernanke and Gertler, 1989; Romer, 1993).

Judging quality by price   Stiglitz (1987) has emphasized another reason why firms may be reluctant to reduce price when faced with a decline in demand. In markets where customers have imperfect information about the characteristics of the products which they wish to buy, the price may be used as a quality signal. By lowering price a firm runs the risk that its customers (or potential customers) may interpret this action as a signal indicating a deterioration of quality.

Having examined several potential sources of real rigidity in the product market, we will now turn to real rigidities in the labour market. If real wages are rigid in the face of demand disturbances this substantially reduces a firm's incentive to vary its price as a response to such disturbances.

7.6.2   Real wage rigidity

Economists have been much better at explaining the consequences of nominal wage rigidity than they have in providing a generally acceptable theoretical explanation of the causes of such inertia. Nominal rigidities allow fluctuations of aggregate demand to have real effects and contribute to a non-market-clearing explanation of business cycles. However Keynesian economists are also concerned to explain the persistently high levels of unemployment which have been a major feature of the labour markets of the major industrial countries since the early 1970s and particularly in Europe during the 1980s (see Table 1.2 and Figure 1.1). In new classical monetary and real business cycle models all agents are price takers. Perfect and instantaneous price and wage flexibility ensures that the labour market always clears at a Walrasian market-clearing real wage. *In a new Keynesian world, where price makers predominate, an equilibrium real wage can emerge which differs from the market-clearing real wage.* Stiglitz (1987) defines a market equilibrium as 'a state where no agents have an incentive to change their behaviour' and in new Keynesian models of real wage rigidity equilibrium may not be characterized by market clearing; that is, demand equals supply. Models involving real wage rigidity are capable of generating involuntary unemployment in long-run equilibrium, in contrast to new classical models where, with everyone on their labour supply function, unemployment in equilibrium is a voluntary phenomenon. Whereas Lucas (1978) argues for the abandonment of the idea that a large part of unemployment is involuntary, Solow (1980) believes that 'what looks like involuntary unemployment is involuntary unemployment'. (See also Hahn, 1987; Blinder, 1988b.)

New Keynesian explanations of real wage rigidity fall into three main groups: (i) implicit contract theories, (ii) efficiency wage theories, and (iii) insider–outsider theories. Since new Keynesian theorists have been mainly associated with the second and third of these, we will provide only a brief comment on implicit contract theory. The reader should consult Rosen (1985) and Timbrell (1989) who provide comprehensive surveys of the implicit contract literature. It should also be noted that Phelps (1990, 1994) treats theories of real wage rigidity as a separate category from new Keynesian theory, belonging instead to what he calls the 'Structuralist School'.

Implicit contract models   The original implicit (non-union) contract models were provided by Bailey (1974), D.F. Gordon (1974) and Azariadis (1975). Following the development of the natural rate hypothesis (Friedman, 1968a; Phelps, 1968) economists devoted more attention to modelling labour market behaviour as the outcome of maximizing behaviour. The main contribution of the 'new' microeconomics literature (Phelps *et al.*, 1970) was to explain why the natural rate of unemployment was positive. However there appears to be much less turnover in the labour market than search theory implies. Furthermore wages frequently diverge from marginal productivities. Implicit contract theory seeks to understand what it is that forms the 'economic glue' that keeps workers and firms together in long-term relationships since such arrangements, rather than the Walrasian auctioneer, dominate the labour market. Because firms seek to maintain the loyalty of their workforce they find it necessary to enter into unwritten (implicit) understandings with their workers. This 'invisible handshake' provides each worker with assurances concerning the terms of the working relationship under a variety of working circumstances. The models of Bailey, Gordon and Azariadis examine the consequences of optimal labour contracts established between risk-neutral firms and risk-averse workers. In these circumstances the wage rate not only represents payment for labour services but also serves as an insurance against the risk of variable income in the face of shocks. A constant real wage smooths the individual worker's consumption stream and firms provide this 'insurance' since they are in a better position than workers to weather economic fluctuations, given their better access to capital and insurance markets. Because firms provide stable wages over time, workers, for their part, accept a real wage which is lower on average than the highly varying rates that would be dictated by market forces.

A major problem with this approach is that it predicts work sharing rather than lay-offs when the economic climate deteriorates. The theory also fails to explain why the firm does not pay lower wages to new recruits. In attempting to remedy these and other weaknesses of this explanation of real wage rigidity, new Keynesian economists have developed efficiency wage and insider–outsider models of wage inertia.

Efficiency wage models Any acceptable account of involuntary unemployment must explain why unemployed workers are unable to bid down wages to a level that will generate full employment. Efficiency wage theories suggest that it is not in a firm's interest to lower real wages because the productivity (effort or efficiency) of workers is not independent of the wage, rather real wages and worker effort are *interdependent*, at least over some meaningful range. Efficiency wage theory, described by Gordon (1990) as the 'rage of the 80s', is surveyed by Yellen (1984), Katz (1986, 1988), Haley (1990) and Weiss (1991).

Solow (1979) provides the basic structure of efficiency wage models. In Solow's model, wage stickiness is in the employer's interest because wage cutting would lower productivity and raise costs. (Henry Ford knew this when he decided to pay his workers $5 per day in 1914.) Because the wage enters a firm's short-run production function in a labour-augmenting way, a cost-minimizing firm will favour real wage rigidity. This can be demonstrated as follows (see Yellen, 1984; Katz, 1988). Assume an economy with identical perfectly competitive firms, each of which has a production function of the form shown in equation (7.6):

$$Q = AF\left(e(w)L\right), \; e'\left(w\right) > 0 \tag{7.6}$$

Here Q is the firm's output, A represents a productivity shift factor, e is effort per worker, w is the real wage and L is the labour input. Effort is assumed to be an increasing function of the real wage and all workers are assumed to be identical. The firm aims to maximize its profits (π) which are given by equation (7.7):

$$\pi = AF[e(w)L] - wL \tag{7.7}$$

Since effort enters the profit equation as $e(w)$, a cut in the real wage below that which generates maximum worker effort will lower the firm's profits. If the firm can hire all the labour it desires at the wage it offers it will maximize its profits by offering an efficiency wage of w^* which satisfies two conditions. The first condition is that the elasticity of effort with respect to the wage is unity. Restated this means that the firm should set a wage which will *minimize labour costs per efficiency unit of labour*. This is illustrated in Figure 7.5. In the upper frame the effort curve indicated by E shows the relationship between the effort of workers and the real wage. The higher the real wage the greater the effort of workers. Initially there is a region of increasing returns where increases in the real wage rate elicit a more than proportionate increase in worker effort (productivity). Effort per pound (dollar) of real wage is measured by e/w. This ratio is maximized at point M where OX is tangential to the effort function. Since the slope of the effort curve (e/w) is the inverse of wage costs per efficiency unit (w/e), as the slope of E increases the wage cost per efficiency unit falls and vice versa. The relationship between w/e and w is shown in the lower frame of Figure 7.5. Since e/w is maximized at M with an efficiency wage of w^* the wage cost per efficiency unit also reaches a minimum at a real wage of w^* (see Stiglitz, 1987, p. 5).

The second condition for profit maximization is that the firm should hire labour up to the point where its marginal product is equal to the efficiency wage. If the aggregate demand for labour at w^* is less than the aggregate supply of labour then the market equilibrium will entail involuntary unemployment. Since the optimal wage rate w^* does not depend on either the level of employment or the productivity shift parameter (A), a shock which shifts the aggregate demand for labour will lead to a change in employment but no change in the rigid real (efficiency) wage. These points are illustrated in Figure 7.6. Here D_{L1} shows the marginal product of labour for a *given* level of effort (e^*). If the efficiency wage exceeds the market clearing wage (w) then the market equilibrium is consistent with involuntary unemployment shown by U. If a shock shifts the labour demand curve to D_{L2} then involuntary unemployment will increase, since the efficiency wage remains at w^*. Only if the market-clearing (Walrasian) wage exceeds the efficiency wage will involuntary unemployment be absent (see Abel and Bernanke, 1992). With $w > w^*$ firms would be forced to pay the market-clearing wage but, for reasons discussed in the following section, w^* is always likely to be greater than the market-clearing wage. If an increase in unemployment influences the effort of employed workers then the effort curve will shift up, which lowers the wage at which e/w is maximized. This possibility is illustrated in Figure 7.5 by a shift of the effort curve from E to E_1. The e/w ratio is now maximized at M_1, with a new efficiency wage of w_1^*.

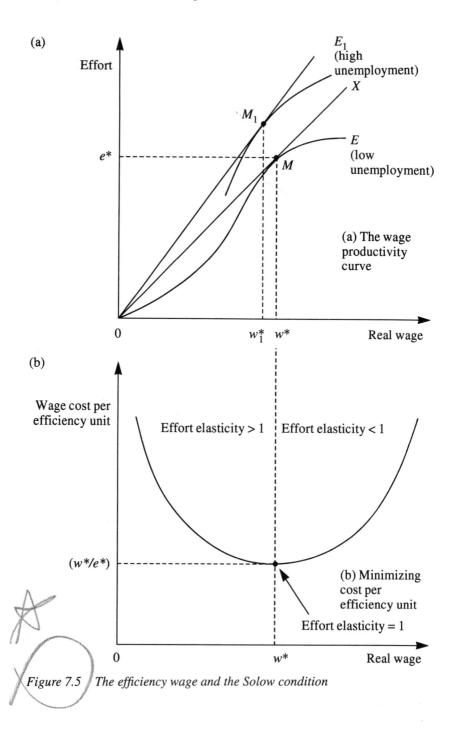

(a)

Effort

E_1
(high
unemployment)

X

M_1

$e*$

E
(low
unemployment)

(a) The wage
productivity
curve

M

0   w_1^* $w*$ Real wage

(b)

Wage cost per
efficiency unit

Effort elasticity > 1 | Effort elasticity < 1

$(w*/e*)$

(b) Minimizing
cost per
efficiency unit

Effort elasticity = 1

0     $w*$ Real wage

Figure 7.5 The efficiency wage and the Solow condition

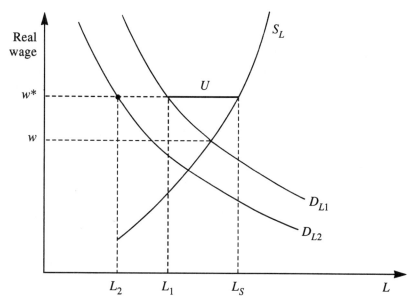

Figure 7.6 Involuntary unemployment in the efficiency wage model

So far we have assumed that effort is positively related to the real wage rate. Now we must examine the reasons which have been advanced by new Keynesian theorists to explain this relationship. The idea that worker productivity and real wages might be positively related over some range was clearly recognized by Alfred Marshall, who observed that 'highly paid labour is generally efficient and therefore not dear labour' (Marshall, 1920). More recently this idea reappeared in the literature relating to developing economies (Leibenstein, 1957; Bardhan, 1993). In this context higher wages increase the physical well-being of workers through higher nutrition, and by reducing malnourishment higher real wages improve labour efficiency. In the developed country context, where most workers have adequate nutrition, a different rationale is needed. The modern efficiency wage theories which have been put forward relate in general to the issues of *selection* and *incentives* and four categories of efficiency wage theory can be identified: (i) the adverse selection model (for example, Weiss, 1980); (ii) the labour turnover model (for example, Salop, 1979); (iii) the shirking model (for example, Shapiro and Stiglitz, 1984); and (iv) the fairness model (for example, Akerlof, 1982). We will examine each of these in turn. The reader should note that the papers referred to above (i–iv) are all collected in Akerlof and Yellen (1986).

The adverse selection model   In the adverse selection model, firms that offer higher wages will attract the best workers. Because the labour market is populated by heterogeneous individuals, firms have *imperfect information* about the productivity characteristics of job applicants; the labour market is an excellent example of a market where *asymmetric information* predominates. When there is asymmetric information one party to a transaction has more information than the other party. In this case workers have more information about their own abilities, honesty and commitment than employers before they are hired and will attempt to send signals to potential employers that convey information about their qualities, such as educational qualifications, previous employment record and current wage if employed (see Spence, 1974, for a discussion of job market signalling). Because of the non-trivial hiring and firing costs firms prefer not to hire workers then find they need to fire those with low productivity. The firm may also need to invest considerable resources in training new employees before it becomes clear that they are not up to scratch. One way of avoiding this problem is for the firm to send a signal to the labour market in the form of offers of high wages. In the model presented by Weiss (1980) the wage offered by a firm influences both the number and quality of job applicants. If worker's abilities are closely connected to their reservation wage then higher wage offers will attract the most productive job applicants and any applicant who offers to work for less than the efficiency wage will be regarded as a potential 'lemon'. Firms will also be reluctant to lower wage rates even if faced with an excess supply of labour wishing to work at the prevailing wage offer because this would in all likelihood induce the most productive workers to quit voluntarily. As a result of these influences an underemployment equilibrium is attained. To avoid adverse selection problems firms will attempt to introduce screening devices, but these measures involve costs, as will the continuous monitoring of workers after they have been appointed.

The labour turnover model   A second reason why firms may offer an efficiency wage in excess of the market-clearing wage is to reduce costly labour turnover. This approach received inspiration from the pioneering work of Phelps (1968 and Phelps *et al.*, 1970) in the development of explanations of the natural rate of unemployment and search behaviour. The idea here is that worker's willingness to quit a job will be significantly reduced if a firm pays above the going rate. With quitting rates a decreasing function of the real wage, firms have an incentive to pay an efficiency wage to reduce costly labour turnover. In the model developed by Salop (1979), labour market equilibrium entails involuntary unemployment since all firms need to raise their wages to deter workers from quitting. In situations where unemployment increases the wage premium necessary to deter labour turnover will fall.

The shirking model In most occupations labour contracts are incomplete, which allows workers to exercise discretion with respect to their effort levels. Because contracts cannot specify every aspect of a worker's performance and duties there is *effort discretion* (see Leibenstein, 1979, for a similar approach). Since the collection of information relating to the productivity of individual workers and the continual monitoring of workers is very costly to the firm, the payment of an efficiency wage in excess of the market-clearing equilibrium wage can act as an incentive which will deter the worker from shirking. Such behaviour may be particularly difficult to detect and monitor when teamwork characterizes the workplace.

The possibility that workers may vary their effort is a further example of the type of problem that can arise when there is an informational asymmetry present. Workers know more about their effort levels than do their employers. This asymmetry creates a *principal–agent* problem. An agency relationship develops whenever there is a relationship between economic actors and the welfare of one person depends on the actions of the other party, that is, when the welfare of the principal is influenced by the action (or inaction) of the agent. In the labour market case the principal is the owner of an enterprise and the managers and other workers are the agents. One way of reducing the problem of shirking in this context is to pay an efficiency wage.

The threat of dismissal is not an effective deterrent in a labour market where workers can quickly find a new job at the same wage rate. However, if a firm pays a wage in excess of that available elsewhere, or if there is unemployment, workers have an incentive not to shirk, since there is now a real cost to being fired and shirking becomes more risky for each worker. In the Shapiro–Stiglitz (1984) model, the payment of an efficiency wage acts as a disincentive to shirking and involuntary unemployment in equilibrium is an outcome of the problems firms face when monitoring is imperfect: 'With imperfect monitoring and full employment workers will choose to shirk.' By being paid more than the going rate, workers now face a real penalty if they are caught shirking. But, as Shapiro and Stiglitz (1984) note, 'if it pays one firm to raise its wage it will pay all firms to raise their wages'. Since a rise in the general level of real wages raises unemployment, even if all firms pay the same efficiency wage, workers again have an incentive not to shirk because if caught they will now face the possibility of prolonged unemployment. The 'reserve army' of the unemployed act as a disincentive device. Hence the effort (productivity) of the worker hired by the ith firm, e_i, is a function of the wage it pays, w_i, the wage paid by all other firms, w_{-i}, and the rate of unemployment, u. This is shown in equation (7.8):

$$e_i = e_i (w_i, w_{-i}, u) \tag{7.8}$$

When all firms pay the same wages ($w_i = w_{-i}$) shirking depends positively on the level of employment. The no shirking constraint (*NSC*) indicates the minimum wage at each level of employment below which shirking will occur, and is shown in Figure 7.7. In Figure 7.7 the market clearing wage is w. However, as is evident from the diagram, *no shirking is inconsistent with full employment*. As an incentive not to shirk, a firm must offer an efficiency wage greater than w. With all firms offering a wage of w^*, workers are deterred from shirking by the risk of becoming unemployed. The diagram also shows that the need to pay a wage greater than w decreases as unemployment increases and that the efficiency wage w^* and level of employment L_0 are associated with an equilibrium level of *involuntary* unemployment indicated by $L_F - L_0$. As the *NSC* will always lie above and to the left of the labour supply curve, there will always be some involuntary unemployment in equilibrium.

The *NCS* will shift to the left if the firm reduces its monitoring intensity and/or the government increases unemployment benefit. In each case the wage necessary to deter shirking at each level of employment is higher. A change in the *NSC* brought about by either of the above reasons is shown in Figure 7.7 as a shift of *NSC* from NSC_0 to NSC_1. The equilibrium following this shift is indicated by E_1, showing that the model predicts an increase in the efficiency wage and an increase in the equilibrium rate of involuntary unemployment as a result of these changes.

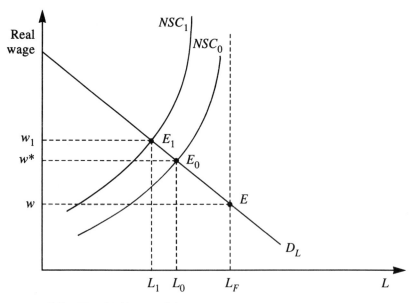

Figure 7.7   The shirking model

The fairness model   In recent years several economists have examined the adverse effects of 'unfair wages' and wage cuts on worker effort via the impact such cuts will have on the *morale* of the workforce. Sociological models stress such factors as the importance of wage relativities, status, relative deprivation, loyalty, trust and equity. In a series of papers, Akerlof (1982, 1984) and Akerlof and Yellen (1987, 1988, 1990) have taken up Solow's (1979, 1980) 'piece of home-made sociology' and developed models where feelings about equity and fairness act as a deterrent to firms to offer too low wages in the labour market. Thurow (1983), Blinder (1988b) and Solow (1990) have also indicated that this socioeconomic line of inquiry could prove fruitful as an explanation of persistent unemployment.

Many economists are critical of models where the labour market is modelled in much the same way as a commodity or financial market. The flexible price–auction model employed by new classical economists does not seem to resemble observed labour market behaviour. There are fundamental differences between labour inputs and other non-human inputs into the production process:

1. workers have preferences and feelings; machines and raw materials do not;
2. workers need to be motivated, machines do not;
3. the productivity of a machine is reasonably well known before purchase, so that problems of asymmetric information relating to quality are much less significant;
4. workers can strike and 'break down' because of ill health (stress and so on); machines can break down but never strike for higher pay or more holidays;
5. the human capital assets of a firm are more illiquid and risky than its capital assets;
6. workers normally require training, machines do not;
7. human capital cannot be separated from its owner, non-human capital can;
8. workers' utility functions are interdependent, not independent.

Because of these crucial differences, *worker productivity is a discretionary variable*; the effort or output of a worker is not given in advance and fixed for the future, irrespective of changes which take place in working conditions. A machine does not get angry when its price fluctuates, nor does it feel upset if it is switched off. In contrast, workers are not indifferent to their price, nor are they unmoved by becoming unemployed against their will. For these and other reasons, the notion of *fairness* would seem to be an important factor in determining outcomes in the labour market. As Solow (1990) has argued,

'The most elementary reason for thinking that the concept of fairness, and beliefs about what is fair and what is not, play an important part in labour market behaviour is that we talk about them all the time.' The words 'fair' and 'unfair' have even been used by neoclassical economists at university departmental meetings!

The first formal model to bring in sociological elements as an explanation of efficiency wages was the seminal paper by Akerlof (1982) where issues relating to fairness lie at the centre of the argument. According to Akerlof, the willing cooperation of workers is something which must usually be obtained by the firm because labour contracts are incomplete and teamwork is frequently the norm. The essense of Akerlof's gift exchange model is neatly summed up in the phrase, 'A fair day's work for a fair day's pay'. Everyday observation suggests that people have an innate psychological need to feel fairly treated, otherwise their morale is adversely affected. In Akerlof's model workers' effort is a positive function of their morale and a major influence on their morale is the remuneration they receive *for a given work standard which is regarded as the norm*. If a firm pays its workers a wage above the going market rate, workers will respond by raising their group work norms, providing the firm with a *gift* of higher productivity in *exchange* for the higher wage.

In subsequent work Akerlof and Yellen (1990) have developed what they call the '*fair wage effort hypothesis*' which is derived from equity theory. In the workplace personal contact and potentially conflicting relationships within a team of workers are unavoidable. As a result issues relating to fairness are never far away. Since there is no *absolute* measure of fairness, people measure their treatment by reference to other individuals within their own reference group. Fairness is measured by making comparisons with workers similarly situated (inside and outside the firm). Thus an individual worker's utility function can be summarized as equation (7.9):

$$U = U(w / \varpi, e, u) \qquad (7.9)$$

The utility of this worker (U) is dependent on the real wage (w) relative to the perceived 'fair' wage (ϖ), the worker's effort (e) and the unemployment rate (u). Assuming the worker wishes to maximize this function, the effort expended will depend on the relationship between w and ϖ for a given level of unemployment. Workers who feel unfairly treated ($w < \varpi$) will adjust their effort accordingly. 'The ability of workers to exercise control over their effort, and their willingness to do so in response to grievances, underlies the fair wage–effort hypothesis' (Akerlof and Yellen, 1990, p. 262). Just as firms face a no-shirking constraint in the Shapiro–Stiglitz model, they face a 'fair wage constraint' in the fairness version of the efficiency wage model. Since the fair wage exceeds the market-clearing wage, this framework generates an equilibrium with involuntary unemployment.

The essence of this innovative approach to explaining real wage rigidity is that the morale of a firm's human capital can easily be damaged if workers perceive that they are being unfairly treated. Firms who attach importance to their *reputation* as an employer and who wish to generate high morale and loyalty from their workforce will tend to pay efficiency wages which are perceived as fair.

Insider–outsider models   Why don't unemployed workers offer to work for lower wages than those currently paid to employed workers? If they did so wages would be bid down and employment would increase. There appears to be an unwritten eleventh commandment: 'Thou shalt not permit job theft by underbidding and stealing the jobs of thy comrades.' The insider–outsider theory also attempts to explain why wage rigidity persists in the face of involuntary unemployment (see Ball, 1990, for a review).

The insider–outsider approach to real wage rigidity was developed during the 1980s in a series of contributions by Lindbeck and Snower (1985, 1986, 1988a, 1988b). In this model the *insiders* are the incumbent employees and the *outsiders* are the unemployed workers. Whereas in efficiency wage models it is firms who decide to pay a wage higher than the market–clearing wage, in the insider–outsider approach the focus shifts to the power of the insiders who at least partially determine wage and employment decisions. No direct effects of wages on productivity are assumed.

Where does the insider power come from? According to Lindbeck and Snower, insider power arises as a result of *turnover costs*. These include hiring and firing costs such as those associated with costs of searching the labour market, advertising and screening, negotiating conditions of employment, mandatory severance pay and litigation costs. Other important costs are production-related and arise from the need to train new employees. In addition to these well known turnover costs, Lindbeck and Snower (1988a) also emphasize a more novel form of cost, the insider's ability and incentive to cooperate with or harass new workers coming from the ranks of the outsiders. If insiders feel that their position is threatened by outsiders they can refuse to cooperate with and train new workers, as well as make life at work thoroughly unpleasant. By raising the disutility of work, this causes the outsiders' reservation wage to rise, making it less attractive for the firm to employ them. To the extent that cooperation and harassment activities lie within the control of workers, they can have a significant influence on turnover costs by their own behaviour.

Because firms with high rates of turnover offer both a lack of job security and few opportunities for advancement, workers have little or no incentive to build reputations with their employers. Low motivation damages productivity and this represents yet another cost of high labour turnover.

Because it is costly to exchange a firm's current employees for unemployed outsiders, the insiders have leverage which they can use to extract a share of the economic rent generated by turnover costs (the firm has an incentive to pay something to avoid costly turnover). Lindbeck and Snower assume that workers have sufficient bargaining power to extract some of this rent during wage negotiations. Although unions are not necessary for insider power they enhance it with their ability to threaten strikes and work-to-rule forms of non-cooperation (For a discussion of union bargaining models and unemployment, see McDonald and Solow, 1981; Nickell, 1990; Layard *et al.*, 1991).

Although the insider–outsider theory was originally put forward as an explanation of involuntary unemployment, it also generates some other important predictions (see Lindbeck and Snower, 1988b). First, insider–outsider theory implies that pronounced aggregate shocks which shift the demand for labour may have *persistent* effects on wages, employment and unemployment. In countries with large labour turnover costs and powerful unions, this 'effect persistence' will be significant. Second, in cases where the shocks are mild, firms with high turnover costs have an incentive to hoard labour and this reduces employment variability. Third, the insider–outsider model can provide a rationale for many features associated with 'dual labour markets'. Fourth, this model has implications for the *composition* of unemployment. Lindbeck and Snower (1988b) argue that 'unemployment rates will be comparatively high for people with comparatively little stability in their work records'. This offers an explanation for the relatively high unemployment rates which are frequently typical among the young, the female population and various minority groups.

Although the insider–outsider theory and efficiency wage theories provide different explanations of involuntary unemployment they are not incompatible but complementary models, since the amount of involuntary unemployment 'may depend on what firms are willing to give and what workers are able to get' (Lindbeck and Snower, 1985).

7.7   New Keynesian Business Cycle Theory

New Keynesian economists accept that the source of shocks which generate aggregate disturbances can arise from the supply side or the demand side. However new Keynesians argue that there are frictions and imperfections within the economy which will amplify these shocks so that large fluctuations in real output and employment result. The important issue for new Keynesians is not so much the source of the shocks but how the economy responds to them.

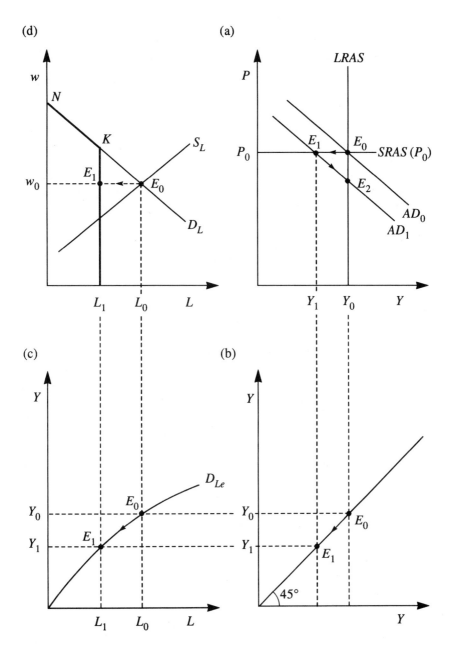

*Figure 7.8   The impact of an aggregate demand shock in the new Keynes-
ian model*

Within new Keynesian economics there have been two strands of research relating to the issue of aggregate fluctuations. The predominant approach has emphasized the importance of nominal rigidities. The second approach follows Keynes (1936) and Tobin (1975) and explores the potentially destabilizing impact of wage and price flexibility. We will examine each in turn. Consider Figure 7.8. In panel (a) we illustrate the impact of a decline in the money supply which shifts aggregate demand from AD_0 to AD_1. If a combination of menu costs and real rigidities make the price level rigid at P_0, the decline in aggregate demand will move the economy from point E_0 to point E_1 in panel (a). The decline in output reduces the effective demand for labour. In panel (c) the effective labour demand curve (D_{Le}) shows how much labour is necessary to produce different levels of output. As the diagram shows, L_1 amount of labour is required to produce Y_1 amount of output. With prices and the real wage fixed at P_0 and w_0, respectively, firms move off the *notional* demand curve for labour, D_L, operating instead along their *effective* labour demand curve indicated by NKL_1 in panel (d). At the rigid real wage of w_0, firms would like to hire L_0 workers, but they have no market for the extra output which would be produced by hiring the extra workers. The aggregate demand shock has produced an increase in involuntary unemployment of $L_0 - L_1$. The new Keynesian short-run aggregate supply curve $SRAS$ (P_0) is perfectly elastic at the fixed price level. Eventually downward pressure on prices and wages would move the economy from point E_1 to E_2 in Panel (a), but this process may take an unacceptably long period of time. Therefore new Keynesian economists, like Keynes, advocate measures which will push the aggregate demand curve back towards E_0. In the new Keynesian model, monetary shocks clearly have non-neutral effects in the short run, although money remains neutral in the long run, as indicated by the vertical long-run aggregate supply curve ($LRAS$).

The failure of firms to cut prices even though this would in the end benefit all firms is an example of a *coordination failure*. A coordination failure occurs when economic agents reach an outcome that is inferior to all of them because there are no private incentives for agents jointly to choose strategies that would produce a much better (and preferred) result (see Mankiw, 1994). The inability of agents to coordinate their activities successfully in a decentralized system arises because there is no incentive for a single firm to cut price and increase production, given the assumed inaction of other agents. Because the optimal strategy of one firm depends on the strategies adopted by other firms, a *strategic complementary* is present, since all firms would gain if prices were reduced and output increased (Alvi, 1993). To many Keynesian economists the fundamental causes of macroeconomic instability relate to problems associated with coordination failure (see Ball and Romer, 1991; Leijonhufvud, 1992) .

The second brand of new Keynesian business cycle theorizing suggests that wage and price rigidities are not the main problem. Even if wages and prices were fully flexible, output and employment would still be very unstable. Indeed price rigidities may well reduce the magnitude of aggregate fluctuations, a point made by Keynes in Chapter 19 of the *General Theory*, but often neglected (see Chapter 2 above, and *General Theory* p. 269). A reconsideration of this issue followed Tobin's (1975) paper (see Sheffrin, 1989, for a discussion of this debate). Tobin himself remains highly critical of new Keynesian theorists who continue to stress the importance of nominal rigidities (Tobin, 1993) and Greenwald and Stiglitz have been influential in developing new Keynesian models of the business cycle which do not rely on *nominal* price and wage inertia, although *real* rigidities play an important role.

In the Greenwald and Stiglitz model (1993a, 1993b) firms are assumed to be *risk-averse*. Financial market imperfections generated by asymmetric information constrain many firms from access to equity finance. Equity-rationed firms can only partially diversify out of the risks they face. Their resultant dependence on debt rather than new equity issues makes firms more vulnerable to bankruptcy, especially during a recession when the demand curve facing most firms shifts to the left. Faced with such a situation a risk-averse equity-constrained firm prefers to reduce its output because the uncertainties associated with price flexibility are much greater than those from quantity adjustment. Greenwald and Stiglitz argue that, as a firm produces more, the probability of bankruptcy increases and since bankruptcy imposes costs these will be taken into account in firms' production decisions. The *marginal bankruptcy cost* measures the *expected* extra costs which result from bankruptcy. During a recession the marginal bankruptcy risk increases and risk-averse firms react to this by reducing the amount of output they are prepared to produce at each price (given wages). Any change in a firm's net worth position or in their perception of the risk they face will have a negative impact on their willingness to produce and shifts the resultant *risk-based aggregate supply curve* to the left. As a result demand-induced recessions are likely to induce leftward shifts of the aggregate supply curve. Such a combination of events could leave the price level unchanged, even though in this model there are no frictions preventing adjustment. Indeed price flexibility, by creating more uncertainty, would in all likelihood make the situation worse. In the Greenwald–Stiglitz model aggregate supply and aggregate demand are interdependent and 'the dichotomy between "demand" and "supply" side shocks may be, at best, misleading' (Greenwald and Stiglitz, 1993b, p. 103).

In Figure 7.9 we illustrate the impact of an aggregate demand shock which induces the aggregate supply curve to shift to the left. The price level remains

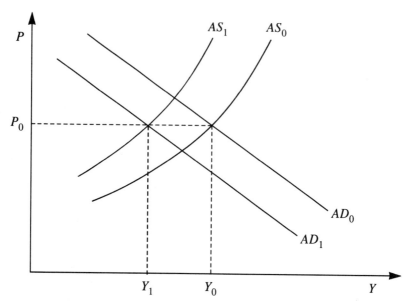

Figure 7.9   The risk-based aggregate supply curve

at P_0, even though output falls from Y_0 to Y_1. A shift of the aggregate supply curve to the left as the result of an increase in perceived risk will also shift the demand curve of labour to the left. If real wages are influenced by efficiency wage considerations, involuntary unemployment increases without any significant change in the real wage.

In addition to the above influences, new Keynesians have also examined the consequences of credit market imperfections which lead risk-averse lenders to respond to recessions by shifting their portfolio towards safer activities. This behaviour can magnify an economic shock by raising the real costs of intermediation. The resulting credit squeeze can convert a recession into a depression as many equity-constrained borrowers find credit expensive or difficult to obtain and bankruptcy results. Because high interest rates can increase the probability of default, risk-averse financial institutions frequently resort to *credit rationing*. Bernanke (1983) argues that the severity of the Great Depression was in large part due to the breakdown of the economy's credit facilities, rather than a decline in the money supply (see Jaffe and Stiglitz, 1990, for a survey of the literature on credit rationing).

7.8   Hysteresis Effects and Unemployment

During the late 1960s, Friedman and Phelps independently put forward expectations-augmented models of the Phillips curve. In Friedman's model the market-clearing rate of unemployment is called the natural rate of unemployment and is associated with a stable rate of inflation (see Chapter 4). According to the *natural rate hypothesis*, fluctuations of aggregate demand cannot exercise any influence over the natural rate of unemployment which is determined by real supply-side influences. Aggregate demand can influence the *actual* rate of unemployment in the short run, but, as inflationary expectations adjust, unemployment returns to its long-run equilibrium (natural) value. In new classical models, if the change in aggregate demand is unanticipated, the combined effect of continuous market clearing and rational expectations ensures that unemployment will quickly return to its natural rate. Many Keynesians have preferred to use what they call the NAIRU (non-accelerating inflation rate of unemployment) rather than the natural rate to describe the rate of unemployment consistent with stable inflation. The crucial difference between these concepts relates to their micro foundations. Friedman's natural rate is a *market-clearing* concept, whereas the NAIRU is that rate of unemployment which generates consistency between the *target* real wage of workers and the *feasible* real wage determined by labour productivity and the size of a firm's mark-up. Since the NAIRU is determined by the balance of power between workers and firms, the micro foundations of the NAIRU relate to theories of imperfect competition in the labour and product markets (see Carlin and Soskice, 1990; Layard *et al.*, 1991).

The dramatic rise in unemployment rates, particularly in Europe during the 1980s, suggested that the natural rate of unemployment (or NAIRU) must have risen and estimates made by econometricians confirmed this view. Two explanations have been put forward to explain this high level of unemployment. The first view explains it as a result of specific changes which have reduced the flexibility of the labour market; more powerful trade unions, higher unemployment compensation, minimum wage laws, excessive regulations and higher taxation are favourite candidates. However, while some of these factors may account for rising unemployment in the 1970s, many economists do not believe that they offer a plausible and complete explanation of the unemployment experienced in the 1980s (union power, for example, has been significantly reduced in the UK).

The simultaneous rise in the actual and equilibrium rates of unemployment has led some new Keynesian economists to explore a second explanation which allows aggregate demand to influence the natural rate (or NAIRU). Models which embody the idea that the natural rate depends on the *history* of the equilibrium rate are called *hysteresis* theories. It was Phelps (1972) who suggested that the natural rate equilibrium will be partly influenced by the path taken to reach equilibrium. Phelps called this path dependency 'hysteresis', a term borrowed from physics, where it is used to describe the lagging of magnetic induction behind the source of magnetism.

In hysteresis models the natural rate of unemployment (or NAIRU) will increase if the actual rate of unemployment in the previous period exceeds the former time period's natural rate (Hargreaves-Heap, 1980). This can be expressed as follows:

$$U_{Nt} = U_{Nt-1} + a\ (U_{t-1} - U_{Nt-1}) + b_t \qquad (7.10)$$

In equation (7.10) U_{Nt} is the natural rate of unemployment at time t, U_{Nt-1} is the previous period's natural rate of unemployment, U_{t-1} is the previous period's actual rate of unemployment and b_t captures other influences on the natural rate such as unemployment compensation. If we assume $b_t = 0$ then equation (7.10) can be rearranged as (7.11):

$$U_{Nt} - U_{Nt-1} = a(U_{t-1} - U_{Nt-1}) \qquad (7.11)$$

From equation (7.11) it can be seen that $U_{Nt} > U_{Nt-1}$ if $U_{t-1} > U_{Nt-1}$. In other words, the shifting actual rate of unemployment acts like a magnet, pulling the natural rate of unemployment in the same direction.

Theories of hysteresis fall into two main categories, namely duration theories and insider–outsider theories. Duration theories point out that, when $U_t > U_{Nt}$, the problem of structural unemployment is exacerbated because the unemployed suffer a depreciation of their human capital (skills) and as a result become increasingly unemployable. A high rate of unemployment also tends to generate an increasing number of long-term unemployed who exercise little influence on wage bargaining, which also raises the NAIRU. Insider–outsider theories emphasize the power of insiders which prevents the downward adjustment of wages in the face of high unemployment. As a result, outsiders are unable to price their way back into jobs following a rise in unemployment (see Blanchard and Summers, 1986, 1988). If hysteresis effects are important the sacrifice ratio associated with disinflation and recessions is much greater than is suggested by the original natural rate hypothesis, since high unemployment will tend to persist. (For an extended discussion of the issues raised in this section, the reader is referred to Cross, 1988; Cross et al., 1993, Layard et al., 1991; Gordon, 1993).

7.9 New Keynesian Economics and the Stylized Facts

The new Keynesian model is relatively successful in explaining many of the business cycle stylized facts (see Abel and Bernanke, 1992).

1. New Keynesian analysis is consistent with the procyclical behaviour of employment as well as procyclical consumption, investment and government expenditures and productivity (see Chapter 6 for a discussion of procyclical productivity).
2. The non-neutrality of money in new Keynesian models is consistent with the stylized fact that money is procyclical and leading.
3. More controversial (see Chapter 6) is the new Keynesian prediction that inflation will tend to be procyclical and lagging. Procyclical inflation is consistent with new Keynesian models which emphasize aggregate demand disturbances. However this stylized fact has in recent years been challenged (see Kydland and Prescott, 1990; Chapter 6).
4. New Keynesian models, unlike the old Keynesian models, do not imply a counter-cyclical real wage. When sticky nominal prices are introduced, the real wage in new Keynesian models can be procyclical or acyclical (see Mankiw, 1990). If the efficiency wage is sensitive to the rate of unemployment then real wages will tend to be mildly procyclical in such models (see Shapiro and Stiglitz, 1984).

Greenwald and Stiglitz (1988) in their survey of macroeconomic theories conclude that no model successfully explains all the data, but the new Keynesian model does better than either the traditional Keynesian or real business cycle alternatives. For those economists who see involuntary unemployment as a stylized fact in need of explanation, the new Keynesian models rooted in imperfect competition are 'impressively better' than the new classical or real business cycle alternatives (Carlin and Soskice, 1990).

7.10 Policy Implications

Following the contributions of Fischer (1977), Phelps and Taylor (1977) it was clear that the new classical conclusion that government demand management policy was ineffective did not depend on the assumption of rational expectations but rather on the assumption of instantaneous market clearing. In new Keynesian models which emphasize sticky prices, money is no longer neutral and policy effectiveness is, at least in principle, re-established. Since greater price flexibility exacerbates the problems of economic fluctuations in the Greenwald–Stiglitz model new Keynesians have also demonstrated the potential role for corrective demand management policies even if prices are flexible (but not instantaneously so). In a world where firms set prices and wages in an uncoordinated way, and where they are uncertain of the consequences of their actions, it is not surprising that considerable inertia with respect to prices and wages results.

In a market economy endogenous forces can frequently amplify the disturbing impact of exogenous shocks. As Stiglitz (1993) points out, new Keynesians are more concerned with they way an economy responds to shocks than with the source of the shocks. Experience during the past quarter-century has confirmed that economies can be disturbed from the supply side as well as the demand side. Indeed, as Benjamin Friedman (1992) has recently observed, it is often practically and conceptually difficult to draw a clear distinction between what is and what is not the focal point of any disturbance. Because in new Keynesian models fluctuations are irregular and unpredictable, new Keynesians are not enthusiastic supporters of government attempts to 'fine-tune' the macroeconomy. Many new Keynesians (such as Mankiw) accept the monetarist criticisms relating to old-style Keynesianism as well as the problems raised by dynamic consistency (see section 5.4.3). There is no unified new Keynesian view on the extent of discretionary action that a government may take in response to aggregate fluctuations. However *most* new Keynesians do see a need for government action because of market failure, especially in the case of a deep recession. Because of uncertainty with respect to the kinds of problems an economy may confront in the future, few new Keynesians favour the fixed rules approach advocated by equilibrium theorists and the majority of monetarists. The consensus among new Keynesian economists is perhaps best captured by Stiglitz (1993, p. 1069) who argues:

> Changing economic circumstances require changes in economic policy, and it is impossible to prescribe ahead of time what policies would be appropriate. ... The reality is that no government can stand idly by as 10, 15, or 20 percent of its workers face unemployment. ... New Keynesian economists also believe that it is virtually impossible to design rules that are appropriate in the face of a rapidly changing economy.

If the monetarists and new classicists successfully undermined the case for fine tuning, new Keynesians have championed the case for '*coarse-tuning*' – policies designed to offset or avoid serious macro level problems (see Lindbeck, 1992). The lesson from new Keynesian analysis is that policy intervention will be necessary in the face of huge shocks which lead to *persistence* because the adjustment process in market economies works too slowly.

For those new Keynesians who have been developing various explanations of real wage rigidity a number of policy conclusions emerge which are aimed specifically at reducing highly persistent unemployment. The work of Lindbeck and Snower (1988b) suggests that institutional reforms are necessary in order to reduce the power of the insiders and make outsiders more attractive to employers. Theoretically conceivable power-reducing policies include:

1. a softening of job security legislation in order to reduce the hiring and firing (turnover) costs of labour;
2. reform of industrial relations in order to lessen the likelihood of strikes.

Policies which would help to 'enfranchise' the outsiders would include:

1. retraining outsiders in order to improve their human capital and marginal product;
2. policies which improve labour mobility; for example, a better functioning housing market;
3. profit-sharing arrangements which bring greater flexibility to wages;
4. redesigning of the unemployment compensation system so as to encourage job search.

Weitzman (1985) has argued forcefully the case for profit-sharing schemes on the basis that they offer a decentralized, automatic and market incentive approach to encourage wage flexibility, which would lessen the impact of macroeconomic shocks. Weitzman points to the experience of Japan, Korea and Taiwan with their flexible payment systems which have enabled these economies to ride out the business cycle with relatively high output and employment levels (see Layard *et al.*, 1991, for a critique).

The distorting impact of the unemployment compensation system on unemployment is recognized by many new Keynesian economists. A system which provides compensation for an indefinite duration without any obligation for unemployed workers to accept jobs offered seems most likely to disenfranchise the outsiders and raise efficiency wages in order to reduce shirking (Shapiro and Stiglitz, 1984). In the shirking model the equilibrium level of involuntary unemployment will be increased if the amount of unemployment benefit is raised. Layard *et al.* (1991) also favour reform of the unemployment compensation system (see Atkinson and Micklewright, 1991, for a survey of the literature).

Some new Keynesians (particularly the European branch) favour some form of incomes policy to modify the adverse impact of an uncoordinated wage bargaining system; for example, Layard *et al.* (1991) argue that 'if unemployment is above the long-run NAIRU and there is hysteresis, a temporary incomes policy is an excellent way of helping unemployment return to the NAIRU more quickly'. However such policies remain extremely contentious and many new Keynesians do not feel that incomes policies have a useful role to play (for example, Mankiw).

7.11   Criticisms of New Keynesian Economics

The new Keynesian research programme has been driven by the view that the orthodox Keynesian model lacked coherent micro foundations with respect to wage and price rigidities. As a result the new Keynesian literature has been, until recently, heavily biased towards theoretical developments. Many economists have been critical of the lack of empirical work and Fair (1992) suggests that this literature has moved macroeconomics away from its econometric base and advises new Keynesians to 'entertain the possibility of putting their various ideas together to produce a testable structural macroeconometric model'. Laidler (1992a) also argues forcefully for the reinstatement of empirical evidence as a research priority in macroeconomics.

In response, new Keynesians can point to the non-orthodox but interesting and innovative research by Blinder (1991) into the pricing behaviour of firms, the empirical work related to testing the efficiency wage hypothesis (for example, Drago and Haywood, 1992; Capelli and Chauvin, 1991) and the influential paper by Ball, Mankiw and Romer (1988) testing menu cost models using cross-country data. In seeking an answer to the important question 'Why are prices sticky?' Blinder's research utilizes the data collected from interviews to discriminate between alternative explanations of price stickiness which is regarded as a stylized fact by Keynesian economists (see Carlton, 1986, for evidence on price rigidities). Preliminary results give some support to Keynesian explanations which feature coordination failures, cost-plus pricing and implicit contracts. Similar work by Bhaskar *et al.* (1993), utilizing data collected in the UK during the 1980s, confirms that most firms tend not to increase prices in booms or reduce them in recessions, but quantity adjustment responses via variations in hours, shift work, inventories or customer rationing are 'overwhelmingly important'.

A second major problem with the new Keynesian literature is that it has yielded numerous elegant theories which are often unrelated (Gordon, 1990). This makes the pulling together of these ideas in order to produce a testable new Keynesian model all the more difficult. New Keynesians have themselves recognized this problem, with Blanchard (1992) reflecting that 'we have constructed too many monsters' with 'few interesting results'. The fascination with constructing a 'bewildering array' of theories with their 'quasi religious' adherence to micro foundations has become a disease. Because there are too many reasons for wage and price inertia, no agreement exists on which source of rigidity is the most important. (For a critique of efficiency wage theory, see Katz, 1986; Weiss, 1991).

A third line of criticism relates to the menu cost literature. Critics doubt that the small costs of price adjustment can possibly account for major contractions of output and employment (Barro, 1989a). Caplin and Spulber (1987) also cast doubt on the menu cost result by showing that, although menu costs may be important to an individual firm, this influence can disappear in the aggregate. In response to these criticisms, new Keynesians argue that the emerging literature which incorporates real rigidities widens the scope for nominal rigidities to have an impact on output and employment (see Ball and Romer, 1990). A further weakness of models incorporating small costs of changing prices is that they generate *multiple equilibria*. Rotemberg (1987) suggest that 'if many things can happen the models are more difficult to reject' and 'when there are multiple equilibria it is impossible to know how the economy will react to any particular government policy'.

A fourth criticism of new Keynesian economics relates to the emphasis it gives to deriving rigidities from micro foundations. Tobin (1993) denies that Keynesian macroeconomics 'asserts or requires' nominal and/or price rigidity. In Tobin's view, wage and price flexibility would, in all likelihood, exacerbate a recession and he supports Keynes's (1936) intuition that rigidity of nominal wages will act as a stabilizing influence in the face of aggregate demand shocks. Tobin also reminds the new Keynesians that Keynes had a 'theoretically impeccable' and 'empirically realistic' explanation of nominal wage rigidity based on workers' concern with wage relativities. Since a nominal wage cut will be viewed by each group of workers as a relative real wage reduction (because workers have no guarantee in a decentralized system of knowing what wage cuts other groups of workers are accepting) it will be resisted by *rational* workers. Summers (1988) has taken up this neglected issue and suggests relative wage influences give rise to significant coordination problems. Greenwald and Stiglitz (1993b) have also developed a strand of new Keynesian theorizing which highlights the destabilizing impact of price flexibility.

A fifth criticism relates to the acceptance by many new Keynesians of the rational expectations hypothesis. Phelps (1992) regards the rational expectations hypothesis as 'unsatisfactory' and Blinder (1992a) notes that the empirical evidence in its favour is 'at best weak and at worst damning'. However, until someone comes up with a better idea, it seems unlikely that this line of criticism will lead to the abandonment of the rational expectations hypothesis in macroeconomics.

A sixth problem identified with new Keynesian economics relates to the continued acceptance by the 'new' school of the 'old' IS–LM model as the best way of understanding the determinants of aggregate demand. King (1993) argues that the IS–LM model has 'no greater prospect of being a viable analytical vehicle for macroeconomics in the 1990s than the Ford Pinto has of being a sporty, reliable car for the 1990s'. The basic problem identified by King is that, in order to use the IS–LM model as an analytical tool, economists must essentially ignore expectations, but 'we now know that this simplification eliminates key determinants of aggregate demand' (King, 1993, p. 68). King advises macroeconomists and policy makers to ignore new Keynesian advertising because, despite the new packaging, the new product is as unsound as the original one.

7.12   An Assessment of New Keynesian Economics

How successful have new Keynesian economists been in their quest to develop coherent micro foundations for sticky price models? Barro's (1989a) main conclusion regarding new Keynesian economics (for which he uses the acronym NUKE) is that, although some of these ideas may prove to be useful as elements in real business cycle models, NUKE models have 'not been successful in rehabilitating the Keynesian approach'. In sharp contrast, Mankiw and Romer (1991, p. 15) conclude that 'The new classical argument that the Keynesian assumption of nominal rigidities was incapable of being given theoretical foundations has been refuted.'

Keynesian economics has displayed a remarkable resilience during recent years, given the strength of the theoretical counter-revolutions launched against its essential doctrines, particularly since the early 1970s. This resilience can be attributed to the capacity of Keynesian analysis to adapt to both theoretical innovations and new empirical findings (see Shaw, 1988). Not only has Keynesian economics proved capable of absorbing the natural rate hypothesis and expectations-augmented Phillips curve, it has also managed to accommodate the rational expectations hypothesis. This fundamental metamorphosis has continued, with new Keynesian theorists attempting to rebuild the micro foundations of Keynesian economics. By emphasizing a variety of imperfections in the labour, product and capital markets, new Keynesian economics is viewed by its advocates as an 'exciting' and 'dynamic research programme' (Stiglitz, 1992). To the critics, new Keynesians have achieved little more than reintroduce 'old wine in new bottles'. It remains to be seen how successful the rehabilitation of Keynesian economics will be.

GREGORY MANKIW

Gregory Mankiw was born in 1958 in Trenton, New Jersey and graduated from Princeton University in 1980 before obtaining his PhD in economics from the Massachusetts Institute of Technology in 1984. Since 1985 he has been teaching at Harvard University, where he is Professor of Economics.

Gregory Mankiw is a leading exponent of the new Keynesian school of macroeconomics. His books include: *New Keynesian Economics. Vol. 1, Imperfect Competition and Sticky Prices*, (MIT Press, 1991), co-edited with David Romer, *New Keynesian Economics, Vol. 2, Coordination Failures and Real Rigidities,* (MIT Press, 1991), co-edited with David Romer, and *Macroeconomics* (Worth Publishers, 1994).

Professor Mankiw's best known articles include: 'Intertemporal Substitution in Macroeconomics', *Quarterly Journal of Economics* (1985), co-authored with Julio Rotemberg and Laurence Summers, 'Small Menu Costs and Large Business Cycles: A Macroeconomic Model of Monopoly', *Quarterly Journal of Economics* (1985), 'The New Keynesian Economics and the Output–Inflation Trade-off', *Brookings Papers on Economic Activity* (1988), co-authored with Lawrence Ball and David Romer, 'Real Business Cycles: A New Keynesian Perspective', *Journal of Economic Perspectives* (1989), 'International Evidence on the Persistence of Economic Fluctuations' *Journal of Monetary Economics* (1989), co-authored with John Campbell, 'A Quick Refresher Course in Macroeconomics', *Journal of Economic Literature* (1990) and 'The Reincarnation of Keynesian Economics', *European Economic Review* (1992).

We interviewed Professor Mankiw in his office at Harvard University on 18 February 1993.

Why do you think we have so much controversy in macroeconomics compared to microeconomics?

That is a hard question. It is certainly true that there is more agreement among microeconomists as to how they approach things. Most microeconomists start off with utility and profit maximization as the underlying motives. Macroeconomics is in some ways harder since you are dealing with the whole economy; the field therefore requires more simplifying assumptions to make anything manageable. I think there is disagreement as to which simplifying assumptions are the most useful.

How important do you think it is for macroeconomics to have neoclassical choice-theoretic foundations?

It is certainly true that all macro phenomena are the aggregate of many micro phenomena; in that sense macroeconomics is inevitably founded on microeconomics. Yet I am not sure that all macroeconomics necessarily has to start off with microeconomic building-blocks. We have a lot of models like the IS–LM model which are very useful, even though those models don't start off with the individual unit and build up from there.

Which papers or books do you feel have had the biggest impact on the development of macroeconomics over the last 25 years?

The biggest impact has undoubtedly come from Lucas. He put the cracks into the Keynesian consensus that existed in the 1960s. He really pulled macroeconomics apart. The disagreements today among macroeconomists have largely arisen from the critiques of Lucas and of his followers.

Where did you draw inspiration for your own work?

It's been a combination of influences. Part comes from the older generation of macroeconomists. I view a lot of the work I do as building on the work of Tobin, Modigliani and Friedman. I also take the problems that Lucas pointed out very seriously. We need to address the concerns of Lucas while still maintaining the element of truth in the neoclassical synthesis.

Why do you think there are so many conflicting interpretations of the General Theory*?*

Keynes had a lot of different ideas. Some people grab onto one set of ideas and say that this is really what is central to what Keynes was saying, and other people grab onto another set of ideas. There is so much in the *General Theory* that it is hard to comprehend it all at once. Disagreements come by choosing different pieces of Keynes's world-view and emphasizing those.

Do you think that, if Keynes had still been living in 1969, he would have received the first Nobel Prize in Economics?
Oh, undoubtedly. I think there are a few very very important economists of the century, and there is no question that Keynes has got to be on anybody's short list.

Do you regard yourself as a Keynesian?
I do, but I'm always nervous about the term because the term 'Keynesian' can mean different things to different people. Recently I have tried to avoid using the term at all, on the grounds that it is more confusing than illuminating. I think of myself as a Keynesian in the sense of believing that the business cycle represents some sort of market imperfection on a grand scale. Milton Friedman was also a Keynesian in that sense. Some people take the word 'Keynesian' as meaning a belief in fine-tuning the economy. Other people take it as a belief that deficit spending is not a bad thing. I don't subscribe to either of those views. I think that the broad theme of the *General Theory* is that the business cycle is something that we really need to worry about because it is a sign of a market imperfection. In that way I am a Keynesian, but as I said before, so is Milton Friedman.

What would you summarize as being the central propositions of new Keynesian macroeconomics?
The central propositions are largely theoretical rather than policy-oriented. New Keynesians accept the view of the world summarized by the neoclassical synthesis: the economy can deviate in the short run from its equilibrium level, and monetary and fiscal policy have important influences on real economic activity. The new Keynesian school has tried to fix those theoretical problems raised by Lucas and also to accept his argument that we need models supported by better microeconomic foundations.

So you wouldn't subscribe to arguments in favour of incomes policies advocated by Post-Keynesians?
No, not at all. When the government gets in the business of setting wages and prices it is not very good at it. The setting of wages and prices should be left to free markets.

So you are no Galbraithian?
Absolutely not [*laughter*].

Was the breakdown of the Phillips curve fatal for orthodox Keynesianism?
It highlighted the absence of a good theory of aggregate supply. What orthodox Keynesians had was a pretty good theory of aggregate demand, the IS–LM model. The problem is once you've got aggregate demand – a downward-sloping curve in P–Y space – you still need a good story for the aggregate supply curve. The Phillips curve came out of nowhere; it is really just a summary of the data. We never had a good theory of that empirical relationship, and the breakdown of the Phillips curve made that very apparent. It also provided room for the more general critique that Lucas put forward.

Do you regard new classical macroeconomics as a separate school of thought from monetarism?
I think so. My impression is that monetarism is a school of thought that says fluctuations in the money supply are the primary cause of fluctuations in aggregate demand and in aggregate income, whereas new classicism is a particular theory as to why fluctuations in aggregate demand may have real effects through an unanticipated price surprise. New classicism is really the next step after monetarism. More recently, new classical economists have turned their attention to real business cycle theory, which is the antithesis of monetarism.

Do you think that overall the new classical contributions have had a beneficial effect on the development of macroeconomics?
Debate is healthy, and the new Keynesian school arose largely in response to the new classical school. A lot of the specific contributions, especially real business cycle theory, are probably not going to survive the test of time. The literature on the time inconsistency of policy is a contribution that will survive the test of time, and has probably been one of the most important contributions to policy analysis in the past two decades.

How important is the rational expectations hypothesis?
It is important in the sense that it has now become the working hypothesis of all practising macroeconomists. It would be peculiar for us to assume that people are rational except when they come to form expectations. I don't think the rational expectations hypothesis is important in the sense of having all the sweeping implications, as was at first believed, such as monetary policy being ineffective.

Much research in the 1980s was directed at providing more rigorous microeconomic foundations for the central elements of Keynesian economics. How successful do you think that research has been?

It has been successful at the theoretical level. There are now several microeconomic models of wage and price rigidities that people can pull off the shelf. The theoretical challenge of Lucas and his followers has been met. It is less clear whether it is going to be successful as an empirical matter. The jury is still out on that one. There is a small empirical literature, but so far research has not been as empirically motivated as I would like.

In your recent edited volumes of collected papers on new Keynesian economics you say that 'new Keynesian macroeconomics could just as easily be labelled new monetarist economics'. What exactly did you mean?

The challenge raised by the real business cycle school is the question of whether money is neutral and, if not, why not? Friedman and Tobin agreed on the proposition that the Federal Reserve was an important player in the economy, that what it did really mattered. The real business cycle school has challenged that by writing down models without any real effects of monetary policy. What the new Keynesian models have tried to do is establish why money is not neutral and what microeconomic imperfections are necessary to explain monetary non-neutrality at the macro level. In this sense, these models are trying to support both traditional Keynesian and monetarist views.

In your work you've argued that the literature on time inconsistency has provided a persuasive case for a commitment to some sort of rule for monetary policy. Do you also support fiscal rules?

Fiscal rules have to be well crafted. A balanced budget amendment that is too strict could be a disaster. At certain times, like recessions and wars, it is appropriate to run budget deficits. So any fiscal rule has to take into account special situations where budget deficits are the appropriate policy response.

Isn't one of the problems with devising rules that if the economy is hit by an unforeseen shock then the government may not want to have in place a rule which is really binding?

What we want to do is write down a rule that will be good in response to normal kinds of shocks, that is based on the kinds of shocks experienced in the past. Unless something completely unforeseeable happens you stick by the rule. So I don't think a recession *per se* is one of those extraordinary events that make you want to break the rule. But some events are completely unexpected: for example, before 1973 people never imagined an OPEC supply shock. This is the type of situation where you might want to rethink the rule. Now that we know what OPEC is capable of, we can write down a rule that takes this into account.

How important is the theory of imperfect competition to new Keynesian macroeconomics?
A large part of new Keynesian economics is trying to explain why firms set the prices that they do. Firms that have some ability to set their prices are those firms with market power: they are imperfectly competitive. Imperfect competition is therefore central to new Keynesian economics.

Given that Joan Robinson and Keynes were both at Cambridge during the 1930s, why has it taken so long to bring imperfect competition into macroeconomics?
I don't think that Keynes was as worried about building his model based on micro foundations as we are today. Joan Robinson was building the microeconomics that would later prove to be very useful for addressing the macroeconomics of Keynes. Keynes, not having read Robert Lucas yet, wasn't worried about building the microeconomics of aggregate supply [*laughter*].

In a sense haven't the Post-Keynesians been ahead of you here? People like Paul Davidson have for years taken imperfect competition as their micro foundation.
Yes, they do have a broad theme of imperfect competition but the details are not very similar. My impression is that the new Keynesian economics is much more in line with the neoclassical synthesis than with the Post-Keynesian analysis.

An important distinction seems to be made by new Keynesians between real rigidities and nominal rigidities. Why is it important to make this distinction?
A real rigidity is not a reason for monetary non-neutrality. Unions, for example, could set rigid real wages away from equilibrium. That would cause unemployment, but not monetary non-neutrality. To get monetary non-neutrality, which is a central challenge for macro theorists, you need some nominal rigidity, such as sticky prices. Having said that, there do seem to be a variety of real rigidities in the world; the question is whether nominal and real rigidities interact. The work of Larry Ball and David Romer [1990] shows that real and nominal rigidities seem to reinforce each other.

Critics of the menu cost literature have suggested that this is a small peg on which to hang an explanation of the business cycle. How can small menu costs have such large real effects on the macroeconomy?

It is clear that menu costs are quite small: firms don't bear huge costs when they change their prices. Yet it is also clear that recessions are very costly events. This literature shows that price adjustments by firms have external effects. When a firm decides to keep prices sticky, this could well be costly for the economy in a way that is not costly for the firm.

How do efficiency wage and insider–outsider theories fit into new Keynesian thinking?
These theories provide particular explanations for real rigidities, such as why real wages don't move to the equilibrium level in labour markets. As I said before, real rigidities and nominal rigidities can complement each other. That is, the insider–outsider and efficiency wage explanations for rigid real wages in some senses complement the menu cost story of rigid prices.

Is the idea of hysteresis crucial to new Keynesian macroeconomics?
I don't think of it as being crucial. It is an interesting idea that a recession can have long-lived effects on the economy after the initial cause of the recession has gone. For example, the high unemployment in Europe in the 1980s persisted far longer than anyone could explain with standard models.

Do you see the concept of NAIRU, and the natural rate, as one and the same idea?
I see them as being basically the same. Most new Keynesian models involve some sort of natural rate; in that sense Milton Friedman has won the debate. Except for a small group of people working with hysteresis, the natural rate hypothesis is pretty well entrenched.

Under what circumstances do you think a government should actually stimulate demand?
Governments should stimulate aggregate demand when it is too low to maintain full employment or when there is reason to believe that unemployment is going to rise above the natural rate. But even if you accept everything that new Keynesians say about prices being sluggish, there is still the question of how good the government is at responding in a timely fashion to the shocks. I am sceptical personally about the usefulness of fiscal policy in fine-tuning the economy. In that debate, I side to a large extent with Milton Friedman. The government is very bad at recognizing shocks and when they do respond they often do so quite late and counter-productively. I see the business cycle as a form of market failure which a government is very limited in its ability to fix. However, in a very deep recession, along the lines of the Great Depression, there is certainly room for the government to do something.

Can we trust politicians to use fiscal and monetary levers in the right way?
This is a serious concern, but there are ways of fixing that problem. Countries with more independent central banks tend to have lower inflation. When you have less independence in the central bank there is more likely to be political pressure and therefore a greater possibility of following a policy of inflating too much. An independent central bank would be better at fine-tuning the economy, to the extent we fine-tune it at all, compared to fiscal policy which is always run by politicians.

How important do you think it is to take into account fairness when you are looking at the labour market? The work of George Akerlof, Janet Yellen and Robert Solow suggests that perhaps new Keynesians should start looking more closely at the psychology and sociology literature.
Some of the papers that they have written have been extremely interesting, but there is not a lot of compelling evidence yet that we need to abandon neoclassical assumptions. I'm not doing so yet in my work, but I'm certainly happy to read the work of others who are doing so [*laughter*].

You have questioned the argument that the disinflation experience of the early 1980s both in the USA and in Britain provided decisive evidence against the new classical claim of painless disinflation. Is that because the deflation was unanticipated?
The real business cycle view says that money anticipated or unanticipated doesn't matter. That is completely at variance with the evidence. Larry Ball [1994] has a paper that shows that for a large number of countries whenever you have a major disinflation it is associated with a period of low output and high unemployment. The evidence is completely clear on that issue. You're right that to a large extent the disinflation was unanticipated even in the United States. People didn't believe that Volcker was going to disinflate as fast as he did, and expectations of inflation did not come down until after the recession was well under way. I am sympathetic to the view that credibility is one determinant of how costly a disinflation will be.

Peter Howitt has talked about a Keynesian recovery, Alan Blinder about a Keynesian restoration, you seem to prefer the term 'reincarnation'; is there something important in the different terms used?
I chose the term 'reincarnation' because it means rebirth into another body. While there are many similarities between new and old Keynesian economics, there are also a lot of differences as well, and I wanted to emphasize that. In some senses the spirit of Keynes has been brought back, but it doesn't look like the old Keynes. In fact Keynes might not recognize the new Keynesians as Keynesians at all [*laughter*].

Do you think Keynes would have been a new Keynesian?
I don't know; I think Keynes was a very unpredictable fellow. I guess he would see some things in it he would like, and some things in it he wouldn't.

Do budget deficits matter?
I think they matter a lot, not for short-run macroeconomic reasons but for long-run reasons that are best described by growth models. The evidence as I see it is that large budget deficits reduce national saving and that low saving leads to low growth. That is a big problem for the United States today.

James Tobin [1988] *has suggested that good papers in economics contain surprises. What surprises have new Keynesian papers uncovered?*
One of the big surprises is that one can go a lot further with menu cost models than people had once thought. The complementarity between real and nominal rigidities is a surprise. But one of the disappointing features so far of the new Keynesian literature is that it hasn't been as empirical as I would have liked. That is a problem being remedied right now in some research.

What are your main objections to real business cycle theory?
My objections are mainly empirical. Theoretically they are very elegant models, and that is a large part of their appeal.

Doesn't the procyclical behaviour of the real wage provide support for real business cycle theories? How do new Keynesians explain the movement of real wages over the business cycle?
My understanding is that real business cycle theories predict very procyclical real wages, but my reading of the evidence is that real wages are only mildly procyclical. This makes it hard to reconcile this model with the evidence. The real wage evidence is not really that hard to explain. If you believe in a world where wages and prices are sticky, the cyclical behaviour of the real wage is really a question of whether wages or prices are more sticky.

How do Keynesians explain procyclical productivity?
The procyclical behaviour of productivity is a puzzle for people who don't believe in technology shocks. The traditional explanation is labour hoarding. In recessions firms keep on workers they don't really need so that they can have the workers still available when the next boom comes, and that tends to give the appearance of procyclical productivity.

Lucas [1978] *has suggested that we should abandon* the *concept of involuntary unemployment. What are your views on this?*

I think there is involuntary unemployment. Part of the new Keynesian literature has come up with models of the labour market to explain why involuntary unemployment exists, why real wages don't adjust to equilibrate labour
markets. There is a lot of truth to the efficiency wage theories and the
insider–outsider theories, for example.

Do you see any signs of an emerg. g consensus in macroeconomics?
I change my mind on that a lot, depending on what conference I go to
[*laughter*]. There are certainly groups within the profession that are agreeing
with each other, new Keynesian people like Olivier Blanchard, Larry Ball,
David Romer, George Akerlof, Alan Blinder and so on. Whether we as a
group are coming to agreement with some of the real business cycle group is
hard to say. I'm delighted that some of the people who previously worked
closely with the real business cycle models are now trying to incorporate
monetary effects into those models. That provides a hope that somewhere
down the line the new Keynesian models and the real business cycle models
are going to merge to some grand synthesis that incorporates the strengths of
both approaches. That hasn't happened yet; that is just a hope.

*If you were advising Clinton about macroeconomic policy for the next three
or four years what would be the kinds of policies you feel are necessary?*
My reaction to President Clinton's speech [17 February 1993] is that I don't
think we need the fiscal stimulus that he is proposing. Recovery is already on
its way. I am happy that he is worried about the budget deficit, as low
national saving is an important macro problem in the long term in the United
States, but I am disappointed that he is putting so much emphasis on tax
increases rather than spending cuts. That is really a view not so much about
macroeconomics as about the size of government. So I give him a mixed
review.

EDMUND PHELPS

Edmund Phelps was born in 1933 in Evanston, Illinois and graduated with a BA from Amherst College in 1955 before obtaining an MA and PhD from Yale University in 1957 and 1959, respectively. After teaching at Yale (1960–62) MIT (1963–5) and the University of Pennsylvania (1966–71) he joined Columbia University, where he is currently McVickar Professor of Political Economy.

Professor Phelps is one of the United States' leading macroeconomic theorists and an architect of the new Keynesian school. In recent years his research interests have focused on structural rigidities in the labour market. Among his best known books are: *Microeconomic Foundations of Employment and Inflation Theory* (W.W. Norton, 1970), *Inflation Policy and Unemployment Theory* (W.W. Norton, 1972), *Studies in Macroeconomic Theory: Employment and Inflation* (Academic Press, 1979), *Individual Forecasting and Aggregate Outcomes: 'Rational Expectations' Examined* (Cambridge University Press, 1983), edited and co-authored by Roman Frydman, *Political Economy: An Introductory Text* (W.W. Norton, 1985) and *Seven Schools of Macroeconomic Thought* (Oxford University Press, 1990).

Among the numerous articles he has written, his best known include: 'Phillips Curves, Expectations of Inflation and Optimal Unemployment Over Time', *Economica* (1967), 'Money Wage Dynamics and Labour Market Equilibrium', *Journal of Political Economy* (1968), 'Stabilizing Powers of

Monetary Policy Under Rational Expectations', *Journal of Political Economy* (1977), co-authored with John Taylor, 'Causes of the 1980s Slump in Europe', *Brookings Papers on Economic Activity* (1986), co-authored with Jean-Paul Fitoussi, 'Testing Keynesian Unemployment Theory Against Structuralist Theory: Global Evidence of the Past Two Decades', in *Issues in Contemporary Economics Vol. 2*, edited by Mark Nerlove (Macmillan, 1991).

We interviewed Professor Phelps in his office at the European Bank for Reconstruction and Development in London on 8 March 1993.

Which papers or books do you feel have had the most important impact on the development of macroeconomics since 1945 – excluding your own contributions?
I was all set to say the *Microeconomic Foundations* [1970] volume [*laughter*]. Well I would have to say the Phillips [1958] article because with that paper we see the beginnings of – not properly expressed – a notion of an equilibrium level of unemployment. Implicit in that paper is a zero inflation equilibrium, when unemployment is below this equilibrium level there's inflation – actually it's unexpected inflation but Phillips didn't really bring that out – and when unemployment is above the equilibrium level there's deflation. A tremendous literature followed, but I would say that was the main paper in getting us to think constructively about the whole supply side of macroeconomic models.

Which literature in addition to that associated with the Phillips paper has particularly influenced your own work?
There were two strands of literature that had an influence on me. One was the role of expectations in determining what individual actors or agents do. I was brought up on that in graduate school by William Fellner, a wonderful Hungarian economic theorist who transmitted to me the whole continental tradition of emphasizing expectations. I was amazed to realize that this began with Alfred Marshall, who defined equilibrium in terms of correct expectations, as did Gunnar Myrdal and Hayek. Somewhere along the line this notion was forgotten. When the econometricians and mathematicians took over, equilibrium became a steady-state notion, so the whole idea was lost. But people like Fellner, Abba Lerner and a few others remembered the old notion of equilibrium and kept the flame alive. The other influences on me came out of the labour economics literature on wage setting that pre-dated the Phillips curve literature.

What in your view is the central message of Keynes's General Theory, *and is that message still valid?*

People never get tired of asking that question, maybe because the answers keep changing from decade to decade [*laughter*]. One good answer is that if the expected profitability of capital is very low then the operation of the economy at anything like its normal equilibrium level may be impossible because you may need negative money rates of interest. Almost everything else in Keynes is now very controversial. But that hard core proposition has survived.

If Keynes had still been alive in 1969, would he have received the first Nobel Prize in Economics?
Oh, absolutely. He had insights into so many problems about the equilibration of the economic system. He illuminated the fact that, when there is so much uncertainty and expectations are so unpredictable and arbitrary, it is very difficult for the price- and wage-setting mechanism to find its equilibrium level. Even if it ever does find it, the equilibrium may have already moved off somewhere else. That's a very big proposition in Keynes, but there are many others.

Keynesian ideas spread very quickly in the USA, but how influential have these ideas actually been for macroeconomic policy making?
The controversial Keynesian notion that fiscal stimulus can be used to change the level of economic activity was tremendously influential in the United States. Some observers also think that it helps to account for the rise of the public sector in the post-war years. People believed it was insurance against depression.

Do you think that the neoclassical synthesis tidied up or undermined Keynes's theoretical contribution?
It introduced some constraints, or rules, into Keynesian policy doctrine. It suggested that the size of the public sector should be governed, not by employment considerations, but by Pigouvian welfare considerations. Deficits should be governed by Ramseyan growth considerations, while monetary policy should be responsible for either employment or inflation. Although it was a big change, the Keynesians I knew, most of whom were neoclassical synthesizers like Paul Samuelson and Jim Tobin, didn't lose their zeal for stabilizing the economy – they thought of themselves as real Keynesian activists. On balance the synthesis was an improvement, as it increased the clarity of Keynesian thinking and also served to unify Keynesian ideas with the earlier ways of thinking of Pigou and Ramsey.

Wasn't the neoclassical synthesis interpretation of Keynes deficient in that it gave insufficient emphasis to the issue of uncertainty?

The synthesis took the optimistic line that you can meet the Pigouvian and Ramsey conditions and that monetary policy can deliver full employment on a platter every day of the week. The Keynesian synthesis people lost sight of the basic theoretical insights that Keynes had come up with, such as uncertainty and difficulties of forecasting. Here's where Milton Friedman, ironically, was more true to Keynes's way of looking at the problem.

In the period 1967–8 both Milton Friedman and yourself provided a fundamental critique of the long-run stable Phillips curve. Were there any significant differences between Friedman's analysis and your own?
Yes. One difference is that Milton Friedman did not really produce a theory of the natural rate of unemployment. He was talking about a neoclassical setting in which employment is determined by the supply of and demand for labour and said that suppliers of labour don't know that the price level has gone up in relation to their money wage rates, so that they will supply more labour than they otherwise would. There would be a false equilibrium at an inflated level of employment. But there's nothing about unemployment there. I think that my theory was better in that it had the rudiments of a theory of unemployment in macroeconomic equilibrium. The basic idea was that if unemployment was very low then firms would have a big turnover problem – too much quitting. Every firm would be trying to outpay all the others. That's a disequilibrium situation in the expectational sense because all the firms will be disappointed to find that they are not succeeding in outpaying the others. The only way to have equilibrium in the sense of correct expectations about wages is to have the unemployment rate sufficiently high, so that the quitting problem is under control. I thought that was an awful lot better way of thinking about the determination of the natural rate.

Do you regard your expectations-augmented version of the Phillips curve as having fundamentally undermined the orthodox Keynesian position?
Well, I didn't think so at the time because I hadn't imagined that anyone would propose that expectations were rational. After they did I worked harder at trying to explain why I thought that wasn't a good premise to operate from. I elaborated a point made more fully in my 1970 paper in the *Microfoundations* book, that not all wage rates are revised every day. I like to think in terms of some periodicity in the way a firm's wage scale is reviewed. There is a staggered wage-setting process, so that if there is a shock calling for a drop in money wage rates to a new equilibrium then there will be a problem because money wages cannot jump down to that level even with rational expectations. The development of this idea was mainly done at Columbia with my colleagues John Taylor and Guillemero Calvo. Later I began to feel that I had not done justice to my original work because why should we swallow this

premise of rational expectations anyway? So I began to argue that prices would not jump to the new equilibrium level even if each individual thought he knew the equilibrium level. As individuals do not know what everyone else thinks the new equilibrium level is, they do not reduce their wage rates the way they should. That led to work, some of it with Roman Frydman [1983], on non-rational expectations.

How important do you think it is for macroeconomics to have neoclassical choice-theoretic foundations?
That's a tough question [*laughter*]. I certainly feel more comfortable having a choice theoretic basis for the way I describe microeconomic behaviour, as I feel that it is more robust than it otherwise would be. Let's try and mine the rational choice models first and see how far we get.

There appears to be more agreement over microeconomic issues rather than macroeconomic issues. Why do you think that is the case?
Maybe that's a delusion, because the really tough operational questions in microeconomics are not so settled. One of the things I have to worry about here at the bank is what sort of institutional changes have to be made in eastern Europe so that those countries can grow rapidly. That gets you into some basic questions about capitalism about which there is considerable disagreement. Is the East Asian model good, is industrial policy useful, do we just need private enterprise? And so on. Once you get down to comparable sorts of operational questions I am not sure if there is any greater agreement on the micro than on the macro side.

What role do you think the Microfoundations *volume* [1970] *played in the development of new classical macroeconomics?*
The island parable that I talked about in my (1969) paper and the elaboration of that in the introduction to the *Microeconomic Foundations* volume certainly had an influence on the work of Bob Lucas and some later work by Lucas and Prescott. I think there was a more basic influence, though. Before there could be rational expectations in macro there first had to be expectations in macro and that conference volume put expectations into the supply side of macro. The new classical movement simply specializes in a particular kind of expectations and simplifies the supply side in such a way as to get certain answers.

Do you think that the new classical contributions have changed macro-economics for the better?
Well, I think they have had a very instructive influence. In a sense they showed what it looks like under one lamppost, so we now know not to look any more under that one [*laughter*]. We need to look under others [*laughter*]!

What are your views on real business cycle models?
They are different from the new classical analysis – most of them are simply neoclassical. I think it's a really interesting line of development but doomed to fail. One thing it suffers from is that it doesn't naturally make room for unemployment. Secondly, it's probably way off the mark on a number of matters having to do with the real rate of interest.

In the late 1970s your work together with that of Stanley Fischer and John Taylor showed that rational expectations does not necessarily imply policy ineffectiveness. In retrospect do you think those papers marked the beginning of a Keynesian revival after a decade of crisis?
Well, they did try and resuscitate Keynesian doctrine. They did not, however, rekindle a great deal of fiscal activism in the Keynesian sense. I guess they gave Milton Friedman a bit of a fight with regard to monetary policy. At the Federal Reserve Board in Washington there are a number of followers of that way of modelling wages and prices who take it quite seriously.

Why are nominal wages sticky?
The answer that Taylor, Calvo, Fischer and I gave was that for the individual firm they become completely unstuck, but only once a year. As a consequence the average level is sticky. It can move only gradually in response to changes in the equilibrium level. Why that's the case is complex. One reason is that the head of a firm has better things to do than spend a good part of each day tinkering with his price list and wage scale.

In your book, Seven Schools of Macroeconomic Thought [1990], *how did you arrive at the number seven?*
Well, actually, I just wrote down the number of schools I felt like talking about and when I saw that they added up to seven I was pretty happy because that's a nice number [*laughter*]. It resonates with the seven pillars of wisdom and so forth. I thought it was pretty neat [*laughter*].

Over the years your work seems to have evolved towards what we would now classify as a new Keynesian position. Do you regard yourself as a new Keynesian?
Yes and no. I have moved on from it now. There is an important message in that work. But I am inclined to think that we are kidding ourselves in supposing that we can describe fluctuations in terms of departures of unemployment from an invariant natural rate. I have been trying over the past five or six years to work out a family of models that together capture as much as I can the kinds of shocks that are capable of moving the natural rate.

What are your views on the menu cost literature?
I wasn't terribly attracted to that way of looking at things. It's a competitor to the scheduled staggering view that some of us took in the 1970s, but that's not why I resisted it. Part of the rationale for the schedule staggering view was that the firm doesn't always want to be monitoring and thinking about its wages – whether they are too far above or below the equilibrium wage. Under the Ss policy that's precisely what they are doing – they are constantly looking at the difference between their own wages and their estimate of the equilibrium wage. That seems a very unrealistic view. Of course, if a firm began to get some idea that the equilibrium wage was way off from its current wages then it might stop to review its wages ahead of schedule, but that's not the norm.

What important lessons were learned from the monetary policy experiments carried out in both the UK and USA in the period 1979–82?
The lessons are a bit uncertain because so much was going on at that time. There was the second oil shock in late 1979 and the fiscal stimulus legislated by the US Congress with encouragement from the Reagan administration in September 1981. Maybe there were more things going on in the world economy than we were aware of. So it wasn't exactly a pure experiment. I don't think the lessons leap out at us. I had the feeling that the profession was drawing the wrong lesson and saying 'Gee, when you have tight money it sure takes a long time to get back to the natural rate.' I made a mistake – I underestimated in my thinking how long it would take. I think the profession was wrong not to recognize that the natural rate itself must have kicked up to a much higher level in the 1980s.

Why is it so difficult to reduce inflation without large costs in terms of lost output and higher unemployment?
Well, the issue is, how difficult is it? The profession drew the conclusion from the 1980s that it really is very difficult. I think it is far more difficult than the monetarists ever recognized. It's probably more difficult than I myself thought it was around that time. But I want to stress that I don't think that's the whole story of the 1980s – a big part of the story of the 1980s is a rise in the natural rate. The staggering of wages and prices can potentially create a problem for inflation stabilization, but it doesn't necessarily create a problem in every case. The more general problem is an expectational one in that people are not convinced that the monetary authorities are serious – the credibility problem. There is the related problem that the credibility that the monetary authorities have is not necessarily common knowledge. Nobody can be sure how optimistic the others are about how serious the monetary authorities are. This is like Keynes's beauty contest problem.

*Why does the responsiveness of wages vary so much across different econo-
mies?*
The institutions that are in place make a difference for the speed with which
the wage level can go up or down, or slow down. If there are unions there
will be more of a tendency to have long-term contracts. The whole fiscal
treatment of wages, unemployment and employment differs tremendously
from country to country. In my own recent econometric research I have found
that Japan is not qualitatively so different from other countries, it's just as if
the units are different. Japan's unemployment rate moves in just the same
way in response to shocks as it does in other countries – it just doesn't move
very much.

*Do you think the supply side-inspired monetary and fiscal mix adopted in the
USA in the early 1980s has been the main factor responsible for the emergence of structural budget deficits?*
I guess the supply-side theory provided a note of legitimacy to giving in to
the temptation to have tax cuts even though the expenditure cuts were not
clearly around the corner.

What is your view of the Ricardian approach to budget deficits?
One of the by-products of some recent research I have done on the determination of national unemployment rates around the world is that the world
public debt makes a significant difference for the world real rate of interest.
That's an anti-Ricardian finding.

*Do you think President Clinton is moving in the right direction with respect
to the budget deficit problem?*
I worry that the rise of tax revenue is going to prove to be imaginary. Also,
for some motives that I can sympathize with, the pressure is on to increase
public expenditure. They are probably not going to be able to cut further the
military budget as much as they had hoped. So that they are not really going
to make much progress on reducing the budget deficit.

*How important have efficiency wage and insider–outsider theories been in
recent macroeconomic analysis?*
I don't think that the profession has taken the efficiency wage theories very
seriously. You can read an entire macroeconomics textbook and will only see
a perfunctory passage that is almost an aside on shirking – maybe I am just
imagining this and it's not even there [*laughter*]. If you look at Hall and
Taylor [1993], a relatively analytical textbook at an intermediate level, there's
something about efficiency wage theory there but it's just sort of dumped in
without much commentary, as a sort of back-up to the notion of the natural

rate. I am sure the profession will think I'm crazy to take it so seriously, but I have been trying to see how, with a quitting or shirking theory of the natural rate, the natural rate changes in response to shocks.

What are the policy implications of efficiency wage and insider–outside theories?
I do strongly believe that it's a good idea to subsidize work, not non-work. So I find myself arguing more and more energetically for a programme of subsidies especially for the hiring of low-wage workers. That's where a lot of the unemployment is. It may also be necessary to reduce or remove most of the subsidy to unemployment in the form of unemployment compensation.

What is your explanation of the high level of European unemployment since 1980?
At first it was mostly due to the tightening of monetary policy. Increasingly it came to reflect a rise in the natural rate of unemployment itself. Part of that was due to the rise in the real price of oil in the early 1980s. Part of it was due to a rise in world real rates of interest, which is an external factor impinging on Europe – and most of that rise in the world real rate of interest resulted from the fiscal stimulus in the United States – that's the Fitousi–Phelps [1986] hypothesis. One thing I discovered in my recent econometric research is that tax rates make a lot of difference. While we talk about the Thatcher–Reagan revolution, which I guess means reducing tax rates, in fact tax rates kept on going up, though maybe more slowly than before. Taxes on employment, labour and wage income are very bad for the unemployment rate.

What are the implications for the natural rate of unemployment of hysteresis effects?
If a long slump has almost permanent effects on the unemployment rate then that's clearly a significant qualification to the natural rate idea. It doesn't mean throwing the idea out of the window. Even in my [1968] paper I emphasized turnover and hiring costs and so on as the underlying explanation of unemployment. Because of the presence of these costs there are frictions so that, if you start off with a high unemployment rate, it will take a long time for it to fall down to its normal or steady state equilibrium level. I guess that's what we call 'persistence' and some people mean by hysteresis only that. Others mean something more permanent.

Is the distinction between voluntary and involuntary unemployment a useful one in macroeconomic analysis?
Most of us now use the term 'involuntary unemployment' to mean a job-rationing phenomenon with wage rates above the market-clearing level. In

my work this rationing arises because wage rates are used as a defence against quitting and turnover – in the shirking model they are used as a defence against shirking. It seems to me that's a good way to model unemployment – I guess I like to model things the way I think they are, rather than model them in a way which is so remote that it's unrecognizable [*laughter*].

Do you agree with Lucas [1978] that we should think of unemployment as a voluntary activity?
He was writing at a time when he did not have any faith or sympathy with incentive wage ideas. The Chicago view is that wages will never be raised as a defence mechanism against quitting or shirking because firms can always find more clever means of dealing with those problems – by using various penalties on the worker. You don't have to be nice to workers to get them to quit less or shirk less. I think that accounts for the stubbornness with which Chicago economists maintain that the only unemployment out there must be voluntary. I don't know whether they still believe that – they do tend to come around eventually [*laughter*].

Do you see any signs of an emerging consensus in macroeconomics?
No, I think we are a long way from an emerging consensus. I hope that it's going to be something like new Keynesianism plus a moving natural rate. I think that's the way to go. Maybe it won't turn out that way, though.

As an American economist working in the UK at the moment, what are your observations on the recent conduct of macroeconomic policy in this country?
Isn't it surprising how little communication there is about the reasoning behind the expressed policy preferences and objectives of the government? They are just laid out as self-evident truths with no discussion. A month or two ago Prime Minister Major was talking as if all we have to do in this country is get the inflation rate down and everything will be fine. What sort of economics is that – I don't think that corresponds to any of our seven schools [*laughter*]. In the US we have our crazies, certainly, both from the left and the right, and every other direction – but at least there is usually a little bit of rhetoric so you have some sense of where they are coming from, what their perspective is, what they think. If you disagree, you can argue with them and question their assumptions. But I don't know how you would argue with Major. It's very strange [*laughter*].

8.   The Austrian and Post-Keynesian schools

> It is even possible that in the end it will turn out that there exists less difference between Mr Keynes's views and my own than I am at present inclined to assume. (Hayek, 1931b)

8.1   Introduction

This chapter considers the Austrian and Post-Keynesian schools as non-mainstream approaches to macroeconomics which represent an important part of that '25 per cent dissenting penumbra around a 75 per cent core of orthodoxy' (Blaug, 1988). Both research traditions have had a varied, but still quite limited, impact upon macroeconomic analysis as a whole. While the Austrian and Post-Keynesian schools represent minority views, there is much to be gained from examining the two approaches in tandem. Several arguments can be advanced in support of the proposition that, at the very least, both research traditions would benefit from talking to, rather than past, each other.

First, they share many similar concerns and criticisms of orthodoxy. For example, both the Austrian and Post-Keynesian approaches seriously explore the implications of *un*knowledge (ignorance that cannot be removed), non-neutral money which completely permeates production and exchange, and the adjustment problems confronting an economy where uncertainty, time and money matter. Such considerations are generally neglected by the mainstream sleight of hand which effectively reduces the problem of uncertainty to one of risk, a monetary economy to one characterized by barter, and transitional states to that of equilibrium.

Second, much can be gained from viewing the contributions of Keynes and Hayek (and their respective research traditions) as *complements* to each other rather than as rivals. A large amount of the work of Shackle has been directed at forging an intellectual bridge between Keynes and Hayek (see Lachmann, 1976; Harcourt, 1981). Both Hicks (1967b, 1982) and Gilbert (1982) have made the case for increased integration. It should also be noted that Durbin (1934) and Haberler (1937) argued, during the Keynes–Hayek debate of the interwar period, that a synthesis of such views should be taken, rather than reliance upon one approach in its entirety.

Third, such contact would allow the trading of strengths. The Post-Keynesian monetary frameworks developed by Minsky (1975, 1978), Davidson (1978) and Rotheim (1981), alongside the 'Keynesian project' of Barrere (1988), share many of the Austrian concerns with integrating money into the real economy. Likewise, the Austrian emphasis upon subjectivism, uncertainty, ignorance and historical time mirrors Post-Keynesian (especially fundamentalist) interests. Both groups could gain from increased intellectual trade: the Austrians from Post-Keynesian insights into the money-debt payments structure and the Post-Keynesians from Austrian insights concerning the structure of the money-pricing process (for a more detailed elaboration of such arguments, see Wynarczyk, 1990).

8.2   The Austrian Research Tradition

During the past 20 years Austrian economics has witnessed a major sustained revival in its fortunes. In the main, this is due to the commitment and tenacity of Mises and Hayek, alongside the salvaging and development of inherited ideas by Lachmann, Rothbard and Kirzner. It has also benefited from the contributions of a new generation of Austrian economists, such as Vaughn, Lavoie, Langlois, Rizzo, O'Driscoll and Garrison, engaged in spreading Austrian doctrines throughout the USA at such university bases as New York, Auburn and George Mason.

Menger, Böhm-Bawerk and von Wieser were instrumental in establishing, articulating and extending the early Austrian research tradition during the so-called 'marginalist revolution' and its immediate aftermath. It was Menger's approach, in particular, which provided Austrian economics with both a distinctive and a modern framework that remains central to its current development (see Vaughn, 1990).

The unique identity and international reputation of the Austrian school has been undermined on two separate occasions this century. The first took place around the time of Menger's death in 1921, when many of its central ideas were perceived to have been *incorporated* by the neoclassical mainstream (see Mises, 1969; Grinder, 1977). Austrian economics was not only threatened by this increasing loss of distinctiveness but also by the fading of its intellectual momentum. Keynes (1914) perceptively alluded to this when he referred to the Austrian tradition as 'once of great eminence, but now losing its vitality'. The school was temporarily rejuvenated by its clashes with the other two major neoclassical research traditions, namely (i) the possibility of economic calculation under socialism (fought against the Walrasian school) and (ii) the nature of economic crises (in opposition to the Marshallian school). This helped to sustain the Austrian research tradition during the interwar period when it was losing its academic location in Vienna following the forced international scattering of many of its most promising economists (see Craver, 1986). These clashes with their neoclassical rivals offered little more than a brief respite, given that the Austrian school was perceived to have lost both these confrontations by the close of the 1930s. This marked the second serious challenge based upon the *rejection*, rather than the incorporation, of Austrian ideas by the mainstream. The sustained revival of the school's fortunes from this low point, and its remarkable resurgence during the last couple of decades, owe much to its successful overturning of these interwar defeats.

It is appropriate, at this point, to consider the current standing of Austrian economics against the Walrasian orthodoxy that continues to dominate economics. Reference has already been made to the methodologies of Lakatos and Laudan (see section 1.7) and of the failure of the former to consider conceptual issues adequately when applying his methodology of scientific research programmes (MSRP). This is a serious shortcoming often neglected by economists in their application of the Lakatosian framework. For example, Rizzo (1982) and Langlois (1982) fail to recognize both the priority accorded by MSRP to empirical matters and the poverty of Austrian and Walrasian economics in this area. One needs to focus upon the conceptual well-foundedness of both research traditions, and MSRP is decidedly found wanting here. On conceptual grounds, the Walrasian research tradition has been successful in technical elaboration and refinement; but Austrians would maintain that this has been mainly achieved by neglecting such problematics as time, money, knowledge, production and adjustment processes. Austrian economics has also been conceptually progressive, directly because of, rather than in spite of, the inclusion of such Walrasian problematics. Not only is the Walrasian treatment of microeconomics seen as a limiting case of the more general Austrian approach (Vaughn, 1980; Murrell, 1983) but the latter is also seen to provide a far richer background for macroeconomics (Garrison, 1984, 1989).

8.3   The Austrian Theory of Business Fluctuations

The Austrian approach to the nature of economic crises highlights time, money, capital structure and coordination failures. Not only does it take what Garrison has referred to as the 'two universals' of macroeconomic theorizing (time and money) seriously, but also, by concentrating upon coordination problems, it does not draw too sharp a distinction between micro and macro analysis. In addition, by focusing upon the heterogeneity of the capital structure it provides a theory of capital which not only takes the existence of both capital and capitalists seriously but also allows for the integration of the theory of growth with that of cyclical fluctuations by removing the distinction between the two (see Lachmann, 1956).

In what follows we shall focus upon the contribution of Mises and Hayek. Mises provided the initial sketch of the Austrian theory of the business cycle, with Hayek later providing the detailed drawing. In his classic, *The Theory of Money and Credit* (1971), first published in 1912, Mises endeavoured to integrate money into the general economic framework. He provided an early model of Austrian business cycle theory which was later extended and elaborated by Hayek to demonstrate how monetary disturbances can lead to misallocations and coordination problems. Money was given a distinctive and key role in the pricing and production process; monetary disturbances affected relative prices and the real side of the economy by altering the time structure of production. Hayek, as Mises's most distinguished disciple, developed and refined the characteristically Austrian theory of money and industrial fluctuations and its integrated money–real approach in two key works, *Monetary Theory and the Trade Cycle* (1929), translated into English in 1933, and *Prices and Production* (1931a). These two contributions should be viewed as complements to each other, with the former concentrating upon the 'monetary causes which start the cyclical fluctuations' and the latter dealing with the 'successive changes in the real structure of production, which constitute those fluctuations' (Hayek, 1966). Although these two works represent the kernel of Hayek's views on the matter of money and fluctuations, he also wrote a number of important papers during the mid-1920s and 1930s, collected together in *Money, Capital and Fluctuations* (1984).

What we may term the Mises–Hayek approach to business fluctuations owes a considerable debt to the contributions of earlier economists both from within and outside the Austrian fold. Menger was an important source of inspiration. He anticipated Keynes in providing a brand of monetary theory which dealt with uncertainty, disequilibrium and the essential properties of money (see Streissler, 1973). Menger not only recognized the all-pervasive nature of money but emphasized the interdependency and complementarity between goods of various orders by exploring the temporal relation between goods of a 'lower' and 'higher' order (consumer goods and investment goods, respectively). The influence of Wicksell's distinction between the natural and market rates of interest and the general price level consequences following their inequality, alongside Böhm-Bawerk's theory of interest and capital, are also acknowledged. Indeed the problems related to the Wicksellian and Böhm-Bawerkian inheritance were especially significant in the Austrian debate with Keynes. Knut Wicksell's profound influence upon the development of monetary theory in the 20th century is undeniable. He guided the subject toward a saving-investment approach which was to prove extremely fruitful, especially in the interwar period, influencing the Swedish, Austrian and Cambridge traditions (see Leijonhufvud, 1981, pp. 131–202). Whilst Wicksell's approach highlighted general price level movements, the Austrians turned their attention towards both the output and relative price adjustment consequences of natural rate–market rate of interest inequalities.

8.4 The Mises–Hayek Model

Austrian business cycle theory revolves around the notion of a disproportionality arising between the supply of consumers' and producers' goods in relation to the demand for them. It attempts to show how the monetary and real sectors are integrated in such a way that a disturbance in one would have an impact on the other. In what follows we present, in a *highly simplified* form, the fundamental and most salient features of the Mises–Hayek model of industrial fluctuations.

8.4.1 The non-neutrality of money

For the Austrians, not only the size of the change in the money supply but the *route* by which money enters, and makes its way through, the economic system affect real variables and the final market outcome. These Cantillon distribution effects highlight the path of money injections and ensure that *money always matters*, in the sense that it is not neutral in its impact on the real sector. As Mises (1990) argues:

> The additional quantity of money does not find its way at first into the pockets of all individuals; not every individual of those benefited first gets the same amount and not every individual reacts to the same additional quantity in the same way.

Mises recognized not only that different commodities are not affected to the same extent by monetary injections but that any 'progressive depreciation' will alter the distribution of income and wealth. Money affects the real side of the economy by altering relative prices and the time structure of production. It causes resources to be increasingly reallocated from the nearest stages of production (consumption goods) towards the furthest stages (investment goods). Such temporal reallocations cannot be sustained, however, because they are not underpinned by a shift in consumers' preferences towards the future. There will come a time when such monetary disturbances will necessarily lead to an economic crisis and the restoration of a sustainable time structure of production reflecting the choices of all economic agents. Austrians are keen to emphasize that, while 'monetary factors cause the cycle ... real phenomena constitute it' (Machlup, 1976).

8.4.2 Money-induced distortions

If the natural rate (n_r) and market rate (m_r) of interest are equal, there will be no disproportional development in the production of capital goods relative to consumption goods and the macroeconomy will be in equilibrium. Saving and investment will be matched in the loanable funds market, so that all investment is backed up by voluntary saving. This is indicated by point E in Figures 8.1 and 8.2. Disproportional development can only arise if there is an inequality between the two rates of interest brought about, for example, by an increase in the money supply. Hayek (1966) recognized that a misdirection of production 'can arise only through the independence of the supply of free money capital from the accumulation of savings; which in turn arises from the elasticity of the volume of money'.

It is this putting out of action of the interest rate brake which enables disproportionality to develop between the output of capital goods and consumption goods in a money credit economy. Figure 8.1 presents *a highly simplified picture* of the impact upon the structure of production of the divergence between the natural and money rates (for a more elaborate presentation of Austrian diagrammatics, see Garrison, 1978).

When the natural rate of interest (the return on capital) is above the market rate of interest (the cost of borrowing) this will lead to a level of investment I_1 greater than the supply of voluntary saving (with this addition being financed by an injection of the money supply). This is shown in panel (a) of Figure 8.1. Total investment is being financed partly by voluntary savings and partly by forced savings. Such forced saving represents an involuntary reduction in consumption given by the movement from $Y_F - I_0$ to $Y_F - I_1$, following the lengthening of the time structure of production from C to C', in panel (b) of Figure 8.1. The granting of producers' credits by the banking system enables increased investment to take place without the support of *all* economic agents, since *artificially* induced capital accumulation (or forced saving) depends upon the frustration of consumption plans. In this case, actual available consumption is less than desired. A rise in capital creation is taking place at the cost of consumption, through the granting of additional credit, without voluntary action on the part of individuals who have to forgo consumption. This forgoing of consumption takes place because the fall in the general value of money diminishes consumers' purchasing power, and enables resources freed through the inflationary process to be used by those producers who have been granted credits.

The essential point to note is that if the market rate of interest is below the natural rate this will lead to a lengthening of the period of production, a lengthening that can only continue so long as consumption is not allowed to return to its former level. If the increased demand for capital goods had been caused by an increased desire to save (that is, a shift of the saving schedule to the right) then the change to a longer period of production would be *permanent* and *sustainable*. Increased investment would have been financed and justified by the voluntary saving choices of economic agents, reflecting their

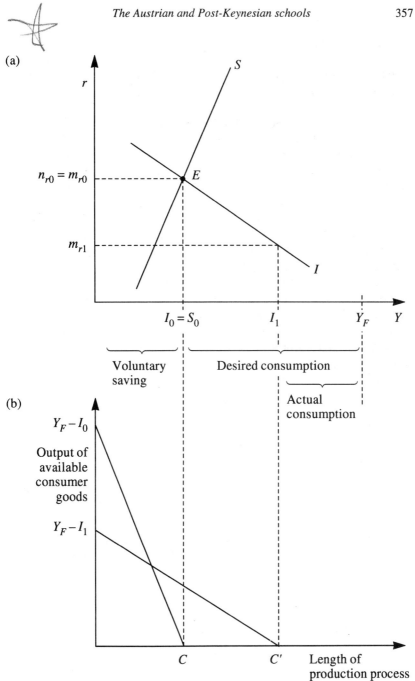

Figure 8.1   A simplified presentation of the Austrian business cycle

willingness to abstain from consumption. Unfortunately, in the scenario we are considering, this is not the case. Economic agents will attempt to restore their former consumption level and this will eventually lead to a *shrinkage* of the structure of production at a rate in excess of the completion of the unfinished investment processes.

8.4.3   The inevitability of the slump

It is a leading maxim of Austrian business cycle theory that the creation of an artificial boom *must* be followed by a slump. In addition, there appears to be an iron law of retribution whereby, the longer one permits an artificial boom to persist, the longer and more intense will be the ensuing slump (see Mises, 1971, pp. 365–6). The monetary disturbance curve illustrated in Figure 8.2 indicates that the greater the natural-market rate of interest inequality the more severe the inevitable reaction. The greater the degree of monetary disturbance in an economy, taking it further away from point E, the greater will be the necessary adjustments required to restore equilibrium. To the right of point E, forced saving will take place (given by I_{fs}) whereas to the left of point E capital consumption will occur (given by I_{cc}). Capital consumption takes place when there is a transition to a less roundabout structure of production which is not backed by the preferences of economic agents. In this case, actual available consumption is greater than desired and the capital

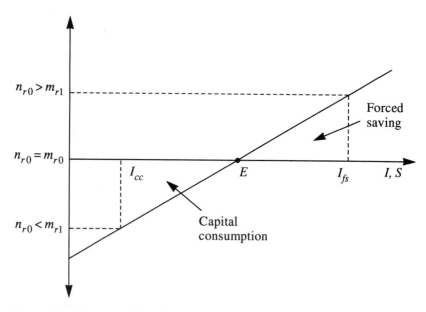

Figure 8.2   Monetary disturbance curve

stock is being run down. Problems are further intensified by the length of time such interest rate differentials are permitted to persist. Booms caused artificially by the increase of credits to producers sow the seeds of their own destruction or, as Hayek (1966) maintains, contain within themselves 'the seeds of an inevitable reaction', since they set up forces which will lead to a reversal. Hayek (1975) recognized that there was no escape: unemployment must follow inflation.

If we look in more detail at what is happening to relative prices we can see why a depression will inevitably follow an artificial boom. Hayek, in his analysis, begins with the assumption of full employment. An increase in credit emanating from the banking system will allow the market rate of interest to fall below the natural rate. Entrepreneurs receive and act upon this misleading price signal by reallocating resources from consumption towards investment. Hayek (1939) identified a 'cluster of errors' whereby entrepreneurs as a group 'simultaneously make mistakes in the same direction'. False expectations will be formed over the relative profitability of more roundabout processes, given that the public's time preference has not changed. This increased investment cannot be sustained and must result in eventual disappointment. For a short time consumer goods production will not be too badly affected. After a time, however, consumer goods prices will begin to rise relative to producer goods, given that they are becoming increasingly scarce relative to the demand for them. The output of consumer goods production falls as goods from the higher stages bid labour and other productive factors from the lower stages. The money channelled to the producers as credits now flows through the economic system. Those receiving the increased income *in money terms* wish to restore their former real consumption levels. So long as money flows to producers as credits, at *an increasing rate*, consumption will be constrained. Economic agents will be unwilling to permit this *involuntary* reduction of consumption indefinitely. As Hayek (1931a) argues: 'It is highly improbable that individuals should put up with an unforeseen retrenchment of their real income without making an attempt to overcome it by spending more money on consumption.'

Consumers wish to return to less capitalistic methods of production. Only so long as money injections continue going to producers as credits – at a rate exceeding or equivalent to the speed at which money flows are going to consumers – will forced saving continue. There are limits, however. Credits granted to producers will have to stop expanding and the market rate of interest will have to rise if the banks are to maintain their liquidity positions. Even if the monetary system was a pure fiat one, the process could not go on indefinitely because it would finally lead to hyperinflation.

8.4.4 The crisis and the onset of depression

The rise in the price of consumers' goods causes prices in the lower stages to rise relative to those in the higher stages and signals the need for a reallocation of the time structure of production back towards less roundabout processes. The rise in the relative price of consumers' goods will cause problems as the system tries to readjust towards an equilibrium path. As Hayek maintained (1931a): 'These temporary scarcity prices of consumers goods will, furthermore, have the effect that at first production will tend to shrink to fewer stages than will be necessary after equilibrium prices of consumers goods have established themselves.'

This means that when the crisis is acute, the capitalist processes may shrink by *more* than is required, or indeed warranted, by the situation. The shrinkage must occur, and the possibility that capital consumption could occur must not be discounted. In terms of Figure 8.2, there is unlikely to be a smooth or rapid restoration of equilibrium to point *E*, rather the economy will find itself to the left of point *E* with an inappropriate, and much less roundabout, structure of production. If an attempt is made to combat the crisis by means of stimulating consumers' spending this will make the situation *worse*, not better. Any increase in consumer credits would cause a *greater* shrinkage of the production process and most probably lead to capital consumption, as well as increased unemployment and uncertainty. The case of Kahn's overcoat, with Hayek's refusal to accept the argument that the purchase of an additional overcoat would aid recovery, suggesting instead that it would hinder it, neatly demonstrates this point (see Robinson, 1978, pp. 2–3). The crisis will be marked not only by a shrinkage in the structure of production but also by an increase in unemployment. These unemployed resources will only be able to be reabsorbed by the economy gradually. Their reabsorption will take time, as entrepreneurs may refrain from enterprise until the uncertainty as regards which lines of production will be the profitable ones to follow is dispelled. Austrian economists view public works or government investment programmes as damaging, since they will lead to further distortions and prevent the necessary adjustments to the capital structure from taking place.

8.4.5 Allowing the depression to run its course

The crisis will be reached when the market rate of interest has to be raised and those investments that were made profitable when forced saving was taking place are now rendered unprofitable. Policy makers should do nothing, except perhaps help the liquidation of unprofitable plants to take place as quickly as possible. Once the crisis begins, they should allow the recession to cure itself through the natural recuperative mechanisms of the market. The best course of action is to stop a crisis before it begins. As Hayek (1975) more recently reaffirmed, 'the time to prevent the coming of a depression is the boom'.

In the Austrian approach, emphasis is given to the need to try and keep the money supply firmly under control so that monetary disturbances will be minimal. Having a neutral monetary policy is seen by Hayek as a theoretical ideal that is difficult to pursue in practice, given the lack of knowledge on how to make the necessary adjustments for such factors as a changing demand for money. Hayek felt that any attempt to fine-tune the money supply to enable its impact to be neutral was theoretically possible but practically utopian. There was a need for both caution and the recognition of the difficulties involved in fine-tuning. As Hayek (1931a) argued:

> It is highly important that we should become fully conscious of the enormous difficulties of the problem of the elimination of disturbing monetary influences, difficulties which monetary reformers are always so inclined to underrate. We are still very far from the point when either our theoretical knowledge or the education of the general public provide justification for revolutionary reform or hope of carrying such reforms to a successful conclusion.

Hayek (1984) originally placed his faith in the gold standard as (relatively) the most appropriate monetary system available, since it created 'fewest disturbances for the natural formation of prices'. He wished to make the monetary system 'knave-proof' by limiting the damage that governments can do. This was also the logic behind his endorsement of fixed exchange rates. Hayek (1978b) questioned whether such rules adequately 'depoliticize' money, arguing, in their stead, that the government monopoly of money should be abolished in favour of competing currencies and the free market reversal of Gresham's maxim, with 'good money driving out bad' (see Dowd, 1988). In the real world, money would always exert an influence on the course of the economic process, but one should contain, as well as one is able, its potentially evil effects.

8.5 Evaluating the Mises–Hayek Model

The Austrian approach to industrial fluctuations, outlined above, was viewed as *the* serious alternative to Keynes's analysis during the interwar period. Lionel Robbins was an important convert who played a key role in establishing an Austrian base at the London School of Economics. His classic work *The Great Depression* (1934), asked the question, 'How does this theory fit the facts of the present depression?' and concluded that it performed rather well. More recent support for the interpretation has come from Rothbard (1975) who has argued that the Austrian explanation of the Great Depression was appropriate. However it is the case that in the post-1945 period a non-

Austrian consensus emerged which questioned the general applicability of the Austrian approach, especially its relevance as an explanation of the 1930s deflationary slump. Even Robbins (1971) conceded that:

> Confronted with the freezing deflation of those days, the idea that the prime essential was the writing down of mistaken investments and the easing of capital markets by fostering the disposition to save and reducing the pressure on consumption was completely inappropriate. Assuming that the original diagnosis of excessive financial ease and mistaken real investment was correct ... to treat what developed subsequently in the way which I then thought valid was as unsuitable as denying blankets and stimulants to a drunk who has fallen into an icy pond, on the ground that his original trouble was overheating.

A number of key conceptual problems exposed within the Austrian business cycle approach diminished its attractiveness to the economics profession. The notion of a single unambiguous natural rate of interest has increasingly been questioned since the early 1930s; the neutral money doctrine was uncongenial to English habits of thought and action, given its excessively ascetic and non-operational features; the real-world correspondence of such notions as forced savings was questioned; problems with the Hayekian geometry were identified alongside criticisms relating to the well-foundedness of Austrian capital theory; the Austrian framework appeared alien and there was a great deal of Kuhnian communication failure. Finally it lacked an attractive political action programme (for the time) since it failed to endorse interventionism.

The Austrian approach also displays a number of important strengths. The original Mises–Hayek framework not only *predicted* the major interwar downturn of the American economy *ex ante*, but also explained how a large amount of unemployment could be *generated* (in the sense of a Lakatosian novel fact). This point was recognized at the time by Shackle (1933, p. 37). Those approaches which concentrated upon the general price level indicator alone (such as those of Keynes and Fisher) failed to recognize that a sustained inflationary boom had been permitted to develop from the mid–1920s because the general price level had remained relatively stable. As Rothbard (1975) maintains:

> the designation of the 1920s as a period of inflationary boom may trouble those who think of inflation as a rise in prices. Prices generally remained stable and even fell slightly over the period. But we must realise that two great forces were at work on prices during the 1920s – the monetary inflation which propelled prices upward and the increase in productivity which lowered costs and prices.

This brings out strongly the clash between Austrian and monetarist explanations of the Great Depression and their respective views on the kind of monetary policy being pursued before and after the Great Crash of 1929. Friedman and Schwartz (1963, pp. 414–19) follow Irving Fisher in seeing Benjamin Strong, the governor of the New York Bank and dominant figure in the Federal Reserve System, as the missing hero of the monetary drama. In their view it was his policies which had been responsible for the earlier prosperity, and his untimely death in 1928 which robbed the monetary system of a bulwark against the severe monetary contraction that ensued. In sharp contrast, Austrians, such as Rothbard, tend to view Strong more as a villain, since he presided over the mismanagement of monetary policy during the 1920s and helped sow the seeds of an inevitable and violent reaction.

There were other important problems with the Austrian approach to business cycles which seriously disadvantaged it during the debates of the 1930s and beyond. Although the Austrian model did receive some empirical support for its explanation of why the depression *occurred*, it had to introduce other factors, such as wage and price rigidities, to account for its *severity and sustained nature*. The Austrians failed to consider seriously the dangers posed by secondary depressions, where a downturn brought about by primary maladjustments of the Austrian type can be worsened by the collapse of financial institutions and the resulting deflation of credit and money (see Lachmann, 1943, 1956). The model may be viewed as *ad hoc*, given that malinvestment and forced saving are dependent upon expectational and wage lags in a less than instantaneously adjusting economy, but these mechanisms are never clearly identified or systematically elaborated upon. The Austrian theory is less than general, given that malinvestment, prompted by misleading information, depends upon elastic expectations (see Lachmann, 1943, 1945). The cluster of entrepreneurial errors and the resultant intertemporal misallocation depends upon both the absence of perfect foresight and the inability to distinguish between monetary and real factors so that entrepreneurs *will* respond to interest rate changes.

8.6 Inflation and the Revival of the Austrian School

The revival of interest in Hayek's views date from the late 1960s and early 1970s, following the onset of increasing inflation alongside rising unemployment. Hayek remained consistent in his belief that inflation misdirects capital and labour by making certain investments and jobs temporarily attractive. An inflationary economy was in the unenviable position of holding a 'tiger by the tail'. Government commitment to the policy of 'full employment at any price' allowed labour unions to increase their wage demands without the cost of pricing their members out of jobs. Inflation created a maldistribution of capital and labour, with the real underlying demands of the economy being constantly undermined by sustained monetary expansion. Hayek (1975, 1978a) has compared inflation to both overeating and drug-taking, with the expressed opinion that the economy needed to go through a dramatic drying-out process to remove inflation from the system, even if it meant a substantial amount of *temporary* unemployment in the short term. According to his analysis there is no choice between inflation and unemployment; rather the selection is 'between some unemployment in the near future and more unemployment at a later date' (Hayek, 1975). Hayek believed in the need to completely eradicate inflation from the system, viewing it as a serious threat to the freedom of the individual. Inflation allows the state to confiscate resources and prevents the price-signalling mechanism from working effectively to guide action. Both its consequences serve to frustrate individual economic agents.

One may contrast his view with that of the orthodox monetarists, especially Friedman, outlined in Chapter 4. Hayek and Friedman have a common faith in the ultimate truth of the quantity theory of money and the inability to fine-tune. In addition, Friedman accepts the Hayekian point that an increasing rate of inflation will increase the amount of noise in market signals and lead to rising unemployment. The price system loses its coordinating efficiency, since 'the broadcast about relative prices is, as it were, being jammed by the noise coming from the inflation broadcast' (Friedman, 1977).

Friedman and Hayek differ in that the former takes a more gradualist stance on the need to purge inflation from the system and remains committed to a monetary growth rule constraint upon governments. Hayek has consistently argued against Keynesian–monetarist formalism, with its tendency to aggregation and concealment of all that really matters. He has questioned whether there is such a thing as *the* price level and argued that conventional faith in such a concept led economists, both before and after the Second World War, to neglect the underlying conditions of the economy with regard to changes in the structure of production. Likewise Friedman's more explicit application of the quantity theory is challenged by Hayek, since it relies upon the relationship between two mythical and misused magnitudes, namely, *the* quantity of money and *the* price level. For Hayek (1978b) there is 'no such thing as *the* quantity of money'. Finally both Austrians and monetarists accept that there is no permanent trade-off between unemployment and inflation and make great play of the confusing price signals engendered by inflation. Monetarists utilize the expectations-augmented Phillips curve framework and focus upon the market for labour, whilst the Austrians adopt some variant of the Hayekian geometry and attend to the market for capital (see Bellante and Garrison, 1988).

If the Hayekian framework was considered by the economics profession as generally inappropriate for the pre-war deflationary slump, it appears far more relevant for the post-war inflationary boom (Hicks, 1967b). Indeed

Shand (1990) has recently commented that 'Keynes was right about employment in the 1930s and Hayek has been right since 1960.' There has been a noticeable turnaround in the fortune of the Mises–Hayek model. Just as the perceived failure of Keynesianism from the 1960s led to doubts over its relevance for the 1930s, so the revival of interest in Austrian economics since the 1970s has led, in turn, to a reassessment of its interwar viability. A number of empirical studies have re-examined the validity of the Mises–Hayek model (Gallaway and Vedder, 1987; Smiley, 1987; Skousen, 1987). In addition the contributions of Gunning (1985) and Garrison (1985, 1989) argue the merits of Austrian macroeconomics *vis-à-vis* its past and present rivals.

8.7 The Austrian Critique of Rational Expectations

Austrian business cycle theory relies upon a non-rational expectations approach, *otherwise the industrial fluctuations it examines could not take place.* However a number of rational expectations commentators have suggested that there is a strong Austrian connection. Kantor (1979) has claimed that Lachmann anticipated some of the flavour of rational expectations and that there are crucial similarities between the work of Hayek and Lucas. Colander and Guthrie (1980) have also argued that the idea of rational expectations has an Austrian flavour, a view shared by Burton (1982) and Fletcher (1987). Laidler (1981) has maintained that the work of Barro, Lucas, Sargent and Wallace (amongst others) is 'neo-Austrian'. It is possible, however, to reject such claims, on the grounds that they tend to ignore crucial differences between the Austrian and Walrasian research traditions (see Hoover, 1988).

One may contrast the rational expectations position of Lucas and others and their 'equilibrium always' with the tradition of Mises and Hayek emphasizing the tendency towards, and the difficulties of actually attaining and maintaining, equilibrium. Even further removed is the radical subjectivism of Lachmann and his highlighting of fundamental *un*knowability, with its 'equilibrium never' (Garrison, 1986a). The Austrian emphasis upon genuine uncertainty, non-neutral money, economic process, the production, acquisition, distribution and diversity of knowledge and *reasonable* rather than rational expectations is all completely at odds with the rational expectations approach. The Austrian vision of rational (read 'purposeful') behaviour, human action on the basis of limited partial knowledge, with change as *the* economic problem, provides a rich tapestry for the decision-making process. Austrians, not unlike Keynes, advocate a reasonable expectations theory whereby individuals make the best use of information, subject to various constraints of time, place and resources. In assuming that the subjective probability of economic agents matches the objective probability distributions, the rational expectations theorists have extended the pure logic of choice at the cost of denying one of the fundamental problems of Austrian economics – that of knowledge coordination. Knowledge and information are not given equally to all agents, on the contrary, from the disaggregated approach of Austrian economics it is maintained that individual agents possess unique, diverse and partial, knowledge–information sets. The question of the correspondence between the subjective and objective data which underpins human action remains one of the most fundamental topics on the Austrian research agenda and cannot be defined away by assuming the fictitious state of equilibrium (Hayek, 1937, 1945). Furthermore under conditions of genuine uncertainty the basis for forming the subjective probabilities of rational expectations does not exist.

Although Hayek made use of general equilibrium theorizing, as the starting point for his trade cycle analysis, his reflections on the appropriateness of the equilibrium concept underwent substantial revision and transformation during the interwar period. He came to recognize its inherent limitations in failing to capture the problems with which he was becoming increasingly concerned – those associated with the dynamics of historical time and the constraints on knowledge (see Butos, 1985; Caldwell, 1988). It may be conjectured that Hayek's intellectual development was marked by a movement away from equilibrium theorizing, whilst that of Lucas and the rational expectations approach is a movement back towards Walras. Rational expectations theorists assume not only that agents optimally use information but, in addition that they use the correct theories and models of economic reasoning to make their predictions. The Hayekian distinction between knowledge *of* and knowledge *within* the structure is quite critical here, separating as it does the economist's knowledge from the economic agent's knowledge, by refusing to conflate theoretical and entrepreneurial knowledge (see Garrison, 1986b). Economic agents, as Mises (1943) realized, do not 'view things with the eye of an economist', nor do they appraise macroeconomic policies in the same way. On the contrary, different agents react differently (Haberler, 1980). For Austrians, the informational noise which agents face is not digestible into distinguishable parts, whether into monetary or non-monetary factors – a point made by Menger long ago (see Marget, 1966, vol. 2, p. 69). Nor can it be handled in such a mechanical manner as implied by rational expectations theory (see Lachmann, 1943). The Austrian and rational expectations theories just do not mix.

It should be remembered that Hayek wished to emancipate monetary theory from its limited domain, relating to the value of money, to the far wider task of explaining 'changes in the relative height of particular prices which are conditioned by the introduction of money' (Hayek, 1966). His contribution should be viewed as an attempt to bring the theory of money into harmony with the theory of production, as the realization and demonstration that 'money will always exert a determining influence on the course of economic events' (Hayek, 1931a). Hayek's theoretical system allows us to carry out real analysis in money terms. So completely does money pervade the realm of the real economy that monetary injections are far more complex and unfathomable than merely throwing money out of helicopters. The new classicists follow Friedman (1972) in denying the importance of Cantillon distribution effects and accept the highly aggregated approach of mainstream Keynesian–monetarist analysis. They follow the prevailing orthodoxy in neglecting the capital structure and focus their attention on wage rates and the intertemporal nature of the labour–leisure trade-off. We shall find that a number of the Austrian criticisms of rational expectations are echoed in the Post-Keynesian critique of this approach, especially those related to the *amount* and *type* of knowledge available.

8.8 The Post-Keynesian School

The Post-Keynesian school represents a relatively young and distinctive, but rather less than unified, approach to macroeconomics. The main elements of the approach can be traced back to the contributions of its founders, with Keynes providing the monetary perspective, Kalecki the real analysis and Sraffa the value and distribution component. It is possible, however, to locate earlier influences, especially the Marshallian impact upon Keynes, and the classical and Marxian thread running through the work of Kalecki and Sraffa. For a historical overview and survey of the literature, see Hamouda and Harcourt (1988) and Sawyer (1991). The approach represents the coming together of several identifiable strands which gained much of its initial impetus from the sustained efforts to 'generalize the *General Theory*' and apply its underlying vision to such matters as growth (Harrod, 1939), accumulation (Robinson, 1956) and distribution (Kaldor, 1956).

At the outset it is important to stress that Post-Keynesians are 'hardly a cohesive group' (Eichner, 1979) and are in fact a rather 'heterogeneous lot' (Harcourt, 1982) connected together by little more than the desire to present a popular front against orthodoxy. Indeed it can be argued that, while the Post-Keynesian school offers 'important and substantial insights', it has yet to reach 'a coherent steady state' (see Harcourt, 1982).

During its evolution and development Post-Keynesianism has failed to display the necessary degree of coherence, comprehensiveness and robustness which is to be expected of a rival to mainstream economics. The increasing tension recently witnessed within the Post-Keynesian camp is hardly surprising, given the revival of the neoclassical orthodoxy and the heterogeneity of the Post-Keynesian roots. A principal source of divergence has its origins in the major differences in the fundamentalist and surplus school sub-sets (see Dutt and Amadeo, 1990). This has led the more radical elements to argue that the Post-Keynesian synthesis should be dissolved into its respec-tive strands, with the Post-Kaleckian (Sawyer, 1985) and Post-Sraffian (Eatwell and Milgate, 1983) aspects clearly distinguished from Keynes.

In what follows we shall examine the shared common themes of Post-Keynesian macroeconomics (section 8.9) with our main focus directed to-ward those two universals of time and money alluded to earlier. Given this, and the fact that much of our discussion is directed towards considerations of the short period, matters relating to growth, income distribution, develop-ment and value will not be covered here. In addition there will be no need to further discuss internal disagreements between those espousing a short-period approach and those upholding a long-period framework (see Dow, 1985; Bortis, 1986). We will, however, explore the essence of the Keynesian revolution in more detail, in terms of fundamentalist Keynesianism and the uncertainty–money–unemployment link (section 8.10). This is followed by a discussion of the Post-Keynesian critique of rational expectations (section 8.11). We conclude (section 8.12) with a comparison of Post-Keynesian and Austrian economics by drawing together and contrasting their theoretical analysis and policy implications.

8.9   Common Post-Keynesian Themes

We begin by considering a number of shared Post-Keynesian themes relating to effective demand failures, the micro foundations of macroeconomics, in-flation and endogenous money.

8.9.1   Effective demand failures

Although the Post-Keynesian approach is marked by both its diversity of view and increasing fragmentation it can be argued (see the foreword by Chick, in Amadeo, 1989) that the principle of effective demand remains the central *shared* concern.

For fundamentalist Keynesians, such a principle was grounded in the prob-lems associated with time and money. Keynes is seen to provide an elabora-tion of the linked Marshallian themes that 'time is at the centre of the chief difficulty of almost every economic problem' and that time is irreversible, so that 'man is not the same at the beginning as at the end of it' (Marshall, 1920). In such an uncertain world, action is based upon *un*knowledge or ignorance that cannot be overcome, since full knowledge is unattainable (see Frowen, 1990). This inevitably leads to mistakes which cannot be easily or costlessly undone. The existence of a perfectly liquid generalized asset (money) allows economic agents to postpone purchases of specific producible commodities (especially investment goods) during periods of disquiet. Keynes paid particular attention to the investment component of effective demand and the role of 'animal spirits' as the prime motivator of change. Those Post-Keynesians who follow Sraffa's lead, and his restoration of the classical (Ricardo–Marx) approach, attend more to problems associated with the creation, accumulation and allocation of the economic surplus. In this approach the contribution of Keynes's theory of effective demand is seen in terms of its role in filling an important gap left by the classics, namely, the determination of the normal levels of output and employment which they had taken as given.

Klein (1951) and Robinson (1978) have credited Kalecki with simultaneously discovering (alongside Keynes) the principle of effective demand (see Patinkin, 1982, for an examination and rejection of such claims). In a series of papers originally published *before* 1936, Kalecki (1969) highlighted the important role of investment (along with capitalist consumption, government spending and the trade surplus) in generating profits and the business cycle. Whilst Keynes's theory of effective demand highlights changes in output, the approach of Kalecki concentrates upon changes in capitalists' profits. One can present Kalecki's argument in orthodox Keynesian terms (see Toporowski, 1993) by expressing the general equation for profits in the economy as:

$$\Pi = I + (G - T) + (X - I_m) + C_c - S_w \tag{8.1}$$

with Π representing capitalists' profits, I investment, G government expenditure, T taxes, X exports, I_m imports, C_c capitalists' consumption and, finally, S_w denoting the savings of workers out of wages. It is important to emphasize that the causal relationship is from expenditure to profits. Increases and decreases in capitalists' profits leads to similar directional movements in output, since in the simple Kaleckian model, where 'workers spend what they get, and capitalists get what they spend', output is equal to capitalists' profit and workers' consumption (wages). Unlike Keynes's approach, Kalecki's involved no 'long struggle of escape' from the marginalist orthodoxy since its class-based focus owes a debt to the earlier classical–Marxian tradition. In contrast to Keynes, Kalecki generally ignored issues related to uncertainty and money in the investment decision (apart from the need for a responsive banking sector), placing emphasis instead upon such objective factors as actual current profitability and the cost of borrowing.

In focusing upon effective demand failures, whether in the short period or in the long, Post-Keynesians have paid particular attention to investment. There is the recognition of Keynes's (1973, Vol. VII) insights that it is extremely difficult to undo investment once made and 'Our knowledge of the factors which will govern the yield of an investment some years hence is usually very slight and often negligible.' Chick (1983) maintains that, for Keynes, the investment decision is substantially dominated by animal spirits. Post-Keynesians effectively replace the centrality of the relative price variable of mainstream economics with the investment variable; this further permits them to reverse the conventional ranking of substitution and income effects in favour of the latter. The role of investment in Post-Keynesian models also provides the link between their integrated explanation of economic growth and income distribution, with changes in the rate of investment having an impact upon both the growth process and relative factor shares between profits and wages (see Eichner and Kregel, 1975).

The *ability* to invest is just as important as the *willingness* to do so. Fluctuations in investment explain much of the inherent dynamic of capitalism and are occasioned by changes in long-term expectations and financial conditions. Post-Keynesians emphasize both the sophisticated nature of capitalist financial institutions and the ability of oligopolistic firms to set product prices. They recognize the enabling function of financial institutions in accommodating capitalists' demand for credit which facilitates investment expenditures independently of current savings (see Chick, 1986). Post-Keynesians also acknowledge that firms have the power to set prices at a level sufficient to generate internal funds for investment purposes. Oligopolistic enterprises have a preference for internal finance 'on the basis of lower cost and limitation of outside interference' (Sawyer, 1991).

8.9.2   Post-Keynesian micro foundations of macroeconomics
A second key feature of Post-Keynesian economics has been its concern with the relationship between microeconomics and macroeconomics. An emphasis is placed upon the *symbiotic* relationship between these two separable elements. Post-Keynesians tend to adopt a dual approach whereby macro influences upon micro are given equal standing to the more conventional one-way influence of micro foundations upon the macro superstructure. In addition the conjunction of micro and macro analysis gives rise to a number of paradoxes relating to the fallacy of composition (Dow, 1988). For example, an individual firm can succeed in lowering costs by cutting wages, but such a policy would fail if carried out by all firms in the economy since it must result in a reduction of prices and/or sales as workers lose the wherewithal to purchase.

Post-Keynesians endeavour to establish a firm microeconomic base which has a large degree of correspondence with reality. They embrace Hicks's (1974) distinction between flex-price markets (raw material and agricultural products) and fix-price markets (manufactured goods), the crucial point being that in fix-price markets prices need not change in response to excess supply or demand; changes in demand are generally met by changes in the volume of output. Kalecki distinguished between cost-determined and demand-determined prices, with each sharing a similarity with Okun's (1981) notion of 'customer' markets and 'auction' markets, respectively. The manufacturing/industrial goods sector is seen to operate with an elastic supply, given the existence of excess capacity. Much of the Post-Keynesian interest in administered pricing follows Kalecki's work in the 1930s and the argument that prices represent a mark-up over costs, with the latter determined by the 'degree of monopoly' (see Kriesler, 1987). Harris (1974) argues that the size of the mark-up is also influenced by the normal rate of capacity utilization and the planned level of investment. Prices are set by calculating the short-run average costs of production and adding a mark-up for profit:

$$P = ATC + NPM \qquad (8.2)$$

with P representing the firm's product price, ATC average total cost (composed of average variable and average fixed costs so that $ATC = AVC + AFC$) and NPM the net profit margin per unit of output.

Such a model is illustrated in Figure 8.3, where price has been set at P and the firm's desired level of output established at Q_d (with capacity output given by Q_c). This would yield target profits equivalent to $AB \times 0Q_d$ if the demand for the product coincided with this output level. Any increase in demand beyond this level (up to Q_c) will lead to an increase in profits whilst a

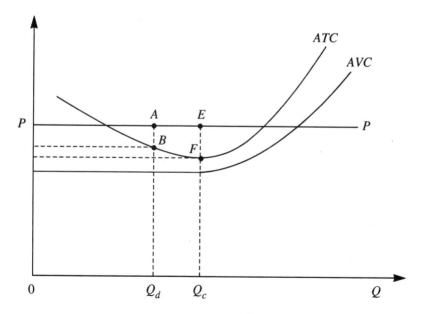

Figure 8.3   The average cost pricing model

decrease will lead to a lowering of profits. Profits (up to Q_c) represent an increasing function of capacity utilization or level of demand. The flat stretch of the *AVC* curve shows that the firm is operating with excess capacity. Within such 'customer' markets, firms are unwilling to raise prices when demand increases because they are interested in 'repeat' sales and do not wish to spoil the market by damaging customer goodwill. This leads Post-Keynesians such as Harcourt and Kenyon (1976) to argue that: 'It is predominantly output and not price which fluctuates with the level of demand in the course of the business cycle.' Empirical support for such a position can be found in Godley and Nordhaus (1972) and Coutts *et al.* (1978).

8.9.3   Inflation: cause and cure
The use of the mark-up at the micro level is complemented by the use of a mark-up at the macro level. The ability of oligopolistic firms and trade unions to set (or influence) product prices and money wages is a reflection of underlying power relationships. Sidney Weintraub (1978) presents a general wage cost mark-up (WCM) of the form:

$$P = mW/q \qquad\qquad (8.3)$$

with *P* representing the general price level, *m* the average economy-wide mark-up over unit labour costs or gross profit margin, *W* the average money wage, and *q* denoting average labour productivity. The evidence suggests that *m* tends to be remarkably stable, so that rising prices are the result of money wage increases being permitted to advance above labour productivity gains, as shown by equation (8.4):

$$\dot{P} = \dot{W} - \dot{q} \qquad\qquad (8.4)$$

In Post-Keynesian models inflation is seen to be the result of conflict over the distribution of income (Rowthorn, 1977) with trade union power strongest at times of full employment. The use of traditional demand management policies to control inflation is seen to have a direct impact upon output and employment levels, while intensifying the degree of conflict by reducing the amount of income available for distribution. Post-Keynesians, such as Weintraub (1978), maintain that the adoption of a tight monetary stance by, for example, the adoption of some monetary growth rule below the current rate of inflation, will intensify unemployment and be unlikely to moderate wage demands:

> By creating enough unemployment, the monetary authority may be able to induce some tapering in the money wage-salary rise, imparting an *indirect* hamper on the

price level. But the toll in human suffering can be onerous. Even then, under union wage adamancy, it may hardly deflect the price tide.

Post-Keynesians argue the need for incomes policy as a necessary and *permanent* adjunct to traditional demand management policies, on the grounds that this will allow a more stable price and output mix within oligopolistic price-making environments. As argued above, pronounced periods of stagflation are seen as a reflection of the failure to deal adequately with inflation by appropriate means. Post-Keynesians point to a dilemma in that *only any two* of the following appear to be achievable simultaneously: (i) full employment; (ii) price stability; and (iii) free collective bargaining. This was clearly recognized by Robinson (1943) when she argued: 'If free wage bargaining, as we have known it hitherto, is continued in conditions of full employment, there would be a constant upward pressure upon money wage rates.'

8.9.4 The endogeneity of money

Post-Keynesians argue that in a modern credit economy the money supply is largely endogenous. The money supply is seen to 'accommodate itself to the needs of trade' (Kaldor, 1970) so that there is a reversal of the direction of causality between money and expenditure usually espoused by orthodox monetarists. This 'enabling' view of money appears to have a long tradition, going back to the anti-Bullionist and Banking schools of the first half of the nineteenth century (see O'Brien, 1975) with their emphasis upon the 'real bills doctrine' (recently revived by Davidson, 1989) and their reversal of the normal quantity theory causality.

The observed close statistical relationship between movements in the stock of money and money income is explained by Post-Keynesians in terms of the endogenous nature of the money supply process within a sophisticated banking–financial framework. The fact that money supply changes *precede* those of money income does nothing to establish the monetarist inference on cause and effect. Post-Keynesians emphasize that *planned* increases in expenditures need to be financed if they are to take place. Such 'preparatory business actions', signalling an *ex ante* desire for loans from the banking system, can only be put into effect if the banks create the necessary amount of credit. The banking system is in the active position of accommodating or frustrating these private sector expenditure plans. Keynes recognized this directly when he introduced his concept of 'the finance motive' (see Davidson, 1965), as did Kalecki, in his discussion of the business cycle, when he emphasized the need for a pliable banking system since any investment would generate the necessary profits to validate the incurred debts. There is an income-generating finance process whereby planned expenditures are transformed via bank credit into *actual* expenditures. Moore (1989) summarizes the Post-Keynesian case when he argues:

> The evidence appears overwhelmingly consistent with the proposition that the direction of causation runs from commercial bank loans to the money stock to the monetary base. This in turn clearly implies the much noted and documented empirical relationship between money and income reflects primarily 'reverse causation' running from income to money.

It is interesting to note, given our discussion of the WCM, that Kaldor (1970) suggested that two principal factors govern changes in the money supply: the rate of change in money incomes and the rate of wage inflation. Consequently Post-Keynesians tend to view the growth in the money stock as 'a response to, and not a cause of, inflation' (Sawyer, 1991). This is brought out clearly by Moore (1979a) when he maintains that the growth in the money supply *validates* rather than causes the rise in wages and prices: 'The Post-Keynesian position that the money stock responds endogenously to changes in the demand for credit treats the rate of money wage change as the key exogenous variable, to which both prices and the money stock adjust.'

Post-Keynesians, such as Moore (1979b), recognize that there is a need to separate the support and control functions of central banks. Whilst the supply of money is subject to policy control, actual control is extremely difficult in a complex and sophisticated money credit economy where such supply is largely endogenous (see Desai, 1987). Moore (1979a) highlights the dilemma faced by the monetary authorities: either accommodate to the needs of trade (including wage-push pressure) or intensify unemployment with an uncompromising policy of monetary restraint. Such a dilemma arises because the banking system does not normally distinguish between increased private expenditure requirements based upon intended business activity ('real bills') and those associated with increased money wages ('inflation bills'). As Davidson (1989) has argued:

> Any healthy banking apparatus which meets the needs of trade can be subverted to create an elastic currency of 'inflation bills' rather than 'real bills', and any deliberate policy aimed at restricting the banking system's ability to issue 'inflation bills' will therefore ~~concurrently limit its~~ ability to supply sufficient 'real bills' to maintain full employment.

The Post-Keynesian argument on the endogeneity of the money supply reinforces its policy commitment to an incomes policy to underpin a sustainable full employment strategy. The banking system would then be in a more sound position to respond to the real demands of trade without the threat of monetary stringency later.

8.10 Fundamentalist Keynesianism: the Uncertainty–Money–Unemployment Link

The fundamentalist Keynesians represent an important sub-set of Post-Keynesianism. They locate the 'essence' of Keynes's revolution in Chapters 12 and 17 of the *General Theory* and his 1937 *Quarterly Journal of Economics* article, 'The General Theory of Employment'. Post-Keynesians argue that an examination of Keynes's *Collected Writings*, in particular his *Treatise on Probability* and the early drafts of the *General Theory*, suggests that Keynes's fundamental break from the classical orthodoxy was far wider than first thought.

Keynes identified and rejected three *linked* core assumptions of classical economics on his way to constructing the *General Theory*. In so doing, he was led to emphasize the uncertainty–money–unemployment link developed by the fundamentalists. Classical theory made the following assumptions.

1. Economic agents' knowledge of the future was such that situations of uncertainty can be reduced to situations of risk. Keynes clearly distinguished between situations involving uncertainty from those involving risk, with emphasis given to the former.
2. A monetary economy can be analysed as if it were a barter economy so that money is neutral. Keynes clearly distinguished between money-using and barter economies by highlighting the all-pervasive nature of money.
3. The economy faces no serious adjustment problems or obstacles to achieving full employment, given a flexible price mechanism. In sharp contrast, Keynes's attention was directed towards transition states and those features of capitalism which make full employment unlikely.

Fundamentalist Keynesians have identified these core assumptions as important *continuing* strands in orthodox thinking. They stress the need to revive Keynes's revolution by elaborating and developing themes associated with historical time (section 8.10.1) and a monetary theory of production (section 8.10.2). A succinct statement of the fundamentalist position is provided by Chick (1978), when she writes: 'the *General Theory* presents a model of a *production* economy, using *money*, moving through *time*, subject to *uncertainty* and the possibility of *error*'.

8.10.1 Uncertainty and historical time
Fundamentalist Keynesians, along with others, identify one of the key contributions of Keynes to be his placing of uncertainty firmly at the centre of the economic stage (see Weintraub, 1975; Peterson, 1977; Shapiro, 1978; Vickers, 1979–80; Fitzgibbons, 1988). Minsky (1975) neatly captured this aspect of

Keynes in his remark that 'Keynes without uncertainty is like Hamlet without the prince'. Keynes's recognition that economies operate in historical rather than logical time – so that the difference between today and tomorrow is 24 hours but that between today and yesterday is an eternity – with economic agents facing an *irreversible* and *unknowable*, but not *unimaginable*, future is seen as one of the glittering achievements of the 1930s (see Shackle, 1967). Within such a 'non-ergodic' (unique and non-repetitive) world, where the rules of probability do not apply, marked by 'kaleidic' change and fundamental discontinuities, the existence of money, conventions and contracts takes on added significance (see Shackle, 1972, 1974; Davidson, 1984, 1991; Palley, 1993).

Keynes's *Treatise on Probability* was published in the same year as Frank Knight's *Risk, Uncertainty and Profit* (1921). A major feature of both contributions is that each author made the same distinction between risk and uncertainty: risk was seen as both measurable and insurable, whereas uncertainty was neither. Risk was seen to characterize a situation where the probability distribution was known, quantitatively specifiable, closed and complete. In contrast, genuine uncertainty has no known probability distribution, is unspecifiable and open to the likelihood of 'potential surprise' and novelty (see Georgescu-Roegen, 1971, 1979, for an elaboration of these distinctions).

The calculus of probability was seen as a blunt weapon for dealing with the problem of human conduct in a world of uncertainty. The foundations of our actions were presented by Keynes as being often 'extremely precarious', 'fluctuating', 'flimsy', 'vague' and 'open to dramatic revision'. This led both Keynes and Knight to emphasize, and rationalize, the adoption of conventions by economic agents as partial solutions to the uncertainty problem. Some stability is provided by conventions which assume that economic agents 'judge the future by the past' (Knight, 1933) and expect 'that the existing state of affairs will continue indefinitely' (Keynes, 1973, Vol. VII) unless we have good cause to believe otherwise. The very existence of uncertainty explains the volatility of investment and the rationale for money, and, in turn, the fluctuations in the demand and supply of output as a whole. The decision to invest, to commit resources to an asset that is durable, often highly specific and unalterable, is based upon conjecture, intuition and *animal spirits*. It is hardly surprising that, in such a world, expectations may well be disappointed. The decision to hold money, itself a convention, allows one to remain liquid and so postpone making irreversible decisions when ignorance is too great. Much of Shackle's work has been concerned with highlighting the problems faced by decision makers under conditions of genuine uncertainty. Economic agents can face novel situations which, by definition, they have never faced before, and the outcome of the decisions they make, once realized, cannot be overturned.

Shackle (1968) illustrates the essence of this problem with his concept of the 'crucial experiment':

> Napoleon could not repeat the battle of Waterloo a hundred times in the hope that, in a certain proportion of cases, the Prussians would arrive too late. His decision to fight ... was what I would call a crucial experiment, using the word crucial in the sense of a parting of the ways. Had he won, repetition would for a long time have been unnecessary; when he lost, repetition was impossible.

If uncertain situations could be simply reduced to those of risk, by assuming that knowledge of the future *is* available today, then many of the problems addressed by Keynes and macroeconomists would disappear.

8.10.2   A monetary theory of production

Keynes attached substantial importance to the need for a monetary theory of production which would explain the fluctuations in effective demand that occur in a world characterized by uncertainty. The *General Theory* demonstrated the way in which money affects the exchange and production process of an economy functioning in historical time. Keynes (1973, Vol. XIII) had realized as early as 1932 that conventional thinking lacked a monetary theory of production where money was not neutral. The early 1933 drafts of the *General Theory* distinguish a monetary economy from those where money is absent or merely a fiction (Keynes, 1979, Vol. XXIX) and, although Keynes made the fundamental role of money less explicit in the finished version, it is clear that the problems he examined would not arise in a non-monetary Walrasian economy.

In Chapter 17 of the *General Theory* money takes its *special* place within a general asset classificatory scheme. For Keynes, money had a zero yield alongside a substantial liquidity premium in excess of its negligible carrying cost. Money was seen to possess two particular characteristics: it had a zero, or very small, elasticity of production, alongside an elasticity of substitution equal, or nearly equal, to zero. Both characteristics were crucial to Keynes's explanation of effective demand failures. An increased demand for money, due to an increased demand for liquidity in the face of greater uncertainty, will not lead to an increased demand for labour in money production or its substitutes. It will, however, result in a *diminished demand for non-money production and labour*. Keynes took the view that an economic system without money will automatically reach a full employment equilibrium. Thus, in the absence of money, classical theory would come back into its own again, as it does in both neo-Walrasian and even 'after-Keynes' Cambridge contributions (Kregel, 1985).

These important insights of Keynes have been developed and elaborated upon by a number of Post-Keynesians, most notably Paul Davidson (1978,

1984), who sees Keynes's revolution as being directed towards overthrowing (i) the gross substitution axiom (defined as the dominance of substitution effects over income effects); (ii) the axiom of reals (where economic agents only act on the basis of non-nominal magnitudes such as commodities, leisure and effort); and (iii) the axiom of an ergodic (probabilistic) economic world. Davidson (1980) has followed Keynes's line in emphasizing time-related markets and money contracts. Money's liquidity premium is seen to be enhanced by the fact that contracts are fixed in terms of money and that money wages are usually quite stable. The relationship between money and money wages is seen by Keynes as both reciprocal and symbiotic. The very liquidity of money makes wages fixed in terms of it, rather than in terms of some other commodity, more sticky *and* the very fact that money wages are relatively stable provides the necessary anchor for the continued existence of a monetary economy.

Much of the above explains Keynes's aversion to a policy of wage and price flexibility as a means to restore full employment equilibrium. He believed such a policy was messy, unbalanced, and struck at the 'sanctity of contract'; the gains to be expected were limited and could not be guaranteed, whilst the costs were enormous in terms of redistributional and expectational consequences. Minsky (1978, 1982) has followed Keynes (and, for that matter, Irving Fisher) in emphasizing the cash flow–cash commitment nexus and the problems posed by a debt-deflation process upon the inherited structure of contractual obligations. He highlights the centrality and necessity of profit flows within capitalism to validate outstanding debts, adopting the Kaleckian framework captured by equation (8.1). A deflation is, by definition, unbalanced for Minsky, since it results in both a decrease in cash flows (as prices and/or sales fall) and a rise in cash commitments (debts). The debt-deflation process makes production units (firms) increasingly financially fragile and susceptible to bankruptcy.

The Post-Keynesian and classical positions are illustrated in Figure 8.4, where the economy is initially at point A with an output of Y_0; that is, the intersection of AD_0 and AS_0. The orthodox stance on downward price–wage flexibility is that it will result in a rightward shift in the AS curve (following wage reductions) and a movement along the AD curve (Pigou 'real balance' price effect) to an eventual full employment equilibrium at point E. Following Kalecki (1944), little faith is placed in the mechanism of the Pigou effect when the money stock is largely composed of bank credit (inside) money. Taking Keynes's expectational and distributional effects seriously means that the AD curve is more likely to move to the left (that is, from AD_0 to AD_1) so that *at the very least* output and employment will remain substantially unchanged (that is, at point B). Indeed, most Post-Keynesians would go further and maintain that a deflationary policy will lead to *more* unemployment and output losses, with a new 'equilibrium' to the left of Y_0 (see, for example, the

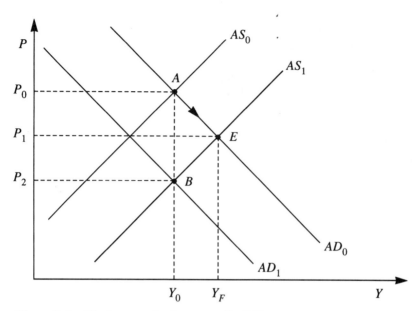

Figure 8.4   The impact of price–wage flexibility

interesting arguments of Dutt, 1986–7; Dutt and Amadeo, 1990; Amadeo, 1992; where it is suggested that historical time, uncertainty and money make the *AD* curve '*upward rising* and shifting', hence necessarily resulting in output and employment reductions). Of course more orthodox Keynesians, notably Tobin, have seriously doubted the stabilizing impact of price and wage flexibility (see Tobin, 1980a, 1993; and Chapters 3 and 7).

8.11   The Post-Keynesian Critique of Rational Expectations

Much of the Post-Keynesian critique of rational expectations echoes Austrian concerns presented in section 8.7. This is hardly surprising, given that they both emphasize non-neutral money, historical time and economic agents' ignorance. Post-Keynesians reject the Walrasian research tradition's adoption of a market-clearing definition of equilibrium. Post-Keynesians, apart from the Sraffian sub-set, tend to employ the equilibrium concept in terms of 'a state of rest'. They criticize orthodoxy for denying history (Robinson), for playing down many of the instabilities associated with positive feedback, such as unstable growth (Harrod), and dynamic increasing returns and cumulative causation (Kaldor).

The critique of Post-Keynesians is directed at the *strong* version of rational expectations. They, not unlike the Austrians, accept a reasonable approach to expectations, captured by Locke and quoted approvingly *twice* by Keynes (1973, Vol. VIII) in the same work: 'He that judges without informing himself to the utmost that he is capable, cannot acquit himself of judging amiss.' Gomes (1982) believes that the strong version of rational expectations cannot hold in the real world, since it depends upon economic agents knowing *the* true economic model when economists clearly do not. The possession of such knowledge, *if it were available*, could be passed on to economists for the price of a Nobel prize. The key weakness according to Gomes is that: 'monetarists of the rational expectations faith assume not only that every entrepreneur is an economist. They also assume that everybody, entrepreneurs and workers alike, is a *monetarist economist*'. Wible (1982–3) makes similar criticisms when he argues that economic agents are presumed to share *the same* economic theory and to apply it like the *most proficient* economist. Rational expectations, as the Austrians maintain, is guilty of conflating theoretical and entrepreneurial knowledge by reducing the latter to the former.

Davidson (1982–3, 1991) argues that rational expectations requires both that agents' subjective beliefs match the underlying reality, and the existence and dominance of ergodic processes. Both points were clearly anticipated within the Austrian critique. The strong version of rational expectations denies the epistemics of time and genuine uncertainty by presuming that the objective probability distribution contains the full scope of future possibilities *today* (see Bausor, 1983). It denies the risk–uncertainty distinction made by Keynes. As recognized by Hoover (1988), rational expectations is used as a means of 'closing the future' and so 'generating determinate solutions'. Rational expectations theorists follow the rules of their parental Walrasian research tradition by reducing pervasive uncertainty to situations of risk. Lucas (1977) has conceded that the rational expectations hypothesis can best handle situations which display stable structures and recurrent events, but that it cannot adequately deal with kaleidic change and crucial experiments.

8.12   Comparing the Austrian and Post-Keynesian Schools

On a theoretical and conceptual level, the Austrian and Post–Keynesian (fundamentalist) approaches share some commonalities related to time and money. Their respective founders, Menger and Keynes, highlighted the special marketability or liquidity properties of money and emphasized the historical time framework of action characterized by *un*knowledge and irreversibility. The followers of both approaches have developed and elaborated these insights to demonstrate why money matters by having an impact upon the production and exchange process. They obviously differ as to *how* money matters; the Austrians emphasize the structure of the money-pricing process, whilst the Post–Keynesians emphasize the money-debt payments structure. Likewise, at a methodological level, they both assert that the assumptions one makes are important, in the sense that they need to be realistic. In all of this, they are quite unlike orthodoxy.

Of course the main area of difference between Austrians and Post-Keynesians *in general* is in their policy prescriptions. Whilst they share the belief that governments can make a difference, they disagree over what that difference is, with the Austrians taking a negative view and the Post-Keynesians a positive view of the state . The Austrians favour free markets and invisible hand mechanisms. This is in direct contrast to the Post-Keynesian position, where markets *need* state assistance to function *more* effectively. Such differences can be overdone, however. Lachmann's recognition (1939, 1956) that a downturn can be magnified by a debt-deflation process means that some Austrians are willing to combat such secondary depressions by means of active government policy. Haberler (1980), for instance, has accepted much of this argument in situations where chain reactions and cumulative processes dominate to transform a situation radically.

A notable area of disagreement on the policy front relates to incomes policy. Austrians question the merits of such a policy by demonstrating its disastrous consequences for the workings of the price mechanism. They argue that incomes policies are mere palliatives inherently doomed to failure in theory and practice. There was a proliferation of such unsuccessful schemes in the 1960s and 1970s in the UK and elsewhere. Shand (1990) captures Austrian scepticism about incomes policy when he argues: 'It was found necessary to call successive ventures by different names in order to allay scepticism born of experience and to whip up enthusiasm for the latest scheme.' The Austrians appear correct in their argument that traditional incomes policies have had their day. Even Moore (1979b) conceded that no successful permanent incomes policy had been applied and that such policies necessarily distort market allocation processes.

Some Post-Keynesians, most notably Davidson (1982–3), wish to distinguish their position from that of the Austrians. Davidson has argued that, whilst they have common ground on the matter of pervasive uncertainty, there are important differences. He maintains that the Austrians believe that no policy can be developed to provide economic stability in an uncertain world. This is to be distinguished from the Post-Keynesian position which favours a government role directed to reducing, wherever possible, such instability; so that one should not confuse 'instability with uncertainty'. It is possible to argue that this is less than fair to the Austrian position, given its emphasis upon rules and conventions in an uncertain world (see O'Driscoll and Rizzo, 1985). It can also be argued that this view ignores much of the theoretical and practical nihilism of Shackle, a notable fundamentalist (see Coddington, 1976).

If Austrians were once 'derided as dinosaurs' (Shand, 1984) then they have made a dramatic comeback, somewhat akin to the recent box-office success of Spielberg's film, *Jurassic Park*! The Post-Keynesians, however, continue to search for some unifying theme and identity. Both schools offer important insights and alternatives to mainstream macroeconomics.

The essence of the Austrian and Post-Keynesian views on uncertainty is, perhaps, best captured by recalling the conversation between two of J.K. Galbraith's (1990) fictional characters in his *A Tenured Professor* (Houghton Mifflin):

Professor Grierson: A good model has predictive value.

Professor McCrimmon: If predictions aren't reliable, of what value are they?

Professor Grierson: To put it simply, the American businessman, in his business planning, has to have something better than a guess.

Professor McCrimmon: So a wrong prediction is better than a guess?

Professor Grierson: A prediction is something to go on ... It narrows the range of uncertainty for the business firm.

Professor McCrimmon: You're saying that uncertainty is reduced by a wrong prediction but increased by a wrong guess?

Evidently McCrimmon had read his Hayek and Shackle!

ROGER GARRISON

Roger Garrison was born in 1944 in Missouri and graduated in electrical engineering in 1967 at the Missouri School of Mines and Metallurgy, Rolla, before obtaining his MA in economics at the University of Missouri at Kansas City in 1974 and his PhD at the University of Virginia in 1981. Since 1978 he has taught at Auburn University, where he is Associate Professor of Economics.

Professor Garrison is widely known for his Austrian-oriented writings on capital, money, and business cycles. His best known articles include: 'Austrian Macroeconomics: A Diagrammatical Exposition', in *New Directions in Austrian Economics* (Sheed, Andrews and McMeel, 1978), edited by Louis M. Spadaro, 'Time and Money: The Universals of Macroeconomic Theorizing', *Journal of Macroeconomics* (1984), 'Intertemporal Co-ordination and the Invisible Hand: An Austrian Perspective on the Keynesian Vision', *History of Political Economy* (1985), 'Hayekian Trade Cycle Theory: A Reappraisal', *Cato Journal* (1986), 'Phillips Curves and Hayekian Triangles: Two Perspectives on Monetary Dynamics', *History of Political Economy* (1988), co-authored with Don Bellante, 'The Austrian Theory of the Business Cycle in the Light of Modern Macroeconomics', *Review of Austrian Economics* (1989) and 'New Classical and Old Austrian Economics: Equilibrium Business Cycle Theory in Perspective', *Review of Austrian Economics* (1991).

Professor Garrison's contributions in the area of business cycle theory are well represented in Stephen Littlechild, (ed.), *Austrian Economics* (Edward Elgar, 1990) and he co-authored, with Israel M. Kirzner, the entry on F.A. Hayek for the *New Palgrave Dictionary of Economics* (1987). Professor Garrison is currently working on a book, *Time and Money: the Macroeconomics of Capital Structure*.

We corresponded with Roger Garrison in May 1993.

How important do you think it is for macroeconomic models to have choice-theoretic roots?
Choice-theoretic roots are necessary but not sufficient. Explaining economic phenomena in terms of the choices and actions of individuals is – or should be – the primary business of economics. Nowadays this proposition is almost as widely accepted among macroeconomists as among microeconomists. It is simply no longer respectable to 'let the data speak for themselves' or to posit specific relationships among macroeconomic magnitudes while remaining agnostic about the 'transmission mechanism'.

But having choice-theoretic roots does not, by itself, confer respectability on a macroeconomic theory. A number of modern constructions – I'm thinking of some of the new classical theories and so-called 'real business cycle' theories – involve highly artificial, or deliberately fictitious, environments in which agents make choices. These theories, sometimes apologetically called 'parables', are defended on the basis of their involving choice in a mathematically tractable setting. All too often, though, such virtues come at too heavy a cost – losing sight of the economic phenomena to be explained. The trunk and branches have been traded for roots. It isn't clear to me, for instance, that a one-good choice-theoretic model can shed any light on the problems of inflation and business cycles. In their more candid moments, the leading architects of this general class of models admit that the link between the operating characteristics of such models and the actual performance of real-world economies involves a large element of faith.

What are the key features of Austrian methodology which you would endorse?
The Austrians' methodological individualism – choice-theoretic roots, as you say – is among the most important. Choices of individuals made in the context of perceived opportunities and constraints are the basic building-blocks of the theory. Austrian subjectivism, which emphasizes the word 'perceived' in the previous sentence, is important too, but can be pushed too far. Shackle and Lachmann, who use the term 'radical subjectivism', all but deny the existence of any underlying economic realities. It seems to me that

many aspects of Austrian theory involve a play-off of perceptions against realities. I might add that most Austrian writers have a healthy attitude about mathematical economics. If I were in the business of issuing methodological taboos, I would say, 'Don't let the applicability of mathematics define the scope of economics.' This sounds like a fairly mild imperative, but a survey of macroeconomic literature over the last several years reveals that it is violated with increasing frequency.

What do you consider to be the key papers/books which have had a major impact on the development of your ideas?
The one book that stands out is F.A. Hayek's *Prices and Production* (1935) – although I should say that, by the time I first read it, I had already read a lot of Mises and Rothbard and was ready for Hayek's triangles. Austrian macroeconomics features the economy's capital structure and particularly the time dimension of capital. Lengthening one leg of a Hayekian triangle at the expense of the other represents a fundamental intertemporal trade-off in which the creation of capital goods in temporally remote stages of production requires a sacrifice of consumer goods in the current period. This capital-theoretic analysis of the intertemporal allocation of resources impressed me early on – especially in comparison to the conventional macroeconomic constructions I was exposed to in my early graduate courses. There is just too much going on within the economy's investment sector to be captured by a single aggregate.

By giving play to the time element, Hayek's triangles greatly enriched the theoretical possibilities. Shifting resources among the temporally defined stages of production changes the intertemporal pattern of final output. If a shift from, say, near-final to more remote stages is the market's reaction to a change in intertemporal consumption preferences, then the economy experiences sustainable growth; if instead a similar shift is spurred by central bank policy in the absence of any preference change, then the economy experiences an unsustainable boom. This critical distinction between preference-induced growth and policy-induced booms, so prominent in Austrian theorizing, seemed to be aggregated out of existence in the more conventional macroeconomic formulation. The theoretical possibilities that flow from disaggregating the investment sector intertemporally underlie much of my own writing.

How healthy is the current state of macroeconomics, given the level of controversy? Do you see any signs of an emerging consensus in macroeconomics and, if so, what form will it take?
What is widely seen within the economics profession as the cutting edge of macroeconomics is becoming increasingly divorced from economic reality

and policy relevance. Building models of the economy has come to be treated as an end in itself. Insistence on mathematical methods and attention to technique has virtually crowded out concern for whether or not the models are actually 'of the economy'. The so called 'Fully Articulated Artificial Economies' are all too often treated as vehicles for displaying some new modelling technique.

Not long ago I listened to a visiting scholar present a paper immodestly entitled 'Six Macroeconomic Models'. Common to all six models was the assumption of rational expectations. Although the modeller himself claimed not to know which, if any, of his half-dozen offerings reflected economic reality, he was willing to proceed on the assumption that the 'agents' populating each model did know – or behaved as if they knew – that the model in question was correct. In my attempt to point up the irony or incongruity of this manner of theorizing, I asked, 'What if model number 2 captures the underlying structure of the economy while agents form expectations in accordance with model number 5?' Our visiting scholar took the question not as a criticism of his approach but as a suggestion for expanding his research agenda. He now had 36 macroeconomic models! The emphasis on technique and the general lack of concern about relevance is not conducive to consensus.

How do you view the rational expectations revolution? Did it make a significant and meaningful contribution? Did it owe any debt to the Austrians?
The most significant positive effect of the rational expectations revolution has been to require macroeconomic theorists to make explicit their assumptions about expectations. Before the revolution, all too many theoretical results hinged on some critical but unstated assumption of systematic expectational error. Sometimes simply articulating an assumption, for instance that workers take the cost of living to be constant when in fact it is steadily increasing, reveals its implausibility. But if the word 'rational' is stipulated to mean consistent with – or, at least, not systematically inconsistent with – the underlying structure of the economy, then the rationality of expectations does not guarantee or even imply plausibility. How do agents know – or behave as if they know – the structure of the economy? Adam Smith has taught us that markets can work despite the fact that agents have little or no appreciation of theoretical economics. All I'm suggesting here is that replacing know-nothing agents with know-it-all agents is not always an improvement. We need to theorize in terms of know-all-they-can-plausibly-know agents.

The rational expectations revolution does owe a debt to the Austrians. Lucas makes regular payments on that debt by acknowledging Hayek's early contributions in the area of economics and knowledge. But the clearest antecedent is in the 1953 addendum to *The Theory of Money and Credit* (1912), where Mises captures the kernel of truth in the rational expectations hypothesis in his critical analysis of inflationary finance. Mises offered his own insightful treatment of expectations as an application of Lincoln's Law: 'You can't fool all of the people all of the time.'

How would you classify the Austrian approach to expectations? If it is neither rational nor adaptive, then how is it best classified?
The Austrian treatment of expectations is guided by considerations about what kind of knowledge market participants can plausibly have. Hayek often makes use of the distinction between two kinds of knowledge. Theoretical knowledge, or knowledge of the structure of the economy, is contrasted with entrepreneurial knowledge, or the knowledge of the particular circumstances of time and place. Economists have some of the first kind of knowledge but not much of the second; market participants have some of the second kind of knowledge but not much of the first. There is a certain formal parallel, here, with the two kinds of knowledge (global and local) in typical island parables as told by new classicists. The difference between the two constructions reflects a more general contrast between Austrian real-worldliness and new classical other-worldliness.

Beyond the constraint imposed by considerations of plausibility, the Austrians, starting with Menger, have tried to give free play to expectations so as not to be second-guessing the entrepreneur. There are, however, some implicit assumptions underlying it all – that some market participants have greater entrepreneurial foresight than others, that the market systematically rewards superior entrepreneurship and that reality eventually asserts itself.

It's worth pointing out that the Hayekian distinction between theoretical and entrepreneurial knowledge helps identify the limits of both rational planning and rational expectations. Trying to push beyond the limits reflects erroneous views about who can plausibly have what kind of knowledge: advocates of rational planning believe that planners or their economists can have as much – if not more – of the second kind of knowledge as can market participants. Proponents of the more extreme versions of rational expectations assume that market participants have, or behave as if they have, as much of the first kind of knowledge as do economists.

In your contribution to the Spadaro volume, New Directions in Austrian Economics *(1978), you provide a diagrammatical exposition of Austrian macroeconomics. What impact did this have within Austrian economics, and did it lead to an improved dialogue with the Keynesians?*
That piece had a very limited audience. Readers who were comfortable with the interlocking graphs didn't know enough about Austrian capital theory and Austrian monetary theory to make sense of them, and readers with a strong

Austrian background were unwilling to cope with – and even were offended by – the graphs. I seem to remember getting some hate mail from people who thought that any attempt to express Austrian ideas graphically was a sacrilege to Mises. But there were a few people – mostly graduate students – who were receptive to both Austrian ideas and graphical analysis. For them, my exposition served its purpose. It demonstrated that all the individual pieces drawn from the Austrian literature fit together in an analytically consistent way. The market for loanable funds, the intertemporal structure of capital, and the inverse relationship between the rate of interest and the degree of 'roundaboutness' all come together as key elements in the Austrian vision of the macroeconomy. These elements set the stage for demonstrating that monetary injections through credit markets lead to systematic but unsustainable distortions in the market process that governs the intertemporal allocation of resources.

Do you think that one can adequately model the Austrian approach, given the emphasis upon uncertainty, historical time, and non-neutral money?
Well, my diagrammatical exposition was the best I could do. And, admittedly, diagrams by their very nature tend to conceal the features that you mention. I can't imagine an Austrian model in the sense of a set of structural relationships that yield determinate values for current output, investment, production time, future output and so on, or in the sense of a Fully Articulated Artificial Economy. I think of a worthwhile model, though, as one that provides a stylized representation of the Austrian vision of the macroeconomy. It is not a substitute for verbal argument but rather a framework for formulating and presenting the argument.

Given your emphasis on the role of capital, what are the major significant contributions of Austrian economics in this area? Why do you think the work of both Hayek and Lachmann on capital and its structure have been generally neglected by both orthodox and not-so-orthodox (Neo-Ricardian/Sraffian) economists?
Two of the most fruitful contributions in the area of capital theory were Hayek's *Prices and Production* (1935), which treated in the simplest and most abstract form the notion that the economy's capital structure has both a time and a value dimension, and Lachmann's *Capital and Its Structure* (1956), which emphasized the extreme heterogeneity of capital goods and the complex lattice-work of relationships among them.

Hayek and Lachmann have been ignored by mainstream macroeconomists precisely because of their attention to pattern or structure as opposed to some aggregate quantity of capital or of investment. The success of the Keynesian Revolution is partly attributable, I think, to its liberating effect in this respect.

After Keynes, it became respectable to press on with macroeconomics without having to think about capital theory. Unfortunately the monetarist counter-revolution didn't challenge this aspect of Keynesianism. Both schools continue to ignore capital, but for opposite reasons. For the Keynesians, capital markets are so *ill*-behaved that nothing much *can* be said about them; for the monetarists, capital markets are so *well*-behaved that nothing much *need* be said about them. I have argued that the Austrians occupy a comfortable middle ground here. Capital markets work, but are particularly vulnerable to monetary disturbances and thus should be a major focus of macroeconomic analysis.

The Neo-Ricardian/Sraffian economists, as you call them, were unreceptive from the beginning to Austrian capital theory, as evidenced by Sraffa's ill-tempered attack on Hayek's *Prices and Production*. Although the Neo-Ricardians clearly incorporate a certain intertemporal trade-off in their distinguishing between corn-for-eating and corn-for-planting, their capital has no structure. It's all corn – as generalized in Sraffa's *Production of Commodities by Means of Commodities* (1960). I think Lachmann used to call this book 'Capital Theory without Capital'.

In more recent years, the Post-Keynesians, who combine Ricardian production theory with Keynesian theory of demand deficiencies, differ from the Austrians in terms of questions asked as much as answers offered. The Post-Keynesians seem to be concerned largely – if not exclusively – with the functional and personal distribution of income rather than with the intertemporal allocation of resources.

What are the major strengths and weaknesses of the Austrian approach to macroeconomics?
Its weaknesses as well as its strengths derive from the capital theory on which it is based. It is the focus on capital and interest that gives the Austrian approach a certain directness and real-worldliness that is missing in alternative formations. For instance, when the central bank initiates a monetary expansion, the new money enters the economy through loan markets and therefore impinges initially on interest rates and in capital markets. It has always struck me as odd that alternative treatments of monetary expansion – I'm thinking here of the dynamics associated with short-run/long-run Phillips curve analysis – so readily skip over this direct effect and deal instead with labour markets and wage rates as affected by asymmetries in perceptions and expectations. Key simplifying assumptions, such as the one that replaces real-world monetary injections through credit markets with the fanciful notion that new money is dispensed by a helicopter, should have served as a red flag: something important has been left out of account. Such fictitious constructions, I think, are designed to postpone – if not avoid altogether – having

to deal with the thorny issues of capital and interest. But all too often the other-worldliness thus created is simply accepted uncritically as the appropriate arena for macroeconomic theorizing. Edmund Phelps has recently identified *Seven Schools of Macroeconomic Thought* (1990) by distinguishing them in terms of the fixity or flexibility of wages and prices and the nature of expectations about wages and prices. I am inclined to lump all these theories together as macroeconomic schools of thought that focus on labour markets and wage rates and contrast them with the Austrian school, which focuses on capital markets and the interest rate.

The directness and real-worldliness of the Austrian approach, however, comes at the expense of ambiguity and complexity. Unlike labour, which can be reckoned in worker hours, capital has no physical unit of measure. But the alternative of dealing with capital in value terms makes its 'quantity' definitionally dependent upon its price. Further, Austrian capital theory disaggregates this 'quantity' into stages of production that are related to one another through a pattern of intertemporal complementarities and substitutabilities. Theorizing about capital can easily get out of hand, as is demonstrated by Hayek's *Pure Theory of Capital* (1941). And producing a direct empirical counterpart to Austrian capital theory and business cycle theory has proved difficult – although some anecdotal evidence and broad historical accounts of booms and busts are enough, in my judgement, to give plausibility to the Austrian views.

How close is Austrian economics to fundamentalist Keynesianism? Does the work of Shackle and Lachmann not demonstrate that there is an intellectual bridge between the two schools which may lead to cross-fertilization?
I think of fundamentalist Keynesianism as one of two extreme positions that help to locate the Austrian view as a middle ground position. Shackle and, following him, Lachmann use the kaleidoscope as their model of asset markets: changes in the pattern of prices in asset markets are no more predictable than changes in the pattern of cut glass in a kaleidoscope. In stark contrast, hard-drawn versions of new classicism treat the price mechanism as a clockwork rather than a kaleidoscope. The clockwork suggests an equilibrium-always approach; the kaleidoscope suggests an equilibrium-never approach. The Austrian view is somewhere between clockwork and kaleidoscope. Asset markets exhibit equilibrium tendencies but, because of the time element and the critical role of expectations, are particularly subject to disruptions. It is true that, like the Austrians, the fundamentalists emphasize such things as uncertainties, historical time and the subjectivity of expectations. And these are the very ideas that are needed to jar the new classicists away from their extreme position.

Streissler has suggested that Menger anticipated Keynes in emphasizing the uniqueness of money among commodities. Would you agree? Would you also not agree that one can comprehend Chapter 17 of the General Theory *more easily if one reads, as a companion piece, Menger's classic 1892* Economic Journal *paper on money?*

Menger was concerned with the origins of money and with how money facilitates exchange. Forty-four years later, Keynes was concerned with the perversities of money and with how hoarding money can frustrate exchange. The 'story of money' had a happy ending for one and a tragic ending for the other. It is true that both believed money to be unique and that Menger's saleability and Keynes's liquidity can be thought of as synonymous. I think that reading the two stories as companion pieces helps identify just where and how the Keynesian plot turns sour. For Keynes, the alternative to holding money is holding bonds – a view reflecting his belief that the decision about *how much* to save and the decision about *what form* the saving will take are made *seriatim*. The speculative demand for money, then, hinged specifically on speculation about movements in the interest rate. And the interest rate, according to Keynes, is not well anchored in economic reality. This construction led Keynes to psychological explanations of liquidity preference. For Menger, the alternative to holding money is holding any commodity for which money can be exchanged. Speculative demand – Menger didn't use the term – would have to reflect speculation on the part of the money holder that opportunities for making exchanges might present themselves. Menger, never mentioning the rate of interest even once in the entire article, had no reason to resort to psychological arguments and certainly never suggested anything in the way of a saleability fetish.

What do you think was Keynes's major legacy to economics?

From a practical standpoint, Keynes's legacy is the institutionalization of demand management policies. According to Marshall, prices adjust to supply and demand conditions; according to Keynes, demand must be adjusted to supply and price conditions. The Full Employment Act of 1946 provided the mandate for government to make the appropriate adjustments. The monetary and fiscal policy levers, as well as the system for collecting the data that tell policy makers which way to pull on the levers, are tailor-made for the Keynesian framework. As a result, the ideological leanings of the policy makers don't count for much. The principle at work here is that those in power tend to pull on the levers they find before them.

Modern 'stimulant packages' are typically gauged in terms of their magnitude – $30 billion worth of stimulus – with little or no regard for specifics. Keynes himself had a decided preference for stimulating investment rather than consumption but was not concerned – as the Austrian theorists would be

– about intertemporal allocation within the investment sector. Keynes simply believed that investment demand was chronically weak and prone to fluctuations because of the 'dark forces of time and ignorance that envelop our future'.

Where the Austrians had focused their theorizing on the intertemporal allocation of resources (as depicted by Hayek's triangles), Keynes – still under the influence of the Marshallian tradition – simply divided time into the short run and the long run (Chapters 5 and 12, respectively, of the *General Theory*). In judging the workability of the market system, he saw no problem in the short run and no solution in the long run. His legacy, then, was to leave it to the state, which he supposed was in a position to calculate on the basis of long-run social advantage, to manage demand so as to compensate for the perceived failings of the market.

Had Keynes still been living in 1969, do you think he would have been awarded the first Nobel Prize in Economics? Would he have received your vote?

In the second and third years in which the Nobel prize was awarded in economics, the recipients were Paul Samuelson (1970), whose 'Keynesian cross' became the centre-piece of textbook Keynesianism, and Simon Kuznuts (1971), who gave us the system of national income accounts and hence added the empirical dimension to the Keynesian research agenda. Many other recipients and even Milton Friedman, whose work on the consumption function was cited by the Nobel committee, have won the prize for their clarifications, extensions or reformulations of Keynesian theory. It would have been inexplicable, then, not to have awarded the first Nobel prize in economics to Keynes himself.

Would Keynes have had my vote? Well, Hayek and Myrdal shared the prize in 1974. Maybe Mises and Keynes should have shared it in 1969. I would relish reading the back-to-back Nobel lectures. (Incidentally, we might want to acknowledge that Tinbergen and Frisch, who actually did receive the prize in 1969, were both very worthy recipients.)

How important are Cantillon effects to the Austrian examination of the money transmission mechanism?

Austrian writers like to cite Cantillon as having been the first to emphasize – in mid-eighteenth century – that inflation does not affect all prices at once. Prices change in some sequence along with the spending and respending of new money. During the process in which prices are adjusting, relative prices are changing, and hence some quantity adjustments are occurring. *How* money is injected into the economy, then, may be as important as *how much* is injected. This is what I mean when I say that the Friedmanian helicopter should serve as a red flag signalling that something important has been left out of account.

The Austrians embrace wholeheartedly the general idea of Cantillon effects but have gone beyond it to recognize that, if money enters the economy through loan markets, then the price and quantity adjustments will exhibit a systematic – not to say determinate – intertemporal pattern. Although possibly softened by the effects of expectations, a low rate of interest attributable to credit expansion raises the prices of long-term capital goods relative to the prices of consumer goods and short-term capital goods and brings about a corresponding reallocation of resources.

Are there any key lags in the Austrian business cycle approach which explain why such cycles occur and recur?
The focus on time and money and, more specifically, on capital gives the Austrian theory a built-in lag structure. As I like to say it, 'capital gives money time to cause trouble'. This aphorism summarizes a lot of Austrian insights. Market participants have intertemporal consumption preferences, which we take as given; the structure of capital, as guided by interest rates and factor prices, will yield output in some particular intertemporal pattern. It takes time to discover whether or not the intertemporal pattern of output is consistent with the intertemporal consumption preferences. A systematic mismatch, such as that created by an artificially low rate of interest, will eventually become apparent, but by that time the economy may be faced with the necessity of a major capital restructuring.

In identifying the nature of the lag, the monetary aspect is important too. Suppose, for instance, that the interest rate were forced downward by decree. The legislature simply installs a cap on the interest rate a point or two below its market-clearing level. What would happen? There would be an obvious and immediate shortage of credit. No lag. Now compare the effects of a legislated credit cap with the effects of credit expansion initiated by the central bank. Whichever policy is used, the interest rate is artificially low. It is inconsistent with intertemporal consumption preferences. But credit expansion eliminates the obviousness and immediacy by papering over the shortage. As a result, there will be lots of quantity adjustments within the investment sector, lots of capital restructuring, before the intertemporal mismatch reveals itself.

Although the time-and-money approach gives the theory a built-in lag, it is not a determinate lag. The length of the lag depends upon specific strengths and patterns of intertemporal complementarities and substitutabilities within the capital structure and on the quality of entrepreneurship and, more generally, of expectations of market participants. It depends importantly on the extent to which market participants try to understand the effects of policy and to anticipate policy changes. All of these considerations can affect the length of the lag between boom and bust, but only the most extreme and implausible assumption about them would completely eliminate the lag. Changes over time in the way market participants form their expectation will virtually ensure that each cyclical episode will differ in detail from previous episodes, but there are no grounds in the Austrian formulation for believing, as some critics seem to believe, that a business cycle anticipated is a business cycle avoided.

You have argued in the Journal of Macroeconomics *(1984) that the two universals of macroeconomics are time and money. Apart from the Austrians, which other schools of thought handle these universals in an appropriate way?*
We can find other schools that have promising approaches to one or the other – but not both – of these aspects of the macroeconomy. For instance, the time-to-build feature of some new classical models has yet to be fully exploited. Recognizing that an investment in Period 1 may influence the decision to make some complementary investment in Period 2 brings capital structure – or at least a hint of it – back into macroeconomics. Hayek entitled one of his early articles, 'Investment that Raises the Demand for Capital' (1937), to emphasize the essential intertemporal complementarities that characterize the capital structure. Unfortunately the new classicists seem to limit the time-to-build concept to intra-firm complementarities, which tends to trivialize it, and have introduced this concept in the context of real rather than monetary disturbances. Note, though, that neither time-to-build nor Hayek's title concept has a home in modern income–expenditure analysis.

The money part of time and money is best handled, I think, in the framework of monetary disequilibrium as set out by Clark Warburton and developed most recently by Leland Yeager. The economy has to adjust piecemeal to monetary disturbances. And because of the implied changes in relative prices during the time-consuming process of adjustment, quantities adjust too. Monetary causes, then, have real consequences. But there is little or no allowance in monetary disequilibrium theory for time-to-build or for any other sort of intertemporal capital structure. I suspect that, in a world with no significant intertemporal complementarities, money-induced disequilibrium would be relatively mild and adequately explained in the Warburton–Yeager framework.

What are the strengths and significant contributions of non-Austrian macroeconomics since Keynes?
Apart from contributions I have already mentioned, I would say that the application of public choice to policy analysis has been significant. But it was

Hayek, I think, who first offered a proto-public choice theory of inflation in his *Constitution of Liberty* (1960). In their *Calculus of Consent* (1962), Buchanan and Tullock credited Hayek and went on to apply choice-theoretic economics more broadly to political issues. The built-in lags that separate the implementation of a policy and its ultimate (negative) effects make for a natural blending of Austrian macroeconomics and public choice.

Also I think that a lot of good economics has come out of attempts to make sense of the *General Theory*. I'm thinking in particular of Leijonhufvud's reconstruction of Keynes. This Swedish–American make-over had Keynes looking more like a cross between Knut Wicksell and William H. Hutt, but it's good economics independent of any connection to the original Keynesian vision. Incidentally I think that Alan Meltzer's book, *Keynes's Monetary Theory: A Different Interpretation* (1988) provides the best true-to-Keynes interpretation of the *General Theory*.

Did the Austrian approach to business cycles adequately explain the interwar experience?

I think it is correct to say that the boom of the 1920s and subsequent bust is the clearest and cleanest illustration of the kind of intertemporal discoordination identified by the Austrians. The newness of the Federal Reserve and the general absence of Fed-watching even in financial circles allowed the monetary expansion to keep interest rates artificially low for an extended period of time. The Austrian theory, then, accounts adequately for the misallocation of resources within the capital structure – the malinvestment – during the upswing and hence for the inevitability of the bust. Other considerations must be added to the story to account adequately for the depth of the downturn and the duration of the depression. What Hayek called the 'secondary deflation' is an income-constrained process in which the economy can spiral downwards far in excess of any needed liquidation. Milton Friedman's insights about the ineptness of the Federal Reserve throughout the 1929–33 period and again in 1937 come into play here. Also the duration of the depression is to be accounted for largely in terms of the perverse effects of New Deal policies, which were well understood by the Austrians and others, but were not really a part of Austrian business cycle theory.

Given your work on Austrian business cycle theory, what insights do Austrian economists offer to explain the behaviour of the US and UK economies in recent years?

Let me confine my answer to the US experience. The boom and bust of recent years is similar in form but different in particulars in comparison to the boom and bust of the interwar period. I have made the argument that, while in the earlier period policy-induced resource allocation was inconsistent with underlying *time* preferences, in the latter period policy-induced resource allocation was inconsistent with underlying *risk* preferences. In each instance, the focus is on the corresponding component of interest rates – the basic rate of time discount for the interwar episode, the risk premium for the recent episode. In the earlier episode, investment undertakings were excessively long-term; in the latter episode, excessively speculative. But in both episodes, the boom was artificial and hence the bust inevitable.

The 1980s boom was financed largely by debt sold abroad. The chronically high budgetary and trade deficits created uncertainties about future market conditions throughout the economy. The success of private business depended importantly on the ability of entrepreneurs to forecast exchange rates, interest rates and inflation rates – all of which can be dramatically affected by the disposition of the deficit. Will our trading partners continue to lend to our government? Will the government begin to borrow more heavily in domestic credit markets? Will the Federal Reserve become more accommodating?

The mere potential for debt monetization kept the default-risk premium off Treasury bills while junk bonds and other highly leveraged transactions became ways of betting one way or another about the inflation that actual debt monetization would entail. The uncertainties stemming from deficit finance were compounded by the government's subsidized deposit insurance and other irregularities and perversities in the particular way that financial institutions were deregulated in the early 1980s. By 1990 the policy-induced risk taking began to turn into losses and bankruptcies, which put an end to the boom. The junk bond market collapsed; the financial institutions are in crisis. The federal budget deficit has yet to be dealt with.

I'm simply suggesting here that there is an Austrian story to be told about the recent behaviour of the US economy. Even if not Hayekian in its particulars, the focus on capital markets and the underlying notion of a policy-induced artificial boom qualify it as a variation on a theme.

What are the key present research agendas of modern Austrian economics?
For several years now, my own research agenda has consisted largely of putting capital theory back into macroeconomics. There is lots of room for development on this front. I think that a well developed capital-based macroeconomics can compare favourably with modern income–expenditure models and with the new classical parables.

More recently, I've begun to pay attention to the problem of chronically high deficits. These fiscal excesses should get more attention from Austrian-oriented economists for two reasons. First, as I've already indicated, the boom of the 1980s was deficit-financed rather than inflation-financed. Understanding the deficit, then, becomes prerequisite to understanding the nature of the boom and subsequent bust. Second, the economics profession seems to be divided between those who (still!) believe that deficits stimulate the economy (the Keynesians) and those who believe that deficits are irrelevant (the new classicists, monetarists and supply-siders). More often than not, debate centres on what we mean by deficit, how to measure it, and whether it is high, low, or actually a surplus. The Austrians are in a good position to step in and argue that the deficit is large and disruptive.

Lastly I think the Austrian research agenda should include free banking. I have not contributed in this area except by reviewing books by Austrian-oriented economists who have. Although there is controversy within the Austrian school about the economics of free banking, it seems to me that competitive note issue is compatible with many other Austrian views. Thinking in terms of the equation of exchange, Hayek argued early on that macro-economic stability is best promoted by a constant MV. The implied monetary rule, then, is: increase M to offset decreases in V, but allow decreases in P to accommodate increases in Q. Central banks lack both the will and the ability to implement such a rule, but in a system of free banking, if I understand it correctly, it is precisely this rule that would get implemented automatically by competitive forces.

VICTORIA CHICK

Victoria Chick was born in 1936 in Berkeley, California, from where she graduated with a BSc in 1958, before obtaining an MA in 1960. Since 1963 she has taught at University College London, becoming a reader in 1984 and a professor in 1993.

Victoria Chick has, despite her dislike of labels, become known as a Post-Keynesian economist, making notable contributions in that area. Her books include: *The Theory of Monetary Policy* (Gray-Mills, 1973; 2nd edn, Blackwell, 1977), *Macroeconomics After Keynes: A Reconsideration of the General Theory* (Philip Allan, 1983) and *On Money, Method and Keynes: Selected Essays by Victoria Chick* (Macmillan/St Martin's Press, 1992), edited by P. Arestis and S.C. Dow.

Her best known articles include: 'The Nature of the Keynesian Revolution: A Reassessment', *Australian Economic Papers* (1978), 'Monetary Increases and their Consequences: Streams, Backwaters and Floods', in A. Ingham and A.M. Ulph (eds), *Demand, Equilibrium and Trade: Essays in Honour of Ivor F. Pearce* (Macmillan, 1984), 'The Evolution of the Banking System and the Theory of Saving, Investment and Interest', *Economies et Sociétés* (1986), 'A Post Keynesian Perspective on the Relation between Banking and Regional Development', co-authored with S.C. Dow, in P. Arestis (ed), *Post Keynesian Monetary Economics: New Approaches to Financial Modelling* (Edward Elgar, 1988) and 'Hicks and Keynes on

Liquidity Preference: A Methodological Approach', *Review of Political Economy* (1991).

We interviewed Victoria Chick in her office at University College, London on 8 March 1993.

Why are there so many varied interpretations of the General Theory*? Do you think this demonstrates the strength or weakness of the book?*
I am inclined to the view that it demonstrates the richness of the book and this is one of its strengths. One always interprets a book according to what one brings to it, additionally, a book like the *General Theory* is full of ambiguity which leaves the way open for a variety of interpretations to a far greater extent than any other work in economics. Some may view such ambiguity as a weakness, I do not. There are facets of the economy which are themselves ambiguous which Keynes was trying to capture – in a way that an artist may endeavour to capture the essence of something rather than draw a perfect replica – and it is partly this which has led to the divergence of interpretation. Bill Gerrard has written very interesting stuff on your question.

In your reconsideration of the General Theory *you have argued that 'the* General Theory *gives a far richer understanding of the structure of macroeconomic interactions and methods of analysing them than much of what has been written since'. How do you justify that particular view?*
Take, for example, IS–LM in its various forms. It had the perceived characteristic of encapsulating, in a few equations the essence of the *General Theory*. There the solution takes place at once, whereas in the *General Theory* proper you have a kind of wheels-within-wheels arrangement with several different time horizons – the very short time horizon of the speculator, the short time horizon of the producer and the much longer time horizon of that same person when engaged in the investment decision. It is very difficult to capture such time sensitivity in a set of simultaneous equations.

Further the *General Theory* is capable of moving around the subject. Take its presentation of the theory of investment, where one gets the clinical and precise set alongside the messy and fuzzy. Such a non-mathematical approach is able to take account of two facets of investment which are sharply opposed but which complement each other. There are many things like that which one could refer to. Keynes rejected the kind of *either/or mode* of thought (to use Sheila Dow's phrase) and went for *both/and*. There is *both* speculation *and* long-term financial investment. There is a rigorous side to the theory of investment and animal spirits, and both of them have a role to play in the whole story. There is a theory of production and a theory of accumulation. You do not get much of that sort of thing in IS–LM.

Given what you have said, Why did Keynes make so little direct criticism of Hicks's IS–LM presentation of the General Theory*?*

That has always been a problem. I do not think that Keynes was as aware as he might have been of the sharp methodological difference between himself and other people. He could not see, with anything like the kind of clarity that Hugh Townshend saw, that Hicks was profoundly subversive of the Keynesian project. It is a curious thing to say, in connection with Keynes's methodology, given his extensive background in probability, but by the time he had written the *General Theory* he had moved on and developed, probably without realizing it, the kind of methodology which we are only working out now. In the context of the theory of probability, Keynes was worried about not being able to assess the consequences of one's actions. That takes you a fair way into the *General Theory* – specifically with regard to investment – but there is so much else there. The whole attitude of the *General Theory*, its entire mode of thought, is far removed from Hicks's Walrasian–Paretian approach. The IS–LM interpretation proved congenial to those who wanted something to hang on to, whereas the *General Theory* was very slippery. Keynes seemed unaware of just how damaging the IS–LM apparatus was to his intellectual agenda. Also I believe Keynes was encouraging a bright, young economist – Hicks – and he had no desire to load him with a pile of criticism. I think that did play a part.

What do you regard as the most original elements in Keynes's General Theory*?*

Keynes figured out exactly what he could and could not keep of traditional theory. He did not accept the idea that small firms could take prices – they always operated under conditions of uncertainty. This led to the 'principle of effective demand', which is the key concept in the whole book. Keynes argued that you must start from macro effective demand and work out the implications for firms. Aggregate demand could change autonomously because investment depended not only upon long-term expectations but also on bank money finance. The crucial element here is that banks can create money without prior saving and so reverse the causality between saving and investment, which is the key in Keynesian theory to autonomous fluctuations in aggregate demand. There are two really great debates in the history of economic thought pulled together in that statement – one is the whole question of whether banks can create credit (that is multiplicatively) and the other is the role of saving (active or passive) in the growth of the economy. Dennis Robertson was the first to realize these implications. Keynes, in the *General Theory*, provided a careful analysis of speculation which pulled apart the money rate of interest and the rate of profit once and for all, whereas in Wicksell the divergence of those two elements was only temporary. In Keynes, there is no expectation whatsoever that the money rate of interest has to bear any particular relation to the rate of profit.

Was Keynes worthy of a Nobel Prize?
Ah well, of that there is no question [*laughter*]. In so far as you think Nobel Prizes are worth chasing [*further laughter*].

Why were both Marshallian and Walrasian methods inadequate for Keynes's purpose when writing the General Theory?
I have already provided part of an answer on Walras in connection with my comments on Hicks. Marshall, in my view, was actually a very strong influence upon the structure of the *General Theory*. Take, for instance, one strong proposition of Marshall, that the demand for labour was derived from the demand for the output that labour produced. The principle of effective demand generalizes that at the aggregate level – that's what gives you the result that the market for labour does not have to clear. You start with effective demand, which provides your labour implications, without implying market clearing as a necessary result. So in that regard Marshall was not absent. It is also true that the *General Theory* used a lot of the technique of partial equilibrium. It is not the Walrasian mode of argument, where all the economy's problems have to be settled at once. Keynes endeavoured to tell a dynamic story expressed in partial equilibrium terms and which was very Marshallian in its tone. He wanted to show that there was an equilibrium, to demonstrate that a situation of unemployment could persist. Keynes carried Marshall forward and made something macro out of it. Walras was not really on the agenda at that particular time and was really only put there subsequently by Hicks and others. The first serious challenge to Hicksian Keynesianism came from Hugh Townshend [1937]. I believe that his interpretation of Keynes is the best that has ever been.

You are regarded as a Post-Keynesian economist. What are the main propositions of Post-Keynesian economics?
As a Post-Keynesian macroeconomist, I would say that the principle of effective demand is the major proposition. Embodied within that principle are other propositions about the impossibility of knowing the future, uncertainty and imperfect information. I think even calling the future 'imperfect information' is a bit of a contradiction of language since we do not know what that information is. As a result of all of that there can be persistent unemployment, with the economy often failing to right itself. These are key macro propositions. In microeconomics, where I am much less expert, Post-Keynesians have done a fine job in moving away from the stereotypical profit-maximizing small firm and developing both oligopoly and monopoly theory, and other modes of pricing.

How important is endogenous money to Post-Keynesian economics?

That is a difficult and terribly complicated issue. I think that at the time that Keynes was writing it was not inconsistent to say that the money supply would increase when investment was financed by bank money – that was very important to Keynes's story. Yet the monetary authorities, at that time, also had an enormous power and control over the money supply if they chose to exercise it – any money entering the system which they did not wish to leave around could be mopped up. From that point of view, I do not think that it was as inconsistent as some people have maintained that Keynes's primacy of investment over saving actually relied on bank credit to get investment up while still maintaining that the money supply was exogenous or more appropriately policy-determined. That was perfectly possible.

Who are the important founding figures of Post Keynesian economics, apart from Keynes?
Joan Robinson, Kaldor and Kalecki are the three key figures. Shackle is slightly different, but very congenial to a Post-Keynesian way of thinking. He starts from a different point of view and perspective. His perspective is much closer, in a way, to the Austrian mode of thought with the individual making the crucial decision. That is there in Keynes and Post-Keynesian economics, but not highlighted to anything like the same extent. Then there are the later strong interpreters such as Minsky, Davidson, Kregel and Harcourt, amongst others. More recently, on the methodological side, there is a very important group of people doing work which has not really been done at that kind of level before – Sheila Dow started it off in a way, followed by Fitzgibbons [1988], Carabelli [1988], O'Donnell [1989] and now this marvellous book by Vercelli [1991].

Do you agree with Sheila Dow that Joan Robinson is the key figure because her work is a blend of all the elements which we now call Post-Keynesian economics?
Yes and no. The comprehensiveness and scale of her work is matched by Kaldor – he had as much range as she did. Robinson is quite a contrast to Keynes in a funny sort of way. Michael Anyadike-Danes took a leaf out of *Zen and the Art of Motorcycle Maintainence* and said that Keynes was the romantic and Joan the classic. I think this is quite a good characterization of the two of them. George Krimpas said that Joan Robinson wanted to teach and Keynes wanted to tease – which is even better [*laughter*]. Joan Robinson and Keynes were very different personalities and their work manifested that. Her accumulation theorems are very classical or neoclassical in their approach but not in their intent – which was to demonstrate how difficult it was to have a stable path for growth.

Is there a reasonable degree of similarity between the views of the Austrians and Post-Keynesians?
Certainly. In the sense that the Austrians would emphasize an uncertain future and an evolutionary approach. The one place where they diverge very strongly is at the same place that Shackle diverges from Post-Keynesian economics; that is to say, they focus upon individual decisions only and have no truck with macroeconomics, in the sense that, when no decision maker can be identified, they sort of go glassy-eyed and say that's not theory.

Do you accept the view that macroeconomics requires microeconomic foundations?
This is a very interesting little topic! What people usually mean by that – and they are usually neoclassical people – is that one must have a system that begins from axioms of individual behaviour. I am not at all convinced of the axiomatic approach to microeconomics generally – whether that microeconomics is to serve as micro foundations for macroeconomics or simply on its own. The antithesis to the axiomatic approach is Keynes's consumption function, which is a very practical/simple stroke of something approaching genius. It does not strike us that way now because we are so accustomed to it. But, if you remember, it knocked him over. The consumption function with an *mpc*<1 proved that the economy would not necessarily tend towards full employment. It cut the aggregate supply curve from above and the equilibrium point, the point of effective demand, was therefore stable, so that output would not expand further towards full employment. We think of the consumption function as so banal now, but it was terribly important and it had no particular micro foundations at all. Other people gave it micro foundations. If you can extend the rigour of the micro foundations underlying the *General Theory* I am all in favour of it and I do not care how neoclassical it may look.

So I am not convinced of the relevance of an axiomatic approach which neoclassical economists are utterly convinced about; for them it is an absolutely fundamental article of faith that you must give axioms of individual behaviour, but it is not part of my baggage. One can push the microeconomics as far as one can and get something out of doing that but, in the end, what makes macroeconomics a viable subject is that the microeconomic decisions which you get from all the micro foundations do not add up. You have a fallacy of composition. If you do not admit the fallacy of composition, do Walras.

The short answer to your question is no [*laughter*]! I do not believe that macroeconomics can only survive if its propositions can be grounded in microeconomic foundations. I think it has a much higher survival value than that, for two reasons: the axiomatic approach is not necessarily relevant and there is the fallacy of composition.

Do you think it is possible to marry together the contributions of Keynes and Sraffa?

Well, in one respect no, but in other respects probably yes. For as long as neo-Ricardians, Sraffians, or whatever one wants to call them, insist that the only thing that marks theory is a concern with long-run points of gravitation then there is no reconciliation, in my view, between them and the Post-Keynesians. Again, if I can go back to the Marshallian foundations stuff and the Marshallian market, short and long periods – which were used in the *General Theory* – there is only one aspect to long-period theorizing in the *General Theory* and that is the demand side of the investment equation, not the supply side. Whether or not it turns out in the long run to have been a good idea to make that investment or not is simply never discovered. It is not a question which ever comes up, and so the mechanism which would drive you in a surplus approach to an equalized profit equilibrium is simply not present; it is not there. And that is all that some Sraffians care about, arguing if you are not concerned with this long-run tendency you are not actually doing theory – I cannot accept that. If one is only concerned with the long period one is wasting one's time. On this matter, the ground between us is enormous, so that bridging it would be very difficult. Of course there are other aspects of the Sraffa approach which are very congenial to Post-Keynesian economists – especially its valuable contribution of challenging a number of the presumptions of neoclassical economics. I think the task of merging the two is extremely difficult. Dutt and Amadeo tried in their book [1990], *Keynes's Third Alternative?* Those two are bright enough to pull the two approaches together if anybody can, so watch that space [*laughter*].

Which papers/books have most influenced the development of macroeconomics in general in recent years?

I would not have any idea because macroeconomics in general is mainstream macroeconomics, and I keep myself as far away from that material as I can manage [*laughter*].

Expectations play a major role in economic analysis. What are your views of the rational expectations hypothesis?

Rational expectations is a way of bringing Walras back through the back door. In Walras everything was established at one point in time and no false trading or false production took place. All that rational expectations is doing, in its strong form, is dismantling time yet again and saying that if we know the true theory we can proceed on that basis. Now weak rational expectations – of the kind where people search for information up to a point – is an attempt to make it more palatable because in its strong form it is sort of mad [*laughter*]. But we need to realize that we cannot know what happens in the future, no matter how much we are willing to pay or search to find out. Rational expectations is part of the Walrasian project with a sugared pill in its weaker form, but the weaker form not solving the essential problem.

In your view have the new classical contributions added anything to our understanding of the macro economy?
I am sure they have but I feel in a very weak position to say exactly what. I am on a weak wicket where Lucas is concerned.

Do you not think that they have forced Keynesians of the mainstream variety to go back and look at Keynes and rethink their ideas?
Well, I wish they had. If they had that impact then I think it would have been marvellous, but I am not at all convinced that they have. They have put the monetarists in a very peculiar position, which might be a contribution [*laughter*].

Would you not agree that the Post-Keynesian view is too fragmented?
No. The Post-Keynesian project has moved from the 1970s aura of a strong critique of neoclassical economics to a positive approach branching out into new fields. Much of the early stuff, on the micro side, had been to develop and enhance the insights of Kalecki, whilst, on the macro side, it had been to reinstate Keynes. Now you see Post-Keynesian economics moving into such areas as development economics, taxation, organizational and behavioural theories of the firm. What you might think is fragmentation is actually people applying the basic principles of Post-Keynesian economics to a wide range of fields.

What about fragmentation in the sense that the distinct roots of Post-Keynesian economics remain separate and increasingly pull in different directions?
I do not see it that way. I have already acknowledged that the Sraffa stream remains a problem, for the reasons outlined earlier. Clearly there are different streams feeding into the same pool of what we now call Post-Keynesian economics and there still remains a great deal of work to be done on coherency between the respective roots. What you have is a disparate group of economists working towards a very similar aim, which is to put economics on a footing which is not axiomatic, not formalistic, which embodies intuition and art as well as science and yet is logical and comes up with conclusions one can have some confidence in. That seems to me to be the Post-Keynesian project. Of course on matters of detail we do argue. What fun would there be in life if one could not argue [*laughter*]? There are wide divergences of view, but it still somehow hangs together. It all comes down to how much variety and ambiguity you can tolerate.

Are we any nearer an integration of monetary and value theory than we were in Keynes's day?
I think Keynes did a lot to bring that integration about. I have to mention Townshend again but the person who has really picked up on his integration of money and value theory – though not quite in the way you expect – is Roy Rotheim.

What have been the landmarks in after-Keynes monetary theory?
The contributions of Minsky, Kregel, Dow and, I would like to think, myself. You are now asking about monetary theory *per se* rather than the combination or confluence of monetary theory and value theory. I think the really important thing about Post-Keynesian monetary theory is that we deal with money as it is and not with real balances or some other construction. I take a very strong evolutionary view of the monetary system and would like to propose that monetary theory has to keep pace with changes in institutions, and the art of that is to know when enough important changes have taken place to demand a change in theory.

Why do economists seem to disagree less over microeconomic issues than they do over macroeconomic issues?
Well, is that really true? Neoclassical microeconomists do not disagree too much but I am not so sure that Post-Keynesian economists do not disagree quite a lot about microeconomics. Macroeconomics is harder to separate from politics, which is always contentious. There is plenty of ideology in microeconomics, but it is not overt.

How do you react to the recent survey of economists' opinions in the AER [1992] *which suggested that they appeared to agree more on micro issues?*
The questions and answers were largely based on neoclassical theory. Neoclassical economists always manage to agree quite closely, for reasons not hard to find. It is not surprising as they start with a certain set of shared premises. Microeconomics is the best place for a neoclassical economist to function. If one does not believe in the fallacy of composition there is really not much scope to do macroeconomics. So they ought to stay out of macroeconomics [*laughter*]. But they are quite good at microeconomics and I admire many of the things that they do.

What are the policy implications of Post-Keynesian economics?
The obvious one is that unemployment can persist. Another is that you cannot ignore transition states. I remember Patrick Minford saying once that you can cut wages and prices and there will be no problem, there will not be any substantial unemployment, because he had this idea that you go from one

equilibrium to another virtually without a transition. If you were a Post-Keynesian you would know that the only way to get wages and prices down is to create unemployment. I often say that Margaret Thatcher's great experiment was Keynesianism with all the signs reversed [*laughter*].

Given the many failed attempts to operate an incomes policy in the UK, do you think that we should abandon all hope of using that as an instrument in the future?
One of the reasons that incomes policy has failed, basically everywhere it has been tried, as far as I know, is that nobody faces up to the fact that it poses a problem. If you are going to run an incomes policy, you are doing something with income distribution, with relative shares, which has always been sorted out by stealth and by the political process. Take the 1970s when the trade unions were putting in enormous wage claims. All of a sudden the middle classes realized they had lost out relative to the workers and voted Margaret Thatcher into office. That is the political process redoing income distribution. Look at the 1920s when monetary stringency had to be imposed in order to get back on the gold standard: the rentiers shot ahead and the workers were slammed into the ground. These policies always have an income-redistributive effect, so unless you can get some amount of agreement about relative shares you cannot run an incomes policy.

Do you see any signs of an emerging consensus in macroeconomics?
No [*laughter*].

How do you view the recent conduct of macroeconomic policy in the UK?
[*Further laughter.*]

9. Conclusions and reflections

> Creating a new theory is not like destroying an old barn and erecting a skyscraper in its place. It is rather like climbing a mountain, gaining new and wider views, discovering new connections between our starting point and its rich environment. But the point from which we started still exists and can be seen, although it appears smaller and forms a tiny part of our broad view gained by the mastery of the obstacles on our adventurous way up. (Attributed to Albert Einstein, cited in Parkin, 1992)

9.1 Introduction

The analogy suggested by Parkin (1992) that macroeconomic theorists are like mountaineers is a useful one. We have seen how various teams (schools) of mountaineers have attempted to scale the macro mountain in order to gain a better view of the economic landscape. However no participant has ever managed to see the top of the mountain, which is continuously shrouded in mist. Each team, confident in its own map-reading skills, decides to take a different route up the same mountain, feeling assured that they have identified the most appropriate route to the summit. During the ascent the teams frequently find that their chosen paths come into close contact, only to part again after some brief exchange of information. The teams may, on occasion, come across the frozen remains of pioneers in the field in need of temporal defrosting. Sometimes a team member wanders off, never to be seen again, or defects to a competing group which appears to be making a speedier ascent. Although some routes prove to be cul-de-sacs, this too is useful information, in that teams now know not to try that particular path. On occasion a team claims to have reached the summit, only to discover, as the clouds lift, that there remain still higher and more treacherous peaks to climb. All groups are constantly under the threat of being swept down the mountain by an avalanche of unfavourable empirical evidence. Although those left behind at base camp endeavour to remain in contact, they often lose sight of teams as they are forced to change course because of unforeseen obstacles which block their chosen route.

From the discussion of the preceding chapters we hope to have conveyed to the reader that modern macroeconomics is both an exciting and a controversial subject. This is most forcefully demonstrated by the contrasting answers given in the interviews by leading exponents of the main schools of macroeconomic thought. The purpose of this concluding chapter is to draw together our discussion of these competing schools by briefly commenting on *why* economists disagree (section 9.2) and *where* economists disagree (section 9.3). Finally, in section 9.4, we tentatively contemplate the likely future direction of macroeconomics.

9.2 Why Economists Disagree

The perception that economists do nothing but disagree is part of common folklore. Public indignation at the fact that a group of *n* economists is likely to result in at least *n* + 1 opinions goes back at least as far as Keynes, who was often charged with holding two contradictory opinions simultaneously. The gibe that, if all the economists that ever lived were placed end to end, they still would not reach a conclusion neatly captures the contemporary mood. Economists are often accused of being guilty of assuming either too much or too little. While such criticisms contain a grain of truth, they fail to recognize important areas of consensus and agreement between economists.

In the immediate post-Second World War period, with the dominance of Keynesianism in theory and policy alongside positivism in methodology, economics appeared to have achieved real scientific status. This view was reinforced by the introduction in 1969 of a Nobel Prize in Economic Science. Exaggerated claims about the credentials of economics have often been made, suggesting that the discipline was almost as 'hard' as the physical sciences and far removed from the other 'softer' social sciences. This perception helped to sustain an illusion that, perhaps, there was only one approach and answer to any economic problem. Many economists yearned for the white garment of the scientist rather than that of the more humble dentist alluded to by Keynes (1972, Vol. IX) in his essay on 'Economic Possibilities for Our Grandchildren'. Even notable philosophers of science were taken in. Popper (1961) pointed to the fact that, whereas the backward social sciences have yet to find a Galileo, economics had already experienced its Newtonian revolution. Likewise Kuhn (1970) argued that economics displayed maturity, being relatively more coherent and consensual than the other social sciences. The inherent weaknesses and practical failings of both Keynesianism and economic positivism highlighted in the late 1960s and early 1970s led to the demise of much of the old orthodoxy without its replacement by any single dominant new approach. Any continuing 'submerged' competition between rival macroeconomic explanations became more open and pronounced. The revival of much of the 'old economics', in a traditional (Austrian) or new form (monetarist, new classical and real business cycle approaches), undermined much of the 'new economics' of orthodox Keynesianism, which in turn encouraged the development of alternative Post-Keynesian and new Keynesian accounts.

In the preceding chapters we have examined the nature and extent of contemporary disagreement within macroeconomics resulting from this great ungluing of the Keynesian orthodoxy. Macroeconomists have largely been engaged in emphasizing their differences rather than their similarities. They have often been more concerned with differentiating their intellectual products in the academic arena alongside a willingness to display conflicts over policy advice in the public arena. The continued survival of rival schools in macroeconomics necessarily depends upon their ability to demarcate their approach from the competition successfully. There has been a tendency to emphasize uniqueness of identity, which in turn, has led to both diversity and labelling. Such discrimination at the theoretical level naturally spills over into policy matters where economists are keen to play the part of 'hired-guns', or as Brittan (1973) puts it, engage in 'gladiatorial combat' directly in front of the public. In short, macroeconomic debate, both at the theory and policy level, enables economists to distinguish and advertise their product. What appears to the public as excessive disagreement and squabbling is the inevitable outcome of competition and widening theoretical and policy choice. Furthermore, given that the majority of economists who ever lived are still alive today, such product differentiation is likely to continue.

Economics is marked by its pronounced inability to reject rather than retain, by its substantial number of conjectures piled high against its paucity of refutations, and the fact that there is 'no final criterion that ends all discussion' (Klamer, 1988) and arbitrates between rival accounts. Theories in economics often get displaced but rarely disappear. This allows disagreement to persist. Friedman's (1953) faith that many of the fundamental disputes within economics in general, and macroeconomics in particular, would be resolved by empirical testing has not as yet been borne out. Neither has Schumpeter's (1954) belief that much of the ideological component of economics would be systematically jettisoned. Substantial differences remain with regard to the interpretation of empirical evidence, ethical considerations, hard core propositions, degree and type of ideological commitment, and much else besides. Of course disagreement is not unique to economics, it is, at the very least, just as widespread, pronounced and deep-rooted in the other social sciences. Even the physical sciences experience such conflicts and are, in reality, much 'softer' than they are usually presented.

Much of the contemporary disagreement within macroeconomics has its roots in the Keynesian episode and events since. Macroeconomics has largely consisted of an attempt to come to terms with Keynes and his *General Theory*. This is brought out clearly in the main text and interviews where the shadow of Keynes generally continues to loom large. Indeed nearly all of the economists we interviewed believe that, if Keynes had been alive around the time of the introduction of the Nobel Prize in Economics, he would have been a likely recipient of either the first, or a subsequent, award. Macroeconomists have been engaged in understanding, extending, correcting or rejecting Keynes's message, a message which was fertile, multifaceted and ambiguous. Not only does one find 'more than enough ammunition in Keynes for many varied points of view' (see Hutchison, 1977, p. 48) but, as Yeager (1973) suggests, Keynes was 'riding several different horses in different parts of the same book'. Keynes was not adverse to using a wide array of arguments to sustain his position and he, and other economists subsequently, recognized the importance of the art of persuasion or rhetoric. Much of the attraction of Keynes's role, as the capitalist redeemer, was in his success at 'turning stones into bread'; rhetoric was an important weapon in the acceptance of this Keynesian miracle, even if it was derided as 'cheap tricks' (Mises, 1977) by his opponents.

The rise and fall of orthodox Keynesian economics owed a great deal to its problem-solving effectiveness. It appeared to provide a robust explanation of a severe empirical problem, namely mass unemployment – which had persisted long enough not to be easily explained away as a minor anomaly. In addition it offered an attractive political action programme for the resolution of the diagnosed problem. Whilst it contained a number of serious conceptual problems, for example inconsistencies and ambiguities of presentation alongside more radical elements, these were effectively submerged by the neoclassical synthesis process. Keynes's *General Theory* was grafted onto the rising Walrasian research tradition, rather than the declining Marshallian research tradition which had inspired it. The mainstream development of macroeconomics after Keynes has been led by schools within the Walrasian research tradition. It has been the non-mainstream schools which have been located elsewhere, with the Post-Keynesians having some allegiance to Marshall and the Austrians rooted in Menger.

The demise of orthodox Keynesianism was in large part the result of its failure to deal adequately with the major new empirical problem posed by stagflation in the 1970s. Conceptually much of its 'heuristic power' had 'petered out' and 'run dry' (Leijonhufvud, 1968). As Klamer (1984) concedes, 'the 70s were a decade of retreat, defense, and frustration' for Keynesian economics. It was, of course, faced by a potent rival, monetarism, which was better able to explain the empirical anomaly in a more consistent fashion. Monetarism, in turn, experienced a period of progress, before being faced with problems of its own. Its failure to account satisfactorily for such a phenomenon as 'the quadrupling of the UK unemployment rate during 1975–81' (Cross, 1982a), was to seriously undermine it. During the early 1970s a new classical counter-revolution took place which was subsequently followed by the development of the real business cycle and new Keynesian approaches. While new classical macroeconomics evolved out of the monetarist approach, it in fact provided a sustained challenge to the monetarist as well as the Keynesian orthodoxies.

New classical macroeconomics displayed important conceptual progress by nurturing a rational expectations revolution, which was subsequently widely incorporated into the macroeconomic mainstream, and highlighting the role of aggregate supply. However important criticisms were increasingly directed at new classical macroeconomics concerning certain conceptual, empirical and policy deficiencies. Its empirical results have been, at best, somewhat mixed and inconclusive. Contrary to its early claims, both unanticipated *and* anticipated policy changes appear to affect output and employment, while several economies have experienced real costs of announced disinflation. New classical macroeconomics has certainly left its mark, and both real business cycle theory and new Keynesian economics can be viewed as a response to issues raised by Robert Lucas Jr. and other prominent new classicists. The real business cycle theorists have been engaged in developing some of the positive parts of the new classical programme. Likewise the new Keynesians are endeavouring to rationalize price and wage rigidities and areas of policy effectiveness . The jury is still out with regard to the contributions of these two most recent mainstream schools. It is still too early to appraise their performance, especially since a large amount of their effort has been directed towards conceptual and theoretical matters.

Of course the demise of orthodox Keynesianism also permitted the revival of interest in such non-mainstream accounts as that of the Austrians and the salvaging of Keynes's fundamental ideas by the Post-Keynesians.

The success of rival schools in macroeconomics depends upon their ability to explain adequately macroeconomic phenomena. What is clear is that 'no model, no single argument, is unexceptional and problem-free' (Klamer, 1984). Macroeconomists do disagree over the relative weights they attach to empirical and conceptual problems, but reasons need to be advanced and communicated to explain why particular economists are concerned with some problems rather than others, and which demonstrate the effectiveness of the different solutions offered (see Laudan, 1984). The competing schools in macroeconomics deal with many common shared problems, such as fluctuations in output, employment and the price level, in different ways. Table 9.1 highlights some of the important features of the schools explored in this book. The mainstream development of macroeconomics can be read from top to bottom; that is, from orthodox Keynesian to new Keynesian. The Austrian and Post-Keynesian approaches represent the most important non-mainstream approaches. Two points should be borne in mind when consulting this table. First, *within* each school identified, there are differences of opinion and emphasis: the table merely characterizes the view most commonly held on particular issues. Second, as is evident from a close scrutiny of the table, there is a considerable degree of *overlap* between the various schools on a number of issues. This suggests that, in practice, the dividing line between schools is becoming increasingly blurred on many issues.

If Keynes provided a major revolution in macroeconomics, it would be difficult to deny that we have had other, perhaps smaller-scale, revolutions subsequently. The fall of orthodox Keynesianism has been followed by the rise of alternative macroeconomic frameworks such that economists 'in the field feel obliged to consider [them] seriously as a contender for the allegiance of themselves or their colleagues' (Laudan, 1977).

9.3 Where Economists Disagree

Throughout our presentation of the development of macroeconomics since Keynes's *General Theory* we have focused upon the areas of disagreement and agreement between the rival macroeconomic schools. Reasons were advanced in the previous section to account for some of the major sources of disagreement. We shall now consider *where*, rather than *why*, economists disagree and, once again, pay particular attention to the macro sphere. A number of studies have been carried out which attempt to explore economists' opinions and identify whether there is an economic consensus at the national and international level. The usual measure of the degree of consensus is to use relative entropy ranging from 0 (perfect consensus) to 1 (no consensus) with respondents equally distributed across response options.

In the United States there have been two major studies carried out and subsequently published (Kearl *et al.*, 1979; Alston *et al.*, 1992). An examination of these respective surveys will not only help to identify whether there has been any noticeable shift in American economic opinion over time but also allow us to compare the results with studies carried out elsewhere, especially in Britain.

The original Kearl *et al.* (1979) study attempted to address the issue of the problem of widespread perceived disagreement among economists. It outlined two main *ex ante* hypotheses: (i) that there would be greater consensus on microeconomic rather than macroeconomic questions; (ii) that there would be greater consensus on *can* questions (positive statements) rather than *ought* questions (normative statements). The results of the Kearl *et al.* study supported both of these hypotheses. Consensus was seen to be largely centred upon microeconomic issues involving the price mechanism, with disagreement located in macroeconomic and normative issues. *Within* macroeconomics there were notable areas of agreement and consensus relating to the fact that fiscal policy *could* stimulate the economy and that wage–price controls *should not* be used to control inflation. There was a large diversity of opinion expressed over whether there was a short-run trade-off between inflation and

Table 9.1 Some areas of agreement and disagreement in macroeconomics

Schools in macroeconomics	Dominant source of instability	Expectations	Price adjustment	Market adjustment	Notion of equilibrium	Dominant time frame	Rules v. discretion	Role of incomes policy
Orthodox Keynesian	Fluctuations in autonomous expenditure	Adaptive	Relatively inflexible	Weak	State of rest probably below full employment	Short	Discretion	Some support
Orthodox monetarist	Monetary disturbances	Adaptive	Flexible	Strong	Market clearing at natural rate	Short and Long	Rules	Irrelevant and distorting
New classical	Monetary disturbances	Rational	Extremely flexible	Very strong	Market clearing at natural rate	Long = short	Rules	Irrelevant and distorting
Real business cycle	Supply shocks (mainly technological)	Rational	Extremely flexible	Very strong	Market clearing at moving natural rate	Long = short	Rules	Irrelevant and distorting
New Keynesian	Demand and supply shocks (eclectic)	Rational	Emphasis on price rigidities	Slow	Consistent with involuntary unemployment	Predominantly short	No clear consensus	Predominantly against
Austrian	Monetary disturbances	Reasonable	Flexible	Strong	Tendency towards	Short and long	Rules	Harmful and distorting
Post-Keynesian	Fluctuations in autonomous expenditure	Reasonable	Sticky	Very weak	State of rest, probably below full employment	Short	Discretion	Essential and beneficial

414

"My PhD thesis was a pioneering attempt to create a new synthesis by constructing a new-classical over-lapping generations equilibrium business cycle model with Austrian roots which nevertheless contained Keynesian price rigidities, neutrality properties, involuntary unemployment, outsider power, decreasing returns to scale, irrational expectations and maximising agents operating in a world of fundamentalist uncertainty, repeatedly hit by endogenous technical progress. When the model generated neo-Marxian predictions I just flipped!"

(Cartoon drawn by Steven Tucker, aged 12¼)

unemployment. The Kearl *et al.* survey concluded that the perception of *widespread* disagreement among economists was 'simply wrong'.

The Alston *et al.* study (1992) investigated whether there was a consensus amongst US economists in the 1990s. It also explored whether there had been any significant shift in economists' opinions since the Kearl study. The authors argue that differences were identified with regard to the role of money in the economy. Economists appeared to be *less* inclined to view the money supply target as more important than interest rates but *more* inclined to view inflation as primarily a monetary phenomenon. In addition *greater* disagreement was expressed over the short-run Phillips curve trade-off than in the earlier study. One area of monetary policy where opinion remained unchanged was related to the adoption of a rule for a fixed rate of monetary growth where a relatively strong consensus to reject this proposition continued. Likewise wage–price controls were still viewed with suspicion by a large majority of the economists surveyed. The Alston survey corroborated the findings of the Kearl study when it concluded that consensus is stronger on micro than macro propositions and on positive rather than normative matters. It is interesting to note that the leading economists we interviewed were generally of the opinion that there was no clearly emerging consensus in macroeconomics and that greater disagreement there, rather than in microeconomics, *if it existed*, was due to the nature of the subject, its history and policy orientation. While Alston *et al.* identified 'much consensus' amongst economists, they pointed out that economists had 'substantially altered' their collective view on monetary matters. An interesting result of the Alston *et al.* survey was their finding that economists' responses to macroeconomic propositions were affected by their degree 'vintage', with orthodox Keynesianism generally being endorsed by those who obtained their highest degree before or during the 1960s.

We can contrast the American findings on economists' opinions with those in Britain and Europe. The first British survey of economic attitudes was published by Brittan (1973). It was unique in questioning not only economists but also members of parliament and political commentators. With regard to the responses of economists, Brittan found a 'high degree of agreement', especially on such issues as demand management, budget deficits and monetary policy. In highlighting the 'substantial degree of consensus' among economists, Brittan made a number of interesting points. First, he recognized that the differences between economists were much less than those between politicians, even when the latter belonged to the same party! Second, a large number of economists displayed 'an extreme preoccupation' with the distribution of income. This led Brittan to suggest that such a concern was more pronounced than that experienced elsewhere in the capitalist West. Third, most economists were found to have an intellectual commitment to the price mechanism. Finally, much of the agreement between economists, *especially* with regard to macro questions, was related to the continued dominance of Keynesian theory. As Brittan (1973) argued, 'the much discussed "monetarist" critique of Keynesian economics has penetrated only skin-deep as far as the great majority of British economists are concerned'.

These results can be compared to the recent detailed investigations into *British Economic Opinion* carried out by Ricketts and Shoesmith (1990) and recently summarized in their 1992 *American Economic Review* paper. The Ricketts and Shoesmith study not only reinforces several of the points made in the earlier Brittan survey but serves to highlight important differences between British economists and their American counterparts.

With regard to Brittan's (1973) contribution, many of his original findings continue to be reflected in British economists' opinions. The proportion of British economists supporting a redistributive role for government was found to be 'higher in the UK than in any other country' (Ricketts and Shoesmith, 1990). In addition British economists not only *combined* respect for the workings of the price mechanism with this redistributive role for government, but also endorsed a positive view of government intervention in general. Keynesianism appears to remain alive and well in Britain, since the proposition that 'fiscal policy has a significant stimulative impact on a less than fully employed economy' produced the highest level of consensus in comparison with surveys carried out elsewhere. Indeed Ricketts and Shoesmith (1990) echo Brittan's earlier remark regarding 'macro theoretical inertia' when they maintain: 'British opinion appears less influenced by the "rational expectations" thinking of the later 1970s and early 1980s and is more conventionally "Keynesian"'.

While Ricketts and Shoesmith (1990, 1992) largely reinforce Brittan's findings, they do allude to a number of differences between their results and those obtained in the USA. They argue that economists' opinions in the UK are 'structured differently from those in the USA and elsewhere'. Unlike the Kearl *et al.* study (1979), they found *no* evidence to support the hypothesis that there was greater consensus on micro than on macro matters, although they did find evidence to corroborate the US study's finding that positive statements generate less disagreement than normative propositions. A noticeable area of difference for Ricketts and Shoesmith (1992) between British and American economists related to the proposition that 'wage–price controls should be used to control inflation'. This produced disagreement in the UK but a relatively hostile consensus in the USA. On the other hand, the proposition that 'in the short run, unemployment can be reduced by accepting an increase in the rate of inflation' displayed greater support from UK economists (with low entropy) compared to US economists (high entropy).

The study by Frey *et al.* (1984) examined the extent of consensus and dissension among economists in the USA and Europe. They found evidence to challenge the claims of Kearl *et al.* (1979) related to the level of consensus on micro/macro and positive/normative propositions. They maintain that the results for the USA do not apply to their survey of German, Swiss, French and Austrian (in the sense of nationality rather than intellectual affiliation) economists. It could not be confirmed that micro and positive propositions had a higher degree of consensus than macro and normative propositions. Economists, internationally speaking, were found to agree on matters apper-taining to the effectiveness and desirability of the price mechanism. Frey *et al.* found that there was a noticeable difference between US, West German and Swiss economists compared to those in Austria and France. The first group supported the market and competition, and resisted government inter-vention, whilst the second group favoured such interventions and were less convinced of the merits of the price mechanism.

The more recent paper by Frey and Eichenberger (1992) endeavours to provide some rationale for the differences between US and European econo-mists. They believe that the fact that US and European economists deviate on micro/macro and positive/normative statements can be explained by differ-ences in incentives (see Colander, 1988) and academic markets. It may be the case, certainly as compared to the UK, that there is a more robust differentia-tion of the macroeconomic product in the USA, which allows for greater disagreement relative to microeconomics. The alternatives to orthodox Keynesianism are better defined and more solidly established in the USA than elsewhere. The centres and channels for confrontation between rivals, in both the academic and policy arenas, are also further developed. It is, per-haps, no accident that the mainstream development of macroeconomics *since* Keynes is, quite simply, 'born in the USA'.

9.4   The Future Direction of Macroeconomics

At the present moment macroeconomics lacks the degree of consensus it once had under orthodox Keynesianism. There is a large amount of competi-tion between the rival schools in economics and an emphasis placed upon differences rather than similarities. The apparent lack of consensus in macroeconomics should be seen in a positive rather than a negative light, and many would agree with Lucas's response (Chapter 5), in his interview, that 'consensus for a research area as a whole is equivalent to stagnation, irrel-evance and death'. Much disagreement reflects the excitement and rich diver-sity of current macroeconomics. John Milton, the 17th-century poet, captured this point in his work *Samson Agonistes*, when he wrote, 'In prosperous days they swarm, but in adverse withdraw their head.' It is an intellectually pros-perous time for macroeconomics.

While there does not appear to be any clearly emerging consensus on the horizon we should not be surprised if a synthesis develops in the future, possibly even from disparate schools. With the benefit of hindsight, differences have often been exaggerated. Take, for example, the orthodox Keynesian–monetarist debate which now appears much more like a family squabble than a clash between rival clans. Stanley Fischer's illuminating analogy, of the distinction he could once draw in the 1950s between a Chev and a Ford, and the fact they look extremely similar now, makes this very point. One thing we can be sure about, with regard to the future direction of macroeconomics, is that it will continue to surprise us just as much as it has done in the past. Few could have anticipated the revival of the 'old' neoclassical macroeconomics and the subsequent fall and rise of Keynesian economics, albeit in new bottles. For the moment, 'Macroeconomics these days is virtually balkanised, though passports are issued' (Phelps, 1992).

Bibliography

Titles marked with an asterisk are particularly recommended for student reading

Abel, A. and Bernanke, B.S. (1992), *Macroeconomics*, New York: Addison Wesley.

Ackley, G. (1966), *Macroeconomic Theory*, New York: Collier-Macmillan.

Akerlof, G.A. (1982), 'Labour Contracts as Partial Gift Exchange', *Quarterly Journal of Economics*, November.

Akerlof, G.A. (1984), 'Gift Exchange and Efficiency Wage Theory: Four Views', *American Economic Review*, May.

Akerlof, G.A. and Yellen, J.L. (1985a), 'A Near-Rational Model of the Business Cycle, with Wage and Price Inertia', *Quarterly Journal of Economics*, Supplement.

Akerlof, G.A. and Yellen, J.L. (1985b), 'Can Small Deviations from Rationality Make Significant Differences to Economic Equilibria?', *American Economic Review*, September.

Akerlof, G.A. and Yellen, J.L. (eds) (1986), *Efficiency Wage Models of the Labour Market*, Cambridge: Cambridge University Press.

Akerlof, G.A. and Yellen, J.L. (1987), 'Rational Models of Irrational Behavior', *American Economic Review*, May.

Akerlof, G.A. and Yellen, J.L. (1988), 'Fairness and Unemployment', *American Economic Review*, May.

*Akerlof, G.A. and Yellen, J.L. (1990), 'The Fair Wage–Effort Hypothesis and Unemployment', *Quarterly Journal of Economics*, May.

Aldcroft, D.H. (1986), *The British Economy: The Years of Turmoil 1920–51*, Brighton: Wheatsheaf.

Aldcroft, D.H. (1993), *The European Economy, 1914–1990*, 3rd edn, London: Routledge.

*Alesina, A . (1989), 'Politics and Business Cycles in Industrial Democracies', *Economic Policy*.

Alesina, A. and Roubini, N. (1992), 'Political Cycles in OECD Economies', *Review of Economic Studies*, October.

*Alesina, A. and Summers, L.H. (1993), 'Central Bank Independence and

Macroeconomic Performance: Some Comparative Evidence', *Journal of Money, Credit and Banking*, May.

Alogoskoufis, G.S., Lockwood, B. and Philippopoulos, A. (1992), 'Wage Inflation, Electoral Uncertainty and the Exchange Rate Regime: Theory and UK Evidence', *Economic Journal*, November.

Alston, R., Kearl, J.R. and Vaughan, M.B. (1992), 'Is There a Consensus Among Economists in the 1990s?' *American Economic Review*, May.

Altonji, J.G. (1986), 'Intertemporal Substitution in Labour Supply: Evidence from Micro Data', *Journal of Political Economy*, June.

Alvi, E. (1993), 'Near Rationality/Menu Costs, Strategic Complementarity and Real Rigidity: An Integration', *Journal of Macroeconomics*, Fall.

Amadeo, E.J. (1989), *Keynes's Principle of Effective Demand*, Aldershot: Edward Elgar.

Amadeo, E.J. (1992), 'Equilibrium Unemployment in Keynes's *General Theory*: Some Recent Debates', *Contributions to Political Economy*.

Ando, A. and Modigliani, F. (1965), 'The Relative Stability of Monetary Velocity and the Investment Multiplier', *American Economic Review*, September.

Arrow, K.J. (1962), 'The Economic Implications of Learning By Doing', *Review of Economic Studies*.

Atkinson, A.B. and Micklewright, J. (1991), 'Unemployment Compensation and Labour Market Transitions: A Critical Review', *Journal of Economic Literature*, December.

Attfield, C.L.F., Demery, D. and Duck, N.W. (1985), *Rational Expectations in Macroeconomics: An Introduction to Theory and Evidence*, Oxford: Basil Blackwell.

Azariadis, C. (1975), 'Implicit Contracts and Underemployment Equilibria', *Journal of Political Economy*, December.

Backus, D. and Driffill, J. (1985), 'Inflation and Reputation', *American Economic Review*, June.

Backus, D.K. and Kehoe, P.J. (1992), 'International Evidence on the Historical Properties of Business Cycles', *American Economic Review*, September.

Backus, D.K., Kehoe, P.J. and Kydland, F.E. (1992), 'International Real Business Cycles', *Journal of Political Economy*, August.

Bailey, M.N. (1974), 'Wages and Unemployment Under Uncertain Demand', *Review of Economic Studies*, January.

Balke, N.S. and Gordon, R.J. (1989), 'The Estimation of Pre-War GNP: Methodology and New Evidence', *Journal of Political Economy*, February.

Ball, L. (1990), 'Insiders and Outsiders: A Review Essay', *Journal of Monetary Economics*, December.

Ball, L. (1991), 'The Genesis of Inflation and the Costs of Disinflation', *Journal of Money, Credit and Banking*, August.

Ball, L. (1994), 'What Determines the Sacrifice Ratio?' in N.G. Mankiw (ed.), *Monetary Policy*, Chicago: University of Chicago Press.

Ball, L. and Cecchetti, S.G. (1988), 'Imperfect Information and Staggered Price Setting', *American Economic Review*, December

Ball, L. and Romer, D. (1989), 'Are Prices Too Sticky?', *Quarterly Journal of Economics*, August.

Ball, L. and Romer, D. (1990), 'Real Rigidities and the Non-Neutrality of Money', *Review of Economic Studies*, April.

Ball, L. and Romer, D. (1991), 'Sticky Prices as Coordination Failure', *American Economic Review*, June.

*Ball, L., Mankiw, N.G. and Romer, D. (1988), 'The New Keynesian Economics and the Output–Inflation Trade-off', *Brookings Papers on Economic Activity*.

Bardhan, P. (1993), 'Economics of Development and the Development of Economics', *Journal of Economic Perspectives*, Spring.

Barrere, A. (ed.) (1988), *The Foundations of Keynesian Analysis*, New York: St Martin's Press.

Barro, R.J. (1972), 'A Theory of Monopolistic Price Adjustment', *Review of Economic Studies*, January.

Barro, R.J. (1974), 'Are Government Bonds Net Wealth?', *Journal of Political Economy*, November/December.

Barro, R.J. (1976), 'Rational Expectations and the Role of Monetary Policy', *Journal of Monetary Economics*, January.

Barro, R.J. (1977a), 'Unanticipated Money Growth and Unemployment in the United States', *American Economic Review*, March.

Barro, R.J. (1977b), 'Long Term Contracting, Sticky Prices and Monetary Policy', *Journal of Monetary Economics*, July

Barro, R.J. (1978), 'Unanticipated Money, Output and the Price Level in the United States', *Journal of Political Economy*, August.

*Barro, R.J. (1979), 'Second Thoughts on Keynesian Economics', *American Economic Review*, May.

Barro, R.J. (1981), 'Output Effects of Government Purchases', *Journal of Political Economy*, December.

*Barro, R.J. (1984), 'Rational Expectations and Macroeconomics in 1984', *American Economic Review*, May.

*Barro, R.J. (1986), 'Recent Developments in the Theory of Rules Versus Discretion', *Economic Journal*, Supplement.

*Barro, R.J. (1989a), 'New Classicals and Keynesians, or the Good Guys and the Bad Guys', *Schweiz Zeitschrift für Volkswirtschaft und Statistik*.

*Barro, R.J. (1989b), 'The Ricardian Approach to Budget Deficits', *Journal of Economic Perspectives*, Spring.

Barro, R.J. (ed.) (1989c), *Modern Business Cycle Theory*, Cambridge, Mass.: Harvard University Press.

Barro, R.J. (1991), 'Economic Growth in a Cross Section of Countries', *Quarterly Journal of Economics*, May.

Barro, R.J. (1993), *Macroeconomics*, 4th edn, New York: John Wiley.

Barro, R.J. and Fischer, S. (1976), 'Recent Developments in Monetary Theory', *Journal of Monetary Economics*, April.

Barro, R.J. and Gordon, D.B. (1983a), 'Rules, Discretion and Reputation in a Model of Monetary Policy', *Journal of Monetary Economics*, July.

Barro, R.J. and Gordon, D.B. (1983b), 'A Positive Theory of Monetary Policy in a Natural Rate Model', *Journal of Political Economy*, July.

Barro, R.J. and Grossman, H. (1971), 'A General Disequilibrium Model of Income and Employment', *American Economic Review*, March.

Barro, R.J. and Grossman, H. (1976), *Money, Employment and Inflation*, New York: Cambridge University Press.

Baumol, W.J. (1977), 'Say's (at least) Eight Laws, or What Say and James Mill May Really Have Meant', *Economica*, May.

Bausor, R. (1983), 'The Rational Expectations Hypothesis and the Epistemics of Time', *Cambridge Journal of Economics*, March.

Begg, D.K.H. (1982), *The Rational Expectations Revolution in Macroeconomics: Theories and Evidence*, Oxford: Philip Allan.

Begg, D.K.H., Dornbusch, R. and Fischer, S. (1991), *Economics*, 3rd edn, Maidenhead: McGraw-Hill .

*Bellante, D. and Garrison, R.W. (1988), 'Phillips Curves and Hayekian Triangles: Two Perspectives on Monetary Dynamics', *History of Political Economy*, Summer.

Bénassy, J.P. (1993), 'Nonclearing Markets: Microeconomic Concepts and Macroeconomic Applications', *Journal of Economic Literature*, June.

Bernanke, B.S. (1983), 'Non-Monetary Effects of the Financial Crisis in the Propagation of the Great Depression', *American Economic Review*, June.

Bernanke, B.S. and Gertler, M. (1989), 'Agency Costs, Net Worth and Business Fluctuations', *American Economic Review*, March.

Bernanke, B.S. and Mishkin, F.S. (1992), 'Central Bank Behaviour and the Strategy of Monetary Policy: Observations From Six Industrialised Countries', *NBER Macroeconomics Annual*.

Bernanke, B.S. and Parkinson, M.L. (1991), 'Procyclical Labour Productivity and Competing Theories of the Business Cycle: Some Evidence from Interwar US Manufacturing Industries', *Journal of Political Economy*, June.

Bhaskar, V., Machin, S. and Reid, G.C. (1993), 'Price and Quantity Adjustment Over the Business Cycle: Evidence From Survey Data', *Oxford Economic Papers*, April.

Black, F. (1987), *Business Cycles and Equilibrium*, Oxford: Basil Blackwell.

Blackburn, K. (1987), 'Macroeconomic Policy Evaluation and Optimal Control Theory: A Critical Review of Some Recent Developments', *Journal of Economic Surveys*.

*Blackburn, K. (1992), 'Credibility and Time-Consistency in Monetary Policy', in K. Dowd and M . K. Lewis (eds) *Current Issues in Financial and Monetary Economics*, Basingstoke: Macmillan.

*Blackburn, K. and Christenson, M. (1989), 'Monetary Policy and Policy Credibility', *Journal of Economic Literature*, March.

Blackburn, K. and Ravn, M.O. (1992), 'Business Cycles in the UK: Facts and Fictions', *Economica*, November.

Blanchard, O.J. (1984), 'The Lucas Critique and the Volcker Deflation', *American Economic Review*, May.

Blanchard, O.J. (1990a), 'Why Does Money Affect Output? A Survey', in B.M. Friedman and F.H. Hahn (eds), *Handbook of Monetary Economics*, New York: North Holland.

Blanchard, O.J. (1990b), 'Comment on B.T. McCallum, New Classical Macroeconomics: A Sympathetic Account', in S. Honkapohja (ed.), *The State of Macroeconomics*, Oxford: Basil Blackwell.

*Blanchard, O.J. (1992), 'For a Return to Pragmatism', in M. Belongia and M. Garfinkel (eds), *The Business Cycle: Theories and Evidence*, London: Kluwer Academic Publishers.

Blanchard, O.J. and Fischer, S. (1989), *Lectures on Macroeconomics*, Cambridge: MIT Press.

Blanchard, O.J. and Kiyotaki, N. (1987), 'Monopolistic Competition and the Effects of Aggregate Demand', *American Economic Review*, September.

Blanchard, O.J. and Quah, D. (1989), 'The Dynamic Effects of Aggregate Demand and Supply Disturbances', *American Economic Review*, September.

Blanchard, O.J. and Summers, L.H. (1986), 'Hysteresis and the European Unemployment Problem', *NBER Macroeconomics Annual*.

Blanchard, O.J. and Summers, L.H. (1987), 'Hysteresis in Unemployment', *European Economic Review*, February/March.

Blanchard, O.J. and Summers, L.H. (1988), 'Beyond the Natural Rate Hypothesis', *American Economic Review*, May.

Blaug, M. (1976), 'Kuhn versus Lakatos or Paradigms versus Research Programmes in the History of Economics', in S.J. Latsis (ed.), *Method and Appraisal in Economics*, Cambridge: Cambridge University Press.

Blaug, M. (1980), *The Methodology of Economics; or, How Economists Explain*, Cambridge: Cambridge University Press.

Blaug, M. (1988), *Economics Through the Looking Glass: The Distorted Perspective of the New Palgrave Dictionary of Economics*, IEA Occasional Paper No. 78, London: Institute of Economic Affairs.

*Blaug, M. (1991), 'Second Thoughts on the Keynesian Revolution', *History of Political Economy*, Summer.

Bleaney, M. (1985), *The Rise and Fall of Keynesian Economics*, London: Macmillan.

Blinder, A.S. (1979), *Economic Policy and the Great Stagflation*, London: Academic Press.

Blinder, A.S. (1986), 'Keynes After Lucas', *Eastern Economic Journal*, July/September.

*Blinder, A.S. (1987), 'Keynes, Lucas and Scientific Progress', *American Economic Review*, May.

*Blinder, A.S. (1988a), 'The Fall and Rise of Keynesian Economics', *Economic Record*, December.

Blinder, A.S. (1988b), 'The Challenge of High Unemployment', *American Economic Review*, May.

*Blinder, A.S. (1991), 'Why Are Prices Sticky? Preliminary Results From An Interview Study', *American Economic Review*, May.

Blinder, A.S. (1992a), 'Déjà Vu All Over Again', in M. Belongia and M. Garfinkel (eds), *The Business Cycle: Theories and Evidence*, London: Kluwer Academic Publishers.

Blinder, A.S. (1992b), 'A Keynesian Restoration is Here', *Challenge*, September/October.

Blinder, A.S. and Solow, R.M. (1973), 'Does Fiscal Policy Matter?', *Journal of Public Economics*, November.

Booth, A. (1985), 'The Keynesian Revolution and Economic Policy-making – A Reply', *Economic History Review*, February.

Booth, A. and Glynn, S. (1975), 'Unemployment in the Interwar Period: A Multiple Problem', *Journal of Contemporary History*, October.

Booth, A. and Glynn, S. (1983), 'Unemployment in Interwar Britain: A Case for Re-Learning the Lessons of the 1930's', *Economic History Review*, August.

Bortis, H. (1986), 'An Essay on Post Keynesian Economics', Fribourg, Switzerland, mimeo.

Bridel, P. (1987), *Cambridge Monetary Thought*, New York: St Martin's Press.

*Brimmer, A.F. (1983), 'Monetary Policy and Economic Activity: Benefits and Costs of Monetarism', *American Economic Review*, May.

Brittan, S. (1973), *Is There an Economic Consensus?*, London: Macmillan.

Bronfenbrenner, M. (ed.) (1969), *Is the Business Cycle Obsolete?*, New York: Wiley.

Brown, E.C. (1956), 'Fiscal Policy in the Thirties: A Reappraisal', *American Economic Review*, December.

*Brunner, K. (1968), 'The Role of Money and Monetary Policy', *Federal Reserve Bank of St. Louis Review*, July.

*Brunner, K. (1970), 'The Monetarist Revolution in Monetary Theory', *Weltwirtschaftliches Archiv*, March.

Buchanan, J.M. (1976), 'Barro on the Ricardian Equivalence Theorem', *Journal of Political Economy*, April.

Buchanan, J.M. and Wagner, R.E. (1978), 'Democracy and Keynesian Contributions: Political Biases and Economic Consequences', in J.M. Buchanan, J. Burton and R.E. Wagner, *The Consequences of Mr Keynes*, London: Institute of Economic Affairs.

*Buchanan, J.M., Burton, J. and Wagner, R.E. (1978), *The Consequences of Mr Keynes*, London: Institute of Economic Affairs.

Buiter, W.H. (1980), 'The Macroeconomics of Dr. Pangloss: A Critical Survey of the New Classical Macroeconomics', *Economic Journal*, March.

Burton, J. (1982), 'The Varieties of Monetarism and their Policy Implications', *The Three Banks Review*, June.

Butos, W.N. (1985), 'Hayek and General Equilibrium Analysis', *Southern Economic Journal*, October.

Cagan, P. (1956), 'The Monetary Dynamics of Hyperinflation', in M. Friedman (ed.), *Studies in the Quantity Theory of Money*, Chicago: University of Chicago Press.

Cagan, P. (1993), 'Does Endogeneity of the Money Supply Disprove Monetary Effects on Economic Activity?', *Journal of Macroeconomics*, Summer.

Cairncross, F. and Cairncross, A. (eds) (1992), *The Legacy of the Golden Age: The 1960s and their Economic Consequences*, London: Routledge.

Caldwell, B.J. (1982), *Beyond Positivism: Economic Methodology in the Twentieth Century*, London: Allen and Unwin.

Caldwell, B.J. (1988), 'Hayek's Transformation', *History of Political Economy*, Winter.

Campbell, J.Y. and Mankiw, N.G. (1987), 'Are Output Fluctuations Transitory?', *Quarterly Journal of Economics*, November.

Campbell, J.Y. and Mankiw, N.G. (1989), 'International Evidence on the Persistence of Economic Fluctuations', *Journal of Monetary Economics*, March.

Capelli, P. and Chauvin, K. (1991), 'An Interplant Test of the Efficiency Wage Hypothesis', *Quarterly Journal of Economics*, August.

Caplin, A.S. and Spulber, D.F. (1987), 'Menu Costs and the Neutrality of Money', *Quarterly Journal of Economics*, November.

Carabelli, A.M. (1988), *On Keynes's Method*, New York: St Martin's Press.

Carlin, W. and Soskice, D. (1990), *Macroeconomics and the Wage Bargain*, Oxford: Oxford University Press.

Carlson, K.M. and Spencer, R.W. (1975), 'Crowding Out and Its Critics', *Federal Reserve Bank of St. Louis Monthly Review*, December.

Carlton, D.W. (1986), 'The Rigidity of Prices', *American Economic Review*, September.

*Carter, M. and Maddock, R. (1984), *Rational Expectations: Macroeconomics for the 1980s?*, London: Macmillan.

Chadha, B. and Prasad, E. (1993), 'Interpreting the Cyclical Behavior of Prices', *IMF Staff Papers*, June.

Chadha, B., Masson, P.R. and Meredith, G. (1992), 'Models of Inflation and the Costs of Disinflation', *IMF Staff Papers*, June.

Chamberlin, E.H. (1933), *The Theory of Monopolistic Competition*, Cambridge, Mass.: Harvard University Press.

Chick, V. (1977), *The Theory of Monetary Policy*, 2nd edn, Oxford: Basil Blackwell.

*Chick, V. (1978), 'The Nature of the Keynesian Revolution: A Reassessment', *Australian Economic Papers*, June.

*Chick, V. (1983), *Macroeconomics After Keynes: A Reconsideration of the General Theory*, Oxford: Philip Allan.

Chick, V. (1986), 'The Evolution of the Banking System and the Theory of Saving, Investment and Interest', *Economies et Sociétés*.

Chow, G.C. (1975), *Analysis and Control of Dynamic Economic Systems*, New York: John Wiley.

Christiano, L.J. and Eichenbaum, M. (1992), 'Current Real Business Cycle Theories and Aggregate Labor Market Fluctuations', *American Economic Review*, June.

Chrystal, K.A. (ed.) (1990), *Monetarism: Vols I and II*, Aldershot: Edward Elgar.

*Clower, R.W. (1965), 'The Keynesian Counter-Revolution: A Theoretical Appraisal', in F.H. Hahn and F.P.R. Brechling (eds), *The Theory of Interest Rates*, London: Macmillan.

Clower, R.W. (ed.) (1969), *Monetary Theory*, Harmondsworth: Penguin.

Coddington, A. (1976), 'Keynesian Economics: The Search for First Principles', *Journal of Economic Literature*, December.

*Coddington, A. (1983), *Keynesian Economics: The Search For First Principles*, London: Allen and Unwin.

*Colander, D.C. (1988), 'The Evolution of Keynesian Economics: From Keynesian to New Classical to New Keynesian', in O.F. Hamouda and J.N. Smithin (eds), *Keynes and Public Policy After Fifty Years, Vol 1: Economics and Policy*, Aldershot: Edward Elgar.

Colander, D.C. and Guthrie, R.S. (1980), 'Great Expectations: What the

Dickens do "Rational Expectations" Mean?', *Journal of Post Keynesian Economics*, Winter.

Cooper, R. and John, A. (1988), 'Coordinating Coordination Failures in Keynesian Models', *Quarterly Journal of Economics*, August.

Cornwall, J. (ed.) (1984), *After Stagflation*, Oxford: Basil Blackwell.

Corry, B.A. (1962), *Money, Saving and Investment in English Economics, 1800–1850*, London: Macmillan.

Coutts, K.J., Godley, W.A.H. and Nordhaus, W.D. (1978), *Industrial Pricing in the United Kingdom*, Cambridge: Cambridge University Press.

Craver, E. (1986), 'The Emigration of the Austrian Economists', *History of Political Economy*, Spring.

Cross, R. (1982a), *Economic Theory and Policy in the U.K.: An Outline and Assessment of the Controversies*, Oxford: Martin Robertson.

Cross, R. (1982b), 'The Duhem–Quine Thesis, Lakatos and the Appraisal of Theories in Macroeconomics', *Economic Journal*, June.

Cross, R. (ed.) (1988), *Unemployment, Hysteresis and the Natural Rate Hypothesis*, Oxford: Basil Blackwell.

Cross, R. *et al.* (1993), 'The NAIRU', *Journal of Economic Studies*.

Cukierman, A. and Meltzer, A.H. (1986), 'A Positive Theory of Discretionary Policy, The Cost of Democratic Government and the Benefits of a Constitution', *Economic Inquiry*, July.

Culbertson, J.M. (1960), 'Friedman on the Lag in Effect of Monetary Policy', *Journal of Political Economy*, December.

Culbertson, J.M. (1961), 'The Lag in Effect on Monetary Policy: Reply', *Journal of Political Economy*, October.

Cunningham Wood, J. (1983), *John Maynard Keynes: Critical Assessments*, Vols 1–4, Beckenham: Croom Helm.

Dalziel, P.C. (1991), 'Theoretical Approaches to Monetary Disinflation', *Journal of Economic Surveys*.

Danthine, J.P. and Donaldson, J.B. (1993), 'Methodological and Empirical Issues in Real Business Cycle Theory', *European Economic Review*, January.

Davidson, P. (1965), 'Keynes's Finance Motive', *Oxford Economic Papers*, March.

*Davidson, P. (1978), *Money and the Real World*, 2nd edn, London: Macmillan.

Davidson, P. (1980), 'The Dual-Faceted Nature of the Keynesian Revolution', *Journal of Post Keynesian Economics*, Spring.

Davidson, P. (1982–3), 'Rational Expectations: A Fallacious Foundation for Studying Crucial Decision-Making Processes', *Journal of Post Keynesian Economics*, Winter.

Davidson, P. (1984), 'Reviving Keynes's Revolution', *Journal of Post Keynesian Economics*, Summer.

Davidson, P. (1989), 'Keynes and Money', in R. Hill (ed.), *Keynes, Money and Monetarism*, London: Macmillan.

*Davidson, P. (1991), 'Is Probability Theory Relevant for Uncertainty? A Post Keynesian Perspective', *Journal of Economic Perspectives*, Winter.

Davis, M.D. (1983), *Game Theory: A Non Technical Introduction*, New York: Basic Books.

Deane, P. (1978), *The Evolution of Economic Ideas*, Cambridge: Cambridge University Press.

Deane, P. (1983), 'The Scope and Method of Economic Science', *Economic Journal*, March.

De Long, B. and Summers, L.H. (1986), 'The Changing Cyclical Variability of Economic Activity in the United States', in R.J. Gordon (ed.), *The American Business Cycle*, Chicago: University of Chicago Press.

Dennison, E.F. (1985), *Trends in American Economic Growth*, Washington: The Brookings Institution .

De Prano, M. and Mayer, T. (1965), 'Tests of the Relative Importance of Autonomous Expenditure and Money', *American Economic Review*, September.

Desai, M. (1987), 'Endogenous and Exogenous Money', in J. Eatwell, M. Milgate and P. Newman (eds), *The New Palgrave: A Dictionary of Economics*, London: Macmillan.

Deutscher, P. (1990), *R.G. Hawtrey and the Development of Macroeconomics*, Basingstoke: Macmillan.

Diamond, P.A. (1982), 'Aggregate Demand Management in Search Equilibrium', *Journal of Political Economy*, October.

Dixon, H. and Rankin, N. (1994), 'Imperfect Competition and Macroeconomics: A Survey', *Oxford Economic Papers*, April.

Dorfman, R. (1989), 'Thomas Robert Malthus and David Ricardo', *Journal of Economic Perspectives*, Summer.

Dornbusch, R. and Fischer, S. (1994), *Macroeconomics*, 6th edn, New York: McGraw-Hill.

*Dow, S.C. (1985), *Macroeconomic Thought: A Methodological Approach*, Oxford: Basil Blackwell.

Dow, S.C. (1988), 'Post Keynesian Economics: Conceptual Underpinnings', *British Review of Economic Issues*, Autumn.

Dowd, K. (1988), *Private Money: The Path to Monetary Stability*, Hobart Paper No. 112, London: Institute of Economic Affairs.

Drago, R. and Heywood, J.S. (1992), 'Is Worker Behaviour Consistent with Efficiency Wages?', *Scottish Journal of Political Economy*, May.

Driffill, J. (1988), 'Macroeconomic Policy Games with Incomplete Information: A Survey', *European Economic Review*, March.

Dunlop, J.G. (1938), 'The Movement of Real and Money Wages', *Economic Journal*, September.

Durbin, E.F.M. (1934), *Purchasing Power and Trade Depression*, London: Jonathan Cape.

Durlauf, S.N. (1989), 'Output Persistence, Economic Structure, and the Choice of Stabilisation Policy', *Brookings Papers on Economic Activity*.

Dutt, A.K. (1986–7), 'Wage Rigidity and Unemployment: The Simple Diagrammatics of Two Views', *Journal of Post Keynesian Economics*, Winter.

*Dutt, A.K. and Amadeo, E.J. (1990), *Keynes's Third Alternative?*, Aldershot: Edward Elgar.

Eatwell, J. and Milgate, M. (eds) (1983), *Keynes's Economics and the Theory of Value and Distribution*, London: Duckworth.

Eichenbaum, M. (1991), 'Real Business Cycle Theory: Wisdom or Whimsy?', *Journal of Economic Dynamics and Control*, October.

Eichenbaum, M. and Singleton, K.J. (1986), 'Do Equilibrium Real Business Cycle Theories Explain Postwar US Business Cycles?', *NBER Macroeconomics Annual*.

*Eichner, A.S. (ed.) (1979), *A Guide to Post-Keynesian Economics*, London: Macmillan.

*Eichner, A.S. and Kregel, J.A. (1975), 'An Essay on Post-Keynesian Theory: A New Paradigm in Economics', *Journal of Economic Literature*, December.

Eijffinger, S. and Schaling, E. (1993), 'Central Bank Independence in Twelve Industrial Countries', *Banca Nazionale Del Lavaro Quarterly Review*, March.

Fair, R. (1992), 'The Cowles Commission Approach, Real Business Cycle Theories and New Keynesian Economics', in M. Belongia and M. Garfinkel (eds), *The Business Cycle: Theories and Evidence*, London: Kluwer Academic Publishers.

Fama, E. (1980), 'Banking in the Theory of Finance', *Journal of Monetary Economics*, January.

Fay, J.A. and Medoff, J.L. (1985), 'Labour and Output Over the Business Cycle', *American Economic Review*, September.

Feldstein, M. (1982), 'Government Deficits and Aggregate Demand', *Journal of Monetary Economics*, February.

Fellner, W. (1976), 'Towards a Reconstruction of Macroeconomics – Problems of Theory and Policy', *American Enterprise Institute*.

Fellner, W. (1979), 'The Credibility Effect and Rational Expectations: Implications of the Gramlich Study', *Brookings Papers on Economic Activity*.

Feyerabend, P. (1978), *Against Method: Outline of an Anarchistic Theory of Knowledge*, London: Verso.

Fischer, S. (1977), 'Long-Term Contracts, Rational Expectations, and the Optimal Money Supply Rule', *Journal of Political Economy*, February.

Fischer, S. (ed.) (1980), *Rational Expectations and Economic Policy*, Chicago: University of Chicago Press.

*Fischer, S. (1988), 'Recent Developments in Macroeconomics', *Economic Journal*, June.

Fischer, S. (1990), 'Rules Versus Discretion in Monetary Policy', in B.M. Friedman and F.H. Hahn (eds), *Handbook of Monetary Economics Vol. II*, Amsterdam: North Holland.

Fisher, I. (1907), *The Rate of Interest*, New York: Macmillan.

Fisher, I. (1933), *Booms and Depressions*, London: Allen and Unwin.

Fitousi, J.P. and Phelps, E.S. (1986), 'Causes of the 1980s Slump in Europe', *Brookings Papers on Economic Activity*.

*Fitzgibbons, A. (1988), *Keynes's Vision*, Oxford: Oxford University Press.

Fletcher, G.A. (1987), *The Keynesian Revolution and Its Critics*, New York: St Martin's Press.

Frenkel, J.A. and Johnson, H.G. (eds) (1976), *The Monetary Approach to the Balance of Payments*, London: Allen and Unwin.

Frenkel, J.A. and Johnson, H.G. (eds) (1978), *The Economics of Exchange Rates*, Reading, Mass.: Addison-Wesley.

Frey, B.S. and Eichenberger, R. (1992), 'Economics and Economists: A European Perspective', *American Economic Review*, May.

Frey, B.S. and Schneider, F. (1988), 'Politico-Economic Models of Macroeconomic Policy: A Review of the Empirical Evidence', in T.D. Willett (ed.), *Political Business Cycles*, Durham: Duke University Press.

Frey, B.S., Pommerehne, W.W., Schneider, F. and Gilbert, G. (1984), 'Consensus and Dissension Among Economists: An Empirical Inquiry', *American Economic Review*, December.

*Friedman, B.M. (1988), 'Lessons of Monetary Policy from the 1980s', *Journal of Economic Perspectives*, Summer.

Friedman, B.M. (1992), 'How Does It Matter?', in M. Belongia and M. Garfinkel (eds), *The Business Cycle: Theories and Evidence*, London: Kluwer Academic Publishers.

Friedman, M. (1953), *Essays in Positive Economics*, Chicago: University of Chicago Press.

Friedman, M. (1956), 'The Quantity Theory of Money, A Restatement', in M. Friedman (ed.), *Studies in the Quantity Theory of Money*, Chicago: University of Chicago Press.

Friedman, M. (1958), 'The Supply of Money and Changes in Prices and Output', reprinted in *The Optimum Quantity of Money and Other Essays*, Chicago: Aldine, 1969.

Friedman, M. (1959), 'The Demand for Money – Some Theoretical and Empirical Results', *Journal of Political Economy*, June.

Friedman, M. (1966), 'Interest Rates and the Demand for Money', *Journal of Law and Economics*, October.

*Friedman, M. (1968a), 'The Role of Monetary Policy', *American Economic Review*, March.

Friedman, M. (1968b), 'Money: Quantity Theory', in D. Sills (ed.), *The International Encyclopedia of the Social Sciences*, New York: Macmillan Free Press.

Friedman, M. (1970a), 'A Theoretical Framework For Monetary Analysis', *Journal of Political Economy*, March/April.

*Friedman, M. (1970b), *The Counter-Revolution in Monetary Theory*, IEA Occasional Paper No. 33, London: Institute of Economic Affairs.

Friedman, M. (1972), 'Comments on the Critics', *Journal of Political Economy*, September/October.

Friedman, M. (1974), *Monetary Correction*, IEA Occasional Paper No. 41, London: Institute of Economic Affairs.

*Friedman, M. (1977), 'Inflation and Unemployment', *Journal of Political Economy*, June.

Friedman, M. (1983), 'A Monetarist Reflects', *The Economist*, 4 June.

Friedman, M. (1984), 'Lessons from the 1979–82 Monetary Policy Experiment', *American Economic Review*, May.

Friedman, M. and Meiselman, D. (1963), 'The Relative Stability of Monetary Velocity and the Investment Multiplier in the United States, 1897–1958', in *Commission on Money and Credit: Stabilization Policies*, Englewood, Cliffs, NJ: Prentice-Hall.

Friedman, M. and Schwartz, A.J. (1963), *A Monetary History of the United States, 1867–1960*, Princeton: Princeton University Press.

Friedman, M. and Schwartz, A.J. (1982), *Monetary Trends in the United States and the United Kingdom: Their Relation to Income, Prices and Interest Rates*, Chicago: University of Chicago Press.

Frisch, R. (1933), 'Propagation and Impulse Problems in Dynamic Economics', in *Essays in Honour of Gustav Cassel*, London: Allen and Unwin.

Frowen, S. (ed.) (1990), *Unknowledge and Choice in Economics*, London: Macmillan

Frydman, R. and Phelps, E.S. (eds) (1983), *Individual Forecasting and Aggregate Outcomes: 'Rational Expectations' Examined*, Cambridge: Cambridge University Press.

Fulton, G. (1984), 'Research Programmes in Economics', *History of Political Economy*, Summer.

Galbraith, J.K. (1967), *The New Industrial State*, Boston, Mass.: Houghton Mifflin.

Galbraith, J.K. (1977), *The Age of Uncertainty*, Boston, Mass.: Houghton Mifflin.

Gallaway, L. and Vedder, R.K. (1987), 'Wages, Prices and Employment: von Mises and the Progressives', *Review of Austrian Economics*.

Garrison, R.W. (1978), 'Austrian Macroeconomics: A Diagrammatical Exposition', in L.M. Spadaro (ed.), *New Directions in Austrian Economics*, Kansas City: Sheed, Andrews and McMeel.

*Garrison, R.W. (1984), 'Time and Money: The Universals of Macroeconomic Theorizing', *Journal of Macroeconomics*, Spring.

Garrison, R.W. (1985), 'Intertemporal Co-ordination and the Invisible Hand: An Austrian Perspective on the Keynesian Vision', *History of Political Economy*, Summer.

Garrison, R.W. (1986a), 'From Lachmann to Lucas: On Institutions, Expectations, and Equilibrating Tendencies', in I.M. Kirzner (ed.), *Subjectivism, Intelligibility and Economic Understanding*, New York: New York University Press.

Garrison, R.W. (1986b), 'Hayekian Trade Cycle Theory: A Reappraisal', *Cato Journal*, Fall.

*Garrison, R.W. (1989), 'The Austrian Theory of the Business Cycle in the Light of Modern Macroeconomics', *Review of Austrian Economics*.

Georgescu-Roegen, N. (1971), *The Entropy Law and the Economic Process*, Cambridge, Mass.: Harvard University Press.

Georgescu-Roegen, N. (1979), 'Methods in Economic Science', *Journal of Economic Issues*, June.

*Gerrard, B. (1991), 'Keynes's General Theory: Interpreting the Interpretations', *Economic Journal*, March.

Gilbert, J.C. (1982), *Keynes's Impact on Monetary Economics*, London: Butterworth.

Glahe, F. R. (1973), *Macroeconomics: Theory and Policy*, New York: Harcourt Brace Jovanovich.

Godley, W.A.H. and Nordhaus, W.D. (1972), 'Pricing in the Trade Cycle', *Economic Journal*, September.

Gomes, G.M. (1982), 'Irrationality of "Rational Expectations"', *Journal of Post Keynesian Economics*, Fall.

Goodhart, C. and Presley, J. (1991), 'Real Business Cycle Theory: A Restatement of Robertsonian Economics?', *Economic Research Paper*, Loughborough University.

Goodwin, C.D. (1988), 'The Heterogeneity of the Economists' Discourse: Philosopher, Priest, and Hired Gun', in A. Klamer, D.N. McCloskey and R.M. Solow (eds), *The Consequences of Economic Rhetoric*, Cambridge: Cambridge University Press.

Gordon, D.F. (1974), 'A Neoclassical Theory of Keynesian Unemployment', *Economic Inquiry*, December.

Gordon, R.A. (1974), *Economic Instability and Growth: The American Record*, New York: Harper and Row.

Gordon, R.J. (1972), 'Wage Price Controls and the Shifting Phillips Curve', *Brookings Papers on Economic Activity*.

Gordon, R.J. (1975), 'Alternative Responses to External Supply Shocks', *Brookings Papers on Economic Activity*.

Gordon, R.J. (1976), 'Recent Developments in the Theory of Inflation and Unemployment', *Journal of Monetary Economics*, April.

*Gordon, R.J. (1978), 'What Can Stabilisation Policy Achieve?', *American Economic Review*, May.

*Gordon, R.J. (1981), 'Output Fluctuations and Gradual Price Adjustment', *Journal of Economic Literature*, June.

Gordon, R.J. (1982a), 'Price Inertia and Policy Ineffectiveness in the United States, 1890–1980', *Journal of Political Economy*, December.

Gordon, R.J. (1982b), 'Why US Wage and Employment Behaviour Differs From That in Britain and Japan', *Economic Journal*, March.

Gordon, R.J. (1988), 'Hysteresis in History: Was There Ever a Phillips curve?', *American Economic Review*, May.

*Gordon, R.J. (1990), 'What Is New-Keynesian Economics?', *Journal of Economic Literature*, September.

Gordon, R.J. (1993), *Macroeconomics*, 6th edn, New York: Harper Collins.

Grandmont, J.M. (1990), 'Keynesian Issues and Economic Theory', in S. Honkapohja (ed.), *The State of Macroeconomics*, Oxford: Basil Blackwell.

*Greenwald, B.C. and Stiglitz, J.E. (1987), 'Keynesian, New Keynesian and New Classical Economics', *Oxford Economic Papers*, March.

Greenwald, B.C. and Stiglitz, J.E. (1988), 'Examining Alternative Macroeconomic Theories', *Brookings Papers on Economic Activity*.

*Greenwald, B.C. and Stiglitz, J.E. (1993a), 'New and Old Keynesians', *Journal of Economic Perspectives*, Winter.

Greenwald, B.C. and Stiglitz, J.E. (1993b), 'Financial Markets, Imperfections and Business Cycles', *Quarterly Journal of Economics*, February.

Grilli, V., Masciandaro, D. and Tabellini, G. (1991), 'Political and Monetary Institutions and Public Finance Policies in the Industrialised Countries', *Economic Policy*.

Grinder, W.E. (1977), 'Introduction' to L. Lachmann, *Capital Expectations, and the Market Process*, Kansas City: Sheed, Andrews and McMeel.

Grossman, H.I. (1980), 'Rational Expectations, Business Cycles and Government Behaviour', in S. Fischer (ed.), *Rational Expectations and Economic Policy*, Chicago: University of Chicago Press.

Gunning, J.P. (1985), 'Causes of Unemployment: the Austrian Perspective', *History of Political Economy*, Summer.

Haberler, G. (1937), *Prosperity and Depression*, Cambridge, Mass.: Harvard University Press.

Haberler, G. (1963), *Prosperity and Depression*, 4th edn, New York: Atheneum.

Haberler, G. (1980), 'Critical Notes on Rational Expectations', *Journal of Money, Credit and Banking*, November.

Hahn, F.H. (1987), 'On Involuntary Unemployment', *Economic Journal*, Supplement.

Haley, J. (1990), 'Theoretical Foundations of Sticky Wages', *Journal of Economic Surveys* .

Hall, R.E. (1991), 'Labour Demand, Labour Supply and Employment Volatility', *NBER Macroeconomics Annual.*

Hall, R.E. and Taylor, J.B. (1993), *Macroeconomics*, 4th edn, New York: W.W. Norton.

Hamilton, J.D. (1983), 'Oil and the Macroeconomy Since World War II', *Journal of Political Economy*, April.

*Hamouda, O.F. and Harcourt, G.C. (1988), 'Post Keynesianism: From Criticism to Coherence', *Bulletin of Economic Research*, January.

Hands, D.W. (1985), 'Second Thoughts on Lakatos', *History of Political Economy*, Spring.

Hansen, A. (1949), *Monetary Theory and Fiscal Policy*, New York: McGraw-Hill.

Hansen, A.H. (1953), *A Guide to Keynes*, New York: McGraw-Hill.

Hansen, G.D. and Prescott, E.C. (1993), 'Did Technology Cause the 1990–1991 Recession?', *American Economic Review*, May.

Harcourt, G.C. (1981), 'Notes on an Economic Querist: G.L.S. Shackle', *Journal of Post Keynesian Economics*, Fall.

*Harcourt, G.C. (1982), 'Post Keynesianism: Quite Wrong and/or Nothing New', *Thames Papers in Political Economy*, Summer.

Harcourt, G.C. and Kenyon, P. (1976), 'Pricing and the Investment Decision', *Kyklos*, September.

*Hargreaves-Heap, S.P. (1980), 'Choosing the Wrong Natural Rate: Accelerating Inflation or Decelerating Employment and Growth?', *Economic Journal*, September

Hargreaves-Heap, S.P. (1992), *The New Keynesian Macroeconomics: Time Belief and Social Interdependence*, Aldershot: Edward Elgar.

Harrington, J.E. Jr. (1993), 'Economic Policy, Economic Performance and Elections', *American Economic Review*, March.

Harris, D.J. (1974), 'The Price Policy of Firms, the Level of Employment and Distribution of Income in the Short Run', *Australian Economic Papers*, June.

Harrod, R. (1939), 'An Essay in Dynamic Theory', *Economic Journal*, March.

Harrod, R. (1951), *The Life of John Maynard Keynes*, London: Macmillan.

Hayek, F.A. (1931a), *Prices and Production*, London: Routledge and Sons.

Hayek, F.A. (1931b), 'Reflections on the Pure Theory of Money of Mr. J.M. Keynes', *Economica*, August.

Hayek, F.A. (1933), *Monetary Theory and the Trade Cycle*, London: Jonathan Cape.

Hayek, F.A. (1935), *Prices and Production*, 2nd edn, London: Routledge and Kegan Paul.

Hayek, F.A. (1937), 'Economics and Knowledge', *Economica*, February.

Hayek, F.A. (1939), *Profits Interest and Investment: and Other Essays on the Theory of Industrial Fluctuations*, London: Routledge and Kegan Paul.

Hayek, F.A. (1945), 'The Use of Knowledge in Society', *American Economic Review*, September.

*Hayek, F.A. (1948), *Individualism and Economic Order*, London: Routledge and Kegan Paul.

Hayek, F.A. (1966), *Monetary Theory and the Trade Cycle*, New York: Augustus M. Kelley.

Hayek, F.A. (1975), *Full Employment at Any Price?*, IEA Occasional Paper No. 45, London: Institute of Economic Affairs.

*Hayek, F.A. (1978a), *A Tiger By the Tail: The Keynesian Legacy of Inflation*, 2nd edn, London: Institute of Economic Affairs.

Hayek, F.A. (1978b), *Denationalisation of Money*, Hobart Paper No. 70, London: Institute of Economic Affairs.

Hayek, F.A. (1983), 'The Austrian Critique', *The Economist*, 11 June.

Hayek, F.A. (1984), *Money, Capital and Fluctuations* (ed. R. McCloughry), London: Routledge and Kegan Paul.

Henry, S.G.B. and Ormerod, P.A. (1978), 'Incomes Policy and Wage Inflation: Empirical Evidence for the U.K. 1961–1977', *National Institute Economic Review*, August.

Hibbs, D.A. (1977), 'Political Parties and Macroeconomic Policy', *American Political Science Review*, December.

Hicks, J.R. (1937), 'Mr. Keynes and the "Classics": A Suggested Interpretation', *Econometrica*, April.

Hicks, J.R. (1950), *A Contribution to the Theory of the Trade Cycle*, Oxford: Oxford University Press.

Hicks, J.R. (1967a), *Critical Essays in Monetary Theory*, Oxford: Oxford University Press.

Hicks, J.R. (1967b), 'The Hayek Story', in *Critical Essays in Monetary Theory*, Oxford: Oxford University Press.

Hicks, J.R. (1974), *The Crisis in Keynesian Economics*, Oxford: Basil Blackwell.

Hicks, J.R. (1976), '"Revolutions" in Economics', in S.J. Latsis (ed.), *Method and Appraisal in Economics*, Cambridge: Cambridge University Press.

Hicks, J.R. (1982), *Money, Interest and Wages*, Oxford: Basil Blackwell.

Hicks, J.R. (1989), *A Market Theory of Money*, Oxford: Clarendon Press.

Holden, K., Peel, D.A. and Thompson, J.L. (1985), *Expectations: Theory and Evidence*, London: Macmillan.

*Hoover, K.D. (1984), 'Two Types of Monetarism', *Journal of Economic Literature*, March.

*Hoover, K.D. (1988), *The New Classical Macroeconomics*, Oxford: Basil Blackwell.

Hoover, K.D. (1991), 'The Causal Direction Between Money and Prices', *Journal of Monetary Economics*, June.

Hoover, K.D. (ed.) (1992), *The New Classical Macroeconomics*, Aldershot: Edward Elgar.

Howitt, P.W. (1986), 'The Keynesian Recovery', *Canadian Journal of Economics*, November.

Howitt, P.W. (1990), *The Keynesian Recovery*, Oxford: Philip Allan.

Hume, D. (1752), 'Of Money', reprinted in *Money and Banking* (ed. A.A. Walters), Harmondsworth: Penguin.

Hutchison, T.W. (1977), *Keynes v The Keynesians*, London: Institute of Economic Affairs.

Jackman, R. (1974), 'Keynes and Leijonhufvud', *Oxford Economic Papers*, July.

Jaffe, D. and Stiglitz, J.E. (1990), 'Credit Rationing', in B.M. Friedman and F.H. Hahn (eds), *Handbook of Monetary Economics*, Vol. II, Amsterdam: North Holland.

Johnson, E.S. (1973), 'John Maynard Keynes: Scientist or Politician?', in J. Robinson (ed.), *After Keynes*, Oxford: Basil Blackwell.

Johnson, E.S. (1978), 'Keynes as a Literary Craftsman', in E.S. Johnson and H.G. Johnson (eds), *The Shadow of Keynes*, Oxford: Basil Blackwell.

Johnson, H.G. (1964), *Money, Trade and Economic Growth*, London: Allen and Unwin; excerpt from Chapter 5 reprinted in R.W. Clower (ed.), *Monetary Theory*, Harmondsworth: Penguin (1969) – page reference in text refers to reprint.

Johnson, H.G. (1969), 'Inside Money, Outside Money, Income, Wealth and Welfare in Monetary Theory', *Journal of Money, Credit and Banking*, February.

*Johnson, H.G. (1971), 'The Keynesian Revolution and the Monetarist Counter-Revolution', *American Economic Review*, May.

Johnson, H.G. (1972a), 'The Monetary Approach to Balance of Payments Theory', in H.G. Johnson (ed.), *Further Essays in Monetary Economics*, London: Macmillan.

Johnson, H.G. (1972b), 'Inflation: A Monetarist View', in H.G. Johnson (ed.), *Further Essays in Monetary Economics*, London: Macmillan.

Jonson, P.D. (1976), 'Money Prices and Output: An Integrative Essay', *Kredit und Kapital*.

Kahn, R. (1931), 'The Relation of Home Investment to Unemployment', *Economic Journal*, June.

Kahn, R.F. (1983), 'Malinvaud on Keynes', in J. Eatwell and M. Milgate (eds), *Keynes's Economics and the Theory of Value and Distribution*, London: Duckworth.

Kahn, R.F. (1984), *The Making of Keynes's General Theory*, Cambridge: Cambridge University Press.

Kaldor, N. (1956), 'Alternative Theories of Distribution', *Review of Economic Studies*, February.

Kaldor, N. (1970), 'The New Monetarism', *Lloyds Bank Review*, July.

Kalecki, M. (1944), 'Professor Pigou on "The Classical Stationary State": A Comment', *Economic Journal*, April.

Kalecki, M. (1969), *Studies in the Theory of Business Cycles, 1933–39*, Oxford: Basil Blackwell.

*Kantor, B. (1979), 'Rational Expectations and Economic Thought', *Journal of Economic Literature*, December.

Kareken, J. and Solow, R.N. (1963), 'Monetary Policy: Lags versus Simultaneity', in *Commission on Money and Credit: Stabilization Policies*, Englewood Cliffs, NJ: Prentice-Hall .

Katz, L.F. (1986), 'Efficiency Wage Theories: A Partial Evaluation', *NBER Macroeconomics Annual*.

*Katz, L.F. (1988), 'Some Recent Developments in Labour Economics and Their Implications for Macroeconomics', *Journal of Money, Credit and Banking*, August.

Kearl, J.R., Pope, C.L., Whiting, G.C. and Wimmer, T.C. (1979), 'A Confusion of Economists?', *American Economic Review*, May.

Keegan, W. (1984), *Mrs Thatcher's Economic Experiment*, Harmondsworth: Penguin.

Keuzenkamp, H.A. (1991), 'A Precursor to Muth: Tinbergen's 1932 Model of Rational Expectations', *Economic Journal*, September.

Keynes, J.M. (1914), 'Review of Mises', *Economic Journal*, September.

Keynes, J.M. (1923), *A Tract on Monetary Reform*, London: Macmillan.

Keynes, J.M. (1936), *The General Theory of Employment, Interest and Money*, London: Macmillan .

*Keynes, J.M. (1937), 'The General Theory of Employment', *Quarterly Journal of Economics*, February.

Keynes, J.M. (1939), 'Relative Movements in Real Wages and Output', *Economic Journal*, March.

Keynes, J.M. (1972), Vol. IX, *Essays in Persuasion*, London: Macmillan.

Keynes, J.M. (1972), Vol. X, *Essays in Biography*, London: Macmillan.

Keynes, J.M. (1973), Vol. VII, *The General Theory of Employment, Interest and Money*, London: Macmillan.

Keynes, J.M. (1973), Vol. VIII, *A Treatise on Probability*, London: Macmillan.

Keynes, J.M. (1973), Vol. XIII, *The General Theory and After: Part 1, Preparation*, London: Macmillan.

Keynes, J.M. (1979), Vol. XXIX, *The General Theory and After: A Supplement*, London: Macmillan.

Kindleberger, C.P. (1973), *The World in Depression 1929–39*, London: Penguin.

King, J.E. (1988), *Economic Exiles*, London: Macmillan.

King, R.G. (1993), 'Will the New Keynesian Macroeconomics Resurrect the IS–LM Model?', *Journal of Economic Perspectives*, Winter.

King, R.G. and Plosser, C.I. (1984), 'Money, Credit and Prices in a Real Business Cycle', *American Economic Review*, June.

King, R.G., Plosser, C.I. and Rebelo, S.T. (1988a), 'Production Growth and Business Cycles: I. The Basic Neoclassical Model', *Journal of Monetary Economics*, March.

King, R.G., Plosser, C.I. and Rebelo, S.T. (1988b), 'Production Growth and Business Cycles: II. New Directions', *Journal of Monetary Economics*, May.

Kirman, A.P. (1992), 'Whom or What Does the Representative Individual Represent?', *Journal of Economic Perspectives*, Spring.

*Klamer, A. (1984), *The New Classical Macroeconomics*, Brighton: Wheatsheaf.

Klamer, A. (1988), 'Negotiating a New Conversation About Economics', in A. Klamer, D.N. McCloskey and R.M. Solow (eds), *The Consequences of Economic Rhetoric*, Cambridge: Cambridge University Press.

Klamer, A. and McCloskey, D.N. (1988), 'Economics in the Human Conversation', in A. Klamer, D.N. McCloskey and R.M. Solow (eds), *The Consequences of Economic Rhetoric*, Cambridge: Cambridge University Press.

Klamer, A., McCloskey, D.N. and Solow, R.M. (eds) (1988), *The Consequences of Economic Rhetoric*, Cambridge: Cambridge University Press.

Klein, L.R. (1947), *The Keynesian Revolution*, New York: Macmillan.

Klein, L.R. (1951), 'Review of Roy Harrod, *The Life of John Maynard Keynes*', *Journal of Political Economy*, October.

Klein, L.R. (1968), *The Keynesian Revolution*, 2nd edn, London: Macmillan.

Knight, F.H. (1933), *Risk, Uncertainty and Profit*, London: London School of Economics, reprint; first published in 1921.

Kregel, J.A. (1985), 'Hamlet Without the Prince: Cambridge Macroeconomics Without Money', *American Economic Review*, May.

Kriesler, P. (1987), *Kalecki's Microanalysis: the Development of Kalecki's Analysis of Pricing and Distribution*, Cambridge: Cambridge University Press.

Kuhn, T.S. (1970), *The Structure of Scientific Revolutions*, Chicago: University of Chicago Press.

Kuhn, T.S. (1977), *The Essential Tension*, Chicago: University of Chicago Press.

Kydland, F.E. and Prescott, E.C. (1977), 'Rules Rather Than Discretion: The Inconsistency of Optimal Plans', *Journal of Political Economy*, June.

Kydland, F.E. and Prescott, E.C. (1980), 'A Competitive Theory of Fluctuations and the Feasibility and Desirability of Stabilization Policy', in S. Fischer (ed.), *Rational Expectations and Economic Policy*, Chicago: University of Chicago Press.

Kydland, F.E. and Prescott, E.C. (1982), 'Time to Build and Aggregate Fluctuations', *Econometrica*, November.

*Kydland, F.E. and Prescott, E.C. (1990), 'Business Cycles: Real Facts and the Monetary Myth', *Federal Reserve Bank of Minneapolis Quarterly Review*, Spring.

Kydland, F.E. and Prescott, E.C. (1991), 'Hours and Employment Variation in Business Cycle Theory', *Economic Theory*.

Lachmann, L. (1939), 'On Crisis and Adjustment', *The Review of Economic Statistics*, May.

Lachmann, L. (1943), 'The Role of Expectations in Economics as a Social Science', *Economica*, February.

Lachmann, L. (1945), 'A Note on the Elasticity of Expectations', *Economica*, November.

Lachmann, L. (1956), *Capital and Its Structure*, London: Bell and Sons.

Lachmann, L. (1976), 'From Mises to Shackle: An Essay on Austrian Economics and the Kaleidic Society', *Journal of Economic Literature*, March.

*Laidler, D.E.W. (1976), 'Inflation in Britain: A Monetarist Perspective', *American Economic Review*, September.

*Laidler, D.E.W. (1981), 'Monetarism: An Interpretation and an Assessment', *Economic Journal*, March.

Laidler, D.E.W. (1982), *Monetarist Perspectives*, Oxford: Philip Allan.

*Laidler, D.E.W. (1986), 'The New Classical Contribution to Macroeconomics', *Banca Nazionale Del Lavoro Quarterly Review*, March.

Laidler, D.E.W. (1990), *Taking Money Seriously*, Oxford: Philip Allan.

Laidler, D.E.W. (1991), *The Golden Age of the Quantity Theory: The Development of Neoclassical Monetary Economies 1870–1914*, Oxford: Philip Allan.

*Laidler, D.E.W. (1992a), 'The Cycle Before New Classical Economics', in

M. Belongia and M. Garfinkel (eds), *The Business Cycle: Theories and Evidence*, London: Kluwer Academie Publishers.

Laidler, D.E.W. (1992b), 'Issues in Contemporary Macroeconomies', in A. Vercelli and N. Dimitri (eds), *Macroeconomies: A Survey of Research Strategies*, Oxford: Oxford University Press.

*Laidler, D.E.W. (1993), *The Demand for Money: Theories, Evidence and Problems*, 4th edn, New York: Harper Collins.

Laidler, D.E.W. and Parkin, M. (1975), 'Inflation: A Survey', *Economic Journal*, December.

Laing, D. (1993), 'A Signalling Theory of Nominal Wage Inflexibility', *Economic Journal*, November.

Lakatos, I. (1978), *The Methodology of Scientific Research Programmes*, Cambridge: Cambridge University Press.

Langlois, R.N. (1982), 'Austrian Economics as Affirmative Science: Comment on Rizzo', in I.M. Kirzner (ed.), *Method, Process and Austrian Economics*, Lexington, Mass.: D.C. Heath and Co.

Laudan, L. (1977), *Progress and Its Problems*, London: Routledge and Kegan Paul.

Laudan, L. (1981), 'A Problem-Solving Approach to Scientific Progress', in I. Hacking (ed.), *Scientific Revolutions*, Oxford: Oxford University Press.

Laudan, I. (1984), *Science and Values*, Berkeley: University of California Press.

Lawson, T. and Pesaran, H. (eds) (1985), *Keynes's Economics: Methodological Issues*, London: Croom Helm.

Layard, R., Nickell, S. and Jackman, R. (1991), *Unemployment, Macroeconomic Performance and the Labour Market*, Oxford: Oxford University Press.

Lee, S.P. and Passell, P. (1979), *The New Economic View of American History*, New York: W.W. Norton.

Leibenstein, H. (1957), *Economic Backwardness and Economic Growth*, New York: Wiley.

Leibenstein, H. (1979), 'A Branch of Economics Is Missing: Micro–Micro Theory', *Journal of Economic Literature*, June.

Leijonhufvud, A. (1967), 'Keynes and the Keynesians: A Suggested Interpretation', reprinted in R.W. Clower (ed.), *Monetary Theory*, London: Penguin, 1969.

Leijonhufvud, A. (1968), *On Keynesian Economics and the Economics of Keynes*, London: Oxford University Press.

Leijonhufvud, A. (1976), 'Schools, "Revolutions" and Research Programmes in Economic Theory', in S.J. Latsis (ed.), *Method and Appraisal in Economics*, Cambridge: Cambridge University Press.

*Leijonhufvud, A. (1981), *Information and Co-ordination: Essays in Macroeconomic Theory*, Oxford: Oxford University Press.

*Leijonhufvud, A. (1992), 'Keynesian Economics: Past Confusions, Future Prospects', in A. Vercelli and N. Dimitri (eds), *Macroeconomics: A Survey of Research Strategies*, Oxford: Oxford University Press.

Lekachman, R. (1969), *The Age of Keynes*, Harmondsworth: Pelican.

Leslie, D. (1993), *Advanced Macroeconomics Beyond IS–LM*, Maidenhead: McGraw-Hill.

Lilien, D.M. (1982), 'Sectoral Shifts and Cyclical Unemployment', *Journal of Political Economy*, August.

Lindbeck, A. (1992), 'Macroeconomic Theory and the Labour Market', *European Economic Review*, April.

*Lindbeck, A. and Snower, D.J. (1985), 'Explanations of Unemployment', *Oxford Review of Economic Policy*, Spring.

Lindbeck, A. and Snower, D.J. (1986), 'Wage Setting, Unemployment, and Insider–Outsider Relations', *American Economic Review*, May.

Lindbeck, A. and Snower, D.J. (1988a), 'Cooperation, Harassment and Involuntary Unemployment: An Insider–Outsider Approach', *American Economic Review*, March.

Lindbeck, A. and Snower, D.J. (1988b), *The Insider–Outsider Theory of Employment and Unemployment*, Cambridge: MIT Press.

Lipsey, R.G. (1960), 'The Relationship Between Unemployment and the Rate of Change of Money Wage Rates in the U.K. 1862–1957: A Further Analysis', *Economica*, February.

*Lipsey, R.G. (1978), 'The Place of the Phillips Curve in Macroeconomic Models', in A.R. Bergstrom (ed.), *Stability and Inflation*, Chichester: John Wiley.

Lipsey, R.G. (1981), 'The Understanding and Control of Inflation: Is There a Crisis in Macroeconomics?', *Canadian Journal of Economics*, November.

Litterman, B. and Weiss, L. (1985), 'Money, Real Interest Rates and Output: A Reinterpretation of Postwar U.S. Data', *Econometrica*, January.

Littleboy, B. and Mehta, G. (1983), 'The Scientific Method of Keynes', *Journal of Economic Studies*, Special Issue.

Long, J.B. and Plosser, C.I. (1983), 'Real Business Cycles', *Journal of Political Economy*, February.

Lovell, M.C. (1986), 'Tests of the Rational Expectations Hypothesis', *American Economic Review*, March.

Lucas, R.E. Jr. (1972), 'Expectations and the Neutrality of Money', *Journal of Economic Theory*, April.

Lucas, R.E. Jr. (1973), 'Some International Evidence on Output–Inflation Tradeoffs', *American Economic Review*, June.

Lucas, R.E. Jr. (1975), 'An Equilibrium Model of the Business Cycle', *Journal of Political Economy*, December.

Lucas, R.E. Jr. (1976), 'Econometric Policy Evaluation: A Critique', in K. Brunner and A. Meltzer (eds), *The Phillips Curve and Labor Markets*, Amsterdam: North Holland, Carnegie-Rochester Series on Public Policy.

*Lucas, R. E. Jr. (1977), 'Understanding Business Cycles', in K. Brunner and A.H. Meltzer (eds), *Stabilization of the Domestic and International Economy*, Amsterdam and New York: North Holland.

*Lucas, R.E. Jr. (1978), 'Unemployment Policy', *American Economic Review*, May.

Lucas, R.E. Jr. (1980), 'The Death of Keynesian Economics: Issues and Ideas', *University of Chicago*, Winter.

Lucas, R.E. Jr. (1981), *Studies in Business Cycle Theory*, Oxford: Basil Blackwell.

Lucas, R.E. Jr. (1987), *Models of Business Cycles*, Oxford: Basil Blackwell.

Lucas, R.E. Jr. (1988), 'On the Mechanics of Economic Development', *Journal of Monetary Economics*, July

Lucas, R.E. Jr. (1993), 'Making a Miracle', *Econometrica*, March.

Lucas, R. E. Jr. and Rapping, L.A. (1969), 'Real Wages, Employment and Inflation', *Journal of Political Economy*, September/October.

*Lucas, R.E. Jr. and Sargent, T.J. (1978), 'After Keynesian Macroeconomics', in *After the Phillips Curve: Persistence of High Inflation and High Unemployment*, Boston, Mass.: Federal Reserve Bank of Boston.

Machlup, F. (1976), 'Hayek's Contribution to Economics', in F. Machlup (ed.), *Essays on Hayek*, Hillsdale, Michigan: Hillsdale College Press.

Maddison, A. (1979), 'Long Run Dynamics of Productivity Growth', *Banca Nazionale Del Lavoro Quarterly Review*, March.

Maddison, A. (1980), 'Western Economic Performance in the 1970s: A Perspective and Assessment', *Banca Nazionale Del Lavoro Quarterly Review*, September.

*Maddison, A. (1987), 'Growth and Slowdown in Advanced Capitalist Economies: Techniques of Quantitative Assessment', *Journal of Economic Literature*, June.

*Maddock, R. and Carter, M. (1982), 'A Child's Guide to Rational Expectations', *Journal of Economic Literature*, March.

Malinvaud, E. (1977), *The Theory of Unemployment Reconsidered*, Oxford: Basil Blackwell.

Mankiw, N.G. (1985), 'Small Menu Costs and Large Business Cycles: A Macroeconomic Model of Monopoly', *Quarterly Journal of Economics*, May.

*Mankiw, N.G. (1989), 'Real Business Cycles: A New Keynesian Perspective', *Journal of Economic Perspectives*, Summer.

*Mankiw, N.G. (1990), 'A Quick Refresher Course in Macroeconomics', *Journal of Economic Literature*, December.

*Mankiw, N.G. (1992), 'The Reincarnation of Keynesian Economics', *European Economic Review*, April.

Mankiw, N.G. (1994), *Macroeconomics*, New York: Worth.

Mankiw, N.G. and Romer, D. (eds) (1991), *New Keynesian Economics*, Cambridge: MIT Press.

Mankiw, N.G., Rotemberg, J.J. and Summers, L.H. (1985), 'Intertemporal Substitution in Macroeconomics', *Quarterly Journal of Economics*, February.

Marget, A.W. (1966), *The Theory of Prices*, New York: Augustus M. Kelley.

Marris, R. (1991), *Reconstructing Keynesian Economics with Imperfect Competition*, Aldershot: Edward Elgar.

Marshall, A. (1920), *Principles of Economics*, London: Macmillan.

Matthews, K. and Minford, P. (1987), 'Mrs Thatcher's Economic Policies 1979–87', *Economic Policy*.

Matthews, R.C.O. (1968), 'Why has Britain had Full Employment Since the War?', *Economic Journal*, September.

Mayer, T. (1978a), 'Money and the Great Depression: A Critique of Professor Temin's Thesis', *Explorations in Economic History*, April.

Mayer, T. (1978b), *The Structure of Monetarism*, New York: W.W. Norton.

Mayer, T. (1980), 'David Hume and Monetarism', *Quarterly Journal of Economics*, August.

*Mayer, T. (1990), *Monetarism and Macroeconomic Policy*, Aldershot: Edward Elgar.

Mayes, D.G. (1981), 'The Controversy over Rational Expectations', *National Institute Economic Review*, May.

McCallum, B.T. (1986), 'On Real and Sticky-Price Theories of the Business Cycle', *Journal of Money, Credit and Banking*, November.

McCallum, B.T. (1989), 'Real Business Cycle Models', in R.J. Barro (ed.), *Modern Business Cycle Theory*, Cambridge, Mass.: Harvard University Press.

McCallum, B.T. (1990), 'New Classical Macroeconomics: A Sympathetic Account', in S. Honkapohja (ed.), *The State of Macroeconomics*, Oxford: Basil Blackwell.

McCallum, B.T. (1992), 'Real Business Cycle Theories', in A. Vercelli and N. Dimitri (eds), *Macroeconomics: A Survey of Research Strategies*, Oxford: Oxford University Press.

McCloskey, D.N. (1983), 'The Rhetoric of Economics', *Journal of Economic Literature*, June.

McCloskey, D.N. (1985), *The Rhetoric of Economics*, Wisconsin: University of Wisconsin Press.

McDonald, I.M. (1992), *Macroeconomics*, New York: John Wiley.

McDonald, I.M. and Solow, R.M. (1981), 'Wage Bargaining and Employment', *American Economic Review*, December.

Mehta, G. (1977), *The Structure of the Keynesian Revolution*, London: Martin Robertson.

*Meltzer, A.H. (1988), *Keynes's Monetary Theory: A Different Interpretation*, Cambridge: Cambridge University Press.

Mendoza, E.G. (1991), 'Real Business Cycles in a Small Open Economy', *American Economic Review*, September.

Mill, J.S. (1982), *On Liberty*, Harmondsworth: Penguin English Library.

*Minford, A.P.L. (1991), *The Supply Side Revolution in Britain*, Aldershot: Edward Elgar.

Minford, A.P.L. and Peel, D.A. (1983), *Rational Expectations and the New Macroeconomics*, Oxford: Martin Robertson.

Minford, A.P.L., Brech, M. and Matthews, K.G.P. (1980), 'A Rational Expectations Model of the UK Under Floating Exchange Rates', *European Economic Review*, September.

Minford, A.P.L., Ashton, P., Peel, M., Davies, D. and Sprague, A. (1985), *Unemployment: Cause and Cure*, 2nd edn, Oxford: Basil Blackwell.

Minsky, H.P. (1975), *John Maynard Keynes*, New York: Columbia University Press.

*Minsky, H.P. (1978), 'The Financial Instability Hypothesis: A Restatement', *Thames Papers in Political Economy*, Autumn.

Minsky, H.P. (1982), 'The Financial Instability Hypothesis: Capitalist Processes and the Behaviour of the Economy', in C.P. Kindleberger and J-P. Laffargue (eds), *Financial Crises: Theory, History and Policy*, Cambridge: Cambridge University Press.

Mises, L. (1943), '"Elastic Expectations" and the Austrian Theory of the Trade Cycle', *Economica*, August.

Mises, L. (1969), *The Historical Setting of the Austrian School of Economics*, New Rochelle, NY: Arlington House.

Mises, L. (1971), *The Theory of Money and Credit*, New York: Foundation for Economic Education.

Mises, L. (1977), 'Stones into Bread, the Keynesian Miracle', in H. Hazlitt (ed.), *The Critics of Keynesian Economics*, Rochelle, NY: Arlington House Publishers.

Mises, L. (1990), 'The Non-Neutrality of Money', in R.M. Ebeling (ed.), *Money, Method and the Market Process: Essays by Ludwig von Mises*, Ludwig von Mises Institute: Praxeology Press.

Mishkin, F.S (1982), 'Does Anticipated Monetary Policy Matter? An Econometric Investigation', *Journal of Political Economy*, February.

Modigliani, F. (1944), 'Liquidity Preference and the Theory of Interest and Money', *Econometrica*, January.

Modigliani, F. (1977), 'The Monetarist Controversy, or Should We Forsake Stabilization Policies?', *American Economic Review*, March.

Modigliani, F. (1986), *The Debate Over Stabilisation Policy*, Cambridge: Cambridge University Press.

Moggridge, D. (1992), *John Maynard Keynes: An Economist's Biography*, London: Routledge.

Moore, B.J. (1979a), 'The Endogenous Money Stock', *Journal of Post Keynesian Economics*, Fall.

Moore, B.J. (1979b), 'Monetary Factors', in A.S. Eichner (ed.), *A Guide to Post-Keynesian Economics*, London: Macmillan.

Moore, B.J. (1989), 'The Endogeneity of Credit Money', *Review of Political Economy*, March.

Morgan, B. (1978), *Monetarists and Keynesians: Their Contribution to Monetary Theory*, London: Macmillan.

Muellbauer, J. and Portes, R. (1978), 'Macroeconomic Models with Quantity Rationing', *Economic Journal*, December.

Mullineux, A.W. (1984), *The Business Cycle After Keynes*, Brighton: Wheatsheaf.

*Mullineux, A.W. and Dickinson, D.G. (1992), 'Equilibrium Business Cycles: Theory and Evidence', *Journal of Economic Surveys*.

Murrell, P. (1983), 'Did the Theory of Market Socialism Answer the Challenge of Ludwig von Mises?, *History of Political Economy*, Spring.

Musgrave, A. (1976), 'Method or Madness?', in R.S. Cohen, P.K. Feyerabend and M.W. Wartofsky (eds), *Essays in Honour of Imre Lakatos*, Dordrecht: Reidel.

Mussa, M. (1976), 'The Exchange Rate, The Balance of Payments and Monetary and Fiscal Policy under a Regime of Controlled Floating', *Scandinavian Journal of Economics*.

Muth, J.F. (1961), 'Rational Expectations and the Theory of Price Movements', *Econometrica*, July.

Naish, H.F. (1993), 'Imperfect Competition as a Micro Foundation for Keynesian Economics: A Graphical Analysis', *Journal of Macroeconomics*, Spring.

Nelson, C.R. and Plosser, C.I. (1982), 'Trends and Random Walks in Macroeconomic Time Series: Some Evidence and Implications', *Journal of Monetary Economics*, September.

Nickell, S . (1990), 'Unemployment: A Survey', *Economic Journal*, June.

Nordhaus, W.D. (1975), 'The Political Business Cycle', *Review of Economic Studies*, April.

Nordhaus, W.D. (1989), 'Alternative Approaches to the Political Business Cycle', *Brookings Papers on Economic Activity*.

O'Brien, D.P. (1975), *The Classical Economists*, Oxford: Clarendon Press.

O'Donnell, R.M. (1982), 'Keynes: Philosophy and Economics', Unpublished PhD, University of Cambridge.

O'Donnell, R.M. (1989), *Keynes: Philosophy, Economics and Politics*, London: Macmillan.

*O'Driscoll, G.P. and Rizzo, M.J. (1985), *The Economics of Time and Ignorance*, Oxford: Basil Blackwell.

Okun, A. (1975), 'Inflation: Its Mechanics and Welfare Cost', *Brookings Papers on Economic Activity*.

*Okun, A. (1980), 'Rational Expectations with Misperceptions as a Theory of the Business Cycle', *Journal of Money, Credit and Banking*, November.

*Okun, A. (1981), *Prices and Quantities: a Macroeconomic Analysis*, Oxford: Basil Blackwell.

Palley, T.I. (1993), 'Uncertainty, Expectations, and the Future: If We Don't Know the Answers, What are the Questions?', *Journal of Post Keynesian Economics*, Fall.

Parkin, M. (1986), 'The Output–Inflation Tradeoff When Prices Are Costly to Change', *Journal of Political Economy*, February.

Parkin, M. (1992), 'Where Do We Stand?', in M. Belongia and M. Garfinkel (eds), *The Business Cycle: Theories and Evidence*, London: Kluwer Academic Publishers.

Parkin, M. and Bade, R. (1982), 'Central Bank Laws and Monetary Policy', unpublished, University of Western Ontario.

*Patinkin, D. (1948), 'Price Flexibility and Full Employment' *American Economic Review*, September.

Patinkin, D. (1956), *Money, Interest and Prices: An Integration of Monetary and Value Theory*, Evanston, Illinois: Row Peterson.

Patinkin, D. (1965), *Money, Interest and Prices*, 2nd edn, New York: Harper and Row.

Patinkin, D. (1969), 'The Chicago Tradition, the Quantity Theory, and Friedman', *Journal of Money, Credit and Banking*, February.

Patinkin, D. (1976), *Keynes's Monetary Thought: A Study of its Development*, Durham: Duke University Press.

Patinkin, D. (1982), *Anticipations of the General Theory?*, Oxford: Blackwell.

Patinkin, D. (1990a), 'In Defence of IS–LM', *Banca Nazionale Del Lavoro Quarterly Review*, March.

*Patinkin, D. (1990b), 'On Different Interpretations of the General Theory', *Journal of Monetary Economics*, October.

Patinkin, D. (1993), 'On the Chronology of the General Theory', *Economic Journal*, May.

Persson, T. (1988), 'Credibility of Macroeconomic Policy: An Introduction and a Broad Survey', *European Economic Review*, March.

Pesek, B. and Saving, T.R. (1967), *Money, Wealth and Economic Theory*, London: Macmillan.

Peterson, W.C. (1977), 'Institutionalism, Keynes and the Real World', *Journal of Economic Issues*, June.

Phelps, E.S. (1967), 'Phillips Curves, Expectations of Inflation and Optimal Unemployment Over Time', *Economica*, August.

Phelps, E.S. (1968), 'Money Wage Dynamics and Labour Market Equilibrium', *Journal of Political Economy*, August.

Phelps, E.S. (1972), *Inflation Policy and Unemployment Theory: The Cost–Benefit Approach to Monetary Planning*, New York: W.W. Norton.

Phelps, E.S. (1978), 'Commodity-Supply Shock and Full Employment Monetary Policy', *Journal of Money, Credit and Banking*, May.

*Phelps, E.S. (1985), *Political Economy: An Introductory Text*, New York: W.W. Norton.

*Phelps, E.S. (1990), *Seven Schools of Macroeconomic Thought*, Oxford: Oxford University Press.

Phelps, E.S. (1992), 'Expectations in Macroeconomics and the Rational Expectations Debate', in A. Vercelli and N. Dimitri (eds), *Macroeconomics: A Survey of Research Strategies*, Oxford: Oxford University Press.

Phelps, E.S. (1994), *Structural Slumps: The Modern Equilibrium Theory of Unemployment, Interest and Assets*, Cambridge, Mass.: Harvard University Press.

Phelps, E.S. and Taylor, J.B. (1977), 'Stabilizing Powers of Monetary Policy Under Rational Expectations', *Journal of Political Economy*, February.

Phelps, E.S. *et al.* (1970), *Microeconomic Foundations of Employment and Inflation Theory*, New York: W.W. Norton.

Phillips, A.W. (1958), 'The Relation Between Unemployment and the Rate of Change of Money Wage Rates in the United Kingdom, 1861–1957', *Economica*, November.

Pigou, A.C. (1941), *Employment and Equilibrium*, London: Macmillan.

Pigou, A.C. (1943), 'The Classical Stationary State', *Economic Journal*, December.

Pigou, A.C. (1947), 'Economic Progress in a Stable Environment', *Economica*, August.

Pindyck, R. and Rubinfeld, D.L. (1989), *Microeconomics*, London: Macmillan.

*Plosser, C.I. (1989), 'Understanding Real Business Cycles', *Journal of Economic Perspectives*, Summer.

Poole, W. (1988), 'Monetary Policy Lessons of Recent Inflation and Disinflation', *Journal of Economic Perspectives*, Summer.

Popper, K.R. (1959), *The Logic of Scientific Discovery*, London: Hutchinson.

Popper, K.R. (1961), *The Poverty of Historicism*, London: Routledge and Kegan Paul.

*Prescott, E.C. (1986), 'Theory Ahead of Business Cycle Measurement', *Federal Reserve Bank of Minneapolis Quarterly Review*, Fall.

Presley, J.R. (1986), 'J.M. Keynes and the Real Balance Effect', *The Manchester School*, March.

Purvis, D.D. (1980), 'Monetarism: A Review', *Canadian Journal of Economics*, February.

Ricketts, M. and Shoesmith, E. (1990), *British Economic Opinion: A Survey of a Thousand Economists*, London: Institute of Economic Affairs.

Ricketts, M. and Shoesmith, E. (1992), 'British Economic Opinion: Positive Science or Normative Judgement?', *American Economic Review*, May.

Rizzo, M.J. (1982), 'Mises and Lakatos: A Reformulation of Austrian Methodology', in I.M. Kirzner (ed.), *Method, Process and Austrian Economics*, Lexington, Mass.: D.C. Heath and Co.

Robertson, D.H. (1926), *Banking Policy and the Price Level*, London: P.S. King.

Robertson, D.H. (1954), 'Thoughts on Meeting Some Important Persons', *Quarterly Journal of Economics*, May.

Robbins, L. (1934), *The Great Depression*, London: Macmillan.

Robbins, L. (1971), *Autobiography of an Economist*, London: Macmillan.

Robinson, J. (1933), *The Economics of Imperfect Competition*, London: Macmillan.

Robinson, J. (1943), 'Planning Full Employment', reprinted in *Collected Economic Papers*, Vol. 1, Oxford: Basil Blackwell, 1966.

Robinson, J. (1956), *The Accumulation of Capital*, London: Macmillan.

Robinson, J. (1962), *Economic Philosophy*, Harmondsworth: Penguin.

Robinson, J. (1971), *Economic Heresies*, London: Macmillan.

Robinson, J. (1972), 'The Second Crisis of Economic Theory', *American Economic Review*, May.

Robinson, J. (1978), *Contributions to Modern Economics*, Oxford: Blackwell.

Rogoff, K. (1985), 'The Optimal Degree of Commitment to an Intermediate Monetary Target', *Quarterly Journal of Economics*, November.

Romer, C.D. (1986a), 'Spurious Volatility in Historical Unemployment Data', *Journal of Political Economy*, March.

Romer, C.D. (1986b), 'New Estimates of GNP and Unemployment', *Journal of Economic History*, June.

Romer, C.D. (1986c), 'Is the Stabilisation of the Postwar Economy a Figment of the Data?', *American Economic Review*, June.

*Romer, C.D. (1992), 'What Ended the Great Depression?', *Journal of Economic History*, December.

Romer, C.D. (1993), 'The Nation in Depression', *Journal of Economic Perspectives*, Spring.

*Romer, C.D. and Romer, D.H. (1989), 'Does Monetary Policy Matter? A

New Test in the Spirit of Friedman and Schwartz', *NBER Macroeconomics Annual*.

*Romer, D. (1993), 'The New Keynesian Synthesis', *Journal of Economic Perspectives*, Winter.

Romer, P. (1986), 'Increasing Returns and Long Run Growth', *Journal of Political Economy*, October.

Roper, B. and Snowdon, B. (eds) (1987), *Markets, Intervention and Planning*, London: Longman.

Rosen, S. (1985), 'Implicit Contracts: A Survey', *Journal of Economic Literature*, September.

Rotemberg, J.J. (1987), 'The New Keynesian Microfoundations', *NBER Macroeconomics Annual*.

Rotemberg, J.J. and Summers, L.H. (1990), 'Inflexible Prices and Procyclical Productivity', *Quarterly Journal of Economics*, November.

Rotemberg, J.J. and Woodford, M. (1991), 'Markups and the Business Cycle', *NBER Macroeconomics Annual*.

Rothbard, M.N. (1975), *America's Great Depression*, Kansas City: Sheed and Ward.

Rotheim, R.J. (1981), 'Keynes's Monetary Theory of Value (1933)', *Journal of Post Keynesian Economics*, Summer.

Routh, G. (1977), *The Origin of Economic Ideas*, London: Macmillan.

Rowley, C.K. (1983), 'Unemployment: Is Government Macroeconomic Policy Impotent?', *Economic Affairs*, January.

Rowley, C.K. (1984), 'Rejoinder', *Economic Affairs*, October–December.

Rowthorn, R. (1977), 'Conflict, Inflation and Money', *Cambridge Journal of Economics*, September.

*Rush, M. (1987), 'Real Business Cycles', *Federal Reserve Bank of Kansas City Economic Review*, February.

*Salant, W.S. (1988), 'The Spread of Keynesian Doctrines and Practices in the United States', in O.F. Hamouda and J.N. Smithin (eds), *Keynes and Public Policy After Fifty Years, Vol 1: Economics and Policy*, Aldershot: Edward Elgar.

Salop, S.C. (1979), 'A Model of the Natural Rate of Unemployment', *American Economic Review*, March.

Samuelson, P.A. (1939), 'Interactions Between the Multiplier Analysis and the Principle of Acceleration', *Review of Economics and Statistics*, May.

Samuelson, P.A. (1946), 'Lord Keynes and the General Theory', *Econometrica*, July.

Samuelson, P.A. (1947), *Foundations of Economic Analysis*, Cambridge, Mass.: Harvard University Press.

Samuelson, P.A. (1948), *Economics*, New York: McGraw Hill.

Samuelson, P.A. (1983), 'The Keynes Centenary: Sympathy From the Other Cambridge', *The Economist*, 25 June.

Samuelson, P.A. (1988), 'In the Beginning', *Challenge*, July/August.

Samuelson, P.A. and Solow, R.M. (1960), 'Analytical Aspects of Anti-Inflationary Policy', *American Economic Review*, May.

*Santomero, A.M. and Seater, J.J. (1978), The Inflation–Unemployment Trade-Off: A Critique of the Literature', *Journal of Economic Literature*, June.

Sargent, T.J. (1973), 'Rational Expectations, the Real Rate of Interest and the Natural Rate of Unemployment', *Brookings Papers on Economic Activity*.

Sargent, T.J. (1976), 'A Classical Macroeconomic Model for the United States', *Journal of Political Economy*, April.

Sargent, T.J. (1993), *Rational Expectations and Inflation*, 2nd edn, New York: Harper Collins.

Sargent, T.J. and Wallace, N. (1975), 'Rational Expectations, the Optimal Monetary Instrument and the Optimal Money Supply Rule', *Journal of Political Economy*, April.

Sargent, T.J. and Wallace, N. (1976), 'Rational Expectations and the Theory of Economic Policy', *Journal of Monetary Economics*, April.

Sargent, T.J. and Wallace, N. (1981), 'Some Unpleasant Monetarist Arithmetic', *Federal Reserve Bank of Minneapolis Quarterly Review*, Autumn.

Sargent, T.J. and Wallace, N. (1985), 'Some Unpleasant Monetarist Arithmetic', *Federal Reserve Bank of Minneapolis Quarterly Review*, Winter.

Sawyer, M.C. (1985), *The Economics of Michal Kalecki*, London: Macmillan.

Sawyer, M.C. (1991), 'Post-Keynesian Macroeconomics', in D. Greenaway, M. Bleaney and I. Stewart (eds), *Companion to Contemporary Economic Thought*, London: Macmillan.

Say, J.B. (1821), *A Treatise on Political Economy*, London: Longmans.

Schumpeter, J.A. (1939), *Business Cycles*, New York: McGraw-Hill.

Schumpeter, J.A. (1954), *A History of Economic Analysis*, London: Allen and Unwin.

Schwartz, A.J. (1992), *Monetarism and Monetary Policy*, IEA Occasional Paper No. 86, London: Institute of Economic Affairs.

Shackle, G.L.S. (1933), 'Some Notes on Monetary Theory of the Trade Cycle', *Review of Economic Studies*, October.

Shackle, G.L.S. (1967), *The Years of High Theory*, Cambridge: Cambridge University Press.

Shackle, G.L.S. (1968), *Uncertainty in Economics*, Cambridge: Cambridge University Press.

Shackle, G.L.S. (1972), *Epistemics and Economics*, Cambridge: Cambridge University Press.

*Shackle, G.L.S. (1974), *Keynesian Kaleidics*, Edinburgh: Edinburgh University Press.

*Shand, A.H. (1984), *The Capitalist Alternative*, Brighton: Wheatsheaf.

Shand, A.H. (1990), *Free Market Morality*, London: Routledge.

Shapiro, C. and Stiglitz, J. (1984), 'Equilibrium Unemployment as a Discipline Device', *American Economic Review*, June.

Shapiro, N. (1978), 'Keynes and Equilibrium Economics', *Australian Economic Papers*, December.

*Shaw, G.K. (1984), *Rational Expectations: An Elementary Exposition*, Brighton: Wheatsheaf.

*Shaw, G.K. (1988), *Keynesian Economics: The Permanent Revolution*, Aldershot: Edward Elgar.

Sheffrin, S.M. (1983), *Rational Expectations*, Cambridge: Cambridge University Press.

Sheffrin, S. (1989), *The Making of Economic Policy*, Oxford: Basil Blackwell.

Sims, C.A. (1972), 'Money, Income, and Causality', *American Economic Review*, September.

Sims, C.A. (1980), 'Comparisons of Interwar and Postwar Business Cycles: Monetarism Reconsidered', *American Economic Review*, May.

Sims, C.A. (1983), 'Is There a Monetary Business Cycle?', *American Economic Review*, May.

*Skidelsky, R. (1983), *John Maynard Keynes: Hopes Betrayed 1883–1920*, London: Macmillan.

*Skidelsky, R. (1992), *John Maynard Keynes: The Economist As Saviour 1920–1937*, London: Macmillan .

Skousen, M. (1987), 'Saving the Depression: A New Look at World War II', *Review of Austrian Economics*.

Smiley, G. (1987), 'Some Austrian Perspectives on Keynesian Fiscal Policy and the Recovery in the Thirties', *Review of Austrian Economics*.

*Smith, D. (1987), *The Rise and Fall of Monetarism: The Theory and Politics of an Economic Experiment*, Harmondsworth: Penguin.

Smith, R.T. (1992), 'The Cyclical Behaviour of Prices', *Journal of Money, Credit and Banking*, November.

Snowdon, B. and Vane, H.R. (1995), 'New Keynesian Economics Today: The Empire Strikes Back', *American Economist*, Spring.

Snowdon, B. and Wynarczyk, P. (1984), 'Have the Keynesians been Vanquished?', *Economic Affairs*, October–December.

Snowdon, B. and Wynarczyk, P. (1985), 'Can Keynesianism be Falsified?', *Economic Affairs*, December–January.

Solow, R.M. (1956), 'A Contribution to the Theory of Economic Growth', *Quarterly Journal of Economics*, February.

Solow, R.M. (1957), 'Technical Change and the Aggregate Production Function', *Review of Economics and Statistics*, August.

Solow, R.M. (1979), 'Another Possible Source of Wage Stickiness', *Journal of Macroeconomics*, Winter.

Solow, R.M. (1980), 'On Theories of Unemployment', *American Economic Review*, March.

*Solow, R.M. (1990), *The Labour Market as a Social Institution*, Oxford: Basil Blackwell.

Sowell, T. (1972), *Say's Law: An Historical Analysis*, Princeton: Princeton University Press.

Spence, M. (1974), *Market Signalling*, Cambridge, Mass.: Harvard University Press.

Sraffa, P. (1926), 'The Law of Returns Under Competitive Conditions', *Economic Journal*, December.

Stadler, G.W. (1990), 'Business Cycle Models with Endogenous Technology', *American Economic Review*, September.

Stadler, G. W. (1993), 'Real Business Cycle Theory: A Survey', *Newcastle Discussion Papers in Economics*, University of Newcastle, England.

Stein, H. (1969), *The Fiscal Revolution in America*, Chicago: University of Chicago Press.

Stein, J.L. (1982), *Monetarist, Keynesian and New Classical Economics*, Oxford: Basil Blackwell.

Stevenson, A., Muscatelli, V. and Gregory, M. (1988), *Macroeconomic Theory and Stabilization Policy*, Oxford: Philip Allan.

*Stewart, M. (1986), *Keynes and After*, 3rd edn, Harmondsworth: Penguin.

Stiglitz, J.E. (1984), 'Price Rigidities and Market Structure' *American Economic Review*, May.

*Stiglitz, J.E. (1987), 'The Causes and Consequences of the Dependency of Quality on Prices', *Journal of Economic Literature*, March.

*Stiglitz, J.E. (1992), ' Methodological Issues and the New Keynesian Economics', in A. Vercelli and N. Dimitri (eds), *Macroeconomics: A Survey of Research Strategies*, Oxford: Oxford University Press.

Stiglitz, J.E. (1993), *Economics*, New York: W.W. Norton.

Stock, J.H. and Watson, M.W. (1988), 'Variable Trends in Economic Time Series', *Journal of Economic Perspectives*, Summer.

Streissler, E. (1973), ' Menger's Theories of Money and Uncertainty – A Modern Interpretation', in J.R. Hicks and W. Weber (eds), *Carl Menger and the Austrian School of Economics*, Oxford: Oxford University Press.

Summers, L.H. (1986), 'Some Sceptical Observations on Real Business Cycle Theory', *Federal Reserve Bank of Minneapolis Quarterly Review*, Fall.

Summers, L.H. (1988), 'Relative Wages, Efficiency Wages, and Keynesian Unemployment', *American Economic Review*, May.

Tarshis, L. (1939), 'Changes in Real and Money Wages', *Economic Journal*, March.

*Taylor, H. (1985), 'Time Inconsistency: A Potential Problem for Policymakers', *Federal Reserve Bank of Philadelphia Business Review*, March/April.

Taylor, J. (1980), 'Aggregate Dynamics and Staggered Contracts', *Journal of Political Economy*, February.

Taylor, J. (1992), 'Synchronised Wage Determination and Macroeconomic Performance in Seven Large Countries', in A. Vercelli and N. Dimitri (eds), *Macroeconomics: A Survey of Research Strategies*, Oxford: Oxford University Press.

Temin, P. (1976), *Did Monetary Forces Cause the Great Depression?*, New York: W.W. Norton.

*Thirlwall, A.P. (1993),'The Renaissance of Keynesian Economics', *Banca Nazionale Del Lavoro Quarterly Review*, September.

Thurow, L.C. (1983), *Dangerous Currents: The State of Economics*, New York: Random House.

Timbrell, M. (1989), 'Contracts and Market Clearing in the Labour Market', in D. Greenaway (ed.), *Current Issues in Macroeconomics*, Basingstoke: Macmillan.

Tinbergen, J. (1952), *On The Theory of Economic Policy*, Amsterdam: North Holland.

Tobin, J. (1958), 'Liquidity Preference as Behaviour Towards Risk', *Review of Economic Studies*, February.

Tobin, J. (1970), 'Money and Income: Post Hoc, Ergo Propter Hoc', *Quarterly Journal of Economics*, May.

Tobin, J. (1972a), 'Friedman's Theoretical Framework', *Journal of Political Economy*, September/October.

*Tobin, J. (1972b), 'Inflation and Unemployment', *American Economic Review*, March.

Tobin, J. (1975), 'Keynesian Models of Recession and Depression', *American Economic Review*, May.

*Tobin, J. (1977), 'How Dead is Keynes?', *Economic Inquiry*, October.

Tobin, J. (1980a), *Asset Accumulation and Economic Activity*, Oxford: Basil Blackwell.

Tobin, J. (1980b), 'Are New Classical Models Plausible Enough to Guide Policy?' *Journal of Money, Credit and Banking*, November.

*Tobin, J. (1981), 'The Monetarist Counter-Revolution Today – An Appraisal', *Economic Journal*, March.

*Tobin, J. (1987), *Policies For Prosperity: Essays in a Keynesian Mode*, P.M. Jackson (ed.), Brighton: Wheatsheaf.

Tobin, J. (1988), '"Comment" on David Romer's paper on "What Are the Costs of Excessive Deficits?"', *NBER Macroeconomics Annual*.

Tobin, J. (1989), 'Keynesian Theory: Is It Still a Useful Tool in the Economic Reality of Today?', *Revista Di Politica Economica*, April.

*Tobin, J. (1993), 'Price Flexibility and Output Stability: An Old Keynesian View', *Journal of Economic Perspectives*, Winter.

Tomlinson, J.D. (1984), 'A Keynesian Revolution in Economic Policy-Making?', *Economic History Review*, May.

Toporowski, J. (1993), 'Profits in the UK Economy: Some Kaleckian Models', *Review of Political Economy*, January.

Townshend, H. (1937), 'Liquidity-Premium and the Theory of Value', *Economic Journal*, March.

Trevithick, J.A. (1975), 'Keynes, Inflation and Money Illusion', *Economic Journal*, March.

*Trevithick, J.A. (1978), 'Recent Developments in the Theory of Employment', *Scottish Journal of Political Economy*, February.

*Trevithick, J.A. (1992), *Involuntary Unemployment: Macroeconomics from a Keynesian Perspective*, London: Harvester-Wheatsheaf.

Trevithick, J.A. and Stevenson, A. (1977), 'The Complementarity of Monetary Policy and Incomes Policy', *Scottish Journal of Political Economy*, February.

Vane, H.R. (1992), 'The Thatcher Years: Macroeconomic Policy and Performance of the UK Economy, 1979–1988', *National Westminster Bank Quarterly Review*, May.

Vane, H.R. and Thompson, J.L. (1979), *Monetarism: Theory, Evidence and Policy*, Oxford: Martin Robertson.

Vane, H.R. and Thompson, J.L. (1992), *Current Controversies in Macroeconomics*, Aldershot: Edward Elgar.

Vaughn, K. (1980), 'Economic Calculation under Socialism: The Austrian Contribution', *Economic Inquiry*, October.

Vaughn, K. (1990), 'The Mengerian Roots of the Austrian Revival', in B.J. Caldwell (ed.), *Carl Menger and his Legacy in Economics*, Durham: Duke University Press.

Vercelli, A. (1991), *Methodological Foundations of Macroeconomics: Keynes and Lucas*, Cambridge: Cambridge University Press.

Vickers, D. (1979–80), 'Uncertainty, Choice and Marginal Efficiencies', *Journal of Post Keynesian Economics*, Winter.

*Walsh, C.E. (1986), 'New Views of the Business Cycle: Has the Past Emphasis on Money Been Misplaced?', *Federal Reserve Bank of Philadelphia Business Review*, February.

Weintraub, E. R. (1975), 'Uncertainty and the Keynesian Revolution', *History of Political Economy*, Winter.

Weintraub, E.R. (1979), *Microfoundations*, Cambridge: Cambridge University Press.

Weintraub, S. (1966), *A Keynesian Theory of Employment, Growth and Income Distribution*, Philadelphia: Chilton.

Weintraub, S. (1978), *Keynes, Keynesians and Monetarists*, University of Pennsylvannia Press.

Weiss, A. (1980), 'Job Queues and Layoffs in Labour Markets with Flexible Wages', *Journal of Political Economy*, June.

Weiss, A. (1991), *Efficiency Wages: Models of Unemployment, Layoffs and Wage Dispersion*, Oxford: Clarendon Press.

Weitzman, M.L. (1985), 'Profit Sharing as Macroeconomic Policy', *American Economic Review*, May.

Whynes, D.K. (1989), 'The Political Business Cycle', in D. Greenaway (ed.), *Current Issues in Macroeconomics*, Basingstoke: Macmillan.

Wible, J.R. (1982–3), 'The Rational Expectations Tautologies', *Journal of Post Keynesian Economics*, Winter.

Wicksell, K. (1958), 'Ends and Means in Economics', in his *Selected Papers on Economic Theory* (ed. E. Lindahl), London: Allen and Unwin.

Wilson, T. (1980), 'Robertson, Money and Monetarism', *Journal of Economic Literature*, December.

Worrall, J. (1978), 'The Ways in Which the Methodology of Scientific Research Programmes Improves on Popper's Methodology', in G. Radnitzky and G. Andersson (eds), *Progress and Rationality in Science*, Boston: Reidel Publishers.

Wynarczyk, P. (1990), 'Economic Crisis and the Crisis in Economics: Internal and External Historical Aspects of the Development of Monetary Thought in the Interwar Period – A Methodological Appraisal', unpublished PhD, University of Kent at Canterbury, UK.

Yeager, L.B. (1973), 'The Keynesian Diversion', *Western Economic Journal*, June.

*Yellen, J.L. (1984), 'Efficiency Wage Models of Unemployment', *American Economic Review*, May.

*Zarnowitz, V. (1992a), 'What is a Business Cycle?', in M. Belongia and M. Garfinkel (eds), *The Business Cycle: Theories and Evidence*, London: Kluwer Academic Publishers .

Zarnowitz, V. (1992b), *Business Cycles: Theory, History, Indicators and Forecasting*, Chicago: University of Chicago Press.

Subject index